1989

INTRODUCTION TO ALGORITHMS
A Creative Approach

INTRODUCTION TO ALGORITHMS

A Creative Approach

UDI MANBER
University of Arizona

ADDISON-WESLEY PUBLISHING COMPANY
Reading, Massachusetts • Menlo Park, California • New York
Don Mills, Ontario • Wokingham, England • Amsterdam
Bonn • Sydney • Singapore • Tokyo • Madrid • San Juan

Library of Congress Cataloging-in-Publication Data

Manber, Udi.
    Introduction to algorithms.

    Includes bibliographies and index.
        1. Data structures (Computer science)
2. Algorithms. I. Title.
QA76.9.D35M36   1989   005.7 ' 3   88–2186
ISBN 0–201–12037–2

Reproduced by Addison-Wesley from camera-ready copy supplied by the author.

The programs and applications presented in this book have been included for their instructional value. They have been tested with care, but are not guaranteed for any purpose. The publisher does not offer any warranties or representation, nor does it accept any liabilities with respect to the programs or applications.

To my parents Eva and Meshulam

PREFACE

This book grew out of my frustrations with not being able to explain algorithms clearly. Like many other teachers, I discovered that not only is it hard for some students to solve (what seemed to me) simple problems by themselves, but it is also hard for them to understand the solutions that are given to them. I believe that these two parts — the creation and the explanation — are related and should not be separated. It is essential to follow the steps leading to a solution in order to understand it fully. It is not sufficient to look at the finished product.

This book emphasizes the creative side of algorithm design. Its main purpose is to show the reader how to design a new algorithm. Algorithms are not described in a sequence of "problem X, algorithm A, algorithm A', program P, program P'," and so on. Instead, the sequence usually (although not always) looks more like "problem X, the straightforward algorithm, its drawbacks, the difficulties overcoming these drawbacks, first attempts at a better algorithm (including possible wrong turns), improvements, analysis, relation to other methods and algorithms," and so on. The goal is to present an algorithm not in a way that makes it easier for a programmer to translate into a program, but rather in a way that makes it easier to understand the algorithm's principles. The algorithms are thus explained through a creative process, rather than as finished products. Our goals in teaching algorithms are to show not only how to solve particular problems, but also how to solve new problems when they arise in the future. Teaching the thinking involved in designing an algorithm is as important as teaching the details of the solution.

To further help the thinking process involved in creating algorithms, an "old–new" methodology for designing algorithms is used in this book. This methodology covers many known techniques for designing algorithms, and it also provides an elegant intuitive framework for explaining the design of algorithms in more depth. It does not, however, cover all possible ways of designing algorithms, and we do not use it exclusively. The heart of the methodology lies in an analogy between the intellectual process of proving mathematical theorems by induction and that of designing combinatorial algorithms. Although these two processes serve different purposes and achieve different types of results, they are more similar than they may appear to be. This analogy has been observed by many people. The novelty of this book is the degree to which this analogy is exploited. We show that the analogy encompasses many known algorithm-design techniques, and helps considerably in the process of algorithm creation. The methodology is discussed briefly in Chapter 1 and is introduced more formally in Chapter 5.

v

Consider the following analogy. Suppose that you arrive at an unfamiliar city, rent a car, and want directions to get to your hotel. You would be quite impatient if you were told about the history of the city, its general layout, the traffic patterns, and so on. You would rather have directions of the form "go straight for two blocks, turn right, go straight for three miles," and so on. However, your outlook would change if you planned to live in that city for a long time. You could probably get around for a while with directions of the second form (if you find someone who gives you those directions), but eventually you will need to know more about the city. This book is not a source of easy directions. It does contain explanations of how to solve many particular problems, but the emphasis is on general principles and methods. As a result, the book is challenging. It demands involvement and thinking. I believe that the extra effort is well worthwhile.

The design of efficient nonnumeric algorithms is becoming important in many diverse fields, including mathematics, statistics, molecular biology, and engineering. This book can serve as an introduction to algorithms and to nonnumeric computations in general. Many professionals, and even scientists not deeply involved with computers, believe that programming is nothing more than grungy nonintellectual work. It sometimes is. But such a belief may lead to straightforward, trivial, inefficient solutions, where elegant, more efficient solutions exist. One goal of this book is to convince readers that algorithm design is an elegant discipline, as well as an important one.

The book is self-contained. The presentation is mostly intuitive, and technicalities are either kept to a minimum or are separated from the main discussion. In particular, implementation details are separated from the algorithm-design ideas as much as possible. There are many examples of algorithms that were designed especially to illustrate the principles emphasized in the book. The material in this book is not presented as something to be mastered and memorized. It is presented as a series of ideas, examples, counterexamples, modifications, improvements, and so on. Pseudo-codes for most algorithms are given following the descriptions. Numerous exercises and a discussion of further reading, with a relevant bibliography, follow each chapter. In most chapters, the exercises are divided into two classes, **drill exercises** and **creative exercises.** Drill exercises are meant to test the reader's understanding of the specific examples and algorithms presented in that chapter. Creative exercises are meant to test the reader's ability to use the techniques developed in that chapter, *in addition* to the particular algorithms, to solve new problems. Sketches of solutions to selected exercises (those whose numbers are underlined) are given at the end of the book. The chapters also include a summary of the main ideas introduced.

The book is organized as follows. Chapters 1 through 4 present introductory material. Chapter 2 is an introduction to mathematical induction. Mathematical induction is, as we will see, very important to algorithm design. Experience with induction proofs is therefore very helpful. Unfortunately, few computer-science students get enough exposure to induction proofs. Chapter 2 may be quite difficult for some students. We suggest skipping the more difficult examples at first reading, and returning to them later. Chapter 3 is an introduction to the analysis of algorithms. It describes the process of analyzing algorithms, and gives the basic tools one needs to be able to perform simple analysis of the algorithms presented in the book. Chapter 4 is a brief introduction to data structures. Readers who are familiar with basic data structures and who have a basic mathematical background can start directly from Chapter 5 (it is always a good idea to read the introduction though). Chapter 5 presents the basic ideas behind the approach of designing algorithms through the analogy to induction proofs. It gives several examples of simple algorithms, and describes their creation. If you read only one chapter in this book, read Chapter 5.

There are two basic ways to organize a book on algorithms. One way is to divide the book according to the subject of the algorithms, for example, graph algorithms, geometric algorithms. Another way is to divide the book according to design techniques. Even though the emphasis of this book is on design techniques, I have chosen the former organization. Chapters 6 through 9 present algorithms in four areas: algorithms for sequences and sets (e.g., sorting, sequence comparisons, data compression), graph algorithms (e.g., spanning trees, shortest paths, matching), geometric algorithms (e.g., convex hull, intersection problems), and numerical and algebraic algorithms (e.g., matrix multiplication, fast Fourier transform). I believe that this organization is clearer and easier to follow.

Chapter 10 is devoted to reductions. Although examples of reductions appear in earlier chapters, the subject is unique and important enough to warrant a chapter of its own. This chapter also serves as an opening act to Chapter 11, which deals with the subject of NP-completeness. This aspect of complexity theory has become an essential part of algorithm theory. Anyone who designs algorithms should know about NP-completeness and the techniques for proving this property. Chapter 12 is an introduction to parallel algorithms. It contains several interesting algorithms under different models of parallel computation.

The material in this book is more than can be covered in a one-semester course, which leaves many choices for the instructor. A first course in algorithm design should include parts of Chapters 3, 5, 6, 7, and 8 in some depth, although not necessarily all of them. The more advanced parts of these chapters, along with Chapters 9, 10, 11, and 12, are optional for a first course, and can be used as a basis for a more advanced course.

Acknowledgments

First and foremost I thank my wife Rachel for helping me in more ways than I can list here throughout this adventure. She was instrumental in the development of the methodology on which the book is based. She contributed suggestions, corrections, and — more important than anything else — sound advice. I could not have done it without her.

Special thanks are due to Jan van Leeuwen for an excellent and thorough review of a large portion of this book. His detailed comments, numerous suggestions, and many corrections have improved the book enormously. I also thank Eric Bach, Darrah Chavey, Kirk Pruhs, and Sun Wu, who read parts of the manuscript and made many helpful comments, and the reviewers Guy T. Almes (Rice University), Agnes H. Chan (Northeastern University), Dan Gusfield (University of California, Davis), David Harel (Weizmann Institute, Israel), Daniel Hirschberg (University of California, Irvine),

Jefferey H. Kingston (University of Iowa), Victor Klee (University of Washington), Charles Martel (University of California, Davis), Michael J. Quinn (University of New Hampshire), and Diane M. Spresser (James Madison University).

I thank the people at Addison-Wesley who failed to supply me with any examples of horror stories that authors are so fond of telling. They were very helpful and incredibly patient and understanding. In particular, I thank my production supervisor Bette Aaronson, my editor Jim DeWolf, and my copy editor Lyn Dupré, who not only guided me but also let me do things my way even when they knew better.

The book was designed and typeset by me. It was formatted in troff, and printed on a Linotronic 300 at the Department of Computer Science, University of Arizona. I thank Ralph Griswold for his advice, and John Luiten, Allen Peckham, and Andrey Yeatts for technical help with the typesetting. The figures were prepared with *gremlin* — developed at the University of California, Berkeley — except for Fig. 12.22, which was designed and drawn by Gregg Townsend. The index was compiled with the help of a system by Bentley and Kernighan [1988]. I thank Brian Kernighan for supplying me the code within minutes after I (indirectly) requested it. The cover was done by Marshall Henrichs, based on an idea by the author.

I must stress, however, that the final manuscript was prepared by the typesetter. He was the one who decided to overlook many comments and suggestions of the people listed here. And he is the one who should bear the consequences.

Tucson, Arizona   Udi Manber
                                            (Internet address: udi@arizona.edu.)

CONTENTS

CHAPTER 1

INTRODUCTION

Great importance has been rightly attached to this process of "construction," and some claim to see in it the necessary and sufficient condition of the progress of the exact sciences. Necessary, no doubt, but not sufficient! For a construction to be useful and not mere waste of mental effort, for it to serve as a stepping-stone to higher things, it must first of all possess a kind of unity enabling us to see something more than the juxtaposition of its elements.

Henri Poincaré, 1902

The Webster's Ninth New Collegiate dictionary defines an *algorithm* as "a procedure for solving a mathematical problem (as of finding the greatest common divisor) in a finite number of steps that frequently involves a repetition of an operation; or *broadly*: a step-by-step procedure for solving a problem or accomplishing some end." We will stick to the broad definition. The design of algorithms is thus an old field of study. People have always been interested in finding better methods to achieve their goals, whether those be starting fires, building pyramids, or sorting the mail. The study of computer algorithms is of course new. Some computer algorithms use methods developed before the invention of computers, but most problems require new approaches. For one thing, it is not enough to tell a computer to "look over the hill and sound the alarm if an army is advancing." A computer must know the exact meaning of "look," how to identify an army, and how to sound the alarm (for some reason, sounding an alarm is always easy). A computer receives its instructions via well-defined, limited primitive operations. It is a difficult process to translate regular instructions to a language that a computer understands. This necessary process, called *programming*, is now performed on one level or another by millions of people.

Programming a computer, however, requires more than just translating well-understood instructions to a language a computer can understand. In most cases, we need to devise totally new methods for solving a problem. It is not just learning the weird language in which we "talk" to a computer that makes it hard to program; it is knowing what to say. Computers execute not only operations that were previously performed by humans; with their enormous speed, computers can do much more than was ever possible. Algorithms of the past dealt with dozens, maybe hundreds of items, and, at most, with thousands of instructions. Computers can deal with billions, or even trillions, of bits of information, and can perform millions of (their primitive) instructions per second. Designing algorithms on this order of magnitude is something new. It is in many respects counterintuitive. We are used to thinking in terms of things we can see and feel. As a result, there is a tendency when designing an algorithm to use the straightforward approach that works very well for small problems. Unfortunately, algorithms that work well for small problems may be terrible for large problems. It is easy to lose sight of the complexity and inefficiency of an algorithm when applied to large-scale computations.

There is another aspect to this problem. The algorithms we perform in our daily life are not too complicated and are not performed too often. It is usually not worthwhile to expend a lot of effort to develop the perfect algorithm. The payoff is too small. For example, consider the problem of unpacking grocery bags. There are obviously less efficient and more efficient ways of doing it, depending on the contents of the bags and the way the kitchen is organized. Few people spend time even thinking about this problem, much less developing algorithms for it. On the other hand, people who do large-scale commercial packing and unpacking must develop good methods. Another example is mowing the lawn. We can improve the mowing by minimizing the number of turns, the total time for mowing, or the length of the trips to the garbage cans. Again, unless one really hates mowing the lawn, one would not spend an hour figuring out how to save a minute of mowing. Computers, on the other hand, can deal with very complicated tasks, and they may have to perform those tasks many times. It is worthwhile to spend a lot of time designing better methods, even if the resulting algorithms are more complicated and harder to understand. The potential of a payoff is much greater. (Of course, we should not overoptimize, spending hours of programming time to save overall a few seconds of computer time.)

These two issues — the need for counterintuitive approaches to large-scale algorithms and the possible complexities of these algorithms — point to the difficulties in learning this subject. First, we must realize that straightforward intuitive methods are not always the best. It is important to continue the search for better methods. To do that, we need of course, to learn new methods. This book surveys and illustrates numerous methods for algorithm design. But it is not enough to learn even a large number of methods, just as it is not enough to memorize many games of chess in order to be a good player. One must understand the principles behind the methods. One must know how to apply them and, more important, when to apply them.

A design and implementation of an algorithm is analogous to a design and construction of a house.[1] We start with the basic concepts, based on the requirements for the house. It is the architect's job to present a plan that satisfies the requirements. It is the engineer's job to make sure that the plan is feasible and correct (so that the house will not collapse after a short while). It is then the builder's job to construct the house based on these plans. Of course, all along the way, the costs associated with each step must be analyzed and taken into account. Each job is different, but they are all related and intertwined. A design of an algorithm also starts with the basic ideas and methods. Then, a plan is made. We must prove the correctness of the plan and make sure that its cost is effective. The last step is to implement the algorithm for a particular computer. Risking oversimplification, we can divide the process into four steps: design, proof of correctness, analysis, and implementation. Again, each of these steps is different, but they are all related. None of them can be made in a vacuum, without a regard to the others. One rarely goes through these steps in linear order. Difficulties arise in all phases of the construction. They usually require modifications to the design, which in turn require another feasibility proof, adjustment of costs, and change of implementation.

This book concentrates on the first step, the design of algorithms. Following our analogy, the book could have been entitled *The Architecture of Algorithms*. However, computer architecture has a different meaning, so using this term would be confusing. The book does not, however, ignore all the other aspects. A discussion of correctness, analysis, and implementation follows the description of most algorithms — in detail for some algorithms, briefly for others. The emphasis is on methods of design.

It is not enough to learn many algorithms to be a good architect and to be able to design new algorithms. One must understand the *principles* behind the design. We employ a different way of explaining algorithms in this book. First, we try to lead the reader to find his or her own solution; we strongly believe that the best way to learn how to create something is to try to create it. Second, and more important, we follow a methodology for designing algorithms that helps this creative process. The methodology, introduced in Manber [1988], provides an elegant intuitive framework for explaining the design of algorithms in more depth. It also provides a unified way to approach the design. The different methods that are encompassed by this methodology, and their numerous variations, are instances of the same technique. The process of choosing among those many possible methods and applying them becomes more methodical. This methodology does not cover all possible ways of designing algorithms. It is useful, however, for a great majority of the algorithms in this book.

The methodology is based on mathematical induction. The heart of it lies in an analogy between the intellectual process of proving mathematical theorems and that of designing combinatorial algorithms. The main idea in the principle of mathematical induction is that a statement need not be proven from scratch: It is sufficient to show that the correctness of the statement follows from the correctness of the same statement for smaller instances and the correctness of the statement for a small base case. Translating this principle to algorithm design suggests an approach that concentrates on extending

---

[1] The two wonderful books by Tracy Kidder, *The Soul of a New Machine* (Little Brown, 1981), and *House* (Houghton Mifflin, 1985), inspired this analogy.

solutions of small problems to solutions of large problems. Given a problem, if we can show how to solve it by using a solution of the same problem for smaller inputs, then we are done. The basic idea is to concentrate on extending a solution rather than on building it from scratch. As we will show in the following chapters, there are many ways of doing this, leading to many algorithm design techniques.

We use mathematical induction mainly as a tool for explaining and designing high-level algorithms. We make little attempt to formalize or axiomize the approach. This has been done by several people, including Dijkstra [1976], Manna [1980], Gries [1981], Dershowitz [1983], and Paull [1988], among others. This book complements these other books. Our goal is mainly pedagogical, but of course whenever something can be explained better it is usually understood better. Among the proof techniques we discuss are strengthening the induction hypothesis, choosing the induction sequence wisely, double induction, and reverse induction. The significance of our approach is two-fold. First, we collect seemingly different techniques of algorithm design under one umbrella; second, we utilize known mathematical proof techniques for algorithm design. The latter is especially important, since it opens the door to the use of powerful techniques that have been developed for many years in another discipline.

One notable weakness of this approach is that it is not a universal approach. Not all algorithms can or should be designed with induction in mind. However, the principle of induction is so prevalent in the design of algorithms that it is worthwhile to concentrate on it. The other principles are not ignored in this book. A common criticism of almost any new methodology is that, although it may present an interesting way to explain things that were already created, it is of no help in creating them. This is a valid criticism, since only the future will tell how effective a certain methodology is and how widely used it becomes. I strongly believe that induction is not only just another tool for explaining algorithms, but it is necessary in order to understand them. Personally, even though I had a good experience in developing algorithms without following this methodology, I found it helpful, and, at least in two cases, it led me to develop new algorithms more quickly (Manber and McVoy [1988], Manber and Myers [1989]).

Notation for Describing Algorithms

In addition to describing the algorithms through the creative process of their development, we also include pseudocodes for many algorithms. The purpose of including programs is to enhance the descriptions. We have not made a great effort to optimize the programs, and we do not recommend simply copying them. In some cases, we made a conscious decision not to include the most optimized version of the program, because it introduces additional complexity, which distracts from the main ideas of the algorithm. We sometimes do not explain in detail how we translate the algorithmic ideas into a program. Such translations sometimes are obvious and sometimes are not. The emphasis in this book, as we mentioned, is on the principles of algorithm design.

For the most part, we use a Pascal-like language (sometimes even pure Pascal). In many cases, we include high-level descriptions (such as ''insert into a table,'' or ''check whether the set is empty'') inside a Pascal code to make it more readable. One notable exception we make to the rules of Pascal is the use of **begin** and **end** to encompass blocks. We include these statements *only* at the beginning and end of the programs, and let the indentation separate the blocks. This convention saves space without causing ambiguities. We usually do not include precise declarations of variables and data types in cases where such declarations are clear (e.g., we may say that G is a *graph*, or that T is a *tree*).

Exercises

Exercises whose numbers are underlined have solutions at the back of the book. Exercises that are marked by a star are judged by the author to be substantially more difficult than other exercises.

The exercises in this chapter do not require any previous knowledge of algorithms. They address relatively simple problems for specific inputs. The reader is asked to find the answers by hand. The main purpose of these exercises is to illustrate the difficulty in dealing with a very large number of possibilities. In other words, one of the goals of these exercises is to cause frustration with straightforward methods. The problems given here will be discussed in the following chapters.

1.1   Write down the numbers 1 to 100 each on a separate card. Shuffle the cards and rearrange them in order again.

1.2   Write down the following 100 numbers each on a separate card and sort the cards. Think about the differences between this exercise and Exercise 1.1.

    32918 21192 11923 4233 88231 8312 11 72 971 8234 22238 49283 3295
    29347 3102 32883 20938 2930 16 823 9234 9236 29372 2218 9222 21202
    83721 9238 8221 30234 93920 81102 1011 18152 2831 29133 9229 10039
    9235 48395 2832 37927 73492 8402 48201 38024 2800 32155 2273 82930
    2221 3841 311 3022 38099 29920 28349 74212 7011 1823 903 2991 9335
    29123 28910 29281 3772 20012 70458 30572 38013 72032 28001 83835
    3017 92626 73825 29263 2017 262 8362 77302 8593 3826 9374 2001
    83261 48402 4845 79794 27271 39992 22836 444 2937 37201 37322
    49472 11329 2253

1.3   Consider the following list of numbers. Your job is to erase as few of those numbers as possible such that the remaining numbers appear in increasing order. For example, erasing everything except the first two numbers leaves an increasing sequence; erasing everything except for first, third, sixth, and eighth numbers, does the same (but fewer numbers are erased).

    9 44 32 12 7 42 34 92 35 37 41 8 20 27 83 64 61 28 39 93 29 17 13 14 55
    21 66 72 23 73 99 1 2 88 77 3 65 83 84 62 5 11 74 68 76 78 67 75 69 70 22
    71 24 25 26

1.4   Solve Exercise 1.3, such that the remaining numbers are in decreasing order.

1.5   Suppose that in a strange country there are five types of coins with denominations of 15, 23, 29, 41, and 67 (all cents). Find a combination of these coins to pay the sum of 18 dollars and 8 cents (1808 cents). You have enough coins of each type in your pocket.

1.6 The input is a list of pairs of integers given below. The meaning of a pair (x, y) is that x is waiting for an answer from y. When x is waiting, it cannot do anything else, and, in particular, it cannot answer any questions from others that may be waiting for it. The problem is to find a sequence of pairs $(x_1 x_2), (x_2 x_3), \cdots, (x_{k-1} x_k), (x_k x_1)$, for some $k > 1$ (any k will do). If such a sequence exists, then there is a **deadlock**. No one can proceed, since everyone is waiting for someone else.

You can use a pencil and a piece of paper, and make any kind of computation, involving numbers (e.g., comparisons, creating tables); however, you cannot draw any kind of a figure. (You may draw figures, unrelated to this particular input, to help you design a *general* method of solving such a problem.)

> 1 16, 2 21, 2 25, 2 22, 23 50, 23 47, 24 1, 25 10, 35 7, 36 45, 36 37, 38 42,
> 39 41, 12 37, 12 23, 12 3, 12 20, 14 25, 41 9, 42 3, 43 5, 43 22, 29 2, 30 48,
> 31 15, 32 17, 6 45, 6 1, 5 35, 5 20, 5 28, 5 11, 48 4, 48 10, 49 32, 7 31, 7 4,
> 5 33, 6 29, 6 12, 6 11, 6 3, 6 17, 45 27, 47 34, 48 20, 7 40, 7 34, 8 11, 9 19,
> 11 30, 11 4, 11 22, 11 25, 20 24, 21 23, 21 46, 22 47, 23 49, 3 39, 3 34, 4
> 14, 4 37, 5 42, 5 8, 15 2, 15 50, 15 4, 15 37, 16 13, 17 38, 18 28, 19 8, 26
> 15, 26 42, 27 18, 28 35, 13 36, 13 50, 13 34, 13 22, 29 34, 29 38, 29 30, 29
> 16, 44 33, 44 36, 44 7, 44 3, 44 32, 44 21, 33 9, 33 21, 33 35, 33 19, 33 41,
> 26 10, 26 44, 26 16, 26 39, 26 17

1.7 The input is the two-dimensional 15 by 15 table given in Fig. 1.1. The ith row and the ith column (for any i) correspond to the same *place*. Each entry in the table indicates the *direct distance* between the places in the corresponding row and column. The "-" symbol indicates that there is no direct link between the two places. The direct distance may not be the shortest distance. There may be a shorter path between two places going through a third place (or several places). For example, the shortest route between 1 and 6 is through 5 and 12. Find the shortest route between 1 and 15, between 4 and 3, and between 15 and 8.

1.8 Consider the table in Fig. 1.1. Find the shortest route between 5 and all other places.

1.9 Consider the graph shown in Fig. 1.2. Find a closed route along the edges of the graph which includes every vertex exactly once. (This graph corresponds to the edges of a dodecahedron; this puzzle was first described by the Irish mathematician Sir William R. Hamilton, and we discuss it further in Section 7.12.)

1.10 The following is a regular **maze problem,** with the exception that the maze is given in numeric representation (rather than a picture). The maze is contained in a rectangle with 11 rows and columns, numbered from 0 to 10. The maze is traversed along the rows and columns — up, down, right, or left. The starting point is 0,0 and the target is 10,10. The following points are obstacles you cannot traverse through:

> (3,2) (6,6) (7,0) (2,8) (5,9) (8,4) (2,4) (0,8) (1,3) (6,3) (9,3) (1,9) (3,0) (3,7)
> (4,2) (7,8) (2,2) (4,5) (5,6) (10,5) (6,2) (6,10) (4,0) (7,5) (7,9) (8,1) (5,7)
> (4,4) (8,7) (9,2) (10,9) (2,6)

a. Find a path from the starting point to the target that does not include any of the obstacles.

b. Find a *shortest* path from the starting point to the target that does not include any of the obstacles.

	1	2	3	4	5	6	7	8	9	10	11	12	13	14	15
1	0	2	3	-	1	9	6	2	1	7	4	2	8	3	-
2	7	0	2	-	-	-	-	2	1	6	9	1	7	2	8
3	8	-	0	8	9	3	6	8	5	7	-	8	-	3	-
4	-	8	-	0	-	5	4	-	-	1	1	9	-	8	-
5	9	-	8	-	0	3	2	7	5	8	-	1	-	4	2
6	3	2	-	3	6	0	5	3	2	-	8	7	2	-	8
7	2	-	-	2	8	-	0	6	2	-	8	8	2	-	4
8	1	1	-	-	2	3	8	0	-	1	1	-	2	7	-
9	4	-	9	-	2	9	-	2	0	4	9	3	-	-	-
10	-	-	-	-	1	8	-	7	1	0	3	-	-	-	2
11	3	8	7	1	-	-	3	8	-	-	0	2	9	2	1
12	3	-	1	2	8	1	1	-	5	1	9	0	2	-	9
13	7	-	3	1	6	-	-	2	-	3	-	9	0	2	-
14	2	9	6	-	7	-	9	-	3	-	1	1	9	0	-
15	2	9	2	1	-	-	1	-	4	3	6	5	1	-	0

Figure 1.1 The table for Exercises 1.7 and 1.8.

1.11 Find the **greatest common divisor** of 225277 and 178794. (The greatest common divisor of two integers is the largest number that divides both of them.)

1.12 Compute the value of 2^{64}. Try to find a way to minimize the number of multiplications.

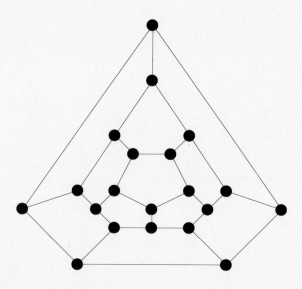

Figure 1.2 Hamilton's puzzle.

1.13   The following list represents the number of electoral votes for each state in the 1988 Presidential election (the candidate receiving the majority of the votes in a state collects all the electoral votes for that state). There are altogether 538 electoral votes. Determine whether it is (mathematically) possible for the election to end up in a tie. (This problem is known as the **partition problem**, and it is a special case of the **knapsack problem** discussed in Section 5.10.)

Alabama	9	Alaska	3	Arizona	7
Arkansas	6	California	47	Colorado	8
Connecticut	8	Delaware	3	Florida	21
Georgia	12	Hawaii	4	Idaho	4
Illinois	24	Indiana	12	Iowa	8
Kansas	7	Kentucky	9	Louisiana	10
Maine	4	Maryland	10	Massachusetts	13
Michigan	20	Minnesota	10	Mississippi	7
Missouri	11	Montana	4	Nebraska	5
Nevada	4	New Hampshire	4	New Jersey	16
New Mexico	5	New York	36	North Carolina	13
North Dakota	3	Ohio	23	Oklahoma	8
Oregon	7	Pennsylvania	25	Rhode Island	4
South Carolina	8	South Dakota	3	Tennessee	11
Texas	29	Utah	5	Vermont	3
Virginia	12	Washington	10	Washington, D.C.	3
West Virginia	6	Wisconsin	11	Wyoming	3

CHAPTER 2

MATHEMATICAL INDUCTION

No one believes an hypothesis except its originator, but everyone believes an experiment except the experimenter.

Anon

Obviousness is always the enemy of correctness.

Bertrand Russell (1872–1970)

2.1 Introduction

We will see in the following chapters that induction plays a major role in algorithm design. In this chapter, we present a brief introduction to mathematical induction through examples. The examples range from easy to quite difficult. Readers who have not seen many induction proofs may find this chapter to be relatively hard. We claim that the processes of constructing proofs and constructing algorithms are similar, and thus experience with induction proofs is very helpful.

Mathematical induction is a very powerful proof technique. It usually works as follows. Let T be a theorem that we want to prove. Suppose that T includes a parameter n whose value can be any natural number (a natural number is a positive integer). Instead of proving directly that T holds for all values of n, we prove the following two conditions:

1. T holds for $n = 1$

2. For every $n > 1$, if T holds for $n - 1$, then T holds for n

The reason these two conditions are sufficient is clear. Conditions 1 and 2 imply directly that T holds for $n = 2$. If T holds for $n = 2$, then condition 2 implies that T holds for $n = 3$, and so on. The induction principle itself is so basic that it is usually not proved; rather, it

9

is stated as an **axiom** in the definition of the natural numbers.

Condition 1 is usually simple to prove. Proving condition 2 is easier in many cases than proving the theorem directly, since we can use the assumption that T holds for $n-1$. This assumption is called the **induction hypothesis**. In some sense, we get the induction hypothesis for free. It is enough to *reduce* the theorem to one with smaller value of n, rather than proving it from scratch. We concentrate on this reduction. Let's start right away with an example.

□ Theorem 2.1

For all natural numbers x and n, $x^n - 1$ is divisible by $x - 1$.

Proof: The proof is by induction on n. The theorem is trivially true for $n=1$. We assume that the theorem is true for $n-1$; namely, we assume that $x^{n-1} - 1$ is divisible by $x-1$ for all natural numbers x. We now have to prove that $x^n - 1$ is divisible by $x-1$. The idea is to try to write the expression $x^n - 1$ using $x^{n-1} - 1$, which, by the induction hypothesis, is divisible by $x-1$:

$$x^n - 1 = x(x^{n-1} - 1) + (x-1).$$

But the left term is divisible by $x-1$ by the induction hypothesis, and the right term is just $x-1$. □

The induction principle is thus defined as follows:

If a statement P, with a parameter n, is true for $n=1$, and if, for every $n > 1$, the truth of P for $n-1$ implies its truth for n, then P is true for all natural numbers.

Instead of using $n-1$ and n, we sometimes use n and $n+1$, which is completely equivalent:

If a statement P, with a parameter n, is true for $n=1$, and if, for every $n \geq 1$, the truth of P for n implies its truth for $n+1$, then P is true for all natural numbers.

The proof of Theorem 2.1 illustrates a simple application of induction. Over the years, many variations of induction have been developed. For example, the following variation, called **strong induction**, is very common.

If a statement P, with a parameter n, is true for $n=1$, and if, for every $n > 1$, the truth of P for all natural numbers $< n$ implies its truth for n, then P is true for all natural numbers.

The difference is that we can use the assumption that the statement is true for all numbers $< n$ in proving the statement for n. In many cases, this stronger assumption can be very useful. Another simple variation is the following:

If a statement P, with a parameter n, is true for n = 1 and for n = 2, and if, for every n > 2, the truth of P for n − 2 implies its truth for n, then P is true for all natural numbers.

This variation "works" in two parallel tracks. The base case for $n = 1$ and the induction step imply P for all odd numbers; the base case for $n = 2$ and the induction step imply P for all even numbers. Another common variation is the following:

If a statement P, with a parameter n, is true for n = 1, and if, for every n > 1, such that n is an integer power of 2, the truth of P for n/2 implies its truth for n, then P is true for all natural numbers that are integer powers of 2.

This variation follows from the first one by writing the parameter n as 2^k, and carrying out the induction for the parameter k (starting from $k = 0$).

Induction can also be used in many different ways to prove properties of structures other than numbers. In most cases, the induction is on some number n that measures the size of the instance of the problem. Finding the right measure to which the induction should be applied is not straightforward. (For example, we could have applied induction to x in the previous example, rather than to n; this would have made the proof much more complicated.) Sometimes, this measure is not natural, and it has to be invented just for the purpose of the induction. The common thread to all these proofs is the *extension* of claims for smaller structures to claims for larger structures.

2.2 Three Simple Examples

The problem is to find the expression for the sum of the first n natural numbers $S(n) = 1 + 2 + \cdots + n$. We prove the following theorem.

□ Theorem 2.2

The sum of the first n natural numbers is n(n + 1)/2.

Proof: The proof is by induction on n. If $n = 1$, then the claim is true because $S(1) = 1 = 1 \cdot (1 + 1)/2$. We now assume that the sum of the first n natural numbers $S(n)$ is $n(n + 1)/2$, and prove that this assumption implies that the sum of the first $n + 1$ natural numbers is $S(n + 1) = (n + 1)(n + 2)/2$. We know from the definition of $S(n)$ that $S(n + 1) = S(n) + n + 1$. But, by the assumption, $S(n) = n(n + 1)/2$, and therefore $S(n + 1) = n(n + 1)/2 + n + 1 = (n + 2)(n + 1)/2$, which is exactly what we wanted to prove. □

We continue with a slightly more complicated sum. Suppose that we want to compute the sum $T(n) = 8 + 13 + 18 + 23 + \cdots + (3 + 5n)$. The sum in the previous example, $S(n)$, is equal to $n^2/2 + n/2$. Each of the elements in the current example is slightly more than five times the corresponding element in the previous example. Hence, it is reasonable to guess that $T(n)$ is also a quadratic expression. Let's try the implicit guess $G(n) = c_1 n^2 + c_2 n + c_3$. That is, we introduce the parameters c_1, c_2, and c_3, and determine their values when it is convenient to do so. For example, we can determine the parameters by checking the first few terms. If $n=0$, the sum is 0, so c_3 must be 0. For $n=1$ and $n=2$, we get the following two equations:

(1) $1 \cdot c_1 + 1 \cdot c_2 = 8$

(2) $4 \cdot c_1 + 2 \cdot c_2 = 13 + 8$

If we multiply (1) by 2 and subtract it from (2), we get $2c_1 = 5$, which implies that $c_1 = 2.5$, and $c_2 = 5.5$. We therefore guess that $G(n) = 2.5n^2 + 5.5n$ is the right expression. We now try to prove that $G(n) = T(n)$ by induction. We have already verified a base case. We assume that $G(n) = T(n)$, and we try to prove that $G(n+1) = T(n+1)$:

$$T(n+1) = T(n) + 5(n+1) + 3 = \text{(by induction) } G(n) + 5(n+1) + 3$$

$$= 2.5n^2 + 5.5n + 5n + 8 = 2.5n^2 + 5n + 2.5 + 5.5n + 5.5$$

$$= 2.5(n+1)^2 + 5.5(n+1) = G(n+1).$$

We have proved the following theorem.

□ **Theorem 2.3**

The sum of the series

$$8 + 13 + 18 + 23 + \cdots + (3 + 5n)$$

is $2.5n^2 + 5.5n$.   □

We end this section with another simple example.

□ **Theorem 2.4**

If n is a natural number and $1 + x > 0$, then

$$(1 + x)^n \geq 1 + nx. \tag{2.1}$$

Proof: The proof is by induction on n. If $n = 1$, then both sides of (2.1) are equal to $1 + x$. We assume that $(1+x)^n \geq 1 + nx$ for all x such that $1 + x > 0$, and consider the case of $n + 1$. We have to prove that $(1+x)^{n+1} \geq 1 + (n+1)x$, for all x such that $1 + x > 0$:

$$(1+x)^{n+1} = (1+x)(1+x)^n \geq \text{(by induction) } (1+x)(1+nx)$$

$$= 1 + (n+1)x + nx^2 \geq 1 + (n+1)x.$$

Notice that we were able to multiply the inequality (implied by the induction) by $(1+x)$ because of the assumption that $1 + x > 0$. The last step was possible because nx^2 is clearly nonnegative.   □

2.3 Counting Regions in the Plane

A set of lines in the plane is said to be in **general position** if no two lines are parallel and no three lines intersect at a common point. The next problem is to compute the number of regions in the plane formed by n lines in general position. Good hints for the right guess can be obtained from small cases. When $n = 1$, there are 2. Two intersecting lines form 4 regions; three lines that do not intersect at a point form 7 regions. It seems, at least for $i \leq 3$, that the ith line adds i regions. If this is true for all i, then the number of regions can be easily computed from $S(n)$, which was computed in the previous section. Therefore, we concentrate on the growth of the number of regions when one more line is added. The claim we are trying to prove is the following:

> **Guess**: *Adding one more line to $n - 1$ lines in general position in the plane increases the number of regions by n.*

As we have already seen, the guess is true for $n \leq 3$. We can now use the guess as our induction hypothesis, and try to prove that adding one line to n lines in general position increases the number of regions by $n + 1$. Notice that the hypothesis does not deal directly with the number of regions, but rather with the growth of the number of regions when one line is added. Even if the hypothesis is true, we will still need to compute the total number of regions, but this part will be straightforward.

How can a new line increase the number of regions? Consider Fig. 2.1. Since all lines are in general position, a line cannot just touch a region at the border; it can either cut a region into two parts (in which case one more region is formed), or be disjoint from it. Consequently, we need only to prove that the $(n + 1)$th line intersects exactly $n + 1$ existing regions. It is possible to prove the theorem directly at this point, but we want to illustrate another technique of induction proofs. Let's remove for the moment the nth line. By the induction hypothesis, without the nth line, the $(n + 1)$th line is adding n new regions. Thus, we need only to prove that the presence of the nth line causes the $(n + 1)$th line to add one additional region. Let's put the nth line back. Since all lines are in general position, the nth and $(n + 1)$th lines intersect at a point p, which must be inside a

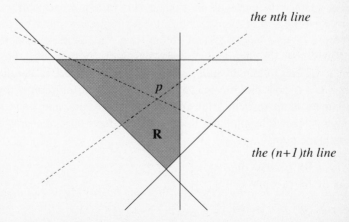

Figure 2.1 $n + 1$ lines in general position.

region R. Both lines thus intersect R. Each line separately cuts R into two pieces, but together they cut R into four pieces! So, the addition of the $(n+1)$th line, when the nth line is *not* present, cuts R into two regions. But, the addition of the $(n+1)$th line, when the nth line is present, affects R by adding two more regions (R is cut from two to four regions) instead of just adding one. Furthermore, R is the only region so affected, since the two lines meet at only one point. Hence, the $n+1$th line adds n regions without the presence of the nth line, but it adds $n+1$ regions with the nth line, and the proof is complete.

□ Theorem 2.5

The number of regions in the plane formed by n lines in general position is
$n(n+1)/2+1.$

Proof: We have already proved that the nth line adds n more regions. The first line introduces two regions; hence, the total number of regions (for $n>1$) is $2+2+3+4+5+ \cdots +n$. We have seen in the previous section that $1+2+3+ \cdots +n=n(n+1)/2$; therefore, the total number of regions is $n(n+1)/2+1.$ □

Comments   There are two interesting points in this proof. First, the hypothesis dealt with the growth of the function we were after, rather than directly with the function. As a result, the induction proof concentrated on the growth of the growth of the function. There is no need to define the hypothesis such that it proves the theorem directly. We can achieve the proof in two or more steps. As long as we are learning more about the situation, we are making progress. There is no need to hurry, or to attempt too much too quickly. Patience usually pays. Second, the same induction hypothesis was used twice in two different configurations: once for the nth line and once for the $(n+1)$th line "acting" as an nth line. This double use is not uncommon, and the lesson it teaches is that we should utilize our assumptions to their fullest.

2.4 A Simple Coloring Problem

Consider again n distinct lines in a plane, this time not necessarily in general position. We are interested in assigning colors to the regions formed by these lines such that neighboring regions have different colors (two regions are considered neighbors if and only if they have an edge in common). We will say that "it is possible to color" the regions if we can follow this rule, and we call the assignment of colors a *valid coloring*. In general, it is possible to color any planar map with four colors (the proof of this fact has occupied mathematicians for about a hundred years, and was found only recently). The regions formed by (infinite) lines, however, have special characteristics, as is shown in the next theorem.

□ Theorem 2.6

It is possible to color the regions formed by any number of lines in the plane with only two colors.

Proof: We use the natural induction hypothesis.

Induction hypothesis: *It is possible to color the regions formed by $< n$ lines in the plane with only two colors.*

It is clear that two colors are necessary and sufficient for $n = 1$. Assume the induction hypothesis, and consider n lines. Again, the only question is how to modify the coloring when the nth line is added. Divide the regions into two groups according to which side of the nth line they lie. Leave all regions on one side colored the same as before, and reverse the colors of all regions on the other side. To prove that this is a valid coloring, we consider two neighboring regions R_1 and R_2. If both are on the same side of the nth line, then they were colored differently before the line was added (by the induction hypothesis). They may have the reverse colors, but they are still different. If the edge between them is part of the nth line, then they belonged to the same region before the line was added. Since the color of one region was reversed, they are now colored differently.

$\square$

Comments   The general method illustrated in this example is the search for flexibility, or for more degrees of freedom. The idea is usually to stretch the hypothesis as much as possible in order to get the most out of it. In this case, the key idea was that, given a valid coloring, we can reverse all colors and still have a valid coloring. This idea was used to handle the formation of new regions by the added line.

2.5 A More Complicated Summation Problem

The next example is more complicated. Consider the following triangle.

$$
\begin{array}{rcccccccl}
1 & & & & & & & = & 1 \\
3 & + & 5 & & & & & = & 8 \\
7 & + & 9 & + & 11 & & & = & 27 \\
13 & + & 15 & + & 17 & + & 19 & = & 64 \\
21 & + & 23 & + & 25 & + & 27 & + & 29 & = & 125
\end{array}
$$

The problem is to find an expression for the sum of the ith row, and prove its correctness.

The sums of the rows seem to follow a regular pattern; They look like a sequence of cubes.

Induction hypothesis: *The sum of row i in the triangle is i^3.*

The problem and the hypothesis are defined in terms of a picture. It is not easy to define the problem precisely, let alone to solve it. In practice, it is not uncommon for problems to be vaguely defined. A major part of any solution is to extract the right problem. Therefore, we will make some assumptions that are consistent with the picture, and solve the problem accordingly. (It is possible to make other assumptions.) The ith row contains i numbers. The numbers are the odd numbers in order. Again, let's concentrate on the difference between two consecutive rows. To prove that the sum of row i is indeed i^3, we need only to show that the difference between row $i+1$ and row i is $(i+1)^3 - i^3$ (we have already seen that the hypothesis is true for $i \leq 4$).

What is the difference between the first number in row $i+1$ and the first number in row i? Since the numbers are the odd numbers in order and there are i of them in row i, the difference is $2i$. This is also the difference between the second number in row $i+1$ and the second number in row i, the third number, the fourth number, and so on. Overall, there are i differences, each of size $2i$. There is also the last element at the end of row $i+1$, which is not matched to any number in the previous row. Hence, the difference between the two rows is $2i^2$ plus the value of the last number in row $i+1$. Since $(i+1)^3 - i^3 = 3i^2 + 3i + 1$, we need only to prove that the value of the last number in row $i+1$ is $3i^2 + 3i + 1 - 2i^2 = i^2 + 3i + 1$. This is where the guess that the sum is i^3 comes to play. We have reduced the problem of finding the sum to a problem of finding an element. We prove the last statement again by induction.

Nested induction hypothesis: *The last number in row $i + 1$ is $i^2 + 3i + 1$.*

The claim is true for $i = 1$. Now, it is sufficient, by induction, to check only the differences. That is, we have to prove that the difference between the last number in row $i+1$ and the last number in row i is equal to

$$[\,i^2 + 3i + 1\,] - [\,(i-1)^2 + 3(i-1) + 1\,] = 2i + 2.$$

But we already know that the difference between any corresponding numbers in row $i+1$ and i is $2i$. The guess has thus been established.

Comments This proof illustrates again that we should not always try to achieve the whole proof in one step. It is a good policy to advance in stages, as long as we are making progress. This proof also illustrates the method of ''going backward'' to arrive at a proof. Instead of starting from a simpler problem and working our way toward the final problem, we start with the final problem and simplify it by reducing it to simpler and simpler problems. This is a very common method (not only in mathematics).

2.6 A Simple Inequality

In this section, we prove the following inequality.

□ Theorem 2.7

$$\frac{1}{2} + \frac{1}{4} + \frac{1}{8} + \cdots + \frac{1}{2^n} < 1, \tag{2.2}$$

for all $n \geq 1$.[1]

Proof: We want to prove the theorem by induction. The theorem is clearly true for $n = 1$. We assume that (2.2) is true for n, and we consider $n + 1$. The only information we get from the induction hypothesis is that the sum of the first n terms is

---

[1]This inequality is usually written as a fact about convergence of infinite series, but we do not assume any knowledge of series; this formulation is completely finite.

less than 1. How can we extend it to include the $n+1$th term? Adding $1/2^{n+1}$ to the left hand side may potentially increase the sum to more than 1. The trick here is to apply the induction in a different order. Given the sum

$$\frac{1}{2} + \frac{1}{4} + \frac{1}{8} + \cdots + \frac{1}{2^n} + \frac{1}{2^{n+1}},$$

we look at the *last n* terms:

$$\frac{1}{4} + \frac{1}{8} + \cdots + \frac{1}{2^n} + \frac{1}{2^{n+1}} = \frac{1}{2}\left[\frac{1}{2} + \frac{1}{4} + \frac{1}{8} + \cdots + \frac{1}{2^n}\right] < \frac{1}{2}$$

by the induction hypothesis. But now we can add 1/2 to both sides and get the expression (2.2) for $n+1$. □

Comments   It is not necessary to consider the last element as the $(n+1)$th element in the induction proof. Sometimes it is easier to consider the first element. There are other instances where it is better to let the $(n+1)$th element be a special element satisfying some special properties. If you run into problems, be flexible, and consider as many options as you can. The following examples extend this notion further.

2.7 Euler´s Formula

The next proof is for a theorem known as **Euler's Formula**. Consider a connected planar map with V vertices, E edges, and F faces. (A face is an enclosed region. The outside region is counted as one face, so, for example, a square has four vertices four edges and two faces.) The map in Fig. 2.2 has 11 vertices, 19 edges, and 10 faces. Two vertices of a map are said to be **connected** if it is possible to go from one vertex to the other by traversing edges of the map. A map is called connected if every two vertices in it are connected. Intuitively, a map is connected if it consists of one part.

□ Theorem 2.8

The number of vertices (V), edges (E), and faces (F) in an arbitrary connected planar map are related by the formula V + F = E + 2.

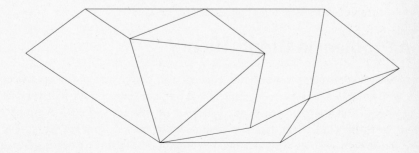

Figure 2.2   A planar map with 11 vertices, 19 edges, and 10 faces.

Proof: We will prove this theorem by a variation of induction known as **double induction**. The induction proceeds first on the number of vertices and then on the number of faces.

Consider first a map with only one face. Such a map does not contain a cycle because, otherwise, the cycle would form at least one face and the outside would form another face. A connected map without a cycle is called a **tree**. We first prove that, for all trees, $V + 1 = E + 2$.

First induction hypothesis: *A tree with n vertices has n − 1 edges.*

The base case is trivial. Assume that trees with n vertices have $n − 1$ edges, and consider trees with $n + 1$ vertices. There must be at least one vertex v connected to only one edge. Otherwise, if all vertices are connected to at least two edges and if we traverse the tree along the edge, starting from any vertex, then we are guaranteed to return to a vertex already visited without getting stuck. But this means that there is a cycle, which is a contradiction. We can remove the vertex v along with the edge connected to it. The resulting map is still connected; thus, it is still a tree. But it has one less vertex and one less edge, which implies the claim.

This serves as a base case for an induction on the number of faces.

Main induction hypothesis: *Any planar map with n faces has E edges and V vertices such that $V + n = E + 2$.*

Consider a map with $n + 1$ faces. It must have a face f, which is a neighbor of the outside face. Since f is a face, it is surrounded by a cycle. Removing one edge of this cycle will not disconnect the map. We remove one of the edges that separates f from the outside. We now have one less face and one less edge and the theorem follows.   □

Comments   This theorem included three parameters. The proof used induction on one parameter (the number of faces), but the base case required another induction on another parameter (the number of vertices). The proof shows that we have to be careful about choosing the right sequence of induction. Sometimes, the induction switches from one parameter to another; sometimes, it is based on a combined value of several parameters; and sometimes, it is applied to two different parameters at the same time. Choosing the right sequence can make a big difference in the difficulty of the proof. As we will see in the following chapters, choosing the right sequence of induction can also make a big difference in efficiency of algorithms.

2.8 A Problem in Graph Theory

We first need to introduce some basic concepts of graph theory (these concepts are discussed in detail in Chapter 7). A graph $G = (V, E)$ consists of a set V of **vertices** and a set E of **edges**. Each edge corresponds to a pair of distinct vertices. A graph can be **directed** or **undirected**. The edges in a directed graph are ordered pairs: The order between the two vertices the edge connects is important. In this case, we draw an edge as an arrow pointing from one vertex (the tail) to another (the head). The edges in an undirected graph are unordered pairs. We deal with directed graphs in this section. The **degree** of a vertex v is the number of edges incident to v. A **path** is a sequence of vertices $v_1, v_2, ..., v_k$ that are connected by the edges $(v_1, v_2), (v_2, v_3), ..., (v_{k-1}, v_k)$ (these edges are also usually considered to be part of the path). Vertex u is said to be **reachable** from vertex v if there is a path from v to u. Let $G = (V, E)$ be a graph, and U a set of vertices $U \subseteq V$. The **subgraph induced by U** is a subgraph $H = (U, F)$ such that F consists of all the edges in E both of whose vertices belong to U. An **independent set** S in a graph $G = (V, E)$ is a set of vertices such that no two vertices in S are adjacent.

□ Theorem 2.9

Let $G = (V, E)$ be a directed graph. There exists an independent set $S(G)$ in G such that every vertex in G can be reached from a vertex in $S(G)$ by a path of length at most 2.

Proof: The proof is by induction on the number of vertices.

Induction hypothesis: *The theorem is true for all directed graphs with $< n$ vertices.*

The theorem is trivial for $n \leq 3$. Let v be an arbitrary vertex in V. Let $N(v) = \{v\} \cup \{w \in V \mid (v, w) \in E\}$. $N(v)$ is the **neighborhood** of v. The graph H induced by the set of vertices $V - N(v)$ has fewer vertices than does G; thus, we can use the induction hypothesis for H. Let $S(H)$ be the independent set of H implied by the induction hypothesis. There are two cases.

1. $S(H) \cup \{v\}$ is independent. In this case, we can set $S(G)$ to be $S(H) \cup \{v\}$, because every vertex in $N(v)$ is reachable from v with distance 1. The vertices not in $N(v)$ are reachable from a vertex in $S(H)$ with distance at most 2 by the induction hypothesis.

2. $S(H) \cup \{v\}$ is not independent. In this case, there must be a vertex $w \in S(H)$ that is adjacent to v. Now, $w \in S(H)$ implies that $w \in V - N(v)$, which implies that (v, w) is not an edge of G. But, since we assumed that w is adjacent to v, (w, v) must be an edge of G. In that case, however, every vertex in $N(v)$ can be reached from w (through v) with distance at most 2. We can set $S(G)$ to be $S(H) \cup \{w\}$, which completes the proof.   □

Comments   The amount of ''reduction'' in this proof was not fixed. That is, we reduced the size of the problem from n to a smaller number *depending on the instance of the problem*. Furthermore, the smaller problem was not an arbitrary problem of smaller size. It depended heavily on the particular larger problem. We removed just enough vertices to make the proof feasible. There is a very fine balance in such proofs between removing too many vertices, in which case the hypothesis is too weak, and removing too few vertices, in which case the hypothesis is too strong. Finding this balance is, in many cases, the heart of the induction proof. Notice also that we used the strong induction principle, because it was required to assume the theorem for all instances of smaller size.

2.9 Gray Codes

We are given a set of n objects and we want to name them. Each name is represented by a unique string of bits. There may be many different objectives for a "good" naming scheme. We deal with only one objective in this example. We would like to arrange the names in a circular list such that each name can be obtained from the previous name by changing exactly one bit. Such a scheme is called a **Gray code**.[2] There are several applications of Gray codes. For example, a sensor may scan some objects. It is better to be able to change representations quickly from one object to the next. The purpose of this section is to find out whether it is possible to construct a Gray code for any number of objects. The objects themselves play no part in the problem; we care only about their number.

A good way to visualize the relationship between the names is by using graphs. The names correspond to the vertices of the graph, and two names are connected if they differ by only one bit. A Gray code corresponds to a cycle containing all the vertices.

We start by trying small values of n. The cases of $n = 1$ and $n = 2$ are trivial. What about $n = 3$? It is not hard to see that it is impossible to find a Gray code of length 3. If we start with any string and change one bit twice, we either get the same string or another string with a two-bit difference; we cannot get the same string after three changes. In fact, this observation implies that it is impossible to construct a Gray code of any odd length. What about $n = 4$? The following is a Gray code of length 4: 00, 01, 11, 10. The corresponding graph is of course a square. We are now ready for our first attempt.

□ Theorem 2.10

There exists a Gray code of length 2k for any positive integer k.

Proof: The proof is by induction on k. The case of $k = 1$ is trivial. Assume that there exists a Gray code of size $2k$ and consider $2(k + 1)$. Let $s_1, s_2, ..., s_{2k}$ correspond to a Gray code of size $2k$. Clearly, if we add a leading 0 or a leading 1 to all the strings, the result is still a Gray code. The following is thus a Gray code of size $2k + 2$ (see Fig. 2.3):

$$0s_1, \ 1s_1, \ 1s_2, \ 0s_2, \ 0s_3, \ 0s_4, \ ..., \ 0s_{2k}. \qquad \square$$

Although the proof is complete, the construction is not very satisfactory. The length of each string in the code is at least one-half of the number of objects. In general, it is possible to represent n objects with $\lceil \log_2 n \rceil$ bits. Can we construct Gray codes of size n with fewer than $n/2$ bits? To achieve a logarithmic number of bits, we need to add one bit whenever the number of objects is doubled. Let's assume that we know how to construct Gray codes for all even numbers $2k$, such that $k < n$. Given $2n$ objects, we try to construct the code from two smaller codes each of size n.

We immediately run into a problem. Although $2n$ is even, and thus there is a Gray code of that size, n may be odd, and there is no odd-size Gray code. Consequently, we

---

[2] Gray codes usually refer to the case where the number of objects is a power of 2. We use it for all values of n.

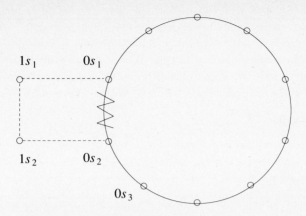

Figure 2.3 Constructing a Gray code of size $2k$.

may not be able to use the induction hypothesis whenever n is odd. Let's restrict ourselves to values of n that are powers of 2. We assume that we know how to construct short (we will see later how short) Gray codes for all powers of 2 less than n, and consider n. Let $s_1, s_2, ..., s_{n/2}$ correspond to a Gray code of size $n/2$. We can again add leading 0s or 1s, such that the two sequences $0s_1, 0s_2, ..., 0s_{n/2}$, and $1s_1, 1s_2, ..., 1s_{n/2}$ also correspond to Gray codes. We can then merge these two sequences into one in the following way (see Fig. 2.4):

$$1s_2, 0s_2, 0s_3, ..., 0s_{n/2}, 0s_1, 1s_1, 1s_{n/2}, 1s_{n/2-1}, ..., 1s_2.$$

For example, we can extend the Gray code for $n=4$ to a Gray code for $n=8$ as follows. The two sequences are 000, 001, 011, 010, and 100, 101, 111, 110. The combined sequence is 101, 001, 011, 010, 000, 100, 110, 111. We constructed a Gray code for n with only one more bit than we used for the Gray code for $n/2$. Hence, the length of each string will be $\log_2 n$.

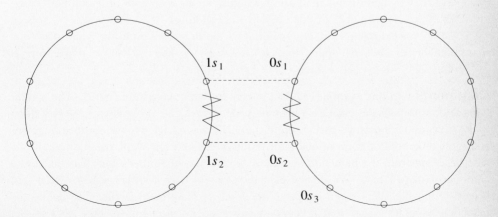

Figure 2.4 Constructing a Gray code from two smaller ones.

How do we extend this construction to any even value of n? Recall that the problem with constructing odd Gray codes was that it was impossible to close the cycle. Looking back at Fig. 2.4, we can see that it is not necessary to have two closed cycles; it is sufficient to have two open sequences. If we can construct an *open* Gray code (namely, one with exactly two names that differ by more than one bit) of odd length, then it may be sufficient for the general construction. We now have two cases.

□ Theorem 2.11

There exist Gray codes of length $\lceil \log_2 k \rceil$ for any positive integer k. The Gray codes for the even values of k are closed, and the Gray codes for odd values of k are open.

Proof: We prove both cases with one *stronger* induction hypothesis.

Induction hypothesis: *There exist Gray codes of length $\lceil \log_2 k \rceil$ for all values $k < n$. If k is even, then the code is closed; if k is odd, then the code is open.*

The base of the induction is trivial. We now construct a Gray code of size n. There are two cases:

1. n is even: The reduction in this case is similar to the reduction for the case where n was a power of 2. By the induction hypothesis, there exists a Gray code of length $n/2$ (either open or closed). We can construct two copies of this code, one with leading 0s and one with leading 1s, and connect them into a cycle (as in Fig. 2.4). Also by the induction hypothesis, the number of bits in the smaller codes is $\lceil \log_2(n/2) \rceil$. We add one bit and double the number of objects; thus, the number of bits for the new code is $\lceil \log_2(n/2) \rceil + 1 = \lceil \log_2 n \rceil$.

2. n is odd: Let $n = 2k + 1$. Construct two Gray codes of size k, and connect them in the same way as before. If $2k$ is not a power of 2, then there are some strings of length $\lceil \log_2(2k) \rceil$, which have not been used as names. One of these strings is connected to one of the strings that has been used. We can now break the cycle of length $2k$ by adding this new string, resulting in an open path of length $2k + 1$ (see Fig. 2.5). The number of bits satisfies the condition. If $2k$ is a power of 2, there are no unused strings left, and we need to add one more bit to the code. The total number of bits is thus $\lceil \log_2(2k) \rceil + 1$. But since $2k$ is a power of 2, $\lceil \log_2(2k) \rceil = \log_2(2k)$, and $\log_2(2k) + 1 = \lceil \log_2(2k + 1) \rceil$.   □

Comments   In this example, we had a theorem with two distinct cases. The natural thing to do is to consider each case separately. However, this is not always the best thing to do. Even though the two cases were different, it was easier to consider them together and to include both of them in one induction hypothesis. This way, the solution of one case benefited from the induction hypothesis concerning the other case. It is much like climbing with two feet. We do not plan the steps of each foot separately. Each foot benefits from the steps taken by the other foot. It is sometimes better to define the induction hypothesis such that it covers a more general problem. In this example, the generalized problem merely included two cases. In the next section, we present an

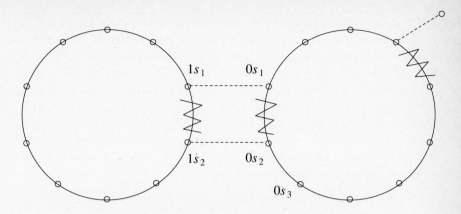

Figure 2.5 Constructing an open Gray code.

example where it is easier to solve the problem by solving an extended problem dealing with more general structures. The advantage to working on a more general problem is that the induction hypothesis is stronger and can be used more effectively. There is an obvious tradeoff. We need to prove the induction statement for $n+1$ assuming that the statement for n is correct. If the statement for n is stronger, then it is easier to use it in the proof. But, on the other hand, there is more to prove. We discuss this issue further in the next section and in Section 5.10. Notice also that we included in the hypothesis *all* values less than $2n$, rather than just $2n-2$.

2.10 Finding Edge-Disjoint Paths in a Graph

Let $G=(V, E)$ be a connected undirected graph. Two paths in G are said to be **edge disjoint**, if they do not contain the same edge. Let O be the set of vertices in V with odd degrees. We first claim that the number of vertices in O is even. To prove this claim, we notice that, by summing up the degrees of all vertices, we get exactly twice the number of edges (since each edge is counted twice). But, since all vertices of even degree contribute an even number to this sum, there must be an even number of vertices of odd degree. We now prove the following theorem.

□ Theorem 2.12

Let $G=(V, E)$ be a connected undirected graph, and let O be the set of vertices with odd degrees. We can divide the vertices in O into pairs and find edge-disjoint paths connecting vertices in each pair.

Proof: The proof is by induction on the number of edges. The theorem is clearly true for $m=1$.

Induction hypothesis: *The theorem is true for all connected undirected graphs with $< m$ edges.*

Consider a connected undirected graph G with m edges, and let O be the set of odd vertices. If O is empty, then the theorem is trivially true. Otherwise, take any two vertices in O. Since G is connected, there is a path connecting them. Remove the whole path from G. The remaining graph has fewer edges. We would like to use the induction hypothesis, to find the paths for the rest of the odd vertices, and to complete the proof. The problem, however, is that, by removing the path, we may have disconnected the graph. The induction hypothesis applied only to connected graphs. We have to be very careful about using the induction hypothesis correctly. We can avoid this difficulty in this case in an ingenious way — we will change the hypothesis and adapt it to our needs!

The problem we encountered was with the connectivity requirement. Let's remove it. We now have the following induction hypothesis:

> **Revised induction hypothesis**: *The theorem is true for all undirected graphs having $< m$ edges.*

This is obviously a stronger theorem. Its proof, on the other hand, is simpler. Consider again an undirected graph with m edges, and O as before. The graph may not be connected. In this case, the graph is partitioned into several connected **components**. We will take two odd vertices *from the same component*. Since each component is a connected graph by itself, it must have an even number of odd vertices. Hence, if there are any odd vertices, we can find two of them in the same component. So now we are basically done. Since the two chosen vertices are in the same component, we can connect them by a path. We then remove the path. The graph has now less than m edges, and we can use the induction hypothesis because it does not require connectivity. Thus, in the remaining graph, we can pair the odd vertices in edge disjoint paths. We can then add the path we removed and complete the proof.

We actually proved a stronger theorem than the one we sought! We proved that the connectivity requirement is unnecessary. And the proof was easier.   □

Comments   This is an example of a very powerful technique we call **strengthening the induction hypothesis**. It is similar in some sense to the method used in the previous section. The main trick is to change the hypothesis to fit our needs. Even though the theorem becomes stronger, the proof may be easier to obtain. Polya calls this principle the **inventor paradox** (Polya [1954]). The reason we can achieve this apparent paradox is that, although we attempt to prove more, we have more on which to base the proof, because the induction hypothesis is also stronger. We will see additional examples of this method of strengthening the induction hypothesis throughout the book. This method is very important.

2.11 Arithmetic versus Geometric Mean Theorem

The next example is a beautiful proof, attributed to Cauchy, of the arithmetic versus geometric mean theorem. It employs an elegant nonstandard use of induction, which we will use later.

□ Theorem 2.13

If $x_1, x_2, ..., x_n$ are all positive numbers, then

$$(x_1 x_2 \cdots x_n)^{\frac{1}{n}} \leq \frac{x_1 + x_2 + \cdots + x_n}{n}. \tag{2.3}$$

Proof: The proof is by induction on n. The induction hypothesis is identical to (2.3). The interesting part of the proof comes from the fact that the induction proceeds backward. Instead of proving a base case and then extending an assumption for smaller values of n to one for larger values of n, we use the following **reversed induction principle**:

> *If a statement P is true for an infinite subset of the natural numbers, and if its truth for n implies its truth for $n-1$, then P is true for all natural numbers.*

This principle holds because the fact that the statement holds for an infinite set guarantees that for every natural number k, there is a greater number m in the set; we can then use the reversed induction step to go backward from m to k.

We will prove the theorem in two steps. In the first step, we use regular induction to prove the theorem only for values of n that are powers of 2. The powers of 2 is the infinite set we need. In the second step, we use reversed induction to prove the theorem for all n. Consider first all values of n that are powers of 2. The theorem is trivial for $n = 1$. Consider $n = 2$. The claim becomes

$$\sqrt{x_1 x_2} \leq \frac{x_1 + x_2}{2},$$

which we can verify easily by squaring both sides. Assume now that (2.3) is true for $n = 2^k$, and consider $2n = 2^{k+1}$. We rewrite the left-hand side of (2.3) as follows:

$$(x_1 x_2 \cdots x_{2n})^{\frac{1}{2n}} = \sqrt{(x_1 x_2 \cdots x_n)^{\frac{1}{n}} (x_{n+1} x_{n+2} \cdots x_{2n})^{\frac{1}{n}}}. \tag{2.4}$$

We can now use the theorem for $n = 2$ with $y_1 = (x_1 x_2 \cdots x_n)^{1/n}$, and $y_2 = (x_{n+1} x_{n+2} \cdots x_{2n})^{1/n}$. The expression (2.4) becomes

$$(x_1 x_2 \cdots x_{2n})^{\frac{1}{2n}} = \sqrt{y_1 y_2} \leq \frac{y_1 + y_2}{2}.$$

But, by the induction hypothesis for n, we have

$$\frac{y_1 + y_2}{2} \leq \frac{\dfrac{x_1 + x_2 + \cdots + x_n}{n} + \dfrac{x_{n+1} + x_{n+2} + \cdots + x_{2n}}{n}}{2},$$

and the claim follows immediately.

132,979

We are now ready to use reversed induction to prove the theorem for all n. Assume that (2.3) is true for an arbitrary n, and consider $n-1$. Define

$$z = \frac{x_1 + x_2 + \cdots + x_{n-1}}{n-1}.$$

The theorem is assumed to be true for any n positive numbers, so, in particular, it is true for $x_1, x_2, \ldots, x_{n-1}, z$. That is,

$$(x_1 x_2 \cdots x_{n-1} z)^{\frac{1}{n}} \le \frac{x_1 + x_2 + \cdots + x_{n-1} + z}{n} = \frac{(n-1)z + z}{n} = z.$$

(z was chosen especially to "collapse" the right-hand side of this expression.) Hence, we have

$$(x_1 x_2 \cdots x_{n-1} z)^{\frac{1}{n}} \le z,$$

which implies that

$$x_1 x_2 \cdots x_{n-1} z \le z^n,$$

and

$$(x_1 x_2 \cdots x_{n-1})^{\frac{1}{n-1}} \le z = \frac{x_1 + x_2 + \cdots + x_{n-1}}{n-1},$$

which is exactly the same as (2.3) for $n-1$.   □

2.12 Loop Invariants: Converting a Decimal Number to Binary

Induction is very useful for proving correctness of algorithms. Consider a program that contains a loop that is supposed to compute a certain value. We want to prove that the result of executing the loop is indeed the intended result. We can use induction on the number of times the loop is executed. The induction hypothesis should reflect the relationships between the variables during the loop execution. Such an induction hypothesis is called a **loop invariant**. We illustrate the use of loop invariants with the algorithm in Fig. 2.6, which converts a decimal number n into a binary number represented by the array b (which is initially zero).

Algorithm Convert_to_Binary consists of one loop with three statements. The first statement increments k, which is an index to the array b. The second statement computes $t \bmod 2$, which is the reminder of the division of t by 2 (namely, 1 if t is odd, and 0 otherwise). The third statement divides t by 2, using an integer division (namely, ignoring fractions).

□ Theorem 2.14

When Algorithm Convert_to_Binary terminates, the binary representation of n is stored in the array b.

Algorithm Convert_to_Binary (*n*) ;
Input: *n* (a positive integer).
Output: *b* (an array of bits corresponding to the binary representation of *n*).

begin
> *t* := *n* ; *{ we use a new variable t to preserve n }*
> *k* := 0 ;
> **while** *t* > 0 **do**
>> *k* := *k* + 1 ;
>> *b[k]* := *t mod 2* ;
>> *t* := *t div 2* ;

end

Figure 2.6 Algorithm *Convert_to_Binary*.

Proof: The proof is by induction on k, the number of times the loop is executed. The induction hypothesis does not have to be the same as the theorem statement. It can apply to only a part of the algorithm. In this case, the main part is the loop, and we use the induction hypothesis to verify the execution pattern of the loop. The hypothesis, in this case, can be thought of as an **invariant**. It is a statement about the variables that is correct independent of the number of times we execute the loop. The most difficult part of the proof is finding the right induction hypothesis. Consider the following hypothesis.

> **Induction hypothesis:** *If m is the integer represented by the binary array*
> $b[1..k]$, *then* $n = t \cdot 2^k + m$.

The expression $t \cdot 2^k + m$ is the heart of the loop invariant, and is also the heart of the algorithm. The hypothesis states that the value of this expression is independent of the number of times the loop is executed. It captures the idea behind the algorithm. At step k of the loop, the binary array represents the k *least significant bits* of n, and the value of t, when shifted by k, corresponds to the rest of the bits.

To prove the correctness of this algorithm, we have to prove three conditions: (1) the hypothesis is true at the beginning of the loop, (2) the truth of the hypothesis at step k implies its truth for step $k+1$, and (3) when the loop terminates, the hypothesis implies the correctness of the algorithm. At the beginning of the loop, $k=0$, $m=0$ (by definition, since the array is empty), and $n=t$. Assume that $n=t \cdot 2^k + m$ at the start of the kth loop, and consider the corresponding values at the end of the kth loop. There are two cases. First, assume that t is even at the start of the kth loop. In this case, $t \bmod 2$ is 0. Thus, there is no contribution to the array (namely, m is unchanged), t is divided by 2, and k is incremented. Hence, the hypothesis is still true. Second, assume that m is odd. In this case, $b[k+1]$ is set to 1, which contributes 2^k to m, t is changed to $(t-1)/2$, and k is incremented. So, at the end of the kth loop, the corresponding expression is $(t-1)/2 \cdot 2^{k+1} + m + 2^k = (t-1) \cdot 2^k + m + 2^k = t \cdot 2^k + m = n$, which is exactly what we need to prove. Finally, the loop terminates when $t=0$, which implies, by the hypothesis, that $n=0\cdot 2^k+m=m$.   □

2.13 Common Errors

We finish this chapter with a few warnings and examples of common traps one can easily fall into by using induction hastily. Many wrong proofs come from strong convictions. If one believes strongly in the theorem, one tends to take as evident certain seemingly trivial "facts" implied by it. In induction proofs, this phenomenon often takes the following form. Since the theorem is "evident," one sometimes *implicitly* adds to the hypothesis several evident "facts." The proof of the step from n to $n+1$ uses these assumptions. Thus, the induction hypothesis is implicitly strengthened, but the stronger assumptions are never proven. For example, one may overlook the fact that the graphs in the theorem were assumed to be connected, and forget to check the reduced graphs for connectivity. Such an omission could be very subtle, and, of course, could lead to a very wrong proof. It is important to state the induction hypothesis precisely.

Another common error is the following. The main step in an induction proof is showing that the truth of the theorem for n implies its truth for $n+1$. We can either start with the $n+1$ instance and show that it follows from the n instance, or start with the n instance and show that it implies the $n+1$ instance. Both approaches are valid. However, the $n+1$ instance must be an *arbitrary* instance! The proof will be wrong if we start with an n instance and extend it to an $n+1$ instance that has some special properties. For example, consider the following wrong proof of Theorem 2.8. We start with an arbitrary map with n faces, and assume, by induction, that $V+n=E+2$. We take an arbitrary face and add a new edge with two new vertices that cuts the face in two. Adding two new vertices "cuts" two old edges, each one into two new edges. Overall, we added one more face, three more edges, and two more vertices. But, $V+2+n+1=E+3+2$, and the claim is true for $n+1$ faces. The reason this is not a valid proof is that the addition of the edge was done in a special way. An edge can also be added between existing vertices, or between one existing vertex and one new vertex. In fact, the graphs we get by adding edges only between new vertices have vertices only of degree 3 or less, so they are very special indeed. In general, it is safer to start with an arbitrary instance and try to prove it using the induction hypothesis, rather than the other way around.

Another dangerous trap involves exceptions to the theorem. It is common to have minor exceptions of the form $n\geq 3$, or "n is not a prime less than 30." The induction principle depends on the ability to imply the hypothesis for $n=2$ from the hypothesis for $n=1$, the hypothesis for $n=3$ from the hypothesis for $n=2$, and so on. If even one of these steps fails, the whole proof fails. We present two examples of this trap. The first example is a simple amusing anecdote; the second example is a more serious one. Consider the following claim.

Ridiculous claim: *Given n lines in the plane, no two of which are parallel to each other, all lines must have one point in common.*

This claim is clearly wrong, but let's look at a ''proof'' of it. The claim is obviously true for one line. Let's even be a little more careful and consider two lines; the claim is still true. Assume that the claim is true for n lines, and consider $n+1$ lines. By the hypothesis, the first n lines have a point in common. But, also by the hypothesis, the last n lines (including the $(n+1)$th line) have a point in common. The common point of the first n lines and the last n lines must be common to all $n+1$ lines, because lines having two points in common are equal. But, in that case, the $(n+1)$th line passes through the same point, and the claim is proven.

What is wrong with this proof? Actually very little. The only wrong step is that the proof unintentionally (or in this case very intentionally) ignores the fact that n must be at least 3 for the argument to work. That is, the claim is true for $n=1$, $n=2$, and also, if it is true for $n=3, 4, \cdots$, then it is true for $n+1=4, 5, \cdots$. The only problem is the step from $n=2$ to $n=3$. This small exception is enough to make the whole proof, and the claim in this case, very wrong. The reader may think that this example is too obvious to miss. Let's look at another example that is not so obvious

Consider the following claim:

$$n = \sqrt{1 + (n-1)\sqrt{1 + n\sqrt{1 + (n+1)\sqrt{1 + (n+2)\cdots}}}}. \tag{2.5}$$

(The expression goes to infinity.) Here is a proof of (2.5) by induction. First, we have to show that the expression converges for all n, so that the claim is meaningful. We omit this part (it is correct). If $n=1$, then (2.5) becomes $1 = \sqrt{1 + 0(\cdots)}$, which is true (since the expression in parenthesis converges). Assume that (2.5) is correct for n, and consider $n+1$. If we square both sides of (2.5) we get

$$n^2 = 1 + (n-1)\sqrt{1 + n\sqrt{1 + (n+1)\sqrt{1 + (n+2)\cdots}}}.$$

Rearranging terms, we get

$$\frac{n^2 - 1}{n - 1} = n + 1 = \sqrt{1 + n\sqrt{1 + (n+1)\sqrt{1 + (n+2)\cdots}}},$$

which is exactly (2.5) for $n+1$. The proof is now complete. Or is it? The only wrong step was dividing by $n-1$ without verifying that this value is not 0. But, $n-1=0$ when $n=1$, which is the first step in the induction! Again, everything works except for one implication — the one that goes from $n=1$ to $n=2$ — and this is enough to invalidate the whole proof. In this case, by the way, the claim is correct, but the proof is not that easy.

2.14 Summary

Mathematical induction is a rich technique. We have seen many variations of induction, and explored some of the methods for using it. The first step is to define the induction hypothesis. We have to decide to which parameter we apply the induction. In many cases, there is only one parameter, and the choice is clear. In other cases, however, we have a fair amount of flexibility. The parameter may be even a newly defined one, introduced especially for the proof. As we have seen, the induction hypothesis does not always follow directly from the theorem statement. Sometimes, we apply induction in several steps, each leading us closer to the proof. At other times, we strengthen the hypothesis such that it implies a stronger theorem.

There are two steps in every induction proof: the base case and the reduction step. The base case is usually, but not always, easy. Because it is easy, there is a tendency to ignore it. The reduction step is the heart of the induction proof. There are many ways to achieve the reduction. The most common way is to reduce a claim involving n to the same claim involving $n-1$. It is also common to "go" from $n+1$ to n. A *strong induction* reduces a claim involving n to one or several claims involving values smaller than n (but not necessarily $n-1$). Other variations include going from $2n$ to n, and *reversed induction*, in which the claim for n is implied from a claim for $n+1$ and a base case consisting of an infinite set is proved. The key to any reduction is that it must preserve the exact statement of the claim. No additional assumptions can be made about the reduced claim, unless they are specifically included in the induction hypothesis.

The reduction step can also be regarded as an *extension* step. We extend the claim from a smaller value of the parameter to a larger value. We have to ensure that the extension "covers" all possible values of the parameter, and that the extended claim is a general claim of the theorem without any additional assumptions or constraints. In Chapter 5, we will see that there is a direct analogy between the variations of induction introduced in this chapter and several algorithm design techniques.

Bibliographic Notes and Further Reading

The discovery of the mathematical induction principle is attributed to the Italian mathematician Franciscus Maurolycus (b. 1494). The history of mathematical induction is described in Bussey [1917] (see also Vacca [1909]). It is interesting to note that a principle very similar to mathematical induction was used in the 12th century in interpretation to the Talmud (this observation is due to J. Gillis). The problem was to interpret a rule that specifies a date as "3 days before a holiday." At the time of the writing of the Talmud, it was not uncommon, when one said "x days before a holiday," to include the holiday itself as part of the x days. The question was whether or not the holiday should be included as part of the 3 days specified in the rule. The interpretation was that the 3 days do not include the holiday because doing so would lead to ambiguities. An inductive argument was used to arrive at that conclusion. The base case was 1 day. It makes no sense to say "1 day before a holiday" when we mean the holiday itself. Therefore, "1 day before a holiday" does not include the holiday. Now, "2 days before a holiday" must also exclude the holiday, because otherwise it will have the same meaning as "1 day before a holiday." Therefore, "3 days before a holiday" does not include the holiday. This is clearly an inductive argument.

The summation problem given in Section 2.5 is from Polya [1957]. A brilliant discussion on the generalization of Euler's formula to three-dimensional objects is given by Lakatos [1976]. It is warmly recommended. The example in Section 2.8 is from

Lovász [1979]. Gray codes were introduced by Gray [1953]. More on coding theory can be found in Hamming [1986]. The proof of the arithmetic versus geometric mean theorem is due to Cauchy (see, for example, Polya and Szego [1972] or Beckenbach and Bellman [1961]). A bibliography for graph theory is given in Chapter 7. More on loop invariants can be found in Gries [1981]. The example of the proof of (2.5) was shown to us by Darrah Chavey.

Further material on mathematical induction can be found in Polya's wonderful books [1954; 1957; 1981]. Additional examples can be found in Sominskii [1963], Golovina and Yaglom [1963], and, of course, throughout this book.

Exercises

2.1   Prove that $x^n - y^n$ is divisible by $x - y$ for all natural numbers x, y ($x \neq y$), and n.

2.2   Extend the solution in Section 2.2 to general arithmetic sums. That is, find the sum $a_1 + a_2 + \cdots + a_n$, where $a_n = c_1 n + c_2$, and c_1, c_2 are constants.

2.3   Find the following sum and prove your claim:

$$1 \cdot 2 + 2 \cdot 3 + \cdots + n(n+1).$$

2.4   Find the following sum and prove your claim:

$$\frac{1}{2} + \frac{1}{4} + \frac{1}{8} + \cdots + \frac{1}{2^n}$$

2.5   Find the sum of the squares of the first n natural numbers and prove your claim.

2.6   Prove that

$$1^2 - 2^2 + 3^2 - 4^2 \cdots + (-1)^{k-1} k^2 = (-1)^{k-1} k(k+1)/2.$$

2.7   Given a set of $n+1$ numbers out of the first $2n$ natural numbers $1, 2, ..., 2n$, prove that there are two numbers in the set, one of which divides the other.

2.8   Let a, b, and n be positive integers. Prove that

$$2^{n-1}(a^n + b^n) \geq (a+b)^n.$$

2.9   Prove by induction that a number, given in its decimal representation, is divisible by 3 if and only if the sum of its digits is divisible by 3.

2.10   Find an expression for the sum of the ith row of the following triangle, which is called the **Pascal triangle**, and prove the correctness of your claim. The sides of the triangle are 1s, and each other entry is the sum of the two entries directly above it.

```
              1
           1     1
        1     2     1
     1     3     3     1
  1     4     6     4     1
```

2.11   Find an expression for the sum of the ith row of the following triangle, and prove the correctness of your claim. Each entry in the triangle is the sum of the three entries directly above it (a nonexisting entry is considered 0).

$$
\begin{array}{ccccccccc}
 & & & & 1 & & & & \\
 & & & 1 & 1 & 1 & & & \\
 & & 1 & 2 & 3 & 2 & 1 & & \\
 & 1 & 3 & 6 & 7 & 6 & 3 & 1 & \\
1 & 4 & 10 & 16 & 19 & 16 & 10 & 4 & 1
\end{array}
$$

2.12   Prove that, for all $n > 1$,

$$
\frac{1}{n+1} + \frac{1}{n+2} + \cdots + \frac{1}{2n} > \frac{13}{24}.
$$

*2.13   Prove that, for all $n > 1$,

$$
1 + \frac{1}{2} + \frac{1}{3} + \cdots + \frac{1}{n} = \frac{k}{m},
$$

where k is an odd number and m is an even number.

2.14   Consider the following series, 1, 2, 3, 4, 5, 10, 20, 40, ..., which starts as an arithmetic series, but after the first 5 terms becomes a geometric series. Prove that any positive integer can be written as a sum of distinct numbers from this series.

2.15   Consider the following series, 1, 2, 3, 6, 12, 24, 54, 84, 114, ..., which starts as an arithmetic series, after the first 3 terms it becomes a geometric series, and then, after 3 more terms, it becomes an arithmetic series again. Does your proof of Exercise 2.14 fit this problem? If it does, find the error in it since, for example, 81 cannot be written as a sum of distinct numbers this series. What is the subtle point in the proof of Exercise 2.14?

2.16   Consider $n \geq 3$ lines in general position in the plane. Prove that at least one of the regions they form is a triangle.

2.17   Consider $n \geq 3$ lines in general position in the plane. Prove that these lines form at least $n - 2$ triangles.

2.18   Given a set of n points in the plane such that any three of them are contained in a unit-size cycle, prove that all n points are contained in a unit-size cycle.

2.19   Prove that the regions formed by n circles in the plane can be colored with two colors such that any neighboring regions are colored differently.

2.20   Prove that the regions formed by n circles in the plane, each with one chord (see Fig. 2.7), can be colored with three colors such that any neighboring regions are colored differently.

2.21   Prove that the regions formed by a planar map all of whose vertices have even degree can be colored with two colors such that no two neighboring regions have the same color.

2.22   Prove that a planar map can be colored with three colors, such that every two neighboring regions are colored with different colors, if and only if each region has an even number of neighboring regions. Two regions are considered neighbors if they have an edge in common.

Figure 2.7 Circles with one chord.

*2.23 The **lattice** points in the plane are the points with integer coordinates. Let P be a polygon that does not cross itself (such a polygon is called **simple**) such that all of its vertices are lattice points (see Fig. 2.8). Let p be the number of lattice points that are on the boundary of the polygon (including its vertices), and let q be the number of lattice points that are inside the polygon. Prove that the area of the polygon is $p/2 + q - 1$.

2.24 We can define **anti-Gray codes** in the following way. Instead of minimizing the difference between two consecutive strings, we can try to maximize it. Is it possible to design an encoding for any even value of objects such that each two consecutive strings differ by k

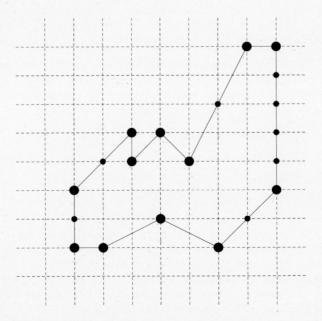

Figure 2.8 A simple polygon on the lattice points.

bits (where is k is the number of bits in each string)? How about $k-1$ bits (or $k-2$, $k-3$, etc.)? If it is possible, find an efficient construction.

2.25   Given a tree T and k subtrees of T such that each pair of subtrees has at least one vertex in common, prove that there is at least one vertex in common to all the subtrees.

2.26   Let $d_1, d_2, ..., d_n$, $n \geq 2$, be positive integers. Prove that, if

$$d_1 + d_2 + \cdots + d_n = 2n - 2,$$

then there exists a tree with n vertices whose degrees are exactly $d_1, d_2, ..., d_n$.

*2.27   Put n points on the boundary of a circle, and connect each point to all the others by a line segment. Assume that no three line segments meet at a point. Calculate the number of regions formed by these line segments inside the circle, and prove your claim.

*2.28   Let $T = (V, E)$ be an undirected tree. Let f be a function that maps vertices to vertices, which satisfies the following condition: If (v, w) is an edge in E, then either $(f(v), f(w))$ is an edge in E or $f(v) = f(w)$. In other words, the function either maps an edge to an edge, or it contracts an edge to a single vertex. Prove that there exists either a vertex v in V such that $f(v) = v$, or an edge (v, w) in E such that $f(v) = w$ and $f(w) = v$ (in other words, there is either a vertex or a edge that the function maps to itself).

2.29   The **pigeonhole principle** (in its simplest variation) states the following: If $n+1$ balls ($n \geq 1$) are put inside n boxes, then at least one box will contain more than one ball. Prove this principle by induction.

2.30   A **complete binary tree** is defined inductively as follows. A complete binary tree of height 0 consists of 1 node which is the root. A complete binary tree of height $h+1$ consists of two complete binary trees of height h whose roots are connected to a new root. Let T be a complete binary tree of height h. The **height** of a node in T is h minus the node's distance from the root (e.g., the root has height h, whereas a leaf has height 0). Prove that the sum of the heights of all the nodes in T is $2^{h+1} - h - 2$.

2.31   Let $F(n)$ be the nth Fibonacci number, which is defined inductively as follows: $F(1) = F(2) = 1$. $F(n) = F(n-1) + F(n-2)$, for $n > 2$. Prove that $F(n)^2 + F(n+1)^2 = F(2n+1)$. (Hint: Strengthen the induction hypothesis by proving two seemingly separate theorems at the same time, as is done in the section on Gray codes.)

2.32   Let n and m be integers such that $1 \leq m \leq n$. Prove by induction that

$$n^2 - m(n+1) + 2n + m^2 \leq n^2 + n.$$

(Hint: Use a "two sided" induction on m. Prove two base cases, $m = 1$ and $m = n$, and go either forward from $m = 1$ or backward from $m = n$.)

2.33   A **bridge** in an undirected graph is an edge whose removal disconnects the graph. Let $G = (V, E)$ be a connected undirected graph without a bridge. Prove that G has the following "ear decomposition" (see Fig. 2.9). The edges of G can be partitioned into disjoint sets $E_1, E_2, ..., E_k$, such that E_1 is a cycle, and, for each i, $1 < i \leq k$, E_i is a path whose endpoints are vertices that already appear in a previous E_j, $j < i$, and its other vertices (if any) have not appeared in previous E_js. (The path may be a closed one, in which case it includes only one previous vertex.)

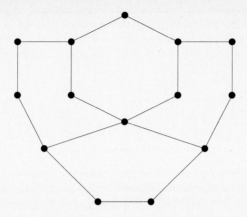

Figure 2.9 An ear decomposition.

*2.34 Let K_n denote the complete undirected graph with n vertices (namely, every two vertices are connected), and let n be an even number. Prove that the edges of K_n can be partitioned into exactly $n/2$ spanning trees. (A spanning tree is a connected subgraph that contains all vertices and no cycles.)

*2.35 Given an undirected graph $G = (V, E)$, a **matching** is a set of edges no two of which have a vertex in common. A **perfect matching** is one in which all vertices are matched. Construct a graph G with $2n$ vertices and n^2 edges such that G has exactly one unique perfect matching.

2.36 Let $a_1, a_2, ..., a_n$ be positive real numbers such that $a_1 a_2 \cdots a_n = 1$. Prove, without using the arithmetic versus geometric inequality, that

$$(1 + a_1)(1 + a_2) \cdots (1 + a_n) \geq 2^n.$$

(Hint: Try a reduction by introducing another variable that replaces two specially chosen numbers from the sequence.)

2.37 Consider the recurrence relation for Fibonacci numbers $F(n) = F(n - 1) + F(n - 2)$. Without solving this recurrence, compare $F(n)$ to $G(n)$ defined by the recurrence $G(n) = G(n - 1) + G(n - 2) + 1$. It seems obvious that $G(n) > F(n)$ (because of the extra 1). Yet the following is a seemingly valid proof (by induction) that $G(n) = F(n) - 1$. We assume, by induction, that $G(k) = F(k) - 1$ for all k such that $1 \leq k \leq n$, and we consider $G(n + 1)$:

$$G(n + 1) = G(n) + G(n - 1) + 1 = F(n) - 1 + F(n - 1) - 1 + 1 = F(n + 1) - 1.$$

What is wrong with this proof?

2.38 The following is another proof of the arithmetic versus geometric mean inequality. The proof has a major weakness, which makes it incomplete in general. Describe this weakness and then define the restrictions on the theorem that are needed to make this proof correct.

Let $S = x_1 + x_2 + \cdots + x_n$. To find a contradiction to the theorem, we need to exhibit n numbers whose sum is S and whose geometric mean is larger than S/n. It makes sense to look for a set of numbers whose sum is S and whose product is *maximum* over all such sets. In other words, we fix the sum (S) and try to maximize the product. Let $\{x_1, x_2, ..., x_n\}$ be a set that maximizes the product, and whose sum is S. If $x_1 \neq x_2$, then we can replace both x_1 and x_2 with their average $(x_1 + x_2)/2$. The sum remains the same, but the product grows, because

$$x_1 x_2 \leq \left[\frac{x_1 + x_2}{2} \right]^2$$

with equality holding only if $x_1 = x_2$. If all the numbers are equal, then the theorem holds. Otherwise, this is a contradiction to the maximality assumption of the set.

2.39   Design an algorithm to convert an binary number to a decimal number. The algorithm should be the opposite of algorithm *Convert_to_Binary* (see Fig. 2.6). The input is an array of bits b of length k, and the output is a number n. Prove the correctness of your algorithm by using a loop invariant.

2.40   Modify algorithm *Convert_to_Binary* (see Fig. 2.6) such that it converts a number given in base 6 to a binary number. The input is an array of base-6 digits, and the output is an array of bits. Prove the correctness of your algorithm by using a loop invariant.

CHAPTER 3

ANALYSIS OF ALGORITHMS

It does not depend on size, or a cow would catch a rabbit.

Pennsylvania German Proverb

He is a fool who looks at the fruit of lofty trees,
but does not measure their height.

Quintus Curtius Rufus

3.1 Introduction

The purpose of algorithm analysis is to predict the behavior, especially the running time, of an algorithm without implementing it on a specific computer. The advantages of doing so are clear. It is much more convenient to have simple measures for the efficiency of an algorithm than to implement the algorithm and test the efficiency every time a certain parameter in the underlying computer system changes. Furthermore, a complicated program usually includes many different "small" algorithms. It would be too much work to test thoroughly all different alternatives for each part of the program.

Unfortunately, it is usually impossible to predict the **exact** behavior of an algorithm. There are too many influencing factors. Instead, we try to extract the main characteristics of the algorithm. We define certain parameters and certain measures that are the most important for the analysis. Many details concerning the exact implementation are ignored. The analysis is thus only an *approximation*; it is not perfect. On the other hand, even a rough approximation can yield significant information about the algorithm. Most important, using this analysis, we can compare different algorithms to determine the best one for our purposes. We can use an analogy to car mileage claims, and attach a disclaimer saying "Use for comparison only — your running times may vary."

In this chapter, we describe one methodology for predicting the approximate running times of algorithms and for comparing different algorithms. The main feature of this approach is that we ignore constant factors and concentrate on the behavior of the algorithm as the size of the input goes to infinity. For example, if the input is an array of size n, and if the algorithm consists of $100n$ steps, then we ignore the constant 100 and say that the running time is approximately n (we will introduce precise notation shortly). If the number of steps is $2n^2 + 50$, then we ignore the constants 2 and 50 and say that the running time is approximately n^2. Since n^2 is larger than n, we say that the second algorithm is slower, even though for $n = 5$, for example, the first algorithm requires 500 steps, whereas the second one requires only 100 steps. This approximation is valid, however, if n is large enough. The second algorithm is indeed slower than the first one for all $n \geq 50$. On the other hand, suppose that the running time of the first algorithm was $100n^{1.8}$. Again, the first algorithm seems better, since $n^{1.8}$ is smaller than n^2. In this case, however, n will have to be approximately 300,000,000 for $100n^{1.8}$ to be smaller than $2n^2 + 50$. Fortunately, most algorithms have small constants in the expression of their running times. Thus, even though the asymptotic approach can be misleading sometimes, it works well in practice. In most cases, looking at only the asymptotic behavior is sufficient as a first approximation and indication of efficiency.

The result of our analysis should indicate how long the algorithm in question is expected to run for a particular input. However, we cannot list the precise running times for all inputs, unless the algorithm is very simple. The number of different possibilities of inputs is enormous, and most algorithms behave differently for different inputs. Instead, we attach a measure to the input, called the **size** of the input, and present analysis relative to that size. The algorithm will not behave exactly the same for all inputs of equal size, but we hope that the variation will be reasonable. The size is usually defined as a measure of the amount of space required to store the input. We will not try to introduce one general definition of size of the input for all algorithms, because we will be mainly interested in comparing different algorithms for the *same* problem. In most cases, the definition of size will be straightforward. We will see some examples shortly. Unless specified otherwise, the size will be denoted by n.

Given a problem and a definition of size, we want to find an expression that gives the running time of the algorithm relative to the size. (The precise definition of "running time" will be given in Section 3.3.) As we said earlier, there is usually not just one value for all inputs of equal size. Consequently, we must choose, among all inputs of the same size, the input we want to use as our indicator. The most common choice is the worst-case input. This may seem peculiar. Why not use the best input, or the average input?

The best input is usually ruled out because, in most cases, it is not representative; there is usually an input for which the problem is trivial. The average-case input may be a good choice, but it is sometimes very hard to measure effectively. First, it is generally not clear what an "average" input is. We can average over many different parameters in many different ways. If we are not careful, the average can contain many cases that never occur in practice, thus making this measure irrelevant. Another serious problem with taking the average case is the mathematical difficulty in analyzing average-case performance. We are still very far from having comprehensive, relatively easy-to-use techniques for average-case analysis. We will discuss average-case analysis for few problems, but we will mainly resort to worst-case analysis. Choosing the worst input as an indicator turns out to be very useful. In some cases, the worst input is very close to the average input and to experimental observations. In other cases, even though the worst input is substantially different from the average input, the algorithm that achieves the best performance for the worst input also performs very well for all cases. Unless specified otherwise, we will use worst-case analysis throughout this book.

In summary, both asymptotic analysis and worst-case analysis are only *approximations* of the running time of a particular algorithm under a particular input. They definitely do not give the whole story. They are, however, very good indicators in most cases.

3.2 The O Notation

As we have already said, our approach will be to ignore constant factors when trying to evaluate the running time of a particular algorithm. To do that effectively we need special notation. We say that a function $g(n)$ is $O(f(n))$ for another function $f(n)$ (pronounced "Oh," or sometimes "Big Oh," of $f(n)$), if there exist constants c and N, such that, for all $n \geq N$, we have $g(n) \leq cf(n)$. In other words, for large enough n, the function $g(n)$ is no more than a constant times the function $f(n)$. The function $g(n)$ may be less than $cf(n)$, even substantially less; the O notation bounds it only from above. For example, $5n^2 + 15 = O(n^2)$, since $5n^2 + 15 \leq 6n^2$ for $n \geq 4$. At the same time, $5n^2 + 15 = O(n^3)$, since $5n^2 + 15 \leq n^3$ for all $n \geq 6$.

The O notation allows us to ignore constants conveniently. Although we can include constants within the O notation, there is no reason to do that. We always write $O(n)$ instead of, say, $O(5n+4)$. Similarly, we write $O(\log n)$ without specifying the base of the logarithm, because changing bases changes the logarithm only by a constant. We write $O(1)$ to denote a constant. We can also use the O notation if we want to specify the constants only in parts of the expression. For example, we may write $T(n) = 3n^2 + O(n)$, or $S(n) = 2n \log_2 n + 5n + O(1)$.

In general, determining whether a certain function $g(n)$ is $O(f(n))$ may not be easy. Most of the functions involved in the analysis of algorithms in this book are relatively simple. With some simple rules, we can cover the majority of (but not all) cases. The most useful rule is the following: We say that a function $f(n)$ is **monotonically growing** if $n_1 \geq n_2$ implies that $f(n_1) \geq f(n_2)$.

□ **Theorem 3.1**

For all constants $c > 0$ and $a > 1$, and for all monotonically growing functions $f(n)$,

$$(f(n))^c = O(a^{f(n)}).$$

In other words, an exponential function grows faster than does a polynomial function.   □

This rule can be used to compare many functions. For example, if we substitute n for $f(n)$ in Theorem 3.1, we get that, for all constants $c > 0$ and $a > 1$,

$$n^c = O(a^n). \tag{3.1}$$

Another example comes from substituting $\log_a n$ for $f(n)$. For all constants $c > 0$ and $a > 1$

$$(\log_a n)^c = O(a^{\log_a n}) = O(n). \tag{3.2}$$

We can add and multiply with the O notation using the following rules.

□ Lemma 3.2

1. If $f(n) = O(s(n))$ and $g(n) = O(r(n))$ then $f(n) + g(n) = O(s(n) + r(n))$.
2) If $f(n) = O(s(n))$ and $g(n) = O(r(n))$ then $f(n) \cdot g(n) = O(s(n) \cdot r(n))$.

Proof: By definition, there are constants c_1, N_1, c_2, and N_2, such that $f(n) \leq c_1 s(n)$ for $n \geq N_1$, and $g(n) \leq c_2 r(n)$ for $n \geq N_2$. The largest of c_1 and c_2, and the largest of N_1 and N_2 can be used to show both claims. □

Since the O notation corresponds to the "≤" relation, however, it is not possible to subtract or divide. That is, *it is not true* in general that $f(n) = O(s(n))$ and $g(n) = O(r(n))$ imply that $f(n) - g(n) = O(s(n) - r(n))$ or that $f(n)/g(n) = O(s(n)/r(n))$ (see Exercises 3.15 and 3.16).

The importance of concentrating on the asymptotic behavior is illustrated in Table 3.1, which contains several typical running times and the time the corresponding algorithms consume for a problem of size $n = 1000$ for different computer speeds. The speeds differ by a constant of 2 from column to column, from 1000 steps per second to 8000 steps per second. We can clearly see the improvements we gain by speeding up the computer (or the algorithm) by a constant factor versus the improvements we gain by changing to a faster asymptotic algorithm (i.e., going up the table). An exponential algorithm will require astronomical time (billions and billions of years) to handle $n = 1000$ (unless the base is very close to 1).

The O notation is used to denote upper bounds on the running times of algorithms; however, using only upper bounds is not sufficient. All the algorithms in this book, for example, have running times of $O(2^n)$. That is, they do not require *more than* exponential time. However, $O(2^n)$ is a very crude upper bound for most of these algorithms — they are much faster than that. We are interested not only in upper bounds, but also in an expression that is as close to the actual running time as possible. In cases where it is too difficult to find the exact expression, we would like to find at least upper and lower bounds for it. Obtaining lower bounds is more difficult than is obtaining upper bounds. An upper bound on the running time of an algorithm implies only that there exists some algorithm that does not use more time than indicated. A lower bound must imply that *no* algorithm can achieve a better bound for the problem. It is impossible, of course, to consider all possible algorithms one by one. We need mechanisms to model problems and algorithms in a way that enables us to prove lower bounds. Lower bounds are discussed further in Section 6.4.6. There is a similar notation to handle lower bounds

running times	*time* $_1$ 1000 steps/sec	*time* $_2$ 2000 steps/sec	*time* $_3$ 4000 steps/sec	*time* $_4$ 8000 steps/sec
$\log_2 n$	0.010	0.005	0.003	0.001
n	1	0.5	0.25	0.125
$n \log_2 n$	10	5	2.5	1.25
$n^{1.5}$	32	16	8	4
n^2	1,000	500	250	125
n^3	1,000,000	500,000	250,000	125,000
1.1^n	10^{39}	10^{39}	10^{38}	10^{38}

Table 3.1 Running times (in seconds) under different assumptions ($n=1000$).

while ignoring constants. If there exist constants c and N, such that for all $n \geq N$ the number of steps $T(n)$ required to solve the problem for input size n is at least $cg(n)$, then we say that $T(n) = \Omega(g(n))$. So, for example, $n^2 = \Omega(n^2 - 100)$, and also $n = \Omega(n^{0.9})$. The Ω notation thus correspond to the "$\geq$" relation.

If a certain function $f(n)$ satisfies both $f(n) = O(g(n))$ and $f(n) = \Omega(g(n))$, then we say that $f(n) = \Theta(g(n))$. For example, $5n \log_2 n - 10 = \Theta(n \log n)$. (The base of the logarithm can be omitted in the expression $\Theta(n \log n)$, since different bases change the logarithm only by a constant factor.) The constants used to prove the O part and the Ω part need not be the same.

The O, Ω, and Θ correspond (loosely) to "$\leq$", "$\geq$", and "$=$". Sometimes we need notation corresponding to "$<$" and "$>$". We say that $f(n) = o(g(n))$ (pronounced "$f(n)$ is little oh of $g(n)$") if

$$\lim_{n \to \infty} \frac{f(n)}{g(n)} = 0.$$

For example, $n / \log_2 n = o(n)$, but $n / 10 \neq o(n)$. Similarly, we say that $f(n) = \omega(g(n))$ if $g(n) = o(f(n))$.

We can strengthen Theorem 3.1 by replacing big O with little o:

□ **Theorem 3.3**

For all constants $c > 0$ and $a > 1$, and for all monotonically growing functions $f(n)$, we have $(f(n))^c = o(a^{f(n)})$. In other words, an exponential function grows faster than does a polynomial function. □

The ∞ Symbol

The O notation has received a lot of criticism over the years. The main objection to it is, of course, that in reality constants do matter. The wide use of the O notation makes it convenient to forget about constants altogether. It is essential to remember that the O notation gives only a first approximation. As such, it serves a useful purpose, and its use has prompted the development of many algorithms that are practical by all measures. It was also instrumental in the development of complexity theory, which sheds light on many aspects of algorithm efficiency.

It is, however, important to distinguish between the case where the constants ignored by the O notation are prohibitively large and the case where they are small and the corresponding algorithm is efficient in practice. To make this distinction, we introduce in this book a new symbol. It is not meant to be a precise mathematically defined notation — it is meant only to replace some prose that accompanies (or at least should accompany) some algorithms whose running times, as measured by the O notation, are of theoretical value only. We suggest to denote by $\mathcal{OO}(f(n))$ (pronounced "Oh Oh of $f(n)$") a function that is $O(f(n))$, but with constants that are too large for most practical uses. (This notation should be easy to remember since it resembles a big ∞.)

The use of the $\mathcal{OO}$ notation should be left to the judgment of the writer. Whether or not a certain constant leads to a "practical use" is not well defined. We have no intention of attempting to tighten our definition. The main purpose is to indicate to the reader the opinion of the writer in a concise form. Another goal in introducing this symbol is to stress that the O notation is not the whole story.

3.3 Time and Space Complexity

How do we analyze an algorithm's running time without running the algorithm? We need to count the number of steps the algorithm performs. The problem is that there are many different types of steps, and each may require a different amount of time. For example, a division may take longer to compute than an addition does. One way to analyze an algorithm is to count the number of different steps separately. But listing all the types of steps separately will be, in most cases, too cumbersome. Furthermore, the implementation of the different steps depends on the specific computer or the programming language used in the implementation. We are trying to avoid that dependency.

Instead of counting all steps, we focus on the one type of step that seems to us to be the **major step**. For example, if we are analyzing a sorting algorithm, then we choose comparisons as the major step. Intuitively, comparing elements is the essence of sorting; all the rest can be regarded as overhead. Of course, we have to make sure that comparisons indeed constitute the major part of the algorithm. Since we will ignore constant factors anyway, it suffices to check that the number of all other operations is proportional to the number of comparisons. If this is true, and if $O(f(n))$ is a bound for the number of comparisons, then $O(f(n))$ is also a bound for the total number of steps. We say that the **time complexity** of the algorithm, or the **running time**, is $O(f(n))$. This approach also solves the problem of different steps that require different computation time, as long as the difference is no more than a constant.

The **space complexity** of an algorithm indicates the amount of temporary storage required for running the algorithm. In most cases, we do not count the storage required for the input or for the output as part of the space complexity. This is so, because the space complexity is used to compare different algorithms for the same problem, in which case the input/output requirements are fixed. Also, we cannot do without the input or output, and we want to count only the storage that may be saved. We also do not count the storage required for the program itself, since it is independent of the size of the input. Like time complexity, space complexity refers to worst case, and it is usually denoted as an asymptotic expression in the size of the input. Thus, an $O(n)$-space algorithm requires a constant amount of memory per input primitive. An $O(1)$-space algorithm requires a constant amount of space independent of the size of the input.

Counting the number of major steps may not be easy. In the next sections we discuss briefly several mathematical techniques for computing running times. In contrast, estimating the space complexity of a particular algorithm is usually straightforward, and, in most cases, we will not discuss it.

3.4 Summations

If an algorithm is composed of several parts, then its complexity is the sum of the complexities of its parts. In many cases, this is not as simple as it sounds. The algorithm may consist of a loop executed many times, each time with a different complexity. We need techniques for summing expressions in order to analyze such cases. Probably the simplest case is a loop of size n, such that the ith step $(i \leq n)$ requires i operations. The total number of operations is thus $1 + 2 + \cdots + n$. We denote sums with the sigma notation. The above sum is written as $\sum_{i=1}^{n} i$, which means ''sum of the term i, where i goes from 1 to n.'' As we have seen in Section 2.2, this sum is equal to $n(n+1)/2$. We can compare this sum to the case where each step requires exactly n operations, and we observe that, by cutting the running time of the ith step from n to i, we save a factor of about 2.

□ **Example 3.1**

Consider now the case of executing a loop in which the ith step requires i^2 operations. In other words, we are looking for the summation

$$S_2(n) = \sum_{i=1}^{n} i^2 .$$

It is clear that $S_2(n) \leq n^3$, since n^3 is equal to running the loop for n^2 operations in each step. Judging from this example, we can guess that the differences between $S_2(n)$ and n^3 are within a constant. We can prove our guess, and find the constants, by induction. We guess that $S_2(n) = P(n) = an^3 + bn^2 + cn + d$. $P(n)$ must satisfy $P(1) = 1$ and the induction step $P(n+1) = P(n) + (n+1)^2$. The induction step implies that

$$a(n+1)^3 + b(n+1)^2 + c(n+1) + d - (an^3 + bn^2 + cn + d) = n^2 + 2n + 1,$$

which implies (since coefficients of the same power of n must be equal) that

$3a + b - b = 1$ the coefficient of n^2 ,

$3a + 2b + c - c = 2$ the coefficient of n ,

and

$a + b + c + d - d = 1$ the coefficient of 1 .

These equations imply that $a = 1/3$, $b = 1/2$, and $c = 1/6$. The value of d comes from the initial condition $(P(1) = 1)$, which implies that $a + b + c + d = 1$. Hence $d = 0$. Combining all the terms, we get

$$S_2(n) = \frac{n^3}{3} + \frac{n^2}{2} + \frac{n}{6} = \frac{n(n+1)(2n+1)}{6} . \tag{3.3}$$

Again, it is interesting to note that by reducing the size of the ith step from n^2 to i^2, we save a factor of about 3. □

There is another way to arrive at expression (3.3). It is a general technique that we will use several times. If we guess that $S_2(n)$ is a third-degree polynomial, then we can try to express $S_2(n)$ as a combination of such polynomials. We then arrive at the solution for $S_2(n)$ by solving an equation involving it and other explicit polynomials. Consider the sum

$$S_3(n) = \sum_{i=1}^{n} i^3 . \tag{3.4}$$

We will first write (3.4) in a different way:

$$S_3(n) = \sum_{i=1}^{n} i^3 = \sum_{i=1}^{n} (i - 1 + 1)^3 = \sum_{i=0}^{n-1} (i+1)^3 = \sum_{i=0}^{n-1} (i^3 + 3i^2 + 3i + 1). \tag{3.5}$$

In other words, we shift the summation, so that the sum goes from 0 to $n-1$ instead of from 1 to n. This shift is illustrated in Fig. 3.1. We can now equate the left side and the right side of (3.5), and expand:

$$\sum_{i=1}^{n} i^3 = \sum_{i=0}^{n-1} (i^3 + 3i^2 + 3i + 1). \tag{3.6}$$

The i^3 terms for i ranging from 1 to $n-1$ are common to both sides of (3.6), and can be canceled. We then write an equation involving the rest of the terms from both sides.

	1^3	+	2^3	+	$\cdots$	+	$(n-1)^3$	+	n^3
$(0+1)^3$	+	$(1+1)^3$	+	$(2+1)^3$	+	$\cdots$	+	$(n-1+1)^3$	

Figure 3.1 Computing a summation by shifting.

$$n^3 = 0^3 + \sum_{i=0}^{n-1} (3i^2 + 3i + 1).$$

We already know that $\sum_{i=0}^{n-1} i = n(n-1)/2$, and it is clear that $\sum_{i=0}^{n-1} i^2 = S_2(n) - n^2$ (the only difference is in the nth term). Hence,

$$n^3 = 3(S_2(n) - n^2) + 3n(n-1)/2 + n.$$

We can now solve for $S_2(n)$:

$$n^3 - 3n(n-1)/2 - n = 3(S_2(n) - n^2),$$

which implies that

$$S_2(n) = \frac{n^3 - 3n(n-1)/2 - n}{3} + n^2 = \frac{n^3}{3} + \frac{3n^2}{6} + \frac{n}{6} = \frac{n(n+1)(2n+1)}{6},$$

which is, of course, exactly the same expression as (3.3).

The main trick in this derivation was to use a particular sum ($S_3(n)$ in this example) in two different ways, such that they mostly cancel each other. Many other sums exhibit the same behavior. If we consider the difference between a sum $f_1 + f_2 + \cdots + f_n$ and a shifted sum $f_2 + f_3 + \cdots + f_{n+1}$, we see that most of the coefficients cancel each other. Only the boundary terms are left. We present three more examples of this technique.

□ Example 3.2

We want to compute the following sum:

$$F(n) = \sum_{i=0}^{n} 2^i = 1 + 2 + 4 + \cdots + 2^n.$$

We would like to compare $F(n)$ to another expression involving $F(n)$ by shifting terms and by canceling most of them. The difference between consecutive terms in $F(n)$ is a factor of 2, so let's multiply the whole expression by 2 (which will allow us to shift):

$$2F(n) = 2 + 4 + 8 + \cdots + 2^n + 2^{n+1}.$$

We can now get an expression involving $F(n)$:

$$2F(n) - F(n) = 2^{n+1} - 1.$$

But, this implies that $F(n) = 2^{n+1} - 1$.   □

□ Example 3.3

Consider now the following slightly more difficult sum:

$$G(n) = \sum_{i=1}^{n} i2^i = 1 \cdot 2^1 + 2 \cdot 2^2 + 3 \cdot 2^3 + \cdots + n \cdot 2^n.$$

We can apply the same technique:

$$2G(n) = 1 \cdot 2^2 + 2 \cdot 2^3 + 3 \cdot 2^4 + \cdots + n \cdot 2^{n+1}$$

(we simply incremented the power). By subtracting the two expressions, we eliminate the effect of the i factor:

$$G(n) = 2G(n) - G(n) = n \cdot 2^{n+1} - (1 \cdot 2^1 + 1 \cdot 2^2 + \cdots + 1 \cdot 2^n)$$

$$= n \cdot 2^{n+1} - (2^{n+1} - 2) = (n-1) 2^{n+1} + 2.$$

□

□ Example 3.4

Finally, we consider the following sum, which will appear in Section 6.4.5 in the analysis of heapsort:

$$G(n) = \sum_{i=1}^{n} i 2^{n-i} = 1 \cdot 2^{n-1} + 2 \cdot 2^{n-2} + 3 \cdot 2^{n-3} + \cdots + n \cdot 2^0.$$

We can apply the same technique:

$$2G(n) = 1 \cdot 2^n + 2 \cdot 2^{n-1} + 3 \cdot 2^{n-2} + \cdots + n \cdot 2^1.$$

Again, by subtracting the two expressions, we eliminate the effect of the i factor:

$$G(n) = 2G(n) - G(n) = 2^n + 1 \cdot 2^{n-1} + 1 \cdot 2^{n-2} + \cdots + 1 \cdot 2^1 - n \cdot 2^0.$$

$$= 2^{n+1} - 2 - n.$$

□

3.5 Recurrence Relations

A **recurrence relation** is a way to define a function by an expression involving the same function. Probably the most famous recurrence relation is the one defining the Fibonacci numbers

$$F(n) = F(n-1) + F(n-2), \quad F(1) = 1, \quad F(2) = 1. \tag{3.7}$$

This expression uniquely defines the function. We can compute from this expression the value of the function at every number k. For example, $F(3) = F(2) + F(1) = 2$, $F(4) = F(3) + F(2) = 3$, and so on. However, if we compute the value of the function by following the definition, we would need $k - 2$ steps to compute $F(k)$. It is much more convenient to have an explicit (or closed-form) expression for $F(n)$. That would enable us to compute $F(n)$ quickly, and to compare $F(n)$ to other known functions. This is called solving the recurrence relation. We sometimes call a recurrence relation simply a *recurrence*.

Recurrence relations appear frequently in the analysis of algorithms. We briefly discuss here a useful technique for solving recurrence relations, and present general solutions of two classes of recurrences that are among the most common recurrences involved in analyzing algorithms. These recurrences will be used later in the book.

3.5.1 Intelligent Guesses

Guessing a solution may seem like a nonscientific method, but, keeping our pride aside, it works very well for a wide class of recurrence relations. It works even better when we are trying to find not the exact solution, but only an upper bound. The main reason that guessing is useful is that proving that a certain bound is valid is easier than computing the bound. Consider the following recurrence which is defined only for values of n that are powers of 2:

$$T(2n) \le 2T(n) + 2n - 1, \quad T(2) = 1. \tag{3.8}$$

We wrote this recurrence as an inequality rather than equality. This is consistent with our modest goal of finding only an upper bound (in the form of the O notation), and with the fact that the right-hand side represents the worst case. We want to find a function $f(n)$ such that $T(n) = O(f(n))$, but we also want to make sure that $f(n)$ is not too far from the actual $T(n)$.

Given a guess for $f(n)$, say $f(n) = n^2$, we prove that $T(n) = O(f(n))$ by induction on n. First, we check the base of the induction. In this case, $T(2) = 1 \le f(2) = 4$. We then prove that $T(n) \le f(n)$ implies that $T(2n) \le f(2n)$. We need to prove that

$$T(n) \le n^2 \quad \text{implies} \quad T(2n) \le (2n)^2.$$

The proof is as follows:

$$T(2n) \le 2T(n) + 2n - 1, \quad \text{(by the definition of the recurrence)}$$

$$\le 2n^2 + 2n - 1, \quad \text{(by the induction hypothesis)}$$

$$< (2n)^2,$$

which is exactly what we wanted to prove. Thus, $T(n) = O(n^2)$. Is n^2 a good estimate for $T(n)$? In the last step of the proof, $2n^2 + 2n - 1$ was substituted by the greater $4n^2$. But there is a substantial gap (about $2n^2$) between these two expressions, which gives us a hint that maybe n^2 is a high estimate for $T(n)$.

Let's try a smaller estimate, say, $f(n) = cn$ for some constant c. It is clear, however, that cn grows more slowly than $T(n)$ does, since $c2n = 2cn$, and there is no room for the extra $2n - 1$. Hence, $T(n)$ is somewhere between cn and n^2.

Let's try now $T(n) \le n \log_2 n$. Clearly, $T(2) < 2\log_2 2$. Assume that $T(n) \le n \log_2 n$, and consider $T(2n)$:

$$T(2n) \le 2T(n) + 2n - 1, \quad \text{(by the definition of the recurrence)}$$

$$\le 2n \log_2 n + 2n - 1, \quad \text{(by the induction hypothesis)}$$

$$< 2n (\log_2 2n),$$

which is exactly what we wanted to prove. The leeway in the proof is only 1 now, so we are very close. Later, we will prove that this is actually the exact solution to within a constant.

The recurrence relation (3.8) is defined only for values of n that are powers of 2. We can define a similar recurrence for all values of n in the following way:

$$T(n) \le 2T(\lfloor n/2 \rfloor) + n - 1, \quad T(2) = 1. \tag{3.9}$$

(Notice that the floor symbol is necessary, because $T(n)$ is defined only for integers.) The recurrence relation (3.9) is more general than (3.8), since it is defined for all values of n, but, for values of n that are powers of 2, (3.9) is exactly the same as (3.8). Therefore, we already know that, for values of n that are powers of 2, $T(n) = O(n \log n)$. We now show that the same bound applies to all values of $T(n)$. It is clear that $T(n)$ is a monotonically increasing function. If n is not a power of 2, $T(n)$ is no more than $T(2^k)$, where 2^k is the first power of 2 that is greater than n. That is, let $2^{k-1} < n < 2^k$; clearly, $T(2^{k-1}) \le T(n) \le T(2^k)$. We proved that $T(2^k) \le c 2^k \log_2 2^k$ for some constant c. Hence,

$$T(n) \le c 2^k \log_2 2^k \le c(2n) \log_2(2n) \le c_1 n \log_2 n.$$

for another constant c_1, which implies that $T(n) = O(n \log n)$ for all n. It is usually sufficient to assume that n is a power of 2 when we are looking for an asymptotic expression.

Let's summarize the steps used in an inductive proof of a solution to a recurrence relation. Suppose that we have a general recurrence relation of the following form:

$$T(g(n)) = E(T, n), \tag{3.10}$$

where $g(n)$ is a function of n (which defines the growth of the recurrence), and E is some expression involving $T(n)$ and n. For example, in (3.8), $g(n) = 2n$, and $E(T, n) = 2T(n) + 2n - 1$. Suppose further that we guess that $T(n) \le f(n)$, for some function $f(n)$. To prove our guess, we need to substitute $g(n)$ for n in $f(n)$, then to substitute $f(n)$ for each occurrence of $T(n)$ in E. We then have to show that $f(g(n))$ is *greater* than or equal to the value substituted for $E(T, n)$. In other words, we have to prove that

$$f(g(n)) \ge E(f, n). \tag{3.11}$$

For example, in (3.8) we guessed that $f(n) = n \log_2 n$; thus, we had to show that $(2n)(\log_2(2n)) \ge 2(n \log_2 n) + 2n - 1$.

A common mistake is to try to prove the opposite — that is, to replace "greater than" with "less than." An intuitive, and easy to remember, explanation is the following. We are trying to prove that $f(n)$ grows more quickly than $T(n)$ does. Hence, if we substitute $g(n)$ for n in $f(n)$, we should get a value larger than what we get by substituting $g(n)$ for n in $T(n)$. But, $T(g(n)) = E(T, n)$ (this is exactly the recurrence relation); thus, we can replace $T(g(n))$ with $E(f, n)$. This process may have to be repeated several times with different functions (guesses) until the proof of the inequality becomes reasonably tight.

Another common mistake is to use the O notation when guessing. That is, we guess that the solution is $O(f(n))$, and we try to substitute $O(f(n))$ for n. However, the O notation *cannot* be used in that way. The problem with using the O notation is that, even though we do not care about the constants at the end, we cannot ignore them through the proof. For example, if we try to prove that the solution of (3.8) is $O(n)$, by substituting $O(n)$ for n, we get the following (the base case is trivial):

$$T(2n) \leq 2T(n) + 2n - 1, \qquad \text{(by the definition of the recurrence)}$$

$$\leq O(n) + 2n - 1, \qquad \text{(by the induction hypothesis)}$$

$$= O(n),$$

which is *wrong*, as we have seen earlier. The error lies in the fact that different constants were used (or rather ignored) at different stages of the "proof." The correct approach is to include the constants explicitly. When we want to guess that the solution is $O(f(n))$, we guess that it is $cf(n)$ for some constant c, and determine the value of c later.

Let's try now to solve the Fibonacci relation by guessing. Again, we are given that

$$F(n) = F(n-1) + F(n-2), \quad F(1) = 1, \quad F(2) = 1. \tag{3.12}$$

Since the value of $F(n)$ is the sum of two previous values, a reasonable guess would be that $F(n)$ is doubled every time; namely, it is approximately 2^n. Let's try $F(n) = c2^n$. Substituting $c2^n$ in (3.12), we get

$$c2^n = c2^{n-1} + c2^{n-2}.$$

This equality is clearly impossible, since c is canceled and the left side is always greater than the right side. So we learned that $c2^n$ is too large, and that the multiplicative constant c plays no role in the induction step.

The next attempt could be another exponential function, but with a smaller base. Instead of guessing different bases, it is easier to introduce a parameter as a base and to compute its value through the verification. We will try $F(n) = a^n$, where a is a constant. Substituting a^n in (3.12), we get

$$a^n = a^{n-1} + a^{n-2},$$

which implies that

$$a^2 = a + 1. \tag{3.13}$$

The two solutions for (3.13) are $a_1 = (1 + \sqrt{5})/2$ and $a_2 = (1 - \sqrt{5})/2$. So, in particular, we now know that $F(n) = O((a_1)^n)$, since $(a_1)^n$ satisfies the recurrence, and we can easily find a constant c such that $c(a_1)^n$ is greater than the given values for $n = 1$ and $n = 2$.

If we want to find the exact value for $F(n)$, we will need to consider the initial values more carefully. Since both $(a_1)^n$ and $(a_2)^n$ solve the recurrence, any linear combination of them does. So the general solution of the recurrence is

$$c_1(a_1)^n + c_2(a_2)^n.$$

We need to compute the values of c_1 and c_2 so that the expression fits the values of $F(1)$ and $F(2)$. It is a simple exercise to verify that $c_1 = 1/\sqrt{5}$, and $c_2 = -1/\sqrt{5}$. Therefore, the exact solution of the Fibonacci relation is

$$F(n) = \frac{1}{\sqrt{5}} \left[\frac{1+\sqrt{5}}{2} \right]^n - \frac{1}{\sqrt{5}} \left[\frac{1-\sqrt{5}}{2} \right]^n.$$

The equation $a^2 = a + 1$, which we encountered in our search for a solution to the recurrence relation (3.12), is called the **characteristic equation** of the recurrence relation. The same technique is the basis for solving any recurrence of the form

$$F(n) = b_1 F(n-1) + b_2 F(n-2) + \cdots + b_k F(n-k)$$

for a constant k.

3.5.2 Divide and Conquer Relations

In a divide-and-conquer algorithm, the problem is divided into smaller subproblems, each subproblem is solved recursively, and a *combine* algorithm is used to solve the original problem. Assume that there are a subproblems, each of size $1/b$ of the original problem, and that the algorithm used to combine the solutions of the subproblems runs in time cn^k, for some constants a, b, c, and k. The running time $T(n)$ of the algorithm thus satisfies

$$T(n) = aT(n/b) + cn^k. \tag{3.14}$$

We assume, for simplicity, that $n = b^m$, so that n/b is always an integer (b is an integer greater than 1). We first try to expand (3.14) a couple of times to get the feel of it:

$$T(n) = a(aT(n/b^2) + c(n/b)^k) + cn^k = a(a(aT(n/b^3) + c(n/b^2)^k) + c(n/b)^k) + cn^k.$$

In general, if we expand all the way to $n/b^m = 1$, we get

$$T(n) = a(a(\cdots T(n/b^m) + c(n/b^{m-1})^k) + \cdots) + cn^k.$$

Let's assume that $T(1) = c$ (a different value would change the end result by only a constant). Then,

$$T(n) = ca^m + ca^{m-1}b^k + ca^{m-2}b^{2k} + \cdots + cb^{mk},$$

which implies that

$$T(n) = c\sum_{i=0}^{m} a^{m-i}b^{ik} = ca^m \sum_{i=0}^{m} (\frac{b^k}{a})^i.$$

But, this is a simple geometric series. There are three cases, depending on whether (b^k/a) is less than, greater than, or equal to 1.

Case 1: $a > b^k$

In this case, the factor of the geometric series is less than 1, so the series converges to a constant even if m goes to infinity. Therefore, $T(n) = O(a^m)$. Since $m = \log_b n$, we get $a^m = a^{\log_b n} = n^{\log_b a}$ (the last equality can be easily proven by taking logarithm of base b of both sides). Thus,

$$T(n) = O(n^{\log_b a}).$$

Case 2: $a = b^k$

In this case, the factor of the geometric series is 1, and thus $T(n) = O(a^m m)$. Notice that $a = b^k$ implies that $\log_b a = k$ and $m = O(\log n)$. Thus,

$$T(n) = O(n^k \log n).$$

Case 3: $a < b^k$

In this case, the factor of the geometric series is greater than 1. We use the standard expression for summing a geometric series. Denote b^k / a by F (F is a constant). Since the first element of the series is a^m, we obtain

$$T(n) = a^m \frac{F^{m+1} - 1}{F - 1} = O(a^m F^m) = O((b^k)^m) = O((b^m)^k) = O(n^k).$$

These three cases are summarized in the following theorem.

□ Theorem 3.4

The solution of the recurrence relation $T(n) = aT(n/b) + cn^k$, where a and b are integer constants, $a \geq 1$, $b \geq 2$, and c and k are positive constants, is

$$T(n) = \begin{cases} O(n^{\log_b a}) & \text{if } a > b^k \\ O(n^k \log n) & \text{if } a = b^k \\ O(n^k) & \text{if } a < b^k \end{cases}.$$

□

The result of Theorem 3.4 applies to many divide-and-conquer algorithms. It should be memorized. This result is also very helpful in the design stage, since it can be used to predict the running time. Generalizations of this formula are given in the exercises.

3.5.3 Recurrence Relations with Full History

A **full-history recurrence relation** is one that depends on all the previous values of the function, not just on a few of them. One of the simplest full-history recurrence relations is

$$T(n) = c + \sum_{i=1}^{n-1} T(i), \tag{3.15}$$

where c is a constant and $T(1)$ is given. We can solve this recurrence by using the same method we used to compute sums. We will try to write the recurrence in such a way that most of the terms will be canceled. (This method is sometimes called **elimination of history**.) For the recurrence (3.15), we compare $T(n+1)$ to $T(n)$:

$$T(n+1) = c + \sum_{i=1}^{n} T(i). \tag{3.16}$$

If we subtract (3.15) from (3.16), we get $T(n+1) - T(n) = T(n)$. So, $T(n+1) = 2T(n)$, which clearly implies that $T(n+1) = T(1) 2^n$. (This claim is true for $T(1)$, and, by induction, if the claim is true for $T(n)$, then it is true for $T(n+1)$, since we double the value every time.)

This argument may be "clear," but it is incorrect! We can, for example, set $T(1)=1$ and $c=5$, and see that $T(2)=6 \neq 2T(1)$. This is another example of carelessly going through an induction proof ignoring the base case. The error results from the fact that the proof does not work for $T(2)$, since $T(1)$ is not necessarily canceled by c. One should be very suspicious when a parameter (c in this case) that appears in the expression does not appear in the final solution. To solve this problem correctly, we note that $T(2)=T(1)+c$ (by definition), and that the proof above is correct for all $n>2$. Hence, $T(n+1)=(T(1)+c)2^{n-1}$.

This recurrence is very simple. The next one is not so simple, but it is very important. It appears in the analysis of the average case of quicksort which we discuss in Section 6.4.4. The recurrence relation is

$$T(n) = n-1 + \frac{2}{n} \sum_{i=1}^{n-1} T(i), \text{ (for } n \geq 2). \quad T(1)=0. \tag{3.17}$$

We use the shifting and canceling terms technique. We want to cancel most of the $T(i)$ terms. Let's look at the corresponding expression for $T(n+1)$:

$$T(n+1) = (n+1)-1 + \frac{2}{(n+1)} \sum_{i=1}^{n} T(i) \quad (n \geq 2). \tag{3.18}$$

For convenience, we multiply both sides of (3.17) by n, and both sides of (3.18) by $n+1$:

$$n T(n) = n(n-1) + 2 \sum_{i=1}^{n-1} T(i) \quad (n \geq 2). \tag{3.19}$$

$$(n+1) T(n+1) = (n+1)n + 2 \sum_{i=1}^{n} T(i) \quad (n \geq 2). \tag{3.20}$$

We can now subtract (3.19) from (3.20), and obtain

$$(n+1)T(n+1) - nT(n) = (n+1)n - n(n-1) + 2T(n) = 2n + 2T(n) \quad (n \geq 2),$$

which implies that

$$T(n+1) = \frac{n+2}{n+1} T(n) + \frac{2n}{n+1} \quad (n \geq 2).$$

This recurrence is easier to solve. First, we substitute 2 for $\frac{2n}{n+1}$, and get a close approximation:

$$T(n+1) \leq \frac{n+2}{n+1} T(n) + 2 \quad (n \geq 2). \tag{3.21}$$

If we expand (3.21), we get

$$T(n) \le 2 + \frac{n+1}{n}\left[2 + \frac{n}{n-1}\left[2 + \frac{n-1}{n-2}\left[\cdots \frac{4}{3}\right]\right]\right]$$

$$= 2\left[1 + \frac{n+1}{n} + \frac{n+1}{n}\frac{n}{n-1} + \frac{n+1}{n}\frac{n}{n-1}\frac{n-1}{n-2} + \cdots + \frac{n+1}{n}\frac{n}{n-1}\frac{n-1}{n-2}\cdots\frac{4}{3}\right]$$

$$= 2\left[1 + \frac{n+1}{n} + \frac{n+1}{n-1} + \frac{n+1}{n-2} + \cdots + \frac{n+1}{3}\right]$$

$$= 2(n+1)\left[\frac{1}{n+1} + \frac{1}{n} + \frac{1}{n-1} + \cdots + \frac{1}{3}\right]$$

$$= 2(n+1)(H(n+1)-1.5),$$

where $H(n) = 1 + 1/2 + 1/3 + \cdots + 1/n$ is the Harmonic series. The Harmonic series has a simple approximation, which we will not prove, $H(n) = \ln n + \gamma + O(1/n)$, where $\gamma = 0.577..$ is **Euler's constant**. Hence, the solution for $T(n)$ is

$$T(n) \le 2(n+1)(\ln n + \gamma - 1.5) + O(1) = O(n \log n).$$

3.6 Useful Facts

In this section, we present, without proof, several equalities and inequalities that are useful in analyzing algorithms.

Arithmetic series

$$1 + 2 + 3 + \cdots + n = \frac{n(n+1)}{2}. \tag{3.22}$$

More generally, if $a_n = a_{n-1} + c$, where c is a constant, then

$$a_1 + a_2 + a_3 + \cdots + a_n = \frac{n(a_n + a_1)}{2}. \tag{3.23}$$

Geometric series

$$1 + 2 + 4 + \cdots + 2^n = 2^{n+1} - 1. \tag{3.24}$$

More generally, if $a_n = ca_{n-1}$, where $c \ne 1$ is a constant, then

$$a_1 + a_2 + a_3 + \cdots + a_n = a_1 \frac{c^n - 1}{c - 1}. \tag{3.25}$$

If $0 < c < 1$, then the sum of the infinite geometric series is

$$\sum_{i=1}^{\infty} a_i = \frac{a_1}{1-c}. \tag{3.26}$$

Sum of squares

$$\sum_{i=1}^{n} i^2 = \frac{n(n+1)(2n+1)}{6}. \tag{3.27}$$

Harmonic series

$$H_n = \sum_{k=1}^{n} \frac{1}{k} = \ln n + \gamma + O(1/n), \tag{3.28}$$

where $\gamma = 0.577..$ is Euler's constant.

Basic rules involving logarithms

$$\log_b a = \frac{1}{\log_a b}. \tag{3.29}$$

$$\log_a x = \frac{\log_b x}{\log_b a}. \tag{3.30}$$

$$b^{\log_b x} = x. \tag{3.31}$$

$$b^{\log_a x} = x^{\log_a b}. \tag{3.32}$$

Sum of logarithms

$$\sum_{i=1}^{n} \lfloor \log_2 i \rfloor = (n+1)\lfloor \log_2 n \rfloor - 2^{\lfloor \log_2 n \rfloor + 1} + 2 = \Theta(n \log n). \tag{3.33}$$

Bounding a summation by an integral

If $f(x)$ is a monotonically increasing continuous function, then

$$\sum_{i=1}^{n} f(i) \le \int_{x=1}^{x=n+1} f(x)dx. \tag{3.34}$$

Stirling's approximation

$$n! = \sqrt{2\pi n} \left[\frac{n}{e}\right]^n (1 + O(1/n)). \tag{3.35}$$

In particular, Stirling's approximation implies that $\log_2(n!) = \Theta(n \log n)$.

3.7 Summary

Niels Bohr once said that "it is very hard to predict; especially the future." It is not *that hard* to predict the behavior of an algorithm, but it is far from being easy. The main method we use is approximation. We ignore many details and attempt to extract only the most important characteristics of the algorithm. The O notation is useful in that respect, but we must never forget that it is only a first approximation. On the other hand, the difficulty in analyzing algorithms should not deter the algorithm designer from attempting this task. It is essential to get at least some indication of the efficiency of an algorithm.

In many cases, especially when recursion is used, we get a recurrence relation. The first thing we should do with a recurrence relation is to look at the first few terms. This will give us some idea of the behavior of the relation, but it is by no means enough. The first few terms help in making the first pass at guessing a solution. Another useful step is to expand the recurrence several times, as we did in Section 3.5.2. Guessing and verifying is a good technique for solving recurrence relations, but it is usually just a first step. We must be careful not to "overguess" — that is, to try an upper bound that is correct, but too pessimistic. There are many other techniques. Fortunately, most algorithms that appear in practice lead to one of a very few classes of recurrence relations, most of which are described in this chapter. It is usually sufficient to assume, as a first step, that n has a special form — in particular, that n is a power of 2.

Bibliographic Notes and Further Reading

The idea of asymptotic analysis was promoted in the early 1970's, and it was met with some resistance. It is by now the major measure for algorithm efficiency. There are several books — mainly on discrete mathematics and combinatorics — that cover techniques for evaluating summations, recurrence relations, and other expressions needed for analyzing algorithms. Brualdi [1977], Bavel [1982], Roberts [1984], and Graham, Knuth, and Patashnik [1989] are just a few examples. There are fewer books that are devoted entirely to algorithm analysis. Knuth [1973a] provides a rich source of material. Additional books and survey papers include Greene and Knuth [1982], Lueker [1980], Purdom and Brown [1985a], Flajolet and Vitter [1987], and Hofri [1987].

Knuth [1976] discusses the relatives of the O notation. Additional techniques for solving recurrence relations can be found in Lueker [1980], and Bentley, Haken, and Saxe [1980]. (The latter contains the solutions to Exercises 3.23 and 3.24.) Tarjan [1985] discusses amortized complexity, which is an elegant method for analyzing the running times of certain algorithms in a more precise way; if a certain part of the algorithm is performed several times, each time with a different running time, then, instead of taking the worst case every time, we amortized the different costs. The recurrence relation in Exercise 3.19 is from Manber [1986]. Exercise 3.21 is from Purdom and Brown [1985a].

Drill Exercises

3.1   Prove that, if $P(n)$ is a polynomial in n, then $O(\log(P(n))) = O(\log n)$.

3.2   Prove that, if $f(n) = o(g(n))$, then $f(n) = O(g(n))$. Is the opposite true?

3.3   Prove, by using Theorem 3.1, that

$$n(\log_3 n)^5 = O(n^{1.2}).$$

3.4   Prove, by using Theorem 3.1, that for all constants $a, b > 0$

$$(\log_2 n)^a = O(n^b).$$

3.5   Compare the following pairs of functions in terms of order of magnitude. In each case, say whether $f(n) = O(g(n))$, $f(n) = \Omega(g(n))$, and/or $f(n) = \Theta(g(n))$.

	$f(n)$	$g(n)$
a.	$100n + \log n$	$n + (\log n)^2$
b.	$\log n$	$\log(n^2)$
c.	$\dfrac{n^2}{\log n}$	$n(\log n)^2$
d.	$(\log n)^{\log n}$	$\dfrac{n}{\log n}$
e.	$n^{1/2}$	$(\log n)^5$
f.	$n\,2^n$	3^n

3.6   Solve the following recurrence relation. Give an exact solution.

$$T(n) = T(n-1) + n/2; \quad T(1) = 1.$$

3.7   Solve the following recurrence relation. Give an exact solution.

$$T(n) = 8T(n-1) - 15T(n-2); \quad T(1) = 1; \quad T(2) = 4.$$

3.8   Prove that $T(n)$, which is defined by the recurrence relation

$$T(n) = 2T(\lfloor n/2 \rfloor) + 2n \log_2 n, \quad T(2) = 4,$$

satisfies $T(n) = O(n \log^2 n)$.

3.9   The following recurrence relation describes the running time of a recursive algorithm for matrix multiplication ([Pan 1978]). What is the asymptotic running time of this algorithm?

$$T(n) = 143640T(n/70) + O(n^2), \quad T(1) = 1.$$

3.10   Find the mistake in the following analysis. Let A be an algorithm that works on complete binary trees (namely, binary trees in which all the leafs are at the same depth). Suppose that A performs $O(k)$ steps for each leaf in the tree, where k is a parameter that has to do with the amount of information stored in the leafs (but is otherwise independent of the tree), and constant time c per each internal node. We claim that the total running time of the algorithm is $O(k)$.

Wrong proof: The ''proof'' is by induction on n, the number of nodes in the tree. If $n = 1$, then the total number of steps is obviously $O(k)$. Assume that the claim is true for all complete binary trees with $< n$ nodes, and consider a tree with n nodes. Such a tree consists of a root and two subtrees, each of size $(n-1)/2$. By the induction hypothesis, the running time for the two subtrees is $O(k)$. Hence, the running time for the tree is $O(k) + O(k) + c$. But this is equal to $O(k)$, and the proof is complete.

3.11   Solve the following full-history recurrence relation:

$$T(n) = \max_i \{T(i)\},$$

where $T(1) = 1$.

3.12   Solve the following full-history recurrence relation:

$$T(n) = n + \sum_{i=1}^{n-1} T(i),$$

where $T(1) = 1$.

3.13   Use (3.34) to prove that, for every positive integer k,

$$\sum_{i=1}^{n} i^k = O(n^{k+1}).$$

3.14   Use (3.34) to prove that, for every positive integer k,

$$\sum_{i=1}^{n} i^k \log_2 i = O(n^{k+1} \log n).$$

Creative Exercises

3.15   Find a counterexample to the following claim: $f(n) = O(s(n))$ and $g(n) = O(r(n))$ imply that $f(n) - g(n) = O(s(n) - r(n))$.

3.16   Find a counterexample to the following claim: $f(n) = O(s(n))$ and $g(n) = O(r(n))$ imply that $f(n)/g(n) = O(s(n)/r(n))$.

*3.17   Find two functions $f(n)$ and $g(n)$, both monotonically increasing, such that $f(n) \neq O(g(n))$ and $g(n) \neq O(f(n))$.

3.18   Consider the recurrence relation

$$T(n) = 2T(n/2) + 1, \ \ T(2) = 1.$$

We try to prove that $T(n) = O(n)$ (we limit our attention to powers of 2). We guess that $T(n) \leq cn$ for some (as yet unknown) constant c, and substitute cn in the expression (see Section 3.5.1). We have to show that $cn \geq 2c(n/2) + 1$. But this is clearly not true. Find the correct solution of this recurrence (you can assume that n is a power of 2), and explain why this attempt failed.

3.19   Find the asymptotic behavior of $S(n)$, which satisfies the following recurrence relation:

$$S(mn) \leq cm \log_2 m \ S(n) + O(mn), \ \ S(2) = 1,$$

where m and c are constant parameters. (The solution should be a function of n, m, and c.)

3.20   Prove that the asymptotic solution for the recurrence relation

$$T(n) = 2T(n - c) + k,$$

where both c and k are integer constants, is $T(n) = O(d^n)$ for some constant d.

3.21   The following recurrence relation appears in divide-and-conquer algorithms in which the problem is divided into unequal size parts:

$$T(n) = \sum_{i=1}^{k} a_i T(n/b_i) + cn.$$

All the a_is and b_is are constants, and they satisfy

$$1 - \sum_{i=1}^{k} a_i/b_i > 0.$$

Find the asymptotic behavior of this recurrence relation (by guessing and verifying).

3.22   Solve the following two recurrence relations. It is sufficient to find the asymptotic behavior of $T(n)$.

    a. $T(n) = 4T\left(\left\lceil \sqrt{n} \right\rceil\right) + 1; \ T(2) = 1.$

    b. $T(n) = 2T\left(\left\lceil \sqrt{n} \right\rceil\right) + 2n; \ T(2) = 1.$

(Hint: Substitute another variable for n.)

3.23   Prove that the solution of the recurrence relation

$$T(n) = kT(n/2) + f(n), \ \ T(1) = c$$

is

$$T(n) = n^{\log k} (c + g(2) + g(4) + \cdots + g(n)),$$

where $g(m)$ is defined as $f(m)/m^{\log k}$. You can assume that n is a power of 2. (This is a more general solution than the one given in Section 3.5.2, since it applies to any function $f(n)$.)

3.24   Prove that the solution of the recurrence relation

$$T(n) = k\,T(n/d) + f(n), \quad T(1) = c,$$

is

$$T(n) = n^{\log_d k}\,(c + g(d) + g(d^2) + \cdots + g(n)),$$

where $g(m)$ is defined as $f(m)/m^{\log k}$. You can assume that n is a power of d.

3.25 Find the asymptotic behavior of the function $T(n)$ defined by the recurrence relation

$$T(n) = T(n/2) + T(\lfloor \sqrt{n} \rfloor) + n, \quad T(1) = 1, \ T(2) = 2.$$

You can consider only values of n that are powers of 2.

3.26 Find the asymptotic behavior of the function $T(n)$ defined by the recurrence relation

$$T(n) = T(n/2) + \sqrt{n}, \quad T(1) = 1.$$

You can consider only values of n that are powers of 2.

3.27 Find the asymptotic behavior of the function $T(n)$ defined by the recurrence relation

$$T(n) = T(n/2) + T\left(\left\lfloor \left\lfloor \frac{n}{\log_2 n} \right\rfloor \right\rfloor\right) + n \ (n > 2), \quad T(1) = 1, \ T(2) = 2.$$

You can consider only values of n that are powers of 2.

3.28 Find the solution of the following recurrence relation. It is sufficient to find the asymptotic behavior of $T(n)$. You should give convincing evidence that the function $f(n)$ you find satisfies $f(n) = \Theta(T(n))$.

$$T(n) = 2T\left(\left\lfloor \left\lfloor \frac{n}{\log_2 n} \right\rfloor \right\rfloor\right) + 3n \ (n > 2), \quad T(1) = 1, \ T(2) = 2.$$

3.29 Although in general it is sufficient to evaluate recurrence relations only for powers of 2, that is not always the case. Consider the following relation:

$$T(n) = \begin{cases} T(n/2) + 1 & \text{if } n \text{ is even} \\ 2T((n-1)/2) & \text{if } n \text{ is odd,} \end{cases}$$

with $T(1) = 1$.

a. Prove that the solution of this recurrence for powers of 2 is $T(2^k) = k + 1$ (namely, for powers of 2, $T(n) = O(\log n)$).

b. Show that, for an infinite number of values of n, $T(n) = \Omega(n)$. Discuss why the usual assumption about the relative behavior for powers of 2 and nonpowers of 2 breaks down for this recurrence.

3.30 Use (3.34) to prove that

$$S(n) = \sum_{i=1}^{n} \lceil \log_2(n/i) \rceil$$

satisfies $S(n) = O(n)$.

3.31 Compute the following sum precisely:

$$S(n) = \sum_{i=1}^{n} \lceil \log_2(n/i) \rceil.$$

You can assume that n is a power of 2.

3.32   The Fibonacci numbers $F(n)$ can be extended to negative values of n using the same definition: $F(n+2) = F(n+1) + F(n)$, and $F(1) = 1$, $F(0) = 0$ (e.g., $F(-1) = 1$, $F(-2) = -1$, and so on). Let $G(n)$ be defined as $F(-n)$. Write a recurrence relation for $G(n)$, and suggest a way to solve it.

3.33   Prove that $G(n) = (-1)^{n+1} F(n)$.

CHAPTER 4

A BRIEF INTRODUCTION TO
DATA STRUCTURES

Science is nothing but trained and organized common sense.
T.H. Huxley, 1878

*I hate intellectuals; they are from the top down;
I am from the bottom up.*
Frank Lloyd Wright (1869–1959)

4.1 Introduction

Data structures are the building blocks of computer algorithms. A design of an algorithm
is like a design of a building. One has to put all the rooms together in a way that is the
most effective for the intended use of the building. To do that, it is not enough to know
about functionality, efficiency, form, and beauty. One needs a thorough knowledge of
construction techniques. Putting a room in midair may achieve the desired effect, but it
is not possible. Other ideas may be possible, but too expensive. In the same way, a
design of an algorithm must be based on a thorough understanding of data structure
techniques and costs.

In this short chapter, we review only the basic data structures used throughout the
book. We do not intend this chapter to provide a comprehensive treatment of data
structures. That would require (at least) a whole book, and indeed, there are many
excellent such books. We expect that most readers have already studied data structures
in some depth. This chapter is intended mostly for quick review.

A useful notion in the study of data structures is that of an **abstract data type**. Normally, when we write a program, we have to specify the data type (e.g., integers, reals, characters). But, in some cases, the data type is not important for the design of the algorithm. For example, we may want to maintain a first-in first-out (FIFO) queue of items. The required operations are *insertions* of items into the queue, and *removals* of items from the queue. In case of removals, the items must be removed in the same order in which they were inserted. It is more convenient and more general to design the algorithms for these operations without specifying the data type of the items. We specify only the required operations. We call the abstract data type that supports these operations a *FIFO queue*. The most important part of an abstract data type is a list of operations that we want to support. Another example of an abstract data type is a queue in which the items have priorities. The removals are not according to the order of insertions, but according to the priorities. That is, the first item to be removed in each step is the item of highest priority among the items in the queue. This abstract data type is called a **priority queue**. Again, we do not specify the data type of the items. (In this case, we do not even have to specify the data type of the priorities; we need only to assume that the priorities are totally ordered and that we can determine that order.)

By concentrating on the operational nature of a data structure, and not on a precise implementation for a particular problem, we make the design more general. The techniques for implementing a priority queue, for example, are for the most part independent of the exact data type. If we realize that our needs correspond to the definition of the abstract data type, we can immediately use it. Abstract data types allow us to make the algorithm-design process more modular.

4.2 Elementary Data Structures

4.2.1 Elements

We use the notion of an **element** throughout this book as a generic name for an unspecified data type. An element can be an integer, a set of integers, a file of text, or another data structure. We use this term whenever the discussion is independent of the type of data. Consider, for example, sorting algorithms. If the only steps the algorithm takes are comparing elements and moving them around, then the same algorithm can be used for sorting integers or names (strings of characters). The implementation (that is, the program) may be slightly different, but the ideas are the same. Since we often concentrate on the ideas rather than on the implementation, it is reasonable to ignore the types of the elements.

The only assumptions we make about elements are the following:

1. Elements can be compared for equality.
2. Elements are taken from a totally ordered set, and it is possible to tell whether one element is "less than" another. We usually are not concerned with the exact definition of the relation "less than," as long as it is a valid total order.
3. Elements can be copied.

All these operations are counted as taking one unit of time. Although the unit is relative to the *size* of the actual elements, we usually will regard these operations as taking constant time. Most of the time, it is easier to think of an element simply as an integer, even though the algorithm may also work for more complicated structures.

4.2.2 Arrays

An **array** is a row of elements of the same type. The **size** of an array is the number of elements in that array. This size must be fixed. Since the size of the array is fixed, and all the elements are of the same type, the amount of memory that should be allocated to store the array is known a priori. For example, if the elements are names with 8 characters each, if each character requires 1 byte of storage, and if the size of the array is 100, then 800 bytes are required to store the array. The storage for an array is always consecutive. If the first byte of the array is stored at location x in memory, then the kth byte of the array is stored at location $x + k - 1$. Consequently, it is easy to compute the starting location of the storage of each element in the array. In our example, if the starting location of the array is at 10000, then the 55th name starts at the 433th byte, which is stored at location 10432, assuming locations are numbered by bytes. (This calculation can be easily modified if locations are numbered differently.)

Arrays are very efficient and very common data structures. Every element of an array can be accessed in constant time. The algorithm designer who uses a high-level language is rarely concerned with location calculations — they are done by the compiler. As a rule of thumb, arrays should be used whenever possible. The main drawbacks for using arrays are their restrictions. Arrays cannot be used to store elements of different types (or sizes), and the size of an array cannot be changed dynamically. We deal with these two restrictions in the following subsections.

4.2.3 Records

Records are similar to arrays, except that we do not assume that all elements are of the same type. A record is thus a list of elements of different types. The exact combination of types is fixed. Like that of an array, the storage size of a record is known in advance. Each element in a record can be accessed in constant time. This is accomplished by keeping an array with the same number of elements, such that for each element the array contains its starting location. This array is needed only to enable a constant time access to any record element. Such access is achieved by consulting the array for the location of the element. The exact program that maintains the array is created automatically by the compiler.

For example, a record may consist of 2 integers, 3 arrays of 20 integers each, 4 more integers, and 2 names each containing 12 characters. (Note that the two array types in the record are considered now to be elements by themselves.) This record is defined in Fig. 4.1. The array stored with the record contains the starting relative locations of all the elements. Thus, if each integer is stored in 4 bytes, Int6, which is the ninth element in the record, starts at byte number 261 ($2 \cdot 4 + 3 \cdot 20 \cdot 4 + 3 \cdot 4 + 1$). Since the sizes of all the elements in the records are known, it is possible to compute the location of each element

```
record example1
begin
        Int1 : integer ;
        Int2 : integer ;
        Ar1  : array [1..20] of integer ;
        Ar2  : array [1..20] of integer ;
        Ar3  : array [1..20] of integer ;
        Int3 : integer ;
        Int4 : integer ;
        Int5 : integer ;
        Int6 : integer ;
        Name1 : array [1..12] of character ;
        Name2 : array [1..12] of character
end
```

Figure 4.1   Definition of a record.

in constant time.   Like that for arrays, the storage for a record is always consecutive; similarly, it is not possible to add elements dynamically.

4.2.4 Linked Lists

There are many applications in which the number of elements is changing dynamically as the algorithm progresses.   It is possible to define all the elements as arrays (or records) large enough to ensure sufficient storage space.   This is often a good solution, but, of course, it is not very efficient to demand storage according to the worst case (and, in many cases, the worst case is unknown).   Furthermore, there are cases where there is a need for insertions and deletions in the *middle* of the list.   If we use arrays and we need to insert an element in the middle, we have to shift all other elements.   This inefficiency is inherent in the consecutive representation of arrays; thus, arbitrary insertions and deletions are very costly for large arrays.   For these cases we need **dynamic data structures**.   We use dynamic data structures extensively throughout this book; a familiarity with them is essential.

Linked lists are the simplest form of dynamic data structures.   Suppose we have a list of elements and we want to be able to insert new elements and to delete old elements efficiently.   The idea is to abandon the consecutive representation of arrays.   Instead, each element is represented separately, and all elements are connected through the use of pointers.   A **pointer** is simply a variable that holds as its value the address of another element.   A **linked list** is a list of pairs, each consisting of an element and a pointer, such that each pointer contains the address of the next pair.   Each such pair is represented by a record.   A linked list can be scanned by following the addresses in the pointers.   Such a scan must be a **linear scan**.   That is, it is not possible to access each element directly — we must traverse the list in order.

There are two major drawbacks to the linked-list representation. First, it requires more space. There is one additional pointer per element. Second, if we want to look at the 30th element, for example, we need to start at the beginning and look at 29 pointers, one at a time. With arrays, we could make a simple calculation and find the 30th element directly. On the other hand, there is one major advantage to this representation. Suppose that we find the 30th element and we now want to insert a new 31st element.[1] All we need to do is to set the pointer associated with the new 31st element to the address of the previous 31st element (this address is stored in the 30th pointer), and set the 30th pointer to point to the new 31st element (see Fig. 4.2). Only two operations are required. With arrays, all elements following the 30th element would need to be moved. A delete operation is also simple. If we want to delete the 31st element, we simply set the 30th pointer to point to the 32nd element, by copying the address stored at the 31st pointer (see Fig. 4.3). Only two operations are required.

The discussion of insertions and deletions in linked lists has ignored several important details that tend to make the implementation of linked lists a little more complicated. The main problem is how to detect the end of the list. Usually, a special

Figure 4.2   Inserting a new element into a linked list.

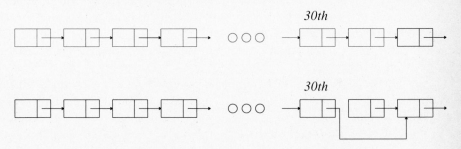

Figure 4.3   Deleting an element from a linked list.

---

[1] The number system is consecutive in nature. It is thus confusing to talk about the new 31st and the old 31st element. We often uses ''30a'' to denote an insertion after 30. This notation causes many problems. If we insert again after the 30th, we may run out of notation ($30a_a$?). This is a good example of the need for dynamic data structures.

address, called **nil**, is provided, such that a nil pointer is a pointer to nowhere; it can be used to indicate an end of a list. Another possibility is to introduce a regular record, but to include in it a key that will guarantee that the search will end there. This additional record, sometimes called a **dummy record**, makes the program simpler, since there are fewer special cases. Dummy records are useful for a variety of data structures.

4.3 Trees

The only structure that arrays and linked lists can capture is the order of the elements they represent. There are numerous applications that require more structure. Trees represent hierarchical structures. They can also serve as a more efficient data structure for certain operations on linear structures. In this section, we will be concerned with only hierarchical trees, also known as rooted trees or arborescences. A **rooted tree** is a set of elements, which we call **nodes** (or vertices), together with a set of edges that connect the elements in a special way (see Fig. 4.4). One node is the root of the tree (the top of the hierarchy). The root is connected to other nodes, which are at level 1 of the hierarchy; they, in turn, are connected to nodes at level 2, and so on. All the connections are thus between nodes and their direct unique ''supervisors'' (usually called **parents** after genealogical trees). Only the root has no parent. The main property of trees is that they do not have cycles. As a result, there is a unique path between any two nodes of a tree.

A node is connected to its parent and to several underlings (again, following the genealogical terminology, we will call the latter **children**). The maximal number of children of any node in the tree is called the **degree** of the tree. We usually order the children of every node, then identify them by their index in that order (the first, second, and so on). In the special case of trees of degree 2, called **binary trees**, we identify the children by **left** (for first) and **right** (for second). A node with no children is called a **leaf** (this time, the terminology comes from real trees). A node that is not a leaf is called an **internal node**. The **height** of a tree is the maximal level of the tree, namely, the

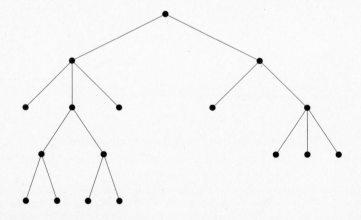

Figure 4.4   A rooted tree.

maximal distance between the root and a leaf. Each node has a **key**, which comes from a totally ordered set (for example, a real number or an integer). We will interchangeably refer to the key and the node as the same when no confusion can arise. For convenience, we assume that we deal with unique keys. Otherwise, we can link together all the elements with the same key in a linked list and have one node with a pointer to that list. Each node usually has a **data** field containing the data (or a pointer to the data) that is associated with the node. The data field depends on the application, and we will generally not deal with it.

In this section, we concentrate on two uses of trees: search trees, and heaps. In both cases, binary trees are used. We start with a discussion of the representation of trees in memory.

4.3.1 Representation of Trees

There are two main representations of trees, an **implicit** representation and an **explicit** representation. In the explicit representation, the connection of one tree node to another is done by a pointer. A node with k children is a record containing an array of k pointers. (In some applications, a node also contains a pointer to its parent.) It is usually more convenient to have all the nodes of the same type. Hence, all nodes have m pointers, where m is the maximal number of children in the tree. Alternately, it is possible to associate only two pointers per node in the following way. The first pointer points to the first child, and the second pointer points to the next sibling. Figure 4.5 illustrates the two representations of the same tree. The main drawback of the second representation is that, to get hold of all the children of a node, we have to traverse a linked list.

No pointers are used in the implicit representation. An array is used to store all the nodes of the tree, and the connections are implied by the positions of the nodes in the array. The most common way of implementing an implicit tree representation is the following. Consider a binary tree T. The root of T is stored in $A[1]$. The left and right children of the root are stored in $A[2]$ and $A[3]$; the two children of the left child of the root are stored in $A[4]$ and $A[5]$; and so on. The array represents a traversal of the tree

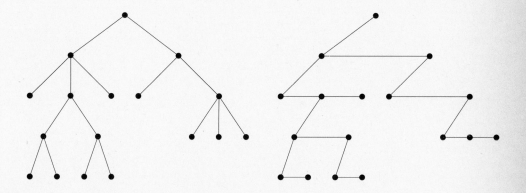

Figure 4.5 Binary representation of a nonbinary tree.

from left to right, level by level. We can define the representation by induction: (1) The root is stored at $A[1]$ (the base case). (2) The left child of a node v that is stored in $A[i]$ is stored in $A[2i]$, and v's right child is stored in $A[2i+1]$. The advantage of this representation is that no pointers are required, which saves storage. On the other hand, if the tree is unbalanced, namely, if some leaves are much farther away from the root than others are, then many nonexisting nodes must be represented. An unbalanced tree is shown in Fig. 4.6; the numbers below each node indicate its position in the array. An array of size 30 is needed to represent 8 nodes. The implicit representation thus may or may not save storage, depending on the tree. Also, since arrays are used, dynamic operations in the middle of the tree are costly. On the other hand, dynamic operations can be reasonably supported if they are limited to nodes that correspond to the end of the array.

4.3.2 Heaps

A heap is a binary tree whose keys satisfy the following *heap property*:

> The key of every node is greater than or equal to the key of any of its children.

By the transitivity law, the heap property implies that the key of every node is greater than or equal to the keys of all that node's descendants. Heaps are useful in implementing a **priority queue**, which is an abstract data type defined by the following two operations:

Insert(x): insert a key x into the data structure.

Remove(): remove the largest key from the data structure.

Heaps can be implemented with either the explicit or the implicit tree representation. We will use the implicit representation, since we can ensure that the heaps will be balanced. We assume that the array is $A[1..k]$, where k is an upper bound on the number of elements the heap will ever contain (if an upper bound is not known, then a linked

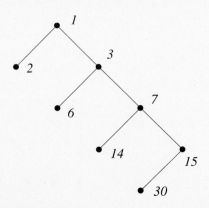

Figure 4.6   Implicit representation of an unbalanced tree.

representation is required). Let n denote the current number of elements in the heap; namely, only the array $A[1..n]$ is of interest at any moment. We now proceed to describe how to implement insert and remove efficiently with the use of heaps.

We start with the *Remove* operation. By the heap property, the node with the largest key in a heap is the root, $A[1]$. So, a *Remove* operation always removes the key from the root. The problem is to restore the heap property after the key of the root has been deleted. We now have an array $A[2..n]$, which corresponds to two separate heaps. We first take the leaf $A[n]$, delete it, and put it in place of the root. That is, we let $A[1] := A[n]$, and decrement the value of n by one. Denote the value of the new $A[1]$ by x. We still have two separate heaps plus a value on top, which may or may not satisfy the heap property. (The only way for x to satisfy the heap property at this point is if the whole path from the root to where x was contained the value x.) To restore the heap property, we now propagate x down the tree, until it reaches a subtree for which it is a maximum. This is done by comparing x with the values of its two children ($A[2]$ and $A[3]$) and, if x is not the maximal among the three, by exchanging $A[1]$ with the largest of them. Assume that $A[2]$ is the maximal. Then, $A[2]$ is clearly the maximal key in the whole heap, so it can be put in the root position. Furthermore, the subtree rooted at $A[3]$ remains unchanged, and thus it also satisfies the heap property. We have to worry only about the subtree rooted at $A[2]$ (because now it has x in its root). But now we can continue inductively in the same way. Assume that we continue for i steps, and that the key x is now at $A[j]$. Only the tree rooted at $A[j]$ may not satisfy the heap property. We again compare x to its two new children, $A[2j]$ and $A[2j+1]$ (if they exist), and exchange if x is not the maximal. The algorithm terminates either when x becomes the maximal of a subtree, or when it reaches a leaf. The maximal number of comparisons required for a deletion is $2\lceil \log_2 n \rceil$, which is twice the height of the tree. The algorithm for removing a maximum element from a heap is given in Fig. 4.7.

An *Insert* operation is similar. We first increment n by one, and insert the new key as the new leaf $A[n]$. We then compare the new leaf with its parent, and exchange if the new leaf is larger than its parent. At this point, the new key is the maximal of its subtree (since the parent was the maximal and it was found to be larger). We assume, inductively, that the tree rooted at $A[j]$ (initially $A[n]$) satisfies the heap condition, and that if we remove this tree the rest of the heap satisfies the heap property. We continue this process, promoting the new key up the tree, until the new key is not larger than its parent (or until it reaches the root). At this point, the whole tree is a valid heap. The maximal number of comparisons required for an insertion is $\lceil \log_2 n \rceil$, which is the height of the tree. The algorithm for inserting an element into a heap is given in Fig. 4.8.

Overall, we can perform any sequence of *Insert* and *Remove* operations in time $O(\log n)$ per operation. On the other hand, it is not possible to perform other operations efficiently with a heap. For example, if we want to *search* for a given key, the hierarchy given by the heap is not useful. A Heap is a good example of an implementation of an abstract data type. A heap supports a limited number of specific operations very efficiently. Whenever we need these particular operations, we can impose the heap structure on the data whatever its type is.

Algorithm Remove_Max_from_Heap (A, n) ;
Input: *A* (an array of size *n* representing a heap).
Output: *Top_of_the_Heap* (the maximal element of the heap), *A* (the new
heap), and *n* (the new size of the heap; if *n* = 0, then the heap is empty).

begin
    if *n* = 0 **then** print "the heap is empty"
    else
        Top_of_the_Heap := A [1] ;
        A [1] *:= A* [*n*] ;
        n := n - 1 ;
        parent := 1 ;
        child := 2 ;
        while *child* ≤ *n - 1* **do**
            if *A[child] < A[child+1]* **then**
                child := child + 1 ;
            if *A[child] > A[parent]* **then**
                swap(A[parent], A[child]) ;
                parent := child ;
                *child := 2*child* ;
            else *child := n* { *to stop the loop* }
end

Figure 4.7 Algorithm *Remove_Max_from_Heap.*

Algorithm Insert_to_Heap (A, n, x) ;
Input: *A* (an array of size *n* representing a heap), and *x* (a number).
Output: *A* (the new heap), and *n* (the new size of the heap).

begin
    n := n + 1 ; { *we assume that the array does not overflow* }
    A [*n*] *:= x* ;
    child := n ;
    parent := n div 2 ;
    while *parent* ≥ *1* **do**
        if *A[parent] < A[child]* **then**
            swap(A[parent], A[child]) ; { *see also Exercise 4.6* }
            child := parent ;
            parent := parent div 2 ;
        else *parent := 0* { *to stop the loop* }
end

Figure 4.8 Algorithm *Insert_to_Heap.*

4.3.3 Binary Search Trees

Binary search trees implement efficiently the following operations:

> *search(x)*: find the key x in the data structure, or determine that x is not there (for simplicity, we will assume that each key appears at most once).
>
> *insert(x)*: insert the key x into the data structure (unless it is already there).
>
> *delete(x)*: delete the key x from the data structure if it is there.

Abstract data types that handle these three operations are called **dictionaries**. Binary search trees implement dictionaries efficiently, as well as other more complicated operations. We will use the explicit representation of trees in this section, since dynamic insertions and deletions are important parts of binary search trees. We do not want to limit ourselves to a given upper bound for the number of elements. We assume that each node in the tree is a record containing at least three fields: *key*, *left*, and *right*, such that *key* holds the key associated with the node, and *left* and *right* are pointers to other nodes (or to nil). Binary search trees are more complicated than heaps, because in heaps only leaves are added or removed and keys exchanged, whereas in binary search trees, any node may be removed and the pointers may be manipulated in many other ways. For simplicity, we assume that all keys are distinct.

Search

As its name suggests, a search tree is a structure to facilitate searching. The structure becomes clear once the search procedure is understood. Assume that we have a key x and we want to know whether it is currently a key of a node in the tree, and if it is, we want to find that node. This operation is called a **search**. We first compare x against the root of the tree, whose value is, say, r. If $x = r$, then we are done. If $x < r$, then we continue the search from the left child; otherwise, we continue the search from the right child. Each key in the search tree serves to divide the range of the keys below it: the keys in the left subtree are all smaller than it, and the keys in the right subtree are all greater than it. This rule defines search trees. We say that the tree is **consistent** if all the keys satisfy this condition. A simple recursive program for searching in a binary search tree is presented in Fig. 4.9.

Insertion

Insertions into binary search trees are also quite simple. Given a key x to insert, a search for x is performed first. If x is already in the tree, then it will be found and the insertion will be aborted. (We assume that we do not want several nodes with the same key.) Otherwise, the search ends (unsuccessfully) at a leaf. A node containing the new key can then be inserted below that leaf (as either a right child or a left child, depending on the value of x). The tree remains consistent, since subsequent searches for x will get to the same leaf and through it to the new node. The search program must be changed slightly so that we find the leaf. We use this opportunity to write a nonrecursive search program, which is given in Fig. 4.10.

Algorithm BST_Search *(root, x)* ;

Input: *root* (a pointer to a root of a binary search tree), and *x* (a number).

Output: *node* (a pointer to the node containing the key *x*, or *nil* if no such node exists).

begin
    if *root = nil or root^.key = x* **then** *node := root*
    { root^ is the record that the pointer root is pointing to. }
    else
        if *x < root^.key* **then** *BST_Search(root^.left, x)*
        else *BST_Search(root^.right, x)*
end

Figure 4.9 Algorithm *BST_search*.

Algorithm BST_Insert *(root, x)* ;

Input: *root* (a pointer to a root of a binary search tree), and *x* (a number).

Output: The tree is changed by inserting a node with the key *x* pointed to by the pointer *child*; if there is already a node with key *x*, then *child* = nil.

begin
    if *root = nil* **then**
        create a new node pointed to by child ;
        root := child ;
        root^.key := x
    else
        node := root ;
        child := root ; *{ to initialize it so that it is not nil }*
        while *node ≠ nil and child ≠ nil* **do**
            if *node^.key = x* **then** *child := nil*
            else
                parent := node ;
                if *x < node^.key* **then** *node := node^.left*
                else *node := node^.right* ;
        if *child ≠ nil* **then**
            create a new node pointed to by child ;
            child^.key := x ;
            child^.left := nil ; *child^right := nil* ;
            if *x < parent^.key* **then** *parent^left := child*
                else *parent^.right := child*
  end

Figure 4.10 Algorithm *BST_insert*.

Deletion

Deletions are generally more complicated. It is easy to delete a leaf; we need only to change the pointer to it to be nil. It is also not hard to delete a node that has only one child; the pointer to the node is changed to point to its child. However, if the node we want to delete has two children, then we need to find a place for the two pointers. Let B be a node with two children whose key we want to delete (see Fig. 4.11). In the first step, we exchange the key of B with a key of another node X, such that (1) X has at most one child, and (2) deleting X (after the exchange) will leave the tree consistent. In the second step, we delete X, which now has the key of B which we wanted to delete. We can easily delete X, because it has at most one child. To preserve the consistency of the tree, the key of X must be at least as large as all the keys in the left subtree of B, and must be smaller than all the keys in the right subtree of B. Notice that the key of X in Fig. 4.11 satisfies these constraints: it is the largest among the keys in the left subtree of B. X is called the **predecessor** of B in the tree. X cannot have a right child, since otherwise it would not have the largest key in that subtree. The deletion algorithm is presented in Fig. 4.12.

Complexity   The running times of search, insert, and delete depend on the shape of the tree and the location of the relevant node. In the worst case, the search path would take us all the way to the bottom. All the other steps in the algorithms require only constant time (e.g., the actual insertion, the exchange of keys in the deletion). So, the worst-case running time is the maximal length of a path from the root to a leaf, which is the height of the tree. If the tree is reasonably balanced (we will define balance shortly), then its height is approximately $\log_2 n$, where n is the number of nodes in the tree. All the operations are efficient in this case. If the tree is unbalanced, then these operations are much less efficient.

If the keys are inserted into a binary search tree in a random order, then the expected height of the tree is $O(\log n)$ — more precisely, $2ln\,n$. In this case, the search and insert operations are efficient. In the worst case, however, the height of the tree can be n (when the tree is a simple linked list). Trees with long paths can result, for example, from insertions in a sorted, or close to sorted, order. Also, deletions may cause problems even if they occur in a random order. The main reason for that is the asymmetry of always using the predecessor to replace a deleted node. If there are frequent deletions,

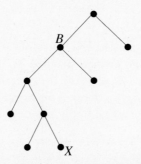

Figure 4.11 Deleting a node with two children.

Algorithm BST_Delete (root, x) ;
Input: *root* (a pointer to a root of a binary search tree), and *x* (a number).
Output: The tree is changed by deleting a node with the key *x*, if it exists.
    { We assume that the root is never deleted, and that all keys are distinct }

begin
    node := root ;
    while *node ≠ nil and node^.key ≠ x* **do**
        parent := node ;
        if *x < node^.key* **then** *node := node^.left*
        else *node := node^.right ;*
    if *node = nil* **then** *print("x is not in the tree") ; halt ;*
    if *node ≠ root* **then**
        if *node^.left = nil* **then**
            if *x ≤ parent^.key* **then**
                parent^.left := node^.right
            else *parent^.right := node^.right*
        else if *node^.right = nil* **then**
            if *x ≤ parent^.key* **then**
                parent^.left := node^.left
            else *parent^.right := node^.left*
        else *{the two children case }*
            node1 := node^.left ;
            parent1 := node ;
            while *node1^.right ≠ nil* **do**
                parent1 := node1 ;
                node1 := node1^.right ;
            { now comes the actual deletion }
            parent1^.right := node1^.left ;
            node^.key := node1^.key
  end

Figure 4.12 Algorithm *BST_delete*.

---

followed by insertions, the tree may have a height of $O(\sqrt{n})$, even for random insertions and deletions. This asymmetry can be avoided if, instead of always choosing the predecessor of the deleted node, we alternate between the predecessor and the successor (which is a smallest key in the right subtree). Fortunately, there are ways to prevent the creation of long paths in binary search trees. We describe one such method in the next section.

4.3.4 AVL Trees

AVL trees (named after Adel'son-Vel'skii and Landis [1962]) were the first data
structures to guarantee $O(\log n)$ running time for search, insert, and delete *in the worst
case* (n is the number of elements). The main idea in AVL trees (and in most other tree
structures that achieve logarithmic bounds) is to spend additional time when inserting and
deleting to *balance* the tree, such that the height of the tree is always bounded by
$O(\log n)$. The time devoted to balancing must not exceed $O(\log n)$, or else insertions
and deletions will be too expensive. The idea is to define balance in such a way that it is
easy to maintain.

> **Definition**: An AVL tree is a binary search tree such that, for every node,
> the difference between the heights of its left and right subtrees is at most 1
> (the height of an empty tree is defined as 0).

This definition guarantees a maximal height of $O(\log n)$, as is shown in the next theorem.

☐ Theorem 4.1

The height h of an AVL tree with n internal nodes satisfies

$$h < 1.4404 \log_2(n+2) - 0.328.$$

Proof: Left as an exercise.   ☐

This theorem implies that search in an AVL tree requires $O(\log n)$ comparisons. The
problem is how to perform insertions and deletions and still to maintain the AVL
property. We start with insertions; again, we assume that all the keys are distinct.

Let x be a new key that we wish to insert into an AVL tree. First, we insert x at the
bottom of the tree in the usual way. If, after the insertion, the tree remains an AVL tree,
then we are done. Otherwise, we need to *rebalance* the tree. There are four possibilities
— two of them are illustrated in Fig. 4.13; the other two are symmetric (to the right).

In part (a) of Fig. 4.13, the new node was inserted into the left subtree, making the
height of B equal to $h+2$, whereas the height of C is h. To remedy this unbalance, we
perform a **rotation**: We move B to the top and change the rest of the tree according to the
binary search property (Fig. 4.14). The height of the new subtree, rooted at B, is now
$h+2$, which is the same as the height of the original subtree before the insertion. As a
result, no more balancing is required. This rotation is called a **single rotation**. It will not
help in part (b) of Fig. 4.13; a **double rotation** is required (Fig. 4.15). Again, the new
subtree has the same height as the original one, so no more balancing is required. An
important property of AVL trees is that one rotation (single or double) is always
sufficient after an insertion. We omit the proof.

The node A in both examples is called the **critical node**. It is the root of the
smallest subtree that becomes a non-AVL subtree as a result of the insertion. To perform
the insertion, we have to find the critical node and to determine which of the cases is
involved. We maintain in each node a **balance factor**, which is equal to the difference
between the heights of the left and right subtrees of this node. For AVL trees, the

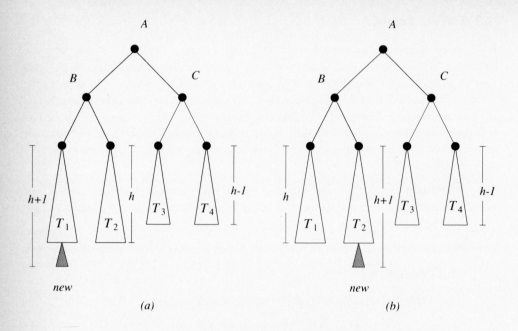

Figure 4.13 Insertions that invalidate the AVL property.

balance factor of each node is 1, −1, or 0. An insertion into a subtree requires rebalancing if the balance factor was either 1 or −1, and the insertion increases the height of a subtree in the "wrong" direction. That implies that the critical node must have a nonzero balance factor. Moreover, if a lower node has a nonzero balance factor, then, after balancing, the heights from that node will be the same as they were before the

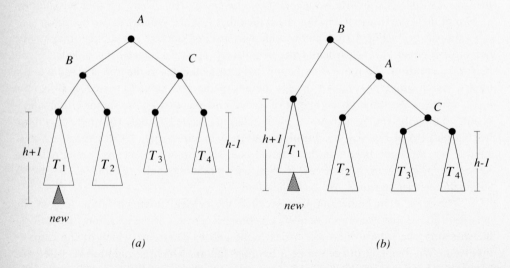

Figure 4.14 A single rotation: (a) Before. (b) After.

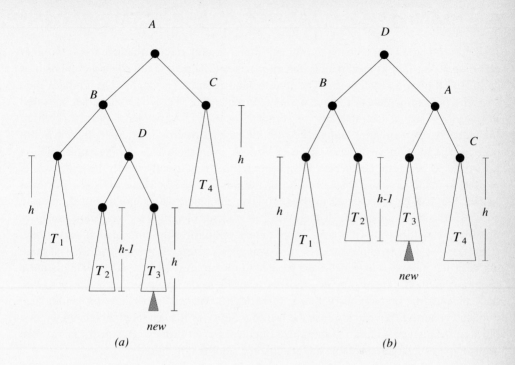

Figure 4.15 A double rotation: (a) Before. (b) After.

insertion (recall that the balancing retains the old heights from the critical node). Hence, the critical node is the lowest ancestor of the new node with nonzero balance factor. On the way down the tree, we look at the balance factors, remembering the last nonzero one. When we reach the leaf, we can easily determine whether we insert to the ''right'' or ''wrong'' direction. We then make another pass (either bottom up or top down — preferably bottom up, since that usually involves less nodes), readjust the balance factors, and perform a rotation if necessary. We omit the details.

Deletions are, as usual, more complicated. It is no longer true that the tree can be rebalanced with only one single or double rotation after a deletion. There are cases where $O(\log n)$ rotations are required, where n is the number of nodes in the tree. Fortunately, each rotation requires only constant number of steps; thus, the worst-case running time of a deletion is still $O(\log n)$. Again, we omit the details.

Comments   AVL trees form an efficient data structure. They perform well in the worst case, requiring at most 45% more comparisons than optimal trees, and even better in the average case. Empirical studies have shown the average search time to be approximately $\log_2 n + 0.25$ comparisons (see Knuth [1973], pp. 460]). The main disadvantages of AVL trees are the need for extra storage for the balance factors, and the fact that the program that implements them is rather complicated. Many other schemes for balanced-search trees have been proposed, including 2-3 trees, B-trees, weight-balance trees, and red-black trees.

4.4 Hashing

Hashing is one of the most (if not *the* most) useful data structures for computer algorithms. Hashing is used mainly for insertions and searches, and some variations of it can also be used for deletions. The idea behind hashing is simple. Designing a data structure for storing data with keys numbered from 1 to n is easy: The data can be stored in an array of size n, such that key i is stored at location i. Any key can thus be accessed immediately. If there are n unique keys in the range 1 to $2n$, for example, then it is still usually best to store them in an array of size $2n$, even though the storage utilization is now only 50 percent. The access is so efficient that it is usually worth the extra space. However, if the keys are integers, say, in the range 1 to M, where M is the maximal integer that can be represented in the particular computer, we cannot afford to allocate space of size M. For example, if there are 250 students identified by their social-security number, we will not allocate an array of size 1 billion to store information about them (there are 1 billion possible social-security numbers). Instead, we can use the last three digits of the numbers, in which case we need only an array of size 1000. This is not a foolproof method. There may be students with the same last three digits (in fact, with 250 students, the probability of that is quite high). We will show how to handle such duplicates shortly. We can also use the last four digits, or the last three digits and the first letter of the student's name, to minimize duplicates even further. However, using more digits requires a larger-size table and results in a smaller utilization.

We assume that we are given a set of n keys taken from a large set U of size M, such that M is much larger than n. We want to store the keys in a table of size m, such that m is not much larger than n. The idea is to use a function, called a **hash function**, to map the keys, which are in the range 1 to M, to new keys in the range 1 to m, so we can store everything in an array of size m. Taking the last three digits of a large integer is such a function. It maps a large set U of size 1 billion to a set of size 1000. Each possible key is thus given a place (index) in a table of size m. We will attempt to store the key in that particular place in the table. If the function is easy to compute, then accessing the key is also easy. However, since the set U is large and the table is small, no matter what function we use, many keys will be mapped into the same place in the table. When two keys are mapped to the same location in the table, we call it a **collision**. We are thus faced with two problems: (1) finding a hash function that minimizes the likelihood of collisions, and (2) handling collisions.

Even though the set U is much larger than the size of the table, the actual set of keys we handle is usually not too large. A good hash function should map the keys uniformly in the table. Of course, no hash function can map all possible sets of keys without collisions. If the size of U is M and the size of the hash table is m, then there must be at least M/m keys that are mapped into the same place. If the mapping is uniform, each location will have approximately M/m keys mapped into it. Hash functions should transform a set of keys uniformly to a set of *random* locations in the range 1 to m. The uniformity and randomness are the essence in hashing. For example, instead of taking the last three digits of the social-security number, we could take the last three digits of the student's year of birth. It is clear that this is an inferior hash function, since it is much more likely that many students were born in the same year than it is that many students have the same last three digits of the social-security number.

Hash Functions

We assume that the keys are integers, and that the size of the hash table is m. A simple and effective hash function is $h(x) = x \bmod m$, where m is a prime number. If the size of the table cannot be adjusted easily to be a prime (it is convenient sometimes to have a size that is a power of 2, for example), then the following hash function can be used: $h(x) = (x \bmod p) \bmod m$, where p is a prime, and $p > m$ (p should be sufficiently larger than m to be effective, but it should also be sufficiently smaller than $|U|$).

As we have already mentioned, no hash function can be good for all inputs. Using primes as described is fairly safe, since most data in practice have no structure related to prime numbers. On the other hand, it is always possible (although unlikely) that, in a certain application, one will want to store results of some experiments made on integers all of which are of the form $r + kp$ for a constant r. All these numbers of course will have the same hash values if p is used as described. We can take the idea of scrambling data with hashing one step further, and use a random procedure to select a hash function! For example, the prime p can be selected at random from a list of primes in the appropriate range. Finding a large list of primes, however, is not easy. Another possibility is the following: At random, select two numbers a and b, such that $a, b < p$, and $a \neq 0$, and let $h(x) = [ax + b \bmod p] \bmod m$. This function is more complicated to compute than the previous one is, but it has the advantage that it is very good *on the average* for all inputs. Of course, the same hash function must be used for all accesses to the same table. In many cases, however, there is a need for many independent tables, or tables that are created and destroyed frequently. In those cases, a different hash function can be used every time a different table is created. The random hash functions described above have certain other desirable properties.

Handling Collisions

The simplest way to handle collisions is to use a method called **separate chaining**. Each entry in the hash table serves as a head of a linked list containing all the keys that are hashed into that entry. To access a key, we hash it and then perform linear search on the appropriate linked list. A new key can be inserted into the beginning of the list (but the list must be searched to ensure that the key is not a duplicate). A search may be inefficient if some lists are long. The lists will be long if the size of the table is small compared to the actual number of keys or if the hash function is bad. Thus, hashing is not a good dynamic structure. It is important to have a good estimate on the number of keys. The main problem with separate chaining is that it requires dynamic memory allocation and more space for the pointers (even if the number of keys is not too large, and the pointers are not used). On the other hand, if for some reason the estimate of the appropriate table size is wrong, separate hashing will still work, whereas other static methods will fail.

Another simple method is **linear probing**. The size of the table is fixed, and there are no pointers. The hash function determines the place of the key in the table. If that place is already occupied, that is, if a collision occurs, then the first empty place after it is taken instead. A search for the key follows the same procedure. (The table is considered in a cyclic order; if the last place is reached and it is full, then the first place is considered next.) An unsuccessful search thus ends at the first empty place. When the table is relatively empty, this simple method works well. If the table is relatively full, there will be many **secondary collisions**, which are collisions that are caused by keys with different hash values. We cannot avoid collisions with keys that have the same hash function, because such keys are mapped into the same place. We should, however, try to minimize secondary collisions. Let's look at an example. Suppose that the ith place is full and that the $(i+1)$th place is empty. A new key, which is mapped to i, will cause a collision, and will be inserted into $i+1$. This case is efficient, since the collision is resolved with minimal effort. However, if a new key is now mapped to $i+1$, there will be a secondary collision and $i+2$ will become full (if it is not full already). Any new key mapped to i, to $i+1$, or to $i+2$ will not only encounter secondary collisions, but will also increase the size of the full segment, causing more secondary collisions later. This effect is called **clustering**. When the table is almost full, the number of secondary collisions with linear probing will be very high, and the search will degrade to linear search.

Deletions cannot be implemented efficiently with linear probing. If an insertion "passes" through a key on its way to an empty slot, and if that key is later deleted, then a future search will be unsuccessful, since it will stop in the new empty slot. If deletions are required, we must have a collision-resolution scheme using pointers.

The clustering effect can be reduced with **double hashing**. When a collision occurs, a second hash value $h_2(x)$ is computed. Instead of searching in a linear order, namely, $i+1, i+2$, and so on, we search the places $i+h_2(x), i+2h_2(x)$, and so on (all in a cyclic order). When another key y is mapped to, say, $i+h_2(x)$, the next attempt will be at $i+h_2(x)+h_2(y)$, instead of at $i+2h_2(x)$. If $h_2(x)$ is independent of $h_2(y)$, then clustering is eliminated. We must be careful, however, to choose the second hash value such that the sequence $i+h_2(x), i+2h_2(x)..., i+nh_2(x)$ spans the whole table (which will happen if the numbers $h_2(x)$ and n are relatively prime).

The main disadvantage of double hashing is that it requires more computation (namely, the selection of a second hash value) for the search. One way to save extra computation is to select a second hash value that is not completely independent of the first hash value, but that still reduces clustering. One such method is to set $h_2(x) = 1$ if $h_1(x)=0$, and $h_2(x) = m - h_1(x)$ otherwise (we assume that m is prime and that $h_1(x) = x \bmod m$).

4.5 The Union-Find Problem

The **union-find problem** (also known as the *equivalence* problem) is a good example of the use of nonstraightforward data structures to improve the efficiency of algorithms. The problem is the following. There are n elements $x_1, x_2, ..., x_n$. The elements are divided into groups. Initially, each element is in a group by itself. There are two kinds of operations performed on the elements and the groups in an arbitrary order:

find (*i*): returns the name of the group that contains x_i

union (*A*, *B*): combines group *A* with group *B* to form a new group with a unique name (any name distinct from the other names will do).

The goal is to design a data structure that will support any sequence of these two operations as efficiently as possible.

Since all the elements are known ahead of time (and they are indexed from 1 to *n*), it is possible to allocate an array $X[1..n]$ for them. The straightforward method of solving the problem is to store the identity of the group containing the *i*th element in $X[i]$. A find operation is thus trivial — we simply look at the array. A union operation takes more time. Assume that union(*A*, *B*) results in a combined group called *A*. Then, it is necessary to change all the entries containing *B* to *A*.

We now present a different approach to this problem. Instead of making the find operation simple, we make the union operation simple. We use indirect addressing. Each entry in the array is a record with the identity of the element and a pointer to another record. Initially all pointers are nil. We perform the operation union(*A*, *B*) by changing the pointer in the record for *B* to point to the record containing *A*, or vice versa (we will discuss this choice shortly). After several unions, the data structure is a set of trees as in Fig. 4.16. Each tree corresponds to a group, and each node corresponds to an element. The element at the root of each tree serves as the name of the group. To find the group that contains element *G*, we follow the path from *G*'s pointer until we reach the root, which is a record whose pointer is nil. This process is similar to someone changing addresses — instead of notifying everyone, it is simpler to leave a forwarding address. Of course, finding the right address is more difficult now, namely, the find operations are less efficient. They are especially inefficient if the union operations form tall trees.

The idea behind the efficient union-find data structure is to balance and collapse the trees. We have already seen that it is worthwhile to expend additional effort to balance the data structure. Consider union(*A*, *B*) in Fig. 4.16. We have two possibilities. We can set *B*'s pointer to point to *A*, or we can set *A*'s pointer to point to *B*. It is clear that the first option leads to a more balanced tree. This idea is formalized in the

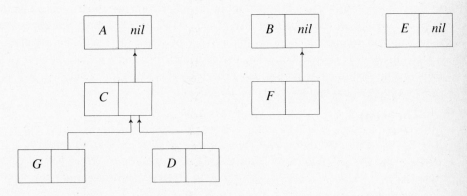

Figure 4.16 The representation for the union-find problem.

following way. We store with each record that corresponds to a root not only the name of the group, but also the number of elements in it.

> **Balancing**: when a union operation is performed, the pointer of the smaller group is set to point to the record of the larger group (ties are broken arbitrarily). The size of the combined group is also computed and placed in the appropriate field in the root.

If the union operation utilizes balancing, then the height of the trees is never more than $\log_2 n$, as is shown in the following theorem.

□ Theorem 4.2

If balancing is used, then any tree of height h must contain at least 2^h elements.

Proof: The proof is by induction on the number of union operations. The theorem is clearly true for the first union, which results in a tree of height 1 with two elements. Consider union(A, B), and assume that A is the larger group, so that B will point to A. Denote by $h(A)$ and $h(B)$ the heights of the trees corresponding to groups A and B, respectively. The height of the combined tree is the maximum of $h(A)$ and $h(B)+1$. If $h(A)$ is larger, then the combined tree has the same height as A's tree with even more elements; hence, the theorem obviously holds. Otherwise, the combined tree has at least twice as many elements as B's tree (since B was assumed to be smaller than A), and its height is one more than B's original height. Again, the theorem is satisfied.   □

Theorem 4.2 implies that a find operation never follows more than $\log_2 n$ pointers. A union operation always take constant time. Consequently, any sequence of m either find or union operations, such that $m \geq n$, takes at most $O(m \log n)$ steps.

It is possible to improve the efficiency of the union-find data structure with the following idea. Consider again the mail-forwarding analogy. If several changes of addresses occur, then the mail will go from one address to another until it reaches the final destination. At that point, it would be a good idea to notify all the forwarding stations about the final destination, so that they can forward the mail directly. After we traverse the pointers from a record to the root of its tree, we change those pointers on the path to point directly to the root (see Fig. 4.17). This is called **path compression**. Traversing the path again only doubles the number of steps; therefore, the asymptotic time complexity of a find operation remains the same. We can use path compression every time a find operation is performed. The following theorem, which we will not prove, gives a good bound on the worst case complexity.

□ Theorem 4.3

If both balancing and path compression are used, then the total number of steps in the worst case for any sequence of $m \geq n$ operations (either find or union) is $O(m \log^* n)$, where $\log^* n$ is the iterated logarithm function, defined below.   □

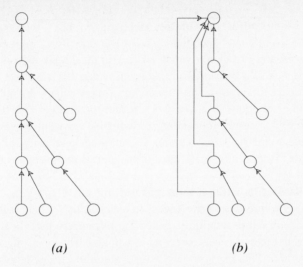

(a)   (b)

Figure 4.17   Path compression: (a) Before. (b) After.

The function $\log^* n$ is defined recursively as follows. $\log^* 1 = \log^* 2 = 1$. For any $n > 2$, $\log^* n = 1 + \log^* (\lceil \log_2 n \rceil)$. For example, $\log^* 4 = 1 + \log^* 2 = 2$, $\log^* 14 = 1 + \log^* 4 = 3$, and $\log^* 60000 = 1 + \log^* 16 = 4$. For any number n, such that $n \le 2^{65536}$, which covers virtually all practical purposes, we have $\log^* n \le 5$. Thus, the complexity of any sequence of unions and finds is almost linear (and is linear in practice). Notice that one particular find operation may still require $O(\log n)$ steps, but, overall, $O(n)$ of them require $O(n \log^* n)$ steps. This is an excellent example of **amortized analysis,** which involves counting all steps together rather than bounding each step separately. Whether it is possible to design a linear time algorithm for this problem is still an open problem.

4.6 Graphs

We devote a whole chapter (Chapter 7) to graph algorithms. In this section, we discuss the data structures used to represent graphs. A graph $G = (V, E)$ consists of a set V of **vertices** (also called **nodes**), and a set E of **edges**. Each edge corresponds to a pair of vertices. The edges represent relationships among the vertices. For example, the graph may represent a set of people, and the edges may connect any two persons who know each other. A graph can be **directed**, or **undirected**. The edges in a directed graph are ordered pairs — the order between the two vertices the edge connects is important. In this case we specify an edge as an arrow pointing from one vertex (the tail) to another (the head). The edges in an undirected graph are unordered pairs. Trees are simple examples of graphs. If we want to indicate a hierarchy in a tree, we can orient all the edges to point away from the root. Such trees are sometimes called **rooted trees**, since it is enough to specify the root in order to define the direction of all the edges. We can also consider undirected trees (sometimes called **free trees**), which do not correspond to a hierarchy.

We will use two main representations of graphs in this book. The first representation uses the **adjacency matrix** of a graph. Let $|V| = n$. The adjacency matrix of G is an $n \times n$ matrix A such that $a_{ij} = 1$ if and only if $(v_i, v_j) \in E$. The ith row of the matrix is thus an array of size n which has a 1 in the jth position if there is an edge leading from v_i to v_j, and a 0 otherwise. Adjacency matrices have one major drawback — they require space of size n^2 no matter how many edges are in the graph. For example, the number of edges in a tree is $n - 1$, and these edges can be represented by one or two pointers per vertex (depending on whether we want to go up or down the tree). With adjacency matrices, each vertex has an associated array of size n. In other words, if the number of edges is small, most of the entries in the adjacency matrix will be 0s.

Instead of having an explicit representation for all of those 0s, we can link the actual number of 1s (representing the edges) in a linked list. There will be one pointer per edge. This second representation is called the **adjacency list**. In the adjacency-list representation, each vertex is associated with a linked list consisting of all the edges adjacent to this vertex. This list is usually sorted according to the labels of the heads of the corresponding edges. The whole graph is represented by an array of lists. Each entry in the array includes the label (or index) of the vertex, and a pointer to the beginning of its list of edges. If the graph is static — that is, if no insertions or deletions are allowed — the lists can be represented by arrays in the following way. We assign an array of size $|V| + |E|$. The first $|V|$ entries correspond to the vertices (in order). Each such entry contains the index in the array where the list of edges emanating from this vertex is started. For example, if there are 20 vertices and 50 edges and vertex 1 has 4 edges emanating from it, then the first entry will be 21 (it is always $|V| + 1$), and the second entry will be 25. The entries corresponding to the edges contain the heads of these edges. In the example above, if the second edge of the second vertex points to the fifth vertex, then entry 26 is equal to 5. The edges are usually stored in a sorted order, although this is not always required. All three representations are illustrated in Fig. 4.18. Adjacency matrices are usually easier to handle than are adjacency lists, and the programs using them are usually simpler. However, adjacency lists are more efficient when the graph has few edges. In practice, most graphs have much fewer than the maximal $n(n-1)/2$ undirected or $n(n-1)$ directed edges. Thus, adjacency lists are more common.

4.7 Summary

Data structures can be divided into static and dynamic structures. Arrays are static structures. The size of an array, or at least a good bound on it, has to be known before we start using it, and it cannot be extended. On the other hand, accessing an array is very efficient. Linked lists are dynamic. They can easily be extended and reduced in size. They can support any size (within the constraints of the total available memory).

Data structures can also be divided into one-dimensional structures and multidimensional structures. Arrays and linked lists are one-dimensional. The only structure they represent is the possible order among the elements. Trees represent a little

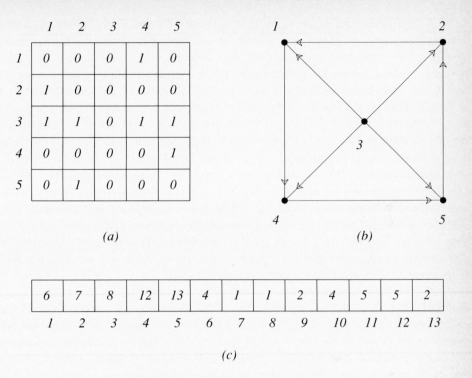

Figure 4.18 Graph representations.

more than one-dimensional structure — they represent hierarchy. Graphs can represent even more elaborate structures. Of course, we can also build multidimensional arrays or multidimensional linked lists.

The concept of abstract data types is very useful. It allows us to concentrate on the operations required from the data structure, and to postpone implementation details that are dependent on the specific data type. We have described implementations for dictionaries, priority queues, and union-find data structures.

If we need only to store data without any structure imposed on them, then hashing is the best option. Hashing cannot be used if the access depends on something besides the explicit key of the element. For example, if we wish to find the minimal key in a hash table, then the whole table must still be scanned.

Bibliographic Notes and Further Reading

The study of data structures is now considered a basic part of computer science education. As a result, many books on data structures have been written. Knuth [1973a] and Knuth [1973b] contain a wealth of information about data structures. Other books include Standish [1980], Aho, Hopcroft, and Ullman [1983], Reingold and Hansen [1983], Gonnet [1984], and Wirth [1986]. A more advanced monograph on data structures and algorithms is by Tarjan [1983].

A comparative study of many data structures for priority-queues was done by Jones [1986]. Jones's paper also includes a comprehensive bibliography on priority queues. The algorithms for insertions and deletions in binary search trees were described, among others, by Hibbard [1962]. This paper proved that the average path length after n random insertions is $2\ln n$. For more information, see Knuth [1973b]. An empirical study on the effects of random insertions and deletions in binary search trees was performed by Eppinger [1983], who conjectured that the length of the average path may be as high as $O(\log^3 n)$. Culberson [1985] proved that, under certain conditions, random deletions and insertions cause the length of the average path to be $O(\sqrt{n})$. A comparison between different balancing schemes is presented in Baer and Schwab [1977]. Balanced trees are also described in Knuth [1973b] and Tarjan [1983]. Sleator and Tarjan [1985] present several new methods for maintaining **self-adjusting trees**. The idea is to adjust the tree by moving the most currently accessed node to the top after every access. Although the trees are not always balanced, they exhibit good performance characteristics in the amortized sense; namely, a single operation may be slow, but over a long period, the average time for each operation is small.

More information about hashing can again be found in Knuth [1973b], and in Gonnet [1984]. A book by Vitter and Chen [1987] describes in great detail one strategy called **coalesced hashing**. Classes of random hash functions called **universal hash functions** are described by Carter and Wegman [1979]. Several interesting applications of this concept can also be found in Wegman and Carter [1979], Karlin and Upfal [1986], and Kurtz and Manber [1987]. There are also extendible hashing schemes that allow dynamic growth of the tables; see, for example, Fagin, Nievergelt, Pippenger, and Strong [1979] and Litwin [1980].

The union-find data structure was first studied by Galler and Fischer [1964], and also by Fischer [1972], and Hopcroft and Ullman [1973] (who obtained the result mentioned in Theorem 4.3), among others. Tarjan [1975] improved the running time to $O(m\alpha(m, n))$, where $\alpha(n)$ is the inverse Ackerman's function, which grows even slower than $\log^* n$. Tarjan and van Leeuwen [1984] studied several simpler variations of path compression that achieve the same running time. For information on graphs, see Chapter 7 and its bibliography.

Drill Exercises

4.1   Write a program to delete an element from a linked list.

4.2   Write a program to reverse the direction of a given linked list. In other words, the pointers should all point backward.

4.3   Convert the simple recursive search procedure for binary search trees to a nonrecursive procedure.

4.4   Design an algorithm to list in order all the keys in a given binary search tree.

4.5   Let $A[1..16]$ be an array that represents a heap (using the implicit representation). What is the minimal number of heap elements that can occupy an array of size 16?

4.6   Algorithm *Insert_to_Heap* may swap elements many times up the heap. Modify the algorithm so that at most one swap will be performed ($O(\log n)$ comparisons are still allowed).

4.7   Suppose that we want to use AVL trees as a priority-queue data structure. What is the complexity of all the operations?

4.8   Show the AVL tree formed by inserting the numbers 1 to 20 in order.

4.9   Show an AVL tree with a node whose deletion results in a non-AVL tree, such that the resulting tree cannot be made an AVL tree by only one (single or double) rotation. Draw the tree, specify the node, and explain why the resulting tree cannot be balanced with one rotation.

Creative Exercises

4.10   Design an implementation of an abstract data type that supports the following operations:

Insert(x): the insertion should be performed even if x is already in the data structure. In other words, the data structure should hold duplicates.

Remove(y): remove *any* element from the data structure and assign it to y. Again, any element will do. If there are several copies of the same element only one of them should be removed.

This abstract data type is called a **pool** (or a *bag*). It is useful for storing jobs, for example. New jobs are generated and inserted into the pool, and when a worker becomes available a job is removed. All the operations should take $O(1)$ time.

4.11   Modify the pool data type of Exercise 4.10 in the following way: Assume now that every element can appear at most once in the data structure. An insertion must now check for duplicates. Implement the same operations as before, but with duplicate checking. What is the complexity of each operation in the worst case? What is a good data structure for the average case?

4.12   Another variant of the pool data type (see Exercises 4.10 and 4.11) is the following: Assume now that all the elements are identified by integers in the range 1 to n, and that n is small enough that you can allocate memory of size $O(n)$. Each element can appear at most once. Design algorithms for *insert* and *remove* (as defined in Exercise 4.10) that work in $O(1)$ time.

4.13   Design an algorithm to construct one heap that contains all the elements of two given heaps of sizes n and m, respectively. The heaps are given in a linked-list representation (each node has links to its two children). The running time of the algorithm should be $O(\log(m+n))$ in the worst case.

4.14   Design an algorithm to construct one heap that contains all the elements of k given heaps. What is the complexity of the algorithm?

4.15   Design an implementation of an abstract data type that supports the following operations:

Insert(x): insert the key x into the data structure only if it is not already there.

Delete(x): delete the key x from the data structure (if it is there).

Find_Next(x): find the smallest key in the data structure that is greater than x.

All these operations should take $O(\log n)$ time in the worst case, where n is the number of elements in the data structure.

4.16   Design an implementation of an abstract data type that supports the following operations:

Insert(x): insert the key x into the data structure only if it is not already there.

Delete(x): delete the key x from the data structure (if it is there).

Find_Smallest(k): find the kth smallest key in the data structure.

All these operations should take $O(\log n)$ time in the worst case, where n is the number of elements in the data structure.

4.17   Design an implementation of an abstract data type that supports the following operations:

Insert(x): insert the key x into the data structure only if it is not already there.

Delete(x): delete the key x from the data structure (if it is there).

Find_Next(x, k): find the kth "right"neighbor smallest key among the keys in the data structure that are larger than x.

All these operations should take $O(\log n)$ time in the worst case, where n is the number of elements in the data structure.

*4.18   The AVL algorithms that were presented in Section 4.3.4 require balanced factors with three possible values, 1, 0, or −1. To represent three values we need 2 bits. Suggest a method for implementing these algorithms (with only a slight modification) with only 1 extra bit per node.

4.19   A **concatenate** operation take two sets, such that all the keys in one set are smaller than all the keys in the other set, and merges them together. Design an algorithm to concatenate two binary search trees into one binary search tree. The worst-case running time should be $O(h)$, where h is the maximal height of the two trees.

4.20   Design an algorithm to concatenate (as defined in Exercise 4.19) two AVL trees into one valid AVL tree. The worst-case running time should be $O(h)$, where h is the maximal height of the two trees.

4.21   Consider an AVL tree formed by a fairly random sequence of insertions and deletions. Assume that each possible balance factor appears with the same probability (namely, a probability of 1/3 for each possibility). Prove that the average length of the path from the critical node to the place of insertion is a constant independent of the size of the tree.

4.22   Determine the general structure of the AVL tree formed by inserting the numbers 1 to n in order. What is the height of this tree?

4.23   Find the "worst AVL tree." That is, construct an AVL tree of height h with the minimal number of nodes. Use this worst AVL tree to prove Theorem 4.1 (Section 4.3.4) regarding the maximal height of an AVL tree with n nodes. (Hint: Try a recursive construction.)

4.24 Let T_1 and T_2 be two arbitrary trees, each having n nodes. Prove that it is sufficient to apply at most $2n$ rotations to T_1 so that it becomes equal to T_2.

4.25 A **join** of two undirected graphs $G = (V, E)$ and $H = (U, F)$ is a new graph $J = (W, D)$ such that $W = V \cup U$ (namely, the vertices of the new graph include the vertices of both graphs), and $D = E \cup F \cup V \times U$ (namely, the edges include all the previous edges plus an edge from each vertex in V to each vertex in U). Suggest a good representation for graphs that allows join operations to be performed efficiently.

4.26 Let $S = \{s_1, s_2, ..., s_m\}$ be a very large set, and assume that S is partitioned into k blocks. Assume that you have a procedure called *which_block* such that given an element s_i, *which_block*(s_i) = number of the block that contains s_i; *which_block* works in constant time (e.g., S may correspond to all street addresses in the United States, and the blocks may correspond to zip codes). You want to maintain a small subset of S, T, and to perform the following operations on T:

> *Insert*(s_i).

> *Delete*(s_i).

> *Delete_block*(j): delete all elements in T that belong to block j.

Initially, T is empty. Each operation should take $O(\log n)$ time in the worst case, where n is the number of elements currently in T. *Delete_block* only removes (disconnects) the elements from the data structure; it need not physically remove each and every one of them. Both m and k are too large, so you cannot afford to use a table of size m or k. However, n is relatively small, and you can use $O(n)$ space.

* 4.27 Let $A[1..n]$ be an array of real numbers. Design algorithms to perform any sequence of the following two operations:

> *Add*(i, y): add the value y to the ith number.

> *Partial_sum*(i): return the sum of the first i numbers, $\sum_1^i A[i]$.

Notice that the number of elements remains fixed (there are no insertions or deletions); the only changes are to the values. Each operation should take $O(\log n)$ steps. You can use one more array of size n as a work space.

* 4.28 Extend the data structure for the problem in Exercise 4.27 to support insertions and deletions. Each element now has a *key* and a *value*. An element is accessed by its key. The addition operation applies to the values (but the elements are accessed by their keys). The *Partial_sum* operation is different.

> *Partial_sum*(y): return the sum of all the elements currently in the set whose value is less than y, $\sum_{x_i < y} x_i$.

The worst-case running time should still be $O(n \log n)$ for any sequence of $O(n)$ operations.

4.29   Design a data structure to maintain a set of elements, each with a key and a value. The following operations should be supported:

Find_value(x): find the value associated with the element x (nil if x is not in the set).

Insert(x, y).

Delete(x).

Add(x, y): add the value y to the current value of the element with key x.

Add_all(y): add the value y to the values of all the elements in the set.

The worst-case running time should be $O(\log n)$ for each of these operations.

4.30   (True story.) A programmer named Guy once encountered an error message from a new compiler he was using indicating that the compiler had run out of memory space while compiling a program. The programmer was baffled, since the program did not use much space. He was able to pinpoint the problem to a certain *case* statement, which is given below. Without this case statement, the program compiled flawlessly. With it, the compiler ran out of space. Determine what data structure the compiler was using that was causing the problem. (The *case* statement is correct and valid; the problem lies with the compiler, which was unable to compile the *case* statement.)

case *i* **of**
1:       Statement(1) ;
2:       Statement(2) ;
4:       Statement(3) ;
256:    Statement(4) ;
65535: Statement(5) ;

CHAPTER 5

DESIGN OF ALGORITHMS

BY INDUCTION

> *Nothing is more important than to see the sources of invention, which are, in my opinion, more interesting than the inventions themselves.*
>
> G. W. Leibniz (1646–1716)

> *Invention breeds invention.*
>
> R. W. Emerson (1803–1882)

5.1 Introduction

In this chapter, we introduce our approach to algorithm design using the analogy to mathematical induction. We include relatively simple examples, and present the basic principles and techniques on which the method is based. The analogous induction techniques have been described in Chapter 2. When appropriate, we repeat the discussion here to make this chapter self contained.

Mathematical induction is based on a **domino principle**. Imagine that we have a line of upended dominoes, and that we wish to knock down all of them by knocking down only the first. To make sure that all dominoes will fall down, we need only to verify that we have pushed the first one and that each domino will topple the next one as it falls. We need not collapse the whole arrangement every time we add a new domino to verify that the new arrangement will work. The same principle can be applied to algorithm design.

> **It is not necessary to design the steps required to solve the problem
> from scratch; it is sufficient to guarantee that (1) it is possible to solve a
> small instance of the problem (the base case), and (2) a solution to every
> problem can be constructed from solutions of smaller problems (the
> inductive step).**

With this principle in mind, we should concentrate on reducing the problem to a smaller
problem (or to a set of smaller problems). The trouble is that it is usually not easy to find
a way to reduce the problem. In this chapter, we present several techniques to facilitate
this process. The examples in this chapter were chosen not because of their importance
(some of them have limited applicability), but because they are simple and yet they
illustrate the principles we want to emphasize. We will present numerous other examples
of this approach throughout the book.

5.2 Evaluating Polynomials

We start with a simple algebraic problem — evaluating a given polynomial at a given
point.

The Problem   Given a sequence of real numbers $a_n, a_{n-1}, ..., a_1, a_0$,
and a real number x, compute the value of the polynomial $P_n(x) = a_n x^n$
$+ a_{n-1} x^{n-1} + \cdots + a_1 x + a_0$.

This problem may not seem to be a natural candidate for an inductive approach.
Nevertheless, we will show that induction can lead directly to a very good solution to the
problem. We start with the most simple (almost trivial) approach, then find variations of
it that lead to better solutions.

The problem involves $n+2$ numbers. The inductive approach is to solve this
problem in terms of a solution to a smaller problem. In other words, we try to reduce the
problem to one with smaller size, which we then solve recursively, or, as we call it, *by
induction*. The first natural attempt is to reduce the problem by removing a_n. We are left
with the problem of evaluating the polynomial

$$P_{n-1}(x) = a_{n-1} x^{n-1} + a_{n-2} x^{n-2} + \cdots + a_1 x + a_0.$$

This is the same problem, except that it has one less parameter. Therefore, we can solve
it by induction.

> **Induction hypothesis:** *We know how to evaluate a polynomial represented
> by the input $a_{n-1}, ..., a_1, a_0$, at the point x (i.e., we know how to compute
> $P_{n-1}(x)$).*

We can now use the hypothesis to solve the problem by induction. First, we have to
solve the base case, which is computing a_0; this is trivial. Then, we must show how to

solve the original problem (computing $P_n(x)$) with the aid of the solution to the smaller problem (which is the value of $P_{n-1}(x)$). This step is straightforward in this case; simply compute x^n, multiply it by a_n, and add the result to $P_{n-1}(x)$:

$$P_n(x) = P_{n-1}(x) + a_n x^n.$$

At this point it may seem that the use of induction in this problem is frivolous — it just complicates a very simple solution. The algorithm implied by the preceding discussion is merely evaluating the polynomial from right to left as it is written. In a moment, however, we will see the power of our approach.

Although the algorithm is correct, it is not efficient. It requires $n + n - 1 + n - 2 + \cdots + 1 = n(n+1)/2$ multiplications and n additions. We now use induction a little differently to obtain a better solution.

We make the first improvement by observing that there is a great deal of redundant computation: The powers of x are computed from scratch. We can save many multiplications by using the value of x^{n-1} when we compute x^n. We make this change by including the computation of x^k in the induction hypothesis.

Stronger induction hypothesis: *We know how to compute the value of the polynomial $P_{n-1}(x)$, and we know how to compute x^{n-1}.*

This induction hypothesis is stronger, since it requires computing x^{n-1}, but it is easier to extend (since it is now easier to compute x^n). We need to perform only one multiplication to compute x^n, then one more multiplication to get $a_n x^n$, then one addition to complete the computation. (The induction hypothesis is not too strong, since we need to compute x^{n-1} anyway.) Overall, there are $2n$ multiplications and n additions. It is interesting to note that, even though the induction hypothesis requires more computation, it leads to less work overall. We will return to this point later. This algorithm looks good by all measures. It is efficient, simple, and easy to implement. However, a better algorithm exists. We discover it by using induction in yet another different way.

Reducing the problem by removing the last coefficient, a_n, is the straightforward step, but it is not the only possible reduction. We can also remove the first coefficient, a_0. The smaller problem becomes the evaluation of the polynomial represented by the coefficients $a_n, a_{n-1}, ..., a_1$, which is

$$P'_{n-1}(x) = a_n x^{n-1} + a_{n-1} x^{n-2} + \cdots + a_1.$$

(Notice that a_n is now the $(n-1)$th coefficient, a_{n-1} is the $(n-2)$th coefficient, and so on.) So we have a new induction hypothesis.

Induction hypothesis (reversed order): *We know how to evaluate the polynomial represented by the coefficients $a_n, a_{n-1}, ..., a_1$ at the point x (i.e., we know how to compute $P'_{n-1}(x)$).*

This hypothesis is more suited to our purposes, because it is easier to extend. Clearly, $P_n(x) = x \cdot P'_{n-1}(x) + a_0$. Therefore, only one multiplication and one addition are required to compute $P_n(x)$ from $P'_{n-1}(x)$. The complete algorithm can be described by the following expression:

$$a_n x^n + a_{n-1} x^{n-1} + \cdots + a_1 x + a_0 = ((\cdots ((a_n x + a_{n-1}) x + a_{n-2}) \cdots) x + a_1) x + a_0.$$

This algorithm is known as **Horner's rule** after the English mathematician W.G. Horner. (It was also mentioned by Newton, see [Knuth 1981], page 467.) The program to evaluate the polynomial is given in Fig. 5.1.

Algorithm Polynomial_Evaluation $(\bar{a}, x)$;
Input: $\bar{a} = a_0, a_1, a_2, ..., a_n$ (coefficients of a polynomial), and x (a real number).
Output: P (the value of the polynomial at x).

begin
   $P := a_n$;
   for $i := 1$ **to** n **do**
      $P := x * P + a_{n-i}$
end

Figure 5.1 Algorithm *Polynomial_Evaluation*.

Complexity   The algorithm requires only n multiplications, n additions, and one extra memory location. Even though the previous solutions seemed very simple and very efficient, we have found it worthwhile to pursue a better algorithm. Not only is this algorithm faster than those described previously, but also its corresponding program is simpler.

Comments   Induction allows us to concentrate on extending solutions of smaller subproblems to those of larger problems. Suppose that we want to solve $P(n)$, which is a problem P that depends on a parameter n (usually its size). We start with an arbitrary instance of $P(n)$, and try to solve it by using the assumption that $P(n-1)$ has already been solved. There are many possible ways to define the induction hypothesis and many possible ways to use it. We will survey several of these methods, and will show their power in designing algorithms.

    This simple example illustrates the flexibility we have when we use induction. The trick that led to Horner's rule was merely considering the input from left to right, instead of the intuitive right to left. Another common possibility is comparing top down versus bottom up (when a tree structure is involved). It is also possible to go in increments of 2 (or more) rather than 1, and there are numerous other possibilities. Moreover, sometimes the best induction sequence is not the same for all inputs. It may be worthwhile to design an algorithm just to find the best way to perform the reduction. We will see examples of all these possibilities.

5.3 Maximal Induced Subgraph

Consider the following problem. You are arranging a conference of scientists from different disciplines and you have a list of people you want to invite. You assume that everyone on the list will agree to come under the condition that there will be ample opportunity to exchange ideas. For each scientist, you write down the names of all other scientists on the list with whom interaction is likely. You would like to invite as many people on the list as possible, but you want to guarantee that each one will have at least k other people with whom to interact (k is a fixed number, independent of the number of invitees). You do not have to arrange the interactions; in particular, you do not have to make sure that there is enough time for them to occur. You just want to lure everyone to the conference. How do you decide whom to invite? This problem corresponds to the following graph-theoretic problem. Let $G = (V, E)$ be an undirected graph. An **induced subgraph** of G is a graph $H = (U, F)$ such that $U \subseteq V$ and F includes all edges in E both of whose incident vertices are in U. A **degree** of a vertex is the number of vertices adjacent to that vertex. The vertices of the graph correspond to the scientists, and two vertices are connected if there is a potential for the two corresponding scientists to exchange ideas. An induced subgraph corresponds to a subset of the scientists.

> **The Problem**   Given an undirected graph $G = (V, E)$ and an integer k, find an induced subgraph $H = (U, F)$ of G of maximum size such that all vertices of H have degree $\geq k$ (in H), or conclude that no such induced subgraph exists.

A direct approach to solving this problem is to remove vertices whose degree is $< k$. As vertices are removed with their adjacent edges, the degrees of other vertices may be reduced. When the degree of a vertex becomes less than k, that vertex should be removed. The order of removals, however, is not clear. Should we remove all the vertices of degree $< k$ first, then deal with vertices whose degrees were reduced? Should we remove first one vertex of degree $< k$, then continue with affected vertices? (These two approaches correspond to breadth-first search versus depth-first search, which are discussed in detail in Section 7.3.) Will both approaches lead to the same result? Will the resulting graph be of maximum size? All these questions are easy to answer; the approach we will describe makes answering them even easier.

Instead of thinking about our algorithm as a sequence of steps that a computer has to take to calculate a result, think of *proving a theorem* that the algorithm exists. We do not suggest attempting a formal proof (at least not at this first stage). The idea is to imitate the steps we take in proving a theorem, in order to gain insight into the problem. We need to find the maximum induced subgraph that satisfies the given conditions. Here is a "proof" by induction.

> **Induction hypothesis:** *We know how to find maximum induced subgraphs all of whose vertices have degrees $\geq k$, provided that the number of vertices is $< n$.*

We need to prove that this "theorem" is true for a base case, and that its truth for $n - 1$ implies its truth for n. The first nontrivial base case occurs when $n = k + 1$, because if $n \leq k$, then all the degrees are less than k. If $n = k + 1$, then the only way to have all the degrees equal to k is to have a **complete graph** (namely, all vertices are connected), which we can detect. So, assume now that $G = (V, E)$ is a graph with $n > k + 1$ vertices. If all the vertices have degrees $\geq k$, then the whole graph satisfies the conditions and we are done. Otherwise, there exists a vertex v with degree $< k$. It is obvious that the degree of v remains $< k$ in any induced subgraph of G; hence, v does not belong to any subgraph that satisfies the conditions of the problem. Therefore, we can remove v and its adjacent edges without affecting the conditions of the theorem. After v is removed, the graph has $n - 1$ vertices — and, by the induction hypothesis, we know how to solve the problem.

We are now done. The algorithm and the answers to the questions we raised earlier are now clear. Any vertex of degree $< k$ can be removed. The order of removals is immaterial. The graph remaining after all these removals must be of maximum size because these removals are *mandatory*. It is also clear that the algorithm is correct, because we designed it by proving its correctness!

Comments   The best way to reduce a problem is to eliminate some of its elements. In this example, the application of induction was straightforward, mainly because it was clear which vertices we should eliminate and how we should eliminate them. The reduction follows immediately. In general, however, the elimination process may not be straightforward. We will see examples of combining two elements into one, causing the number of elements to be reduced (Section 6.6); of eliminating restrictions on the problem rather than eliminating parts of the input (Section 7.7); and of designing a special algorithm to find which elements can be eliminated (Section 5.5). Another example of eliminating the right elements is presented next. It is interesting to note that, if we replace "$\geq$" with "$\leq$" in the statement of the problem (that is, if we look for a maximal induced subgraph all of whose degrees are *at most* k), the problem becomes much more difficult (see Exercise 11.12).

5.4 Finding One-to-One Mappings

Let f be a function that maps a finite set A into itself (i.e., every element of A is mapped to another element of A). For simplicity, we denote the elements of A by the integers 1 to n. We assume that the function f is represented by an array $f[1..n]$ such that $f[i]$ holds the value of $f(i)$ (which is an integer between 1 and n). We call f a *one-to-one* function if, for every element j, there is at most one element i that is mapped to j. The function f can be represented by a diagram, as shown in Fig. 5.2, where both sides correspond to the same set and the edges indicate the mapping. The function in Fig. 5.2 is clearly not a one-to-one function.

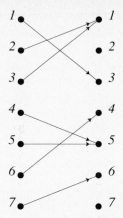

Figure 5.2 A mapping from a set into itself (both sides represent the same set).

> **The Problem**   Given a finite set A and a mapping f from A to itself, find a subset $S \subseteq A$ with the maximum number of elements, such that (1) the function f maps every element of S to another element of S (i.e., f maps S into itself), and (2) no two elements of S are mapped to the same element (i.e., f is one-to-one when restricted to S).

If f is originally one-to-one, then the whole set A satisfies the conditions of the problem, and A is definitely maximal. If, on the other hand, $f(i)=f(j)$ for some $i \neq j$, then S cannot contain both i and j. For example, the set S that solves the problem given in Fig. 5.2 cannot contain both 2 and 3 since $f(2)=f(3)=1$. The choice of which one of them to eliminate cannot be arbitrary. Suppose, for example, that we decide to eliminate 3. Since 1 is mapped to 3, we must eliminate 1 as well (the mapping must be into S and 3 is no longer in S). But if 1 is eliminated, then 2 must be eliminated as well (for the same reason). But, this subset is not maximal, since it is easy to see that we could have eliminated 2 alone. (The solution for Fig. 5.2 is the subset $\{1,3,5\}$.) The problem is to find a general method to decide which elements to include.

Fortunately, we have some flexibility in deciding how to reduce the problem to a smaller one. We can reduce the size of the problem by finding either an element that belongs to S or an element that does not belong to S. We will do the latter. We use the straightforward induction hypothesis.

> **Induction hypothesis:** *We know how to solve the problem for sets of $n-1$ elements.*

The base case is trivial: If there is only one element in the set, then it must be mapped to itself, which is a one-to-one mapping. Assume now that we have a set A of n elements and we are looking for a subset S that satisfies the conditions of the problem. We claim that any element i that has no other element mapped to it cannot belong to S. (In other words, an element i in the right side of the diagram, which is not connected to any edge, cannot be in S.) Otherwise, if $i \in S$ and S has, say, k elements, then those k elements are mapped into at most $k-1$ elements; therefore, the mapping cannot be one-to-one. If there is such an i, then we simply remove it from the set. We now have a set $A' = A - \{i\}$ with $n-1$ elements, which f maps into itself; by the induction hypothesis, we know how to solve the problem for A'. If no such i exists, then the mapping is one-to-one, and we are done.

The essence of this solution is that we *must* remove i. We proved that i cannot belong to S. This is the strength of induction: Once we remove an element and reduce the size of the problem, we are done. We have to be careful, however, that the reduced problem is exactly the same (except for size) as the original problem. The only condition on the set A and the function f was that f maps A into itself. This condition is still maintained for the set $A - \{i\}$, since there was nothing that was mapped to i. The algorithm terminates when no more elements can be removed.

Implementation   We described the algorithm as a recursive procedure. In each step, we found an element such that no other element is mapped to it, removed it, and continued recursively. The implementation, however, need not be recursive. We can maintain a counter $c[i]$ with each element i. Initially, $c[i]$ should be equal to the number of elements that are mapped to i. We can compute $c[i]$, for all i, in n steps by scanning the array and incrementing the appropriate counters. We then put all the elements that have a zero counter in a queue. In each step, we remove an element j from the queue (and the set), decrement $c[f(j)]$, and, if $c[f(j)]=0$, we put $f(j)$ in the queue. The algorithm terminates when the queue is empty. The algorithm is given in Fig. 5.3.

Complexity   The initialization part requires $O(n)$ operations. Every element can be put on the queue at most once, and the steps involved in removing an element from the queue take constant time. The total number of steps is thus $O(n)$.

Comments   In this example, we reduced the size of the problem by eliminating elements from a set. Therefore, we tried to find the easiest way to remove an element without changing the conditions of the problem. Because the only requirement we made was that the function maps A into itself, the choice of an element to which no other element is mapped is natural.

5.5 The Celebrity Problem

The next example is a popular exercise in algorithm design. It is a nice example of a problem that has a solution that does not require scanning all the data (or even a significant part of them). Among n persons, a *celebrity* is defined as someone who is known by everyone but does not know anyone. The problem is to identify the celebrity, if one exists, by asking questions only of the form, "Excuse me, do you know the person over there?" (The assumption is that all the answers are correct, and that even the celebrity will answer.) The goal is to minimize the number of questions. Since there are

---

Algorithm Mapping (f, n) ;
Input: f (an array of integers whose values are between 1 and n).
Output: S (a subset of the integers from 1 to n, such that f is one-to-one on S).

begin
    $S := A$; { A is the set of numbers from 1 to n }
    for $j := 1$ **to** n **do** $c[j] := 0$;
    for $j := 1$ **to** n **do** increment $c[f[j]]$;
    for $j := 1$ **to** n **do**
        if $c[j] = 0$ **then** put j in Queue;
    while Queue is not empty **do**
        remove i from the top of the queue;
        $S := S - \{i\}$;
        decrement $c[f[i]]$;
        if $c[f[i]] = 0$ **then** put $f[i]$ in Queue
end

Figure 5.3 Algorithm *Mapping*.

$n(n-1)/2$ pairs of persons, there is potentially a need to ask $n(n-1)$ questions, in the worst case, if the questions are asked arbitrarily. It is not clear that we can do better in the worst case.

We can use a graph-theoretical formulation. We can build a directed graph with the vertices corresponding to the persons and an edge from person A to person B if A knows B. A celebrity corresponds to a **sink** of the graph (no pun intended). A sink is a vertex with indegree $n-1$ and outdegree 0. Notice that a graph can have at most one sink. The input to the problem corresponds to an $n \times n$ adjacency matrix (whose ij entry is 1 if the ith person knows the jth person, and 0 otherwise).

The Problem   Given an $n \times n$ adjacency matrix, determine whether there exists an i such that all the entries in the ith column (except for the iith entry) are 1, and all the entries in the ith row (except for the iith entry) are 0.

The base case of two persons is simple. Consider as usual the difference between the problem with $n-1$ persons and that with n persons. We assume that we can find the celebrity among the first $n-1$ persons by induction. Since there is at most one celebrity, there are three possibilities: (1) the celebrity is among the first $n-1$, (2) the celebrity is the nth person, and (3) there is no celebrity. The first case is the easiest to handle. We need only to check that the nth person knows the celebrity, and that the celebrity does not know the nth person. The other two cases are more difficult because, to determine whether the nth person is the celebrity, we may need to ask $2(n-1)$ questions. If we ask $2(n-1)$ questions in the nth step, then the total number of questions will be $n(n-1)$ (which is what we tried to avoid). We need another approach.

The trick here is to consider the problem ''backward.'' It may be hard to identify a celebrity, but it is probably easier to identify someone as a noncelebrity. After all, there are definitely more noncelebrities than celebrities. If we eliminate someone from consideration, then we reduce the size of the problem from n to $n-1$. Moreover, we do not need to eliminate someone specific; anyone will do. Suppose that we ask Alice whether she knows Bob. If she does, then she cannot be a celebrity; if she does not, then Bob cannot be a celebrity. We can eliminate one of them with one question.

We now consider again the three cases with which we started. We do not just take an arbitrary person as the nth person. We use the idea in the last paragraph to eliminate either Alice or Bob, then solve the problem for the other $n-1$ persons. We are guaranteed that case 2 will not occur, since the person eliminated cannot be the celebrity. Furthermore, if case 3 occurs — namely, there is no celebrity among the $n-1$ persons — then there is no celebrity among the n persons. Only case 1 remains, but this case is easy. If there is a celebrity among the $n-1$ persons, it takes two more questions to verify that this is a celebrity for the whole set. Otherwise, there is no celebrity.

The algorithm proceeds as follows. We ask A whether she knows B, and eliminate either A or B according to the answer. Let's assume that we eliminate A. We then find (by induction) a celebrity among the remaining $n-1$ persons. If there is no celebrity, the algorithm terminates; otherwise, we check that A knows the celebrity and that the celebrity does not know A.

Implementation   As was the case with the algorithm in the previous section, it is more efficient to implement the celebrity algorithm iteratively, rather than recursively. The algorithm is divided into two phases. In the first phase, we eliminate all but one candidate, and in the second phase we check whether this candidate is indeed the celebrity. We start with n candidates, and, for the purpose of this discussion, let's assume that they are stored in a stack. For each pair of candidates, we can eliminate one candidate by asking one question — whether one of them knows the other. We start by taking the first two candidates from the stack, and eliminating one of them. Then, in each step, we have one remaining candidate, and, as long as the stack is nonempty, we take one additional candidate from the stack, and eliminate one of these two candidates. When the stack becomes empty, one candidate remains. We then check that this candidate is indeed the celebrity. The algorithm is presented in Fig. 5.4 (notice that the stack is implemented explicitly by the use of the indices i, j, and $next$).

Complexity   At most $3(n-1)$ questions will be asked: $n-1$ questions in the first phase to eliminate $n-1$ persons, and then at most $2(n-1)$ questions to verify that the candidate is indeed a celebrity. Notice that the size of the input is not n, but rather $n(n-1)$ (the number of entries of the matrix). This solution shows that it is possible to identify a celebrity by looking at only $O(n)$ entries in the adjacency matrix, even though a priori the solution may be sensitive to each of the $n(n-1)$ entries.

Algorithm Celebrity (Know) ;
Input: *Know* (an $n \times n$ Boolean matrix).
<u>**Output:**</u> *celebrity.*

begin
    i := 1 ;
    j := 2 ;
    next := 3 ;
    { in the first phase we eliminate all but one candidate }
    while *next ≤ n + 1* **do**
        if *Know[i, j]* **then** *i := next*
        else *j := next ;*
        next := next + 1 ;
        { one of either i or j is eliminated }
    if *i = n + 1* **then**
        candidate := j
    else
        candidate := i ;
    { Now we check that the candidate is indeed the celebrity }
    wrong := false ;
    k := 1 ;
    Know[candidate, candidate] := false ;
        { a dummy variable to pass the test }
    while *not wrong and k ≤ n* **do**
        if *Know[candidate, k]* **then** *wrong := true ;*
        if *not Know[k, candidate]* **then**
            if *candidate ≠ k* **then** *wrong := true ;*
        k := k + 1 ;
    if *not wrong* **then** *celebrity := candidate*
    else *celebrity := 0 { no celebrity }*
end

Figure 5.4 Algorithm *Celebrity.*

Comments   The key idea in this elegant solution is to reduce the size of the problem from n to $n - 1$ in a clever way. This example shows that it sometimes pays to expend some effort (in this case — one question) to perform the reduction more effectively. Do not start by simply considering an *arbitrary* input of size $n - 1$ and attempting to extend it. Select a *particular* input of size $n - 1$. We will see more examples where we spend substantial time just constructing the right order of induction — and that time is well spent.

5.6 A Divide-and-Conquer Algorithm: The Skyline Problem

So far, we have seen examples from graph theory and numerical computation. This example deals with a problem of drawing shapes.

> **The Problem**   Given the exact locations and shapes of several rectangular buildings in a city, draw the skyline (in two dimensions) of these buildings, eliminating hidden lines.

An example of an input is given in Fig. 5.5(a); the corresponding output is given in Fig. 5.5(b). We are interested in only two-dimensional pictures. We assume that the bottoms of all the buildings lie on a fixed line (i.e., they share a common horizon). Building B_i is represented by a triple (L_i, H_i, R_i). L_i and R_i denote the left and right x coordinates of the building, respectively, and H_i denotes the building's height. A **skyline** is a list of x coordinates and the heights connecting them arranged in order from left to right. For example, the buildings in Fig. 5.5(a) correspond to the following input:

(1,**11**,5), (2,**6**,7), (3,**13**,9), (12,**7**,16), (14,**3**,25), (19,**18**,22), (23,**13**,29), and (24,**4**,28).

(The numbers in boldface type are the heights.) The skyline in Fig. 5.5(b) is represented as follows:

(1,**11**,3,**13**,9,**0**,12,**7**,16,**3**,19,**18**,22,**3**,23,**13**,29,**0**).

(Again, the numbers in boldface type are heights.)

The straightforward algorithm for this problem is based on adding one building at a time to the skyline. The induction hypothesis is the simple one. We assume that we know how to solve the problem for $n - 1$ buildings, and then we add the nth building.

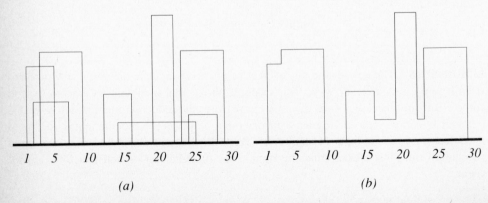

(a)   *(b)*

Figure 5.5 The skyline problem: (a) The input. (b) The skyline.

The problem is trivial for one building. To add a building B_n to the skyline, we need to intersect it with the existing skyline (see Fig. 5.6). Let B_n be (5,9,26). We first scan the skyline from left to right to find where the left side of B_n fits (i.e., we search for the appropriate x coordinate — 5 in this example). In this case, the horizontal line that "covers" 5 is the one from 3 to 9, and its height is 13. We can now scan the skyline, looking at one horizontal line after another, and adjusting whenever the height of B_n is higher than the existing height. We stop when we reach an x coordinate that is greater than the right side of B_n. For this example, we do not adjust the height from 3 to 9, but we do adjust it all the way from 9 to 19, then adjust it once more from 22 to 23. The new skyline is represented by

(1,**11**,3,**13**,9,**9**,19,**18**,22,**9**,23,**13**,29,**0**).

This algorithm is clearly correct, but it is not necessarily efficient. In the worst case, the scan for B_n requires $O(n)$ steps. Hence, the total number of steps will be $O(n) + O(n-1) + \cdots + O(1) = O(n^2)$.

To improve the performance of this algorithm, we use a well-known technique called **divide and conquer**. Instead of using the simple induction principle of extending the solution for $n-1$ to a solution for n, we extend a solution for $n/2$ to a solution for n. (Again, the base case of one building is trivial.) Divide-and-conquer algorithms divide the inputs into smaller subsets, solve (conquer) each subset recursively, and merge the solutions together. Generally, it is more efficient to divide the problem into subproblems of about equal size. As we saw in Chapter 3, the solution of the recurrence relation $T(n) = T(n-1) + O(n)$ is $T(n) = O(n^2)$, whereas that of $T(n) = 2T(n/2) + O(n)$ is $T(n) = O(n \log n)$. Therefore, if we divide the problem into two equal-sized subproblems, then combine the solutions in linear time, the algorithm runs in time $O(n \log n)$. The divide-and-conquer technique is very useful, and we will see many examples of it.

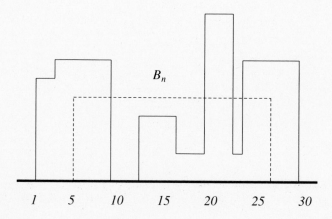

Figure 5.6 Addition of a building (dotted line) to the skyline of Figure 5.5(b) (solid lines).

The key idea behind the divide-and-conquer algorithm in this example is the observation that, in the worst case, it takes linear time to merge one building with the skyline, and also linear time to merge two different skylines. In about the same time, we achieve more using the latter approach. Two skylines can be merged with basically the same algorithm that merges one building into a skyline (Fig. 5.7). We scan the two skylines together from left to right, match x coordinates, and adjust heights when necessary. The merge can be achieved in linear time, and therefore the complete algorithm runs in time $O(n \log n)$ in the worst case. This algorithm is similar to mergesort, which is discussed in detail in Section 6.4.3. Therefore, we do not give the precise algorithm for the skyline algorithm here.

Comments   Always try to get more for your money. There is nothing mysterious or technical about this principle. If the algorithm includes a step that is more general than required, consider applying this step to a more complicated part of the problem. The reason the divide-and-conquer approach is so useful is that it uses the combine step to its fullest. The recurrence relations given in Section 3.5.2 cover the most common divide-and-conquer algorithms. You should memorize these recurrence relations.

5.7 Computing Balance Factors in Binary Trees

Let T be a binary tree with root r. The **height** of a node v is the distance between v and the farthest leaf down the tree. The **balance factor** of a node v is defined as the difference between the height of the node's left subtree and the height of the node's right subtree (we assume that the children of a node are labeled by left or right). In Chapter 4, we discussed AVL trees, in which all nodes have balance factors of -1, 0, or 1. In this section, we consider arbitrary binary trees. Figure 5.8 shows a tree in which each node is labeled with numbers representing h/b, where h is the node's height and b is its balance factor.

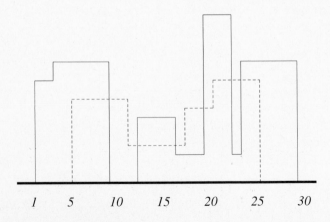

Figure 5.7 Merging two skylines.

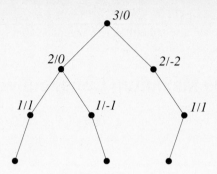

Figure 5.8 A binary tree. The numbers represent h/b, where h is the height and b is the balance factor.

> **The Problem**   Given a binary tree T with n nodes, compute the balance factors of all the nodes.

We use the regular inductive approach with the straightforward induction hypothesis.

> **Induction hypothesis:** *We know how to compute balance factors of all nodes in trees that have $< n$ nodes.*

The base case of $n = 1$ is trivial. Given a tree with $n > 1$ nodes, we remove the root, then solve the problem (by induction) for the two subtrees that remain. We chose to remove the root because the balance factor of a node depends on only the nodes below that node. We now know the balance factors of all the nodes, except for the root. The root's balance factor, however, depends not on the balance factors of the root's children, but rather on their height. Hence, simple induction does not work in this case. We need to know the heights of the children of the root. The idea is to include the height-finding problem within the original problem:

> **Stronger induction hypothesis:** *We know how to compute balance factors **and** heights of all nodes in trees that have $< n$ nodes.*

Again, the base case is trivial. Now, when we consider the root, we can determine its balance factor easily by calculating the difference between the heights of its children. Furthermore, we can also determine the height of the root — it is the maximal height of the two children plus 1.

The key to the algorithm is that it solves a slightly extended problem. Instead of computing only balance factors, we also compute heights. The extended problem turns out to be an easier one to solve, because the heights are easy to compute. In many cases, solving a stronger problem is easier. With induction, we need only to extend a solution of a small problem to a solution of a larger problem. If the solution is broader (because the problem is extended), then the induction step may be easier, since we have more with which to work. It is a common error to forget that there are two different parameters in this problem, and that each one should be computed separately. We will present several examples of such errors later in the book.

5.8 Finding the Maximum Consecutive Subsequence

The following problem is from Bentley [1986] (it also appeared in Bates and Constable [1985]).

The Problem   Given a sequence $x_1, x_2, ..., x_n$ of real numbers (not necessarily positive) find a subsequence $x_i, x_{i+1}, ..., x_j$ (of consecutive elements) such that the sum of the numbers in it is maximum over all subsequences of consecutive elements.

We call such a subsequence a **maximum subsequence**. For example, in the sequence (2, -3, 1.5, -1, 3, -2, -3, 3), the maximum subsequence is (1.5, -1, 3); its sum is 3.5. There may be several maximum subsequences in a given sequence. If all the numbers are negative, then the maximum subsequence is empty (by definition, the sum of the empty subsequence is 0). We would like to have an algorithm that solves the problem and reads the sequence in order only once.

The straightforward induction hypothesis is as follows:

Induction hypothesis: *We know how to find the maximum subsequence in sequences of size $<n$.*

If $n = 1$, then the maximum subsequence consists of the single number if that number is nonnegative, or the empty subsequence otherwise. Consider a sequence $S = (x_1, x_2, ..., x_n)$ of size $n > 1$. By induction, we know how to find a maximum subsequence in $S' = (x_1, x_2, ..., x_{n-1})$. If that maximum subsequence is empty, then all the numbers in S' are negative, and we need to consider only x_n. Assume that the maximum subsequence found by induction in S is $S'_M = (x_i, x_{i+1}, ..., x_j)$, for certain i and j such that $1 \le i \le j \le n-1$. If $j = n-1$ (namely, the maximum subsequence is a *suffix*), then it is easy to extend the solution to S: If x_n is positive, then it extends S'_M; otherwise, S'_M remains maximum. However, if $j < n-1$, then there are two possibilities. Either S'_M remains maximum, or there is another subsequence, which is not maximum in S', but is maximum in S when x_n is added to it.

The key idea here is to **strengthen the induction hypothesis**. We first illustrate the technique by using it to solve the maximum-subsequence problem, then discuss it in more generality in the next section. The problem we had with the straightforward induction hypothesis was that x_n may extend a subsequence that is not maximum in S', and thus may create a new maximum subsequence. Knowing only the maximum subsequence in S' is thus not sufficient. However, x_n can extend only a subsequence that ends at $n-1$ — that is, a suffix of S'. Suppose that we strengthen the induction hypothesis to include the knowledge of the maximum suffix, denoted by $S'_E = (x_k, x_{k+1}, ..., x_{n-1})$.

> **Stronger induction hypothesis:** *We know how to find, in sequences of size < n, a maximum subsequence overall, and the maximum subsequence that is a suffix.*

If we know both subsequences, the algorithm becomes clear. We add x_n to the maximum suffix. If the sum is more than the global maximum subsequence, then we have a new maximum subsequence (as well as a new suffix). Otherwise, we retain the previous maximum subsequence. We are not done yet. We also need to find the new maximum suffix. It is not true that we always simply add x_n to the previous maximum suffix. It could be that the maximum suffix ending at x_n is negative. In that case, it is better to take the empty set as the maximum suffix (such that later x_{n+1} will be considered by itself). The algorithm for finding the sum of the maximum subsequence is given in Fig. 5.9.

Algorithm Maximum_Consecutive_Subsequence (X, n) ;
Input: *X* (an array of size *n*).
Output: *Global_Max* (the sum of the maximum subsequence).

begin
    Global_Max := 0 ;
    Suffix_Max := 0 ;
    for i := 1 to n do
        if x[i] + Suffix_Max > Global_Max then
            Suffix_Max := Suffix_Max + x[i] ;
            Global_Max := Suffix_Max
        else if x[i] + Suffix_Max > 0 then
                Suffix_Max := x[i] + Suffix_Max
            else Suffix_Max := 0
end

Figure 5.9 Algorithm *Maximum_Consecutive_Subsequence*.

5.9 Strengthening the Induction Hypothesis

Strengthening the induction hypothesis is one of the most important techniques for proving mathematical theorems with induction. When attempting an inductive proof, we often encounter the following scenario. Denote the theorem by P. The induction hypothesis can be denoted by $P(<n)$, and the proof must conclude that $P(<n) \Rightarrow P(n)$. In many cases, we can add another assumption, call it Q, under which the proof becomes easier. That is, it is easier to prove $[P \text{ and } Q](<n) \Rightarrow P(n)$ than it is to prove

$P(<n) \Rightarrow P(n)$. The assumption seems correct, but it is not clear how we can prove it. The trick is to include Q in the induction hypothesis. We now have to prove that $[P$ and $Q](<n) \Rightarrow [P$ and $Q](n)$. P and Q is a stronger theorem than just P, but often stronger theorems are easier to prove. This process can be repeated and, with the right added assumptions, the proof becomes tractable. The maximum-subsequence problem is a good example of how this principle is used to improve algorithms.

A nice analogy to this principle is a well-known phenomenon: It is easier to add \$1 million to profits that are based on \$100 million of sales, than it is to add \$1 thousand to profits that are based on \$10 of sales.

The most common error people make while using this technique is to ignore the fact that an additional assumption was added and to forget to adjust the proof. In other words, they prove that $[P$ and $Q](<n) \Rightarrow P(n)$, without even noticing that Q was assumed. This oversight corresponds to forgetting to compute the new maximum suffix in the maximum-subsequence example. In the balance factors example, it corresponds to forgetting to compute the heights separately — which, unfortunately, is a common error. We cannot overemphasize this fact:

It is crucial to follow the induction hypothesis precisely.

We will present more complicated examples of strengthening the induction hypothesis in Sections 6.11.3, 6.13.1, 7.5, 8.3, and 12.3.1 (among others).

5.10 Dynamic Programming: The Knapsack Problem

Suppose that we are given a *knapsack* and we want to pack it fully with items. There may be many different items of different shapes and sizes, and our only goal is to pack the knapsack as full as possible. The knapsack may correspond to a truck, a ship, or a silicon chip, and the problem is to package items. There are many variations of this problem; we consider only a simple one dealing with one-dimensional items. Other variations of the knapsack problem are presented in the exercises, and in Chapter 11.

The Problem   Given an integer K and n items of different sizes such that the ith item has an integer size k_i, find a subset of the items whose sizes sum to exactly K, or determine that no such subset exists.

We denote the problem by $P(n, K)$, such that n denotes the number of items and K denotes the size of the knapsack. We will implicitly assume that the n items are those that are given as the input to the problem, and we will not include their sizes in the notation of the problem. Thus, $P(i, k)$ denotes the problem with the first i items and a knapsack of size k. For simplicity, we first concentrate on only the decision problem, which is to determine whether a solution exists. We start with the straightforward induction approach.

Induction hypothesis (first attempt): *We know how to solve* $P(n-1, K)$.

The base case is easy; there is a solution only if the single element is of size K. If there is a solution to $P(n-1, K)$ — that is, if there is a way to pack some of the $n-1$ items into the knapsack — then we are done; we will simply not use the nth item. Suppose, however, that there is no solution for $P(n-1, K)$. Can we use this negative result? Yes — it means that the nth item must be included. In this case, the rest of the items must fit into a smaller knapsack of size $K - k_n$. We have reduced the problem to two smaller subproblems: $P(n-1, K)$ and $P(n-1, K-k_n)$. To complete the solution, we have to strengthen the hypothesis. We need to solve the problem not only for knapsacks of size K, but also for knapsacks of all sizes at most K.

Induction hypothesis (second attempt): *We know how to solve* $P(n-1, k)$ *for all* $0 \le k \le K$.

The previous reduction did not depend on a particular value of K; it will work for any k. We can use this hypothesis to solve $P(n, k)$ for all $0 \le k \le K$. The base case $P(1, k)$ can be easily solved: If $k = 0$, then there is always a (trivial) solution. Otherwise, there is a solution only if the first item is of size k. We now reduce $P(n, k)$ to the two problems $P(n-1, k)$ and $P(n-1, k-k_n)$. If $k - k_n < 0$, then we ignore the second problem. Both problems can be solved by induction. This is a valid reduction, and we now have an algorithm; however, the algorithm may be inefficient. We reduced a problem of size n to *two* subproblems of size $n-1$! (We also reduced the value of k in one subproblem.) & Each of these two subproblems may be reduced to two other subproblems, leading to an exponential algorithm.

Fortunately, it is possible in many cases to improve the running time for these kinds of problems. The main observation is that the total number of possible problems may not be too high. In fact, we introduced the notation of $P(i, k)$ especially to demonstrate this observation. There are n possibilities for the first parameter and K possibilities for the second one. Overall, there are only nK different possible problems! The exponential running time resulted from doubling the number of problems after every reduction, but if there are only nK different problems, then we must have generated the same problem many many times. The solution is to remember all the solutions and never solve the same problem twice. This approach is a combination of strengthening the induction hypothesis and using strong induction (which is using the assumption that all solutions to smaller cases, and not only that for $n-1$, are known). Let's see now how to implement this approach.

We store all the known results in an $n \times K$ matrix. The (i, k)th entry in the matrix contains the information about the solution of $P(i, k)$. The reduction from the second-attempt hypothesis basically computes the nth row of the matrix. Each entry in the nth row is computed from two of the entries above it. If we are interested in finding the actual subset, then we can add to each entry a flag that indicates whether the corresponding item was selected in that step. This flag can then be traced back from the (n, K)th entry, and the subset can be recovered. The algorithm is given in Fig. 5.10. Figure 5.11 shows the complete matrix for a given input.

Algorithm Knapsack (S, K) ;
Input: *S* (an array of size *n* storing the sizes of the items),
  and *K* (the size of the knapsack).
Output: *P* (a two-dimensional array such that $P[i, k].exist$ = true if there
  exists a solution to the knapsack problem with the first *i* elements and a
  knapsack of size *k*, and $P[i, k].belong$ = true if the *i*th element belongs
  to that solution).
  { See Exercise 5.15 for suggestions about improving this program. }

begin
  $P[0, 0].exist := true$;
  for $k := 1$ **to** K **do**
    $P[0, k].exist := false$;
  { there is no need to initialize $P[i, 0]$ for $i \geq 1$, because it will
    be computed from $P[0, 0]$ }
  for $i := 1$ **to** n **do**
    for $k := 0$ **to** K **do**
      $P[i, k].exist := false$; { the default value }
      if $P[i-1, k].exist$ **then**
        $P[i, k].exist := true$;
        $P[i, k].belong := false$
      else if $k - S[i] \geq 0$ **then**
        if $P[i-1, k-S[i]].exist$ **then**
          $P[i, k].exist := true$;
          $P[i, k].belong := true$
end

Figure 5.10 Algorithm *Knapsack*.

	0	1	2	3	4	5	6	7	8	9	10	11	12	13	14	15	16
$k_1=2$	O	-	I	-	-	-	-	-	-	-	-	-	-	-	-	-	-
$k_2=3$	O	-	O	I	-	I	-	-	-	-	-	-	-	-	-	-	-
$k_3=5$	O	-	O	O	-	O	-	I	I	-	I	-	-	-	-	-	-
$k_4=6$	O	-	O	O	-	O	I	O	O	I	O	I	-	I	I	-	I

Figure 5.11 An example of the table constructed for the knapsack problem. The input
consists of four items of sizes 2, 3, 5, and 6. The symbols in the table are the following:
"I": a solution containing this item has been found; "O": a solution without this item has
been found; "-": no solution has not yet been found. (If the symbol "-" appears in the
last line, then there is no solution for a knapsack of this size.)

The method we just used is an instance of a general technique called **dynamic programming**. The essence of dynamic programming is to build large tables with all known previous results. The tables are constructed iteratively. Each entry is computed from a combination of other entries above it or to the left of it in the matrix. The main problem is to organize the construction of the matrix in the most efficient way. Another example of dynamic programming is presented in Section 6.8.

Complexity   There are nK entries in the table, and each one is computed in constant time from two other entries. Hence, the total running time is $O(nK)$. If the sizes of the items are not too large, then K cannot be too large and nK is much better than an exponential expression in n. (If K is very large or if the sizes are real numbers, then this approach will not work; we discuss this issue in Chapter 11.) If we are interested only in determining whether a solution exists, then the answer is in $P[n, K]$. If we are interested in finding the actual subset, then we can trace back from the (n, K)th entry, using, for example, the *belong* flag in the knapsack program, and recover the subset in $O(n)$ time.

Comments   The dynamic programming approach is effective when the problem can be reduced to several smaller, but not small enough, subproblems. All possible subproblems are computed. We do this computation by maintaining a large matrix. Hence, dynamic programming can work only if the total number of possible subproblems is not too large. Even then, dynamic programming requires building large matrices, and thus it usually requires a large space. (In some cases, as in the program in Fig. 5.10, it is possible to use less space by storing only a small part of the matrix at any moment.) The running times are usually at least quadratic.

5.11 Common Errors

In this section, we briefly mention some common errors in the use of induction to design algorithms. We have already discussed common errors in induction proofs in Section 2.13. All those errors have analogous errors here. For example, forgetting the base case is common. In the case of a recursive procedure, a base case is essential to terminate the recursion. Another common error is to extend a solution for n to a solution of a *special instance* of the problem for $n+1$, instead of an arbitrary instance.

Changing the hypothesis unintentionally is another common mistake. Here is a typical example of it. A graph $G = (V, E)$ is called **bipartite** if its set of vertices can be partitioned into two subsets such that there is no edge connecting two vertices from the same subset. If the graph is connected and bipartite, then the partition is unique (we omit the proof of this fact).

> **The Problem**   Given a connected undirected graph $G = (V, E)$, determine whether it is bipartite and, if it is, partition the vertices accordingly.

A wrong solution: Remove a vertex v and partition the rest of the graph, if possible, by induction. We call the first subset *red*, and the second subset *blue*. If v is connected to only red vertices, add it to the blue subset. If v is connected to only blue vertices, add it to the red subset. If v is connected to vertices from both subsets, then the graph is not bipartite (since the partition is unique).

The main error in this attempted solution, and the one we want to illustrate, is that after we have removed a vertex the graph may not be connected. Hence, the smaller instance of the problem is not the same as the original instance, and induction cannot be used. Had we removed a vertex that does not disconnect the graph, this solution would have been valid. This problem has a better solution, which does not depend on the graph being connected; we leave that solution to the reader (Exercise 7.32). For a similar example and further discussion of this common error, see Section 7.5. A result related to this incorrect algorithm is included in Exercise 5.24.

Changing the hypothesis is sometimes very tempting. If the hypothesis is something of the form "we know how to find such and such," then we are tempted to think that we can find other simple things with the same effort. But we cannot use any such assumption unless it is included specifically in the induction hypothesis. One way to avoid changing the hypothesis unintentionally is to think of it as a black box. Do not make any changes to that black box, unless you are ready to open it (namely, to redefine it explicitly).

5.12 Summary

Several techniques for designing algorithms, all of which are variations of the same approach, were introduced in this chapter. These are by no means all the known methods for designing algorithms. Additional techniques and numerous examples are presented in the following chapters. The best way to learn these techniques is to use them to solve problems. The rest of this book is devoted to precisely that purpose. The principles presented in this chapter are as follows:

- We can use the principle of induction to design algorithms by reducing an instance of a problem to one or more of smaller size. If the reduction can always be achieved, and the base case can be solved, then the algorithm follows by induction. The main idea is to concentrate on reducing a problem, rather than on solving it directly.

- One of the easiest ways to reduce the size of a problem is to eliminate some of its elements. That technique should be the first line of attack. The elimination can take many forms. In addition to simply eliminating elements that clearly do not contribute (as in Section 5.3), it is possible to merge two elements into one, to find elements that can be handled by special (easy) cases, or to introduce a new element that takes on the role of two or more original elements (Section 6.6).

- We can reduce the size of the problem in many ways. Not all reductions, however, lead to the same efficiency. As a result, all possibilities for reductions should be considered. In particular, it is worthwhile to consider different orders for the induction sequence. We have seen examples where it is better to take the largest element first. Sometimes, it is better to take the smallest element first. We will see examples of starting from the middle (Section 6.2). We also will see examples of induction on trees in which the root is removed first (top down), and examples in which the leaves are removed first (bottom up) (Section 6.4.4).

- One of the most efficient ways to reduce the size of a problem is to divide it into two (or more) equal parts. Divide and conquer works effectively if the problem can be divided such that the output of the subproblems can easily generate the output for the whole problem. Divide-and-conquer algorithms are given in Sections 6.4, 6.5, 8.2, 8.4, 9.4, and 9.5.
- Since a reduction can change only the size of the problem, but not the problem itself, we should look for smaller subproblems that are as independent as possible. For example, the problem of finding some ordering among several items can be reduced to finding (and removing) the item that is first in the order; the relative order of the rest of the items is independent of the first item (see Sections 6.4 and 7.5).
- There is one way, however, to overcome the limitation that the reduced problem must be identical to the original problem: Change the problem statement. This is a very important method that we will use often. Sometimes, it is better to weaken the hypothesis and to arrive at a weaker algorithm, which can be used as a step in the complete algorithm (see Section 6.10).
- Finally, we can use all these techniques together, or in various combinations. For example, we can use the divide-and-conquer approach with strengthening the induction hypothesis, so that the different subproblems become easier to combine (see Section 8.4).

Bibliographic Notes and Further Reading

The method presented in this chapter was developed by the author (Manber [1988]). It is by no means new. The use of induction, and in general mathematical proof techniques, in the algorithms area has its origin in the flowcharts of Goldstine and von Neumann (see von Neumann [1963]), but was first fully developed by Floyd [1967]. Dijkstra [1976], Manna [1980], Gries [1981], and Dershowitz [1983] present methodologies similar to ours to develop programs together with their proof of correctness. Their approach addresses program design in a much more rigorous and detailed fashion than the presentation in this chapter. The use of loop invariants, described in Section 2.12, can be considered, in some sense, to be equivalent to the use of induction in this chapter. Recursion, of course, has been used extensively in algorithm design (see, for example, Burge [1975] and Paull [1988]).

The celebrity problem was first suggested by Aanderaa (see Rosenberg [1973]). It is possible to save an additional $\lfloor \log_2 n \rfloor$ questions by being careful not to repeat, in the verification phase, questions asked during the elimination phase (King and Smith-Thomas [1982]). Strengthening the induction hypothesis is probably a very old trick. Polya [1957] calls this technique **the inventor's paradox** (because it is easier to invent, or prove, something that is stronger). It is also sometimes called **generalization**. Dynamic programming was introduced and formalized by Bellman [1957]. It has numerous applications, and many variations. For a detailed description of dynamic programming see, for example, Dreyfus and Law [1977], or Denardo [1982]. The observation leading to Exercise 5.24 was pointed out to us by Tom Trotter.

Drill Exercises

5.1   Design a divide-and-conquer algorithm for polynomial evaluation. How many additions and multiplications does your algorithm require? Can you think of an advantage this algorithm has over Horner's rule?

5.2   Try to follow the steps of inductive reasoning that were used in Section 5.3 to solve the following maximal induced subgraph problem: Given a graph $G = (V, E)$, we are looking for the maximal induced subgraph G' such that all the degrees in G' are *at most* k (as opposed to ''at least'' in the problem in Section 5.3). This version is much more difficult than the original version, and the approach taken for the original version does not work here. Discuss why it does not work. (See Chapter 11 for a discussion of this problem for the simple case of $k = 0$.)

5.3   Consider algorithm *Mapping* (Fig. 5.3). Is it possible that the set S will become empty at the end of the algorithm? Show an example, or prove that it cannot happen.

5.4   Write the appropriate loop invariant for the first while loop in algorithm *Celebrity* (Fig. 5.4).

5.5   You are given a binary tree T. T is called an **AVL tree** (see also Section 4.3.4) if the balance factors of all its nodes are 0, 1, or -1. Assume that the nodes do not have enough space to store the balance factor. Design an efficient algorithm to solve the following decision problem. Given a tree T, the algorithm should determine whether or not T is an AVL tree. The answer should be only yes or no.

5.6   Modify algorithm *Maximum_Consecutive_Subsequence* (Fig. 5.9) such that it finds the actual subsequence and not only the sum.

5.7   Write a program to recover the solution to a knapsack problem using the *belong* flag.

5.8   In algorithm *Knapsack*, we first checked whether the ith item is unnecessary (by checking $P[i-1, j]$). If there is a solution with the $i-1$ items, we take this solution. We can also make the opposite choice, which is to take the solution with the ith item if it exists (i.e., check $P[i, j-k_i]$ first). Which version do you think will have a better performance? Redraw Fig. 5.11 to reflect this choice.

5.9   A given knapsack problem may have many different solutions. What are the special characteristics of the solution obtained from algorithm *Knapsack*? What separates this solution from all the rest? How does your answer change if the choice is made according to the policy of Exercise 5.7?

Creative Exercises

5.10   Solve the following **extended skyline problem**. Suppose that the buildings in the skyline have roofs. Each building is a rectangle with a triangular roof on top. (You can assume for simplicity that all the roofs have 45-degree angles with the buildings.) Again, all the buildings have a common horizon. Design an algorithm to draw the skyline in this case.

5.11   Suppose that there are two different (maybe proposed) skylines: One is projected on a screen with a blue color, and the other is superimposed on the first one with a red color. Design an efficient algorithm to compute the shape that will be colored purple. In other words, compute the intersection of two skylines.

5.12   Let $x_1, x_2, ..., x_n$ be a sequence of real numbers (not necessarily positive). Design an $O(n)$ algorithm to find the subsequence $x_i, x_{i+1}, ..., x_j$ (of consecutive elements) such that the product of the numbers in it is maximum over all consecutive subsequences. The product of the empty subsequence is defined as 1.

5.13   Suppose that a given tree is not an AVL tree. We call a node an **AVL node** if its balance factor is 0, 1, or -1. Design an algorithm to mark the nodes in T that are not AVL nodes, but all of whose descendents are AVL nodes.

5.14   Let $G = (V, E)$ be a binary tree with n vertices. We want to construct an $n \times n$ matrix whose ijth entry is equal to the distance between v_i and v_j. (Since the tree is undirected, the matrix will be symmetric.) Design an $O(n^2)$ algorithm to construct such a matrix for a tree that is given in the adjacency-list representation.

5.15   Let $G = (V, E)$ be a binary tree. The **distance** between two vertices in G is the length of the path connecting these two vertices (neighbors have distance 1). The **diameter** of G is the maximal distance over all pairs of vertices. Design a linear-time algorithm to find the diameter of a given tree.

5.16   Improve the space utilization in algorithm *Knapsack* (Section 5.10). Is there a need for a complete $n \times K$ matrix? What is the space complexity of the improved algorithm?

5.17   Solve the following variation of the knapsack problem: The assumptions are identical to those of Section 5.10, except that there is an unlimited supply of each item. In other words, the problem is to pack items of given sizes in a given-sized knapsack, but each item may appear many times.

5.18   Here is another variation of the knapsack problem: The assumptions are the same as in Exercise 5.17 (n items, unlimited supply, fixed-sized knapsack), but now each item has an associated *value*. Design an algorithm to find how to pack the knapsack fully, such that the items in it have the maximal value among all possible ways to pack the knapsack.

5.19   Here is the most common variation of the knapsack problem: The assumptions are the same as in Exercise 5.17 (n items with sizes and values, unlimited supply, fixed-sized knapsack, and the goal of maximizing the value), but now we are not restricted to filling the knapsack exactly to capacity. We are interested only in maximizing the total value, subject to the constraint that there is enough room for the chosen items in the knapsack.

5.20   Let $x_1, x_2, ..., x_n$ be a set of integers, and let $S = \sum_{i=1}^{n} x_i$. Design an algorithm to partition the set into two subsets of equal sum, or determine that it is impossible to do so. The algorithm should run in time $O(nS)$.

5.21   Suppose that you are given an algorithm as a *black box* — you cannot see how it is designed — that has the following properties: If you input any sequence of real numbers, and an integer k, the algorithm will answer "yes" or "no," indicating whether there is a subset of the numbers whose sum is exactly k. Show how to use this black box to find the subset whose sum is k, if it exists. You should use the black box $O(n)$ times (where n is the size of the sequence).

5.22   The **towers of Hanoi** puzzle is a standard example of a nontrivial problem that has a simple recursive solution. There are n disks of different sizes arranged on a peg in decreasing order of sizes. There are two other empty pegs. (see Fig. 5.12). The purpose of the puzzle is to move all the disks, one at a time, from the first peg to another peg in the following way. Disks are moved from the top of one peg to the top of another. A disk can be moved to a peg only if it is smaller than all other disks on that peg. In other words, the ordering of disks by decreasing sizes must be preserved at all times. The goal is to move all the disks in as few moves as possible.

    a. Design an algorithm (by induction) to find a minimal sequence of moves that solves the towers of Hanoi problem for n disks.

    b. How many moves are used in your algorithm? Construct a recurrence relation for the number of moves, and solve it.

    c. Prove that the number of moves in part b is optimal; that is, prove that there cannot exist any other algorithm that uses less moves.

5.23   Write a nonrecursive program for the towers of Hanoi problem (defined in Exercise 5.22).

5.24   The following is a variation of the towers of Hanoi problem (see Exercise 5.22). We no longer assume that all the disks are initially on one peg. They may be arbitrarily distributed among the three pegs, as long as they are ordered in decreasing sizes on each peg. The purpose of the puzzle remains to move all disks to one specified peg, under the same constraints as the original problem, with as few moves as possible. Design an algorithm to find a minimal sequence of moves that solves this version of the towers of Hanoi problem for n disks.

Figure 5.12 The towers of Hanoi puzzle.

5.25   This exercise is related to the wrong algorithm for determining whether a graph is bipartite, described in Section 5.11. In some sense, this exercise shows that not only is the algorithm wrong, but also the simple approach cannot work. Consider the more general problem of *graph coloring:* Given an undirected graph $G = (V, E)$, a *valid coloring* of G is an assignment of colors to the vertices such that no two adjacent vertices have the same color. The problem is to find a valid coloring, using as few colors as possible. (In general, this is a very difficult problem; it is discussed in Chapter 11.) Thus, a graph is **bipartite** if it can be colored with two colors.

a. Prove by induction that trees are always bipartite.

b. We assume that the graph is a tree (which means that the graph is bipartite). We want to find a partition of the vertices into the two subsets such that there are no edges connecting vertices within one subset. Consider again the wrong algorithm for determining whether a graph is bipartite, given in Section 5.11: We take an arbitrary vertex, remove it, color the rest (by induction), and then color the vertex in the best possible way. That is, we color the vertex with the oldest possible color, and add a new color only if the vertex is connected to vertices of all the old colors. Prove that, if we color one vertex at a time regardless of the global connections, we may need up to $1 + \log_2 n$ colors. You should design a construction that maximizes the number of colors for every order of choosing vertices. The construction can depend on the order in the following way. The algorithm picks a vertex as a next vertex and starts checking the vertex's edges. At that point, you are allowed to add edges incident to this vertex as you desire, provided that the graph remains a tree, such that, at the end, the maximal number of colors will be required. You cannot remove an edge after it is put in (that would be cheating the algorithm, which has already seen the edge). The best way to achieve this construction is by induction. Assume that you know a construction that requires $\leq k$ colors with few vertices, and build one that requires $k + 1$ colors without adding too many new vertices.

CHAPTER 6

ALGORITHMS INVOLVING SEQUENCES AND SETS

Order is a lovely thing;
on disarray it lays its wing,
teaching simplicity to sing.

Anna Hempstead Branch (1875–1937)

6.1 Introduction

In this chapter, we deal with inputs that are either finite sequences or finite sets. The difference between sequences and sets is that in sequences the order in which the elements are given is important whereas in sets it is not. Also, in sets we assume that an element does not appear more than once, whereas there is no such assumption for sequences. Since inputs are usually given in some order, we can regard them as sequences. Nevertheless, we may call an input a set when we are not interested in the given order. Throughout this chapter, unless specified otherwise, the representation of the input is assumed to be an array, and we assume that the size of the array is known. The elements in the sequences or sets are assumed to be taken from a totally ordered set (e.g., integers, reals), so that they can be compared. In this chapter, we consider problems in which the elements are all of the same type. We study issues such as maximality, order, special subsequences, data compression, and similarities of sequences.

This chapter contains many different algorithms with a variety of applications. Our purpose is to give more examples of the design methodology introduced in Chapter 5, and, at the same time, to describe some important algorithms. We include algorithms that are very important and universally applicable (binary search and sorting, for example), algorithms that are very important but have specific applications (file compression and sequence comparisons), and algorithms that are not very important but illustrate interesting techniques (finding the two largest elements in a set, and the stuttering-subsequence problem).

The first example in this chapter is binary search — a basic and elegant algorithm that comes in many forms and appears in many situations. We then discuss sorting — one of the most extensively studied algorithmic problems — order statistics, data compression, two problems involving text manipulation, and probabilistic algorithms. We end this chapter with several examples of elegant algorithms illustrating interesting design techniques.

6.2 Binary Search and Variations

Binary search is to algorithms what a wheel is to mechanics: It is simple, elegant, and immensely important, and it is rediscovered frequently. The basic idea behind binary search is to cut the search space in half (or approximately so) by asking only one question. In this section, we describe several variations of binary search and show its versatility.

Pure Binary Search

> **The Problem**   Let $x_1, x_2, ..., x_n$ be a sequence of real numbers such that $x_1 \leq x_2 \leq \cdots \leq x_n$. Given a real number z, we want to find whether z appears in the sequence, and, if it does, to find an index i such that $x_i = z$.

For simplicity, we look for only one index i such that $x_i = z$. In general, we may be interested in finding all such indices, the smallest one, the largest one, and so on. The idea is to cut the search space in half by checking first the middle number. Assume, for simplicity that n is even. If z is less than $x_{n/2+1}$, then z is clearly in the first half of the sequence; otherwise, z is in the second half. Finding z in either half is a problem of size $n/2$, which can be solved by induction. We handle the base case of $n = 1$ by directly comparing z to the element. The algorithm is given in Fig. 6.1.

Complexity   Each time a comparison is made, the range is cut by one half; therefore, the number of comparisons required to find a given number in a sequence of size n with binary search is $O(\log n)$. This version of binary search delays the equality comparisons to the end. The alternative is to check equality with z in each step. The disadvantage of the version we present is that there is no hope for stopping the search early; the advantage is that only one comparison is made in every step (instead of one equality comparison and one inequality comparison). This search is thus usually faster. Although

---

Algorithm Binary_Search (X, n, z) ;

Input: X (a sorted array in the range 1 to n), and z (the search key).
Output: *Position* (an index i such that $X[i] = z$, or 0 if no such index exist).

begin
    Position := Find(z, 1, n) ;
end

function Find (z, Left, Right) : integer ;
begin
    if Left = Right **then**
        if X [Left] = z **then** *Find := Left*
        else Find := 0
    else
        Middle := $\lceil \frac{1}{2}(Left + Right) \rceil$;
        if z < X [Middle] **then**
            Find := Find (z, Left, Middle-1)
        else
            Find := Find (z, Middle, Right)
end

Figure 6.1 Algorithm *Binary_Search*.

---

it is more convenient to write the program as a recursive program, we can easily convert it to a nonrecursive program. Binary search is not as effective for small values of n as it is for large ns. If n is small, then it is better simply to search the sequence linearly.

Binary Search in a Cyclic Sequence

A sequence $x_1, x_2, ..., x_n$ is said to be **cyclically sorted** if the smallest number in the sequence is x_i for some unknown i, and the sequence $x_i, x_{i+1}, ..., x_n, x_1, ..., x_{i-1}$ is sorted in increasing order.

> **The Problem**   Given a cyclically sorted list, find the position of the minimal element in the list (we assume, for simplicity, that this position is unique).

To find the minimal element x_i in the sequence, we use the idea of binary search to eliminate half the sequence with one comparison. Take any two numbers x_k and x_m, such that $k < m$. If $x_k < x_m$, then i cannot be in the range $k < i \leq m$, since x_i is minimal in the whole sequence. (Notice that we cannot exclude x_k.) On the other hand, if $x_k > x_m$, then i

must be in the range $k < i \leq m$, since the order is switched somewhere in that range. Thus, with one comparison, we can eliminate many elements. By choosing k and m appropriately, we can find i in $O(\log n)$ comparisons. The algorithm is given in Fig. 6.2.

Algorithm Cyclic_Binary_Search (X, n, z) ;

Input: X (a cyclically sorted array in the range 1 to n of distinct elements).
Output: *Position* (the index of the minimal element in $\overline{x}$).

begin
    Position := *Cyclic_Find*$(1, n)$;
end

function Cyclic_Find (*Left, Right*) : *integer* ;
begin
    if *Left* = *Right* **then** *Cyclic_Find* := *Left*
    else
        Middle := $\lfloor \frac{1}{2}(Left + Right) \rfloor$;
        if $X[Middle] < X[Right]$ **then**
            Cyclic_Find := *Cyclic_Find* (*Left, Middle*)
        else
            Cyclic_Find := *Cyclic_Find* (*Middle+1, Right*)
    end

Figure 6.2 Algorithm *Cyclic_Binary_Search*.

Binary Search for a Special Index

In the following search problem, the key is not given; instead, we are looking for an index that satisfies a special property.

The Problem   Given a sorted sequence of distinct integers $a_1, a_2, ..., a_n$, determine whether there exists an index i such that $a_i = i$.

Pure binary search is not applicable here, because the value of the searched element is not given. However, the property we seek is adaptable to the binary search principle. Consider the value of $a_{n/2}$ (assume again that n is even). If this value is exactly $n/2$, then we are done. Otherwise, if it is less than $n/2$, then, since all numbers are distinct, the value of $a_{n/2-1}$ is less than $n/2 - 1$, and so on. No number in the first half of the sequence can satisfy the property, and we can continue searching the second half. The same argument holds if the answer is "greater than." The algorithm is given in Fig 6.3.

Algorithm Special_Binary_Search (A, n) ;

Input: X (a sorted array in the range 1 to n of distinct integers).
Output: *Position* (the index satisfying $A[Position] = Position$, or 0 if no such index exists).

begin
    Position := Special_Find(1, n) ;
end

function Special_Find (Left, Right) : integer ;
begin
    if *Left = Right* **then**
        if *A [Left] = Left* **then** *Special_Find := Left*
        else *Special_Find := 0 { unsuccessful search }*
    else
        Middle := $\lceil \frac{1}{2}(Left + Right) \rceil$ *;*
        if *A [Middle] < Middle* **then**
            Special_Find := Special_Find (Middle + 1, Right)
        else
            Special_Find := Special_Find (Left, Middle)
end

Figure 6.3 Algorithm *Special_Binary_Search.*

Binary Search in Sequences of Unknown Size

Sometimes we use a procedure much like binary search to double the search space rather than to halve it. Consider the regular search problem, but suppose that the size of the sequence is unknown. We cannot halve the search range, since we do not know its boundaries. Instead, we look for an element x_i that is greater than or equal to z. If we find such an element, then we can perform binary search in the range 1 to i. We first compare z to x_1. If $z \leq x_1$, then z can only be equal to x_1. Assume, by induction, that we know that $z > x_j$ for some $j \geq 1$. If we compare z to x_{2j}, then we double the search space with one comparison. If $z \leq x_{2j}$, then we know that $x_j < z \leq x_{2j}$ and we can find z with $O(\log j)$ additional comparisons. Overall, if i is the smallest index such that $z \leq x_i$, then it takes $O(\log i)$ comparisons to find an x_j such that $z \leq x_j$, and another $O(\log i)$ comparisons to find i.

The same algorithm can also be used when the size of the sequence is known, but we suspect that i is very small. This algorithm is an improvement over regular binary search in such cases because its running time is $O(\log i)$ rather than $O(\log n)$. However, there is an extra factor of 2 in the running time of this algorithm, since we perform two binary search like procedures. Therefore, this algorithm is better only when $i = O(\sqrt{n})$.

The Stuttering-Subsequence Problem

The principle of binary search appears even in problems that do not seem to require any search. Let A and B be two sequences of characters from a finite alphabet $A = a_1 a_2 \cdots a_n$ and $B = b_1 b_2 \cdots b_m$, such that $m \leq n$. We say that B is a **subsequence** of A if there are indices $i_1 < i_2 < \cdots < i_m$ such that, for all j, $1 \leq j \leq m$, we have $b_j = a_{i_j}$. In other words, B is a subsequence of A if we can embed B inside A in the same order but with possible holes. It is simple to determine whether B is a subsequence of A. We scan A until we find the first occurrence (if any) of b_1, continue from there until we find b_2, and so on. The proof that this algorithm is correct is easy by induction, and we leave it as an exercise. Since the algorithm involves one linear scan of A and B, its running time is clearly $O(m+n)$. Given a sequence B, we define B^i to be the sequence B with each character appearing i times consecutively. For example, if $B = xyzzx$, then $B^3 = xxxyyyzzzzzzxxx$.

> **The Problem** Given two sequences A and B, find the maximal value of i such that B^i is a subsequence of A.

This problem is called the **stuttering-subsequence problem**. It may seem difficult at first, but it can be solved easily with binary search.

For each given value of i, we can construct the sequence B^i easily. Hence, we can determine whether B^i is a subsequence of A for any specific value of i. Furthermore, if B^j is a subsequence of A, then B^i is a subsequence of A, for $1 \leq i \leq j$. The maximal value of i that needs to be considered cannot exceed n/m, since in that case the sequence B^i would be longer then A. So, we can use binary search. We first set $i = \lceil n/m \rceil /2$, and check whether B^i is a subsequence of A. We then continue with binary search, eliminating the lower range if the answer is yes and the upper range otherwise. It will take $\lceil \log_2(n/m) \rceil$ tests to determine the maximal i. The overall running time is thus $O((n+m)\log(n/m)) = O(n \log(n/m))$. Sequence comparison problems are also discussed in Section 6.8.

This solution suggests a general technique. Whenever we are looking for the maximal i that satisfies some property, it may be sufficient to find an algorithm that determines whether a *given* i satisfies that property. We can do the rest by binary search if we have an upper bound for i, and if the property is such that, whenever i satisfies it, then j satisfies it, for $1 \leq j \leq i$. If we do not know an upper bound for i, we can use the doubling scheme. That is, we can start at $i = 1$ and double the value of i until we find the right range. This search will take longer, but, unless the desired i is extremely large, it will still be efficient. The resulting algorithm, however, may not be optimal. In many cases, such as the stuttering-subsequence problem, it is possible to eliminate the extra $O(\log n)$ factor.

Solving Equations

This subject area does not conform to the subject of this chapter, but it deserves a short mention here. Suppose that we want to find a solution to the equation $f(x)=0$, where f is a continuous function which we can compute. We are given that x is in the range $[a, b]$ (i.e., $a \leq x \leq b$), and that $f(a) \cdot f(b) < 0$ (i.e., one of $f(a)$ and $f(b)$ is positive and the other one is negative). We want to find a solution to the equation within a given precision.

Since the function is continuous, a solution must exist in the range $[a, b]$. We can use a variation of binary search, known as **bisection** or the **Bolzano method**, which works as follows. The function f is evaluated at $x_1 = (a+b)/2$. If $f(x_1)=0$ (within the required precision), then we have a solution. Otherwise, we can select one of the subranges $[a, x_1]$ or $[x_1, b]$, each being one half the size of the original, in which a solution is guaranteed to exist. The selection is done such that the values of the function are positive at one end and negative at the other. We continue in this way until the desired precision is achieved. After k steps, the size of the region that contains a solution is $(b-a)/2^k$.

6.3 Interpolation Search

In binary search, the search space is always cut in half, which guarantees the logarithmic performance. However, if during the search we find a value that is very close to the search number z, it seems more reasonable to continue the search in that "neighborhood" instead of blindly going to the next half point. In particular, if z is very small, we should start the search somewhere in the beginning of the sequence instead of at the halfway point.

Consider the way we open a book when we are searching for a certain page number. Say the page number is 200 and the book looks like an 800-page book. Page 200 is thus around the one-fourth mark, and we use this knowledge as an indication of where to open the book. We will probably not hit page 200 on the first try; suppose that we get page 250 instead. We now cut the search to a range of 250 pages, and the desired page is at about the 80 percent mark between page 1 and 250. We now try to go back about one-fifth of the way. We can continue this process until we get close enough to page 200, that we can flip one page at a time. This is exactly the idea behind interpolation search. Instead of cutting the search space by a fixed half, we cut it by an amount that seems the most likely to succeed. This amount is determined by interpolation, which is illustrated in Fig. 6.4. The first guess is at $X[8]$, which turns out to be larger than z. Another interpolation leads to $X[5]$, and then another finally leads to $X[4]$. The algorithm, including the precise expression used for the interpolation, is given in Fig. 6.5.

Complexity   The performance of interpolation search depends not only on the size of the sequence, but also on the input itself. There are inputs for which interpolation search checks every number in the sequence (see Exercise 6.4). However, interpolation search is very efficient for inputs consisting of relatively uniformly distributed elements (the

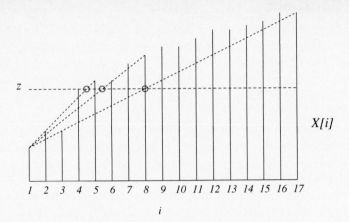

Figure 6.4 Interpolation search.

***

Algorithm Interpolation_Search *(X, n, z)* ;

Input: *X* (a sorted array in the range 1 to *n*), and *z* (the search key).
Output: *Position* (an index *i* such that $X[i] = z$, or 0 if no such index exist).

begin
    if $z < X[1]$ or $z > X[n]$ **then** *Position := 0*
        { unsuccessful search }
    else *Position := Int_Find(z, 1, n)*
end

function Int_Find *(z, Left, Right) : integer* ;
begin
    if $X[Left] = z$ **then** *Int_Find := Left*
    else if $Left = Right$ or $X[Left] = X[Right]$ **then**
      Int_Find := 0
    else

$$Next\_Guess := \left\lceil Left + \frac{(z - X[Left])(Right - Left)}{X[Right] - X[Left]} \right\rceil \ ;$$

    if $z < X[Next\_Guess]$ **then**
      Int_Find := Int_Find (z, Left, Next_Guess − 1)
    else
      Int_Find := Int_Find (z, Next_Guess, Right)
  end

Figure 6.5 Algorithm *Interpolation_Search*.

pages of a book are, of course, uniformly distributed). It can be shown that the average number of comparisons performed by interpolation search, where the average is taken over all possible sequences, is $O(\log \log n)$. Although this seems to be an order of magnitude improvement over the performance of binary search (due to the extra logarithm), interpolation search is not much better than binary search in practice for two main reasons. First, unless n is very large, the value of $\log_2 n$ is small enough that the logarithm of it is not much smaller. Second, interpolation search requires more elaborate arithmetic.

6.4 Sorting

Sorting is one of the most extensively studied problems in computer science. It is the basis for many algorithms, and it consumes a large proportion of computing time for many typical applications. There are numerous variations of the sorting problem, and dozens of sorting algorithms. We cannot cover in this section even a small part of this subject. We mention only several common techniques. As usual, we concentrate on the principles behind the algorithms that can be useful for other problems. We will go into more detail than usual in this section.

> **The Problem** Given n numbers $x_1, x_2, ..., x_n$, arrange them in increasing order. In other words, find a sequence of distinct indices $1 \leq i_1, i_2, ..., i_n \leq n$, such that $x_{i_1} \leq x_{i_2} \leq \cdots \leq x_{i_n}$.

For simplicity, unless specified otherwise, we assume that the numbers are distinct. All the methods described in this section are valid for nondistinct numbers as well. A sorting algorithm is called **in-place** if no additional work space is used besides the initial array that holds the elements.

6.4.1 Bucket Sort and Radix Sort

Perhaps the simplest sorting technique is the "mailroom" sort: allocate a sufficient number of "boxes" — we call them **buckets** — and put each element in the corresponding bucket. This method is called **bucket sort**. If the elements are letters and they need to be sorted according to states, for example, then allocating one bucket per state is sufficient and the resulting algorithm is very efficient. On the other hand, if the letters need to be sorted by zip codes (with 5 digits), then this method requires 100,000 boxes and a very large mailroom. Thus, bucket sort works very well only for elements from a small, simple range that is known in advance. A more detailed description of bucket sort follows.

We assume that there are n elements, all of which are integers in the range 1 to m. We allocate m buckets, and then, for each i, we put x_i in the bucket corresponding to its value. At the end, we scan the buckets in order and collect all the elements. The complexity of this simple algorithm is obviously $O(m+n)$. If $m=O(n)$, then we get a linear-time sorting algorithm. On the other hand, if m is very large relative to n (as may be the case with zip codes), then $O(m)$ is too large. In addition, the algorithm requires $O(m)$ storage, which is an even more serious problem for large m.

A natural extension of this idea is **radix sort**. Consider the zip-code example again. Using bucket sort for zip codes is not effective because the range of zip codes is too large to handle. Can we do something to reduce the range? We use induction on the *range* in the following way. We use several stages. First, we use 10 buckets and sort everything according to only the first digit of the zip code. Each bucket now covers 10,000 different zip codes (corresponding to the remaining four digits). The running time for this stage is $O(n)$. At the end of the first stage, we have 10 buckets, each with elements corresponding to a smaller range. We can now solve the problem for each bucket by induction. Since we reduce the range by a factor of 10 in each stage, and since all zip codes have 5 digits, only 5 stages will be required. Once the buckets are sorted, it is easy to put them together into a sorted list. We leave the details of this algorithm to the reader (Exercise 6.5), since we want to show another variation of the same idea. We note that the range can be divided in any convenient way. In the zip-code example, the range is divided according to the zip codes' decimal representation. If the keys are strings of characters that need to be sorted in a lexicographic order, we can consider one character at a time, leading to a **lexicographic sort**. Both algorithms are similar. The version of radix sort presented here (namely, a left to right scan) is known as **radix-exchange sort**.

A straightforward recursive implementation of radix-exchange sort requires temporary buckets (about 50 buckets will be needed in the zip-code example; see also Exercise 6.5). Another way to achieve radix sort is to apply the induction in the opposite order. That is, the sorting is done from right to left, starting with the least significant parts instead of the most significant parts. We assume that the elements are large integers represented by k *digits*, and each digit is in the range 0 to $d-1$. The induction hypothesis is the straightforward one.

Induction hypothesis: *We know how to sort elements with $< k$ digits.*

The difference between this method and the previous radix-exchange sort is the way we extend the hypothesis. (This idea of applying induction in the opposite order is similar to the one for Horner's rule in Section 5.2.) Given elements with k digits, we first ignore the *most significant digit* and sort the elements according to the rest of the digits by induction. We now have a list of elements sorted according to their $k-1$ least significant digits. We scan all the elements again and use bucket sort, on the most significant digit, with d buckets. Then, we collect all the buckets in order. This algorithm is called **straight-radix sort**. We want to argue that the elements are now sorted according to k digits.

We claim that two elements that are put in different buckets in the last step are arranged in the right order. We do not even need the induction hypothesis for this case, since, by the lexicographic ordering, the most significant digit is the one that determines the order regardless of the other digits. On the other hand, if two elements have the same most significant digit, then, by the induction hypothesis, they are in the right order before the last step. Thus, we have to make sure that they stay in the right order. This is the only subtle part of the algorithm, and it is a good example of the use of the inductive approach to make sure the algorithm is correct. It is essential that elements that are put in the same bucket remain in the same order. This can be achieved by using a queue for each bucket, and by appending the d queues at the end of a stage to form one global queue of all elements (sorted according to the i least significant digits). The precise algorithm is given in Fig. 6.6.

Algorithm Straight_Radix (X, n, k) ;

Input: X (an array of integers, each with k digits, in the range 1 to n).
Output: X (the array in sorted order).

begin
    We assume that all elements are initially in a global queue GQ ;
    { We use GQ for simplicity; it can be implemented through X }
    for *i := 1* **to** *d* **do**
    { d is the number of possible digits; d = 10 in case of decimal numbers }
        initialize queue Q [i] to be empty ;
    for *i := k* **downto** *1* **do**
        while *GQ is not empty* **do**
            pop x from GQ ;
            d := the ith digit of x ;
            insert x into Q [d] ;
        for *t := 1* **to** *d* **do**
            insert Q [t] into GQ ;
    for *i := 1* **to** *n* **do**
        pop X [i] from GQ
end

Figure 6.6 Algorithm *Straight_Radix*.

Complexity   It takes n steps to put all the elements in the queue GC, and d steps to initialize the queues $Q[i]$. The main loop of the algorithm, which is executed k times, pops each element from GC and pushes it into one of the $Q[i]$s. It also concatenates all the $Q[i]$s together. The overall running time of the algorithm is $O(nk)$.

In the remainder of this section, we consider sorting techniques that use direct comparisons between the elements without regard to the "structure" of their keys. Each comparison will thus involve the whole key. These algorithms are more general since they make no assumptions about the types of elements, except that two elements can be compared.

6.4.2 Insertion Sort and Selection Sort

We use a straightforward induction. Suppose that we know how to sort $n-1$ numbers and we are given n numbers. We can sort the $n-1$ numbers and then put the nth number in its correct place by scanning the $n-1$ sorted numbers until the correct place to insert is found. This procedure is appropriately called **insertion sort**. It is simple and effective for small values of n. However, it is not an efficient algorithm for large n. In the worst case, the nth number is compared to all the previous $n-1$ numbers. The total number of comparisons for sorting n numbers may be as high as $1+2+\cdots+n-1 = \frac{1}{2}(n-1)(n-2) = O(n^2)$. Furthermore, inserting the nth number in its correct place involves moving other elements. In the worst case, $n-1$ elements are moved in the nth step; hence, the number of element movements is also $O(n^2)$. We can improve insertion sort by storing the elements in an array, and using binary search on the $n-1$ sorted numbers to find the correct place to insert. The search takes only $O(\log n)$ comparisons per insertion, leading to $O(n \log n)$ comparisons overall. However, the number of data movements remains unchanged, so this is still a quadratic-time algorithm.

We can improve the straightforward induction by selecting a special nth number. For example, we can select the maximal number as the nth number. The maximal is a good choice because we know where to put it — it belongs at the end of the array. The algorithm consists of first selecting the maximal, then putting it in the right place (by swapping it with whatever is there), and then recursively sorting the rest. This algorithm is called **selection sort**. The advantage of selection sort over insertion sort is that only $n-1$ data movements (swaps in this case) are required versus $O(n^2)$ in the worst case for insertion sort. On the other hand, since it takes $n-1$ comparisons to find the maximal element (finding the maximal is discussed in Section 6.5), the total number of comparisons is always $O(n^2)$, whereas insertion sort with binary search requires only $O(n \log n)$ comparisons.

It is also possible to use balanced trees for efficient insertion or selection (see Chapter 4). Using AVL trees, for example, each insertion requires $O(\log n)$ time. Scanning an AVL tree to get a list of its numbers in order takes $O(n)$ time. If we assume by induction that we know how to build an AVL tree for $n-1$ numbers, then all we need to do is to insert, which takes $O(\log n)$ time. Overall, it takes $O(n \log n)$ time to insert n numbers into an empty AVL tree, and $O(n)$ time at the end to list them in sorted order. For large n, this is a much better solution than insertion sort or selection sort, but it requires more space to hold the pointers. It is clearly not an in-place algorithm. It is also quite complicated, and it is not as good as the algorithms we present next. The programs for insertion and selection sorts are simple and are left as exercises.

6.4.3 Mergesort

To improve the efficiency of insertion sort, we notice that in the time it takes to scan the sorted numbers to find the correct place to insert one number, we can find the correct place for many numbers. We have already used this idea in Section 5.6. If we have two sets of numbers that are already sorted, we can merge them together with one scan. The merge involves considering the numbers of the second set in order and finding the correct place in the first set for the smallest number, the second smallest, and so on. More precisely, denote the first set by $a_1, a_2, ..., a_n$, and the second set by $b_1, b_2, ..., b_m$, and assume that both sets are sorted in increasing order. Scan the first set until the right place to insert b_1 is found, and insert it; then continue the scan from that place until the right place to insert b_2 is found, and so on. Since the bs are sorted, we never have to go back. The total number of comparisons, in the worst case, is the sum of the sizes of the sets. What about data movements? It is inefficient to move elements each time an insertion is performed, since the same elements will be moved many times. Instead, since the merge produces the elements one by one in sorted order, we copy them to a temporary array; each element is copied exactly once. Overall, merging two sorted sequences of sizes n and m can be done with $O(n+m)$ comparisons and data movements (provided that additional storage is available).

The merge procedure that we just described can be used as a basis for a divide-and-conquer sorting algorithm, known as **mergesort**. The algorithm works as follows. First, the sequence is divided into two equal or close-to-equal (in case of an odd size) parts. Second, each part is sorted separately recursively. Third, the two sorted parts are merged into one sorted sequence, as described above. The precise algorithm is given in Fig. 6.7. An example of mergesort is shown in Fig. 6.8 (the copying is not shown).

Complexity   Let $T(n)$ be the number of comparisons required by mergesort in the worst case. Let's assume, for simplicity, that n is a power of 2. To calculate $T(n)$, we need to solve the following recurrence relation:

$$T(2n) = 2T(n) + O(n), \ \ T(2) = 1.$$

The solution of this recurrence relation is $T(n) = O(n \log n)$ (see Chapter 3), which is asymptotically better than the $O(n^2)$ running time required for insertion sort or selection sort. The number of data movements is also $O(n \log n)$, which is more than the $O(n)$ data movements required by selection sort.

Although mergesort is better than insertion sort for large n, it still has several drawbacks. First, mergesort is not as easy to implement. Second, the merging step requires additional storage to copy the merged set. Thus, mergesort is not an in-place algorithm. (There are more complicated versions of mergesort that use only constant amounts of extra storage; see the bibliography section.) This copying must be done every time two smaller sets are merged, which makes the procedure slower.

6.4.4 Quicksort

Mergesort and its analysis demonstrate the efficiency of divide and conquer. If we can divide the problem into two equal-sized subproblems, solve each subproblem separately, and combine the solutions, we can get an $O(n \log n)$ algorithm, provided that the division step and the combining step take $O(n)$. The problem with mergesort was the need for extra storage, since the merging is arbitrary and we cannot predict where each element will end up in the order. Can we somehow perform a different divide and conquer so that the position of the elements can be determined? The idea of quicksort is to spend most of the effort in the divide step and very little in the conquer step.

Algorithm Mergesort (X, n) ;
Input: *X* (an array in the range 1 to *n*).
Output: *X* (the array in sorted order).

begin
    M_Sort(1, n)
end

procedure *M_Sort(Left, Right) ;*

begin
    if *Right - Left = 1* **then**
    *{ checking for this case is not necessary, because it will be handled
    correctly anyway, but it makes the program more efficient }*
        if *X[Left] > X[Right]* **then** *swap (X[Left], X[right])*
    else if *Left ≠ Right* **then**
        Middle := $\lceil \frac{1}{2} (Left + Right) \rceil$;
        M_Sort(Left, Middle-1) ;
        M_Sort(Middle, Right) ;
        *{ we now merge the two sorted sequences above into one sorted
        sequence }*
        i := Left ;
        j := Middle ;
        k := 0 ;
        while *(i ≤ Middle − 1) and (j ≤ Right)* **do**
            k := k + 1 ;
            if *X [i] ≤ X [j]* **then**
                TEMP [k] := X [i] ;
                i := i + 1
            else
                TEMP [k] := X [j] ;
                j := j + 1 ;
        if *j > Right* **then**
            { move the rest of the left side to the end of the array }
            { if i ≥ Middle, then the right side is already in the right place }
            for *t := 0* **to** *Middle − 1 − i* **do**
                X [Right − t] := X [Middle − 1 − t] ;
        { we now copy TEMP back into X }
        for *t := 0* **to** *k - 1* **do**
            X [Left + t] := TEMP [t]
end

Figure 6.7 Algorithm *Mergesort.*

6	2	8	5	10	9	12	1	15	7	3	13	4	11	16	14
(2)	(6)	8	5	10	9	12	1	15	7	3	13	4	11	16	14
2	6	(5)	(8)	10	9	12	1	15	7	3	13	4	11	16	14
(2)	(5)	(6)	(8)	10	9	12	1	15	7	3	13	4	11	16	14
2	5	6	8	(9)	(10)	12	1	15	7	3	13	4	11	16	14
2	5	6	8	9	10	(1)	(12)	15	7	3	13	4	11	16	14
2	5	6	8	(1)	(9)	(10)	(12)	15	7	3	13	4	11	16	14
(1)	(2)	(5)	(6)	(8)	(9)	(10)	(12)	15	7	3	13	4	11	16	14
1	2	5	6	8	9	10	12	(7)	(15)	3	13	4	11	16	14
1	2	5	6	8	9	10	12	7	15	(3)	(13)	4	11	16	14
1	2	5	6	8	9	10	12	(3)	(7)	(13)	(15)	4	11	16	14
1	2	5	6	8	9	10	12	3	7	13	15	(4)	(11)	16	14
1	2	5	6	8	9	10	12	3	7	13	15	4	11	(14)	(16)
1	2	5	6	8	9	10	12	3	7	13	15	(4)	(11)	(14)	(16)
1	2	5	6	8	9	10	12	(3)	(4)	(7)	(11)	(13)	(14)	(15)	(16)
(1)	(2)	(3)	(4)	(5)	(6)	(7)	(8)	(9)	(10)	(11)	(12)	(13)	(14)	(15)	(16)

Figure 6.8 An example of mergesort. The first row is in the initial order. Each row illustrates either an exchange operation or a merge. The numbers that are involved in the current operation are circled.

Suppose that we know a number x such that one-half of the elements are greater than or equal to x and one-half of the elements are smaller than x. We can compare all elements to x and partition the sequence into two parts according to the answer. This partition requires $n - 1$ comparisons. Since the two parts are equal in size, one part can occupy the first half of the array and the other the second half. Furthermore, this partition can be accomplished without additional space, as will be shown shortly. This is the divide step. We can now sort each subsequence recursively. The combine step is trivial since the two parts already occupy the correct positions in the array. Therefore, no additional space is required.

Thus far, we have assumed that we know the value of x, which we usually do not. It is easy to see, however, that the same algorithm will work no matter which number is used for the partition. We call the number used in the partition the **pivot**. Our purpose is to partition the array into two parts, one with numbers greater than the pivot and the other with numbers less than or equal to the pivot. We can achieve this partition with the following algorithm. We use two pointers to the array, L and R. Initially, L points to the left side of the array and R points to the right side of the array. The pointers "move" in opposite directions toward each other. The following induction hypothesis (or loop invariant) guarantees the correctness of the partition.

> **Induction hypothesis:** *At step k of the algorithm, pivot $\geq x_i$ for all i such that $i < L$, and pivot $< x_j$ for all j such that $j > R$.*

The hypothesis is trivially true at the beginning (since no i or j satisfies the conditions). Our goal is to move either L to the right or R to the left at step $k + 1$ without invalidating the hypothesis.

When $L = R$, the partition is almost completed except possibly for x_L, with which we deal later. Let's assume that $L < R$. There are two cases. If either $x_L \leq pivot$ or $x_R > pivot$, then the corresponding pointer(s) can move and the hypothesis is preserved. Otherwise, we have $x_L > pivot$ and $x_R \leq pivot$. In this case, we can *exchange* x_L with x_R and move both pointers inward. Both cases involve the movement of at least one of the pointers; hence, the pointers will eventually meet and the algorithm will terminate.

We are left with the problems of choosing a good pivot and dealing with the last step of the algorithm in which the two pointers meet. Divide-and-conquer algorithms work best when the parts have equal sizes, which suggests that the closer the pivot is to the middle, the faster the algorithm runs. It is possible to find the median of the sequence (we discuss median finding in the next section), but it is not worth the effort. As we shall see in the analysis, choosing a random element from the sequence is a good choice. If the sequence is in a random order, then we might as well choose the first element as the pivot. We make this choice, mainly for simplicity, in the algorithm presented in Fig. 6.9.

Algorithm *Partition* (*X, Left, Right*) ;
Input: *X* (an array), *Left* (the left boundary of the array), and *Right* (the right boundary).
Output: *X* and *Middle* such that $X[i] \leq X[Middle]$ for all $i \leq Middle$ and $X[j] > X[Middle]$ for all $j > Middle$.

begin
    pivot := *X*[*Left*] ;
    L := *Left* ; *R* := *Right* ;
    while *L* < *R* **do**
        while *X*[*L*] $\leq$ *pivot* **and** *L* $\leq$ *Right* **do** *L* := *L* + *1* ;
        while *X*[*R*] > *pivot* **and** *R* $\geq$ *Left* **do** *R* := *R* - *1* ;
        if *L* < *R* **then**
            exchange X[*L*] *with X*[*R*] ;
    Middle := *R* ;
    exchange X[*Left*] *with X*[*Middle*]
end

Figure 6.9 Algorithm *Partition*.

When the first element is chosen as the pivot, we can exchange it with x_L at the last step of the partition, which will put the pivot in the middle of the partition as required. We mention other policies in the complexity discussion. In any case, any pivot chosen from the sequence can be exchanged with the first element, and then the algorithm in Fig. 6.9 can be used.

An example of algorithm *Partition* is given in Fig. 6.10. The pivot is the first number (6). The circled numbers are those that have just been exchanged. After three exchanges, p_h points to $X[6] = 1$, and p_l points to $X[7] = 12$. The last exchange involves the middle point (1) and the pivot (6). After this exchange, everything to the left of the pivot is less than or equal to it, and everything to the right is greater than it. The two subsequences (from 1 to 6 and from 7 to 16) can be sorted recursively. Quicksort is thus an in-place algorithm. The algorithm for quicksort is given in Fig. 6.11, and an example of it is presented in Fig. 6.12.

Complexity   The running time of quicksort depends on the particular input and on the selection of the pivot. If the pivot always partitions the sequence into two equal parts,

6	2	8	5	10	9	12	1	15	7	3	13	4	11	16	14
6	2	④	5	10	9	12	1	15	7	3	13	⑧	11	16	14
6	2	4	5	③	9	12	1	15	7	⑩	13	8	11	16	14
6	2	4	5	3	①	12	⑨	15	7	10	13	8	11	16	14
①	2	4	5	3	⑥	12	9	15	7	10	13	8	11	16	14

Figure 6.10 Partition of an array around the pivot 6.

Algorithm Quicksort (X, n) ;
Input: X (an array in the range 1 to *n*).
Output: X (the array in sorted order).

begin
    Q_Sort(1, n)
end

procedure Q_Sort(Left, Right) ;
begin
    if Left < Right **then**
        Partition(X, Left, Right) ;
        Q_Sort(Left, Middle − 1) ;
        Q_Sort(Middle + 1, Right)
end

Figure 6.11 Algorithm *Quicksort*.

6	2	8	5	10	9	12	1	15	7	3	13	4	11	16	14
1	2	4	5	3	(6)	12	9	15	7	10	13	8	11	16	14
(1)	2	4	5	3	(6)	12	9	15	7	10	13	8	11	16	14
(1)	(2)	4	5	3	(6)	12	9	15	7	10	13	8	11	16	14
(1)	(2)	3	(4)	5	(6)	12	9	15	7	10	13	8	11	16	14
(1)	(2)	3	(4)	5	(6)	8	9	11	7	10	(12)	13	15	16	14
(1)	(2)	3	(4)	5	(6)	7	(8)	11	9	10	(12)	13	15	16	14
(1)	(2)	3	(4)	5	(6)	7	(8)	10	9	(11)	(12)	13	15	16	14
(1)	(2)	3	(4)	5	(6)	7	(8)	9	(10)	(11)	(12)	13	15	16	14
(1)	(2)	3	(4)	5	(6)	7	(8)	9	(10)	(11)	(12)	(13)	15	16	14
(1)	(2)	3	(4)	5	(6)	7	(8)	9	(10)	(11)	(12)	(13)	14	(15)	16

Figure 6.12   An example of quicksort. The first line is the initial input. A new pivot is selected in each line. The pivots are circled. When a single number appears between two pivots it is obviously in the right position.

then the recurrence relation is $T(n) = 2T(n/2) + O(n)$, $T(2) = 1$, which implies $T(n) = O(n \log n)$. We will see that we get an $O(n \log n)$ running time even under much weaker conditions. However, if the pivot is very close to one side of the sequence, then the running time is much higher. For example, if the pivot is the smallest element in the sequence, then the first partition requires $n - 1$ comparisons and places only the pivot in the right place. If the sequence is already in increasing order, and we always select the first element as the pivot, then the running time of the algorithm is $O(n^2)$. We can eliminate the quadratic worst case for sequences that are sorted or almost sorted by comparing the first, last, and middle elements, and then taking the median of these three (namely, the second largest) as the pivot. An even safer method is to choose pivots from among the elements in the sequence *at random*. The running time of quicksort will still be $O(n^2)$ in the worst case, because there is still a chance that the pivot is the smallest element in the sequence. However, the likelihood that this worst case occur is very small. We now analyze this case.

We assume that each of the x_i has the same probability of being selected as the pivot. The running time $T(n)$ of quicksort if the ith smallest element is the pivot is

$$T(n) = n - 1 + T(i - 1) + T(n - i).$$

(It takes $n - 1$ comparisons for the partition, and we need to sort two smaller sequences of sizes $i - 1$ and $n - i$.) If each element has the same probability of being selected, then the **average running time** is

$$T(n) = n - 1 + \frac{1}{n} \sum_{i=1}^{n} (T(i-1) + T(n-i))$$

$$= n - 1 + \frac{1}{n} \sum_{i=1}^{n} T(i-1) + \frac{1}{n} \sum_{i=1}^{n} T(n-i)$$

$$= n - 1 + \frac{2}{n} \sum_{i=0}^{n-1} T(i).$$

This is a recurrence relation with full history. We discussed this particular relation in Section 3.5.3, and its solution was shown there to be $T(n) = O(n \log n)$. Hence, quicksort is indeed quick on the average.

In practice, quicksort is very fast, so it well deserves its name. A major reason for its quickness, besides the elegant divide and conquer, is that many elements are compared against the same element (the pivot). The pivot is thus stored in a register and there is no need for a data movement from memory. In most computers, this saves considerable time.

One way to improve the running time of quicksort is to use a technique we call **choosing the base of the induction wisely**. The idea is to start the induction not always from 1. Quicksort, as described above, is called recursively until the base case, which consists of sequences of size 1. However, simple sorting techniques, such as insertion sort or selection sort, perform very well for small sequences, whereas the efficiency of quicksort shows only for large sequences. Therefore, we can define the base case for quicksort to be of size larger than 1 (it seems that 10 to 20 is a good size, but that depends on the specific implementation), and handle the base case by insertion sort. (In other words, we replace the check "if Left < Right" by "if Left < Right - Threshold" and add an "else" part which runs insertion sort.) This change leads to an improvement of the running time of quicksort by a small constant. In Section 6.11.3, we will see how to use the principle of selecting the base of the induction to improve asymptotically the running time of an algorithm.

6.4.5 Heapsort

Heapsort is another fast sorting algorithm. In practice, it is usually not quite as fast as quicksort for large n, but it is not much slower. On the other hand, unlike quicksort, its performance is guaranteed. Like mergesort, the worst-case running time of heapsort is $O(n \log n)$. Unlike mergesort, heapsort is an in–place sorting algorithm. In this section, we emphasize one part of heapsort — building the heap. The algorithm for building the heap illustrates the way design and analysis of algorithms should be interleaved.

Heaps were discussed in Chapter 4. We assume here an implicit representation; specifically, the elements are given in an array $A[1..n]$, which corresponds to a tree in the following way: The root of the tree is stored in $A[1]$, and the children of any node $A[i]$ (if there are any) are stored in $A[2i]$ and $A[2i+1]$. Such an array satisfies the **heap property** if the value of each node is greater than or equal to the values of its children.

Heapsort works as follows. The input is an array $A[1..n]$. First, the elements in the array are rearranged to form a heap. We will discuss how to build a heap later. If A is a heap, then $A[1]$ is the maximal element of the array. We exchange $A[1]$ with $A[n]$ so that $A[n]$ now contains the correct element. We then consider the array $A[1..n-1]$. Again, we rearrange the array to form a heap (we have to worry only about the new $A[1]$), exchange $A[1]$ with $A[n-1]$, and continue with $A[1..n-2]$. Overall, there is one initial step of building a heap, and $n-1$ steps of exchanging elements and rearranging the heap. Rearranging the heap after an exchange is basically the same as algorithm *Remove_Max_from_Heap,* given in Section 4.3.2. Building a heap is an interesting problem on its own, and it is described in detail below. Overall, the running time of heapsort is $O(n \log n)$ ($O(\log n)$ per exchange), plus the running time of the algorithm for building the heap. Heapsort is clearly an in-place sorting algorithm. The algorithm for heapsort is given in Fig. 6.13.

Algorithm Heapsort (X, n) ;
Input: X (an array in the range 1 to n).
Output: X (the array in sorted order).

begin
    Build_Heap (X) ; { see text below }
    for $i := n$ *downto* 2 *do*
        swap (A[1], A[i]) ;
        Rearrange_Heap (i − 1)
        { basically the same procedure as Remove_Max_from_Heap
        in Fig. 4.7 }
end

Figure 6.13 Algorithm *Heapsort.*

Building a Heap

We now concentrate on the problem of building a heap from an arbitrary array.

The Problem   Given an array $A[1..n]$ of elements in an arbitrary order, rearrange the elements so that the array satisfies the heap property.

There are two natural ways to build a heap — top down and bottom up. They correspond respectively to scanning the array representing the heap either from left to right or from right to left. Figure 6.14 illustrates both methods. We first describe both methods with the use of induction. We then show that there is a substantial difference in performance

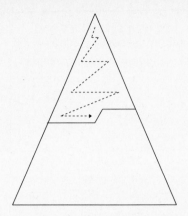 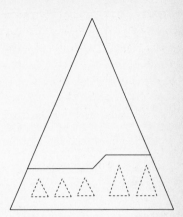

Figure 6.14 Top down and bottom up heap construction.

between the two methods.

Consider scanning the array from left to right (corresponding to top down).

Induction hypothesis (top down): *The array $A[1..i]$ is a heap.*

The base case is trivial, since $A[1]$ by itself is always a heap. The main part of the algorithm is to incorporate $A[i+1]$ into the heap $A[1..i]$. But, this is exactly the same as inserting $A[i+1]$ into the heap (see Chapter 4). $A[i+1]$ is compared to its parent, and exchanges are made until the new parent is larger. The number of comparisons in the worst case is $\lfloor \log_2(i+1) \rfloor$.

Consider now scanning the array from right to left (corresponding to bottom up). We would like to say that the array $A[i+1..n]$ is a heap and to consider adding the element $A[i]$. But the array $A[i+1..n]$ does not correspond to one heap; it corresponds to a collection of heaps. (Note that we consider $A[i+1..n]$ as part of the tree represented by $A[1..n]$, and not as an array by itself.) Therefore, the induction hypothesis is slightly more complicated.

Induction hypothesis (bottom up): *All the trees represented by the array $A[i+1..n]$ satisfy the heap condition.*

$A[n]$ by itself is obviously a heap, so the base case is satisfied. We can do better, however. The whole array $A[\lfloor n/2 \rfloor +1..n]$ represents leaves in the tree. Hence, the trees corresponding to $A[\lfloor n/2 \rfloor +1..n]$ are all singletons, so they satisfy the heap property trivially. We need to start the induction process only at $\lfloor n/2 \rfloor$. This is a good hint that the bottom-up approach may be better. After all, half the work is trivial. (This is also another example for the importance of selecting the base of the induction with care.)

Consider now $A[i]$. It has at most two children ($A[2i+1]$ and $A[2i]$), both serving as roots to valid heaps (by the induction hypothesis). Incorporating $A[i]$ into a heap is straightforward. $A[i]$ is compared to the maximal of its children, and, if necessary, it is exchanged with the larger child. This is similar to a deletion in a heap (see Chapter 4). The exchanges continue down the tree until the old value of $A[i]$ reaches a place where it is larger than both its children. A bottom-up construction is illustrated in Fig. 6.15. Since the height of $A[i]$ is $\lfloor \log_2(n/i) \rfloor$, the number of comparisons in the worst case is $2\lfloor \log_2(n/i) \rfloor$.

Complexity (top down)   The ith step requires at most $\lfloor \log_2 i \rfloor \leq \lfloor \log_2 n \rfloor$ comparisons; hence, the running time is $O(n \log n)$. Moreover, $O(n \log n)$ is not an overestimation of the running time, as the following argument shows.

$$\sum_{i=1}^{n} \lfloor \log_2 i \rfloor \geq \sum_{i=n/2}^{n} \lfloor \log_2 i \rfloor \geq n/2 \lfloor \log_2(n/2) \rfloor = \Omega(n \log n).$$

Complexity (bottom up)   The number of comparisons involved in each step is at most twice the height of the corresponding node (since each node may have to be compared with its two children, exchanged, and so on down the tree). Therefore, the complexity is at most twice the sum of the heights of all nodes in the tree. We want to evaluate this sum. Let's look at complete trees first, and denote by $H(i)$ the sum of heights of all nodes in the complete binary tree of height i. We can derive a recurrence relation for $H(i)$, noting that a tree of height i consists of two trees of height $i-1$ and a root. Hence, $H(i) = 2H(i-1) + i$, and $H(0) = 0$. We can verify (by induction) that the solution of this recurrence is $H(i) = 2^{i+1} - (i+2)$. Since the number of nodes in a complete binary tree of height i is $2^{i+1} - 1$, it follows that the complexity of bottom-up heap construction is $O(n)$ for complete binary trees (namely, heaps with $2^k - 1$ nodes). The complexity for a heap with n nodes such that $2^k \leq n < 2^{k+1} - 1$ is no more than that for a heap with $2^{k+1} - 1$ nodes, which is still $O(n)$. (A more careful analysis shows that the constant is not increased; see Exercise 6.32.) The reason the bottom-up approach is

1	2	3	4	5	6	7	8	9	10	11	12	13	14	15	16
6	2	8	5	10	9	12	1	15	7	3	13	4	11	16	14
2	6	8	5	10	9	12	(14)	15	7	3	13	4	11	16	(1)
2	6	8	5	10	9	(16)	14	15	7	3	13	4	11	(12)	1
2	6	8	5	10	(13)	16	14	15	7	3	(9)	4	11	12	1
2	6	8	5	10	13	16	14	15	7	3	9	4	11	12	1
2	6	8	(15)	10	13	16	14	(5)	7	3	9	4	11	12	1
2	6	(16)	15	10	13	(12)	14	5	7	3	9	4	11	(8)	1
2	(15)	16	(14)	10	13	12	(6)	5	7	3	9	4	11	8	1
(16)	15	(13)	14	10	(9)	12	6	5	7	3	(2)	4	11	8	1

Figure 6.15   An example of building a heap bottom up. The numbers on top are the indices. The circled numbers are those that have been exchanged on that step.

faster than the top-down approach is that there are many nodes at the bottom of the tree and few at the top. Thus, it is better to minimize the work for the bottom nodes rather than to minimize the work for the top nodes.

This is another example where trying a different order of induction leads to a better algorithm. The top-down method is the more straightforward and intuitive, but the bottom-up method turns out to be superior.

Comments   It is hard to summarize sorting in one paragraph. The main techniques that were described in this section are variations of divide and conquer. We have seen that it is worthwhile to spend time for the divide in order to make the conquer easier. In the induction analogy, this translates into trying different orders of induction, and, in particular, applying the induction to special subsets rather than to arbitrary elements. We have also seen that the analysis must go hand in hand with the design. With some experience one learns to develop intuition about efficiency of algorithms even before the analysis is performed. This intuition is helpful in directing the search for a better algorithm. The truth is usually (but not always!) not far removed from the intuition.

6.4.6 A Lower Bound for Sorting

We have started with an $O(n^2)$ algorithm for sorting and improved it to an $O(n \log n)$ algorithm. Is it possible to improve it even further? A lower bound for a particular problem is a proof that *no algorithm* can solve the problem better. It is much harder to prove a lower bound, since we have to address all possible algorithms and not just one approach. We need to define a model that corresponds to an arbitrary (unspecified) algorithm and to prove that the running time of any algorithm that fits the model must be higher than or equal to the lower bound. In this section, we discuss one such model called a **decision tree**. Decision trees model computations that consist mainly of comparisons. Decision trees are not general models of computation, as are Turing machines or random-access machines — hence, lower bounds using them are weaker — but they are simpler in many respects and are easier to work with. There are many variations of decision trees, and many known lower bound proofs utilizing them.

We define decision trees as binary trees with two types of nodes — internal nodes and leaves. Each internal node is associated with a **query** whose outcome is one of two possibilities, each associated with one of the emanating branches. Each leaf is associated with a possible output. We assume that the input is a sequence of numbers $x_1, x_2, ..., x_n$. The computation starts at the root of the tree. At each node, the query is applied to the input and, according to the outcome of the query, either the left or the right branch is taken. When a leaf is reached, the output associated with the leaf is the output of the computation. The worst-case running time associated with a tree T is the height of T, which is the maximal number of queries required by an input. A decision tree thus corresponds to an algorithm. Although decision trees cannot model every algorithm (for example, we cannot compute a square root of a number with a decision tree), they are reasonable models of comparison-based algorithms. A lower bound obtained for decision trees implies that no algorithm *of that form* can perform better. We now use decision trees to prove a lower bound for sorting.

□ Theorem 6.1

Every decision tree algorithm for sorting has height $\Omega(n \log n)$.

Proof: The input for sorting is a sequence $x_1, x_2, ..., x_n$. The output is the same sequence in the sorted order. Another way to look at the output is that it is a *permutation* of the input; namely, the output indicates how to rearrange the elements such that they become sorted. Every permutation is a possible output, since the input can be in any order. A sorting algorithm is correct if it handles all possible inputs. Thus, every permutation (rearrangement) of $(1, 2, ..., n)$ should be represented as a possible output in the decision tree for sorting. The output in a decision tree is associated with the leaves. Since two different permutations correspond to different outputs, they must be associated with different leafs. Therefore, there must be at least one leaf for every possible permutation. The total number of permutations on n elements is $n!$. Since we assume that the tree is a binary tree, the height of the tree is at least $\log_2(n!)$. By Stirling's formula

$$n! = \sqrt{2\pi n} \, (\frac{n}{e})^n (1 + O(1/n)).$$

Hence, $\log_2(n!) = \Omega(n \log n)$, which completes the proof.   □

This kind of a lower bound is called an **information-theoretic** lower bound, because it does not depend at all on the computation (notice that we have not even defined the kind of queries we allow), but only on the amount of information contained in the output. What the lower bound says in this case is that every sorting algorithm requires $\Omega(n \log n)$ comparisons in the worst case, since it needs to distinguish between $n!$ different cases and it can distinguish between only two possibilities at a time. We could have defined a decision tree as a tree with three children (corresponding, for example, to "<," "=," and ">"). In this case, the height would have been at least $\log_3 n!$, which is still $\Omega(n \log n)$. In other words, the $\Omega(n \log n)$ lower bound applies to any decision tree with constant number of branches per node.

This lower bound proof implies only that no comparison-based sorting algorithm can be faster than $\Omega(n \log n)$. It may be possible to sort more quickly by utilizing special properties of the keys and performing algebraic manipulations on the keys. For example, if there are n elements, all integers with values between 1 and $4n$, then bucket sort will produce a sorted list in $O(n)$ time. This is not a contradiction to the lower bound, since bucket sort does not use comparisons. It uses the fact that the values of the numbers can be used efficiently as *addresses* (buckets).

When discussing decision trees, we usually ignore their sizes, and concentrate only on their heights. As a result, even simple linear-time algorithms may correspond to decision trees with an exponential number of nodes. The size is not important, since we do not intend actually to construct the tree. We use the tree only as a tool for lower bound proofs. Ignoring the size makes the proofs more powerful, since they may apply to programs of exponential size. On the other hand, the technique may be too powerful, rendering it useless for deriving lower bounds for problems that cannot be solved by practical-sized programs, but can be solved with an exponential-sized program (e.g., a program with a table for all the possible solutions). Decision trees are **nonuniform** models of computation. The tree depends on n, the size of the input. We can potentially build different trees for different values of n. This is not just a whimsical worry. It turns out that we can build decision trees of polynomial height — but exponential size — for problems that probably require exponential running time, so decision trees are too optimistic sometimes. That is, a decision tree lower bound may fall far below the actual complexity of the problem. On the other hand, if the lower bound is equal to the upper bound of a particular algorithm — as is the case with sorting — then the lower bound implies that even if we use a lot more space, we cannot improve the algorithm.

It is interesting to note that the average running time of any comparison based sorting algorithm is also $\Omega(n \log n)$. We omit the proof, which is much more complicated (see for example Aho, Hopcroft, and Ullman [1974]).

6.5 Order Statistics

Given a sequence $S = x_1, x_2, ..., x_n$ of elements, we say that x_i has **rank** k in S if x_i is the kth-smallest element in S. We can easily determine the ranks of all elements in a sequence by sorting the elements. However, there are many questions about ranks that can be answered without sorting. In this section, we deal with such questions. We start with the problem of finding the maximum and minimum elements, then consider the general problem of finding the kth smallest element.

6.5.1 Maximum and Minimum Elements

Finding the maximum or the minimum element of a sequence is straightforward. If we know the maximum of a sequence of size $n-1$, then we need only to compare this maximum to the nth element to find the maximum of a sequence of size n (finding the maximum of a sequence of size 1 is trivial). This process takes one comparison per element, starting with the second element; hence, the number of comparisons is $n-1$.

Suppose now that we want to find both the maximum *and* the minimum elements.

The Problem   Find the maximum and minimum elements in a given sequence.

The straightforward solution is to solve both problems independently. The total number of comparisons will be $2n-3$: $n-1$ to find the maximum and then $n-2$ to find the minimum (because the maximum need not be considered). Can we do better? Consider again an inductive approach. Assume that we know how to solve the problem for $n-1$ elements, and that we want to find the solution for n elements (the base case is trivial). We have to compare the additional element to the maximum and minimum elements found so far. This requires two comparisons, which implies that the total number of comparisons will again be $2n-3$, since no comparison is required for the first element, and only one comparison is required for the second element. We cannot improve the solution by scanning the elements in a different order, because the position of the elements in the sequence is irrelevant to the problem.

The next attempt can be to extend the solution by more than one element at a time. Let's try to extend the solution by two elements at a time. That is, assume that we know how to solve the problem for $n-2$ elements, and try to solve it for n. (For this approach to be complete, we need two base cases, $n=1$ and $n=2$, so that extending by two will cover all natural numbers.) Consider x_{n-1} and x_n, and let *MAX* (*min*) be the maximum (minimum) of the first $n-2$ elements (known by induction). It is easy to see that finding the new maximum and minimum requires only three comparisons. We first compare x_{n-1} to x_n, then compare the larger of these two values to *MAX*, then compare the smaller of them to *min*. So, overall, we have an algorithm with approximately $3n/2$ comparisons instead of $2n$ comparisons! Can we do better by adding three (or four) elements at a time? Following the same approach leads to the same number of comparisons. It turns out that we cannot reduce the number of comparisons for this problem by any method. It is interesting to note that a divide-and-conquer approach also leads to about $3n/2$ comparisons (Exercise 6.14).

6.5.2 Finding the *k*th-Smallest Element

We now consider the general problem.

> **The Problem**   Given a sequence $S = x_1, x_2, ..., x_n$ of elements, and an integer k such that $1 \leq k \leq n$, find the kth-smallest element in S.

This problem is called **order statistics** or **selection**. If k is very close to 1 or very close to n, then we can find the kth-smallest element by running the algorithm for finding the minimum (maximum) element k times. This approach requires approximately kn comparisons. Sorting would be better than this naive algorithm, unless k is $O(\log n)$ or $n - O(\log n)$. There is, however, another algorithm that finds efficiently the kth smallest element for any value of k.

The idea is to use divide and conquer in the same way as it is done in quicksort, except that only one subproblem has to be solved. In quicksort, the sequence is partitioned by a pivot into two subsequences. The two subsequences are then sorted recursively. Here, we need only to determine which subsequence contains the kth smallest element, and then to continue the algorithm recursively *only for this subsequence*. The rest of the elements can be ignored. The algorithm is given in Fig. 6.16.

Complexity   As in quicksort, choosing poor pivots leads to a quadratic algorithm. Since only one subproblem has to be solved in each recursive call, the running time of this algorithm is lower than that of quicksort. The average number of comparisons is

Algorithm Selection (X, n, k) ;
Input: X (an array in the range 1 to n), and k (an integer).
Output: S (the kth smallest element; the array X is changed).

begin
    if (k < 1) or (k > n) **then** print "error"
    else
        S := Select(1, n, k)
end

procedure Select *(Left, Right, k) ;*
begin
    if Left = Right **then**
        Select := Left
    else
        Partition (X, Left, Right) ; { see Fig. 6.9 }
        Let Middle be the output of Partition ;
        if $Middle - Left + 1 \geq k$ **then**
            Select (Left, Middle, k)
        else
            Select (Middle + 1, Right, k − (Middle − Left + 1))
end

Figure 6.16 Algorithm *Selection*.

$O(n)$, but we will not prove that here. It is also possible to find the kth smallest in $O(n)$ steps in the worst case. However, in practice, the algorithm presented in Fig. 6.16 is more efficient.

Comments   Most applications of order statistics require finding the *median*, that is, the $n/2$-smallest element. Algorithm *Selection* is an excellent median-finding algorithm. There is no simpler algorithm for finding only medians. In other words, extending the median-finding problem to finding any kth-smallest element makes the algorithm simpler! This is another example of strengthening the induction hypothesis since the recursion requires arbitrary values of k.

6.6 Data Compression

Data compression is an important technique for saving storage. Given a file, which we consider as a string of characters, we want to find a compressed file, as small as possible, such that the original file can be reconstructed from the information in the compressed file. Data compression is useful, for example. when access to the file is infrequent, so the work involved in compressing and uncompressing is justified by the storage savings. It is also important in communication problems where the cost of sending information is greater than the cost of processing it. Data compression has many more applications, and it is a very developed field. In this section, we describe only one algorithm for one particular aspect of data compression.

For simplicity the file is assumed to be a sequence of English letters. Each of the 26 characters is represented by a unique string of bits, called the **encoding** of the character. If the length of all encodings is the same (as is the case for most standard encodings), the number of bits representing the file depends only on the number of characters in that file. On the other hand, it is possible to choose smaller bit representations for characters (such as A) that appear more often and larger representations for characters (such as Z) that appear rarely. For example, in ASCII (American Standard Code for Information Interchange), all characters are represented by bit strings of size 7. A is represented by the bit string 1000001, B by 1000010, and so on. (There is room for 128 characters, including lower-case and special characters.) The word ''AND'' (and any other word with three letters) requires 21 bits. If we change the representation of A to, say 1001, we save 3 bits every time A appears. However, not every set of encodings is valid. There may be ambiguities. For example, we cannot choose 1001 as an encoding for A and leave the encoding of M as 1001101, because when we read 1001 we cannot determine whether it is A or is part of M. We could use special delimiters to separate characters, but that would only add to the representation. In general, the prefixes of an encoding of one character must not be equal to a complete encoding of another character. We call this constraint the **prefix constraint**. Whenever we shorten the encoding of one character, we may have to lengthen the encodings of others. The problem is to find the best balance, assuming we know the frequency of appearances of the different characters.

The Problem   Given a text (a sequence of characters), find an encoding for the characters that satisfies the prefix constraint and that minimizes the total number of bits needed to encode the text.

First, we have to compute the number of times each character appears in the text; we call this value the **frequency** of the character. (In many cases, we can use standard frequency tables computed for typical texts, instead of computing the exact frequency table for the particular text.) Denote the characters by $C_1, C_2, ..., C_n$, and denote their frequencies by $f_1, f_2, ..., f_n$. Given an encoding E in which a bit string S_i of length s_i represents C_i, the **length** of the file F compressed by using encoding E is

$$L(E, F) = \sum_{i=1}^{n} s_i \cdot f_i.$$

Our goal is to find an encoding E that satisfies the prefix constraint and minimizes $L(E, F)$.

   The prefix constraint is needed to make the decoding unambiguous, so let's look at a decoding procedure. We need to scan the sequence of bits one by one until we get a sequence that is equal to an encoding of one of the characters. Consider a binary tree in which each node has either two emanating edges labeled by 1 and 0, or no emanating edges. The leaves in this tree correspond to the characters. The sequence of 0s and 1s on the path from the root to a leaf corresponds to the character's encoding (see Fig. 6.17). The prefix constraint says that all characters must correspond to leaves. When the encoded file is scanned and a leaf is reached, we can safely determine the corresponding character. Our problem is to construct such a tree that minimizes $L(E, F)$. The tree representation is not necessary in order to solve the problem. It is useful, however, to have a graphic illustration of the problem (and its constraints).

   The algorithm is based on a reduction of a problem with n characters to a problem with $n-1$ characters (the base case is trivial). As usual, the main difficulty is how to define the induction hypothesis and in which order to eliminate characters. The reduction here is different from the ones we have seen so far. Instead of simply eliminating one character from consideration, we introduce a new "artificially made" character in place of two existing characters. This technique is a little more complicated, but it serves the same purpose — the size of the input is reduced. Let C_i and C_j be two characters with minimal frequency (if there are more than two such characters, then ties are broken arbitrarily). We claim that there exists a tree that minimizes $L(E, F)$ in which these characters correspond to leaves with the maximal distance from the root. Otherwise, if there is a character with higher frequency lower in the tree, it can be exchanged with C_i or C_j decreasing $L(E, F)$. (If its frequency is equal, it can still be exchanged without changing $L(E, F)$.) Since each node in the tree has either two children or no children (or else we can shorten the tree), we can assume that C_i and C_j are together. We now replace C_i and C_j with a new character, called C_{ij}, whose frequency is the sum $f_i + f_j$.

   The problem now has $n-1$ characters ($n-2$ old and one new), and as such can be solved by the induction hypothesis. We obtain the solution of the original problem by substituting an internal node in the reduced problem with two leaves corresponding to C_i and C_j in place of the leaf corresponding to C_{ij}. We leave the proof of optimality as an exercise.

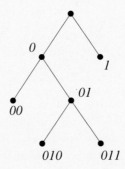

Figure 6.17 The tree representation of encoding.

Implementation   The operations required for Huffman's encoding are (1) insertions into a data structure, (2) deletions of the two characters with minimal frequency from the data structure, and (3) building the tree. A heap is a good data structure for the first two operations, each of which requires $O(\log n)$ steps in the worst case. The algorithm is given in Fig. 6.18. This compression technique is known as **Huffman's encoding** after D. Huffman [1952], who proposed this algorithm.

Algorithm Huffman_Encoding (S, f) ;
Input: S (a string of characters), and f (an array of frequencies).
Output: T (the Huffman tree for S).

begin
    insert all characters into a heap H according to their frequencies ;
    while H is not empty **do**
        if H contains only one character X **then**
            make X the root of T
        else
            pick two characters X and Y with lowest frequencies
                and delete them from H ;
            replace X and Y with a new character Z whose frequency is
                the sum of the frequencies of X and Y ;
            insert Z to H ;
            make X and Y children of Z in T { Z has no parent yet }
end

Figure 6.18   Algorithm *Huffman_Encoding*.

□ Example 6.1

Suppose that the data contains six characters A, B, C, D, E, and F, with frequencies 5, 2, 3, 4, 10, and 1, respectively The Huffman tree corresponding to these characters is given in Fig. 6.19. The internal nodes are numbered according to the time they were created. □

Complexity   Building the tree takes constant time per node. Insertions and deletions take $O(\log n)$ steps each. Overall, the running time of the algorithm is $O(n \log n)$.

6.7 String Matching

Let $A = a_1 a_2 \cdots a_n$ and $B = b_1 b_2 \cdots b_m$, $m \leq n$, be two strings of characters. We assume that the characters come from a finite set. (It is convenient to think of English characters, although it is not necessary.) A **substring** of a string A is a consecutive sequence of characters $a_i a_{i+1} \cdots a_j$ from A We denote by $A(i)$ $(B(i))$ the special substring $a_1 a_2 \cdots a_i$ $(b_1 b_2 \cdots b_i)$.

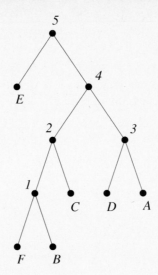

Figure 6.19 The Huffman tree for example 6.1.

The Problem   Given two strings A and B, find the first occurrence
(if any) of B in A. In other words, find the smallest k such that, for all i,
$1 \le i \le m$, we have $a_{k+i} = b_i$.

The most obvious example of this problem is a search for a certain word or pattern in a
text file.[1] Any text editor must contain commands to find patterns. The problem also has
applications to other areas — including molecular biology, where it is useful to find
certain patterns inside large RNA or DNA molecules.

   This problem seems simple at first. We can try to match B inside A by starting at
the first character of A that matches b_1 and continuing (comparing to b_2 and so on) until
we either complete the match or find a mismatch. In the latter case, however, we must go
back to the place from which we started and start again. This process is illustrated in Fig.
6.20 by an example that we will use throughout this section. In this example,
$A = xyxxyxyxyyxyxyxyyxyxyxx$, and $B = xyxyyxyxyxx$. The first mismatch occurs at a_4
since $b_4 \ne a_4$. We now must start comparing b_1 to a_2, which leads to a mismatch right
away. Next, we start at a_3, which is a match, but $a_4 \ne b_2$. The next attempt is more
promising: We have a match from a_4 to a_7, only to have a mismatch at a_8. Now, we
need to backtrack several steps and to compare b_1 to a_5 (mismatch), then b_1 to a_6, and
so on. Eventually, we find a match starting at a_{13}. We may have to backtrack and
compare again a substantial number of times, leading to $O(mn)$ number of comparisons

---

[1]At least, that is the most obvious one to me, as I am currently editing a text file.

$$A = xyxxyxyxyyxyxyxyyxyxyxx. \quad B = xyxyyxyxyxx.$$

```
          1  2  3  4  5  6  7  8  9  10 11 12 13 14 15 16 17 18 19 20 21 22 23
          x  y  x  x  y  x  y  x  y  y  y  x  y  x  y  x  y  y  y  x  y  x  y  x  x

   1:     x  y  x  y  ·  ·  ·
   2:        x  ·  ·  ·
   3:           x  y  ·  ·  ·
   4:              x  y  x  y  y  ·  ·  ·
   5:                 x  ·  ·  ·
   6:                    x  y  x  y  y  x  y  x  y  x  x
   7:                       x  ·  ·  ·
   8:                          x  y  x  ·  ·  ·
   9:                             x  ·  ·  ·
  10:                                x  ·  ·  ·
  11:                                   x  y  x  y  y  ·  ·  ·
  12:                                      x  ·  ·  ·
  13:                                         x  y  x  y  y  x  y  x  y  x  x
```

Figure 6.20 An example of a straightforward string matching.

in the worst case. Notice that a lot of the work is redundant. For example, we find twice that the subpattern $xyxy$ fits inside A starting at a_{11} (lines 6 and 11). In the example of finding a word in a text file, the number of backtracking steps will be very small, since most of the time the mismatch will occur early on. This simple algorithm is fairly good for such applications. In other cases, where the alphabet is small and the patterns have many repetitions, the number of backtracking steps may be large. The algorithm above may compare the same subpattern to the same place in the text many times. We would like to find an algorithm that avoids such worst cases. The problem is to arrange the information we learn throughout the algorithm such that it can be used efficiently later on when the same matches occur in other places.

To improve the straightforward algorithm we must first understand the reasons for its inefficiency. The bad case we discussed was caused by the need to backtrack. A particular bad case will occur if the pattern is $yyyyx$ and the text is $yyyyyyyyyyyx$. We will compare the five ys in the pattern to the text, find the mismatch with the x, move one step to the right, and make four redundant comparisons again and again. (This simple case is easy to handle, but it illustrates the general problem.) On the other hand, consider the pattern $xyyyyy$. To match this pattern in the text, we look for occurrences of x followed by five ys. If the number of ys is not sufficient, there is no need to backtrack. We will need to find the next x, and all the matched ys will not help. The straightforward algorithm, adapted to the pattern $xyyyyy$, runs in linear time since no backtracking is needed.

Let's return now to the original pattern $B = xyxyyxyxyxx$. Suppose that a mismatch occurs when the fifth character of B is scanned (as it is when a_8 is compared to it in line 4 of Fig. 6.20). The preceding two characters in A must have been xy (since they matched). But, xy are also the first characters of B. We now want to "slide" B to the right and compare the current character in A to some character in the middle of B (taking into account the previous matches). We would like to slide B as far to the right as possible (to save comparisons) without bypassing potential matches. In this case, we can slide B two steps to the right. We continue the match by comparing the same character in A that caused the mismatch (a_8 in the example) to b_3, since we already know that b_1 and b_2 matched. (In fact, that is exactly what we did later on, in line 6 of Fig. 6.20, except that it took us three more redundant comparisons — x in line 5, and xy at the beginning of line 6 — to get there.) Notice that this whole discussion is completely independent of A! We know the last few characters in A since they have matched B so far.

In the following discussion, we will not assume that there are only two characters in the text (and pattern), even though, for simplicity, the examples will contain only two characters. It is possible (and that is the subject of Exercise 6.45) to make the algorithm even more efficient in this case.

Let's look at another example by continuing the match. The mismatch at line 6 of Fig. 6.20 is at the last character of B, b_{11}. We can now do a lot more sliding. Consider the subpattern $B(10) = b_1 b_2 \cdots b_{10}$. We know that $B(10)$ is exactly the same as the preceding 10 characters in A; that is, $B(10) = A[6..15]$, because they matched. We want to determine exactly how many steps B can be shifted to the right until there is some hope of another match. We determine this number by looking for a maximum *suffix* of $B(10)$ that is equal to a *prefix* of B. In this case, that suffix is of length 3 (xyx), as is illustrated in Fig. 6.21. In the figure, $B(10)$ is shifted, one step at a time, and is compared to itself, until a prefix matches a suffix. (The last character, b_{11}, is ignored since it is the cause of the mismatch.) Since we know that $B[1..3] = B[8..10]$, we can continue by comparing a_{16} to b_4, and so on, until the complete match occurs. We save all the comparisons on lines 7 to 12 and half those on line 13. The only difference between Fig. 6.21 and Fig. 6.20 is that the information in Fig. 6.21 depends only on B. This is important because we can preprocess B once, and find all the relevant information about it regardless of the text A. We now can take advantage of all the matches done in line 6 of Fig. 6.20; none of them will be repeated.

```
B =   x   y   x   y   y   x   y   x   y   x   x
      x   .   .   .
          x   y   x   .   .       .
              x   .   .       .
                  x   .   .       .
                      x   y   x   y   y
                          x   .   .       .
                              x   y   x
```

Figure 6.21 Matching the pattern against itself.

The preprocessing of B is the essence of the improved algorithm. We will study all the repeating patterns of B and devise a way to handle mismatches when they occur without backtracking. Our scheme is the following. The string A is always scanned forward; there is no backtracking in A, although the same character of A may be compared to several characters of B (when there are mismatches). When a mismatch is encountered, we consult a table to find how far in B we must backtrack. There is an entry in the table for each character in B corresponding to the amount of backtracking (or the number of shifts) required when there is a mismatch involving this character. In a moment, we will show how to construct this table efficiently. We first define the table precisely and show how we use it for the string-matching problem.

The idea behind the table should be clear now. For each b_i we want to find the largest suffix of $B(i-1)$ that is equal to a prefix of $B(i-1)$. If the length of this suffix is j, then the mismatched character in A can be matched against b_{j+1} directly, without going through all the other redundant matches. We already know that the most recent j characters in A match the beginning of B. Furthermore, since this suffix is the *largest* among those that are equal to a prefix, we know that B cannot fit into A any farther to the left. The table is called *next*, and here is a precise definition of the values of its entries:

$next(i)$ = the maximum j $(0 < j < i-1)$ such that $b_{i-j} b_{i-j+1} \cdots b_{i-1} = B(j)$, and 0 if no such j exists.

For convenience we define $next(1) = -1$ to distinguish this case. It is clear that $next(2)$ is always equal to 0 (since there is no j satisfying $0 < j < 2-1$). The values of the *next* table for the pattern B in Fig. 6.21 are given in Fig. 6.22. These values can be computed in a brute force way, as was done in Fig. 6.22. However, there is an elegant way to compute all these values in time $O(m)$. Let's first assume that the values of *next* are given to us, and see how to perform the matching. Afterwards, we will describe how to compute *next*.

The matching proceeds as follows. The characters in A are compared to those in B until there is a mismatch. At that point, say at b_i, the *next* table is consulted and the same character in A is compared against $b_{next(i)+1}$ (since the first $next(i)$ characters already match). If this is a mismatch too, then the next comparison is against $b_{next(next(i)+1)+1}$, and so on. The only exception to this rule is when the mismatch is against b_1; in this case,

$i =$	1	2	3	4	5	6	7	8	9	10	11
$B =$	x	y	x	y	y	x	y	x	y	x	x
$next =$	-1	0	0	1	2	0	1	2	3	4	3

Figure 6.22 The values of *next*.

we want to proceed in A. This case can be determined by the special value of $next(1)$, which is -1. The program for string matching is given in Fig. 6.23.

Algorithm String_Match (A, n, B, m) ;
Input: A (a string of size n), and B (a string of size m).
  { We assume that $next$ has been computed; see Fig. 6.25 }
Output: $Start$ (the first index such that B is a substring of A starting
  at $A[Start]$).

begin
  $j := 1$; $i := 1$;
  $Start := 0$;
  while $Start = 0$ and $i \leq n$ **do**
      if $B[j] = A[i]$ **then**
          $j := j + 1$;
          $i := i + 1$
      else
          $j := next[j] + 1$;
          if $j = 0$ **then**
              $j := 1$;
              $i := i + 1$;
      if $j = m + 1$ **then** $Start := i - m$
end

Figure 6.23 Algorithm *String_Match*.

It remains to find an algorithm to compute the values of the *next* table. We use induction. As we mentioned, $next(2)=0$, which takes care of the base case. We assume that the values of *next* for $1, 2, ..., i-1$ have been computed, and we consider $next(i)$. At best, $next(i)$ can be $next(i-1)+1$, which will happen if $b_{i-1} = b_{next(i-1)+1}$. In other words, the largest suffix that is equal to a prefix is extended by b_{i-1}. This is the easy case. The difficult case is when $b_{i-1} \neq b_{next(i-1)+1}$. We need to find a new suffix that is equal to a prefix. However, we already know how to fit the largest suffix of $B(i-2)$: It fits in $b_1 b_2 \cdots b_{next(i-1)}$ (see Fig. 6.24). But having $b_{i-1} \neq b_{next(i-1)+1}$ is exactly the same as having a regular mismatch at $b_{next(i-1)+1}$! And we already know what to do about that. If there is a mismatch at index j, we go to $next(j)$. So, we have a mismatch at index $next(i-1)+1$, and we go to $next(next(i-1)+1)$. That is, we try to match b_{i-1} to $b_{next(next(i-1)+1)+1}$. If they match, we set $next(i) = next(next(i-1)+1)+1$. Otherwise, we continue in the same fashion until we either get a match or we return to the beginning.

□ **Example 6.2**

Let $B = xyxyyxyxyxx$ (the same as in Fig. 6.21), and consider $next(11)$. We first look at $next(10)$, which is 4, and compare b_{10} to b_5. If they had been the same, then the largest

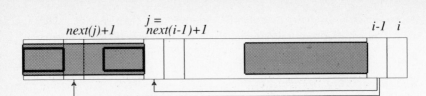

Figure 6.24 Computing next(i).

prefix that is equal to a suffix would have been 5, but they are not. So, we have a mismatch at b_5, and we look at *next* (5) which is 2. We now compare b_{10} to b_3, and they happen to be the same. Hence, *next* (11)=3, which can easily be verified by hand.   □

The algorithm for computing the *next* table is difficult to understand, but it is not difficult to implement. The program is given in Fig. 6.25.

Algorithm Compute_Next (B, m) ;
Input: B (a string of size m).
Output: *next* (an array of size m).

begin
 $next(1) := -1$;
 $next(2) := 0$;
 for $i := 3$ **to** m **do**
  $j := next(i-1) + 1$;
  while $b_{i-1} \neq b_j$ and $j > 0$ **do**
   $j := next(j) + 1$;
  $next(i) := j$
end

Figure 6.25 Algorithm *Compute_Next*.

Complexity   A character of A may be compared against many characters of B. If there is a mismatch, then the same character of A is compared against the character of B pointed to by the *next* table. If there is another mismatch, then we continue comparing against the same character of A until there is either a match or we reach the beginning of B. Nevertheless, we claim that the running time of this algorithm is still $O(n)$. How many times can we backtrack for one character from A, say a_i? Let's assume that the first mismatch involved b_k. Since each backtrack leads us to a smaller index in B, we can backtrack only k times. However, to reach b_k we must have gone *forward* k times without any backtracking! If we assign the costs of backtracking to the forward moves, then we at most double the cost of the forward moves. But there are exactly n forward moves, so the number of comparisons is $O(n)$.

This algorithm was developed by Knuth, Morris, and Pratt [1977], and it is known as the **KMP algorithm**. Another fast algorithm for this problem was developed by Boyer and Moore [1977]. We sketch it briefly. The difference between the algorithms is that the Boyer–Moore algorithm scans B from the end rather than from the beginning. That is, the first comparison will be of b_m against a_m. If there is a match, then the next comparison will be of b_{m-1} against a_{m-1}, and so on. If there is a mismatch, we use the information, much as we did in the previous algorithm, to shift the whole pattern to the right. For example, if $a_m = $ ''Z,'' and Z does not appear at all in B, then the whole pattern can be shifted to the right by m steps, and the next comparison will be of a_{2m} against b_m. If Z does appear in B, say at b_i, then we can shift by $m-i$ steps. The decision how much to shift becomes more complicated when there are several partial matches. On the one hand, we want to utilize the matches already found. On the other hand, it is more efficient to shift the whole pattern as far as possible, even if the same comparisons may have to be performed twice. We omit the details. The interesting characteristic of this algorithm is that it is likely to make fewer than n comparisons (in regular text)! This is because one bad mismatch allows us to shift, without any more comparisons, by m.

6.8 Sequence Comparisons

The subject of sequence comparisons has received a lot of attention lately. The main reason for that attention is the applications to problems in molecular biology. We concentrate here on only one problem — finding the minimum number of edit steps required to change one string into another. The main technique used throughout this section is **dynamic programming** (discussed in Section 5.10).

Let $A = a_1 a_2 \cdots a_n$ and $B = b_1 b_2 \cdots b_m$ be two strings of characters. We assume that the characters come from a finite set (English characters, for example). We would like to change A character by character such that it becomes equal to B. We allow three types of changes (or **edit steps**), and we assign a cost of 1 to each: (1) *insert* — insert a character into the string, (2) *delete* — delete a character from the string, and (3) *replace* — replace one character with a different character. For example, to change the string *abbc* into the string *babb*, we can delete the first *a*, forming the string *bbc*, then insert an *a* between the two *b*s (*babc*), and then replace the last *c* with a *b* for a total of three changes. However, we can also insert a new *b* at the beginning (forming *babbc*), and then delete the last *c*, for a total of two changes. Our goal is to minimize the number of single-character changes.

The string-edit problem has also applications to file comparisons and revisions maintenance. We may have a text file (or a program) and another file that is a modification of the first one. It is convenient to extract the differences between the two files. There may be several versions of the same program, and, if the versions are similar and they need to be archived, it is more efficient to store only the differences instead of storing the whole programs. In such cases, we may allow only insertions and deletions. In other cases, we may assign different costs to each of the edit steps.

There are quite a few possible changes, and it seems difficult to find the best one. As usual, we try induction. We denote by $A(i)$ ($B(i)$) the prefix substrings $a_1 a_2 \cdots a_i$ ($b_1 b_2 \cdots b_i$). Our problem is to change $A(n)$ to $B(m)$ with a minimum number of edit steps. Suppose that we know the best way to change $A(n-1)$ to $B(m)$ by induction. (There may be several different best solutions; we assume only that we know one of them.) With one more deletion, that of a_n, we have a way to change $A(n)$ to $B(m)$. But this may not be the best way of doing it. It could be that it is better to replace a_n with b_m, or better yet, a_n may even be equal to b_m.

We need to consider all the different possibilities of constructing the minimum change from A to B with the aid of the best changes of smaller sequences involving A and B. Denote by $C(i, j)$ the minimum cost of changing $A(i)$ to $B(j)$. Let's assume for now that we are interested only in finding the cost of changing A to B and not in the change itself. We are interested in finding a relation between $C(n, m)$ and $C(i, j)$s for some combination of smaller is and js. It is not hard to see that there are four possibilities, corresponding to the three different edit steps and to doing nothing:

delete: if a_n is deleted in the minimum change from A to B, then the scenario above holds. The best change would be the one from $A(n-1)$ to $B(m)$ and then one more deletion. In other words, $C(n, m) = C(n-1, m) + 1$.

insert: if the minimum change from A to B involves insertion of a character to match b_m, then we have $C(n, m) = C(n, m-1) + 1$. That is, we find (by induction) the minimum change from $A(n)$ to $B(m-1)$ and insert a character equal to b_m.

replace: if a_n is replacing b_m, then we first need to find the minimum change from $A(n-1)$ to $B(m-1)$ and then to add 1 if $a_n \neq b_m$.

match: if a_n is equal to b_m, then $C(n, m) = C(n-1, m-1)$.

Denote

$$c(i, j) = \begin{cases} 0 & \text{if } a_i = b_j \\ 1 & \text{if } a_i \neq b_j. \end{cases}$$

We can now combine these four cases into the following recurrence relation.

$$C(n, m) = \min \begin{cases} C(n-1, m) + 1 & (\text{deleting } a_n) \\ C(n, m-1) + 1 & (\text{inserting for } b_m) \\ C(n-1, m-1) + c(n, m) & (\text{replacing V matching } a_n), \end{cases}$$

with $C(i, 0) = i$ for all i, $0 \leq i \leq n$, and $C(0, j) = j$ for all j, $0 \leq j \leq m$.

It is not difficult to prove that these possibilities are the only ones. Consider a_n. It must be handled somehow. It is either deleted, which is handled by the first case, or it is mapped into some character in B. In the latter case, either a_n is mapped into b_m, which is handled by the third or fourth case, or it is mapped into a character appearing before b_m, in which case something must be inserted after a_n.

The problem with this approach is that we used induction too many times! We reduced a problem of size (n, m) to three problems of only slightly smaller sizes. If we use recursion separately for each smaller problem, we triple the work every time we reduce the size by a constant. That leads to an exponential algorithm. Fortunately, in this case there is no need to solve each subproblem separately. The key to this observation is that there are not too many different subproblems altogether. Each possible subproblem involves computing $C(i, j)$ for some i and j in the ranges $0 \leq i \leq n$, and $0 \leq j \leq m$. There are nm combinations of such is and js, so there should not be a need for more than nm subproblems. This is the same phenomenon we observed in the knapsack problem (Section 5.11). To overcome it, we use **strong induction**. Instead of just extending a problem of size $n - 1$ to a problem of size n, we extend all subproblems of size $< n$ to the problem of size n. This is a two-dimensional problem, so we have to extend all subproblems of sizes $< (n, m)$ to the problem of size (n, m). The notation $< (n, m)$ means "any combination of (i, j) such that at least one of these values is less than the corresponding bound and the other one is no greater than its bound."

We will be able to use strong induction if the solutions of all the subproblems are available to us. We create a table with the results of all subproblems. Consider Fig. 6.26. To compute the value of $C(i, j)$, we need the three other values indicated by shading in the figure. We want to scan the matrix so that, whenever we arrive at an entry, we have already visited the three other entries necessary for its computation. In this case, a row-order traversal (i.e., row by row from left to right) is sufficient. This two-dimensional version of the approach is an example of **dynamic programming**.

Implementation   We maintain a matrix $C[1..n, 1..m]$. Each entry $C[i, j]$ of the matrix holds the value of $C(i, j)$. Let $M[i, j]$ denote the last move (change) that leads to the minimum value of $C[i, j]$. The reason we need only the last change is that we can backtrack and find all the changes from the matrix. This move is any one of $delete(i)$,

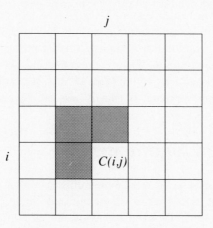

Figure 6.26 The dependencies of $C(i, j)$.

insert(j), or *replace*(i, j). To compute $C[i, j]$, we need to know the values of $C[i-1, j]$, $C[i, j-1]$, and $C[i-1, j-1]$. The last change can be determined according to which of the possibilities leads to the minimum value for $C[i, j]$. The algorithm is given in Fig. 6.27.

Algorithm *Minimum_Edit_Distance* (A, n, B, m) ;
Input: A (a string of size n), and B (a string of size m).
Output: C (the cost matrix).

Begin
    for $i := 0$ **to** n **do** $C[i, 0] := i$;
    for $j := 1$ **to** m **do** $C[0, j] := j$;
    for $i := 1$ **to** n **do**
        for $j := 1$ **to** m **do**
            $x := C[i-1, j] + 1$;
            $y := C[i, j-1] + 1$;
            if $a_i = b_j$ **then**
                $z := C[i-1, j-1]$
            else
                $z := C[i-1, j-1] + 1$;
            $C[i, j] := \min (x, y, z)$
            { $M[i, j]$ can be set appropriately }
  end

Figure 6.27 Algorithm *Minimum_Edit_Distance*.

Complexity It is clear from the program in Fig. 6.27 that the running time is $O(nm)$. One major drawback is the need for an $O(nm)$ space as well.

Comments Dynamic programming is useful in cases where the solution of a problem depends on many solutions of slightly smaller problems. The use of a table to store previous results is common in dynamic programming. The table is usually scanned in some order (usually row order), which leads to at least quadratic running times. Thus the dynamic programming approach is usually less efficient than, say, the divide-and-conquer approach.

6.9 Probabilistic Algorithms

The algorithms we discussed so far were **deterministic** — every step was predetermined. If we use a deterministic algorithm twice for the same input, we will get two identical execution patterns and results. Probabilistic algorithms are different. They include steps that depend not only on the input but also on results of some **random events**. There are many variations of probabilistic algorithms. We will discuss two of them. We start with a simple example and continue with a more formal treatment.

Suppose that we have a set of numbers $x_1, x_2, ..., x_n$, and we want to select one of them that belongs to the "upper half" (i.e., it is greater than or equal to the median). For example, we may want to select a "good" student according to her or his grades. One option is to select the maximum (which is, of course, always in the upper half). We have already seen that finding the maximum requires $n - 1$ comparisons. Another possibility is to start the maximum-finding algorithm and to stop just after the halfway point is reached. A number that is greater than one-half of the numbers is definitely in the upper half. This algorithm requires about $n/2$ comparisons. Can we do better? It is not difficult to prove that it is impossible to guarantee that a number belongs to the upper half by making less than $n/2$ comparisons. So, it may seem that we found an optimal algorithm.

This algorithm, however, is an optimal algorithm only if we insist on a *guarantee*. In many cases, a guarantee is not required; a good likelihood that the solution is correct is enough. For example, in hashing we could not guarantee that no collisions would occur, but we were able to handle them if they did. (Hashing can also be considered a probabilistic algorithm, as will become apparent shortly.) If we do not insist on a guarantee, then a better algorithm exists for finding an element in the upper half. Let's take two random numbers from the set, x_i and x_j, such that $i \neq j$. Assume that $x_i \geq x_j$. The probability that a random number from the set belongs to the upper half is at least 1/2 (it will be more than 1/2 if many numbers are equal to the median). So, the probability that both x_i and x_j do not belong to the upper half is at most 1/4. But, since $x_i \geq x_j$, this probability is the same as the probability that x_i does not belong to the upper half. Thus, the probability that x_i belongs to the upper half is at least 3/4.

Being correct with a probability of 3/4 is usually not good enough. However, the same principle can be easily extended. We can select k numbers at random and pick the maximal among them. By the same argument, the probability that the maximal of the k elements belongs to the upper half is at least $1 - 2^{-k}$. For example, if $k = 10$, we have a success probability of 0.999. If $k = 20$, we have a success probability of 0.999999. If $k = 100$, the probability of error is, for all practical purposes, negligible. The probability of a programming error, of a hardware error, or of an earthquake for that matter, exceeds that. We now have an algorithm that selects a number in the upper half, with overwhelming probability, using at most 100 comparisons regardless of the size of the input. (We assume that choosing an element at random can be done in one operation; we discuss random-number generation in Section 6.9.1.)

This type of algorithm is sometimes called a **Monte Carlo** algorithm. It may give a wrong result with very small probability, but its running time may be better than that of the best deterministic algorithm. Another type of a probabilistic algorithm is one that never gives a wrong result, but its running time is not guaranteed. It may terminate quickly or it may run for an arbitrarily long time. This type of algorithm, which is sometimes called a **Las Vegas** algorithm, is useful if its *expected* running time is low. In Section 6.9.2, we show a Las Vegas algorithm that solves a certain coloring problem. In Section 6.9.3, we describe an elegant technique for transforming some Las Vegas algorithms into deterministic algorithms. We apply the technique to obtain an efficient deterministic algorithm for the coloring problem of Section 6.9.2. This technique, however, cannot transform every efficient Las Vegas algorithm into an efficient deterministic algorithm.

The idea of probabilistic algorithms has direct analogies to mathematical proof techniques. Using probability to prove combinatorial properties is a powerful technique. In a nutshell, the idea is to prove that, among a set of objects, the probability that an object has certain properties is greater than 0, which is an indirect proof that there exists an object with these properties. This method translates to algorithms in the following way. Suppose that we are searching for an object with certain properties, and we know that if we generate a random object it will satisfy the desired properties with nonzero probability (this is a probabilistic proof that the desired object exists). We try to follow the probabilistic proof by generating random events when appropriate, then finding the object with some positive probability. We can repeat this process many times until we succeed. If the probabilities work in our favor, we end up with an effective Las Vegas algorithm.

6.9.1 Random Numbers

Probabilistic algorithms require that we select numbers at random. We must find efficient methods for doing that. However, any deterministic procedure will generate numbers according to some fixed scheme, depending on the steps of the procedure. If the scheme is completely deterministic, then the numbers generated cannot be *random* in the true sense of the word. They will relate to one another in a specific way. Fortunately, this is not a major practical problem. In practice, it is sufficient to use **pseudorandom numbers**. These numbers are generated by a deterministic procedure — and thus are not truly random — but the procedure makes any relationship among the numbers unnoticable by most applications.

It is beyond the scope of this book to discuss this issue in depth. We restrict the discussion to one very effective method, called the **linear congruential method**, for generating pseudorandom numbers. The first step is to choose an integer **seed** $r(1)$, which is a number selected at random by some external means (e.g., the current time in microseconds, the current record of one's favorite team). The rest of the numbers are computed according to the following rule:

$$r(i) = (r(i-1) \cdot b + 1) \bmod t,$$

where b and t are constants. The selection of b and t must be done carefully. Knuth [1981] suggests the following guidelines: t should be quite large, in the millions at least, and can be a power of 2 (or 10) if that is convenient; b should be about one digit less than t, and its decimal representation should end with $x21$, with x even. These (strange) guidelines are designed to avoid hitting some bad cases that cause many repetitions of the same numbers. The numbers generated by the linear congruential method are in the range 0 to $t-1$. We can achieve a different range by multiplying the numbers by the appropriate factor (t should be chosen to be a multiple of that range).

6.9.2 A Coloring Problem

Let S be a set with n elements, let $S_1, S_2, ..., S_k$ be a collection of distinct subsets of S, each containing exactly r elements, such that $k \leq 2^{r-2}$.

The Problem   Color each element of S with one of two colors, red or blue, such that each subset S_i contains at least one red and at least one blue element.

A coloring that satisfies this condition is called a **valid coloring**. It turns out that, under the given conditions on the subsets, there is always a valid coloring. We present a simple probabilistic algorithm that is adapted from a probabilistic proof of existence of such a coloring. The algorithm is almost as simple as possible:

> *Take every element of S and color it either red or blue at random (with probability 1/2) independently of the coloring of the other elements.*

This algorithm obviously does not always lead to a valid coloring. Let's calculate the probability of failure. The probability that all elements of S_i are colored red is 2^{-r}. The probability that at least one of the k subsets is colored only red is no more than $k\,2^{-r} \leq 1/4$ (because of the bound on k). Hence, the probability that a random coloring is not valid is at most 1/2 (since there is also a probability of at most 1/4 of a subset entirely colored blue). This is a proof that a valid coloring always exists (otherwise the probability of failure must be exactly 1). It also implies that the random algorithm is very good. We can easily test the validity of a particular coloring. We simply check the elements of each subset until we find two of different colors. We have a 50–50 chance of success. If we fail, we simply try again. The expected number of times we need to run the algorithm to get a valid coloring is 2. The algorithm is clearly a Las Vegas algorithm, because we check each coloring and terminate only when we find a valid one. This is a simple application of probabilistic methods. Unfortunately, probabilistic algorithms are often not so simple. Next, we show that this algorithm can be modified such that it finds a valid coloring deterministically.

6.9.3 A Technique for Transforming Probabilistic Algorithms into Deterministic Algorithms[2]

We now show how to use induction to transform the probabilistic coloring algorithm into a deterministic algorithm. The technique we present does not work for every Las Vegas algorithm. We do not believe that it is possible to transform efficiently every Las Vegas algorithm into a deterministic algorithm. This technique is interesting, however, because

---

[2] This section can be skipped at first reading.

it employs the idea of strengthening the induction hypothesis in a powerful way. The resulting algorithm will not only be efficient and deterministic, but will also solve a more general problem, removing some of the restrictions imposed on the original problem.

Let S be again a set of n elements, and $S_1, S_2, ..., S_k$ be a collection of distinct subsets of S. The probabilistic algorithm was based on the fact that the probability that we get a valid coloring by coloring each element at random is at least 1/2. Suppose that we can color an element either blue or red such that the probability that we get a valid coloring of the rest of the elements by a random coloring is nonzero. We claim that this will lead to an algorithm by induction on n. If we can color one element such that probability of success remains nonzero, then we can color all elements by induction.

Since we are trying to handle one element at a time, we must strengthen the induction hypothesis such that we no longer require that all subsets be of the same size. The most important condition is that the probability of success remain nonzero. Let s_i denote the size of subset S_i. The probability that S_i is colored with only one color is 2^{-s_i+1}. The probability of *failure* (i.e., the probability that a random coloring of all elements is not a valid coloring) is no more than

$$F(n) = \sum_{i=1}^{k} 2^{-s_i+1}.$$

This probability $F(n)$ is a function of the sizes of the sets, but we write it as a function of n for convenience. We are on solid grounds as long as $F(n) < 1$. Let's try the following induction hypothesis.

> **Induction hypothesis:** *We know how to color a set S with $< n$ elements, provided that $F(n) < 1$.*

If one of the subsets has only one element, then this element contributes 1 to $F(n)$, so $F(n)$ cannot be less than 1. If $n = 2$, then, since the subsets are assumed to be distinct, there can be only one subset with the two elements, and we can color one element blue and one element red. Hence, the base case is established. We now try to reduce the coloring problem for n elements to one for $n-1$ elements.

Let x be an arbitrary element of S. There are two possible ways to color x — blue or red. Suppose that x is colored blue. What is the probability that a random coloring of the other $n-1$ elements is valid? A subset S_i that does not include x has the same probability of failure — namely 2^{-s_i+1}. A subset S_j that includes x has one fewer element, and it only needs to have at least one red-colored element (it already has a blue-colored element). Thus, the probability of failing to color subset S_j is $2^{-(s_j-1)}$. Notice that this probability is the same as it was before we colored x! Therefore, $F(n)$ remains less than 1, and we now have to color only $n-1$ elements. Does that mean that we now have an algorithm? No. It means only that the first choice can be made arbitrarily. After the first choice is made, the problem is different.

We can no longer use the same induction hypothesis, because, after we color the first element, some of the subsets need to be colored with two colors, and some of them need to be colored with only one color. We have to strengthen the induction hypothesis further to reflect this change. Suppose that some elements are already colored. A subset may be in one of four states: (1) the subset has red and blue elements, in which case we do not have to consider it any further; (2) the subset has at least one red element but no blue elements, in which case at least one of the uncolored elements must be colored blue; (3) the subset has at least one blue element but no red elements, in which case at least one of the uncolored elements must be colored red; and (4) the subset has no colored elements. We call a subset in state (2) a *red* subset, a subset in state (3) a *blue* subset, and a subset in state (4) a *neutral* subset. Let u_i be the number of uncolored elements of subset S_i. If S_i is in state (1), then it is already colored successfully. If S_i is red or blue, then the probability of failure in coloring it randomly is 2^{-u_i}. If S_i is neutral, then the probability of failure in coloring it randomly is 2^{-u_i+1}. Let f_i denote the probability of failure in coloring subset S_i randomly. We have to maintain the property that

$$F(n) = \sum_{i=1}^{k} f_i < 1. \tag{6.1}$$

The induction hypothesis must reflect the status of all subsets. We extend the problem to include arbitrary red, blue, and neutral subsets. In other words, the input is now a collection of subsets, each labeled red, blue, or neutral. We assume that condition (6.1) is satisfied.

The Problem   Color each element of S with one of two colors, red or blue, such that each red subset contains at least one blue element, each blue subset contains at least one red element, and each neutral subset contains at least one red element and at least one blue element.

The induction hypothesis is the straightforward hypothesis for this (nonstraightforward) extension of the problem.

   Induction hypothesis: *We know how to color a set S with < n elements to satisfy the conditions of the problem, provided that (6.1) is satisfied.*

The base case is similar to the previous base case. Given a set S with n elements such that (6.1) is satisfied, we need to color one element of S and to leave (6.1) satisfied.

   We again pick an arbitrary element $x \in S$. There are two possible ways to color x, each leading to different statuses of the subsets. If we color x red, then all red subsets containing x remain red (but with one less uncolored element), all blue subsets containing x become successfully colored (and can be removed), and all neutral subsets containing x become red subsets. Subsets that do not contain x are not changed. Coloring x blue leads to similar changes. We can now compute the value of $F(n-1)$, which we denote by $F_R(n-1)$, to indicate that we color x red. We also denote by $F_B(n-1)$ the corresponding value of $F(n-1)$ in the case when x is colored blue. The key to the algorithm is the following lemma.

□ Lemma 6.2

Let $F(n)$ be the probability of failure initially, let $F_R(n-1)$ be the probability of failure after coloring x red, and let $F_B(n-1)$ be the probability of failure after coloring x blue. Then, $F_R(n-1) + F_B(n-1) \leq 2F(n)$.

Proof: A subset that does not contain x remains unchanged. Its contribution to $F_R(n-1)$, $F_B(n-1)$, and $F(n)$ is the same, which is consistent with the claim. We consider now the subsets that contain x. There are three possibilities, according to the subset status. (1) A red subset contributes nothing to $F_B(n-1)$, because it is now successfully colored; its contribution to $F_R(n-1)$ is twice as much as that to $F(n)$, because it has one fewer element. Again, this is consistent with the claim. (2) The case of a blue subset is the same as that of a red subset. (3) A neutral subset with u_i elements contributes 2^{-u_i+1} to $F(n)$. This subset becomes either red or blue with one less element. Thus, it contributes $2^{-(u_i-1)}$ to both $F_R(n-1)$ and $F_B(n-1)$. In either case, its contribution to $F(n)$, $F_R(n-1)$, and $F_B(n-1)$ is the same, establishing the claim.   □

Lemma 6.2 leads directly to the algorithm. The base case of one element is simple, because, for (6.1) to be satisfied, there can be only one red or one blue subset containing the element. If there is only one subset, then we can color the element with the other color. If $F_R(n-1)+F_B(n-1)\leq 2F(n)$, then either $F_R(n-1)\leq F(n)$ or $F_B(n-1)\leq F(n)$ (or both). We can compute these values and color x blue if $F_B(n-1)$ is less than $F_R(n-1)$, and color x red otherwise. By Lemma 6.2, condition (6.1) in the induction hypothesis is satisfied, and the algorithm follows. We leave the implementation of this algorithm to the reader.

6.10 Finding a Majority

Let E be a sequence of integers $x_1, x_2, ..., x_n$. The **multiplicity** of x in E is the number of times x appears in E. A number z is a **majority** in E if its multiplicity is greater than $n/2$.

The Problem   Given a sequence of numbers, find the majority in the sequence or determine that none exists.

For example, an integer can represent a *vote* in an election, and the problem is to find whether someone won the election. If the number of candidates is small, then bucket sort can be used effectively to solve the problem in $O(n)$ time. However, if the number of possible candidates is very large (the sign of the times), then bucket sort cannot be used. We assume here that there is no limit on the number of possible candidates, and that they are represented as arbitrary integers. Voting is also performed in computer systems, for example, to achieve consistency of decisions.

This problem is an excellent example of a straightforward problem whose straightforward solutions are not as efficient as an elegant solution that requires some thinking but is more efficient and simpler to implement. We first discuss several straightforward approaches to the problem, and then present the elegant algorithm.

The most straightforward way to solve this problem is to use sorting. Once the votes are sorted, it is easy to count how many votes each candidate got. Sorting, however, requires $O(n \log n)$ comparisons in the worst case. We will see that it is possible to do better. We can also use a median-finding algorithm. If there is a majority, then it must be equal to the median (the median is the $(n/2)$th smallest element, and the majority appears more than $n/2$ times). Therefore, once the median is found, we can count the number of times it appears, and if the median is not a majority, then there is no majority. Since finding the median is easier than sorting, this is a better approach. Another approach is to use a probabilistic algorithm. We can pick a small random sample of the votes, take the majority of the sample, and count the number of times this sample majority appears in the whole list. However, although it is easy to verify that a given vote is a majority, it is impossible with this algorithm to prove that there is no majority. The outcome of such an algorithm may be "undecided." (This is the method used for public-opinion polls; some election predictions are indeed "too close to call.") It is also not easy to determine the appropriate size of the sample.

We now present a linear-time algorithm to find a majority that can handle any number of candidates. The algorithm is faster and simpler than the median-finding algorithm. As we did in the algorithm for finding a celebrity (Section 5.5), we first try to eliminate as many elements as we can from being candidates for majority. It turns out that we can eliminate all but one element. Finding this one candidate is helped by the following observation, which allows us to reduce the problem to a smaller one:

If $x_i \neq x_j$ and we eliminate both of these elements from the list, then the majority in the original list remains a majority in the new list.

(Notice that the opposite is not true: the list 1,2,5,5,3 has no majority, but if we remove 1 and 2, then 5 becomes a new majority.)

So, if we find two unequal votes, we eliminate both, find the majority in the smaller list, and check whether it is a majority in the original list. What if we do not find unequal votes? If we scan the votes and they are all equal, then we have to keep track of only one possible candidate; once we find a vote that is not equal to this one candidate, we can use the observation above. If all the remaining votes are equal, then we have to check only one candidate. This is the seed of the idea; we now show how to implement it.

The votes are scanned in the order they appear. We use two variables, C (candidate) and M (multiplicity). When we consider x_i, C is the only candidate for majority among $x_1, x_2, ..., x_{i-1}$, and M is the number of times C appeared so far *excluding* the times C was eliminated. In other words, the votes $x_1, x_2, ..., x_{i-1}$ can be divided into two groups of sizes $2k$ and M, such that $2k + M = i - 1$, the first group contains k pairs of unequal votes (which can be eliminated by the observation), and the second group contains C appearing M times. If there is a majority among $x_1, x_2, ..., x_{i-1}$, then it must "survive" this elimination scheme, and so it must be equal to C. (Notice again that the opposite is not true; C may survive the elimination without being the majority.) When we consider x_i we compare it to C, and either increment or decrement the multiplicity depending on whether or not x_i is equal to C. We also have to take care of the case of having no candidate (which will happen, for example, at x_3 if $x_2 \neq x_1$). This case occurs when M is equal to 0, and we simply set $C = x_i$ and $M = 1$. At the end, we have only one candidate C, and we can count the number of times C appears in the list and determine whether it is the majority or whether there is no majority. The algorithm is given in Fig. 6.28.

Algorithm Majority (X, n) ;
Input: X (an array of size n of positive numbers).
Output: *Majority* (the majority in X if it exists, or -1 otherwise).

begin
    $C := X[1]$;
    $M := 1$;
    { *first scan; eliminate all but one candidate C* }
    for $i := 2$ **to** n **do**
        if $M = 0$ **then**
            $C := X[i]$;
            $M := 1$
        else
            if $C = X[i]$ **then** $M := M + 1$
            else $M := M - 1$;
    { *second scan; check whether C is a majority* }
    if $M = 0$ **then** *Majority* $:= -1$
    else
        Count $:= 0$;
        for $i := 1$ **to** n **do**
            if $X[i] = C$ **then** *Count* $:=$ *Count* $+ 1$;
        if *Count* $> n/2$ **then** *Majority* $:= C$
        else *Majority* $:= -1$
end

Figure 6.28 Algorithm *Majority*.

Complexity   We use $n - 1$ comparisons to find a candidate and $n - 1$ comparisons, in the worst case, to determine whether this candidate is a majority. Thus, overall, there are at most $2n - 2$ comparisons. It is possible to reduce the number of comparisons to $3n/2 + 1$, and that is optimal (Fischer and Salzberg [1982]). In any case, since there are constant number of other operations per comparison, the overall running time is $O(n)$.

6.11 Three Problems Exhibiting Interesting Proof Techniques[3]

In this section, we present three unrelated problems involving sequences and multisets. Each algorithm is an example of a different proof technique. The first algorithm utilizes the principle of strengthening the induction hypothesis. We strengthen the induction hypothesis four times during the development of this solution, leading to an efficient algorithm. The second algorithm is an example of an obvious technique — improving the "theorem" by eliminating all unnecessary assumptions. The example shows that this principle is not always straightforward. This third example shows how to improve an algorithm by choosing the base of the induction wisely.

6.11.1 Longest Increasing Subsequence

Let S be a sequence of distinct integers $x_1, x_2, ..., x_n$. An **increasing subsequence (IS)** of S is a subsequence $x_{i_1}, x_{i_2}, ..., x_{i_k}$, with $i_1 < i_2 < \cdots < i_k$, such that, for all $1 \le j < k$, we have $x_{i_j} < x_{i_{j+1}}$. A **longest increasing subsequence (LIS)** of S is an increasing subsequence of maximum length.

> **The Problem**   Find a longest increasing subsequence of a given sequence of distinct integers.

The algorithm we develop in this section is an excellent example of the principle of strengthening of the induction hypothesis. We will strengthen the hypothesis several times, each time as a result of problems encountered in the previous attempt. Consider first the straightforward induction.

> **Induction hypothesis (first attempt):** *Given a sequence of size $< m$, we know how to find a longest increasing subsequence of it.*

The base case consists of sequences of size 1 for which the problem is trivial. Given a sequence of size m, we find an LIS of its first $m - 1$ elements, and consider x_m. If x_m is greater than the last element in the LIS, given by the induction, then x_m can be appended to the LIS, creating a new longer LIS, and we are done. Otherwise, however, it is not clear how to proceed. For example, there may be several different LISs and x_m may extend one of them, but not necessarily the one found by the induction. The next step seems to be a strengthening of the induction hypothesis as follows:

> **Induction hypothesis (second attempt):** *Given a sequence of size $< m$, we know how to find all the longest increasing subsequence of it.*

---

[3] This section can be skipped at first reading.

The base case is still trivial. We use induction in the same way, except that now we can check x_m against *all* of the LISs and find whether a longer IS exists. This attempt solves the previous problem, but it introduces another problem — we now have to find *all* LISs. If x_m cannot extend any LIS, then there may still be an IS of length 1 less than the longest, and x_m can extend it, which will create a new LIS. It seems that we have gotten ourselves into a hole, because we now have to find all ISs of largest and second largest length. But to find all the second largest ISs, we will need to find all the third largest ISs, then all fourth largest, and so on. This is a good example where strengthening the induction hypothesis is overdone.

Let's look back at the stronger induction hypothesis. Do we really need *all* LISs? We need only to know whether x_m can extend one of them. Can we somehow find the "best" one in terms of potential of extension? The answer is positive. The best LIS is the one that ends with the smallest number! If we can extend any LIS, we can surely extend this one. (There may be several different LISs that end with the same number, and they are all equivalent in terms of extension potential. For simplicity, we talk about "the best one" instead of "an arbitrary best one.") Let's try another induction hypothesis, this one a little weaker than the last one:

> **Induction hypothesis (third attempt):** *Given a sequence of size $< m$, we know how to find a longest increasing subsequence of it, such that no other longest increasing subsequence of it has a smaller last number.*

The base case is still trivial. Given x_m, we can determine whether it can be appended to the LIS found by the induction. Assume that the LIS is of length s. If x_m can be added, then we have a new LIS, which is longer than the previous one; thus, this new LIS is unique, so it is definitely the "best" one, and we are done. Otherwise, we know that no longer increasing subsequence exists. But we are still not done. It may be the case that x_m cannot be added to the best LIS (since it is smaller than the last number in that LIS), but it can be added to an IS of length $s - 1$, making the latter an LIS with a smaller last number. To account for this possibility, we need to know the best IS of length $s - 1$. But then again, if the induction hypothesis states that we know the best IS of length $s - 1$, then x_m may extend an IS of length $s - 2$ making it the new best IS of length $s - 1$. We will have to be able to determine whether x_m extends such an IS in order to proceed with the induction. So, we will need to know the best IS of length $s - 2$, $s - 3$, and so on down to the best IS of length 1, which is simply the smallest number in the sequence so far. (Even without using induction, one can see that shorter ISs cannot be discarded arbitrarily — there is always the possibility that one of these ISs is the start of the final LIS.)

Yet again we try to strengthen the induction hypothesis. We denote by BIS(k) the best increasing subsequence of length k — namely, the one that ends with the smallest number (if there is more than one such subsequence we take an arbitrary one). We denote by BIS(k).*last* the last number in the sequence BIS(k).

> **Induction hypothesis (fourth attempt):** *Given a sequence of size $< m$, we know how to find BIS(k) for all $k < m - 1$, if they exist.*

The base case remains trivial. Given x_m, we have to find which of the BISs it can change. x_m extends a certain BIS(k) if and only if the following two conditions occur: (1) $x_m >$ BIS(k).*last*, so x_m can be added to BIS(k), and (2) $x_m <$ BIS($k + 1$).*last*, so BIS(k) with x_m at the end is better than BIS($k + 1$). We claim that BIS(1).*last* < BIS(2).*last* < $\cdots$ < BIS(s).*last*, where s is the size of the LIS. This claim is true because, if BIS(j).*last* $\leq$ BIS($j - 1$).*last* for some j, then the first $j - 1$ numbers of BIS(j) would be better than BIS($j - 1$). The algorithm proceeds as follows. Given x_m, we look at the values of BIS(i).*last*, for $i = s, s - 1, s - 2$, and so on, until we find one, say BIS(j).*last*, which is smaller than x_m. If no such j exists, then x_m is the smallest number in the sequence so far, and it becomes BIS(1). If $j = s$, then we extend BIS(s) with x_m, creating a new BIS($s + 1$). (The previous BIS(s) remains unchanged.) Otherwise, we have BIS(j).*last* $< x_m <$ BIS($j + 1$).*last*. We then replace BIS($j + 1$) with BIS(j)x_m.

This is basically the whole algorithm, and it is quite simple once we use the right induction. Notice that the search can be performed by binary search, because we are searching a sorted set. Hence, each x_m adds at most $O(\log m)$ comparisons, and the total running time is $O(n \log n)$. We leave it to the reader to complete the details of this algorithm, which is not a straightforward task.

6.11.2 Finding the Two Largest Elements in a Set

A common technique, which is important in proving almost any theorem, is to search the proof thoroughly for assumptions or steps that are not essential. Removing such assumptions results in a better theorem. Having inessential assumptions is also sometimes an indication that the proof may be wrong. Quoting Polya and Szego [1927]: "One should scrutinize each proof to see if one has in fact made use of all the assumptions; one should try to get the same consequence from fewer assumptions . . . and one should not be satisfied until counterexamples show that one has arrived at the boundaries of the possibilities." The same is true for algorithms. This principle sounds simple, but many times it is not, as seen in the next example.

The Problem Given a set S of n numbers $x_1, x_2, ..., x_n$, find the first and second largest of them.

We are looking for an algorithm that minimizes only the number of comparisons of elements from the set. We ignore other operations. Furthermore, for simplicity, we assume that n is a power of 2.

We try the usual divide-and-conquer technique, by dividing the set S of size n into two subsets P and Q of size $n/2$. If we use straightforward induction, we assume that we know the first and second largest elements of P and Q, denote them by p_1, p_2, and q_1, q_2 respectively, and we try to find the first and second largest elements of S. It is easy to see that two more comparisons are necessary and sufficient to find the first and second largest elements of S. One comparison is between the two maximals p_1 and q_1, and the other one is between the "loser" and the second largest of the "winner" (see Fig. 6.29). This approach leads to the recurrence relation $T(2n)=2T(n)+2$, $T(2)=1$, whose solution is $T(n)=3n/2-2$. This is better than the straightforward $2n-3$ comparisons, and it is very similar to the problem of finding the maximal and minimal elements presented in Section 6.5.1. We want to do even better.

If the two comparisons are necessary for the inductive step, then how can we improve the total number of comparisons? Looking carefully at the comparisons in Fig. 6.29, we see that q_2 will not be used further in the algorithm. Therefore, the computation leading to its discovery was unnecessary. If we can avoid this computation, then we will save significant number of comparisons. However, until we compare p_1 to q_1, we do not know whether p_2 or q_2 can be ignored. If we had known which subset was going to "lose," then we could have used the regular maximum-finding algorithm for this subset, saving many comparisons. So, we suspect that quite a few comparisons can be avoided, but we do not know which ones they are.

The trick is to delay the computation of the second largest element until the end. We keep only a list of candidates for second largest, and we do not assume that we know the second largest element in the induction hypothesis:

> **Induction hypothesis:** *Given a set of size $< n$, we know how to find the maximum element and a "small" set of candidates for the second maximum element.*

We have not defined a value for "small" in the hypothesis. We will discover the appropriate value when we develop the algorithm.

The algorithm proceeds as follows. Given a set S of size n, we divide it into two subsets P and Q of size $n/2$. By the induction hypothesis, we know the largest elements of the two sets, p_1 and q_1, plus a set of candidates for the second largest, C_P and C_Q. We compare p_1 and q_1 and take the largest, say p_1, to be the maximum of S. We then

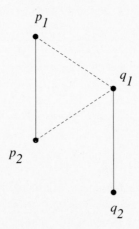

Figure 6.29 Finding the largest and second largest elements (the dashed lines correspond to the comparisons).

discard C_Q, since all elements of C_Q are less than q_1 which is at most the second largest, and add only q_1 to C_P. At the end, we get the largest element and a set of candidates from which we choose the second largest element directly. The number of comparisons for finding the maximum satisfies the recurrence relation $T(n) = 2T(n/2) + 1, \ T(2) = 1$, which implies that $T(n) = n - 1$. It is easy to see that $\log_2 n$ is a sufficient size for the candidate set, because we add one more element to the candidate set when we double the size of the set we consider. Therefore, finding the second largest element requires $\log_2 n - 1$ additional comparisons. The total number of comparisons is thus $n - 1 + \log_2 n - 1$, which, incidently, is the best possible (see [Knuth 1973b]). The induction hypothesis, for the case when n is equal to a power of 2, is thus as follows.

> **Induction hypothesis:** *Given a set of size $< n$, we know how to find the maximum element and a set of at most $\log_2 n$ candidates for the second maximum element.*

Comments   Once an algorithm is constructed, it is a good idea to examine it carefully for parts that do not contribute to the final result. Often, these parts can be eliminated. Even if the redundant operations cannot be eliminated, they may be replaced by simpler operations, which are more efficient.

6.11.3 Computing the Mode of a Multiset

Let $S = (x_1, x_2, ..., x_n)$ be a multiset of (not necessarily distinct) elements from a totally ordered set. A **mode** of a multiset is defined as an element that occurs most frequently in the multiset (there may be more than one mode). The number of times an element occurs is called its **multiplicity**. The mode is thus the element with the highest multiplicity.

The Problem   Find a mode of a given multiset S.

Our goal is to minimize the number of comparisons. One possible way to find the mode is to use sorting. Once the elements are sorted, we can scan the sorted sequence and count the multiplicities (equal elements will be consecutive in the sorted sequence). We will see that sorting is not always necessary. The reason for thinking that sorting may not be required is that finding the majority (Section 6.12) can be done in linear time, whereas sorting requires $O(n \log n)$ time. This leads us to suspect that, if the multiplicity of the mode is high, then there may be a fast way of finding it without sorting.

Let's try the straightforward induction approach. We assume that we know the mode of a multiset with $n - 1$ elements, and try to find the mode of an n element multiset. This is not easy since there may be several elements with the highest multiplicity; the nth element may break the tie. Suppose that the induction hypothesis states that we know *all* the elements with the highest multiplicity. Then, we can determine whether the nth element breaks the tie, but it may also increase the multiplicity of another number, which now has to be added to the list. We have already seen (Section 6.13.1) that keeping track of all different "best" solutions is possible, but the cost will probably be too high. On the other hand, it is not necessary that the nth element be arbitrary — we can choose a special one. Suppose that the nth element is the *maximum* element. We still have basically the same problems as before, but now we are closer to a solution. We can reduce the size of the problem by removing not one but *all* occurrences of the maximal element. We then solve the reduced problem, and compare the multiplicity of the mode of the reduced multiset with the multiplicity of the maximal element.

We now have an algorithm, but unfortunately, it is still too slow. Finding the maximum of a multiset of n elements requires $n-1$ comparisons. If the multiset contains quite a few distinct elements, then too many maximum computations will have to be performed. In particular, if the multiset is in fact a set (i.e., all the elements are distinct), then this algorithm is basically the same as the $O(n^2)$ selection sort.

To improve the performance of the algorithm, we resort to the divide-and-conquer technique. Instead of using one element or a small set of elements in the induction, we try to divide the multiset into two parts of about the same size. The two parts should be disjoint, so that they lead to independent subproblems. How do we divide a multiset into two approximately equal disjoint parts? We can first find the *median* of the multiset and then split the multiset into three parts — less than, equal to, and greater than the median. We have already seen how to find a median in $O(n)$ expected number of comparisons (Section 6.5). It is also possible to find the median in $O(n)$ time in the worst case, although we have not proved this result. We use the median-finding algorithm as a step in our algorithm. Given a multiset of size n, we first find the median and perform the splitting, then solve two subproblems of size no more than $n/2$. The mode of the original multiset can be easily determined from the modes of the two smaller multisets, since the smaller multisets are disjoint. Since finding the median and splitting can be done in linear time, we get the familiar recurrence relation

$$T(n) \leq 2T(n/2) + O(n), \ T(2) = 1,$$

which implies that $T(n) = O(n \log n)$. But this is no better than sorting. In fact, if the splitter element is chosen at random instead of being the exact median, then this algorithm is basically the same as quicksort.

We now come to the heart of this algorithm. To improve the performance, we look at the base of the induction. Suppose that the multiplicity of the mode is M. We claim that we can start the induction from submultisets of size M. In other words, we do not have to continue splitting the multiset into parts smaller than M. Since all parts are disjoint, one of the parts of size M must contain only the mode. At this point, the mode will be discovered because the multiplicity of all other elements cannot exceed M. Therefore, there is no need to divide the multiset any further.

The implementation of this algorithm is not straightforward. We cannot use recursion, because we do not know beforehand how far to carry out the recursion. The recursion should be terminated when the size of the multiset becomes at most M, but the value of M is found during the execution of the algorithm by checking all the smaller multisets. In each step, all the submultisets are checked, and, if none of them contains only one distinct element, then all of them are further divided. If any of the submultisets contains only one distinct element, then we can terminate. We leave the implementation details to the reader.

Complexity   The resulting recurrence relation is modified only in its base:

$$T(n) \leq 2T(n/2) + O(n), \ \ T(M) = O(M),$$

which implies that the number of comparisons is $O(n \log(n/M))$. An intuitive explanation of this expression is that the recursion is carried out only until a multiset of size M is encountered, which is a total of $\log(n/M)$ times. Each time it takes a linear number of comparisons to divide and check all subproblems. In particular, if $M = cn$ for some constant c, then this is a linear-time algorithm. If M is a constant, then this is an $O(n \log n)$ algorithm. This algorithm is thus superior to sorting only if M is fairly high and if the cost of comparisons is also high (there is a significant overhead for remembering subproblems).

6.12 Summary

We touched on quite a few subjects in the this chapter — searching, sorting, order statistics, data compression, string manipulation, probabilistic algorithms, and others. We presented only one or two basic problems in each subject. In practice, problems are often not as clean and simple to define as are the problems presented in this chapter. One should therefore try to abstract the main parts of a given problem. The techniques that we employed in this chapter are quite similar to those introduced in Chapter 5. Induction again plays a major role.

Many of the problems discussed in this chapter have straightforward solutions that can be obtained with little effort — linear search and selection sort are two examples. If the size of the input is small, these solutions are most often not only good enough, but they are also better than sophisticated solutions. Whenever the size of the input is not small (e.g., over 100), it is important to attempt to find better solutions. The use of linear-search and quadratic-sorting algorithms, for example, is quite common. Unfortunately, these and other inefficient algorithms are used too often for large inputs.[4]

Bibliographic Notes and Further Reading

A wealth of material about sorting and searching, including their history, can be found in Knuth [1973b]. Additional algorithms involving sequences and sets, as well as topics in combinatorics, are presented in Stanton and White [1986]. A formal derivation of a binary-search paradigm can be found in Manna and Waldinger [1987]. The stuttering-subsequence problem of Section 6.2 is from Mirzaian [1987], where a linear-time

---

[4]A recent example highlighted this issue unexpectedly when the virus (or worm) that attacked over 6000 computers across the United States on November 2, 1988, slowed down those computers considerably, partly because all the search algorithms in it used linear search (see Spafford [1988]).

algorithm is presented. The average performance of interpolation search was studied by Perl, Itai, and Avni [1978], and some empirical results are given by van der Nat [1979].

Mergesort was probably first developed by von Neumann in 1945, and it was one of the first stored programs to be implemented. An in-place version of mergesort was first developed by Kronrod [1969]; see also Huang and Langston [1988], and Dvorak and Durian [1988]. Quicksort is due to Hoare [1962]. A detailed study of quicksort appears in Sedgewick [1978]. Heapsort was developed by Williams [1964]. A wonderful film containing descriptions of nine major sorting techniques all shown with beautiful animation was produced by the computer graphics group at the University of Toronto [1981]. Even though sorting has been studied extensively for many years, there are still many open problems. The exact number of comparisons required for sorting n numbers is still unknown. The algorithm outlined in Exercise 6.30 is by Ford and Johnson [1959]. It was the "champion" for some time in terms of number of comparisons, but it was proved not to be optimal by Manacher [1979]. Another widely used sorting algorithm is shellsort invented by Shell [1959]. Shellsort is simple and very easy to implement. However, its complexity is still unknown; see Incerpi and Sedgewick [1987] for recent results and empirical observations. Decision trees have been used successfully to prove lower bounds for several basic problems; Moret [1982] presents a survey of their uses.

An analysis of the probabilistic selection algorithm was given by Floyd and Rivest [1975]. A linear-time deterministic algorithm for order statistics was first developed by Blum, Floyd, Pratt, Rivest, and Tarjan [1972]. However, the running time is in fact $\mathcal{O}(n)$ since the constant is very high. Schönhage, Paterson, and Pippenger [1976] presents a median finding algorithm with at most $3n$ comparisons. The best-known lower bound (on the number of comparisons) for finding the median is $2n$ (Bent and John [1985]). This paper contains results for the general order statistic problem; the expressions for the general lower bounds are more complicated.

Data compression has been studied widely due to its great importance. The algorithm in Section 6.6 is due to Huffman [1952] (see also Knuth [1973a]). Variations of Huffman's algorithm that use only one pass are described by Knuth [1985] and Vitter [1985]. Another effective and popular algorithm is due to Ziv and Lempel [1978]. More on data compression in general can be found in Lynch [1985].

The string-matching algorithms presented in Section 6.7 are due to Knuth, Morris, and Pratt [1977], and to Boyer and Moore [1977]. Galil [1979] improved the worst-case running time of the Boyer–Moore algorithm. More on the complexity of the Boyer–Moore algorithm can be found in Guibas and Odlyzko [1980] and in Schaback [1988]. Empirical comparisons between various string matching algorithms can be found in Smit [1982]. A probabilistic string matching algorithm was developed by Karp and Rabin [1987]. This algorithm uses the idea of **fingerprinting** to make short representations of large strings so that they can be compared efficiently. It can also be used with two-dimensional patterns. The string matching problem can be extended to look for patterns more complicated than just strings. For example, "wild cards" are useful; we may want to search for all occurrences of strings of the form $B*C$, where B and C are given strings and * denotes any string. A more general problem is to look for any regular sets of strings. For more on these problems see Aho and Corasick [1975].

Another important problem is to search for strings in a fixed text that has been preprocessed. Suffix trees (Weiner [1973], McCreight [1976]) and Suffix Arrays (Manber and Myers [1989]) allow fast search.

Sequence comparisons and their many applications are covered in a book edited by Sankoff and Kruskal [1983]. Various problems involving strings are included in a book edited by Apostolico and Galil [1985]. The algorithm given in Section 6.8 is due to Wagner and Fischer [1974]. This algorithm can be improved in many ways, including savings of storage (Hirschberg [1975]), improved running times when the sequences are far apart (Hunt and Szymanski [1977]), and when they are close (Ukkonen [1985] and Myers [1986]). A survey of relevant results appears in Hirschberg [1983].

The probabilistic algorithm that finds an element in the upper half is due to Yao [1977]. Random number generation is covered in detail in Knuth [1981]. The probabilistic coloring algorithm given in Section 6.9.2 is based on a probabilistic proof of existence given in Bollobás [1986]. The technique for converting probabilistic algorithms to deterministic algorithms, which was illustrated in Section 6.9.3, is due to Raghavan [1986]. The use of this technique to solve the coloring problem of Section 6.9.2 was pointed out to us by K. Pruhs. The general problem of finding a valid coloring for arbitrary-sized subsets is NP-complete (Lovász [1973]). Erdös and Spencer [1974] present many examples of probabilistic techniques for proving combinatorial properties.

The majority problem was studied, for example, by Misra and Gries [1982]. Using a more sophisticated data structure than the one presented in Section 6.10, Fischer and Salzberg [1982] showed that the number of comparisons (but not the number of other steps) can be reduced to $3n/2+1$ in the worst case, and that this bound is optimal.

An excellent description of a solution to the longest increasing subsequence problem (from which we borrowed heavily) is given by Gries [1981]. Erdös and Szekeres [1935] proved, by a very elegant use of the pigeonhole principle, that every sequence of distinct elements of length n^2+1 must have either an increasing or a decreasing subsequence of length $n+1$. The problem of finding the largest and second largest elements in a set was first suggested, in the context of arranging tennis tournaments, by Lewis Carroll (see [Knuth 1973b]). Another algorithm for finding the mode is given in Dobkin and Munro [1980] (see also Gonnet [1984]).

The solution to Exercise 6.27 is discussed in Aho, Hopcroft, and Ullman [1974]. Exercise 6.34 is from Karp, Saks, and Wigderson [1986]. A solution to Exercise 6.39 is given in Rodeh [1982]. The subject of Exercise 6.42 is discussed in Choueka, Fraenkel, Klein, and Perl [1985]. The notion of realizable sequences (Exercise 6.64) was introduced by Ryser [1957].

Drill Exercises

6.1 Design a good strategy for the following well-known game: One player thinks of a number in the range 1 to n. The other player attempts to find the number by asking questions of the form "is the number less than (greater than) x?" The object is to ask as few questions as possible. (Assume that nobody cheats.)

6.2   Find a strategy to the guessing game in Exercise 6.1 when the range of choice is unknown — that is, the chosen number may be any positive number.

6.3   Suppose that you are using a program that handles large texts, for example, a word processing program. The program takes as input a text, represented as a sequence of characters, and produces some output. Once in a while, the program encounters an error from which it cannot recover. Not only that, but it cannot even indicate what error it is, or where it is. In other words, the only action the program takes is to halt and to output "Error." Assume that the error is local; in other words, it results only from a particular string in the text which the program, for some unknown reason, does not like. The error is independent of the context in which the offending string appears. Suggest a strategy to locate the source of the error.

6.4   Construct an example for which interpolation search will use $\Omega(n)$ comparisons for searching in a table of size n.

6.5   Write the complete program for radix-exchange sort. The input is a sequence of n integers, each with k digits. Each digit is in the range 1 to m. You can assume that $O(m)$ space is available. First, write the program as a recursive procedure. Determine the amount of extra space required by the recursive procedure. Then, design a nonrecursive program and try to minimize the amount of extra space.

6.6   Write the complete programs for insertion sort (with linear search and binary search) and selection sort.

6.7   Count the number of comparisons used to sort the input in Fig. 6.8 (by mergesort), and in Fig. 6.11 (by quicksort). Compute the number of comparisons for the same input for insertion sort and selection sort.

6.8   Prove, by using a loop invariant, that the first if statement in algorithm *Mergesort* (Fig. 6.7) is not necessary. In other words, prove that the result of the algorithm will not change if we remove this if statement, and start the algorithm with the if statement "if *Left* ≠ *Right*."

6.9   Compare mergesort with the solution to the skyline problem in Chapter 5. Try to formalize the similarities. Will it be possible to use one solution almost as a "black box" to solve the other problem?

6.10   Write the appropriate loop invariant for the main loop in Algorithm *Partition* (Fig. 6.9), and prove the correctness of the algorithm.

6.11   Construct an example for which quicksort will use $\Omega(n^2)$ comparisons when the pivot is chosen by taking the median of the first, last, and middle elements of the sequence.

6.12   In some cases, the input for a sorting algorithm is already *almost* sorted, which means that the number of out-of-order elements is small. Describe how the different sorting algorithms suggested in Section 6.4 perform for almost sorted inputs. Which algorithm would you use? (You are encouraged to design your own.)

6.13   Construct a table similar to that in Fig. 6.15 for building a heap top down.

6.14   Design a divide-and-conquer algorithm to find the minimal and maximal elements in a set. The algorithm should use at most $3n/2$ comparisons (for $n = 2^k$). Can you pinpoint the reason this algorithm requires less than the straightforward $2n - 3$ comparisons algorithm?

6.15   Build the Huffman tree for the set of characters in this question. Include all characters. How many bits are saved in the storage of this question using Huffman trees versus a storage based on a fixed-length encoding?

6.16   Construct the *next* table (Section 6.7) for the string *aabbaababababbaabbaabb*.

6.17   Construct the matrices C and M obtained by comparing the sequences *aabccbbaabca* to *baacbabaccaba* using algorithm *Minimum_Edit_Distance* of Fig. 6.27.

6.18   Write the appropriate loop invariant for the first loop in Algorithm *Majority* (Fig. 6.28), and prove the correctness of the first phase of the algorithm.

Creative Exercises

Unless specified otherwise, sequences and sets are assumed to be of size n, and to consist of elements that are real numbers. Algorithms are said to run in *linear time* if they run in time $O(n)$. All the running times are worst case.

6.19   Given an array of integers $A[1..n]$, such that, for all i, $1 \leq i < n$, we have $|A[i] - A[i+1]| \leq 1$. Let $A[1] = x$ and $A[n] = y$, such that $x < y$. Design an efficient search algorithm to find j such that $A[j] = z$ for a given value z, $x \leq z \leq y$. What is the maximal number of comparisons to z that your algorithm makes?

6.20   Prove by using decision trees that the algorithm you developed for Exercise 6.19 is optimal in the worst case (or improve your algorithm until you can prove that it is optimal).

6.21   The input is a set S with n real numbers. Design an $O(n)$ time algorithm to find a number that is *not* in the set. Prove that $\Omega(n)$ is a lower bound on the number of steps required to solve this problem.

6.22   The input is a set S containing n real numbers, and a real number x.

   a. Design an algorithm to determine whether there are two elements of S whose sum is exactly x. The algorithm should run in time $O(n \log n)$.

   b. Suppose now that the set S is given in a sorted order. Design an algorithm to solve this problem in time $O(n)$.

6.23   Given two sets S_1 and S_2, and a real number x, find whether there exists an element from S_1 and an element from S_2 whose sum is exactly x. The algorithm should run in time $O(n \log n)$, where n is the total number elements in both sets.

6.24   Design an algorithm to determine whether two sets are disjoint. State the complexity of your algorithm in terms of the sizes m and n of the given sets. Make sure to consider the case where m is substantially smaller than n.

6.25   Design an algorithm to compute the union of two given sets, both of size $O(n)$. The sets are given as arrays of elements. The output should be an array of distinct elements that form the union of the sets. No element should appear more than once. The worst-case running time of the algorithm should be $O(n \log n)$.

6.26   The input is a sequence of real numbers $x_1, x_2, ..., x_n$, such that n is even. Design an algorithm to partition the input into $n/2$ pairs in the following way. For each pair, we compute the sum of its numbers. Denote by $s_1, s_2, ..., s_{n/2}$ these $n/2$ sums. The algorithm should find the partition that minimizes the *maximum* sum.

*6.27   Modify lexicographic sort to work for variable-length strings. In other words, you can no longer assume that all numbers have exactly k digits. Some numbers may be long and some short. It is possible of course to "pad" all numbers by adding "dummy" (0) digits to make them all of the same length. Find an algorithm that avoids doing that and achieves a running time linear in the total number of digits.

6.28   The input is a sequence $x_1, x_2, ..., x_n$ of integers in an arbitrary order, and another sequence $a_1, a_2, ..., a_n$ of distinct integers from 1 to n (namely $a_1, a_2, ..., a_n$ is a *permutation* of $1, 2, ..., n$). Both sequences are given as arrays. Design an $O(n \log n)$ algorithm to order the first sequence according to the order imposed by the permutation. In other words, for each i, x_i should appear in the position given in a_i. For example, if $x = 17, 5, 1, 9$, and $a = 3, 2, 4, 1$, then the outcome should be $x = 9, 5, 17, 1$. The algorithm should be *in-place*, so you cannot use an additional array.

6.29   The input is d sequences of elements such that each sequence is already sorted, and there is a total of n elements. Design an $O(n \log d)$ algorithm to merge all the sequences into one sorted sequence.

6.30   The following is a brief and incomplete description of a sorting algorithm known as the Ford and Johnson sorting.

1. Arbitrarily form $n/2$ distinct pairs of elements
2. Compare the elements in each pair
3. Recursively sort the $n/2$ larger elements
4. Insert in some order the $n/2$ remaining elements into the sorted list of larger elements

This algorithm uses fewer comparisons than almost any other algorithm, provided that the insertions in step 4 are done in a "good" order. Consider the cases of $n = 5, 6$, and 8. Find a good order in which to insert in step 4. You should end up with an optimal sorting algorithm (in terms of the number of comparisons) for these values of n (in fact, you will get an optimal algorithm for any $n < 12$ with this algorithm).

6.31   The input is a sequence of n integers with many duplications, such that the number of distinct integers in the sequence is $O(\log n)$.

a. Design a sorting algorithm to sort such sequences using at most $O(n \log \log n)$ comparisons in the worst case.

b. Why is the lower bound of $\Omega(n \log n)$ not satisfied in this case?

6.32   Prove that the sum of the heights of all nodes in a balanced binary tree with n nodes is at most $n - 1$. (A balanced binary tree with n nodes is one that corresponds to an implicit representation using an array of size n.) Show a tree whose sum of heights is exactly $n - 1$.

6.33   The sum of the heights of all nodes in a heap (see Section 6.4.5) can also be computed directly by noting that the height of the node corresponding to position i in the array (of size n) is at most $\lceil \log_2(n - i + 1) \rceil$. Find the sum of heights by using this method.

6.34 The input is a heap of size n (in which the largest element is on top), given as an array, and a real number x. Design an algorithm to determine whether the kth smallest element in the heap is greater than or equal to x. The worst-case running time of your algorithm should be $O(k)$, independent of the size of the heap. You can use $O(k)$ space. (Notice that you do not have to find the kth smallest element; you need only determine its relationship to x.)

6.35 The *weighted selection problem* is the following. The input is a sequence of distinct numbers $x_1, x_2, ..., x_n$ such that each number x_i has a positive weight $w(x_i)$ associated with it. Let W be the sum of all weights. The problem is to find, given a value X, $0 < X \le W$, the number x_j such that

$$\sum_{x_i > x_j} w(x_i) < X,$$

and

$$w(x_j) + \sum_{x_i > x_j} w(x_i) \ge X.$$

Design an efficient algorithm to solve the weighted selection problem. (Notice that when all weights are 1, this problem becomes the regular selection problem.)

6.36 Let A be an algorithm that finds the kth largest of n elements by a sequence of comparisons. Prove that A collects enough information to determine which elements are greater than the kth largest and which elements are less than it. (In other words, you can partition the set around the kth largest element without making more comparisons.)

6.37 Consider the problem of finding the kth largest element, and suppose that we are interested only in minimizing space. Each element fills one memory cell. The input is a sequence of elements, given one at a time, inserted into a fixed cell C. That is, in the ith input step x_i is put into C (and C's previous content is erased). You can perform any computation between two input steps (including, of course, moving the content of C to a temporary location). The purpose is to minimize the extra number of cells required by the algorithm. Give an upper bound and a lower bound on the number of memory cells needed to find the kth largest element.

6.38 The goal of this problem is to find the kth smallest element, as in Exercise 6.37, but this time we want to minimize the running time as well as to use very little space (although not necessarily minimal space). The input is again a sequence of elements $x_1, x_2, ..., x_n$, given one at a time. Design an $O(n)$ expected time algorithm to compute the kth smallest element using only $O(k)$ memory cells. The value of k is known ahead of time (so that sufficient amount of memory can be allocated), but the value of n is not known until the last element is seen.

6.39 Let A and B be two sets, both with n elements, such that A resides in computer P and B in Q. P and Q can communicate by sending messages, and they can perform any kind of local computation. Design an algorithm to find the nth smallest element of the union of A and B (i.e., the median). You can assume, for simplicity, that all the elements are distinct. Your goal is to minimize the number of messages, where a message can contain one element or one integer. What is the number of messages in the worst case?

6.40 Given a set of integers $S = \{x_1, x_2, ..., x_n\}$, find a subset $R \subseteq S$, such that

$$\sum_{x_i \in R} x_i \equiv 0 \ (\text{modulo } n).$$

6.41   Use the idea of the information-theoretic bound to prove a lower bound of $\Omega(\log n)$ comparisons for the problem of finding the value of i such that $x_i = i$ in the sequence $x_1, x_2, ..., x_n$, or determining that no such i exists. (This problem is discussed in Sections 6.2 and 6.4.6.)

6.42   Suppose that you want to use Huffman's encoding but that you do not use a programming language that lets you access bits. You can read the sequence of bits as a sequence of bytes (or any other blocks of size k depending on the machine). Each byte (block) corresponds to an integer, and the encoding thus corresponds to a sequence of integers (each less than 2^8). Design a method to translate the sequence of integers such that you can use the Huffman tree and decode the corresponding sequence of bits. Do it by building a table of size $k \times 2^k$, where k is the size of the block (8 in the case of bytes). The table depends on the tree (which is given to you). You can use only multiplication, addition, and subtraction of integers; you cannot use bit operations. The table should allow you to access any bit in a number i taken from the sequence of integers. Now solve the problem again, but this time use a table of size 2×2^k.

6.43   Assume that a Huffman's encoding has been applied to a certain text. The Huffman tree has been constructed and it is available to you. The frequencies of all characters in the text are also known. Assume now that the text has been changed slightly such that the frequency of one (existing) character X has been increased by 1. You want to update the tree so that it remains optimal for the modified text. A friend makes the following suggestion for an algorithm to modify the tree.

First, he notes that an important property of a Huffman tree is that the frequencies associated with the nodes are nondecreasing as the nodes are closer to the root. (In other words, a node with lower frequency cannot be higher in the tree than a node with higher frequency.) The frequency of an internal node v is defined as the sum of all the frequencies of the characters associated with external nodes that are descendants of v. Consequently, he suggests checking whether the increased frequency still satisfies that property by checking the next higher level. If there is no node in the next higher level with a frequency smaller than the frequency of X, then leave X in its place. Otherwise, replace X with the character at the higher level whose frequency is now smaller than that of X. This algorithm may sometimes work, but it is generally incorrect. Describe why it is incorrect and how it can be corrected. You should mention not only what is missing in the algorithm but, more important, discuss why the algorithm does not work, as is, in general. That is, either construct a counterexample under which this algorithm does not construct an optimal tree, or show that, had the algorithm been correct, it would have led to a contradiction (or to some highly suspicious implications). It is not enough to point out that the algorithm does not deal with some cases. It could be that those cases can be ignored. You need to show that the algorithm is definitely wrong.

6.44   The input is two strings of characters $A = a_1 a_2 \cdots a_n$ and $B = b_1 b_2 \cdots b_n$. Design an $O(n)$ time algorithm to determine whether B is a cyclic shift of A. In other words, the algorithm should determine whether there exists an index k, $1 \le k \le n$ such that $a_i = b_{(k+i) \bmod n}$, for all i, $1 \le i \le n$.

6.45   The KMP string matching algorithm can be improved for binary strings in the following way: When constructing the *next* table, in addition to looking at the suffix of the string seen so far, we can add the mismatched character. That is, we look for the longest suffix of $B(i-1)\overline{b_i}$ that matches a prefix of B. ($\overline{b_i}$ is the complement character of b_i.) That way, every character in A is compared to a character in B exactly once.

    a. Give a precise definition of the modified *next* table, and show its new values for the example in Fig. 6.21.

    b. Modify the string matching algorithm to take advantage of this change.

6.46   **An on-line string matching algorithm**: Suppose that the pattern is input one character at a time at a relatively slow pace (e.g., by typing), but the text is already given. We would like to proceed with the matching as much as we can, without waiting until all the pattern is known. In other words, when the kth character is input, we would like to be at the first place in the text that matches the first $k-1$ characters in the pattern. Modify the KMP algorithm to achieve that goal.

6.47   Modify the KMP string matching algorithm to find the largest prefix of B that matches a substring of A. In other words, you do not need to match all of B inside A; instead, you want to find the largest match (but it has to start with b_1).

6.48   Let T and P be two sequences $t_1, t_2, ..., t_n$ and $p_1, p_2, ..., p_k$ of characters, such that $k \leq n$. Design an $O(n)$ algorithm to determine whether P is a subsequence of T. (P is a subsequence of T if there exist a sequence of indices $i_1 < i_2 < \cdots < i_k$ such that for all j, $1 \leq j \leq k$, we have $t_{i_j} = p_j$.)

6.49   Design an algorithm for Exercise 6.48 such that, if there are many subsequences in T that are equal to P, then the algorithm finds the subsequence whose sum of indices is maximum. That is, find the sequence of indices $i_1 < i_2 < \cdots < i_k$ such that for all j, $1 \leq j \leq k$, we have $t_{i_j} = p_j$, and $\sum_{j=1}^{k} i_j$ is maximized.

6.50   Consider Exercise 6.48; assume that each character t_i in T has a *cost* $c(t_i)$ associated with it. Find the matching subsequence that maximizes the sum of costs. That is, find the sequence of indices $i_1 < i_2 < \cdots < i_k$ such that for all j, $1 \leq j \leq k$, we have $t_{i_j} = p_j$, and $\sum_{j=1}^{k} c(t_{i_j})$ is maximized.

6.51   The **largest common subsequence (LCS)** of two sequences T and P is the largest sequence L such that L is a subsequence of both T and P. The **smallest common supersequence (SCS)** of two sequences T and P is the smallest sequence L such that both T and P are subsequences of L.

    a. Design efficient algorithms to find the LCS and SCS of two given sequences.

    b. Let $d(T, P)$ be the smallest edit distance between T and P such that no replacements are allowed (in other words, we have to insert and delete). Prove that $d(T, P) = |SCS(T, P)| - |LCS(T, P)|$, where $|SCS(T, P)|$ $(|LCS(T, P)|)$ is the size of the smallest SCS (LCS) of T and P.

6.52   Generalize the minimal-edit-distance problem presented in Section 6.8 to the case where insertions at the beginning or the end of one of the sequences are not counted. In other words, if B fits inside A, then we do not count the insertions needed to enlarge B; we count only the edit distance of B to the subsequence of A to which it fits. (Notice that, if you insert at the beginning of B without cost, you must count the insertions at the end of A, and vice versa.)

6.53   The sequence comparison problem can be generalized to three (or more) sequences in the following way. In each step, we are allowed to insert, delete, or replace characters from any of the sequences. The cost of a step is 0 if the corresponding characters in all sequences are equal, and 1 otherwise (even if two sequences match and only one insertion or deletion is necessary). For example, suppose that the sequences are *aabb*, *bbb*, and *cbb*. One possible edit sequence is inserting *a* in front of *bbb* and *cbb* (which costs 1), replacing a *b* in *bbb* and a *c* in *cbb* with an *a*, and then the rest matches; the total cost is 2. Design an $O(n^3)$ algorithm to find the minimal edit distance between three given sequences.

6.54   Let $A = a_1 a_2 \cdots a_n$ and $B = b_1 b_2 \cdots b_m$ be two strings of characters. Denote by $A[i]$ the string $a_i a_{i+1} \cdots a_n$ (namely, the ith suffix of A). Let d_i be the minimal edit distance between B and $A[i]$. Design an $O(n^2)$ algorithm to find the minimum value of d_i (among all i, $1 \le i \le n$).

6.55   The input is a sequence of numbers $x_1, x_2, ..., x_n$. Prove that any deterministic algorithm that selects a number from the set which is in the upper half (i.e., greater than or equal to the median) must make at least $\lfloor \frac{1}{2} n \rfloor$ comparisons.

6.56   Determine the expected number of steps required by the probabilistic coloring algorithm of Section 6.9.2, in terms of both k and r.

6.57   Assume that you have a procedure for generating random numbers in the range 1 to k, for every $k \le n$. Design an algorithm to generate a random *permutation* of n numbers. Each possible permutation should be selected with equal probability.

6.58   Public-opinion polls are examples of probabilistic algorithms. Suppose that there are two candidates and n voters. A common algorithm is to ask k random voters and take the average response. Assume that exactly one-half of the voters favor each of the candidates. What is the probability that the results of the survey (with k voters) are in the range of 45 percent to 55 percent? (The result should be an expression with n, k, and the percentages as parameters.)

6.59   The results of public-opinion polls are usually given with an "error" range. For example, they may indicate that candidate X has x percent of the vote, and add that the poll has a ± 3 percent margin of error. Discuss why stating the bounds on the percentage of error as absolute bounds is not precise. What would be the precise way to define the error?

6.60   The purpose of this exercise is to compare Monte Carlo algorithms to Las Vegas algorithms. In a nutshell, Monte Carlo algorithms guarantee the running time, but cannot guarantee correctness; Las Vegas algorithms, on the other hand, guarantee correctness, but cannot guarantee the running time. Suppose that the problem we consider is a decision problem, so the answer is either yes or no. Assume that the error probability in the Monte Carlo algorithm is at most 1/4. (This is enough since we can simply run the algorithm many times and take the majority as the answer, thereby reducing the probability of error significantly.) Which type of algorithm is more powerful? In other words, is it possible to convert one type of algorithm to the other?

6.61   Design an algorithm that, given a list of n elements, finds all the elements that appear more than $n/4$ times in the list. The algorithm should use $O(n)$ comparisons. (Hint: Modify the majority algorithm.)

6.62   You are asked to design a schedule for a round-robin tennis tournament. There are $n = 2^k$ players. Each player must play every other player, and each player must play one match per day for $n-1$ days. Denote the players by $P_1, P_2, .., P_n$. Output the schedule for each player. (Hint: Use divide and conquer in the following way. First, divide the players into two equal groups and let them play within the groups for the first $n/2 - 1$ days. Then, design the games between the groups for the other $n/2$ days.)

*6.63   Design an algorithm to arrange a round-robin tennis tournament (see Exercise 6.62) for any number of players. If the number of players is odd, then in each round one player does not participate.

*6.64   Let $r_1, r_2, ..., r_n$ and $c_1, c_2, ..., c_n$ be two sequences of integers whose sum is equal; namely,

$$\sum_{i=1}^{n} r_i = \sum_{i=1}^{n} c_i.$$

Such sequences are called **realizable** if there is an $n \times n$ matrix all of whose elements are either 0 or 1, such that, for all i, the sum of the ith row is exactly r_i and the sum of the ith column is exactly c_i. Not all sequences are realizable. For example, the two sequences $0, 2$ and $0, 2$ are not realizable since only the second element of the second row can be nonzero, but it cannot be more than 1. Design an algorithm to determine whether two given sequences are realizable, and construct a matrix with the corresponding row and column sums if they are. (Hint: First, strengthen the induction hypothesis to extend the problem to $n \times m$ matrices. Then, use induction on n (the number of rows). Try to place 1s in the first row so that the problem for the other $n-1$ rows can be solved if and only if the original problem can be solved.)

CHAPTER 7

GRAPH ALGORITHMS

A shortcut is the longest distance between two points.

Anon

7.1 Introduction

In the previous chapter, we discussed algorithms involving sets and sequences of objects. The relationships we studied were limited to ordering, multiplicities, overlappings, and so on. In this chapter, we discuss more involved relationships among objects. We use graphs to model these relationships. Graphs can model a large variety of situations, and they have been used in diverse fields ranging from archaeology to social psychology. We present several important basic algorithms to manipulate graphs and to compute certain graph properties.

First let's see examples of modeling by graphs.

1. Finding a good route to a restaurant in a city is a graph-theoretical problem. The streets correspond to the edges (directed edges in the case of one-way streets), and the intersections to the vertices. Each vertex and each edge (street segment) can be associated with an expected time delay, and the problem is to find the "quickest" path between two vertices.

2. Some programs can be partitioned into states. From each state the program may have several possibilities to proceed. Some of the states may be considered undesirable. The problem of finding which states can lead to an undesirable state is a graph-theoretical problem in which the states correspond to the vertices and an edge indicates a possible move from one state to another.

3. The problem of scheduling classes in a university can be viewed as a graph-theoretical problem. The vertices correspond to the classes, and two classes are connected if there is a student who wishes to take them both or they are both taught by the same professor. The problem is to schedule the classes such that the

conflicts are minimized. This is a difficult problem and good solutions to it are hard to find.

4.   Consider a computer system with several user accounts. Each user has a security permission to access his or her account. Users may want to cooperate and to give one another permission to use their account. However, if A has permission to use B's account, and B has permission to use C's account, then A may be able to use C's account as well. The problem of identifying which users can access which accounts is a graph-theoretical problem. The users correspond to the vertices in this case, and there is a directed edge from user A to user B if A gives B permission to use his or her account.

There are quite a few textbooks on graph theory (see the Bibliography section), and numerous other applications.

Representations of graphs were discussed in Section 4.6. For the most part, we will use the adjacency list representation, which is more efficient for sparse graphs (i.e., graphs with relatively few edges). We begin by introducing standard terminology. A graph $G = (V, E)$ consists of a set V of **vertices** (also called **nodes**), and a set E of **edges**. Each edge corresponds to a pair of distinct vertices. (Sometimes self-loops, which are edges from a vertex to itself, are allowed; we will assume that they are not allowed.) A graph can be **directed** or **undirected**. The edges in a directed graph are ordered pairs; the order between the two vertices the edge connects is important. In this case, we draw an edge as an arrow pointing from one vertex (the tail) to another (the head). The edges in an undirected graph are unordered pairs; we draw them simply as line segments. A **multigraph** is a graph with possibly several edges between the same pair of vertices (i.e., E is a multiset). Graphs that are not multigraphs are sometimes called **simple** graphs. Unless specified otherwise, we will assume that the graphs we deal with are simple. The **degree** $d(v)$ of a vertex v is the number of edges incident to v. In a directed graph, we also distinguish between the **indegree**, which is the number of edges for which v is the head, and the **outdegree**, which is the number of edges for which v is the tail.

A **path** from v_1 to v_k is a sequence of vertices $v_1, v_2, ..., v_k$ that are connected by the edges $(v_1, v_2), (v_2, v_3), ..., (v_{k-1}, v_k)$ (these edges are also usually considered to be part of the path). A path is called **simple** if each vertex appears in it at most once. Vertex u is said to be **reachable** from vertex v if there is a path (directed or undirected, depending on the graph) from v to u. A **circuit** is a path whose first and last vertices are the same. A circuit is called **simple** if, except for the first and last vertices, no vertex appears more than once. A simple circuit is also called a **cycle**. (Circuits are sometimes called cycles even if they are not simple; we will assume that cycles are always simple.) The **undirected form** of a directed graph $G = (V, E)$ is the the same graph without directions on the edges. A graph is called **connected** if (in its undirected form) there is a path from any vertex to any other vertex. A **forest** is a graph that (in its undirected form) does not contain a cycle. A **tree** is a connected forest. A **rooted tree** (also known as an **arborescence**) is a directed tree with one distinguished vertex called the **root**, such that all the edges are pointing away from the root.

A **subgraph** of a graph $G = (V, E)$ is a graph $H = (U, F)$ such that $U \subseteq V$ and $F \subseteq E$. A **spanning tree** of an undirected graph G is a subgraph of G that is a tree and that contains all the vertices of G. A **spanning forest** of an undirected graph G is a subgraph of G that is a forest and that contains all the vertices of G. A **vertex-induced subgraph** of a graph $G = (V, E)$ is a subgraph $H = (U, F)$ such that $U \subseteq V$ and F consists of all the edges in E both of whose vertices belong to U. A vertex-induced subgraph is usually simply called an **induced subgraph**. If a graph $G = (V, E)$ is not connected, then it can be partitioned in a unique way into a set of connected subgraphs called the **connected components** of G. A connected component of G is a connected subgraph of G such that no other connected subgraph of G contains it. In other words, a connected component is a maximal connected subgraph. A **bipartite graph** is a graph whose vertices can be divided into two sets such that all edges connect vertices from one set to vertices in the other set. A **weighted graph** is a graph with weights (or costs, or lengths) associated with the edges.

Many definitions for directed and undirected graphs are similar, except for some obvious differences. For example, directed paths and undirected paths are defined in exactly the same way, but, of course, the directions of the edges in directed paths are specified. When we discuss one type of graph we will not specifically use a different notation. So, for example, when we talk about paths in the context of directed graphs we will mean directed paths.

We start with a simple example that is considered to be the first problem in graph theory — walking the bridges of Königsberg. We then discuss how to traverse a graph, how to order a graph, how to find shortest paths in a graph, how to partition the graph into blocks satisfying certain properties, and other problems. Chapter 10 includes a discussion on the relationships of graph algorithms and matrix algorithms. Several more graph algorithms are presented there.

7.2 Eulerian Graphs

The notion of Eulerian graphs is involved in what is considered to be the first solved problem of graph theory. The Swiss mathematician Leonhard Euler encountered the following puzzle in 1736. The town of Königsberg (now Kaliningrad) lay on the banks and on two islands of the Pregel river, as is shown in Fig. 7.1. The city was connected by seven bridges. The question (which many townspeople attempted to solve) was whether it was possible to start walking from anywhere in town and return to the starting point by crossing all bridges exactly once. The solution is obtained by abstracting the problem. The graph in Fig. 7.2 is equivalent, for the purpose of the problem, to the layout of Fig. 7.1. The question becomes the graph-theoretical problem of whether it is possible to find a circuit in the graph that contains each edge exactly once. Another way to pose the question is to ask whether it is possible to draw the graph in Fig. 7.2 — and end at the same place from which we started — without lifting the pencil. Euler solved this problem by proving that such a traversal is possible if and only if the graph is connected and all its vertices have even degrees. Such graphs are called **Eulerian graphs**. Since the graph in Fig. 7.2 contains vertices of odd degrees, it follows that the Königsberg bridges problem is impossible to solve. A proof of this theorem by induction, which corresponds to an efficient algorithm for constructing the closed path, is given next.

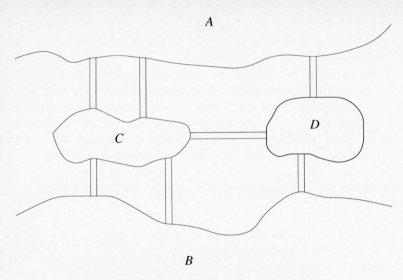

Figure 7.1 The Königsberg bridges problem.

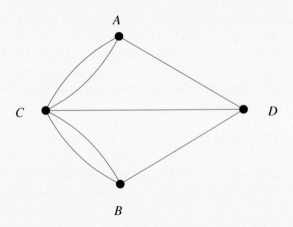

Figure 7.2 The graph corresponding to the Königsberg bridges problem.

The Problem   Given an undirected connected graph $G = (V, E)$ such that all the vertices have even degrees, find a closed path P such that each edge of E appears in P exactly once.

It is easy to prove that all vertices must have even degree for such a closed path to exist: When traversing a closed path, we enter and leave each vertex the same number of times. Since each edge is used exactly once, the number of edges adjacent to each vertex must be even. To prove by induction that the condition is sufficient, we first have to decide which parameter to apply the induction. The first consideration is to be able to reduce the problem without changing it. If we remove a vertex or an edge, the resulting graph may not satisfy the even-degree property. We should remove a set of edges S such that, for each vertex v in the graph, the number of edges from S adjacent to v is even (possibly 0). Any circuit satisfies this requirement, so the question is whether an Eulerian graph always contains a circuit. Suppose that we start traversing the graph, without going through any edge more than once, from an arbitrary vertex v in an arbitrary order. We claim that the traversal will eventually return to v because, whenever we enter another vertex, we reduce the degree of that vertex by 1, making it odd, and therefore we can always leave it. (Note that this circuit may not include all the edges.)

We are now ready to state the induction hypothesis and prove the theorem.

> **Induction hypothesis:** *A connected graph with $< m$ edges, all of whose vertices have even degrees, contains a closed path that includes each edge exactly once, and we know how to find that path.*

(It is easier to state the induction hypothesis in terms of the number of edges rather than the number of closed paths, even though the induction is performed on paths.) Consider a graph $G = (V, E)$ with m edges. Let P be a closed path in G. Let G' be the graph resulting from removals of all the edges of P from G. The degrees of all vertices in G' must be even, since the number of removed edges adjacent to any vertex is even. But we cannot simply apply the induction hypothesis yet, since G' may not be connected. Let $G'_1, G'_2, ..., G'_k$ be the connected components of G'. In each component, the degrees of all vertices are even. Furthermore, the number of edges in each component (indeed, in all of them together) is $< m$. Hence, we can now apply the induction hypothesis to each component. That is, by the induction hypothesis, each component has a closed path that includes every edge exactly once, and we know how to find it. Denote these k closed paths by $P_1, P_2, ..., P_k$. We now need to merge all these paths to one closed path covering the whole graph G. We start with any vertex in P and traverse P until we meet the first vertex v_j belonging to one of the components G'_j. At this point, we traverse the path P_j returning to v_j. We can continue this way, traversing the paths of the components the first time we meet them, until we return to the starting vertex. At this point, all edges will have been traversed exactly once. This closed path is called an **Eulerian circuit**. The algorithm is not yet complete. We still need to find an efficient method to identify the connected components, and an efficient method to traverse the graph. Both of those issues are discussed next. The implementation of the Eulerian circuit algorithm is left as an exercise.

7.3 Graph Traversals

The first problem we encounter when trying to design a graph algorithm is how to look at the input. This was a trivial problem in the previous chapter because of the one-dimensionality of the input — sequences and sets can be easily scanned in linear order. Scanning a graph, or **traversing** it, as we call it, is not straightforward. We present two traversal algorithms — **depth-first search** (DFS), and **breadth-first search** (BFS). Most of the algorithms in this chapter depend, in one way or another, on one of these techniques.

7.3.1 Depth-First Search

The depth-first search algorithms for directed graphs and undirected graphs are almost identical. However, since we also want to explore several graph properties that are different in directed graphs and in undirected graphs, we divide the discussion into two parts.

Undirected Graphs

Suppose that the undirected graph $G = (V, E)$ correspond to an art gallery consisting of an arrangement of corridors where the paintings are hung. The edges of G correspond to the corridors, and the vertices correspond to the intersections of the corridors. We want to walk through the gallery and see all the paintings. We assume that we can see both sides of a corridor when we walk through it in any direction. If the graph is Eulerian, then it is possible to walk throughout the gallery visiting each corridor exactly once. We do not assume here that the graph is Eulerian, and we allow each edge to be traversed more than once (as it turns out, each edge will be traversed exactly twice). The idea behind depth-first search is the following. We walk through the gallery trying to enter new corridors whenever we can. The first time we visit an intersection, we leave a pebble there, and we continue from another corridor (unless it is a deadend). When we arrive at an intersection that already has a pebble, we return through the same corridor from which we came, and try another corridor. If all the corridors leading from the intersection have already been visited, then we remove the pebble from this intersection, and return through the corridor from which we first entered. We will not visit this intersection again. (Removing the pebbles is done only to clean the gallery; it is not an essential part of the algorithm.) We always try to explore new corridors; we return from the corridor from which we first entered an intersection, only if we tried all other corridors. We call this approach **depth-first search** (DFS) to indicate that we first try to visit new edges (going deeper into the gallery). The main reasons for the usefulness of DFS is the way it divides the graph and its adaptability to recursive algorithms.

The description we gave of DFS was in terms of walking and putting down pebbles. Let's see now how DFS is implemented for undirected graphs given in the adjacency list representation. The traversal is started from an arbitrary vertex r, which is called the **root of the DFS**. The root is **marked** as visited. An arbitrary (unmarked) vertex r_1, connected to r, is then picked and a DFS starting from r_1 is performed (recursively). The recursion stops when it reaches a vertex v such that all the vertices connected to v are already marked. If, after the DFS for r_1 terminates, all the vertices adjacent to r are marked, then the DFS for r terminates. Otherwise, another arbitrary unmarked vertex r_2 connected to r is picked, a DFS starting from r_2 is performed, and so on.

There is generally a purpose for traversing the graph. To incorporate different applications with the DFS framework, we associate two types of work, *preWORK* and *postWORK*, with visiting a vertex or an edge; *preWORK* is performed at the time the vertex is marked, and *postWORK* is performed after we backtrack from an edge or find that the edge leads to a marked vertex. Both *preWORK* and *postWORK* depend on the application of DFS. This notation allows us to present several applications by defining only *preWORK* and *postWORK*. The DFS program is given in Fig. 7.3. The starting vertex of the recursive call is *v*. For simplicity, we first assume that the graph is connected. An example is given in Fig. 7.4, where the numbers associated with the vertices indicate the order in which the vertices could be traversed by DFS.

Algorithm Depth_First_Search (*G*, *v*) ;
Input: *G* = (*V*, *E*) (an undirected connected graph), and *v* (a vertex of *G*).
Output: depends on the application.

begin
    mark v ;
    perform preWORK on v ; { preWORK depends on the application of DFS }
    for *all edges* (*v*, *w*) **do**
        if *w is unmarked* **then** *Depth_First_Search(G, w) ;*
        perform postWORK for (v, w)
        { postWORK depends on the application of DFS; it is sometimes
        performed only on edges leading to newly marked vertices. }
end

Figure 7.4 Algorithm *Depth_First_Search*.

□ Lemma 7.1

If G is connected, then all its vertices will be marked by algorithm Depth_First_Search, and all its edges will be looked at at least once during the execution of the algorithm.

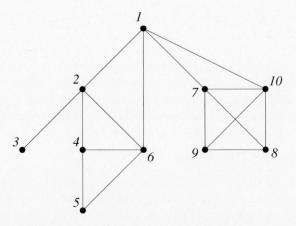

Figure 7.4 A DFS for an undirected graph.

Proof: Suppose the contrary, and let U denote the set of unmarked vertices remaining at the end of the algorithm. Since G is connected, at least one vertex from U must be connected to at least one marked vertex. But this situation cannot happen, since whenever a vertex is visited, all the unmarked vertices adjacent to it are visited (hence marked) too. Since all vertices are visited, and since whenever a vertex is visited all its edges are considered, all edges are considered. □

If a graph $G = (V, E)$ is not connected, we have to modify DFS slightly. If all vertices are marked after the first try, then the graph is connected and we are done. Otherwise, we start with an arbitrary unmarked vertex, perform another DFS, and so on. Thus, we can use DFS to determine whether or not a graph is connected and to find its connected components. The corresponding algorithm is given in Fig 7.5. We will generally consider only connected graphs, because otherwise we can usually deal with each connected component separately. Thus, we will use DFS as it is described in Fig. 7.3, without specifically mentioning that it may have to be run several times as in Fig. 7.5.

Algorithm Connected_Components (G) ;
Input: $G = (V, E)$ (an undirected graph).
Output: v.Component is set to the number of the component containing v,
      for every vertex v.

begin
    Component_Number := 1 ;
    while there is an unmarked vertex v **do**
        Depth_First_Search(G, v) ;
        (using the following preWORK:
            v.Component := Component_Number ;)
        Component_Number := Component_Number + 1
end

Figure 7.5 Algorithm *Connected_Components*.

Complexity   It is easy to see that each edge is looked at exactly twice (once from each end). Therefore, the running time is proportional to the number of edges. However, since the graph may contain many vertices that are not connected to anything (and all of them must be examined), we must include $O(|V|)$ in the expression for the running time. Therefore, the overall running time is $O(|V| + |E|)$.

Constructing the DFS Tree

Next, we present two simple uses of DFS — numbering the vertices with **DFS numbers**, and building a special spanning tree, called the **DFS tree**. The DFS numbers and the DFS tree exhibit special properties that are useful for many algorithms. Even if the tree is not built explicitly, it is easier to understand many algorithms by considering it. To describe these algorithms, we need only to describe either *preWORK* or *postWORK*. The algorithm for numbering the vertices with DFS numbers is given in Fig. 7.6, and the algorithm for building the DFS tree is given in Fig. 7.7. These two algorithms need not be performed separately.

Algorithm DFS_Numbering (G, v) ;
Input: $G = (V, E)$ (an undirected graph), and v (a vertex of G).
Output: for every vertex v, $v.DFS$ is set to the DFS number of v.

Initially DFS_Number := 1 ;
Use DFS with the following preWORK:
preWORK:
    v.DFS := DFS_Number ;
    DFS_Number := DFS_Number + 1 ;

Figure 7.6 Algorithm *DFS_Numbering*.

Algorithm Build_DFS_Tree (G, v) ;
Input: $G = (V, E)$ (an undirected graph), and v (a vertex of G).
Output: T (a DFS tree of G; T is initially empty).

Use DFS with the following postWORK:
postWORK :
    if *w was unmarked* **then** *add the edge* (v, w) *to T ;*
    *{ the statement above can be included in the **if** statement (line 4) of*
        algorithm Depth_First_Search }

Figure 7.7 Algorithm *Build_DFS_Tree*.

A vertex v is called an **ancestor** of a vertex w in a tree T with root r, if v is on the unique path from w to r in T. If v is an ancestor of w, then w is called a **descendant** of v.

□ **Lemma 7.2** (The main property of undirected DFS trees)

Let $G = (V, E)$ be a connected undirected graph, and let $T = (V, F)$ be a DFS tree of G constructed by algorithm Build_DFS_Tree. Every edge $e \in E$ either belongs to T (i.e., $e \in F$), or connects two vertices of G, one of which is the ancestor of the other in T.

Proof: Let (v, u) be an edge of G, and suppose that v is visited by DFS before u. After v is marked, we perform DFS starting from all neighbors of v that have not been marked yet. Since u is a neighbor of v, the DFS will either start from u, in which case (v, u) will belong to T, or the DFS will visit u before it backtracks from v, in which case u is a descendant of v in T.   □

In other words, DFS avoids **cross edges**, which are edges connecting vertices sideways across the tree. Avoiding cross edges is important for recursive procedures performed on the graph, as we will see later.

Since DFS is a very important program, we also include its nonrecursive version. The main tool for implementing a recursive program is a stack, which keeps information needed to ''unfold'' the recursive calls. A compiler maintains all the local data associated with every instance of the recursive procedure on the stack. Hence, when one recursive instance ends, we can get back to the exact point (with the exact information) in the calling procedure (which may be another instance of the same recursive procedure). Frequently, not all local data need to be maintained on the stack, which is one reason why using nonrecursive procedures is more efficient. The nonrecursive version we give next is a good example of a translation from a recursive to a nonrecursive program.

One major difficulty we face in translating a recursive version into a nonrecursive version is that we need explicit bookkeeping. We called DFS recursively inside a *for* loop, and expected the program to remember the right place in the loop from which to continue after the end of the recursive call. In a nonrecursive version, we must maintain this information explicitly. We assume that each vertex v has a linked list of its incident edges in a certain order (DFS will follow this order). The list is pointed to by $v.First$. Each item in the list is a record containing two variables: *Vertex* and *Next*. *Vertex* is the name of the vertex on the other side of the edge, and *Next* points to the next item. *Next* of the last edge on the list points to nil. DFS proceeds as before, traversing down the tree until no new vertices are found. A stack is maintained throughout the search. The stack contains all the vertices on the path from the root to the current vertex (in the order of the path). Between every two vertices *Parent* and *Child*, the stack contains a pointer to the edge from *Parent* that is the next one DFS traverses when it backtracks from *Child*. The nonrecursive version of DFS is given in Fig. 7.8.

Directed Graphs

The procedure for DFS for directed graphs is identical to that for undirected graphs. However, directed DFS trees have different properties. It is no longer true that there are no cross edges, as can be seen in Fig. 7.9. There are now four types of edges — **tree edges**, **back edges**, **forward edges**, and **cross edges**. The first three types of edges connect two vertices one of which is a descendant of the other in the tree: Tree edges connect parents to children in the tree, back edges connect descendants to ancestors, and forward edges connect ancestors to descendants. Only cross edges connect vertices not ''related'' in the tree. Cross edges, however, must cross from ''right to left,'' as is shown in the next lemma.

□ **Lemma 7.3** (The main property of directed DFS trees)

Let $G = (V, E)$ be a directed graph, and let $T = (V, F)$ be a DFS tree of G. If (v, w) is an edge in E such that v.DFS_Number < w.DFS_Number, then w is a descendant of v in the tree T.

Algorithm Nonrecursive_Depth_First_Search (G, v) ;
Input: $G = (V, E)$ (an undirected connected graph), and v (a vertex of G).
Output: depends on the application.
    { We use the Pascal pointer symbol ˆ explicitly here;
    we will not do that in the rest of this chapter. }

begin
    while *there is an unmarked vertex v* **do**
        mark v ;
        perform preWORK on v ;
        Edge := v.First ;
        push v and Edge to the top of the stack ;
        Parent := v ;
        { initialization up to here; now comes the main loop of the recursion }
        while *the stack is not empty* **do**
            remove Edge from the top of the stack ;
            while *Edge ≠ nil* **do**
                Child := Edgeˆ.Vertex ;
                if *Child is unmarked* **then**
                    mark Child ;
                    perform preWORK on Child ;
                    push Edgeˆ.Next to the top of the stack ;
                    { so that we can return to the next edge when we are done
                      with Child }
                    Edge := Child.First ;
                    Parent := Child ;
                    push Parent to the top of the stack ;
                else *{ Edge is a back edge }*
                    perform postWORK for (Parent, Child) ;
                    { this step is skipped if we perform postWORK only on
                      tree edges }
                    Edge := Edgeˆ.Next ;
            remove Child from the top of the stack ;
            if *the stack is not empty* **then**
            { the stack becomes empty when Child is the root }
                let Edge and Parent be at the top of the stack ;
                  { do not remove them }
                perform postWORK for (Parent, Child)
end

Figure 7.8 Algorithm *Nonrecursive_Depth_First_Search.*

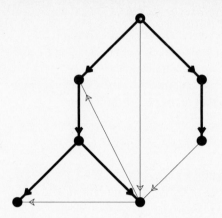

Figure 7.9 A DFS tree for a directed graph.

Proof: Since the DFS number of w is greater than that of v, w was visited after v. Since (v, w) is an edge in E, (v, w) must be considered during the DFS of v. If at that time w was unmarked, (v, w) would be added to the tree; hence, $(v, w) \in F$, and the condition is satisfied. Otherwise, w was marked after v during the recursive call of DFS from v. Hence, w must be a descendant of v in the tree T.   □

DFS for connected undirected graphs, starting from any vertex, traverses the whole graph. This is not so for directed graphs. Consider the directed graph in Fig. 7.10. If DFS starts at a, for example, then only the left column will be traversed. DFS will traversed the whole graph of Fig. 7.10 only if it starts at v. If v and its two incident edges are deleted from the graph, then there is no vertex from which a DFS traverses the whole graph. We must start again from an unmarked vertex, and continue doing so until all vertices are marked. Therefore, whenever we talk about DFS for directed graphs, we assume that it is run until all the vertices are marked and all the edges are considered.

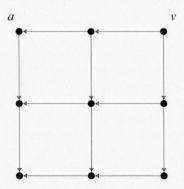

Figure 7.10 An example of a directed DFS that does not traverse the whole graph.

As an example, we show how to use DFS to determine whether or not a graph is acyclic.

The Problem Given a directed graph $G = (V, E)$, determine whether it contains a (directed) cycle.

□ Lemma 7.4

Let $G = (V, E)$ be a directed graph, and let T be a DFS tree of G. Then, G contains a directed cycle if and only if G contains a back edge (relative to T).

Proof: If there is a back edge, then it leads to a vertex higher up in the tree, so it completes a cycle. Conversely, let C be a cycle in G and let v be the vertex in C with the lowest DFS number. We claim that the edge (w, v) leading to v in C is a back edge. It cannot be a forward or a tree edge, since it leads from a higher DFS-numbered vertex to a lower DFS-numbered vertex. Suppose that v is not an ancestor of w in the tree, and let u be the lowest common ancestor of v and w. Since v has a lower DFS number than that of w, it is in a subtree of u that was visited before the subtree of u that contains w. This implies that the only way to reach w from v is through u or an ancestor of u (since it is impossible to go "from left to right"). But, C contains a path from v to w, and C cannot contain an ancestor of v since v has the lowest DFS number in C. □

The algorithm for determining whether a directed graph is acyclic is given in Fig. 7.11.

Algorithm Find_a_Cycle (G) ;
Input: $G = (V, E)$ (a directed graph).
Output: *Find_a_Cycle* (true if G contains a cycle and false otherwise).

Use DFS, starting from an arbitrary vertex, with the following preWORK and postWORK:

preWORK:
    v.on_the_path := true ;
{ x.on_the_path is true if x is on the path from the root to the current vertex }
{ initially x.on_the_path = false for all vertices, and Find_a_Cycle is false }

postWORK:
    if *w.on_the_path* **then** *Find_a_Cycle := true ; halt ;*
    if *w is the last vertex on v's list* **then** *v.on_the_path := false ;*

Figure 7.11 Algorithm *Find_a_Cycle*.

7.3.2 Breadth-First Search

Breadth-first search (BFS) traverses the graph in what seems like a more organized order — it does so level by level. If we start from a vertex v, then all v's children are visited first. The second level includes a visit to all the ''grandchildren,'' and so on (see Fig. 7.12). The traversal is implemented similarly to the nonrecursive implementation of DFS, except that the stack is replaced by a queue. We can associate BFS numbers with vertices similarly to DFS numbers. That is, a vertex w has BFS number k if it was the kth vertex to be marked by BFS. We can build a BFS tree by including only edges that lead to newly visited vertices. The BFS algorithm is given in Fig. 7.13. (The notion of *postWORK* is not as well defined for BFS as it is for DFS, since intuitively the search does not proceed ''down and up,'' but only down; we therefore omit it.)

□ **Lemma 7.5**

If an edge (u,w) belongs to a BFS tree, such that u is a parent of w, then u has the minimal BFS number among vertices with edges leading to w.

Proof: The claim follows from the first-in-first-out property of the queue.   □

□ **Lemma 7.6**

For each vertex w, the path from the root to w in T is a shortest path from the root to w in G.

Proof: Left to the reader.   □

The **level** of a vertex w is the length of the path in the tree from the root to w. BFS traverses the graph level by level.

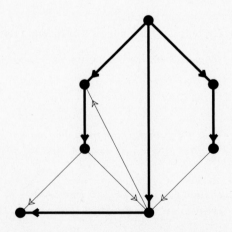

Figure 7.12 A BFS tree for a directed graph.

Algorithm Breadth_First_Search (G, v) ;
Input: $G = (V, E)$ (an undirected connected graph), and v (a vertex of G).
Output: depends on the application.

begin
    mark v ;
    put v in a queue { First In First Out };
    while the queue is not empty do
        remove the first vertex w from the queue ;
        perform preWORK on w ;
           { preWORK depends on the application of BFS }
        for all edges (w, x) such that x is unmarked do
        mark x ;
        add (w, x) to the tree T ;
        put x in the queue
end

Figure 7.13 Algorithm *Breadth_First_Search*.

□ Lemma 7.7

If (v,w) is an edge in E that does not belong to T, then it connects two vertices whose level numbers differ by at most 1.

Proof: Left to the reader. □

Now that we know how to traverse a graph, we present several algorithms involving graphs. We again use the design-by-induction technique very heavily.

7.4 Topological Sorting

Suppose that there is a set of tasks that need to be performed one at a time. Some tasks depend on other tasks and they cannot be started until the other tasks are completed. All the dependencies are known, and we want to arrange a schedule for performing the tasks which is consistent with the dependencies (i.e., every task is scheduled to be performed only after all the tasks on which it is dependent are completed). We want to design a fast algorithm to generate such a schedule. This problem is called **topological sorting**. We can associate a directed graph with the tasks and their dependencies in the following way. Each task is associated with a vertex and there is a directed edge from task x to task y if y cannot start until x is finished. Obviously, the graph must be acyclic; otherwise, some tasks can never be started.

> **The Problem**   Given a directed acyclic graph $G = (V, E)$ with n vertices, label the vertices from 1 to n such that, if v is labeled k, then all vertices that can be reached from v by a directed path are labeled with labels $>k$.

The straightforward induction hypothesis is the following.

> **Induction hypothesis:** *We know how to label all directed acyclic graphs with $< n$ vertices according to the conditions above.*

The base case of one vertex is trivial. As usual, we consider a graph with n vertices, remove one vertex, apply the induction hypothesis, and try to extend the labeling. We are free to choose any vertex as the nth vertex. Therefore, we should choose a vertex that will simplify our work. We need to label vertices. Which vertex is the easiest to label? It is clearly a vertex (task) with no dependencies — namely, a vertex whose indegree is zero. This vertex can be labeled 1 without any problems. Can we always find a vertex of indegree zero? The answer is intuitively yes, since we must be able to start somewhere. The following lemma establishes this fact.

□ Lemma 7.8

A directed acyclic graph always contains a vertex with indegree 0.

Proof: If all the vertices had positive indegrees, then we could traverse the graph "backward" and never have to stop. Since there are finitely many vertices, however, we must go through a cycle, which is impossible in an acyclic graph. (By the same argument, there is a vertex with outdegree 0.)   □

We will see shortly how to find a vertex with indegree 0. Once we find it, we label it 1, remove it with its adjacent edges, and label the rest of the graph — which is still acyclic, of course — with labels 2 to n. (To be completely precise, the induction hypothesis assumed labels of 1 to $n - 1$ instead of 2 to n, but this causes no problems.) Notice that once we decided to select a vertex of indegree 0 for the reduction, the algorithm followed with little effort.

Implementation   The only implementation problems are how to find a vertex with indegree 0 and how to adjust the indegrees when a vertex is removed. We associate a variable *Indegree* with each vertex, such that initially $v.Indegree$ is equal to v's indegree. The *Indegree* variables can be initialized by traversing all the edges in any order (using DFS, for example), and incrementing $w.Indegree$ whenever an edge (v, w) is traversed. The vertices with indegree 0 are put in a queue (a stack will do just as well). By Lemma 7.8, there is at least one vertex v with indegree 0. It is easy to find v — it is simply removed from the queue. Then, for each edge (v, w) coming out of v, the counter of w is decreased by 1. When a counter becomes 0, the vertex is put on the queue. A removal of v leaves the graph still acyclic. Therefore, by Lemma 7.8, there must be at least one vertex of indegree 0 in the remaining graph. The algorithm terminates when the queue becomes empty, in which case all the vertices have been labeled. The algorithm is given in Fig. 7.14.

Complexity   Initializing the *Indegree* variables requires $O(|V| + |E|)$ time. Finding a vertex with indegree 0 takes constant time (accessing a queue). Each edge (v, w) is considered once (when v is taken from the queue). Thus, the number of times the variables need to be updated is exactly equal to the number of edges in the graph. The running time of the algorithm is therefore $O(|V| + |E|)$, which is linear in the size of the input.

7.5 Single-Source Shortest Paths

In this section, we deal with **weighted graphs**. Let $G = (V, E)$ be a directed graph with nonnegative **weights** associated with the edges. We will call the weights *lengths* in this section, because traditionally the problem is called the *shortest* path problem (rather than the *lightest* path problem). (Length of a path also sometimes denotes the number of edges in the path; we will be careful to avoid confusion.) If the graph is undirected, we can think of it as a directed graph such that each undirected edge corresponds to two directed edges (in opposite directions) with the same length. Thus, the discussion in this section applies to undirected graphs as well. The **length of a path** is the sum of the lengths of its edges.

Algorithm Topological_Sorting (G) :
Input: $G = (V, E)$ (a directed acyclic graph).
Output: The *Label* field indicates a topological sorting of G.

begin
    Initialize v.Indegree for all vertices ; { e.g., by DFS }
    G_label := 0 ;
    for i := 1 to n do
        *if v_i.Indegree = 0 **then** put v_i in Queue ;*
    repeat
        remove vertex v from Queue ;
        G_label := G_label + 1 ;
        v.label := G_label ;
        for all edges (v, w) do
            w.Indegree := w.Indegree - 1 ;
            *if w.Indegree = 0 **then** put w in Queue ;*
    until Queue is empty
end

Figure 7.14 Algorithm *Topological_Sorting*.

> **The Problem**   Given a directed graph $G = (V, E)$ and a vertex v, find
> shortest paths from v to all other vertices of G.

For simplicity, we discuss only how to find the length of the shortest paths. The algorithms can be extended to find the actual paths. There are many examples of shortest path problems. For example, the graph may correspond to a road map, and the length of a segment may correspond to its actual length, to the expected time it takes to travel through it, or to the cost of constructing it, depending on the problem.

The Acyclic Case

Let's first assume that the graph G is acyclic. The problem is easier in this case, and its solution will help us to find a solution to the general case. We try induction on the number of vertices. The base case is trivial. Let $|V| = n$. We can use topological sorting as discussed in the previous section. If the label of v is k, then all vertices with labels $< k$ need not be considered. There is no way to reach these vertices from v. Furthermore, the order imposed by the topological sorting is a good order for the induction. Consider the last vertex, namely, the vertex z with label n. Suppose (inductively) that we already know the shortest paths from v to all vertices except for z. Denote the length of the shortest path from v to w by $w.SP$. To find $z.SP$, we need only to check those vertices w with edges leading to z. Since the shortest paths to all other vertices are already known, $z.SP$ is equal to the minimum, over all w with an edge to z, of $w.SP + length(w, z)$. Are we done? We have to be careful that adding z does not shorten the distance to other vertices. But, since z is the last vertex in the topological order, no other vertex in the graph can be reached from z, so no other path is affected. Therefore, by removing z, computing the shortest paths without it, then putting it back, we have solved the problem. The corresponding induction hypothesis is the following.

> **Induction hypothesis:** *Given a topological ordering, we know how to find the lengths of the shortest paths from v to the first $n - 1$ vertices.*

Given an acyclic graph with n vertices in a topological order, we remove the nth vertex, solve the reduced problem by induction, then take the minimum of the values $w.SP + length(w, z)$ over all w such that $(w, z) \in E$. The algorithm is given in Fig. 7.15. We now improve the algorithm such that the topological order can be found hand in hand with the shortest paths. In other words, we want to combine the two passes, one for the topological sorting and one for the shortest paths, into one pass.

Consider the way the algorithm will be executed recursively (after the topological order is found). Assume, for simplicity, that the label of v in the topological order is 1. The first step is the call to the recursive procedure. It will call itself repeatedly until v is reached. At that time, the length of the shortest path to v is set to 0, and the recursion starts to unfold. The vertex u with label 2 will be considered next, and the length of its shortest path will be set to the length of the edge from v to u if it exists; otherwise, there is no path from v to u. The next step will be to check the vertex x with label 3. In this

---

Algorithm Acyclic_Shortest_Paths (G, v, n) ;
Input: $G = (V, E)$ (a weighted acyclic graph), v (a vertex),
    and n (the number of vertices).
Output: For every vertex $w \in V$, $w.SP$ is the length of the shortest path
    from v to w.
{ We assume that a topological sort has already been performed. An improved
algorithm, which computes the topological order as well, is given in Fig. 7.16. }

begin
    let z be the vertex labeled n { in the topological order };
    if $z \neq v$ **then**
        Acyclic_Shortest_Paths (G − z, v, n − 1) ;
        { G − z results from removing z with its incident edges from G }
        for *all w such that* $(w, z) \in E$ **do**
            if $w.SP + length(w, z) < z.SP$ **then**
                $z.SP := w.SP + length(w, z)$;
    else $v.SP := 0$
end

Figure 7.15 Algorithm *Acyclic_Shortest_Paths*.

---

case, there may be edges to x from v and/or from u, and the corresponding paths will be compared. Instead of applying recursion in some sense ''backward,'' we now try to execute the same steps in increasing order of labels.

The induction is applied in increasing order of labels starting from v. This order will eliminate the need to know the labels in advance, and we will be able to run both algorithms at the same time. We assume that the lengths of the shortest paths to vertices labeled 1 to m are known, and we consider the vertex labeled $m + 1$, call it z. To find the shortest path to z, we need to check all edges coming into z. The topological order guarantees that all such edges come from vertices with smaller labels. By the induction hypothesis, these vertices have already been considered; hence, the lengths of the shortest paths to them are already known. For each such edge (w, z), we know the length of the shortest path to w, $w.SP$, hence the shortest path through this edge to z is $w.SP + length(w, z)$. Therefore, the length of the shortest path to z is the minimum, over all w, of $w.SP + length(w, z)$. Furthermore, as before, we need not worry about adjusting shortest paths to vertices with lower labels, since there is no way to reach any of them from z. The improved algorithm is given in Fig. 7.16.

Complexity Each edge is checked once in the initialization of the indegrees and once when its tail is removed from the queue. The queue is accessed in constant time. Each vertex is considered only once. Therefore, the worst-case running time is $O(|V| + |E|)$.

Algorithm Improved_Acyclic_Shortest_Paths (G, v) ;
Input: $G = (V, E)$ (a weighted acyclic graph), v (a vertex of G).
Output: For every vertex w, $w.SP$ is the length of the shortest path from v to w.
{ *This is a nonrecursive version of the previous algorithm, and it includes*
  topological sorting }

begin
    for *all vertices w* **do**
        w.SP := ∞ ;
    Initialize v.indegree for all vertices ; { e.g., by DFS }
    for *i := 1 to n* **do**
        if *v_i.indegree = 0* **then** *put v_i in Queue ;*
    v.SP := 0 ;
    repeat
        remove vertex w from Queue ;
        for *all edges (w, z)* **do**
            if *w.SP + length(w, z) < z.SP* **then**
                z.SP := w.SP + length(w, z) ;
                z.indegree := z.indegree − 1 ;
                if *z.indegree = 0* **then** *put z in Queue ;*
    until *Queue is empty*
end

Figure 7.16 Algorithm *Improved_Acyclic_Shortest_Paths*.

The General Case

When the graph is not acyclic, there is no such thing as a topological order, and the algorithms we just discussed cannot be applied directly. It may be possible, however, to use the ideas of these algorithms for the general case. The simplicity of the algorithms we presented is a result of the following feature of topological order:

> *If z is a vertex with label k, then (1) there are no paths from z to vertices*
> *with labels < k, and (2) there are no paths from vertices with labels > k to*
> *z.*

This feature enables us to find the shortest path from v to z without having to consider the vertices that are after z in the topological order. Can we somehow define an order on the vertices of a general graph that will allow us to do something similar?

The idea is to consider the vertices of the graph in the order imposed by the lengths of their shortest paths from v. We do not know these lengths initially, of course; we will find them during the execution of the algorithm. First, we check all the edges coming out of v. Let (v, x) be the edge of minimum length among them. Since all lengths are positive, the shortest path from v to x is the edge (v, x). All other paths from v are at least as long. So, we know the shortest path to x, and this can serve as the base case for the induction. Let's try one more step. How can we find the shortest path to one more vertex? We choose the vertex that is second closest to v (x is the first closest). The only paths we need to consider are other edges from v or paths consisting of two edges — the first edge is (v, x) and the second is an edge from x. We choose the minimum of $length(v, y)$ ($y \neq x$) or $length(v, x) + length(x, z)$ ($z \neq v$). Again, we do not need to consider any other paths, since this is the shortest way to get out of v (except to x). Here is the general induction hypothesis.

> **Induction hypothesis:** *Given a graph and a vertex v, we know the k vertices that are closest to v and the lengths of the shortest paths to them.*

Notice that the induction is on the number of vertices whose shortest paths have already been computed and not on the size of the graph. Furthermore, it assumes that these are the closest vertices to v and that we can identify them. We know how to find the closest vertex (x above), so the base case, with $k = 1$, is solved. When $k = |V| - 1$, the complete problem is solved.

Denote the set containing v and the k closest vertices to v by V_k. The problem is to find a vertex w that is closest to v among the vertices *not* in V_k, and to find the shortest path from v to w. The shortest path from v to w can go through only the vertices in V_k. It cannot include vertices not in V_k, since they would then be closer to v than w. Therefore, to find w, it is sufficient to consider only edges connecting vertices from V_k to vertices not in V_k; all other edges can be ignored for now. Let (u, z) be an edge such that u is in V_k and z is not. Such an edge corresponds to a path from v to z, which consists of the shortest path from v to u (already known by induction) and the edge (u, z). We need only to compare all such paths, and take the shortest among them.

The algorithm implied by the induction hypothesis is the following. At each iteration, a new vertex is added. It is the vertex w such that the length

$$\min_{u \in V_k} (u.SP + length(u, w)) \tag{7.1}$$

is the minimal over all w not in V_k. By the arguments above, w is indeed the $(k+1)$th closest vertex to v; thus, adding it extends the induction hypothesis.

The algorithm is complete now, but its efficiency can be improved. The main step of the algorithm involves finding the next closest vertex. This is done by computing the minimal path length according to (7.1). However, it is not necessary to check all the values $u.SP + length(u, w)$ in every step. Most of these values are not changed when a new vertex is added; only those that correspond to paths that go through the new vertex may change. We can maintain the lengths of the known shortest paths to all vertices in V_k, and *update* them only when V_k is extended. The only way to find better shortest paths when w is added to V_k is to go through w. Therefore, we need to check all edges coming out of w to vertices not in V_k. For each such edge (w, z), we check the length of $w.SP + length(w, z)$, and update $z.SP$ if necessary. Thus, each iteration involves finding a vertex with minimum SP value, and updating the SP values of some of the remaining vertices.

Implementation   We need to be able to find a minimum among a set of path lengths, and to update path lengths frequently. A heap is a good data structure for finding minimum elements and updating lengths of elements. Since we need to find the vertex with minimum path length, we keep all vertices not yet in V_k in a heap with their current known shortest path lengths from v as their keys. Initially, all but one of the path lengths are ∞, so the heap is ordered in no particular order (except that v is on top). Finding w is easy; we can simply take it from the top of the heap. All the edges (w, u) can be checked and the path lengths can be updated without difficulty. However, when a path length to, say, z is updated, z's place in the heap may change. We need to be able to modify the heap accordingly. To do that, we need to know z's position in the heap. (Remember that a heap is not a search structure; it does not provide any facilities to locate an element.) Locating z in the heap can be done with another data structure connected to the heap. Since the identities of all vertices are known ahead of time, we can put them in an array with pointers to their location in the heap. Finding a vertex in the heap thus requires only accessing the array. Since the elements of the heap are the vertices of the graph, the space requirement is only $O(|V|)$, which is reasonable. Path lengths only decrease. If an element of the heap becomes smaller than its parent, it can be exchanged and moved up until its appropriate position is found. This is exactly the same as the regular heap maintenance procedures (e.g., insert). The shortest paths algorithm is given in Fig. 7.17.

Algorithm *Single_Source_Shortest_Paths* (G, v) ;
Input: $G = (V, E)$ (a weighted directed graph), and v (the source vertex).
Output: for each vertex w, $w.SP$ is the length of the shortest path from v to w.
   { all lengths are assumed to be nonnegative. }

begin
    for all vertices w *do*
        w.mark := false ;
        $w.SP := \infty$;
    $v.SP := 0$;
    while there exists an unmarked vertex *do*
        let w be an unmarked vertex such that $w.SP$ is minimal ;
        w.mark := true ;
        for all edges (w, z) such that z is unmarked *do*
            if $w.SP + \text{length}(w, z) < z.SP$ *then*
                $z.SP := w.SP + \text{length}(w, z)$
    end

Figure 7.17 Algorithm *Single_Source_Shortest_Paths*.

Complexity   Updating the length of a path takes $O(\log m)$ comparisons, where m is the size of the heap. There are $|V|$ iterations, leading to $|V|$ deletions from the heap. There are also at most $|E|$ updates (since each edge can cause at most one update), leading to $O(|E|\log|V|)$ comparisons in the heap. Hence, the running time is $O((|E|+|V|)\log|V|)$. Notice that this algorithm is slower than the same algorithm for acyclic graphs, since the next vertex in the latter algorithm was taken from the (arbitrarily ordered) queue, and no updates were required.

□ Example 7.1

An example of algorithm *Single_Source_Shortest_Paths* is given in Fig. 7.18. The first line includes only paths of one edge from *v*. The shortest path is chosen, in this case, leading to vertex *a*. The second line shows the update of the paths including now all paths of one edge from either *v* or *a*, and the shortest path now leads to *c*. A new vertex is chosen in each line, and the current known shortest paths from *v* are listed to every vertex. The circled distances are those that are known to be the shortest.   □

Comments   This type of algorithm is sometimes called **priority search** — each vertex is assigned a priority (e.g., the current known distance from the source), and vertices are traversed according to that priority. When a vertex is considered, all its

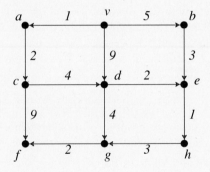

	v	*a*	*b*	*c*	*d*	*e*	*f*	*g*	*h*
a	0	1	5	∞	9	∞	∞	∞	∞
c	0	①	5	3	9	∞	∞	∞	∞
b	0	①	5	③	7	∞	12	∞	∞
d	0	①	⑤	③	7	8	12	∞	∞
e	0	①	⑤	③	⑦	8	12	11	∞
h	0	①	⑤	③	⑦	⑧	12	11	9
g	0	①	⑤	③	⑦	⑧	12	11	⑨
f	0	①	⑤	③	⑦	⑧	12	⑪	⑨

Figure 7.18   An example of the single-source shortest-paths algorithm.

adjacent edges are checked. That check may trigger a change in some priorities. The procedure for making that change is what distinguishes one priority search from another. Priority search is more expensive than regular search. It is useful for problems involving weighted graphs.

We found the shortest paths from v to all other vertices by finding one path at a time. Each additional path was identified by one edge, which led from a previously known shortest path to a new vertex. All those edges together form a tree with v as its root (Exercise 7.8). This tree, called the **shortest path tree**, is important in dealing with a variety of path problems.

7.6 Minimum-Cost Spanning Trees

Consider a network of computers connected through bidirectional links. There is a positive cost associated with sending a message on each of the links. We assume that the cost of sending a message on a specific link does not depend on the direction. We want to broadcast a message to all the computers starting from an arbitrary computer. We assume that the cost of the broadcast is the sum of the costs of the links used to forward the message. (Another possible definition of cost is the time it takes to complete the broadcast; see Exercise 7.63.) The network can be represented by an undirected graph with positive costs on the edges. The problem is to find a fixed connected subgraph (corresponding to the links used in the broadcast), containing all the vertices, such that the sum of the costs of the edges in the subgraph is minimum. It is not difficult to see that this subgraph must be a tree. If any cycle had been present, then we could have broken it by deleting one of its edges; the graph would still be connected, but the cost would be smaller since all costs are positive. This subgraph is called the **minimum-cost spanning tree** (MCST), and it has many uses besides broadcasts. Our goal is to find an efficient algorithm to find an MCST.[1] For simplicity, we assume that the costs are distinct. This assumption implies that the MCST is unique (Exercise 7.11), which makes the problem easier to discuss. The algorithm remains the same without this assumption, except that, when equal-cost edges are encountered, any one of them can be chosen (i.e., ties are broken arbitrarily). The proof of correctness is more complicated in this case.

The Problem   Given an undirected connected weighted graph $G = (V, E)$, find a spanning tree T of G of minimum cost.

(Notice that we now call the weights *costs*.) The straightforward induction hypothesis is the following.

---
[1] We assume here that the whole graph is known to us. The complete topology of a communication network and all current costs are usually unknown only at the local sites; therefore, a **distributed** algorithm is needed.

Induction hypothesis 1: *We know how to find the MCST for connected graphs with $< m$ edges.*

The base case is trivial. Given the MCST problem with m edges, how do we reduce it to a problem with $< m$ edges? We claim that the minimum-cost edge must be included in the MCST. If it is not included, then adding it to the MCST would create a cycle; removing any other edge from this cycle creates a tree again, but with smaller cost, which is a contradiction to the minimality of the MCST. So, we now know one edge that belongs to the MCST. We can remove this edge from the graph, and apply induction to the rest of the graph, which now contains less edges. Is that a valid use of induction?

This is not a valid use of induction, because, after we remove an edge, the problem we need to solve is not the same as the original problem. First, the selection of one edge limits the selection of other edges. Second, after we remove an edge, the graph may not be connected any more. We cannot emphasize this issue too strongly — the induction hypothesis has to be precisely defined and followed.

The solution is to adjust the induction hypothesis. We know how to select the first edge, but we cannot simply remove it and forget about it, since the rest of the selections depend on it. Therefore, instead of removing it, we mark it as being selected and use this fact (its selection) for the algorithm. The algorithm proceeds by selecting one edge at a time to the MCST. Thus, the induction is not on the size of the graph, but rather on the number of edges already selected in a given fixed graph.

Induction hypothesis 2: *Given a connected graph $G = (V, E)$, we know how to find a subgraph T of G with k edges ($k < |V| - 1$), such that T is a tree that is a subgraph of the MCST of G.*

We have already discussed the base case for this hypothesis, which is choosing the first edge. We assume that we have already found the tree T satisfying the induction hypothesis, and we need to extend T by one more edge. How can we find another edge that is guaranteed to be in the MCST? We apply the same argument that was used to find the first edge. T is already known to be part of the MCST. Hence, there must be at least one edge in the MCST connecting T to vertices not in T. We will try to find one such edge. Let E_k be the set of all edges connecting T to vertices not in T. We claim that the edge with minimum cost in E_k belongs to the MCST. Denote this edge by (u, w) (see Fig. 7.19). Since the MCST is a spanning tree, it contains a unique path from u to w (there exists a unique path between every two vertices in a tree). If (u, w) does not belong to the MCST, then it is not included in that path from u to w. But, since u does belong to T and w does not belong to T, there must be at least one edge (x, y) in this path that connects T to a vertex not in T. The cost of this edge is higher than the cost of (u, w), since (u, w) has the minimum cost among all such edges. But now we can use the same argument that we applied to the first selected edge. If we add (u, w) to the MCST and remove the edge (x, y), we get another spanning tree with smaller cost, which is a contradiction.

Implementation   This algorithm is very similar to the single-source shortest-path algorithm presented in the previous section. The first chosen edge is the edge with

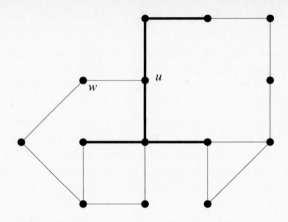

Figure 7.19 Finding the next edge of the MCST.

minimum cost. T is then defined as a tree with only this edge. In each iteration, we need to find the minimum-cost edge connecting T to vertices outside of T. In the shortest-path algorithm we found the minimum-length *path* leading outside of T. Hence, the only difference between the MCST algorithm and the shortest-path algorithm is that the minimum is taken not on the length of a path but on the cost of an edge. The rest of the algorithm is virtually the same. We maintain, for each vertex w not included in T, the minimum-cost edge leading to w from a vertex in T (or ∞ if no such edge exists). In each iteration, we choose the minimum-cost edge and connect the corresponding vertex w to T. We then check all the edges incident to w. If the cost of any such edge (w, z) (for z not in T) is smaller than the cost of the current best edge leading to z, we update z's cost. The algorithm is presented in Fig. 7.20.

Complexity   The complexity of this algorithm is identical to that of the single-source shortest-path algorithm presented in the previous section. The worst-case running time is $O((|V| + |E|) \log |V|)$.

□ **Example 7.2**

An example of algorithm *MCST* is illustrated in Fig. 7.21. The vertex in the first column of the table is the one that is added at that step. The first vertex is v, and the edges connected to v are listed along with their costs. The vertex with the minimum-cost edge is chosen in each line. The current best edges (and their costs) leading to unmarked vertices are updated at each step (only the tails of the edges are listed).   □

Comments   The algorithm for finding an MCST is an example, although not a pure one, of a method called the **greedy method**. Suppose that we are dealing with a set of elements, each with an associated cost, and that we are interested in finding the set of elements with maximum (or minimum) cost satisfying some constraints. In the MCST

Algorithm MCST (G) ;
Input: *G* (a weighted undirected graph).
Output: *T* (a minimum-cost spanning tree of *G*).

begin
    Initially T is the empty set ;
    for *all vertices w* **do**
        w.Mark := false ; { w.Mark is true if w is in T }
        w.Cost := ∞ ;
    let (x, y) be a minimum cost edge in G ;
    x.Mark := true ; { y will be marked in the main loop }
    for *all edges (x, z)* **do**
        z.Edge := (x, z) ; { a minimum cost edge from T to z }
        z.Cost := cost(x, z) ; { the cost of z.Edge }
    while *there exists an unmarked vertex* **do**
        let w be an unmarked vertex such that w.Cost is minimal ;
        if *w.Cost = ∞* **then**
            print "G is not connected" ;
            halt
        else
            w.Mark := true ;
            add w.Edge to T ;
            { we now update the costs of unmarked vertices connected to w }
            for *all edges (w, z)* **do**
                if *not z.Mark* **then**
                    if *cost(w, z) < z.Cost* **then**
                        z.Edge := (w, z) ;
                        z.Cost := cost(w, z)
  end

Figure 7.20 Algorithm *MCST*.

---

problem, the elements were the edges of the graph, and the constraint was that the edges correspond to a spanning tree. The greedy method is to be greedy and take the maximal-cost possible element at any step. In the MCST algorithm, we introduced some more constraints on the selection of edges, specifically, we considered only edges that were connected to the current tree. Therefore, the MCST algorithm is not purely greedy. We can also, however, find the MCST by selecting, at each step, the minimum-cost edge anywhere in the graph, provided that this edge does not form a cycle (Exercise 7.59). The greedy method does not always lead to an optimal solution. It is usually just a *heuristic* to find suboptimal solutions. Sometimes, however, as in the MCST example, the greedy method does lead to the best solution.

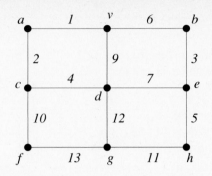

	v	a	b	c	d	e	f	g	h
v	-	v(1)	v(6)	∞	v(9)	∞	∞	∞	∞
a	-	-	v(6)	a(2)	v(9)	∞	∞	∞	∞
c	-	-	v(6)	-	c(4)	∞	c(10)	∞	∞
d	-	-	v(6)	-	-	d(7)	c(10)	d(12)	∞
b	-	-	-	-	-	b(3)	c(10)	d(12)	∞
e	-	-	-	-	-	-	c(10)	d(12)	e(5)
h	-	-	-	-	-	-	c(10)	h(11)	-
f	-	-	-	-	-	-	-	h(11)	-
g	-	-	-	-	-	-	-	-	-

Figure 7.21 An example of the minimum-cost spanning-tree algorithm.

7.7 All Shortest Paths

We now consider the problem of computing shortest paths between *all* pairs of vertices in a graph.

The Problem   Given a weighted graph $G = (V, E)$ (directed or un-directed) with nonnegative weights, find the minimum-length paths between all pairs of vertices.

Again, since we are talking about shortest paths, we refer to the weights as *lengths*. This problem is called the **all-pairs shortest-paths problem**. For simplicity, we discuss how to find only the lengths of the shortest paths, rather than the paths themselves. We assume that the graph is directed; the same arguments hold for undirected graphs. We assume throughout this section that all weights are nonnegative; Exercise 7.73 deals with negative lengths.

As usual, let's start with straightforward induction. We can use induction either on the edges or on the vertices. What is involved in terms of shortest paths in adding a new edge, say (u, w), to a graph? First, the edge may form a shorter path between u and w. Furthermore, there may be other shorter paths that use (u, w). In the worst case, we need to check, for every pair of vertices v_1 and v_2, whether the length of the shortest path from v_1 to u plus the length of (u, w) plus the length of the shortest path from w to v_2 is shorter than the known path from v_1 to v_2. Overall, for every new edge, we may have to make $O(|V|^2)$ checks, leading to a worst-case running time of $O(|E||V|^2)$. (Since the number of edges may be as large as $O(|V|^2)$, this is an $O(|V|^4)$ algorithm.)

What is involved in terms of shortest paths in adding a new vertex u to a graph? We first need to find the lengths of the shortest paths from u to all other vertices and from all other vertices to u. Since all shortest paths that do not involve u are already known, we can find the shortest path from u to w in the following way. We need only to determine the first edge out of u in this path. If this edge is (u, v), then the length of the path from u to w is the length of (u, v) plus the length of the shortest path from v to w (which is already known). We therefore compare these lengths for all vertices adjacent to u, and take the minimum length. The shortest path from w to u can be found similarly. But again, this is not enough. We still have to check, for any pair of vertices, whether there exists a shorter path between the two using the new vertex u. For each pair of vertices v and w, we check the length of getting from v to u plus the length of getting from u to w, and we compare this length to the length of the previously known shortest path. Overall $O(|V|^2)$ comparisons and additions are needed for each added vertex, leading to an $O(|V|^3)$ algorithm. The induction on vertices is thus better than the induction on edges, but there exists an even better induction method for this problem.

The trick is to leave the number of edges and vertices fixed, and to put restrictions on the type of paths allowed. The induction addresses the removals of these restrictions on the paths until, at the end, all possible paths are considered. We label the vertices from 1 to $|V|$. A path from u to w is called a *k-path* if, except for u and w, the highest-labeled vertex on the path is labeled k. In particular, a 0-path is an edge (since no other vertices can appear on the path).

Induction hypothesis: *We know the lengths of the shortest paths between all pairs of vertices such that only k-paths, for some $k < m$, are considered.*

The base of the induction is $m = 1$, in which case only direct edges can be considered and the solution is obvious. We assume the induction hypothesis for m, and we try to extend it to $m + 1$. We now have to consider all k-paths such that $k < m + 1$. So, the only new paths that we need to consider are m-paths. We have to find the shortest m-paths between all pairs of vertices, and to check whether they improve on the k-paths for $k < m$. Denote by v_m the vertex labeled m. Any shortest m-path must include v_m exactly once. The shortest m-path between u and w is the shortest k-path (for some $k < m$) between u and v_m appended by the shortest j-path (for some $j < m$, where j need not be equal to k) between v_m and w. By induction, we already know the lengths of all shortest k-paths for $k < m$; hence, we need only to sum the two lengths above to find the shortest m-path between u to w. Not only is this algorithm faster (by a constant factor) than the one using the straightforward induction on vertices, but it is also simple to program. The algorithm is given in Fig. 7.22.

Algorithm All_Pairs_Shortest_Paths *(Weight)* ;
Input: *Weight* (an $n \times n$ adjacency matrix representing a weighted graph).
{ *Weight* [*x*, *y*] is the weight of the edge (*x*, *y*) if it exists, or ∞ otherwise;
 Weight [*x*, *x*] is 0, for all *x* }
Output: At the end, the matrix *Weight* contains the lengths of the
   shortest paths.

begin
  for *m* := 1 **to** *n* **do**   { *the induction sequence* }
    for *x* := *1* **to** *n* **do**
      for *y* := *1* **to** *n* **do**
        if *Weight[x, m] + Weight[m, y] < Weight[x, y]* **then**
          Weight[x, y] := *Weight[x, m] + Weight[m, y]*
  end

Figure 7.22 Algorithm *All_Pairs_Shortest_Paths.*

The inner two loops of the algorithm are used to check all *pairs* of vertices. Notice that this check can be applied to the pairs of vertices in *any* order, since each check is independent of the others. Such flexibility is important, for example, for parallel algorithms.

Complexity   For each *m*, the algorithm involves only one sum and one comparison per pair of vertices. The induction sequence is of length $|V|$, so the total number of additions (and comparisons) is at most $|V|^3$. Recall that the running time of the single-source algorithm is $O(|E| \log |V|)$. If the graph is dense such that the number of edges is $\Omega(n^2)$, then using this algorithm is better than using the single-source algorithm for every vertex. Although it is possible to implement the single-source algorithm in time $O(|V|^2)$ (Exercise 7.43.), which will lead to an $O(|V|^3)$ algorithm for all-pairs shortest paths, the algorithm in this section is better for dense graphs because it is so simple to implement. On the other hand, if the graph is relatively sparse, then the running time of $O(|E| |V| \log |V|)$, resulting from using the single-source algorithm $|V|$ times, is better.

7.8 Transitive Closure

Given a directed graph $G = (V, E)$, the **transitive closure** $C = (V, F)$ of G is a directed graph such that there is an edge (*v*, *w*) in C if and only if there is a directed path from *v* to *w* in G. The transitive closure is related, for example, to the user-accounts security problem mentioned at the beginning of this chapter. The vertices correspond to the users, and the edges correspond to permissions. The transitive closure identifies for each user all the other users with permission (either directly or indirectly) to use his or her account. There are many other applications of the transitive closure, and so finding it efficiently is important.

The Problem   Given a directed graph $G = (V, E)$, find its transitive closure.

We solve this problem by using a **reduction**. That is, we transform any instance of the transitive closure problem to an instance of another problem that we already know how to solve. We then transform the solution of the other problem to a solution of the transitive closure problem. The reduction is from the all-pairs shortest-paths problem.

Let $G' = (V, E')$ be a complete directed graph (i.e., all vertices are connected in both directions). Each edge e in E' is assigned the length 0 if $e \in E$, and 1 otherwise. We now solve the all-pairs shortest-paths problem for G'. If there is a path from v to w in G, then its length in G' is 0, since all edges of G have length 0 in G'. Therefore, there is a path between v and w if and only if the length of the shortest path between v and w in G' is 0. Thus, an answer to the all-pairs shortest-paths problem can be transformed directly into an answer for the transitive closure problem.

The idea of using reductions between two problems is explored in detail in Chapter 10. We used reduction here mainly to illustrate the technique with a simple example. It is easy to modify the all-pairs shortest-paths algorithm directly to a transitive closure algorithm, as is shown in Fig 7.23.

Algorithm Transitive_Closure (A) ;
Input: A (an $n \times n$ adjacency matrix representing a weighted graph).
{ $A [x, y]$ is true if the edge (x, y) belongs to the graph, and false otherwise;
   $A [x, x]$ is true for all x }
Output: At the end, the matrix A represents the transitive closure of the graph.

begin
   for $m := 1$ **to** n **do**   { *the induction sequence* }
      for $x := 1$ **to** n **do**
         for $y := 1$ **to** n **do**
            if $A [x, m]$ and $A [m, y]$ **then** $A [x, y] := true$
            { *this step is improved in the next algorithm* }
   end

Figure 7.23 Algorithm *Transitive_Closure*.

The fact that we can reduce one problem to another means that the solution of the first problem is general enough to embody the solution of the other. But, more general solutions are usually more expensive. We have seen cases where a more general problem is easier to solve; in many cases, however, the more you get the more you have to pay for it. When a reduction is used we should always try to improve the resulting solution by using the special characteristics of the problem.

Consider the main step of the algorithm: the *if* statement. It consists of two checks, for $A[x, m]$ and for $A[m, y]$. An action is taken only if both of these checks are satisfied. This *if* statement is performed n times for each pair of vertices. Any improvement of this statement would lead to a substantial improvement of the algorithm. Do we really need to perform the two checks all the time? The first check depends on only x and m, whereas the second check depends on only m and y. Therefore, we can perform the first check only once for a certain x and a certain m. If the first check fails, then there is no need to perform the second check for any value of y. If the first check succeeds, then there is no need to perform it again. This change is incorporated in the (improved) algorithm presented in Fig. 7.24. The asymptotic complexity remains unchanged, but this algorithm will run about twice as fast.

Algorithm Improved_Transitive_Closure *(A) ;*
Input: *A* (an $n \times n$ adjacency matrix representing a weighted graph).
{ $A[x, y]$ is true if the edge (x, y) belongs to the graph, and false otherwise;
$A[x, x]$ is true for all x }
Output: At the end, the matrix *A* represents the transitive closure of *G*.

begin
   for $m := 1$ **to** n **do**   { *the induction sequence* }
      for $x := 1$ **to** n **do**
         if $A[x, m]$ **then**
            for $y := 1$ **to** n **do**
               if $A[m, y]$ **then** $A[x, y] := true$
end

Figure 7.24 Algorithm *Improved_Transitive_Closure*.

Implementation   The implementation of the algorithm is straightforward. Notice, however, that the last line has the same effect as an *or* operation on the xth row of the matrix. Each entry (x, y) in the xth row is set to the value of itself *or* that of (m, y). These operations are equivalent to setting the xth row to be the *or* of the xth row and the mth row. Since many computers can perform an *or* operation on many bits at the same time, a row *or* operation can be performed faster than several bit-by-bit operations. So, in practice, the number of steps for this algorithm is $O(n^3/w)$, where w is the word size (the number of bits that can be *or*'d together in one step). This is a very simple example of a parallel algorithm. This issue is also discussed in Section 9.5.3.

7.9 Decompositions of Graphs

We have already seen one form of graph decomposition — the partition into connected components. In general, the idea of graph decomposition is to partition the graph into subgraphs such that each of the subgraphs satisfies a certain desirable property. Then, when we need to design an algorithm that manipulates the graph, it may be possible to consider each subgraph separately and to use its desirable property. For example, we have seen several algorithms that require that the graph be connected. By partitioning the graph into its connected components, we were able to apply these algorithms to each component separately, and thus to avoid many complications. This section presents two other decompositions — biconnected components and strongly connected components. The first one applies to undirected graphs and the second one to directed graphs. Both are useful in designing algorithms. In particular, both decompositions depend heavily on the cycles in the graph (undirected and directed cycles respectively). Therefore, whenever there is a problem that involves cycles in one way or another (and many graph problems involve cycles), it is a good idea to consider these decompositions. They are not always useful, but they should at least be considered. We assume throughout this section that the graphs are connected.

7.9.1 Biconnected Components

The notion of biconnectivity extends the regular connectivity concept in a natural way. An undirected graph is **connected** if there is a path from every vertex to every other vertex. An undirected graph is **biconnected** if there are at least two vertex disjoint paths from every vertex to every other vertex. Biconnected graphs thus exhibit a higher level of connectivity: If for some reason one of the paths connecting two vertices can no longer be used, then the two vertices are still connected. It turns out that, if a graph is not biconnected, then it can be partitioned into subgraphs, each of which is biconnected. We will be mainly interested in that partition. In general, an undirected graph is called **k-connected** if there are at least k vertex disjoint paths between every two vertices. We first study several properties of k-connected graphs.

The first important property of k-connected graphs is a theorem due to Menger [1927] that relates the number of vertex disjoint paths between vertices to the number of vertices required to disconnect the graph.

□ Menger's Theorem

Let $G = (V, E)$ be an undirected connected graph, and let u and v be two nonadjacent vertices in G. The minimum number of vertices whose removal from G disconnects u from v is equal to the maximal number of vertex disjoint paths from u to v. (When a vertex is removed, all its incident edges are removed as well.) □

A simple corollary of Menger's theorem is the following, due to Whitney [1932].

□ **Whitney's Theorem**

An undirected graph is k-connected if and only if at least k vertices must be removed in order to disconnect the graph.   □

Since the condition in Whitney's theorem is equivalent to the condition defining *k*-connectivity, we can use either one of these conditions. For a proof of these theorems, see for example Chartrand and Lesniak [1986]. (One side of the theorems is clear: If there are *k* vertices whose removal disconnects the graph, then there cannot be more than *k* vertex disjoint paths; the other direction is more complicated.)

Menger's theorem is one of the most important theorems in graph theory. For our purposes, the main implication of the two theorems is that a graph is *not* biconnected if and only if there is a vertex whose removal disconnects the graph. Such a vertex is called an **articulation point**. Figure 7.25 illustrates the structure of a nonbiconnected graph. Such a graph contains one or more articulation points. The blocks, "between" the articulation points, which are highlighted in the figure, are by themselves biconnected. These blocks form the biconnected components of the graph. We make this notion more precise next.

> **Definition**: A **biconnected component** is a maximal subset of the edges
> such that its induced subgraph is biconnected (namely, there is no subset
> that contains it and induces a biconnected graph).

A biconnected component is defined as a set of edges. A vertex can belong to several components. Indeed, each articulation point belongs to more than one component. (In

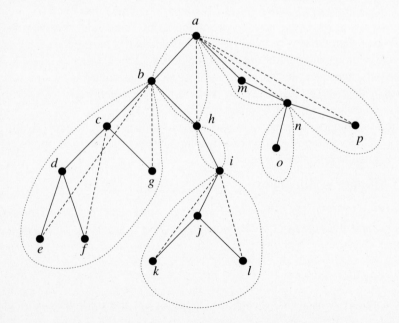

Figure 7.25 The structure of a nonbiconnected graph.

fact, this description provides another characterization of articulation points.) The set of edges of every graph can be partitioned into biconnected components in a unique way. Each edge belongs to exactly one component. The following two claims prove the existence of the partition and its uniqueness.

□ Lemma 7.9

Two edges e and f belong to the same biconnected component if and only if there is a cycle containing both of them. (Note that a biconnected component may consist of only one edge; this claim addresses only biconnected components with at least two edges.)

Proof: First, we show that a cycle is always entirely contained in one biconnected component. If the cycle contains edges from more than one biconnected component, then we can extend each of these components by adding the rest of the cycle. The extended subgraph is still biconnected since a cycle cannot be disconnected by one vertex. This contradicts the maximality of the component. For the other side of the theorem, if the two edges belong to the same biconnected component, then we can obtain the cycle containing them in the following way. We add two new (artificial) vertices to the "middle" of e and f. (That is, if $e = (v, w)$, we add a new vertex z and replace e by the two edges (v, z) and (z, w); we do the same for f.) The component, as a subgraph, remains biconnected since it still contains no articulation points. (Removing any of the new vertices is the same as removing the old edges, which cannot disconnect the component; removing an old vertex has the same effect as before.) Therefore, there are two vertex-disjoint paths between the two new vertices, but these paths exactly complete a cycle containing e and f. □

□ Lemma 7.10

Each edge belongs to exactly one biconnected component.

Proof: Each edge definitely belongs to at least one biconnected component (possibly containing only itself). It cannot belong to more than one biconnected component, since there would be cycles containing it and edges from both components. A combination of the two cycles is one larger cycle containing edges of two components. We have already seen that this is impossible. □

We want to find the partition into biconnected components. Let's start as usual with the straightforward induction hypothesis.

Induction hypothesis: *We know how to find the biconnected components of connected graphs with $< m$ edges.*

A connected graph with one edge is biconnected. Consider a graph with m edges and pick an arbitrary edge x. We remove x from the graph and find, by induction, the biconnected components. We now have to determine what effect adding x would have on the partition. The easiest case is when x connects two vertices from the same component (for example the edge (a, n) in Fig. 7.25). In this case, adding x has no effect on the partition (it only makes that one particular component even more connected). Another easy case is when x completely disconnects the graph (for example the edges (h, i) and (n, o) in Fig. 7.25). In this case, it is clear that both of x's endpoints are articulation points and, as a result, x is a biconnected component by itself. (Such an edge is appropriately called a **bridge**.) Obviously, none of the other components is changed. The difficult case is when x does not disconnect the graph and connects vertices from two different components. An example of such an edge is edge (b, e) in Fig. 7.25. We also illustrated this case in Fig. 7.26(a). It is clear that x merges the two components it connects, plus several other components that are "in between," into one larger component. The problem is thus to find all the "in-between" components and to merge them efficiently.

Looking back at Fig. 7.25 and Fig. 7.26, we can see that the biconnected components define a tree in the following way. Each biconnected component is associated with a node (we call them nodes to distinguish them from the original vertices). We start with an arbitrary component R as the root of the tree (the component containing a, b, and h in Fig. 7.25). The children of R are those biconnected components that have common articulation points with R; the grandchildren are those biconnected components that have not been included in the tree yet, which have common articulation points with the children, and so on. In other words, we construct the trees in a breadth-first fashion. We cannot simply say that two biconnected components are connected if they have an articulation point in common, because an articulation point may be common to more than two biconnected components, and we do not want to form cycles. It is not difficult to prove that a tree is always formed by this construction (Exercise 7.17). This

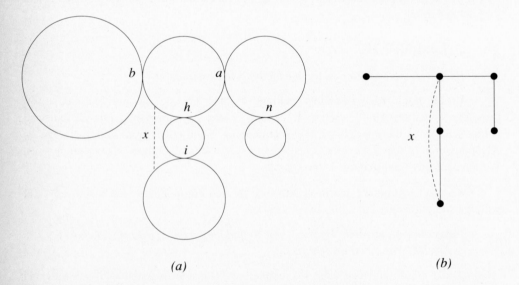

(a)   *(b)*

Figure 7.26 An edge that connects two different biconnected components. (a) The components corresponding to the graph of Fig. 7.25 with the articulation points indicated. (b) The biconnected component tree.

tree is called the **biconnected tree**. Figure 7.26(a) shows the biconnected components of the graph in Fig. 7.25, and Fig. 7.26(b) shows the corresponding biconnected tree. The edge x in Fig. 7.26 illustrates the addition of an edge; it can correspond, for example, to an edge connecting a and k in the original graph.

If we think of the biconnected tree now, we see that an edge connecting vertices from two different components generates a cycle in the tree. All the nodes (corresponding to components) in that cycle must be merged into one component. So we now have an algorithm. We add to the induction hypothesis the assumption that we know how to construct the tree, and then we can handle each of the three cases we discussed earlier. We omit the details because there is a better algorithm.

The problem with the algorithm we just described is the time it takes to find the cycle generated by the added edge in the biconnected tree. Finding a cycle in a tree may require traversing the whole tree, which in the worst case requires looking at all the edges of the tree. There may be as many as $O(|V|)$ edges in the tree, and we have to perform this step for each edge of the original graph. Thus, this algorithm may require $O(|V| \cdot |E|)$ time (this is not a precise analysis). We would like to avoid searching for a cycle in each step.

One common way to improve a straightforward inductive algorithm is to choose carefully the order of induction. In the preceding discussion, we picked an arbitrary edge. We may be able to improve the algorithm if we pick the edges in an order that will make it easier to handle the biconnected tree. A natural first attempt would be to use a good graph traversal. It turns out, as we shall see in a moment, that DFS is excellent for this purpose. Consider again Fig. 7.25. Assume that DFS starts at vertex a, and consider the articulation point b. Let B be the component "below" b which the DFS visits first after visiting b. (In Fig 7.25, this component consists of the edges connecting vertices b, c, d, e, f, and g.) How can we determine that b is indeed an articulation point? By definition, if all paths from B to the rest of the graph pass through b, then b is an articulation point. So, we want to determine whether there are any edges coming out of B to the rest of the graph.

Assume that the vertices in B are visited next by the DFS. If there are no edges out of B, the traversal will be local to B. All of B's edges will be traversed and b will be reached again. Furthermore, since DFS eliminates cross edges, the only edges that may connect B to the rest of the graph are back edges. In other words, b *disconnects B if and only if there are no back edges out of B that reach the tree above b.* (The only exception to this rule occurs at the root of the DFS tree; we discuss this case later.) Let's see now how we can determine this fact.

We want to know how high in the DFS tree we can reach from a subtree. We traverse the graph using DFS. At each vertex v, we first visit one whole subtree below v, then another, and so on. Let T_1 be a subtree rooted at a child of v such that the DFS visits this child first. Suppose that we find not only all the biconnected components in T_1, but also the highest vertex in the tree that is connected to T_1 by a back edge. (This is really just strengthening the induction hypothesis, as will be seen in a moment.) Let's denote by $High(v)$ the highest vertex in the DFS tree that is connected, by a back edge, to either v or a descendent of v (in the DFS tree). Assume that the children of v in the

DFS tree are w_1, w_2, ..., w_k (see Fig. 7.27). We can easily compute $High(v)$ if we know $High(w_i)$ for all w_i: It is simply the highest among all $High(w_i)$ and among all the back edges from v. (We will describe shortly how to determine efficiently whether one vertex is higher than another.) So, if we perform DFS, we can easily compute all the $High$ values. For example, in Fig. 7.27, $High(w_1)=r$, $High(w_2)=v$, and $High(w_3)=w_3$; the highest back edge from v goes to q, hence $High(v)=r$.

Now suppose that we have computed all the $High$ values. We claim that a vertex v is an articulation point if and only if there is a child w_i of v such that $High(w_i)$ is not higher than v. Indeed, if such w_i exists, then there are no edges from vertices in the subtree rooted at w_i to vertices higher than v in the tree; hence, v is an articulation point. (The beauty of DFS is that it traverses the graph in exactly the right order for our purposes.)

Computing the $High$ values goes hand in hand with the DFS, according to the following induction hypothesis.

> **Induction hypothesis:** *When we visit the kth vertex by DFS, we know how to find the High values of vertices that have already been visited and are below this vertex.*

The order of the induction follows the order of DFS. When we reach a vertex v, we perform (recursively) a DFS for all children of v, find (by induction) their $High$ values, and compute $High(v)$ according to the definition. At the same time, we can decide whether a vertex is an articulation point.

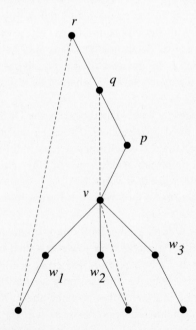

Figure 7.27 Computing the *High* values.

The root of the DFS tree presents a special case. Obviously, no *High* value can exceed the root. It is easy to see that the root is an articulation point if and only if it has more than one child in the DFS tree. Of course, this is easy to determine.

The key to the efficiency of the algorithm for computing the *High* values is that all the necessary information is available when DFS is performed. The only problem we have is how to decide whether one vertex is higher than another in the DFS tree. We use DFS numbers to make this determination. All the vertices involved in the computation of the *High* values are ancestors in the tree. Therefore, they already have a DFS number. Furthermore, the higher an ancestor is, the lower its number is! This is not true for vertices that are not related in the tree; fortunately, however, we care only about back edges. So, a practical way to manipulate the *High* values is to use the DFS numbers. We define *High* (*v*) as before, except that it refers not to the highest vertex itself, but to that vertex's DFS number. It is confusing to describe the algorithm in terms of DFS numbers, because higher vertices correspond to lower DFS numbers. Therefore, we define *decreasing DFS numbers:* the root has a DFS number of $|V|$ and the number is decreased every time we visit a new vertex. We can also use negative numbers: we assign the root a DFS number of -1, and we decrement the number every time we visit a new vertex. The advantage of the latter scheme is that the value of $|V|$ need not be known in advance.

The only remaining task is to find the actual biconnected components. We could find them by brute force, but there is also an elegant way. Let's look back at Fig. 7.25. Notice that, at the point where the algorithm determined that *b* is an articulation point, the edges of *B* were the most recent to be traversed. During the traversal, we put the new vertices on a stack and add the edges as they are encountered. When a vertex is found to be an articulation point, we can remove from the stack all the top edges going back in the stack until that vertex is reached. This is exactly the biconnected component! We can now remove those edges from the graph and continue in the same way. The complete program for biconnected components is given in Fig. 7.28. (The algorithm can be defined merely in terms of preWORK and postWORK of DFS, but, for completeness, we present it fully.)

Complexity   Clearly, the extra amount of work, in addition to the work involved in the DFS, is constant per vertex. Hence, the running time of this algorithm is $O(|V|+|E|)$. The space requirements are also $O(|V|+|E|)$ since the components must be remembered as they are traversed.

□ **Example 7.3**

An example of algorithm *Biconnected_Components* for the graph in Fig. 7.25, which is repeated here, is given in Fig. 7.29. The first line gives the vertices and the second line gives their (decreasing) DFS Numbers. Each successive line presents the *High* numbers as updated when a new call to the recursive procedure is made. A vertex is circled when it is discovered to be an articulation point.   □

---

*Algorithm **Biconnected_Components** (G, v, n)*

Input: $G = (V, E)$ (an undirected connected graph), v (a vertex serving as the root of the DFS tree), and n (the number of vertices in G).

Output: the biconnected components are marked and the *High* values are computed.

begin
    for *every vertex v of G* **do**
        v.DFS_Number := 0 ;
    { the DFS numbers will also serve to indicate whether or not the corresponding vertices have been visited }
    DFS_N := n ;
    { we use decreasing DFS numbers; see the explanation in the text. }
    BC(v)
end

*procedure **BC**(v) ;*

begin
    v.DFS_Number := DFS_N ;
    DFS_N := DFS_N - 1 ;
    insert v into Stack ; { Stack is initially empty }
    v.High := v.DFS_Number ; { initial value }
    for *all edges (v, w)* **do**
        insert (v, w) into Stack ;
        { each edge will be inserted twice (for both directions) }
        if *w is not the parent of v* **then**
            if *w.DFS_Number = 0* **then**
                BC(w) ;
                if *w.High ≤ v.DFS_Number* **then**
                { v disconnects w from the rest of the graph }
                    remove all edges and vertices from Stack until v is
                        reached, and mark the subgraph they form
                        as a biconnected component ;
                    insert v back into Stack ;
                    { v is part of w's component and possibly others }
                v.High := max (v.High , w.High)
            else *{ (v, w) is a back edge or a forward edge }*
                v.High := max (v.High , w.DFS_Number)
  end

Figure 7.28 Algorithm *Biconnected_Components*.

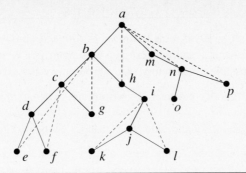

	a	b	c	d	e	f	g	h	i	j	k	l	m	n	o	p
	16	15	14	13	12	11	10	9	8	7	6	5	4	3	2	1
a	16	-	-	-	-	-	-	-	-	-	-	-	-	-	-	-
b	16	15	-	-	-	-	-	-	-	-	-	-	-	-	-	-
c	16	15	14	-	-	-	-	-	-	-	-	-	-	-	-	-
d	16	15	14	13	-	-	-	-	-	-	-	-	-	-	-	-
e	16	15	14	13	15	-	-	-	-	-	-	-	-	-	-	-
d	16	15	14	15	15	-	-	-	-	-	-	-	-	-	-	-
f	16	15	14	15	15	14	-	-	-	-	-	-	-	-	-	-
d	16	15	14	15	15	14	-	-	-	-	-	-	-	-	-	-
c	16	15	15	15	15	14	-	-	-	-	-	-	-	-	-	-
g	16	15	15	15	15	14	15	-	-	-	-	-	-	-	-	-
c	16	15	15	15	15	14	15	-	-	-	-	-	-	-	-	-
(b)	16	15	15	15	14	13	15	-	-	-	-	-	-	-	-	-
h	16	15	15	15	15	14	15	16	-	-	-	-	-	-	-	-
i	16	15	15	15	15	14	15	16	8	-	-	-	-	-	-	-
j	16	15	15	15	15	14	15	16	8	7	-	-	-	-	-	-
k	16	15	15	15	15	14	15	16	8	7	8	-	-	-	-	-
j	16	15	15	15	15	14	15	16	8	8	8	-	-	-	-	-
l	16	15	15	15	15	14	15	16	8	8	8	8	-	-	-	-
j	16	15	15	15	15	14	15	16	8	8	8	8	-	-	-	-
(i)	16	15	15	15	15	14	15	16	8	8	8	8	-	-	-	-
(h)	16	15	15	15	15	14	15	16	8	8	8	8	-	-	-	-
b	16	16	15	15	15	14	15	16	8	8	8	8	-	-	-	-
a	16	15	15	15	15	14	15	16	8	8	8	8	-	-	-	-
m	16	15	15	15	15	14	15	16	8	8	8	8	4	-	-	-
n	16	15	15	15	15	14	15	16	8	8	8	8	4	16	-	-
o	16	15	15	15	15	14	15	16	8	8	8	8	4	16	2	-
(n)	16	15	15	15	15	14	15	16	8	8	8	8	4	16	2	-
p	16	15	15	15	15	14	15	16	8	8	8	8	4	16	2	16
n	16	15	15	15	15	14	15	16	8	8	8	8	4	16	2	16
m	16	15	15	15	15	14	15	16	8	8	8	8	16	16	2	16
(a)	16	15	15	15	15	14	15	16	8	8	8	8	16	16	2	16

Figure 7.29 An example of computing *High* values and biconnected components.

7.9.2 Strongly Connected Components

In this section, we discuss only directed graphs. A directed graph is **strongly connected** if, for every pair of vertices v and w, there is a path from v to w and a path from w to v. In other words, it is possible to reach any vertex from any other vertex.

> **Definition**: A **strongly connected component** is a maximal subset of the vertices such that its induced subgraph is strongly connected (i.e., there is no subset that contains it and induces a strongly connected graph).

Notice that, unlike biconnected components, a strongly connected component is defined as a set of vertices. The vertices of every graph can be partitioned into strongly connected components in a unique way. Each vertex belongs to exactly one component. An edge in the graph may belong to one component, or it may connect two separate components. We prove the existence of the partition by the following two claims, which are similar to the biconnected component case in the previous section.

□ Lemma 7.11

Two vertices belong to the same strongly connected component if and only if there is a circuit containing both of them. (Recall that a circuit is a closed directed path that is not necessarily simple; that is, it may include a vertex more than once. A cycle is a simple circuit.)

Proof: A circuit is by itself strongly connected. A strongly connected component cannot include only a subset of the vertices of a circuit, since it would not be maximal (we can add all the other vertices of the circuit to the component). Now, given any two vertices v and w from the same strongly connected component, we claim that they are contained in a circuit. By the definition of strong connectivity, there is a path from v to w and a path from w to v. Putting together these two paths results in a circuit (but not necessarily in a cycle, since the paths may not be vertex disjoint).   □

□ Lemma 7.12

Each vertex belongs to exactly one strongly connected component.

Proof: If a vertex v belongs to more than one strongly connected component, then there are circuits containing v and vertices from the other components. However, combining those circuits results in another circuit, which, by Lemma 7.11, must be contained in only one strongly connected component. This is a contradiction.   □

We can define the **strongly connected component (SCC) graph** similarly to the biconnected component tree. (This graph is also called a **condensation graph**.) The nodes of the SCC graph (we call them nodes to distinguish them from the original vertices) correspond to the strongly connected components; there is a directed edge from node a to node b if there is a directed edge (in the original graph) from any vertex in the component that corresponds to a to any vertex in the component that corresponds to b. The SCC graph is acyclic since cycles cannot involve more than one component. Figure 7.30 presents a directed graph G and its SCC graph.

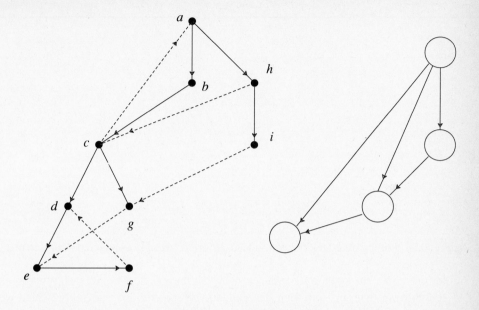

Figure 7.30 A directed graph and its strongly connected component graph.

As was the case with biconnected components, we can design an algorithm by induction.

> **Induction hypothesis:** *We know how to find the strongly connected components of graphs with < m edges, and how to construct their SCC graphs.*

The base case is trivial. Consider a graph with *m* edges and pick an arbitrary edge *x*. We remove *x* from the graph and find, by induction, the strongly connected components. We now have to determine what effect adding *x* would have on the partition. Again, the easy case is when *x* connects two vertices from the same component. In this case, adding *x* has no effect on the partition or on the SCC graph. The difficult case is when *x* connects vertices from two different components. This case is illustrated in Fig. 7.31, in which an edge *x* is connecting two components in the SCC graph of Fig. 7.30. Clearly, *x* merges these two components if and only if it completes a (directed) cycle in the SCC graph. In this case, all the components corresponding to the nodes in the cycle are combined into one component, and we are done. If *x* does not complete a cycle in the SCC graph, then no changes are made to the component. As was the case with biconnected components, we can improve this algorithm by considering the edges in a particular order. Again, DFS plays a major role.

Let's try to follow the same steps as we did in the biconnected component algorithm, and modify them when necessary. When we visit a vertex through DFS, we want to determine whether it is part of a circuit with other vertices — in particular, vertices that are higher than it in the DFS tree. The notion of *High* values can be used in

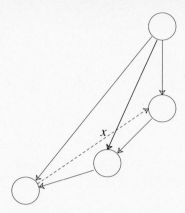

Figure 7.31 Adding an edge connecting two different strongly connected components.

a similar way. We are looking for vertices such that there is no way to reach other parts of the graph from them or from their descendants. We need a mechanism by which we can identify the ''breakpoints'' in a similar way to the articulation points. Consider the DFS tree. The strongly connected components occupy connected parts of the tree (Exercise 7.88). That is, all the vertices in a strongly connected component must belong to one connected subtree of the DFS tree. For a given component, consider its highest vertex in the tree; we call this vertex the **root of the component**. The root is the first vertex of the component to be visited by the DFS. (For example, the roots in Fig. 7.30 are a, d, g, and i.) If we can identify the roots similarly to the way we identified articulation points, then we can find the partition. We will see that the roots are similar to articulation points.

The algorithm is based on induction that follows the order of DFS. Let r be the root of the first component visited in its entirety by the DFS. It is the lowest leftmost component in the usual picture of DFS ($r = d$ in Fig. 7.30). The component must consist of all of r's descendants in the tree (none of the descendants can belong to a smaller component, since that component's traversal would have been completed first). If, during the DFS, we can identify r as the first root, then we can identify the component, remove it from the graph, and continue by induction. This is not as simple as we stated it, but this is the main idea. Let's first see if we can identify r.

First, for a vertex r to be a root of a component, there cannot be any back edges leading from a descendant of r to a vertex higher than r. Such a back edge completes a cycle with the higher vertex, which implies that the higher vertex belongs to the same component as r. We can determine whether such back edges exist similarly to the biconnected component case — using the *High* values. However, we need to be more careful here since DFS in directed graphs does not eliminate cross edges. Consider Fig. 7.32. Vertex g does not have any back edges, but it has a cross edge to e, which is contained in a cycle with a higher vertex b. Consequently, g's parent (f) is not a root of a component, even though there is no back edge from any of its descendants. Thus, we

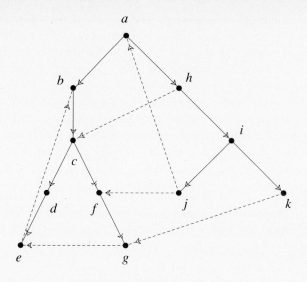

Figure 7.32 The effect of cross edges.

must consider the cross edges as well.

What is the effect of cross edges? Cross edges must go from right to left; in other words, they must point to vertices that have already been visited. Remember that we are looking for the first root. If there is a cross edge from g to e and the root has not been found yet, then we claim that it cannot be f. It must be a vertex which is an ancestor of both f and e. If it had not been an ancestor of f, then it would have been discovered before we reached f. In particular, the fact that the component containing e has not been discovered yet means that there is a way to go higher from e. So, a cross edge from g to a vertex that was visited before f implies that f is not a root. But this is just as easy to take into account as a back edge — we need only to consider DFS numbers! When considering the effect of the edge from g to e, it is not important whether this edge is a back edge. Only the DFS number of e (and its value relative to that of f) is important. We can define the *High* values as in the biconnected component case by looking for an edge leading to a vertex with the lowest DFS number. The *High* value of a vertex is the highest among those of its children and among its back edges or cross edges. *A vertex is the first root if it is the first vertex whose High value is not higher than itself.* Notice that the *High* values do not really point to the highest vertices. The *High* value of g will be the DFS number of e, even though it is possible to reach b from e (and thus from g). We care only whether we can reach a vertex higher than g (or f); it is not important to know the identity of the highest vertex. (Nor do we want to chase pointers once a back edge is encountered.)

Once we find the first root, we can find the first strongly connected component — it consists of all the descendants of the root in the DFS tree. We can then remove this component from the graph. This is done by deleting all the component's vertices and edges, and all the edges that point to them from other vertices. We can ignore edges from other vertices, since there is no way to get outside of the component. The rest can be done by induction since we now have a smaller graph! (The reader should carefully verify that all the assumptions are still valid.) Notice that the definition of the *High* values is dynamic. Since we remove the edges pointing to the newly discovered component, they will play no part in the computation of the *High* values later. (This is different from the "static" definition of the *High* values for the biconnected component case, which did not depend on any of the previous components.) In practice, there is no need to actually remove either vertices or edges. We can simply mark the vertices of each component as they are discovered, and later on ignore edges pointing to marked vertices. The strongly connected component algorithm is given in Fig. 7.33 (we use decreasing DFS numbers again to avoid confusion).

Complexity   The algorithm is similar to the biconnected component algorithm and its complexity is the same. The time and space complexities are $O(|V| + |E|)$.

□ Example 7.4

An example of algorithm *Strongly_Connected_Components* for the graph in Fig. 7.32, which is repeated here, is given in Fig. 7.34. The first line gives the vertices and the second line their (decreasing) DFS numbers. Each successive line presents the *High* numbers as updated when a new call to the recursive procedure is made. A vertex is circled when it is discovered to be a root of a strongly connected component.   □

7.9.3 Examples of the Use of Graph Decomposition

In this short section, we present two examples where the use of graph decomposition significantly simplifies the solutions. The first problem involves undirected graphs and the second one involves directed graphs.

> **The Problem**   Given a connected undirected graph $G = (V, E)$, determine whether it contains a cycle of even length.

We have seen that a cycle must be contained in a biconnected component. Hence, we can first partition the graph into its biconnected components, then consider each component separately. In other words, we can now assume that the graph is biconnected! If the graph is biconnected and it contains more than one edge, then it contains at least one cycle (in fact, every two edges are contained in a cycle). Let's find an arbitrary cycle $C_1 = v_1, v_2, ..., v_k, v_1$. If k is even, we are done. If there are no more edges — that is, the graph consists of exactly one odd cycle — then the answer is obviously negative. Otherwise, there is an edge not in the cycle such that one of its vertices is in the cycle. Let that edge be (v_i, w). Since the graph is biconnected, the edges (v_i, w) and (v_i, v_{i+1}) are contained in another cycle C_2. We traverse C_2 starting at w until we meet C_1 again

Algorithm Strongly_Connected_Components (G, v, n)

Input: $G = (V, E)$ (a directed graph), v (a vertex serving as the root
of the DFS tree), and n (the number of vertices in G).

Output: marking the strongly connected components, and computing
the *High* values.

{ As is always the case with directed DFS, this procedure may
have to be called several times until all vertices have been visited. }

begin
    for *every vertex v of G* **do**
        v.DFS_Number := 0 ;
        v.Component := 0 ;
    Current_Component := 0 ;
    DFS_N := n ;
    { we use decreasing DFS numbers; see the explanation in Section 7.9.1. }
    while *there exists a vertex v such that v.DFS_Number = 0* **do**
        SCC(v)
end

procedure SCC(v) ;

begin
    v.DFS_Number := DFS_N ;
    DFS_N := DFS_N − 1 ;
    insert v into STACK ;
    v.High := v.DFS_Number ; { the initial value }
    for *all edges (v, w)* **do**
        if *w.DFS_Number = 0* **then**
            SCC(w) ;
            v.High := max (v.High , w.High)
        else
           if w.DFS_Number > v.DFS_Number and w.Component = 0 **then**
           { (v, w) is a cross edge or a back edge that we need to consider }
              v.High := max (v.High , w.DFS_Number) ;
    if *v.High = v.DFS_Number* **then** *{ v is a root of a component }*
        Current_Component := Current_Component + 1 ;
        repeat *{ mark the vertices of the new component }*
            remove x from the top of STACK ;
            x.Component := Current_Component ;
        until *x = v*
end

Figure 7.33 Algorithm *Strongly_Connected_Components*.

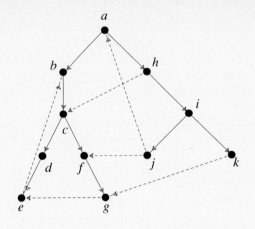

	a	b	c	d	e	f	g	h	i	j	k
	11	10	9	8	7	6	5	4	3	2	1
a	11	-	-	-	-	-	-	-	-	-	-
b	11	10	-	-	-	-	-	-	-	-	-
c	11	10	9	-	-	-	-	-	-	-	-
d	11	10	9	8	-	-	-	-	-	-	-
e	11	10	9	8	10	-	-	-	-	-	-
d	11	10	9	10	10	-	-	-	-	-	-
c	11	10	10	10	10	-	-	-	-	-	-
f	11	10	10	10	10	6	-	-	-	-	-
g	11	10	10	10	10	6	7	-	-	-	-
f	11	10	10	10	10	7	7	-	-	-	-
c	11	10	10	10	10	7	7	-	-	-	-
(b)	11	10	10	10	10	7	7	-	-	-	-
a	11	10	10	10	10	7	7	-	-	-	-
h	11	10	10	10	10	7	7	4	-	-	-
i	11	10	10	10	10	7	7	4	3	-	-
j	11	10	10	10	10	7	7	4	3	11	-
i	11	10	10	10	10	7	7	4	11	11	-
(k)	11	10	10	10	10	7	7	4	11	11	1
i	11	10	10	10	10	7	7	4	11	11	1
h	11	10	10	10	10	7	7	11	11	11	1
(a)	11	10	10	10	10	7	7	11	11	11	1

Figure 7.34 An example of computing *High* values and strongly connected components.

at, say, v_j (see Fig 7.35). Clearly, $v_i \neq v_j$. The path v_i, w, ..., u, v_j defines two cycles, as is shown in Fig. 7.35. It is easy to see that one of the three cycles in the figure must be even. We have proved the following theorem.

□ Theorem 7.13

Every biconnected graph that has more than one edge and is not merely an odd-length cycle contains an even-length cycle.

□

The second problem is a similar one, but for directed graphs.

The Problem   Given a directed graph $G = (V, E)$, determine whether it contains a (directed) cycle of odd length.

Again, we know that a cycle must be contained in a strongly connected component, so we might as well assume that the graph is strongly connected. We perform DFS starting from an arbitrary vertex r and we mark vertices with either *even* or *odd*. We mark r as *even*, then, for each edge (v, w), we mark w with the opposite mark of v. Since r can be reached from any vertex (by the strong-connectivity assumption), we claim that there is a cycle of odd length if and only if we try to mark a vertex that is already marked by the opposite mark (the most notable example is if we reach r again and try to mark it as *odd*). We leave the proof of this fact to the reader. It is strongly dependent on the strong connectivity assumption.

Both of these problems are much more difficult to solve without the decomposition. Since both decompositions can be achieved efficiently in linear time, it is usually worthwhile to start thinking about a given problem with the extra assumption that the graphs in questions are either biconnected or strongly connected. This is especially

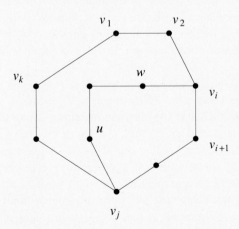

Figure 7.35 Finding an even-length cycle.

true for problems that involve cycles. It is interesting to note that the problem of efficiently determining whether a directed graph contains an even-length cycle is still open (see the Bibliography section).

7.10 Matching

Given an undirected graph $G = (V, E)$, a **matching** is a set of edges no two of which have a vertex in common. The reason for the name is that an edge can be thought of as a match of its two vertices. We insist that no vertex belongs to more than one edge from the matching so that it is a monogamous matching. A vertex that is not incident to any edge in the matching is called **unmatched**. We also say that the vertex does not belong to the matching. A **perfect matching** is one in which all vertices are matched. A **maximum matching** is one with the maximum number of edges. A **maximal** matching, on the other hand, is a matching that cannot be extended by the addition of an edge. Problems involving matching occur in many situations (besides social). Workers may be matched to jobs, machines to parts, and so on. Furthermore, many problems that seem unrelated to matching have equivalent formulations in terms of matching problems.

Matching in general graphs is a difficult problem. In this section, we limit our discussion to two specific matching problems. The first problem is not so important; it involves finding perfect matchings in special very dense graphs. The solution to this problem, however, illustrates an interesting approach, which we then generalize to solve an important problem concerning matching in bipartite graphs.

7.10.1 Perfect Matching in Very Dense Graphs

In this example, we consider a very restricted case of the perfect matching problem. Let $G = (V, E)$ be an undirected graph such that $|V| = 2n$ and the degree of each vertex is at least n. We present an algorithm to find a perfect matching in such graphs. As a corollary, we show that, under these conditions, a perfect matching always exists.

We use induction on the size m of the matching. The base case, $m = 1$, is handled by taking any arbitrary edge as a matching of size one. We will show that we can extend any matching that is not perfect either by adding another edge or by replacing an existing edge with two new edges. In either case, the size of the matching is increased, and the result follows.

Consider a matching M in G with m edges such that $m < n$. We first check all the edges not in M to see whether any of them can be added to M. If we find such an edge, then we are done. Otherwise, M is a maximal matching. Since M is not perfect, there are at least two nonadjacent vertices, v_1 and v_2, that do not belong M. These two vertices have at least $2n$ distinct edges coming out of them. All of these edges lead to vertices that are covered by M, since otherwise such an edge could be added to M. Since the number of edges in M is $< n$ and there are $2n$ edges from v_1 and v_2 adjacent to them, at least one edge from M — say (u_1, u_2) — is adjacent to three edges from v_1 and v_2. Assume, without loss of generality, that those three edges are $(u_1, v_1), (u_1, v_2)$, and (u_2, v_1) (see Fig. 7.36(a)). It is easy to see that, by removing the edge (u_1, u_2) from M

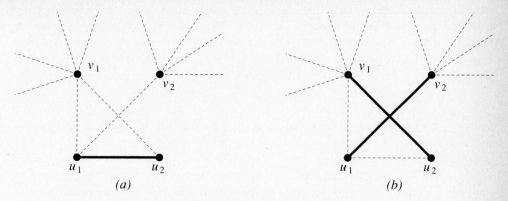

Figure 7.36 Extending a matching.

and adding the two edges (u_1, v_2), and (u_2, v_1), we get a larger matching (Fig. 7.36(b)).

We leave the implementation of this algorithm as an exercise (7.21). This algorithm is another example of a *greedy* approach. At most three edges were involved in each step in the extension of one matching to a larger one. This was sufficient in this case, but, in general, finding a good matching is more difficult. A choice of one edge may affect choices of other edges far away in the graph. Next, we show how to generalize this approach to other matching problems.

7.10.2 Bipartite Matching

Let $G = (V, E, U)$ be a bipartite graph, such that V and U are two disjoint sets of vertices, and E is a set of edges connecting vertices from V to vertices in U.

The Problem Find a maximum-cardinality matching in a bipartite graph G.

We can formulate this problem in terms of real matching: V is a set of girls, U is a set of boys, and E is a set of "possible" pairings; we want to match boys to girls so as to maximize the number of matched boys and girls.

A straightforward approach is to try to match according to some strategy until no more matches are possible, in the hope that the strategy will guarantee optimality, or at least come close. We can try different strategies. For example, we can try a greedy approach by first matching the vertices with small degrees, hoping that the other vertices will be more likely to have unmatched partners later on. (In other words, first match the boys that are the most difficult to match, and worry about the rest later.) Instead of trying to analyze such strategies (which is hard), we try the approach used in the previous problem. Suppose that we start with a maximal matching, which is not necessarily a maximum matching. Can we somehow improve it? Consider Fig. 7.37(a), in which the matching is depicted by bold lines. It is clear that we can improve the matching by replacing the edge *2A* with the edges *1A* and *2B*. This is similar to the transformation we applied in the previous problem. But we are not restricted to replacing one edge with two edges. If we find a similar situation where k edges can be replaced by $k+1$ edges, then we have an improvement. For example, we can improve the matching further by replacing the edges *3D* and *4E* with the edges *3C*, *4D*, and *5E* (Fig. 7.37(b)).

Let's study these transformations. Our goal is to add more matched vertices. We start with an unmatched vertex v and try to find a match for it. If we already have a maximal matching, then all of v's neighbors are already matched, so we must try to break up a match. We choose another vertex u, adjacent to v, which was previously matched to, say, w. We match v to u and break up the match between u and w. We now have to find a match for w. If w is connected to an unmatched vertex, then we are done (this was the first case above); if not, we can continue this way by breaking matches and trying rematches. To translate this attempt into an algorithm, we have to do two things. First, we have to make sure that this procedure terminates, and second, we have to show that, if there is an improvement, then this procedure will find it. First, we formalize this idea.

An **alternating path** P for a given matching M is a path from a vertex v in V to a vertex u in U, both of which are unmatched in M, such that the edges of P are alternatively in $E - M$ and in M. That is, the first edge (v, w) of P does not belong to M (since v does not belong to M), the second edge (w, x) belongs to M, and so on, until the last edge of P, (z, u), which does not belong to M. Notice that alternating paths are exactly what we used already to improve a matching. The number of edges in P must be odd since P starts in V and ends in U. Furthermore, there is exactly one more edge of P in $E - M$ than there is in M. Therefore, if we replace all the edges of P that belong to M by the edges that do not belong to M, we get another matching with one more edge. For example, the first alternating path we used to improve the matching in Fig. 7.37(a) was (*1A*, *A2*, *2B*), which was used to replace the edge *A2* with the edges *1A* and *2B*; the second alternating path was (*C3*, *3D*, *D4*, *4E*, *E5*), which was used to replace the edges *3D* and *4E* with the edges *C3*, *D4*, and *E5*.

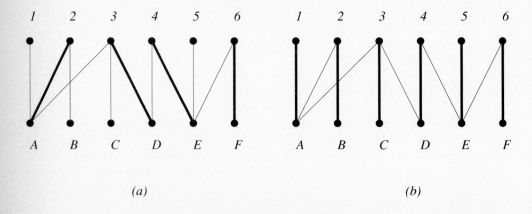

(a)   (b)

Figure 7.37 Extending a bipartite matching.

It should be clear now that, if there is an alternating path for a given matching M, then M is not maximum. It turns out that the opposite is also true.

□ Alternating-Path Theorem

A matching is maximum if and only if it has no alternating paths. □

This claim will be proved, in the context of a more general theorem, in the next section.

The alternating path theorem immediately suggests an algorithm, because any matching that is not maximum has an alternating path and any alternating path can extend a matching. We start with the greedy algorithm, adding as many edges to the matching as possible, until we get a maximal matching. We then search for an alternating path, and modify the matching accordingly until no more alternating paths can be found. The resulting matching is maximum. Since each alternating path extends a matching by one edge and there are at most $n/2$ edges in any matching (where n is the number of vertices), the number of iterations is at most $n/2$. The only remaining problem is how to find alternating paths. We solve this problem as follows. We transform the undirected graph G to a directed graph G' by directing the edges in M to point from U to V and directing the edges not in M to point from V to U. Figure 7.38(a) shows the matching obtained for the graph in Fig. 7.37(a), and Fig. 7.38(b) shows the directed graph G'. An alternating path corresponds exactly to a directed path from an unmatched vertex in V to an unmatched vertex in U. Such a directed path can be found by any graph-search procedure, for example, DFS. The complexity of a search is $O(|V| + |E|)$; hence, the complexity of the algorithm is $O(|V|(|V| + |E|))$.

An Improvement

Since a search can traverse the whole graph in the same worst-case running time that it traverses one path, we might as well try to find several alternating paths with one search. We have to make sure, however, that these paths do not modify one another. One way to guarantee the independence of such alternating paths is to restrict them to be vertex

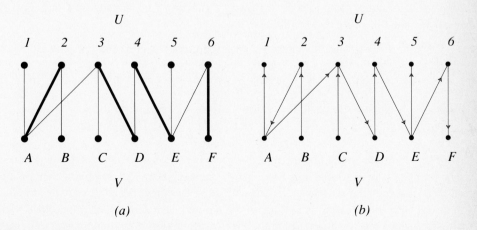

Figure 7.38 Finding alternating paths.

disjoint. If the paths are vertex disjoint, they modify different vertices, so they can be applied concurrently. The new improved algorithm for finding alternating paths is the following. First, we perform BFS in G' from the set of all unmatched vertices in V, level by level, until a level in which unmatched vertices in U are found. Then, we extract from the graph induced by the BFS a *maximal* set of vertex disjoint paths in G' (which are alternating paths in G). This is done by finding any path, removing its vertices, finding another path, removing its vertices, and so on. (The result is not a *maximum* set, but merely a maximal set.) We choose a maximal set in order to maximize the number of edges added to the matching with one search (each vertex-disjoint alternating path adds one edge to the matching). Finally, we modify the matching using this set of alternating paths. This process is repeated until no more alternating paths can be found (i.e., the new directed graph G' disconnects the unmatched vertices in V from the unmatched vertices in U).

Complexity   It turns out that the number of iterations of the improved algorithm is $O(\sqrt{|V|})$ in the worst case. We omit the proof, which is due to Hopcroft and Karp [1973]. The overall worst-case running time is thus $O((|V| + |E|)\sqrt{|V|})$.

7.11 Network Flows

The problem of network flows is a basic problem in graph theory and combinatorial optimization. It has been studied extensively for the last 35 years, and many algorithms and data structures have been developed for it. It has many variations and extensions. Furthermore, many seemingly unrelated problems can be posed as network-flow problems. The basic variation of the network-flow problem is defined as follows. Let $G = (V, E)$ be a directed graph with two distinguished vertices, s (the source) with indegree 0, and t (the sink) with outdegree 0. Each edge e in E has an associated positive weight $c(e)$, called the **capacity** of e. The capacity measures the amount of flow that can pass through an edge. We call such a graph a **network**. For convenience we assign a capacity of 0 to nonexisting edges. A **flow** is a function f on the edges of the network that satisfies the following two conditions:

1. $0 \le f(e) \le c(e)$: The flow through an edge cannot exceed the capacity of that edge.
2.   For all $v \in V - \{s, t\}$, $\sum_u f(u, v) = \sum_w f(v, w)$: The total flow entering a vertex is equal to the total flow exiting this vertex (except for the source and sink).

These two conditions imply that the total flow leaving s is equal to the total flow entering t. The problem is to maximize this flow. (If the capacities are real numbers, then it is not even clear that maximum flows exist; we will show that they indeed always exist.) One way to visualize this problem is to think of the network as a network of water pipes. The goal is to push as much water through the pipes as possible. If too much water is pushed to the wrong area, the pipes will burst.

First, we show that the problem of bipartite matching, discussed in the previous section, can be posed as a network-flow problem. This may seem to be a fruitless exercise, since we already know how to solve the matching problem, but we do not know how to solve the network-flow problem (namely, the reduction is in the wrong direction). The reason we present this wrong-order reduction is that the techniques for solving the network-flow problem are similar to those for solving the bipartite matching problem. Understanding the similarities can be helpful in understanding network-flow algorithms.

Given a bipartite graph $G = (V, E, U)$ in which we want to find a maximum-cardinality matching, we add two new vertices s and t, connect s to all vertices in V, and connect all vertices in U to t. We also direct all the edges in E from V to U (see Fig. 7.39, in which all edges are directed from left to right). We now assign capacities of 1 to all the edges, and we have a valid network-flow problem on the modified graph G'. Let M be a matching in G. There is a natural correspondence between M and a flow in G'. We assign a flow of 1 to all the edges in M and to all the edges connecting s or t to matched vertices in M. All the other edges are assigned a flow of 0. The total flow is thus equal to the number of edges in the matching. It turns out that M is a maximum matching if and only if the corresponding flow is a maximum flow in G'. One side is clear: If the flow is maximum and it corresponds to a matching, then we cannot have a larger matching, since it would correspond to a larger flow. For the other side of the claim we somehow have to adapt the idea of alternating paths to network flows, and to show that, if there are no alternating paths, then the corresponding flow is maximum. We proceed to do just that.

An **augmenting path** with respect to a given flow f is a directed path from s to t which consists of edges from G, but not necessarily in the same direction; each of these edges (v, u) satisfies exactly one of the following two conditions:

1. (v, u) is in the same direction as it is in G, and $f(v, u) < c(v, u)$. In this case, the edge (v, u) is called a **forward edge**. A forward edge has room for

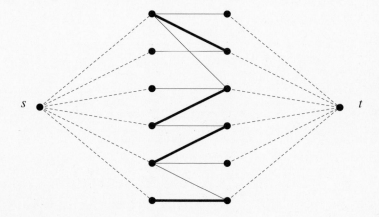

Figure 7.39 Reducing bipartite matching to network flow (the directions of all the edges are from left to right).

more flow. The difference $c(v, u) - f(v, u)$ is called the **slack** of the edge.

2. (v, u) is in the opposite direction in G (namely, $(u, v) \in E$), and $f(u, v) > 0$. In this case, the edge (v, u) is called a **backward edge**. It is possible to borrow some flow from a backward edge.

Augmenting paths are extensions of alternating paths, and they serve the same purpose for network flows as alternating paths do for bipartite matching. If there exists an augmenting path with respect to a flow f (we say that f **admits** an augmenting path), then f is not maximum. We can modify f by moving more flow through the augmenting path in the following way. If all the edges of the path are forward edges, then more flow can be moved through them, and all the constraints are still satisfied. The extra flow in that case is exactly the minimum slack of the edges in the path. The case of backward edges is a little more complicated. Consider Fig. 7.40. Each edge is marked with two numbers a/b, such that a is the capacity and b is the current flow. It is clear that no more flow can be pushed forward, since there is no path from s to t that consists of only forward edges. However, there is a way to extend the flow.

The path $s - v - u - w - t$ is an augmenting path. An additional flow of 2 can reach u from s through this path (2 is the minimum slack over all forward edges until u). We can *deduct* a flow of 2 from $f(w, u)$. The conservation constraint is now satisfied for u, since u had an additional flow of 2 coming in through the augmenting path, and a flow of 2 deducted from the backward edge. We now have an extra flow of 2 at w that needs to be pushed, which is exactly what we want. We can continue pushing flow from w in the same way, pushing it forward on forward edges, and deducting it from backward edges. In this case, there is one forward edge (w, t) that reaches t, and we are done. Since only forward edges can leave s and enter t, the total flow is increased. The increase is equal to the minimum of either the minimal slack of forward edges or the minimal current flow through backward edges. Figure 7.41 shows the same network with the modified flow. (This flow is in fact maximum.)

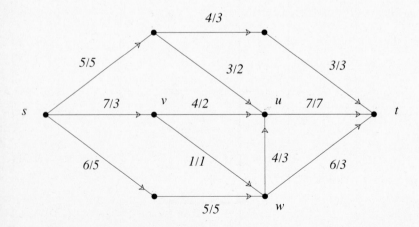

Figure 7.40 An example of a network with a (nonmaximum) flow.

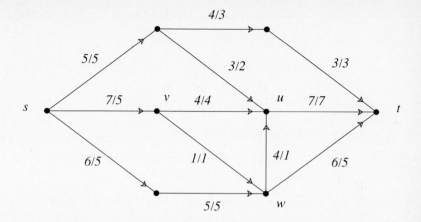

Figure 7.41 The result of augmenting the flow of Fig. 7.40.

The arguments above establish that if there is an augmenting path, then the flow is not maximum. The opposite is also true:

☐ The Augmenting-Path Theorem

A flow f is maximum if and only if it admits no augmenting path.

Proof: We have already shown one direction of the theorem — if the flow admits an augmenting path, then it is not maximum. Let's assume now that a flow f admits no augmenting path, and prove that f is maximum. We use the concept of **cuts**. Intuitively, a cut is a set of edges that separate s from t. More precisely, let A be a set of vertices of V such that $s \in A$ and $t \notin A$. Denote the rest of the vertices by $B = V - A$. A cut is the set of edges $\{(v, w) \in E\}$ such that $v \in A$ and $w \in B$. The capacity of the cut is defined as the sum of the capacities of its edges. It is clear that no flow can exceed the capacity of any cut. (If you disconnect the pipes, no water can flow through them.) Hence, if we find a flow whose value is equal to the capacity of a (any) cut, then this flow must be maximum. We proceed to prove that, if a flow admits no augmenting paths, then it is equal to the capacity of a cut, and hence it is maximum.

Let f be a flow that admits an augmenting path. Let $A \subset V$ be the set of vertices such that for each $v \in A$ there is an augmenting path, with respect to the flow f, from s to v. Clearly, $s \in A$, and $t \notin A$ (since we assumed that f admits no augmenting path). Therefore, A defines a cut. We claim that, for all edges (v, w) in that cut, $f(v, w) = c(v, w)$. Otherwise, (v, w) would be a forward edge and there would be an augmenting path to w, contrary to our assumption that $w \notin A$. By the same argument, there cannot be an edge (w, v) such that $w \notin A$ and $v \in A$, and $f(w, v) > 0$ (since it would be a backward edge and it could extend an augmenting path). Hence, the value of the flow f is equal to the capacity of the cut defined by A, and f is maximum. ☐

We have proved the following fundamental theorem.

□ Max-Flow Min-Cut Theorem

The value of a maximum flow in a network is equal to the minimum capacity of a cut.   □

The augmenting-path theorem also implies the following theorem.

□ The Integral-Flow Theorem

If the capacities of all edges in the network are integers, then there is a maximum flow whose value is an integer.

Proof: The theorem follows directly from the augmenting-path theorem. In fact, any algorithm that uses only augmenting paths will lead to an integral flow if all the capacities are integers. This is obvious since we start with a flow of 0, and each augmenting path adds an integer to the total flow.   □

We now return to the bipartite-matching problem. Clearly, any alternating path in G corresponds to an augmenting path in G', and vice versa. The augmenting-path theorem implies the alternating-path theorem given in the previous section. If M is a maximum matching, then there is no alternating path for it, which implies that there is no augmenting path in G', which implies that the flow is maximum. On the other hand, there is a maximum integral flow, and it clearly corresponds to a matching since each vertex in V is connected by only one edge (with capacity 1) to s; hence, each vertex of V can support a flow of only 1. The same argument holds for the vertices of U. This matching must be maximum since, if it could be extended, then there would be a larger flow.

The augmenting-path theorem immediately suggests an algorithm. We start with a flow of 0, search for augmenting paths, and augment the flow accordingly, until there are no more augmenting paths. We are always making progress since we are increasing the flow. Searching for augmenting paths can be done in the following way. We define the **residual graph**, with respect to a network $G = (V, E)$ and a flow f, as the network $R = (V, F)$ with the same vertices, the same source and sink, and the same edges, but with possibly different directions and different capacities. The edges in the residual graph correspond to the possible edges in an augmenting path. Their capacities correspond to the possible augmenting flow through those edges. More precisely, an edge (v, w) belongs to F if it is either a forward edge, in which case its capacity is $c(v, w) - f(v, w)$, or a backward edge, in which case its capacity is $f(v, w)$. An augmenting path is thus a regular directed path from s to t in the residual graph. Constructing the residual graph requires $|E|$ steps since each edge has to be checked exactly once.

Unfortunately, selecting augmenting paths in an arbitrary way may lead to a very slow algorithm. The worst-case running time of such an algorithm may not even be a function of the size of the graph. Consider the network in Fig. 7.42. The maximum flow is obviously $2M$. However, one might start with the path $s-a-b-t$, which can support a flow of only 1. Then, one might take the augmenting path $s-b-a-t$, which again

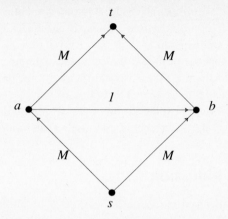

Figure 7.42 A bad example of network flow.

augments the flow by only 1. This process can be repeated $2M$ times, where M may be very large, even though the graph has only four vertices and five edges. (Since the value of M can be represented by $O(\log M)$ bits, this algorithm is exponential, in the worst case, in the size of the input.)

Although the scenario above may be unlikely, we have to take precautions to avoid it. Furthermore, we want to minimize the number of augmentations in order to speed up the algorithm. Edmonds and Karp [1972], for example, suggested (among other things) selecting the next augmenting path by taking the augmenting path with the minimum number of edges. They proved that, if this policy is maintained, then at most $(|V|^3 - |V|)/4$ augmentations are required. This leads to an algorithm whose worst case is polynomial in the size of the input. Many different algorithms have been suggested since then. Some are complicated; others are relatively simple (none are really simple). An upper bound of $O(|V|^3)$ on the complexity of network flow has been achieved by several of these algorithms. We will not describe these algorithms here (references are given in the Bibliography section).

7.12 Hamiltonian Tours

We started this chapter with a discussion of a tour containing all edges of a graph. We end the chapter with a discussion of a tour containing all the vertices of a graph. This is also a famous problem, named after the Irish mathematician Sir William R. Hamilton, who designed a popular game based on this problem in 1857.

> **The Problem**   Given a graph $G = (V, E)$, find a simple cycle in G that includes every vertex of V exactly once.

Such a cycle is called a **Hamiltonian cycle**. Graphs containing such cycles are called **Hamiltonian graphs**. The problem has a directed and an undirected version; we will consider only the undirected version.

Unlike the Eulerian-tour problem, the problem of finding Hamiltonian cycles (or characterizing Hamiltonian graphs) is very difficult. It belongs to the class of NP-complete problems discussed in Chapter 11. In this section, we present a simple example in which we find Hamiltonian cycles in only special graphs that are very dense. The most interesting part of this example is the use of an interesting technique called **reversed induction**.

7.12.1 Reversed Induction

We have already seen reversed induction in Section 2.11. The idea is to use an infinite set S (e.g., $S = \{2^k\}$, $k = 1, 2, ...$) as the base case for the induction. That is, we prove that the theorem $P(n)$ holds for all values of n that belong to S. Then, we go "backward," proving that the validity of $P(n)$ implies the validity of $P(n-1)$. Usually in mathematics, going from n to $n-1$ is not easier than going from $n-1$ to n, and proving an infinite base case is much more difficult than a simple one. When designing algorithms on the other hand, it is almost always easy to go from n to $n-1$, namely, to solve the problem for smaller inputs. For example, we can introduce "dummy" inputs that do not affect the outcome. As a result, it is sufficient in many cases to design the algorithm not for inputs of all sizes, but only for sizes taken from an infinite set. The most common use of this principle is designing algorithms only for inputs of size n which is a power of 2. It makes the design much cleaner and eliminates many "dirty" details. Obviously, these details will have to be resolved eventually. But it is more convenient to solve the main problem first. We use the assumption that n is a power of 2 in several algorithms throughout the book (e.g., Sections 8.2, and 9.4).

The same method is also useful when there is a bound on the number of possible elements. The base case of the theorem can be the instance with the maximal number of elements (rather than the minimal number). The proof can then "go backward." For example, suppose that we want to prove a theorem about graphs and we want to apply induction on the number of edges. We can start with the complete graph, which has the maximal number of edges for a fixed number of vertices. We can then prove that the theorem continues to hold even if we *remove* an edge (as opposed to the usual adding of an edge). This gives us extra flexibility in applying induction. The next algorithm illustrates this principle.

7.12.2 Finding Hamiltonian Cycles in Very Dense Graphs

Let $G = (V, E)$ be a connected undirected graph, and let $d(v)$ denote the degree of the vertex v. The following problem involves finding Hamiltonian cycles in very dense graphs. We will show that the conditions of the problem guarantee that the graph is Hamiltonian. We introduce the problem to illustrate the principle of reversed induction.

The Problem   Given a connected undirected graph $G = (V, E)$ with $n \geq 3$ vertices, such that each pair of nonadjacent vertices v and w satisfies $d(v) + d(w) \geq n$, find a Hamiltonian cycle in G.

The algorithm is based on reversed induction on the number of edges. The base case is the complete graph. Every complete graph with at least three vertices contains a Hamiltonian cycle and it is easy to find one (put all vertices in an arbitrary order and connect them in a cycle).

>   **Induction hypothesis**: *We know how to find a Hamiltonian cycle in graphs satisfying the given conditions with $\geq m$ edges.*

We have to show how to find a Hamiltonian cycle in a graph with $m - 1$ vertices that satisfies the conditions of the problem. Let $G = (V, E)$ be such a graph. Take any pair of nonadjacent vertices v and w in G, and consider the graph G', which is the same as G except that v and w are connected. By the induction hypothesis, we know how to find a Hamiltonian cycle in G'. Let $x_1, x_2, ..., x_n, x_1$ be such a cycle in G' (see Fig. 7.43). If the edge (v, w) is not included in the cycle, then the same cycle is contained in G and we are done. Otherwise, without loss of generality, we can assume that $v = x_1$ and $w = x_n$. By the conditions given for G, $d(v) + d(w) \geq n$. The stage is now set to find a new Hamiltonian cycle.

Consider all the edges in G coming out of v and w. There are at least n of them (by the conditions of the problem). But G contains $n - 2$ other vertices. Therefore, there are two vertices x_i and x_{i+1}, which are neighbors in the cycle, such that v is connected to x_{i+1} and w is connected to x_i. Using the edges (v, x_{i+1}) and (w, x_i), we can now find a new Hamiltonian cycle that does not use the edge (v, w). It is the cycle $v(= x_1), x_{i+1}, x_{i+2}, ..., w(= x_n), x_i, x_{i-1}, ..., v$ (see Fig. 7.43).

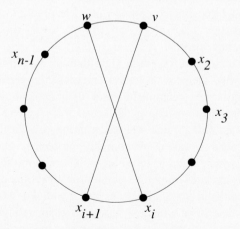

Figure 7.43 Modifying Hamiltonian cycles.

Implementation   The straightforward implementation of this proof starts with the complete graph and replaces one edge at a time. We can do better by starting with a much smaller graph as follows. Take the input graph G, find a large path (e.g., by DFS), and add the edges (not from G) necessary to complete this path to a Hamiltonian cycle. We now have a larger graph G', which has a Hamiltonian cycle. Usually, only few edges will be added. However, even in the worst case, at most $n - 1$ edges will be added. We can apply the proof above iteratively, starting with G', until a Hamiltonian path is obtained for G. The total number of steps to replace an edge is $O(n)$. There are $O(n)$ edges to replace; hence, the algorithm runs in time $O(n^2)$.

7.13 Summary

Graphs are used to model relationships among pairs of objects. Since most algorithms require an examination of the whole input, the first issue involved in graph algorithms is frequently graph traversal. We studied two types of graph traversals: *depth-first search* (DFS), and *breadth-first search* (BFS). We saw several examples where DFS was more suitable than BFS. Therefore, we suggest trying DFS first (although there are many examples where BFS is superior). DFS is especially suited for recursive algorithms on graphs. BFS also usually requires more space (although again, this is not a rule — it depends on the graph). We have also seen an example of *priority search*, which was used to compute shortest paths from a single source. Priority search is more expensive than regular search. It is useful for optimization problems involving weighted graphs.

Cycles usually cause major difficulties for graph algorithms. Therefore, algorithms for trees or directed acyclic graphs are usually much easier to design and faster to execute. It is important to realize that graphs with even a small number of edges can have many different cycles (Exercise 7.54). Algorithms that require checking all or a large fraction of the cycles in a graph can be very slow for most graphs.

Graph decomposition is very useful. Fortunately, it is also usually reasonably inexpensive. We have seen decompositions into connected components, biconnected components, and strongly connected components. Decomposition basically allows us to assume certain properties (such as connectivity), even though the graphs under consideration may not have them.

Another useful technique for graph algorithms is *reduction*. Since graphs can be represented by matrices there is a natural relationship between graph and matrix algorithms. We discuss this relationship and reductions in general in Chapter 10. Network-flow problems and matching problems are excellent source for reductions. Reductions also help us to determine whether a problem is difficult. In Chapter 11, we discuss a class of problems, called NP-complete problems, which probably cannot be solved by algorithms whose running times are polynomial in the size of the input in the worst case. This class includes numerous graph problems. The differences between easy problems and hard problems sometimes seem minuscule. For example, we have seen an efficient algorithm to determine whether a directed graph contains a simple cycle of odd length; the same problem with the extra constraint that the cycle contains a given vertex (or edge) is NP-complete. It is essential to understand and develop an intuitive feeling for these differences. Thus, the material in Chapter 11 is very important for understanding graph algorithms.

Bibliographic Notes and Further Reading

Graph theory is a relatively new field in mathematics. Most of the basic results were discovered only in this century. Nevertheless, by now graph theory is a developed and well-understood field, with thousands of results. Many books on graph theory have been published, among them Berge [1962], Ore [1963], Harary [1969], Berge [1973], Deo [1974], Bondy and Murty [1976], Chartrand [1977], Capobianco and Molluzzo [1978], Bollobás [1979], Tutte [1984], and Chartrand and Lesniak [1986]. There are also several books devoted to graph algorithms, including Even [1979], Golumbic [1980] (which emphasizes perfect graphs and related classes of graphs), Gondran and Minoux [1984] (which emphasizes optimization problems), Gibbons [1985], Nishizeki and Chiba [1988] (which is devoted to planar graphs), and a survey paper by van Leeuwen [1986].

The notion of Eulerian graphs is due to Euler [1736], and it is regarded as the first result in graph theory. An algorithm for finding Eulerian paths can be obtained quite easily from the proof (see, for example, Even [1979] or Ebert [1988]). Depth-first search was first described by Lucas [1882] (describing work by Trémaux) and Tarry [1895], where it was used to design algorithms to traverse a maze. The importance of depth-first search was made evident in the work of Tarjan [1972], who also presented the algorithms for biconnected and strongly connected components.

The minimum-cost spanning tree problem has been studied extensively. The algorithm presented in Section 7.6 (although not its implementation) is due to Prim [1957]. Another algorithm (which is the subject of Exercise 7.59) is due to Kruskal [1956]. Other algorithms for finding the minimum-cost spanning tree were developed by Yao [1975], Cheriton and Tarjan [1976], Fredman and Tarjan [1987], and Gabow, Galil, Spencer, and Tarjan [1986]

The algorithm for single-source shortest paths presented in Section 7.5 was developed by Dijkstra [1959]. The implementation using a heap is due to Johnson [1977] (see also Tarjan [1983]). When the graph is sparse, as is usually the case in practice, this is a fast algorithm. If the number of edges is proportional to $|V|^2$, then the running time of this algorithm is $O(|V|^2 \log |V|)$. A better implementation for dense graphs, with a running time of $O(|V|^2)$, is the subject of Exercise 7.43. The best-known asymptotic running time for this problem (using quite complicated data structures) is $O(|E| + |V| \log |V|)$, a result due to Fredman and Tarjan [1987]. The all-pair shortest-paths algorithm presented in Section 7.7 is due to Floyd [1962]. It works correctly for weighted graphs with possibly negative weights, provided that there are no negative weight cycles (Exercise 7.73). It is possible to find all the shortest paths faster on the average — Spira [1973] presented an algorithm whose average running time is $O(|V|^2 \log^2 |V|)$, and Moffat and Takaoka [1987] used a hybrid of Spira's algorithm and an earlier algorithm by Dantzig [1960] to obtain an algorithm whose average running time is $O(|V|^2 \log |V|)$. For more information on shortest-path algorithms see the survey by Deo and Pang [1984] (which includes, among other things, 222 references).

The transitive closure algorithm presented in Section 7.8 is due to Warshall [1962].

The augmenting-path theorem and its application to network flows were discovered by Ford and Fulkerson [1956]. An excellent description of the data structures and combinatorial algorithms for network flows is given in Tarjan [1983]. A new algorithm for network flow was recently developed by Goldberg and Tarjan [1988]. More information on the network-flow problem and many of its extensions can be found in Ford and Fulkerson [1962], Hu [1969], Christofides [1975], Lawler [1976], Minieka [1978], Papadimitriou and Steiglitz [1982], and Gondran and Minoux [1984]. A book by Lovász and Plummer [1986] covers both the mathematical foundations of matching theory and algorithms for various matching problems. Galil [1986] presents a survey of matching algorithms in bipartite and general graphs. The algorithm in Section 7.12.2 for finding Hamiltonian cycles in dense graphs is based on a theorem (and its proof) by Ore [1960].

Two important subjects in graph algorithms were not discussed here: planarity and graph isomorphism. The problem of characterizing planar graphs and embedding them in the plane is one of the oldest problems in graph theory. Early algorithms for this problem were developed by Auslander and Parter [1961] and Lempel, Even, and Cederbaum [1966]. A linear-time algorithm to determine whether a graph is planar was developed by Hopcroft and Tarjan [1974]. It uses a linear-time (DFS-based) algorithm to decompose a graph into 3-connected components (Hopcroft and Tarjan [1973]). This algorithm motivated the development of many other algorithms and data structures. A polynomial-time algorithm for graph isomorphism has not been found yet. Graph isomorphism is one of the very few major problems whose status (either polynomial or NP-hard) is still unknown (more on that in Chapter 11). For a discussion on this topic see, for example, Hoffman [1982], or Luks [1982].

A discussion on de Bruijn sequences (Exercise 7.28) can be found in Even [1979]. Exercise 7.46 is from Sedgewick and Vitter [1986]. Exercise 7.55 is motivated by an exercise from Bollobás [1986], and Exercise 7.58 is motivated by an exercise from Lovász [1979]. Ford [1956] contains an algorithm that satisfies the requirements of Exercise 7.75. The algorithm for transitive closure hinted in Exercise 7.81 is from Warren [1975]. Exercise 7.97 is from Lovász and Plummer [1986]. Gabow and Tarjan [1988] present an efficient algorithm for the bottleneck problem in Exercise 7.100. The theorem presented in Exercises 7.101 and 7.102 is known as Gomory's theorem. Exercise 7.105 is from Lovász [1979]. Exercise 7.121 is related to a problem of designing space-efficient routing tables, which is solved in Manber and McVoy [1988].

Drill Exercises

7.1   Consider the problem of finding balance factors in binary trees discussed in Section 5.8. Solve this problem using DFS. You need only to define preWORK and postWORK.

7.2   Let $G = (V, E)$ be a connected undirected graph, and let T be a DFS tree of G rooted at v.

a. Let H be an arbitrary induced subgraph of G. Show that the intersection of T and H is not necessarily a spanning tree of H.

b. Let R be a subtree of T, and let S be the subgraph of G induced by the vertices in R. Prove that R could be a DFS tree of S.

7.3 The input is a connected undirected graph $G = (V, E)$, a spanning tree T of G, and a vertex v. Design a algorithm to determine whether T is a valid DFS tree of G rooted at v. In other words, determine whether T can be the output of DFS under some order of the edges starting with v. The running time of the algorithm should be $O(|E| + |V|)$.

7.4 Characterize all undirected graphs that contain a vertex v such that there exists a DFS spanning tree rooted at v that is identical to a BFS spanning tree rooted at v. (Two spanning trees are identical if they contain the same set of edges; the order in which they are traversed is immaterial here. However, both trees must have the same root v.)

7.5 Modify algorithm *Topological_Sorting* (Fig. 7.14) in the following way. Assume that you no longer know whether or not the graph is acyclic. Obviously, if the graph is cyclic, a topological sort is impossible. Design an algorithm that will output the topological-sort labeling if the graph is acyclic, and will output a cycle if the graph is not. The running time of the algorithm should be $O(|E| + |V|)$.

7.6 Consider algorithm *Single_Source_Shortest_Paths* (Fig. 7.17) Prove that the subgraph consisting of all the edges that belong to shortest paths from v, found during the execution of the algorithm, is a tree rooted at v.

7.7 Let $G = (V, E)$ be an undirected weighted graph, and let T be the shortest-paths tree rooted at a vertex v (Exercise 7.6). Suppose now that all the weights in G are increased by a constant number c. Is T still the shortest-paths tree from v?

7.8 Prove or show a counterexample: Algorithm *Single_Source_Shortest_Paths* (Fig. 7.17) works correctly for weighted graphs some of whose edges have negative weights, provided that there are no negative-weight cycles.

7.9 Let $G = (V, E)$ be an undirected weighted graph. Prove that, if all the costs are distinct, then there exists exactly one unique minimum-cost spanning tree.

7.10 Modify algorithm *MCST* (Fig. 7.20) to find a *maximum*-cost spanning tree.

7.11 Prove or show a counterexample: algorithm *MCST* (Fig. 7.20) works correctly for weighted graphs some of whose edges have negative costs.

7.12 a. Give an example of a weighted connected undirected graph $G = (V, E)$ and a vertex v, such that the minimum-cost spanning tree of G is the same as the shortest-path tree rooted at v.

b. Give an example of a weighted connected undirected graph $G = (V, E)$ and a vertex v, such that the minimum-cost spanning tree of G is very different from the shortest path tree rooted at v. Can the two trees be completely disjoint?

7.13 Describe the changes in the biconnected components and biconnected tree resulting from deleting the vertex c from the graph in Fig. 7.25.

7.14 a. Run the biconnected components algorithm on the graph in Fig. 7.44. The algorithm should follow the DFS numbers that are given in the figure. Show the *High* values as computed by the algorithm in each step.

b. Add the edge (4,8) to the graph and discuss the changes this makes to the algorithm.

7.15   Prove that the definition of a biconnected tree in Section 7.9.1 is valid. You have to show that there are no cycles, and that the set of all biconnected components are connected.

7.16   a. Run the strongly connected components algorithm on the graph in Fig. 7.45. The algorithm should follow the DFS numbers that are given in the figure. Show the *High* values as computed by the algorithm in each step.

b. Add the edge (4,1) to the graph and discuss the changes this makes to the algorithm.

7.17   Let $G = (V, E)$ be a strongly connected graph and let T be a DFS tree in G. Prove that, if all the forward edges in G, with respect to T, are removed from G, the resulting graph is still strongly connected.

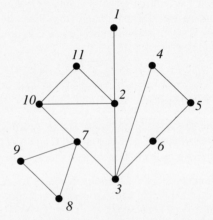

Figure 7.44 An undirected graph with DFS numbers for Exercise 7.14.

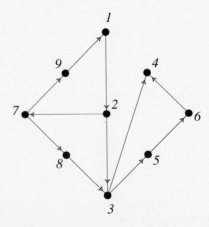

Figure 7.45 A directed graph with DFS numbers for Exercise 7.16.

7.18 a. Prove the correctness of the algorithm for finding an odd length cycle in a directed graph (Section 7.9.4).

b. Show an example of a graph that is not strongly connected for which the algorithm does not work.

7.19 Show an implementation of the algorithm discussed in Section 7.10.2 to find a perfect matching in a graph with $2n$ vertices, each with degree at least n. Your algorithm should run in time $O(|V| + |E|)$ in the worst case.

7.20 This exercise generalizes somewhat the proof of existence of perfect matchings in dense graphs. Suppose that you are given a graph with $2n$ vertices such that not all of them have high degree, but, for any two nonadjacent vertices, the sum of their degrees is at least $2n$. Is it still true that a perfect matching always exists? Is the algorithm obtained in Exercise 7.19 still valid?

Creative Exercises

Unless specified otherwise, we assume that the graphs are given in an adjacency-lists representation. Such a representation requires $O(|V| + |E|)$ space; hence, we say that an algorithm runs in *linear time* if its running time is $O(|V| + |E|)$. Unless specified otherwise, all the running times are worst case. In some cases, a particular running time is given and the exercise requires achieving that time; in other cases, we ask only for an "efficient algorithm." In the latter case, the reader should try to find the best possible algorithm. In practice, of course, the best running time is unknown when a problem is encountered.

7.21 Given an undirected graph $G = (V, E)$ and an integer k, find the maximum induced subgraph H of G such that each vertex in H has degree $> k$, or determine that it does not exist. (An induced subgraph of a graph $G = (V, E)$ is a graph $H = (U, F)$ such that $U \subseteq V$, and F includes all edges in E both of whose vertices are in U.) The algorithm should run in linear time. (This problem is discussed in Section 5.3.)

7.22 Let $G = (V, E)$ be a connected undirected graph. We want to pick a vertex of degree 1 of G, remove it and its incident edge from G, and continue this process (i.e., taking another vertex of degree 1 in the remaining graph, removing it, and so on) until all edges are removed. If this procedure is always possible for certain graphs, then designing algorithms by induction for these graphs may be easier. Characterize connected undirected graphs that satisfy these conditions. In other words, find necessary and sufficient conditions for a graph G on which the procedure described above is possible.

7.23 Describe an efficient implementation of the Eulerian graph algorithm discussed in Section 7.2. The algorithm should run in linear time and space.

7.24 Let $G = (V, E)$ be an undirected graph such that each vertex has an even degree. Design a linear-time algorithm to direct the edges of G such that, for each vertex, the outdegree is equal to the indegree.

7.25 A *directed Eulerian circuit* is a directed circuit that contains each edge exactly once. Prove that a directed graph contains a directed Eulerian circuit if and only if the indegree of each vertex is equal to its outdegree, and the underlying undirected graph is connected. Design an efficient algorithm to find such an Eulerian circuit if it exists.

7.26   Let $G = (V, E)$ be an undirected connected graph with k vertices of odd degrees.

   a. Prove that k is even.

   b. Design an algorithm to find $k/2$ open paths such that each edge in G is included in exactly one of these paths.

7.27   Design an algorithm to find a vertex in a connected undirected graph whose removal *does not* disconnect the graph. The algorithm should run in linear time. (Do not use the biconnected components algorithm.) As a consequence, prove that every connected graph contains such a vertex.

7.28   A **binary de Bruijn sequence** is a (cyclic) sequence of 2^n bits $a_1 a_2 \cdots a_{2^n}$ such that each binary string s of size n is represented somewhere in the sequence; that is, there exists a unique index i such that $s = a_i a_{i+1} \cdots a_{i+n-1}$ (where the indices are taken modulo 2^n). For example, the sequence 11010001 is a binary de Bruijn sequence for $n = 3$. Let $G_n = (V, E)$ be a directed graph defined as follows. The vertex set V corresponds to the set of all binary strings of size $n - 1$ ($|V| = 2^{n-1}$). A vertex corresponding to the string $a_1 a_2 \cdots a_{n-1}$ has an edge leading to a vertex corresponding to the string $b_1 b_2 \cdots b_{n-1}$ if and only if $a_2 a_3 \cdots a_{n-1} = b_1 b_2 \cdots b_{n-2}$. Prove that G_n is a directed Eulerian graph, and discuss the implications for de Bruijn sequences.

7.29   Design an efficient algorithm for the following problem: Given n positive integers $d_1, d_2, ..., d_n$, such that $d_1 + d_2 + \cdots + d_n = 2n - 2$, construct a tree with n vertices of degrees exactly $d_1, d_2, ..., d_n$.

7.30   Let $(i_1, o_1), (i_2, o_2), ..., (i_n, o_n)$ be a sequence of pairs of integers such that

   a. $i_1 = 0$, and $i_k = 1$ for $1 < k \leq n$

   b. $\sum_{j=1}^{n} o_j = n - 1$

   Find a rooted tree with n vertices such that the indegree of vertex k is i_k, and its outdegree is o_k. The algorithm should run in time $O(n)$.

7.31   Let $G = (V, E)$ be a directed graph (not necessarily acyclic). Design an efficient algorithm to label the vertices of the graph with distinct labels from 1 to $|V|$ such that the label of each vertex v is greater than the label of at least one of v's predecessors, or to determine that no such labeling is possible. (A predecessor of v is a vertex w such that $(w, v) \in E$.)

7.32   An undirected graph $G = (V, E)$ is said to be k-colorable if all the vertices of G can be colored using k different colors such that no two adjacent vertices have the same color. Design a linear-time algorithm to color a graph with two colors or determine that two colors are not sufficient.

7.33   Let $G = (V, E)$ be an undirected graph that can be colored with two colors. It may be possible to color G with two colors in several different ways. Use the algorithm in Exercise 7.32 to prove that the coloring of G is *unique* (except for interchanging the colors, which can always be done) if and only if G is connected.

7.34   Let T be an undirected tree (not necessarily binary) whose root is r. Each vertex in T is associated with a character taken from a fixed finite alphabet. The tree is represented by adjacency lists. Let P be a *pattern* string (represented by an array of characters). Design an algorithm to find whether the pattern appears at least once in a path from the root to a leaf. The algorithm should run in time $O(n+m)$ in the worst case, where n is the number of vertices in the tree and m is the size of the pattern.

7.35   Given a connected undirected graph $G=(V, E)$ that contains exactly one cycle, direct the edges such that the indegrees of all vertices are at most 1. (Such directed graphs are called **injective** since they correspond to injective functions.) What is the complexity of your algorithm?

7.36   Let $G=(V, E)$ be an undirected graph. Design an algorithm to determine whether it is possible to direct the edges of G such that the indegree of every vertex is at least 1. If it is possible, then the algorithm should show a way to do it.

7.37   Given a connected undirected graph $G=(V, E)$, direct its edges such that the following two conditions are satisfied:

     a. The resulting directed graph contains a rooted tree (i.e., a tree all of whose edges point away from the root).

     b. Any edge, which does not belong to the tree above, completes a directed cycle with edges of the tree.
     What is the complexity of your algorithm?

7.38   Given a directed acyclic graph $G=(V, E)$, find a simple (directed) path in G that has the maximum number of edges among all simple paths in G. The algorithm should run in linear time.

7.39   a. Solve the problem in Exercise 7.38 for the case of weighted graphs. That is, you are now looking for a path whose weight is the maximum over all paths.

     b. Will your algorithm work for negative cost edges?

     c. Will your algorithm work for general (not necessarily acyclic) graphs?

7.40   Let $G=(V, E)$ be a directed acyclic graph, and let k be the maximal number of edges in a path of G. Design an algorithm to divide the vertices into at most $k+1$ groups such that for each two vertices v and w in the same group there is no path from v to w and there is no path from w to v. The algorithm should run in linear time.

7.41   Let $G=(V, E)$ be a directed graph with the following property. G consists of an acyclic subgraph H, which contains all of G's vertices, and additional *back edges*, such that every simple path in G contains at most one back edge. Design a linear-time algorithm to find all shortest paths from a fixed source to all other vertices of G. (Note that the identity of H is not known.)

7.42   Let $G=(V, E)$ be a directed graph and let v and w be two vertices in G. Design a linear-time algorithm to find the *number* of different shortest paths (not necessarily vertex disjoint) between v and w. (There are no weights on the edges.)

7.43   Design an implementation of algorithm *Single_Source_Shortest_Paths* (Fig. 7.15) which requires running time of $O(|V|^2)$ in the worst case (for any size of E).

7.44 Let $G = (V, E)$ be a weighted directed graph. Design an algorithm to find a cycle in G of minimum weight. The algorithm should run in time $O(|V|^3)$.

7.45 The algorithms for finding shortest paths described in Section 7.5 break ties arbitrarily. Discuss how to modify these algorithms such that, if there are several different paths of the same length, then the one with the minimum number of edges (hops) will be chosen. You can use $O(|E|)$ additional space. (Ties between several paths of the same length *and* the same number of edges can be broken arbitrarily.)

7.46 A **Euclidean graph** is an undirected weighted graph such that each vertex corresponds to a point in the plane and the weight of an edge is equal to the distance between the points it connects. The following heuristic has been suggested to find the shortest path between two given vertices s and t in a Euclidean graph. Use Dijkstra's algorithm for single-source shortest paths, except that, at each iteration, choose the next previously unchosen vertex x that minimizes the sum $dist(s, x) + Euclid\_dist(x, t)$, where $dist$ corresponds to the shortest path and $Euclid\_dist$ corresponds to the Euclidean distance. The algorithm terminates when t is selected, at which point the shortest path from s to t is found.

a. How would you implement this algorithm? You have to mention only the differences from the implementation of Dijkstra's algorithm.

b. Explain why this method will not work for general (non-Euclidean) graphs.

c. Give an example where this heuristic is much faster (by more than a constant) than Dijkstra's algorithm, and an example where it is not faster. What is the worst-case running time in terms of the number of vertices?

7.47 The input is a directed graph $G = (V, E)$ with a distinguished vertex v, such that there is a positive cost $c(w)$ associated with each vertex w. The cost of a directed path $v, x_1, x_2, ..., x_k, u$ is defined as $\sum_{i=1}^{k} c(x_i)$. The costs of the two endpoints v and u are ignored, so if $(v, u) \in E$, the cost of getting from v to u is 0. Design an efficient algorithm to find the minimum-cost paths from v to all other vertices.

7.48 Let $G = (V, E)$ be a directed weighted graph such that all the weights are positive. Let v and w be two vertices in G and $k \leq |V|$ be an integer. Design an algorithm to find the shortest path from v to w that contains exactly k edges. The path need not be simple.

7.49 There is a large class of problems, called **bottleneck problems**, which have the following form. The input is a weighted graph. We are interested a certain property of the graph (in this case, shortest paths). We define the **bottleneck weight** of a subgraph as the weight of the maximum-weight edge in that subgraph, as opposed to the usual definition of sum of the weights. (This maximum-weight edge is the bottleneck.) In this problem, we consider bottleneck shortest paths (i.e., the cost of the path is defined as the maximum cost of an edge in the path).

a. Design an algorithm to solve the single-source shortest-paths problem where the path costs are defined as above. Can you say something special about the tree of shortest paths obtained by this algorithm?

b. Design an algorithm to solve the all-pairs shortest-paths problem where the path costs are defined as above. The algorithm should be a variation of algorithm *All_Pairs_Shortest_Paths* (Fig. 7.22).

7.50   Let $G = (V, E)$ be a weighted acyclic directed graph with possible negative weights. Design a linear-time algorithm to solve the single-source shortest-paths problem from a given source v.

7.51   Let $d(v)$ denote the degree of a vertex v. Design a linear-time algorithm to sort *all* the adjacency lists of a given directed graph $G = (V, E)$ by increasing vertex degrees. That is, if $d(u) < d(v)$, then edges to u precede edges to v in all the adjacency lists that contain both. Ties are broken arbitrarily. The algorithm can use linear space.

7.52   Find necessary and sufficient conditions under which the set of edges E of an undirected graph $G = (V, E)$ can be partitioned into disjoint subsets $E_1, ..., E_k$ such that each E_i corresponds to a simple cycle. Design an efficient algorithm to find such a partition in graphs that satisfy these conditions.

7.53   Given an undirected connected graph $G = (V, E)$, find a simple cycle of minimum length (no weights). The length of the smallest cycle in a graph is called the **girth** of the graph.

7.54   Prove that there are undirected graphs with n vertices and $O(n)$ edges that contain $2^{\Omega(n)}$ different cycles. (This claim implies that even sparse graphs may have an exponential number of cycles; therefore, an algorithm that requires checking all the cycles is inherently inefficient for general graphs.)

7.55   Design an algorithm to solve the following problem:

Input: A directed graph $G = (V, E)$ with $n + 1$ vertices and n edges, whose underlying undirected graph is a tree, where each edge (u, w) is labeled with a unique integer $\lambda(u, w)$ in the range $1, 2, ..., n$.

Output: A function S from vertices to subsets of $\{1, 2, ..., n\}$ such that the following two conditions are satisfied:

1. If $(u, w) \in E$, then $S(w) = S(u) \cup \{\lambda(u, w)\}$

2. If $u \neq w$, then $S(u) \neq S(w)$

(Note: $S(u)$ can be any subset of $\{1, 2, ..., n\}$ including the empty set or the whole set.)

7.56   Consider again the problem in Exercise 7.55. Prove that the problem cannot be solved for any graph (and any labeling) which contains a cycle (not necessarily directed). In other words, prove that the restriction of the problem to trees is necessary.

7.57   A **kernel** in a directed graph $G = (V, E)$ is a subset $V' \subseteq V$ such that no two vertices in V' are connected by an edge, and for every vertex $w \notin V'$ there is an edge (v, w) such that $v \in V'$. The input is a directed graph $G = (V, E)$ with $n + 1$ vertices and n edges, whose underlying undirected graph is a tree. Design an algorithm to find a kernel in G or determine that no kernel exists.

7.58   Let $G = (V, E)$ be a directed graph and let f be a function defined on all edges of G such that $\sum_{i=1}^{k} f(e_k) = 0$ if $e_1, ..., e_k$ is a circuit in G. Find a function p on the vertices of G such that for each edge (v, w), we have $f(v, w) = p(w) - p(v)$.

7.59   Here is a sketch of a different MCST algorithm. Instead of keeping one tree and enlarging it one edge at a time, we keep a collection of disjoint trees (which are all part of the MCST) and combine them, adding one edge at a time. Initially, all the vertices are considered as disjoint trees of size 0. In each step, the algorithm finds the minimum-cost edge that connects two separate trees, and combines these two trees by adding the edge. Prove that such an approach is feasible and correct. Describe an implementation of an algorithm based on this approach. What is the complexity of your algorithm? (Hint: The Union-Find data structure is helpful here.)

7.60   Let $G = (V, E)$ be an undirected weighted graph, and let F be a subgraph of G that is a forest (i.e., F does not contain any cycles). Design an efficient algorithm to find a spanning tree in G that contains all the edges of F, and that has minimum cost among all spanning trees containing F.

7.61   Let $G = (V, E)$ be a connected weighted undirected graph, and let T be a minimum-cost spanning tree of G. Suppose that the cost of one edge e in G is changed. Discuss the conditions under which T is no longer an MCST. Design an efficient algorithm either to find a new MCST or to determine that T is still an MCST. (e may or may not belong to T.)

7.62   Consider a communication network that can be modeled as a weighted undirected connected graph $G = (V, E)$. Each site in the network is represented as a vertex and each line of communication is bidirectional and has a *cost* associated with it. The cost may correspond to the expected delay on the line, or to the tariff for using this line. Each site has only *local* information; that is, it knows only the edges (and vertices) adjacent to it. An MCST of the network can be used to broadcast messages to all sites. If we broadcast the messages by using only the edges of the MCST, then the total cost is minimized. Assume that such an MCST is computed by some method and that each site knows which of the edges adjacent to it belong to the MCST. Assume now that sites in a certain subset $U \subset V$ share between them the information that is known to all of them. In other words, every site in U knows not only about the edges and vertices adjacent to itself, but it also knows all the edges and vertices adjacent to all vertices in U. Furthermore, assume that the partial MCST restricted to U is connected (i.e., it is a tree). Consider an edge $e \in U$, which belongs to the MCST, whose cost has just changed.

   a. Find the conditions under the change in e's cost is guaranteed *not* to affect the MCST. Consider only conditions that can be checked with the information known to the sites in U. In other words, how can the sites in U determine that no action needs to be taken to modify the MCST after the change?

   b. Find the conditions under which the modified MCST is different from the original one only in edges that belong to U (hence, the change can be handled locally). Consider only conditions that can be checked with the information known to the sites in U.

   c. Describe briefly an algorithm to check for the conditions in parts a and b (again only within U), and to modify the MCST accordingly. The algorithm does not need to handle the case where the change to the MCST may be outside U.

7.63   Consider the problem of broadcasting in a network, but assume now that the main interest is fast dissemination of information rather than minimum cost. In other words, the costs correspond to the time it takes to forward a message, and we want to minimize the elapsed time of broadcast. A message can be sent concurrently on separate links. Assume that one message is sent from a fixed source and is forwarded to all other sites such that each site receives only one copy of the message. You can assume that you are a controller with full information about the topology of the network.

a. Design an algorithm to determine the optimal forwarding, assuming that the only delays are associated with the links.

b. Design an algorithm to determine the optimal forwarding when there are also delays associated with the sites. It takes $t(v)$ units of time for site v to forward a message to one of its neighbors. If v forwards the message to k neighbors, then it takes $kt(v)$ time. (The values of $t(v)$ are known for all v.)

7.64 Let $G = (V, E)$ be a connected undirected weighted graph. Assume for simplicity that the weights are positive and distinct. Let e be an edge of G. Denote by $T(e)$ the spanning tree of G that has minimum cost among all spanning trees of G that contain e. Design an algorithm to find $T(e)$ for all edges $e \in E$. The algorithm should run in time $O(|V|^2)$.

7.65 Design an efficient algorithm to find the minimum bottleneck weight spanning tree of a weighted connected undirected graph. (Recall that a bottleneck weight is defined as the maximum weight of an edge in the subgraph.) In other words, you are asked to find a spanning tree in which the maximum weight is minimized.

7.66 Solve a variation of the problem in Exercise 7.65 for directed graphs: The input is a weighted directed graph $G = (V, E)$ with a distinguished vertex v. Find a rooted spanning tree, with v as the root, such that the maximum-cost edge in the tree is minimized. (Recall that in a rooted tree the directions of all edges are away from the root.)

7.67 Let $G = (V, E)$ be an undirected weighted graph, and let T be an MCST of G. Suppose now that all the weights in G are increased by a constant number c. Is T still an MCST? If not, how difficult is it to modify T into an MCST?

*7.68 Let $G = (V, E)$ be a connected weighted undirected graph, and let T be an MCST of G. Suppose that we now add a new vertex v to G, together with some weighted edges from v to vertices of G. Design a linear-time algorithm to find a new MCST that includes v.

7.69 Suppose that the cost of a spanning tree is not the sum of the costs of the tree's edges but rather the *product* of their costs (all costs are positive). Design an efficient algorithm to find a maximum-cost spanning tree under this assumption. (You can assume that all costs are distinct.)

7.70 Let $G = (V, E)$ be a connected undirected graph with n vertices numbered from 1 to n. Design an efficient algorithm to find the smallest k such that successively deleting the vertices numbered $1, 2, ..., k$ (in that order) results in a graph all of whose connected components contain at most $n/2$ vertices. Deleting a vertex also includes deleting all the edges incident to it. (Hint: Use the union-find data structure.)

7.71 Let $G = (V, E)$ be an undirected graph. A set $F \subseteq E$ of edges is called a **feedback-edge set** if every cycle of G has at least one edge in F. Design an algorithm to find a minimum-size feedback-edge set.

7.72 Let $G = (V, E)$ be a weighted undirected graph with positive weights. Design an algorithm to find a feedback-edge set (defined in Exercise 7.71) of G of minimum weight.

7.73 Prove that algorithm *All_Pairs_Shortest_Paths* given in Fig. 7.22 works correctly for weighted graphs with possibly negative weights provided that there are no negative-weight cycles.

7.74 Let $G = (V, E)$ be a weighted directed graph such that some of the weights may be negative but there are no negative-weight cycles (i.e., there are no cycles in which the sum of the edge weights is negative). Let T be a spanning tree of G rooted at v. Design a linear-time algorithm to determine whether the tree T contains only shortest paths from v to all other vertices of G. You need to output only yes or no.

7.75 The following are hints for an algorithm to compute single-source shortest paths in weighted graphs with negative weights but no negative-weight cycles. The algorithm starts with an arbitrary rooted spanning tree, as in Exercise 7.74. It then applies the algorithm in that exercise to determine whether the tree is the shortest path tree. The algorithm obtained in Exercise 7.74 should provide some *evidence* in case the tree is not the desired tree. This evidence is used to make a modification to the tree, and the same procedure is applied until the tree becomes the shortest-path tree.

a. Describe in more detail the exact algorithm.

b. Prove that the algorithm terminates after $O(|V| \cdot |E|)$ steps.

c. Suggest a way to improve the algorithm by selecting a good initial tree. The improvement need not change the worst case, only the "common" case.

7.76 Let $G = (V, E)$ be a weighted directed graph such that some of the weights may be negative. Design an efficient algorithm to determine whether the graph contains a negative-weight cycle. You need to output only yes or no.

7.77 a. Let $G = (V, E)$ be a directed graph, and let v be a vertex of V. Each edge of E is *colored* either black or red. Design a linear-time algorithm to determine whether G has a simple cycle, which includes v, with alternating colors — namely, each red (black) edge in the cycle has two black (red) neighbors. If such a cycle exists, then the algorithm should find at least one.

b. Solve this problem without the restriction that the cycle has to include the special vertex.

7.78 Given a connected undirected graph $G = (V, E)$, find a spanning tree of G with minimum height. (The height of a tree is the maximum distance from a root to a leaf.)

7.79 A **Hamiltonian path** is a simple path that includes all the vertices of the graph. Design an algorithm to determine whether a given acyclic directed graph $G = (V, E)$ contains a Hamiltonian path. The algorithm should run in linear time.

7.80 Algorithm *Improved_Transitive_Closure* given in Fig 7.24 has three nested loops. The first one (the outer one) chooses a column, the second one chooses a row, and the third one operates on the chosen row. Suppose that we exchange the first two loops such that the first one chooses a row and the second one chooses a column. In other words, we simply exchange the first two lines in the program, as is shown in algorithm *WRONG_Transitive_Closure* in Fig. 7.46. Show that this modification does not work, by giving an example for which the transitive closure is not computed.

7.81 Exchanging the order of scanning the matrix for the transitive closure algorithm (which was attempted unsuccessfully in Exercise 7.80) is desired for the following reason. If the matrix is very large and thus cannot be stored in main memory, we need to access it from secondary memory. Assume that the matrix is stored by rows such that each row occupies a page. We want to minimize the number of pages that need to be fetched from secondary

---

Algorithm WRONG_Transitive_Closure (A) ;
Input: *A* (an *n* ×*n* adjacency matrix representing a weighted graph).
{ *A* [*x*, *y*] is true if the edge (*x*, *y*) belongs to the graph, and false otherwise;
   A [*x*, *x*] is true for all *x* }
Output: At the end, the matrix *A* represents the transitive closure of the graph.

begin
    for *x* := 1 to *n* **do**
        for *m* := 1 to *n* **do**
            if *A* [*x*, *m*] **then**
                for *y* := 1 to *n* **do**
                    if *A* [*m*, *y*] **then** *A* [*x*, *y*] := true

Figure 7.46 Algorithm *WRONG_Transitive_Closure*.

---

memory. If the first loop scans the matrix by columns, then we need to bring all the rows to look at each column. On the other hand, if we exchange the first two loops and we find that a certain entry (*x*, *y*) is false, then there is no need to fetch the *y*th row in the next step. Therefore, if the matrix is sparse (i.e., if it contains only a few 1s), fewer pages need to be fetched. The algorithm in Fig. 7.46 is wrong as is, but it can be fixed.

a. Show that, if we run this algorithm $O(\log n)$ times, then it computes the transitive closure correctly.

b. Show that, in fact, it is sufficient to run the algorithm only twice.

7.82 Let $G = (V, E)$ be a **multigraph**, namely, an undirected graph that may have more than one edge between a pair of vertices. *E* is in this case a multiset, and $|E|$ is the total number of edges. Design an $O(|E| + |V|)$ algorithm to delete each vertex *v* of degree 2 by replacing the edges (*u*, *v*) and (*v*, *w*) by an edge (*u*, *w*), and to eliminate multiple copies of edges by repacing them with a single edge. (Note that removing multiple copies of an edge may create a new vertex of degree 2, which has to be removed, and removing a vertex of degree 2 may create multiple edges, which must be removed too.)

7.83 A connected undirected graph $G = (V, E)$ is called **edge-biconnected** if removal of any one edge leaves the graph connected. Design a linear-time algorithm to determine whether a graph is edge-biconnected.

7.84 Given a connected undirected graph $G = (V, E)$, and three edges, *a*, *b*, and *c*, find whether there exists a cycle in *G* that contains both *a* and *b* but *does not* contain *c*. The algorithm should run in linear time.

7.85 Let $G = (V, E)$ be a connected undirected graph and let $T = (V, F)$ be a spanning tree of *G*. Prove that the intersection of *F* with the set of edges of any biconnected component is a set of edges that forms a spanning tree of the component.

7.86 A **biconnected extension** of a graph $G = (V, E)$ is a biconnected graph $G' = (V, E')$ such that $E \subseteq E'$. Given an undirected graph $G = (V, E)$, find the minimum biconnected extension; that is, find a biconnected extension with the minimum number of edges. (Hint: Start by considering very simple graphs, and work your way up to general graphs.)

7.87   Suppose that you are given an undirected graph with a list of all the articulation points. Show how to find the biconnected components without resorting to running the whole biconnected component algorithm.

7.88   Let $G = (V, E)$ be a directed graph, and let T be a DFS tree of G. Prove that the intersection of the edges of T with the edges of any strongly connected component of G form a subtree of T.

7.89   A *High* value computed by algorithm *Strongly_Connected_Components* (Fig. 7.33) does not actually point to the ''highest'' vertex reachable from the vertex under consideration. It serves only as an indication whether a strongly connected component has been found. Design a linear-time algorithm to find, for each vertex v in the graph, the vertex with the largest DFS number (based on a fixed DFS tree with decreasing DFS numbers) reachable from v.

7.90   Let $G = (V, E)$ be a connected undirected graph. Design a linear-time algorithm to determine whether the edges of G can be oriented such that the resulting directed graph is strongly connected. The algorithm should find such an orientation if it exists.

7.91   a. Prove the following theorem: *A directed graph $G = (V, E)$ is strongly connected if and only if there is a circuit in G that includes every edge at least once.* (Note that an edge may appear more than once in that circuit.)

        b. Design an efficient algorithm to find such a circuit in a given strongly connected graph $G = (V, E)$.

7.92   A **vertex basis** of a directed graph $G = (V, E)$ is a minimum-size subset $B \subseteq V$ with the property that, for each vertex v in V, there is a vertex b in B such that there is a path of length 0 or more from b to v. Prove the following two claims, and then use them to design a linear-time algorithm to find a vertex basis in general directed graphs.

        a. A vertex that is not on a cycle and has nonzero indegree cannot be in any vertex basis.

        b. An acyclic directed graph has a unique vertex basis, and it is easy to find it.

7.93   A directed graph $G = (V, E)$ is called **unilateral** if, for any two vertices v and w in G, at least one of them is reachable from the other. In particular, every strongly connected graph is unilateral. On the other hand, there are many unilateral graphs that are not strongly connected. For example, a graph that consists of two vertices connected by one edge is unilateral, but it is not strongly connected. Design a linear-time (and linear-space) algorithm to determine whether a given directed graph is unilateral. (Hint: Consider the strongly connected components graph.)

7.94   A directed graph $G = (V, E)$ is called **unipathic** if, whenever w is reachable from v, there is only one simple path from v to w. Design an efficient algorithm to determine whether a given graph $G = (V, E)$ is unipathic. (Hint: Solve the problem first for acyclic graphs.)

7.95   Design a linear-time algorithm for finding a maximum matching in a tree.

7.96   Prove the alternating-paths theorem directly without the use of network flows or cuts. (Hint: Given two matching M_1 and M_2, study the properties of the symmetric difference between them; namely, the set of all edges that appear in exactly one of them.)

7.97   Let G be an undirected bipartite graph, and let M be an arbitrary matching in G.

   a. Prove the following theorem: *There exists a maximum matching in G that covers all the vertices that M covers.* (A vertex is covered by a matching M if it is incident to one of the edges of M.)

   b. Convert the proof in part a to an algorithm for finding such a maximum matching when G and M are given.

*7.98   Prove that the running time of Hopcroft and Karp bipartite matching algorithm (the improved algorithm in Section 7.10) is $O((m+n)\sqrt{n})$ in the worst case.

7.99   Suppose that we want to find a **nonmonogamous** matching in a graph. In other words, instead of looking for disjoint edges, we are looking for disjoint **star graphs**, which are trees with one vertex (the root) connected to all other vertices. One edge is a special case of a star graph, but one vertex alone with no edges is a trivial graph which we do not consider to be a star graph. Let $G = (V, E)$ be an undirected connected graph. The goal is to design an algorithm that finds a collection of vertex-disjoint stars in G, each with at least two vertices. Each vertex should be included in one of the stars, but not all the edges need to be included. In other words, the stars should cover all the vertices, but not necessarily all the edges. (There are no minimality or maximality constraints.)

   a. Find the error in the following algorithm both by pointing out the wrong argument and by exhibiting a counterexample.

   Wrong algorithm: We use induction. The induction hypothesis is that we know how to solve the problem for a graph with $< n$ vertices. Given a graph $G = (V, E)$ with n vertices, we first pick an arbitrary vertex v and remove v with all its neighbors from the graph. The remaining graph may not be connected, but we can consider each connected component separately and apply the same algorithm by induction.

   b. Design an efficient (and correct) algorithm for this problem.

7.100   Consider the following **bottleneck** problem. The input is a weighted bipartite graph $G = (V, E)$ with n vertices and m edges. We define the **bottleneck weight** of matching M to be the weight of the maximum-weight edge in M. Design an algorithm to find, among all maximum matchings, one with minimum bottleneck weight. The algorithm should run in time $O(\sqrt{n}\, m \log n)$.

7.101   Consider an $N \times N$ board of alternating black and white squares (such as a chess board). Prove, by using the alternating-path theorem, that if one removes one arbitrary black square and one arbitrary white square, then the rest of the board can be covered by dominoes (of size 2×1).

7.102   Prove the theorem in Exercise 7.101 by finding a Hamiltonian cycle in a graph defined by the board in the following way: The vertices are the squares and any two neighboring squares are connected.

7.103   Let $G = (V, E)$ be a connected undirected graph. Given two spanning trees T and R of G, find the shortest sequence of trees $T_0, T_1, ..., T_k$, such that $T_0 = T$, $T_k = R$, and each tree differs from the previous one by an addition of one edge and a deletion of one edge.

7.104 Assume that a round-robin tournament is played among n players. That is, each player plays once against all $n-1$ other players. There are no draws, and the results of all games are given in a matrix. It is not possible in general to sort the players, since A may beat B, B may beat C, and C may beat A (in other words, the results are not necessarily transitive). We are interested in a "weak" sorting as follows. Design an algorithm to arrange the players in an order $P_1, P_2, ..., P_n$ such that P_1 beat P_2, P_2 beat P_3, and so on (concluding with P_{n-1} beating P_n). The algorithm should take the above matrix of results as input, and should run in time $O(n \log n)$ in the worst case. (Any entry in the matrix can be accessed in constant time.)

7.105 Given n integers $0 \le d_1 \le d_2 \le \cdots \le d_n$, such that $d_1 + d_2 + \cdots + d_n$ is even, and, for every $2 \le i \le n$, we have $d_i \le d_1 + d_2 + \cdots + d_{i-1}$. Construct an undirected multigraph with n vertices of degrees exactly $d_1, d_2, ..., d_n$.

*7.106 An **edge coloring** of a graph is an assignment of colors to the edges (one color per edge), such that two edges incident to the same vertex have different colors. Design an algorithm to find an edge coloring with k colors for undirected bipartite graphs all of whose vertices have degree k such that k is a power of 2. The running time of the algorithm should be $O(|E| \log k)$.

7.107 An **edge cover** of an undirected graph $G = (V, E)$ is a set of edges such that each vertex in the graph is incident to at least one edge from the set. Design an efficient algorithm to find a minimum-size edge cover for a given bipartite graph.

7.108 A **vertex cover** of an undirected graph $G = (V, E)$ is a set of vertices U such that each edge in the graph is incident to at least one vertex from U. Design an efficient algorithm to find a minimum-size vertex cover for a given tree. (Vertex covers in general graphs are discussed in Chapter 11.)

7.109 Let $G = (V, E)$ be a tree with weights associated with the vertices such that the weight of each vertex is equal to the degree of that vertex. Design an algorithm to find the **minimum-weight vertex cover** of G, i.e., a vertex cover with minimum weight.

7.110 Design an efficient algorithm to find a minimum-size vertex cover for a given bipartite graph. (Hint: Find a relationship to minimum cuts in the graph.)

7.111 Let $G = (V, E)$ be an undirected graph. An **independent set** in G is a set of vertices no two of which are connected. Design an efficient algorithm to find a maximum-size independent set in a given bipartite graph. (Independent sets in general graphs are discussed in Chapter 11.) (Hint: Find a relationship to Exercise 7.110.)

7.112 Design an algorithm to find a **maximal independent set** (see Exercise 7.111) in a given undirected graph $G = (V, E)$. The set need not have the *maximum* size over all independent sets. It is only required to be maximal in the sense that it cannot be extended by the addition of more vertices to it and still remain independent.

7.113 Let $G = (V, E)$ be a tree such that each vertex v has an associate weight $w(v)$. Design a linear-time algorithm to find an independent set in G (see Exercise 7.111) with maximum weight.

7.114 Let $G = (V, E)$ be a connected undirected graph. Design an algorithm to determine whether G contains a vertex cover (see Exercise 7.108) with at most k vertices, all of which are independent (i.e., no two vertices from the cover are adjacent).

7.115 Design an algorithm to determine whether an undirected graph $G = (V, E)$ has a set of vertices U, such that U is a minimum vertex cover and a maximum independent set at the same time. The algorithm should find such a set if it exists.

7.116 An **interval graph** is an undirected graph whose vertices correspond to intervals on the real line and two vertices are connected if the corresponding intervals intersect. Let $G = (V, E)$ be an interval graph such that the corresponding intervals are known. Design an efficient algorithm to find a maximum independent set in G.

7.117 An undirected graph $G = (V, E)$ is a **split graph** if its vertex set can be partitioned into two disjoint subsets U and W such that the graph induced by U has no edges and the graph induced by W is a complete graph (i.e., all the edges are present). Design a linear-time algorithm to determine whether a given graph is a split graph.

7.118 a. Design an algorithm to determine whether a given undirected graph $G = (V, E)$ contains a triangle as a subgraph. The running time of the algorithm should be $O(|V| \cdot |E|)$.

b. Can your algorithm find *all* the triangles contained as subgraphs in G?

7.119 a. Design an algorithm to determine whether a given undirected graph $G = (V, E)$ contains a square as a subgraph (i.e., a cycle of length 4). The running time of the algorithm should be $O(|V|^3)$.

b. Improve your algorithm to run in time $O(|V| \cdot |E|)$.
You can use the adjacency matrix representation or the adjacency list representation, whichever is more convenient.

7.120 Prove that there is no algorithm that finds *all* squares that are subgraphs of a given undirected graph $G = (V, E)$ whose running time in the worst case is $O(|V| \cdot |E|)$.

*7.121 Let T be a rooted directed tree, not necessarily binary. There is a weight associated with each vertex, such that the weight of a vertex is greater than the weight of the vertex's parent (in other words, the weights satisfy the heap condition with the minimal weight on top). Each vertex can be designated as either a *regular* vertex or a *pivot* vertex. The cost of a pivot vertex is the same as its weight. Regular vertices get *discounts*, however — their cost is their weight minus the weight of the closest ancestor that is a pivot vertex. Thus, selecting a vertex as a pivot vertex may increase its cost, but it will also decrease the costs of some of its descendants. There is no limit on the number of pivot vertices. Design an efficient algorithm to designate every vertex as either a regular vertex or a pivot vertex, such that the total cost of all vertices is minimized.

7.122 Let T be a complete binary tree of height h, and $n = 2^h - 1$ vertices. We want to **embed** T in the plane in the following way. Each vertex corresponds to a unique lattice point (i.e., a point with integral coordinates), adjacent vertices are connected by straight line segments, and no two line segments intersect. Embedding graphs in the plane in this way is an important problem in integrated chip design and especially VLSI design. Our objective in this exercise is to minimize the area enclosing the layout. We define this area to be the minimum-area rectangle along lattice points (which are not occupied) that contains the layout. So, for example, a straight chain with k vertices would be enclosed in a rectangle of area $2(k + 1)$. It is clear that for any graph with n vertices the minimal possible area is of size $\Omega(n)$.

a. Describe a layout for T that requires $O(n)$ area. (Hint: Use divide and conquer; each complete binary tree consists of two smaller complete binary trees, both connected to a new shared root. Assume that you know how to embed trees of height $h-1$, and find the layout of a tree of height h.)

b. Design an algorithm to compute, for each vertex in T, its coordinates in the layout obtained in part a.

CHAPTER 8

GEOMETRIC ALGORITHMS

I paint objects as I think them, not as I see them.

Pablo Picasso (1881–1973)

8.1 Introduction

Geometrical algorithms play an important role in many areas of computer science, including computer graphics, computer-aided design, VLSI design, robotics, and databases. There may be thousands or even millions of points, lines, squares, and circles in a computer-generated picture; a robot may have to make thousands of moves; a design of a computer chip may involve millions of items. All these problems involve the manipulation of geometric objects. Since the size of the input for these problems may be quite large, it is essential to develop efficient algorithms for them.

There are two somewhat separate areas in which geometric algorithms arise; unfortunately, they are both called *computational geometry*. One of them mainly deals with **continuous** aspects of geometric objects; the other one mainly deals with **discrete** properties of geometric objects. The distinction is not strong, and there are many similar problems and techniques. Our emphasis will be on discrete computational geometry. In this chapter, we discuss several basic geometric algorithms. As in other chapters, the scope of this chapter is necessarily limited. We include some of the basic algorithms that appear as building blocks in the design of more complicated algorithms, and that illustrate interesting techniques. We will limit the discussion to two-dimensional objects.

The objects appearing in this chapters are points, lines, line segments, and polygons. The algorithms manipulate these objects and compute certain properties of them. We start with basic definitions and a discussion of data structures used to represent the different objects. A **point** p is represented as a pair of coordinates (x, y) (we assume a fixed coordinate system throughout this chapter). A **line** is represented by a pair of points p and q (which can be any two distinct points on the line), and it is denoted by $-p-q-$. A **line segment** is also represented by a pair of points p and q, but in this case we assume that the points are the segment's endpoints, and we denote the line segment by $p-q$. A **path** P is a sequence of points $p_1, p_2, ..., p_n$, and the line segments $p_1-p_2, p_2-p_3, ..., p_{k-1}-p_k$ connecting them. We will sometimes call the line segments in a path **edges**. A **closed path** is a path whose last point is the same as its first point. A closed path is also called a **polygon**. The points defining the polygon are also called the **vertices** of the polygon. For example, a triangle is a polygon with three vertices. A polygon is represented as a sequence rather than as a set of points because the order in which the points are given is very important. Changing the order, even without changing the points themselves, may result in a different polygon. A **simple polygon** is one whose corresponding path does not intersect itself; that is, no edges of the polygon intersect except for neighboring edges at their common vertex. A simple polygon encloses a region in the plane. We will call this region the **inside** of the polygon. A **convex polygon** is a polygon such that any line segment connecting two points inside the polygon is itself entirely inside the polygon. A **convex path** is a path of points $p_1, p_2, ..., p_n$ such that connecting p_1 with p_n results in a convex polygon.

We assume that the reader is familiar with basic analytic geometry. For example, we will need to compute the intersection point of two line segments, determine whether a given point lies on a certain side of a given line, and compute the distance between two given points. All these operations can be done in constant time with basic arithmetic operations. (We assume for now that square roots can be computed in constant time; we discuss this issue in Section 8.3.)

One inconvenient characteristic of many geometric algorithms is the existence of numerous "special cases." For example, two lines in the plane usually intersect at one unique point, except when the lines are parallel or when they are the same. When we perform a computation on two given lines, we need to consider all three possibilities. More complicated objects can lead to many other types of special cases, requiring special care. Usually, most of these special cases can be handled in a straightforward manner, but the need to consider them makes the design and the description of geometric algorithms tedious sometimes. We occasionally ignore details that are not essential for understanding the main ideas of the algorithm.

8.2 Determining Whether a Point Is Inside a Polygon

We start with a simple problem.

> **The Problem**   Given a simple polygon P and a point q, determine whether the point is inside or outside the polygon.

This problem may seem trivial at first, but when complicated nonconvex polygons are considered, as is the case in Fig. 8.1, the problem is definitely not simple. Trying to solve a problem by hand first is always a good idea. The first intuitive approach is to try somehow to reach the outside boundary from the given point. When we try this approach we see that it is sufficient to count the number of intersections with edges of the polygon until the outside is reached. For example, in Fig. 8.1, going northeast from the given point (following the dashed line in the figure) results in two intersections with the polygon before the outside is reached. Since the first intersection from the outside brings us inside the polygon and the second intersection brings us back outside, the point is outside the polygon. In general (ignoring special cases for the moment), the point is inside the polygon if and only if the number of intersections (as described above) is odd. We now have a sketch of an algorithm, which is presented in Fig. 8.2.

As we mentioned in Section 8.1, there are usually several special cases that need attention. Let s be a point outside the polygon, and let L be the line segment connecting q to s. We are trying to determine whether q is inside P according to the number of intersections of L with edges of P. The line L, however, may overlaps some edges of P. When one edge overlaps another one, do we call this an intersection? Two intersections? In this case, we clearly do not want to count overlaps as intersections. Another special case is the intersection of L with a vertex of P. Figure 8.3(a) gives an example in which the intersection of L with a vertex of P should not count, and Fig. 8.3(b) gives an example in which it should count as an intersection. We leave it to the reader to characterize these cases and to find how to handle them (Exercise 8.2).

In the development of this algorithm, we implicitly assumed that we are looking at pictures. When the input is given as a list of coordinates, as is usually the case in a computer application, the task is different. For example, when we do the work by hand, and we see the polygon with our eyes, it is easy to find a good path (i.e., one with few intersections) from the point to the outside. This is not an easy task, however, when the

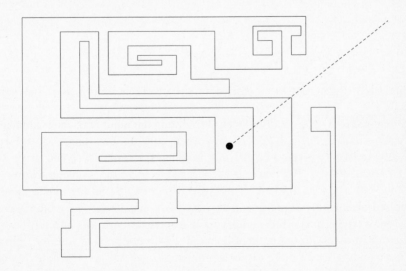

Figure 8.1 Determining whether a point is inside a polygon.

Algorithm Point_in_Polygon_1 *(P, q) ; { first attempt }*
Input: *P* (a simple polygon with vertices $p_1, p_2, ..., p_n$, and edges
    $e_1, e_2, ..., e_n$), and *q* (a point).
Output: *Inside* (a Boolean variable that is set to true if *q* is inside *P* and false
    otherwise).

begin
    Pick an arbitrary point s outside the polygon ;
    Let L be the line segment q−s ;
    count := 0 ;
    for all edges e_i of the polygon **do**
        if *e_i intersects L* **then** *{ We assume that the intersection is not at a*
            vertex nor is the line L overlapping with e_i; see the text }
            increment count ;
    if *count is odd* **then** *Inside := true*
    else *Inside := false*
end

Figure 8.2 Algorithm *Point_in_Polygon_1*.

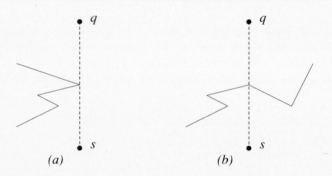

(a)   (b)

Figure 8.3 Special cases for determining whether a point is inside a polygon.

polygon is stored as a series of coordinates. Counting the number of intersections is easy to do visually, but again, it is not as easy when only the coordinates are given. The polygon of Fig. 8.1 is given as a list of coordinates in Fig. 8.4. (The given point is centered at | 368 308 | .) The reader is encouraged to solve the problem now by looking only at Fig. 8.4. Clearly, the bulk of the work is computing all the intersections. This work can be substantially simplified if the line *q−s* is parallel to one of the axes — for example, the vertical axis. The number of intersections with this special line may be much more than that with the optimal line, but we do not need to find the optimal line (which is actually a much more difficult problem — see Exercise 8.3), and computing each intersection is much easier. The modified algorithm is presented in Fig. 8.5.

320.00 368.00 | 320.00 384.00 | 288.00 384.00 | 288.00 380.00 | 308.00 380.00 |
308.00 376.00 | 280.00 376.00 | 280.00 392.00 | 332.00 392.00 | 332.00 364.00 |
364.00 364.00 | 364.00 352.00 | 256.00 352.00 | 256.00 404.00 | 224.00 404.00 |
224.00 332.00 | 352.00 332.00 | 352.00 288.00 | 224.00 288.00 | 224.00 312.00 |
320.00 312.00 | 320.00 300.00 | 256.00 300.00 | 256.00 296.00 | 328.00 296.00 |
328.00 320.00 | 208.00 320.00 | 208.00 280.00 | 384.00 280.00 | 384.00 340.00 |
240.00 340.00 | 240.00 396.00 | 248.00 396.00 | 248.00 348.00 | 416.00 348.00 |
416.00 272.00 | 320.00 272.00 | 320.00 256.00 | 448.00 256.00 | 448.00 320.00 |
432.00 320.00 | 432.00 340.00 | 452.00 340.00 | 452.00 224.00 | 256.00 224.00 |
256.00 244.00 | 320.00 244.00 | 320.00 248.00 | 248.00 248.00 | 248.00 216.00 |
224.00 216.00 | 224.00 240.00 | 232.00 240.00 | 232.00 256.00 | 288.00 256.00 |
288.00 264.00 | 224.00 264.00 | 224.00 272.00 | 192.00 272.00 | 192.00 416.00 |
428.00 416.00 | 428.00 384.00 | 416.00 384.00 | 416.00 400.00 | 424.00 400.00 |
424.00 408.00 | 384.00 408.00 | 384.00 384.00 | 400.00 384.00 | 400.00 396.00 |
388.00 396.00 | 388.00 404.00 | 408.00 404.00 | 408.00 372.00 | 352.00 372.00 |
352.00 404.00 | 264.00 404.00 | 264.00 368.00 |

Figure 8.4 The polygon of Fig. 8.1, given as a sequence of coordinates.

Algorithm Point_in_Polygon_2 (P, q) ; *{ second attempt }*
Input: P (a simple polygon with vertices $p_1, p_2, ..., p_n$, and edges
  $e_1, e_2, ..., e_n$), and $q = (x_0, y_0)$ (a point).
Output: *Inside* (a Boolean variable that is set to true if q is inside P and false
  otherwise).

begin
  count := 0 ;
  for *all edges e_i of the polygon* **do**
      if *the line $x=x_0$ intersects e_i* **then**
      *{ We assume that the intersection is not at a vertex nor is the
          line $x=x_0$ overlapping with e_i }*
          *Let y_i be the y coordinates of the intersection between
              the line $x=x_0$ and e_i ;*
          if $y_i < y_0$ **then** *{ the intersection is below q }*
              increment count ;
      if *count is odd* **then** *Inside := true*
      else *Inside := false*
end

Figure 8.5 Algorithm *Point_in_Polygon_2*.

As an example, let's try to determine whether the point q with coordinates
(368, 308) is inside or outside of the polygon given in Fig. 8.4. We count the number of

intersections with a line segment starting at q and going straight down. We need to look at all the edges, and check, for those edges whose y coordinates are below 308, whether the x coordinate cross 368. There are four edges that cross the line:

(208, 280)–(384, 280) ;
(416, 272)–(320, 272) ;
(320, 256)–(448, 256) ;
(452, 224)–(256, 224).

Hence, the point is outside the polygon.

Complexity   It takes constant time to perform an intersection between two line segments in the plane. The algorithm computes n such intersections (where n is the size of the polygon), and performs other operations that take constant time. Hence, the total running time of this algorithm is $O(n)$.

Comments   In many cases, a simple approach originating from a solution obtained by hand (or eye) calculations is not efficient for large inputs. In some cases, however, such an approach is not only simple, but also efficient. Starting with an "easy-to-visualize" method is always a good idea. There are several observations that can be achieved this way. In this case, by looking at the picture, we observed that we could solve the problem by following some path from the point to the outside, disregarding everything else. This was really the main observation that led to the algorithm.

8.3 Constructing Simple Polygons

A set of points in the plane defines many different polygons, each depending on the order of the points. In this section, we concentrate on finding a simple polygon defined by a set of points.

The Problem   Given a set of n points in the plane, connect them in a simple closed path.

There are several methods to construct simple polygons. We present a method corresponding to the way we would probably approach this problem if we had to solve it by hand. Consider a large circle C that contains all the points. Scan the area of C by a rotating line originating from the center of C (see Fig. 8.6). Let's assume for now that the rotating line never touches more than one point from the set at a time. It seems that, if we connect the points in the order they are encountered in the scan, we get a simple polygon. Let's try to prove this claim. Denote the points, as they appear in the order imposed by the rotating line, by $p_1, p_2, ..., p_n$ (the first point is chosen arbitrarily). For all i, $1 \le i < n$, the edge p_i–p_{i+1} is included in a distinct region of the circle; hence, it does not intersect with any other edge. However, this is not enough to prove that the resulting

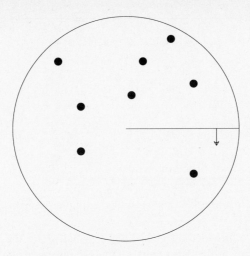

Figure 8.6 Scanning the points.

polygon is simple — in fact, it may not be. The angle between some p_i and p_{i+1} may be greater than 180 degrees, in which case the region corresponding to the edge p_i–p_{i+1} consists of more than one-half of the circle. Thus, the edge p_i–p_{i+1} cuts into the other regions, and it may intersect other edges. (To see that it may, we can consider a circle that is centered somewhere outside of the circle of Fig. 8.6.) This is a good example of the kind of ''special cases'' that arise often in geometrical problems. We have to be careful to make sure that all cases are considered. (Of course, we must do that for any kind of algorithm, but this problem is more prevalent in geometric algorithms.)

    We can overcome this obstacle quite easily. For example, we can take any three points from the set and choose, as a center of the circle, a point inside the triangle formed by these three points. This choice will ensure that the circle does not contain a segment of more than 180 degrees without any points from the set. Another solution, which is the one we will use, is to choose one of the points from the set as the center of the circle. We will choose the point z with the largest x coordinate (and the smallest y coordinate, if there is more than one point with the largest x coordinate). We now use basically the same algorithm. We sort the points according to their position in the circle centered at z. These positions can be computed by sorting the *angles* between a fixed line (e.g., the x axis) and the lines from z to the other points. If two (or more) points have the same angle, they are further sorted according to their distance from z. We then connect z to the point with the smallest angle and to the point with the largest angle, and connect the other points in order. Since all other points lie to the left of z, the bad case we mentioned earlier cannot occur. (There is still one more special case that occurs when all the points lie on a line; in that case, any polygon through the points will have overlapping edges.) The simple polygon obtained by this method for the points in Fig. 8.6 is given in Fig. 8.7.

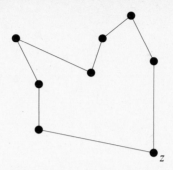

Figure 8.7 Constructing a simple polygon.

We can improve this method in two ways, which share the same principle. First, we do not have to compute the exact angles. We use the angles only to find the order for connecting the points. But the same order is imposed by the *slopes* of the lines (that is, by the ratios of the y differences to the x differences). Computing the slopes is easier than computing the angles (there is no need to compute arctangents). Second, using the same argument, we can avoid computing distances when two points have the same slope. It is sufficient to compute the square of the distances! Therefore, there is no need to compute square roots. The algorithm is presented in Fig 8.8.

Algorithm Simple_Polygon ($p_1, p_2, ..., p_n$) ;
Input: $p_1, p_2, ..., p_n$ (points in the plane).
Output: P (a simple polygon whose vertices are $p_1, p_2, ..., p_n$ in some order).

begin
    for i := 2 to n do
        compute the angle α_i between the line $-p_1-p_i-$ and the x axis ;
        { it is sometimes more desirable to take an extreme point instead of
            p_1, e.g., a point from the set with the largest x coordinate
            (and smallest y coordinate if there are several points with the
            same largest x coordinate) }
    Sort the points according to the angles $\alpha_2, ..., \alpha_n$;
        { break ties according to distances from p_1 }
    P is the polygon defined by the list of points in sorted order
end

Figure 8.8 Algorithm *Simple_Polygon*.

Complexity   The running time of this algorithm is dominated by the sorting, which requires $O(n \log n)$ time.

8.4 Convex Hulls

The **convex hull** of a set of points is defined as the smallest convex polygon enclosing all the points. We would like the convex hull to be represented as a regular polygon, namely, the vertices should be listed in cyclic order.

> **The Problem** Compute the convex hull of n given points in the plane.

Dealing with convex polygons is easier than handling arbitrary polygons. The convex hull serves, in some sense, as the smallest ''convenient'' region encompassing a set of points. The vertices of the convex hull are points from the set. We say that a point *belongs* to the hull if it is a vertex of the hull. A convex hull can contain as little as three and as many as all the points as vertices. Convex hulls have many uses, and consequently, numerous algorithms have been developed to compute them.

8.4.1 A Straightforward Approach

As usual, we start with a straightforward inductive approach. We can easily find the convex hull of three points. We assume that we know how to compute the convex hull of $< n$ points, and we try to find the convex hull of n points. How can the nth point change the convex hull formed by the first $n-1$ points? There are two cases: Either the extra point is inside the convex hull, in which case the hull is unchanged, or the point is outside the hull, in which case the hull is ''stretched'' to reach that point (see Fig. 8.9). So, we need to solve two subproblems. We have to determine whether a point is inside the hull,

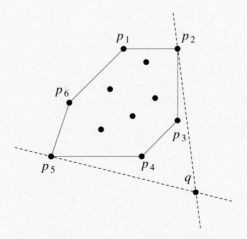

Figure 8.9 Stretching a convex polygon.

and we have to be able to stretch the hull if the point is outside of it. These problems are not easy. We have enough experience by now with the straightforward inductive approach to try some improvements right away. The first improvement is to choose a special nth point rather than an arbitrary one. It is tempting to choose a point inside the hull, so no work will be required to extend the hull. But, of course, some points must belong to the hull, and in some cases all points belong to the hull. Another possible choice, which worked well for the previous problem, is an extreme point — namely, some sort of maximal or minimal point.

We choose again the point with the maximal x coordinate (and the minimal y coordinate, if there are several points with the same maximal x coordinate). Denote this point by q. It is clear that q is guaranteed to be a vertex of the convex hull. Thus, the only problem is how to modify (stretch) the hull to include q. We first need to find the vertices of the old hull that are now inside the new hull (p_3 and p_4 in Fig. 8.9) and to remove them; then, we must insert the new point as a new vertex between two existing vertices (p_2 and p_5 in Fig. 8.9). A **supporting line** of a convex polygon is a line that intersects the polygon at exactly one vertex of the polygon. The polygon thus lies entirely on one side of a supporting line. Consider now the supporting lines $-q-p_2-$ and $-q-p_5-$ (see Fig. 8.9). Usually, only two vertices of the polygon have lines to q which are supporting lines. (We will ignore the special case of two or more points that are on the same line with q.) The polygon lies between the two supporting lines, and that is exactly the way we want to modify it. The supporting lines have the maximal and minimal angles, with, say, the x axis, among all other lines from points in the polygon to q. To find these two vertices, we need to consider the lines from q to all the vertices $p_1, p_2, ..., p_n$, to compute the angles, and to pick the maximal and minimal (see also Exercise 8.4). Once the identity of the two extreme vertices is known, the modified hull can be constructed. (There are several other approaches to modifying the hull, and this is not necessarily the best one; we chose it for its simplicity.) We omit the details concerning this algorithm because we will present a faster algorithm shortly.

Complexity   For each point, we need to compute angles to all the previous points, to find the maximal and minimal angles, and to delete and insert points from the list. Thus, the work involved in processing the kth point is $O(k)$, and we have already seen that the solution of the recurrence relation $T(n) = T(n-1) + O(n)$ is $O(n^2)$. Therefore, the running time of this algorithm is $O(n^2)$. The algorithm also requires sorting, but the running time is dominated by the other operations.

8.4.2 Gift Wrapping

How can we improve this algorithm? When we extend the polygon point by point, we spend a lot of time building convex polygons containing points that may be internal to the final convex hull. Can we avoid doing that? Instead of considering convex hulls of subsets of the set of points, we can start with the whole set and build the hull directly. That is, we can start with an extreme point (which must be on the hull), find its neighbors in the hull by finding the supporting lines, and continue from these neighbors in the same way. This algorithm is known as the **gift wrapping algorithm** for obvious reasons. We start with one vertex of the "gift," and wrap the hull around the gift by finding neighbor after neighbor. The algorithm is given in Fig 8.10. It can be modified to work for higher dimensions as well.

The gift-wrapping algorithm is a straightforward application of the following induction hypothesis (on k):

Induction hypothesis: *Given a set of n points in the plane, we can find a convex path of length $k < n$ that is part of the convex hull of this set.*

With this hypothesis, the emphasis is on extending a *path* rather than on extending the hull. Instead of finding convex hulls of smaller sets, we find a part of the final convex hull.

Algorithm Gift_Wrapping $(p_1, p_2, ..., p_n)$;
Input: $p_1, p_2, ..., p_n$ (a set of points in the plane).
Output: P (the convex hull of $p_1, p_2, ..., p_n$).

begin
    set P to be the empty set ;
    Let p be the point in the set with the largest x coordinate
        (and the smallest y coordinate, if there are several points
        with the same largest x coordinate) ;
    Add p to P ;
    Let L be the line containing p which is parallel to the x axis ;
    while *P is not complete* **do**
        let q be the point such that the angle between the line $-p-q-$ and L
            (in counterclockwise fashion) is minimal among all points ;
        add q to P ;
        L := line $-p-q-$;
        p := q
    end

Figure 8.10 Algorithm *Gift_Wrapping*.

Complexity To add the kth point to the hull, we find the minimum and maximum angles among $n - k$ lines. Therefore, the running time of the gift-wrapping algorithm is $O(n^2)$, which is not better than the stretching algorithm.

8.4.3 Graham's Scan

We now show an algorithm to compute the convex hull in time $O(n \log n)$. The algorithm starts by ordering the points according to angles, similarly to the construction of simple polygons described in Section 8.3. Let p_1 be the point with the maximal x coordinate (and the minimal y coordinate, if there are several other points with the same x

coordinate). For each point p_i, we compute the angle of the line $-p_1-p_i-$ with the x axis, and sort the points according to these angles (see Fig. 8.11). We now scan the points in the order they appear in the polygon and, as before, try to find the vertices of the convex hull. As in the gift-wrapping algorithm, we will maintain a path consisting of a subset of the points scanned so far. This path will be a convex path whose corresponding convex polygon encloses all the points scanned so far. (The corresponding convex polygon is the one formed by connecting the first and last points of the path.) Hence, when all the points are scanned, we find the convex hull. The main difference between this algorithm and the gift-wrapping algorithm is that the convex path we maintain is not necessarily part of the final convex hull. It is only part of the convex hull of the points that were scanned so far. The path may contain points that are not on the final convex hull; these points will be eliminated later. For example, the path from p_1 to q_m in Fig. 8.11 is convex, but q_m and q_{m-1} clearly do not belong to the convex hull. This discussion leads to an algorithm, based on the following induction hypothesis.

> **Induction hypothesis:** *Given a set of n points in the plane, ordered according to algorithm Simple_Polygon (Section 8.3), we can find a convex path among the first k points whose corresponding convex polygon encloses the first k points.*

The case of $k = 1$ is trivial. Denote the convex path obtained (inductively) from the first k points by $P = q_1, q_2, ..., q_m$. We now have to extend the hypothesis to $k+1$ points. Consider the angle between the lines $-q_{m-1}-q_m-$ and $-q_m-p_{k+1}-$ (see Fig. 8.11). If the angle is less than 180 degrees (where the angle is measured from the *inside* of the polygon), then p_{k+1} can be added to the existing path (since the path with it is still convex), and we are done. Otherwise, we claim that q_m is inside the convex polygon obtained by removing q_m from P, adding p_{k+1} to P, and connecting p_{k+1} to p_1. This is so because the points were ordered according to their angles. The line $-p_1-p_{k+1}-$ is on the

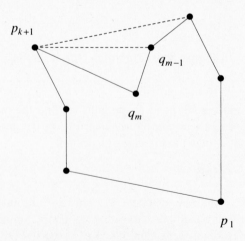

Figure 8.11 Graham's scan.

"left" side of the first k points. Hence, q_m must be inside the convex polygon defined above, q_m can be removed from P, and p_{k+1} can be added. Are we done? Not quite. Although q_m can be eliminated, the modified path is not necessarily convex. Indeed, Fig. 8.11 shows clearly that other points may have to be eliminated as well. For example, q_{m-1} may now be inside the polygon defined by the modified path. We must continue checking the last two edges of the path until we find two that form an angle of less than 180 degrees. The path is then convex, the hypothesis has been extended to $k+1$ points, and we are done. The detailed algorithm is presented in Fig 8.12.

Algorithm Graham's_Scan $(p_1, p_2, ..., p_n)$;
Input: $p_1, p_2, ..., p_n$ (a set of points in the plane).
Output: $q_1, q_2, ..., q_m$ (the convex hull of $p_1, p_2, ..., p_n$).

begin
    Let p_1 be the point in the set with the largest x coordinate
        (and smallest y coordinate if there are several points
        with the same largest x coordinate) ;
    Use algorithm Simple_Polygon to arrange the points around p_1
        in sorted order ; let the order be $p_1, p_2, ..., p_n$;
    $q_1 := p_1$;
    $q_2 := p_2$;
    $q_3 := p_3$;
    { P initially consists of p_1, p_2, and p_3 }
    $m := 3$;
    for $k := 4$ to n **do**
        while *the angle between* $-q_{m-1}-q_m-$ *and* $-q_m-p_k-$ *is* ≥ 180 *degrees* **do**
            $m := m - 1$;
        $m := m + 1$;
        $q_m := p_k$
end

Figure 8.12 Algorithm *Graham's_Scan*.

Complexity   The complexity of the algorithm is dominated by the sorting. All the other steps require only $O(n)$ time. Each point in the set is considered exactly once in the induction step as p_{k+1}. At that time, the point is always added to the convex path. The same point will be considered later (possibly more than once) to verify its inclusion in the current convex path. We call this phase a *backward* test. The number of points involved in a backward test may be high, but all these points except for two (the current point and the point that is found to still belong to the convex path) are eliminated! So, we spend only a constant time to eliminate each point, and a constant time to add it. Overall, $O(n)$ steps are required for this phase. The total running time of the algorithm is thus $O(n \log n)$ due to the sorting.

8.5 Closest Pair

Suppose that we are given the locations of n objects and we want to check that no two of the objects are too close to each other. The objects may correspond, for example, to parts in a computer chip, to stars in a galaxy, or to irrigation systems. In this section, we discuss a variation of this problem, which is an example of a large set of **proximity** problems.

The Problem   Given a set of n points in the plane, find a pair of closest points.

Other proximity problems include finding, for each point in the set, the closest point to it or the k closest points to it, and finding the closest point to a new given point.

A Straightforward Approach

A straightforward solution is to check the distances between all pairs and to take the minimal one. This solution requires $n(n-1)/2$ distance computations and $n(n-1)/2-1$ comparisons. The straightforward solution using induction would proceed by removing a point, solving the problem for $n-1$ points, and considering the extra point. However, if the only information obtained from the solution of the $n-1$ case is the minimum distance, then the distances from the additional point to all other $n-1$ points must be checked. As a result, the total number of distance computations $T(n)$ satisfies the recurrence relation $T(n)=T(n-1)+n-1$, $(T(2)=1)$, and we have already seen that $T(n)=O(n^2)$. In fact, these two straightforward solutions are identical. We want to find a more efficient algorithm for large n.

A Divide-and-Conquer Algorithm

Instead of considering one point at a time, we divide the set into two equal parts. The induction hypothesis can stay the same, but instead of reducing the problem of n points to the problem of $n-1$ points, we reduce it to two problems with $n/2$ points. We assume, for simplicity, that n is a power of 2, so that it is always possible to divide the set into two equal parts. There are many ways to divide a set of points into two equal parts. We are free to choose the best division for our purposes. We would like to get as much useful information as we can from the solution of the smaller problems; thus, we want as much of that information to be still valid when the complete problem is considered. It seems reasonable to divide the set by dividing the plane into two disjoint parts, each containing one-half of the set. After we find the minimal distance in each part, we have to be concerned only with the distances between points close to the boundaries of the sets. The easiest way of dividing the set is to sort all the points according to their x coordinates, for example, and then to divide the plane by the vertical line that bisects the set (see Fig. 8.13). (If several points lie on the vertical line, then we divide them arbitrarily.) We

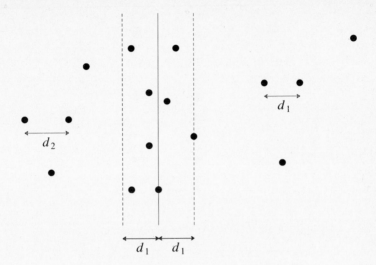

Figure 8.13 The closest pair problem.

choose this division to minimize the work of combining the solutions of the smaller problems. The sorting needs to be performed only once.

For simplicity, we concentrate on finding only the minimal distance among the points. Identifying the actual two closest points will be straightforward from the algorithm. If the set has only two points, then we find their distance directly. Let P be a set of n points, and assume that n is a power of 2. We first divide P into two equal-sized subsets, P_1 and P_2, as described above. We find the closest distance in each subset by induction. Let the minimal distance in P_1 be d_1, and in P_2 be d_2, and assume, without loss of generality, that $d_1 \leq d_2$. We need to find the closest distance in the whole set; namely, we have to see whether there is a point in P_1 with a distance $<d_1$ to a point in P_2. First, we notice that it is sufficient to consider only the points that lie in a strip of width $2d_1$ centered around the vertical separator of the two subsets (see Fig. 8.13). No other point can be of distance less than d_1 from points in the other subset. Using this observation, we can usually eliminate many points from consideration, but, in the worst case, all the points can still reside in the strip, and we cannot ''afford'' to use the straightforward algorithm for them.

Another less obvious observation is that, for any point p in the strips, there is only a small number of points on the other side whose distance to p can be smaller than d_1. This is so because all the points in each strip are at least d_1 apart. If p is a point in the strip with y coordinate y_p, then only the points on the other side with a y coordinate y_q such that $|y_p - y_q| < d_1$ need to be considered. There could be at most six such points on one side of the strip (see Fig. 8.14 for the worst case). As a result, if we sort all points in the strip according to their y coordinates, and scan the points in order, we need to check each point against only a constant number of its neighbors in the order (instead of against all $n - 1$ points). A sketch of the algorithm is given in Fig 8.15.

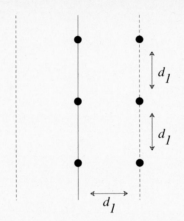

Figure 8.14 The worst case of six points d_1 apart.

Algorithm Closest_Pair_1 $(p_1, p_2, ..., p_n)$; *{ first attempt }*
Input: $p_1, p_2, ..., p_n$ (a set of n points in the plane).
Output: d (the distance between the two closest points in the set).

begin
    Sort the points according to their x coordinates ;
        { this sorting is done only once at the beginning }
    Divide the set into two equal-sized parts ;
    Recursively, compute the minimal distance in each part ;
    Let d be the minimal of the two minimal distances ;
    Eliminate points that lie farther than d apart from the separation line ;
    Sort the remaining points according to their y coordinates ;
    Scan the remaining points in the y order and compute the distances of
        each point to its five neighbors ;
    *if any of these distances is less than d **then***
        update d
end

Figure 8.15 Algorithm *Closest_Pair_1*.

Complexity It takes $O(n \log n)$ steps to sort according to the x coordinates, but this sorting is done only once. We then solve two subproblems of size $n/2$. Eliminating the points outside of the strips can be done in $O(n)$ steps. It then takes $O(n \log n)$ steps to sort according to the y coordinates. Finally, it takes $O(n)$ steps to scan the points inside the strips and to compare each one to a constant number of its neighbors in the order. Overall, to solve a problem of size n, we solve two subproblems of size $n/2$ and use $O(n \log n)$ steps for combining the solutions (plus $O(n \log n)$ steps once at the beginning for sorting the x coordinates). We obtain the following recurrence relation:

$$T(n) = 2T(n/2) + O(n \log n), \quad T(2) = 1.$$

We leave it to the reader to verify that the solution of this recurrence relation is $T(n) = O(n \log^2 n)$. This is asymptotically better than a quadratic algorithm, but we still want to do better than that.

An *O(n log n)* Algorithm

The key idea here is to strengthen the induction hypothesis. The reason we have to spend $O(n \log n)$ time in the combining step is the sorting of the y coordinates. Although we know how to solve the sorting problem directly, doing so takes too long. Can we somehow solve the sorting problem at the same time we are solving the closest-pair problem? In other words, we would like to strengthen the induction hypothesis for the closest-pair problem to include sorting.

> **Induction hypothesis:** *Given a set of < n points in the plane, we know how find the closest distance and how to output the set sorted according to the points' y coordinates.*

We have already seen how to find the minimal distance if the points are sorted in each step according to their y coordinates. Hence, the only thing that we need to do to extend this hypothesis is to sort the set of n points when the two subsets (of size $n/2$) are already sorted. But, this sorting is exactly mergesort (Section 6.3.2). The main advantage of this approach is that we do not have to sort every time we combine the solutions — we only have to merge. Since merging can be done in $O(n)$ steps, the recurrence relation becomes $T(n) = 2T(n/2) + O(n)$, $T(2) = 1$, which implies that $T(n) = O(n \log n)$. The revised algorithm is given in Fig 8.16.

8.6 Intersections of Horizontal and Vertical Line Segments

Intersection problems are common in computational geometry, and they have many applications. We are sometimes interested in computing the intersection of several objects, and we are sometimes interested only in detecting whether the intersection is nonempty. Detection problems are usually easier, although not always substantially easier. In this section, we present one intersection problem that illustrates an important technique of computational geometry. The same technique can be applied to other intersection problems (and to other problems as well), some of which are given as exercises.

> **The Problem**   Given a set of n horizontal and m vertical line segments in the plane, find all the intersections among them.

Algorithm Closest_Pair_2 $(p_1, p_2, ..., p_n)$; *{ An improved version }*
Input: $p_1, p_2, ..., p_n$ (a set of n points in the plane).
Output: d (the distance between the two closest points in the set).

begin
    Sort the points according to their x coordinates ;
        { this sorting is done only once at the beginning }
    Divide the set into two equal-sized parts ;
    Recursively do the following:
        compute the minimal distance in each part ;
        sort the points in each part according to their y coordinates ;
    Merge the two sorted lists into one sorted list ;
    { Notice that we must merge before we eliminate ; we need to
     supply the whole set sorted to the next level of the recursion }
    Let d be the minimal of the minimal distances ;
    Eliminate points that lie further than d apart from the separation line ;
    Scan the points in the y order and compute the distances of each
        point to its five neighbors ;
    if any of these distances is less than d **then**
        update d
end

Figure 8.16 Algorithm *Closest_Pair_2*.

This problem is important, for example, in the design of VLSI circuits. A circuit may contain hundreds of thousands of "wires," and the designer has to make sure that there are no unexpected intersections. It is also important in the context of hidden-line elimination. (The hidden-line elimination problem is usually more complicated, because the lines are not only either horizontal or vertical.) For simplicity, when there is no ambiguity, we call the line segments simply *lines* in this section. An example of the problem is given in Fig. 8.17.

Finding all intersections among either all the vertical lines or all the horizontal lines is a simple problem, which is left as an exercise. We assume, for simplicity, that there are no intersections between two vertical lines or between two horizontal lines. If we try to reduce the problem by removing one line (either vertical or horizontal) at a time, then the removed line will have to be compared against all other lines, and the resulting algorithm will involve $O(mn)$ comparisons. In general, there may be as many as mn intersections, and the algorithm may require $O(mn)$ time just to report them. But the number of intersections may be much smaller than mn. We would like to find an algorithm that performs very well when there are few intersections and not too poorly when there are many. We achieve it by combining two of our favorite techniques: choosing a special order of induction and strengthening the induction hypothesis.

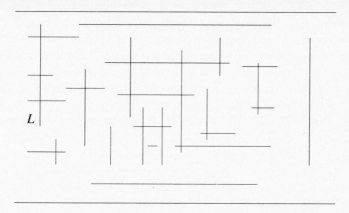

Figure 8.17   Intersections of horizontal and vertical lines.

The order of induction is determined by an imaginary line (an infinite line, not a segment) that "sweeps" the plane from left to right; the line segments are considered in the order in which they intersect with this imaginary line. In addition to computing intersections, we also keep some information about the line segments that we have seen so far. This information will be helpful for computing the next intersections more efficiently. This technique is called the **line-sweep** technique.

Let the imaginary line be a vertical line that sweeps the plane from left to right. To achieve this sweeping effect, we sort all the endpoints of the segments according to their x coordinates. The two endpoints of a vertical line have the same x coordinates, so we need only one of them. We must use, however, the two endpoints of each horizontal line. After all the endpoints are sorted, we consider them one by one in that order. As usual in an inductive approach, we assume that we have already computed the intersections among the previous line segments and have maintained some additional information, and we now try to handle the next line segment and to update the information. The structure of the algorithm is thus as follows. We consider one endpoint at a time in the left-to-right order. We use the information gathered so far (which we have not yet specified) to process the endpoint, find some intersections that it causes, and update the information to be used for the next endpoint. The main part of the algorithm is the definition of the information that we maintain. Let's attempt to run the algorithm and to discover what is needed.

One feature of the induction hypothesis, which seems natural to have, is the knowledge of all the intersections that occurred to the left of the current position of the sweeping line. Is it better to check for intersections when a vertical line is considered or when a horizontal line is considered? It seems better to choose the former. When we look at a vertical line, the horizontal lines that can intersect it are still under consideration (since we have not yet reached their right endpoint). On the other hand, when we look at either the left endpoint or the right endpoint of a horizontal line, we either have not yet seen the vertical lines that intersect it, or we have forgotten about them. Assume that the sweeping line is currently at the x coordinates of the vertical line L (see Fig. 8.17). What kind of information is required to find all intersections involving L? Since all intersections to the left of the current sweeping line are assumed to be already known, there is no need to consider a horizontal line any further if its right endpoint is to the left of the sweeping line. Hence, only those horizontal lines whose left endpoints are to the left of the sweeping line and whose right endpoints are to the right of the sweeping line should be under consideration (there are six such lines in Fig. 8.17). The list of these horizontal lines should be maintained. When L is encountered, it should be checked for intersection against all these horizontal lines. The important point here is that we need not check the x coordinates to determine intersections with L! We already know that all horizontal lines in the list have x coordinates that match that of L. We have to check only the y coordinates of the horizontal lines in the list to see whether they match the y coordinates of L. We are now ready to try an induction hypothesis.

> **Induction hypothesis:** *Given a list of k sorted x coordinates as described (with x_k being the rightmost x coordinates), we know how to report all intersections among the corresponding lines that occur to the left of x_k, and to eliminate those horizontal lines that are to the left of x_k.*

We call the horizontal lines that are still under consideration **candidates**. (These are the horizontal lines whose left endpoints are to the left of the current x coordinate, and whose right endpoints are to the right or at the current x coordinate.) We maintain a data structure containing the set of candidates. The implementation of this data structure will be discussed shortly.

The base case for this induction hypothesis is easy. To extend the hypothesis, we need to handle the $(k + 1)$th endpoint. There are three cases:

1. The $(k + 1)$th endpoint is a right endpoint of a horizontal line, in which case we simply eliminate the line from the set of candidates. As we said, intersections are detected when vertical lines are considered, so we lose no intersections by eliminating the horizontal line. This step thus extends the induction hypothesis.

2. The $(k + 1)$th endpoint is a left endpoint of a horizontal line, in which case we add the line to the set of candidates. Since the line's right endpoint has not been reached yet, the line should not be eliminated, so, by the arguments above, this is a proper way to extend the induction.

3. The $(k + 1)$th endpoint is a vertical line. This is the main part of the algorithm. We can find the intersections involving this vertical line by checking the y coordinates of all the horizontal lines in the set of candidates against the y coordinates of the vertical line.

The algorithm is now complete. The number of comparisons will usually be much smaller than mn. Unfortunately, in the worst case, this algorithm still requires $O(mn)$ comparisons, even if the actual number of intersections is small. If all the horizontal lines stretch from left to right, for example, then each vertical line must be checked against all horizontal lines, resulting in an $O(mn)$ algorithm. This bad case will hold even if no vertical line intersects with a horizontal line.

To improve the algorithm, we need to minimize the number of comparisons between the y coordinates of a vertical line and those of the horizontal lines in the set of candidates. Let the y coordinates of the vertical line we are currently considering be y_L and y_R, and let the y coordinates of the horizontal lines in the set of candidates be $y_1, y_2, ..., y_k$. Suppose that the horizontal lines in the set of candidates are given in sorted order according to their y coordinates (namely, $y_1, y_2, ..., y_k$ is in increasing order). We can find the horizontal lines that intersect with the vertical line by performing two binary searches, one for y_L and one for y_R. Suppose that $y_i < y_L \leq y_{i+1} \leq y_j \leq y_R < y_{j+1}$. The horizontal lines that intersect with the vertical line are exactly $y_{i+1}, y_{i+2}, ..., y_j$. We can also perform only one binary search, say, for y_L, and then scan the y coordinates until we find y_j. Even though the original problem involves two dimensions, finding $y_{i+1}, ..., y_j$ is a one-dimensional problem. Searching for numbers in a given one-dimensional range (in this case, y_L to y_R) is called a *one-dimensional range query*. If the numbers are sorted, then the running time for a one-dimensional range query is proportional to the search time plus the number of items that are found. But, of course, we cannot afford to sort the horizontal lines every time we encounter a vertical line.

Let's review the requirements. We need a data structure that allows us to insert a new element, to delete an element, and to perform a one-dimensional range query efficiently. Fortunately, there are several data structures — for example, balanced trees — that can perform insertions, deletions, and searches in $O(\log n)$ per operation (n being the number of elements in the set), and linear scans in time proportional to the number of elements found. The algorithm is presented in Fig 8.18.

Complexity   Sorting according to x coordinates requires time $O((m+n)\log(m+n))$. Since each insert and delete operation requires $O(\log n)$ steps, the running time for handling the horizontal lines is $O(n \log n)$ overall. Handling the vertical lines requires a one-dimensional range query, which can be performed in time $O(\log n + r)$, where r is the number of intersections involving this vertical line. The running time of the algorithm is thus $O((m+n)\log(m+n)+R)$, where R is the total number of intersections.

8.7 Summary

In some sense, geometric algorithms seem less abstract than, say, graph algorithms, since we are used to seeing and handling geometric objects. But, appearances are sometimes misleading. Dealing with huge number of objects is different from looking at small pictures, and we must be careful that the picture that we have in the back of our minds does not lead us to wrong conclusions. We must deal with many special cases, and make sure that we can cover all of them. The algorithm for determining whether a point is inside a polygon (Section 8.2) is a good example. We usually do not think of a polygon as being like the one given in Fig. 8.1. Furthermore, it is easy to overlook the special cases that may occur. Therefore, special caution must be exercised when designing geometric algorithms.

The techniques for designing (discrete) geometric algorithms are similar to the techniques that we have studied in the previous chapters. Induction plays an important

---

Algorithm Intersection ($(v_1, v_2, ..., v_m), (h_1, h_2, ..., h_n)$) ;
Input: $v_1, v_2, ..., v_m$ *(a set of vertical line segments),*
  and $h_1, h_2, ..., h_n$ (a set of horizontal line segments),
Output: The set of all pairs of intersecting segments.
  { $y_B(v_i)$ ($y_T(v_i)$) denote the bottom (top) y coordinates of line v_i }

begin
  sort all x coordinates in increasing order and place them in Q ;
  V := ∅ ;
    { V is the set of horizontal lines that are currently candidates for
      intersection ; it is organized as a balanced tree according to the
      y coordinates of the horizontal lines }
  while *Q is not empty* **do**
    remove the first endpoint p from Q ;
    if *p is the right endpoint of h_k* **then**
        remove h_k from V
    else if *p is the left endpoint of h_k* **then**
        insert h_k into V
      else if *p is the x coordinate of a vertical line v_i* **then**
          perform a one-dimensional range query for the range
            $y_B(v_i)$ to $y_T(v_i)$ in V
  end

Figure 8.18 Algorithm *Intersection*.

---

role. The line-sweep technique, which is based on induction, is common to several geometric algorithms (one was presented in Section 8.5). The divide-and-conquer approach is also quite common. Geometric algorithms (except for simple ones) seem to require complicated data structures, and many sophisticated and ingenious data structures have been developed for that purpose. We have not covered here any of these special data structures.

Bibliographic Notes and Further Reading

We have seen only a small sample of geometric algorithms in this chapter. Even though discrete computational geometry is a relatively new field, there exists an extensive literature in this area, spanning the last 15 years. Several books concentrate on computational geometry. Preparata and Shamos [1985] and Edelsbrunner [1987] present numerous techniques, examples, and a comprehensive bibliography. Additional books include Mehlhorn [1984] and Toussaint [1984].

The gift-wrapping algorithm for convex hulls is due to Chand and Kapur [1970]. Graham's algorithm is due to Graham [1972]. A bibliography containing 268 papers on convex hull algorithms and other problems of convexity was published by Ronse [1987].

The algorithm for finding the closest pair is due to Shamos and Hoey [1975]. An $O(n \log n)$ algorithm that uses the line-sweep technique is due to Hinrichs, Nievergelt, and Schorn [1988]. A probabilistic algorithm for finding the closest pair, whose expected running time is $O(n)$, was developed by Rabin [1976] (see also Fortune and Hopcroft [1979]). A general technique for proximity problems involves the construction of **Voronoi diagrams**. A Voronoi diagram for a given set of points is a division of the plane into regions such that each region contains all points that are closest to one of the points from the set. Voronoi diagrams can be constructed in $O(n \log n)$ time (Shamos and Hoey [1975]). They are useful for a variety of proximity problems.

The algorithm for reporting intersections among vertical and horizontal lines (presented in Section 8.6) is due to Bentley and Ottmann [1979]. The running time of $O(n \log n + R)$ of this algorithm is the best possible in the worst case (see Preparata and Shamos [1985]). An algorithm for determining whether there are any intersections among an arbitrary set of line segments was developed by Shamos and Hoey [1976]. It also uses the line-sweep technique. This problem can also be solved by a divide-and-conquer algorithm with strengthening the induction hypothesis (Guting and Wood [1984]). There is a large body of literature on intersection problems, and the reader is referred to one of the books listed above. Exercise 8.16 is from Bentley, Faust, and Preparata [1982], and Exercises 8.17–8.18 are discussed in Preparata and Shamos [1985].

Drill Exercises

8.1   Complete algorithm *Point_In_Polygon_1* (Fig. 8.2) by addressing the special cases that arise when the line L intersects a vertex of the polygon or overlaps an edge of the polygon.

8.2   Design an algorithm to determine whether n given points in the plane are all on one line. What is the complexity of your algorithm?

8.3   Let S be an arbitrary set of points in the plane. Is there only one unique simple polygon whose vertices are the set S? Either prove the uniqueness, or show an example of two different simple polygons with the same set of vertices.

8.4   The first algorithm we presented for computing the convex hull (Section 8.4) proceeds by computing the supporting lines from an extreme point to the hull formed by the rest of the points. Suppose that the only thing we know about the extra point q is that it is outside the hull. It may be above the hull, below the hull, or anywhere else. We can still try to find the two supporting lines from q to the hull by computing the angles to all other points, but it is not clear any more how to select the minimum and maximum angle, because these angles can be in any range. Find a method to determine which of the lines from q to points in the hull is a supporting line.

8.5   Let $p_1, p_2, ..., p_n$ be a set of points that are ordered cyclically according to a circle whose center is somewhere inside the convex hull of these points. Modify Graham's scan to work (without additional sorting) on this set of points.

8.6   Graham's scan is applied to a set of points in a certain order. We used algorithm *Simple_Polygon* (Fig. 8.8) to sort the points in the following way. We started with an "extreme" point p (which was guaranteed to be on the hull) and sorted all other points according to the angles between a fixed line (e.g., the x axis) and the line segments connecting the points to p. Prove (by showing a counterexample) that not every point p can be used for that purpose. In other words, show a set of points S and another point p, *not in the set*, such that sorting the points relative to p (using the angles from p to the points in the set) and then applying Graham's scan does not lead to the correct convex hull.

8.7   Show, by an example, that it is possible for algorithm *Graham's_Scan* (Fig. 8.12) to reject p points in a row, one at a time, for every value of p. (In other words, the loop can be executed for p steps without changing the value of m.)

8.8   Show an example of n points in the plane with distinct x coordinates, for which algorithm *Closest_Pair_2* (Fig. 8.16) will take $\Omega(n \log n)$ steps.

8.9   Given a set of n horizontal line segments in the plane, find all the intersections among them. The algorithm should run in time $O(n \log n)$ in the worst case.

Creative Exercises

8.10   The input is a set of n points in the plane and a line. Design a linear-time algorithm to find a line that is parallel to the given line and that separates the set of given points into two equal-sized subsets (if a point lies on the line, then it can be counted as being on either side).

8.11   Let P be a simple (not necessarily convex) polygon enclosed in a given rectangle R, and q be an arbitrary point inside R. Design an efficient algorithm to find a line segment connecting q to any point outside of R such that the number of edges of P that this line intersects is minimum. (This question is motivated by the algorithm for determining whether a point is inside or outside a polygon; see Section 8.2.)

8.12   Let P be a convex polygon given by an array of its vertices in cyclic order. Design an algorithm to determine whether a given point q is inside P. The running time of the algorithm should be $O(\log n)$ in the worst case.

8.13   Many convex-hull algorithms are based on or are similar to sorting algorithms. You are asked to develop a convex-hull algorithm that is similar to an efficient insertion sort. In each iteration, one more point should be considered and possibly should be inserted to the current convex hull, which should consist of the convex hull of the points seen so far. The points should be considered in an arbitrary order (i.e., no sorting should be done initially). The algorithm should be based on an efficient data structure to determine whether a given point is inside a given convex polygon. What is the worst-case running time of your algorithm? (You do not have to supply all the details for all the special cases.)

8.14   Consider the idea of computing the convex hull by stretching the hull one point at a time with the use of supporting lines (see Section 8.4). Design an $O(n \log n)$ algorithm for computing the convex hull based on this idea.

8.15   Assume that you have a black box that finds the convex hull of the union of two disjoint convex polygons P_1 and P_2 in time $O(|P_1| + |P_2|)$ ($|P_i|$ denotes the number of points in P_i). Design an algorithm that uses this black box to find the convex hull of a given set of n points in the plane. The running time of the algorithm should be $O(n \log n)$.

8.16   A **d-approximate convex hull** of a set of points P is a convex polygon all of whose vertices are from P, such that all points in P are either inside it or within distance d from it. (We define the distance of a point from a polygon as the minimum over all lengths of line segments connecting the point to anywhere in the polygon.) Let P be a set of n points such that the maximal difference between the x coordinates of any two points in P is X. Design an algorithm to compute a d-approximate convex hull of P, which runs in time and space $O(n + X/d)$.

8.17   Let P be a set of n points in the plane. We define the **depth** of a point p in P as the number of convex hulls that need to be "peeled" (removed) for p to become a vertex of the convex hull. Design an $O(n^2)$ algorithm to find the depths of all points in P. (Notice that the straightforward algorithm that finds convex hulls and removes them may run for $O(n^2 \log n)$ time, since all hulls may have a constant number of vertices.)

8.18   a. A point p in the plane is said to **dominate** another point q if both the x coordinate and y coordinate of p are greater that or equal to those of q. A point p is a **maximal** point in a given set of points P if no point in P dominates it. Design an $O(n \log n)$ algorithm to find all maximal points of a given set P with n points.

b. Solve the corresponding problem for three dimensions (the definition of dominance is extended to include all dimensions).

8.19   Let S be a set of points in the plane. For each $p \in S$, we define $D(p)$ to be the set of points in S that are dominated by p (see Exercise 8.18). Design an algorithm to compute the sizes of the sets $D(p)$ for all $p \in S$. The running time of the algorithm should be $O(n \log n)$ in the worst case.

8.20   Given n points in the plane, find the pair of points such that the line segment connecting them has the maximal slope. The running time of the algorithm should be $O(n \log n)$ in the worst case.

8.21   The input is a set of n points in the plane, represented as an array of linked lists in the following way. Each entry in the array has two fields: X, which gives the x coordinates, and *Next*, which points to a (nonempty) linked list of all the points in the set whose x coordinates are equal to X, sorted according to their y coordinates. The array is sorted according to the x coordinates. Design an algorithm to find the closest pair of points whose x coordinates are either equal or consecutive in the array. The algorithm should run in time $O(n)$ in the worst case. Is it necessary to compute square roots in this algorithm? Does your algorithm find the closest pair (without any restrictions)?

8.22   The input is a set of line segments in the plane such that all segments are horizontal, vertical, or have a 45-degree angle with the horizon. You are asked to extend the algorithm for reporting all intersections among a set of vertical and horizontal line segments to this case without increasing the asymptotic worst-case running time.

*8.23   Design an algorithm to compute all the intersections among a set of horizontal and vertical line segments by using a divide-and-conquer approach. The running time of the algorithm should be the same as the algorithm discussed in Section 8.6. That is, all intersections should be reported in time $O((m+n)\log(m+n)+R)$ (where R is the number of intersections found).

8.24   The input is a set of n arbitrary line segments in the plane. Design an algorithm to determine whether any two of the line segments intersect. The algorithm needs to output only yes or no. The running time of the algorithm should be $O(n\log n)$ in the worst case. (Hint: Use the line-sweep method similarly to the horizontal and vertical case, but maintain different information.)

8.25   A **grid polygon** is a simple polygon all of whose edges are parallel to either the x axis or the y axis. Design an efficient algorithm to compute the intersection of two given grid polygons (i.e., the area common to both of them). The polygons are given by their vertices in a cyclic order.

8.26   The input is a set of intervals on a line, which are represented by their two endpoints. Design an algorithm to identify all intervals that are contained in another interval from the set. The algorithm should run in time $O(n\log n)$ in the worst case.

8.27   The input is a set of n rectangles all of whose edges are parallel to the axes. Extend the algorithm obtained in Exercise 8.26 to mark all the rectangles that are contained in other rectangles. Can you obtain a running time of $O(n\log n)$?

8.28   The input is a set of n rectangles all of whose edges are parallel to the axes. Design an algorithm to find the intersection of all the rectangles.

8.29   The input is a set of n circles in the plane. Design an algorithm to detect whether there are any two circles in the set with nonempty intersection. The algorithm does not need to compute the intersection, only output yes or no. The running time of the algorithm should be $O(n\log n)$ in the worst case.

8.30   The input is a set of n polygons, each with k vertices. Design an algorithm to detect whether there are any two polygons in the set with nonempty intersection. The algorithm does not need to compute the intersection, only output yes or no. What is the worst-case running time?

8.31   The input is two convex polygons given by their lists of vertices (in a cyclic order). Design a linear-time algorithm to compute the intersection of these polygons. The output, which is also a convex polygon, should be represented by a list of vertices in a cyclic order.

8.32   The input is two convex polygons given by their lists of vertices (in a cyclic order). Design a linear-time algorithm to compute the **union** of the two polygons (i.e., the area enclosed by at least one of the polygons).

8.33   The input is a set of n rectangles all of whose edges are parallel to the axes. Design an algorithm to compute the union of all the rectangles. The union is obviously a polygon. It should be represented by its list of vertices in counterclockwise order. (This problem is an extension to the skyline problem in chapter 5.)

8.34   The input is a set of n triangles in the plane, given by their vertices. Design an $O(n\log n)$ algorithm to compute their intersection (i.e., the area common to all of them).

8.35 The input is a convex polygon given by its list of n vertices in cyclic order. Design a linear-time algorithm to find n triangles whose intersection is the given polygon.

8.36 The input is a set of n points in the plane. Design an $O(n^2 \log n)$ algorithm to determine whether there exist four points in the set that are vertices of a square.

8.37 The input is a set of n points in the plane. Design a polynomial-time algorithm to determine whether there are k points in the set (for some $k \le n$) that are the vertices of a regular polygon. (A regular polygon is a polygon with equal-sized edges and angles.)

8.38 The input is a set of n points all of which have integer coordinates. We are interested in finding a set of parallel lines such that all the points are contained in at least one of the lines in the set. The lines must either be parallel to the axes or have a 45-degree angle with the axes. Design an $O(n \log n)$ algorithm to find a minimum-size set of lines satisfying these conditions. Again, the lines must all be parallel, so, in particular, if one of the lines has a 45-degree angle with the coordinates, then all of them do.

8.39 A line divides the plane into two **half-planes**. The intersection of any number of half-planes is a convex polygon (half-planes are convex and the intersection of convex objects is always convex). The problem is to compute the intersection of n given half-planes and output it as a convex polygon. That is, the output should include the list of the vertices in the cyclic order in which they appear in the polygon. The half-planes are given by the linear inequality that defines them. Design an $O(n \log n)$ algorithm to compute this intersection.

8.40 The input is $2n$ points in general position in the plane (i.e., no three points lie on a common line), such that n points are colored red and n points are colored blue. Design an algorithm to match the blue points to the red points such that (1) each point has a unique match, and (2) none of the line segments connecting matched points intersect. The algorithm need not make use of any graph-matching techniques. It is not evident that such a matching always exists, but it is true. The algorithm should run in polynomial time. (Hint: Use induction: Try to find a red point and a blue point whose connecting line segment poses no problems; if that fails, try to divide the set of points by a straight line such that the problem is divided into two smaller problems.)

CHAPTER 9

ALGEBRAIC AND NUMERICAL ALGORITHMS

One plus one is two.
Two plus two is four.
Four plus four is eight.
Eight plus eight is more than ten.

A child's poem

9.1 Introduction

Whenever we perform an arithmetic operation, we are in fact executing an algorithm. We are usually so familiar with these operations that we take the corresponding algorithms for granted. However, whether it is multiplication, division, or a more complicated arithmetic operation, the straightforward algorithm is not always the best when very large numbers or large sequences of numbers are involved. The same phenomenon that we have seen in the previous chapters occurs here as well: Some algorithms that are good for small input become inefficient when the size of the input grows.

As we have done in previous chapters, we will measure the complexity of an algorithm by the number of "operations" that the algorithm executes. For the most part we will assume that basic arithmetic operations (such as addition, multiplication, and division) take one unit of time. This is a reasonable assumption when the operands can be represented by one or two computer words (e.g., integers that are not too large, single-precision or double-precision real numbers). There are cases, however, when the operands are huge (e.g., 2000 digit integers). In such cases, we have to take into account the size of the operands, or at least to be aware that the basic operations are not simple. It is possible to design algorithms that look very efficient ''on paper,'' by are in fact very inefficient, because the sizes of the operands are ignored.

The meaning of the ''size of the input'' is confusing sometimes. Given an integer n on which we want to perform an arithmetic operation, it is natural to think of the value n as the size of the input. However, this is contrary to our usual convention of using the storage requirements of the input for defining its size. The distinction is very important. Adding two 100-digit numbers can be done quickly, even by hand. On the other hand, counting to a value represented by a 100-digit number cannot be done in reasonable time even by the fastest computer. Since a number n can be represented by $\lceil \log_2 n \rceil$ bits, its **size** is defined as $\lceil \log_2 n \rceil$. For example, an algorithm that requires $O(\log n)$ operations when n is the input (for example, an algorithm for computing $2n$) is considered linear, since $O(\log n)$ is a linear function of the size of the input, whereas an algorithm that requires $O(\sqrt{n})$ operations when n is the input (for example, factoring n by trying all numbers less than or equal to $\sqrt{n}$) is considered exponential.

As usual, we concentrate in this chapter on interesting techniques for designing algorithms. We first discuss how to compute powers of a given number. We then present what is probably the oldest known nontrivial algorithm: Euclid's algorithm for finding the greatest common divisor. It is quite amazing that modern computers use a 2200-year old algorithm. We then discuss algorithms for polynomial multiplication and matrix multiplication, and we end the chapter with one of the most important and most beautiful algorithms — the fast Fourier transform.

9.2 Exponentiation

We start with a basic arithmetic operation.

> **The Problem**   Given two positive integers n and k, compute n^k.

We can easily reduce the problem to that of computing n^{k-1}, since $n^k = n \cdot n^{k-1}$. Therefore, the problem can be solved by induction on k, and the resulting straightforward algorithm is given in Fig. 9.1. We have reduced the value of k, but not its size. The straightforward algorithm requires k iterations. Since the size of k is $\log_2 k$, the number of interation is exponential in the size of k ($k = 2^{\log_2 k}$). This is not bad for very small values of k, but it is unacceptable for large values of k.

Another way to reduce the problem is to use the fact that $n^k = (n^{k/2})^2$. With this observation, we reduce the problem to one with n and $k/2$. Reducing the value of k by half corresponds to reducing its size by a constant. Thus, the number of multiplications will be linear in the size of k. We now have the skeleton of the algorithm — repeated squaring. The simplest case is for $k = 2^j$ for some integer j:

Algorithm Power (*n, k*) ; *{ first attempt }*
Input: *n* and *k* (two positive integers).
Output: *P* (the value of n^k).

begin
    P := *n* ;
    for *i* := 1 **to** *k* − 1 **do**
        P := *n* * *P*
end

Figure 9.1 Algorithm *Power*.

$$n^k = n^{2^j} = \left[\left[n^2\right]^2\right]^{\cdots 2} \Bigg\} \; j \text{ times.}$$

But what if *k* is not a power of 2? Consider again the reduction we just used. We started with two parameters *n* and *k*, and reduced the problem to a smaller one with *n* and *k*/2. This reduction is not always valid since *k*/2 may not be an integer. If *k*/2 is not an integer, the reduced problem does not satisfy the conditions of the original problem. But if *k*/2 is not an integer, then (*k* − 1)/2 is an integer, and the following reduction is appropriate:

$$n^k = n\left[n^{(k-1)/2}\right]^2.$$

We now have an algorithm. If *k* is even, we simply square the solution for *k*/2. If *k* is odd, we square the solution for (*k* − 1)/2 and multiply by *n*. The number of multiplications is at most $2\log_2 k$. The algorithm is given in Fig. 9.2.

Complexity The number of multiplications is $O(\log k)$. As the algorithm progresses, however, the numbers become larger. Therefore, the multiplications become more costly. We leave it to the reader (Exercise 9.12) to analyze the complexity of this algorithm under a more realistic measure for the cost of the multiplications. We now present an application of this algorithm in which the numbers do not grow during the execution of the algorithm.

An Application to Cryptography

The study of cryptography is beyond the scope of this book, and we discuss it briefly. Encryption schemes usually rely on complete secrecy. Any two participants who want to exchange secret messages must agree on the encryption–decryption algorithm and must use secret keys known only to themselves. We want to avoid this need to exchange secret keys between every pair of participants. The following is known as the **RSA public-key encryption scheme** (after Rivest, Shamir, and Adleman [1978], who developed it). The scheme can be used by a group of participants (e.g., computer users)

Algorithm Power_by_Repeated_Squaring (*n, k*) ;
Input: *n* and *k* (two positive integers).
Output: *P* (the value of n^k).

begin
    P := *n* ;
    j := *k* ;
    while *j* > 1 **do**
        P := *P*P* ;
        if *j* mod 2 = 1 **then**
            P := *P*n* ;
        j := *j* div 2
end

Figure 9.2 Algorithm *Power_by_Repeated_Squaring*.

---

who want to communicate by encrypted messages. Each participant has only two keys, one for encryption and one for decryption (independent of the number of other participants). These keys are chosen as follows. A participant *P* in the RSA scheme selects two very large prime numbers *p* and *q* and computes their product *n* = *pq*. He then chooses another very large integer *d*, such that *d* and $(p-1)(q-1)$ have no common divisor. (See the next section for an algorithm to verify that fact; if *d* is a random number, then the condition above is likely to occur.) From *p*, *q*, and *d*, it is possible (although not easy) to compute the value of a number *e* that satisfies

$$e \cdot d \equiv 1 \ (\mathrm{mod} \ (p-1)(q-1)). \tag{9.1}$$

As we shall see next, *e* will be the encryption key and *d* the decryption key. The values of *n* and *e* are publicized by *P* in a central directory that everyone can read. (We assume the availability of a trusted directory such that no other person can forge *P*'s keys.) The value of *d*, as well as the values of *p* and *q*, which are not needed anymore, are kept secret by *P*.

    Let *M* be an integer that corresponds to a message that *P* wants to encrypt (every message can be translated to a sequence of bits, which can be translated to an integer). Assume that *M* is smaller than *n*; otherwise *M* can be broken into several small messages each smaller than *n*. The encryption function E_P that *P* uses is very simple:

$$E_P(M) = M^e \ (\mathrm{mod} \ n).$$

Since both *n* and *e* are made public, everyone can encrypt messages and send them to *P*. The decryption function D_P is just as simple (but it can be performed only by *P*, since the value of *d* is secret):

$$D_P(C) = C^d \ (\mathrm{mod} \ n).$$

One can prove that (9.1) guarantees that $D_P(E_P(M)) = M$, hence these are valid encryption and decryption functions. Both algorithms thus consist of computing only one power (M^e or C^d) and one division (for the congruence), although these operations are performed on very large numbers. The modulo n operation can be applied at *any step* of the algorithm, and not necessarily at the end. This is true because

$$x \cdot y(\bmod n) = [\, x(\bmod n) \cdot y(\bmod n)\,](\bmod n),$$

for all integers x, y, and n. Applying the modulo n operation in each step of the computation is very important, since this way the values of the operands do not grow above n. If we use algorithm *Power_by_Repeated-Squaring* of Fig. 9.2, not only do we require only $O(\log e)$ (or $O(\log d)$) multiplications and divisions for computing the power, but each multiplication and division involves numbers that are less than n. We need to modify algorithm *Power_by_Repeated-Squaring* by only changing each multiplication to a multiplication modulo n. Thus, applying the RSA scheme requires only $O(\log n)$ multiplications and divisions of numbers that are less than n.

There is no known algorithm that can factor a very large number (e.g., of 1000 digits) in a reasonable time (e.g., our lifetime). Thus, the knowledge of the value of n does not imply the knowledge of p and q. It is commonly believed (although there is no known proof of this fact) that it is impossible to compute the function D_P efficiently without the knowledge of any one of d, p, or q.[1] Therefore, by keeping d, p, and q secret, P can receive encrypted messages from anyone without compromising the secrecy of the messages. There are several other advantages of this scheme, which is called a **public-key cryptosystem**.

9.3 Euclid's Algorithm

The **greatest common divisor** of two positive integers n and m, denoted by GCD(n, m), is the unique positive integer k such that (1) k divides both n and m, and (2) all other integers that divide both n and m are smaller than k.

> **The Problem**   Find the greatest common divisor of two given positive integers.

As usual, we try to reduce the problem to one of smaller size. Can we somehow make n or m smaller without changing the problem? Euclid noticed the obvious positive answer: If k divides both n and m, then it divides their difference! If $n > m$, then GCD$(n, m) =$ GCD$(n - m, m)$, and we now have a smaller problem. But, again, we reduced the *values*

---

[1] It is known that an algorithm for computing d from n and e would lead to an efficient probabilistic algorithm for factoring n, which is a strong evidence that d cannot be compromised (see Bach, Miller, and Shallit [1986]). Potentially, however, there may be another way to compute D_P without the knowledge of d.

of the numbers in question, and not their *sizes*. For the algorithm to be efficient, we must reduce the sizes. For example, if n is very large (say 1000 digits) and $m = 24$, we will need to subtract 24 from n approximately $n/24$ times. This computation will take $O(n)$ steps, which is exponential in the size of n.

Let's look at this algorithm again. We subtract m from n and apply the same algorithm to $n - m$ and m. If $n - m$ is still larger than m, we subtract m again. In other words, we keep subtracting m from n until the result becomes less than m. But this is exactly the same as dividing n by m and looking at the remainder. Division can be done quickly. This leads directly to Euclid's algorithm, which is presented in Fig. 9.3.

Complexity   We claim that Euclid's algorithm has linear running time in the size of $n + m$; specifically, its running time (counting each operation as one step independent of the size of the operands) is $O(\log(n + m))$. To prove this claim, it is sufficient to show that the value of a is reduced by half in a constant number of iterations. Let's look at two consecutive iterations of algorithm *GCD*. In the first iteration, a and b ($a > b$) are changed into b and $a \bmod b$. Then, in the next iteration, they are changed into $a \bmod b$ and $b \bmod (a \bmod b)$. So, in two iterations, the first number a is changed to $a \bmod b$. But, since $a > b$, we have $a \bmod b < a/2$, which establishes the claim.

9.4 Polynomial Multiplication

Let $P = \sum\limits_{i=0}^{n-1} p_i x^i$, and $Q = \sum\limits_{i=0}^{n-1} q_i x^i$, be two polynomials of degree $n - 1$. A polynomial is represented by its ordered list of coefficients.

Algorithm GCD *(m, n)*
Input: m and n (two positive integers).
Output: *gcd* (the gcd of m and n).

begin
    $a := max(\ n, m\ )\ ;$
    $b := min(\ n, m\ )\ ;$
    $r := 1\ ;$
    while $r > 0$ *do* { *r is the remainder* }
        $r := a \bmod b\ ;$
        $a := b\ ;$
        $b := r\ ;$
    $gcd := a$
end

Figure 9.3 Algorithm *GCD*.

> **The Problem** Compute the product of two given polynomials of degree $n-1$.

$$PQ = \left[p_{n-1}x^{n-1} + \cdots + p_0 \right] \left[q_{n-1}x^{n-1} + \cdots + q_0 \right] = \tag{9.2}$$

$$p_{n-1}q_{n-1}x^{2n-2} + \cdots + \left[p_{n-1}q_{i+1} + p_{n-2}q_{i+2} + \cdots + p_{i+1}q_{n-1} \right]x^{n+i} + \cdots + p_0 q_0.$$

We can compute the coefficients of PQ directly from (9.2). It is easy to see that, if we follow (9.2), then the number of multiplications and additions will be $O(n^2)$. Can we do better? We have seen by now so many improvements of straightforward quadratic algorithms that it is not surprising that the answer is positive. A complicated $O(n \log n)$ algorithm will be discussed in Section 9.6. But first, we describe a simple divide-and-conquer algorithm.

For simplicity, we assume that n is a power of 2. We divide each polynomial into two equal-sized parts. Let $P = P_1 + x^{n/2} P_2$, and $Q = Q_1 + x^{n/2} Q_2$, where

$$P_1 = p_0 + p_1 x + \cdots + p_{n/2-1}x^{n/2-1}, \quad P_2 = p_{n/2} + p_{n/2+1}x + \cdots + p_{n-1}x^{n/2-1},$$

and

$$Q_1 = q_0 + q_1 x + \cdots + q_{n/2-1}x^{n/2-1}, \quad Q_2 = q_{n/2} + q_{n/2+1}x + \cdots + q_{n-1}x^{n/2-1}.$$

We now have

$$PQ = (P_1 + P_2 x^{n/2})(Q_1 + Q_2 x^{n/2}) = P_1 Q_1 + (P_1 Q_2 + P_2 Q_1)x^{n/2} + P_2 Q_2 x^n.$$

The expression for PQ now involves products of polynomials of degree $n/2$. We can compute the product of the smaller polynomials (e.g., $P_1 Q_1$) by induction, then add the results to complete the solution. Can we use induction directly? The only constraints are that the smaller problems be exactly the same as the original problem, and that we know how to multiply polynomials of degree 1. Both conditions are clearly satisfied. The total number of operations $T(n)$ required for this algorithm is given by the following recurrence relation:

$$T(n) = 4T(n/2) + O(n), \quad T(1) = 1.$$

The factor 4 comes from the 4 products of the smaller polynomials, and the $O(n)$ comes from adding the smaller polynomials. The solution of this recurrence relation is $O(n^2)$ (see Section 3.5.2), which means that we have not achieved any improvement (see Exercise 9.4).

To get an improvement to the quadratic algorithm we need to solve the problem by solving less than four subproblems. Consider the following multiplication table (the reason we use such an elaborate table for this simple notation will become apparent in the next section).

$\times$	P_1	P_2
Q_1	A	B
Q_2	C	D

We want to compute $A + (B+C)x^{n/2} + Dx^n$. The important observation is that we do not have to compute B and C separately; we need only to know their sum! If we compute the product $E = (P_1 + P_2)(Q_1 + Q_2)$, then $B + C = E - A - D$. Hence, we need to compute only three products of smaller polynomials: A, D, and E. All the rest can be computed by additions and subtractions, which contribute only $O(n)$ to the recurrence relation anyway. The new recurrence relation is

$$T(n) = 3T(n/2) + O(n),$$

which implies $T(n) = O(n^{\log_2 3}) = O(n^{1.59})$.

Notice that the polynomials $P_1 + P_2$ and $Q_1 + Q_2$ are related to the original polynomials in a strange way. They are formed by adding coefficients whose indices differ by $n/2$. This is quite a nonintuitive way to multiply polynomials, yet this algorithm reduces the number of operations significantly for large n.

□ Example 9.1

Let $P = 1 - x + 2x^2 - x^3$, and $Q = 2 + x - x^2 + 2x^3$. We compute their product using the divide-and-conquer algorithm. We carry the recursion only one step.

$$A = (1-x) \cdot (2+x) = 2 - x - x^2,$$

$$D = (2-x) \cdot (-1+2x) = -2 + 5x - 2x^2,$$

and

$$E = (3-2x) \cdot (1+3x) = 3 + 7x - 6x^2.$$

From E, A, and D, we can easily compute $B + C = E - A - B$:

$$B + C = 3 + 3x - 3x^2.$$

Now, $P \cdot Q = A + (B+C)x^{n/2} + Dx^n$, and we have

$$P \cdot Q = 2 - x - x^2 + 3x^2 + 3x^3 - 3x^4 - 2x^4 + 5x^5 - 2x^6$$

$$= 2 - x + 2x^2 + 3x^3 - 5x^4 + 5x^5 - 2x^6.$$

Notice that we used 12 multiplications compared to 16 in the straightforward algorithm, and 12 additions and subtractions instead of 9. (We could have reduced the number of multiplications to 9 if we had carried the recursion one more step.) The savings are, of course, much larger when n is large. (The number of additions and subtractions remains within a constant factor of that in the straightforward algorithm, whereas the number of multiplications is reduced by about $n^{0.4}$.)   □

9.5 Matrix Multiplication

The product C of two $n \times n$ matrices A and B is defined as follows:

$$c_{ij} = \sum_{k=1}^{n} a_{ik} \cdot b_{kj}. \tag{9.3}$$

The Problem Compute the product $C = A \times B$ of two $n \times n$ matrices of real numbers.

The straightforward way (and seemingly the *only* way) to compute matrix product is to follow (9.3), which requires using n^3 multiplications and $(n-1)n^2$ additions. Notice that n represents the number of rows and columns in the matrix, rather than the size of the input, which is n^2. We now present two different schemes that show the possibilities for improvements.

9.5.1 Winograd's Algorithm

Assume, for simplicity, that n is even. Denote

$$A_i = \sum_{k=1}^{n/2} a_{i,2k-1} \cdot a_{i,2k}, \quad \text{and} \quad B_j = \sum_{k=1}^{n/2} b_{2k-1,j} \cdot b_{2k,j}.$$

After rearranging terms, we get

$$c_{i,j} = \sum_{k=1}^{n/2} (a_{i,2k-1} + b_{2k,j}) \cdot (a_{i,2k} + b_{2k-1,j}) - A_i - B_j.$$

But the A_is and B_js need to be computed only once for each row or column. To compute all the A_is and B_js requires only n^2 multiplications. The total number of multiplications has thus been reduced to $\frac{1}{2}n^3 + n^2$. The number of additions has increased by about $\frac{1}{2}n^3$. This algorithm is thus better than the straightforward algorithm in cases where additions can be performed more quickly than multiplications.

Comments This algorithm shows that rearranging the order of the computation can make a difference, even for expressions, such as matrix multiplication, which have a simple form. The next algorithm carries this idea much farther.

9.5.2 Strassen's Algorithm

We use the divide-and-conquer method in a way similar to the polynomial multiplication algorithm in Section 9.4. For simplicity, we assume that n is a power of 2. Let

$$A = \begin{bmatrix} A_{1,1} & A_{1,2} \\ A_{2,1} & A_{2,2} \end{bmatrix}, \quad B = \begin{bmatrix} B_{1,1} & B_{1,2} \\ B_{2,1} & B_{2,2} \end{bmatrix}, \quad \text{and} \quad C = \begin{bmatrix} C_{1,1} & C_{1,2} \\ C_{2,1} & C_{2,2} \end{bmatrix},$$

where the $A_{i,j}$s, $B_{i,j}$s, and $C_{i,j}$s are $n/2 \times n/2$ matrices. We can use the divide-and-conquer approach and reduce the problem to computing the $C_{i,j}$s from the $A_{i,j}$s and the $B_{i,j}$s. That is, we can treat the $n/2 \times n/2$ submatrices as *elements* and consider the whole problem as one of computing a product of two 2×2 matrices of elements. (We have to be careful when we substitute elements for submatrices; this is the subject of Exercise 9.23.) The algorithm for the 2×2 product can be converted to an $n \times n$ product algorithm by substituting a recursive call each time a product of elements appears. The regular algorithm for multiplying two 2×2 matrices uses 8 multiplications. Substituting each multiplication by a recursive call, we get the recurrence relation $T(n) = 8T(n/2) + O(n^2)$, which implies that $T(n) = O(n^{\log_2 8}) = O(n^3)$. This is not surprising since we are using the regular algorithm. If we could only compute the product of two 2×2 matrices with less than 8 multiplications, we would get an algorithm that is asymptotically faster than cubic.

The most important part of the recursion is how many multiplications are required to compute the product of two 2×2 matrices. The number of additions is not as important since they always contribute $O(n^2)$ to the recurrence relation, which is not a factor in determining the asymptotic complexity. (It does affect the constant factor, however.) Strassen found that 7 multiplications are sufficient to compute the product of two 2×2 matrices. Instead of simply writing down the equations leading to Strassen's algorithm, we sketch a method that *could have* been used by Strassen to find it. This method can be used for similar problems.

Computing the product

$$\begin{bmatrix} a & b \\ c & d \end{bmatrix} \begin{bmatrix} e & g \\ f & h \end{bmatrix} = \begin{bmatrix} p & s \\ r & t \end{bmatrix}$$

is equivalent to computing the product

$$\begin{bmatrix} a & b & 0 & 0 \\ c & d & 0 & 0 \\ 0 & 0 & a & b \\ 0 & 0 & c & d \end{bmatrix} \begin{bmatrix} e \\ f \\ g \\ h \end{bmatrix} = \begin{bmatrix} p \\ r \\ s \\ t \end{bmatrix}. \tag{9.4}$$

We write (9.4) as $A \cdot X = Y$. We are looking for ways to minimize the number of multiplications required to evaluate Y. Let's look for special matrix products that are easy to compute. As it turns out, we need four types of such special products (the last two of which are very similar). They are as follows:

Type	Product	No. of Multiplications
α)	$\begin{bmatrix} a & a \\ a & a \end{bmatrix} \begin{bmatrix} e \\ f \end{bmatrix} = \begin{bmatrix} a(e+f) \\ a(e+f) \end{bmatrix}$	1

$$\beta) \qquad \begin{bmatrix} a & a \\ -a & -a \end{bmatrix} \begin{bmatrix} e \\ f \end{bmatrix} = \begin{bmatrix} a(e+f) \\ -a(e+f) \end{bmatrix} \qquad\qquad 1$$

$$\gamma) \qquad \begin{bmatrix} a & 0 \\ a-b & b \end{bmatrix} \begin{bmatrix} e \\ f \end{bmatrix} = \begin{bmatrix} ae \\ ae+b(f-e) \end{bmatrix} \qquad 2$$

$$\delta) \qquad \begin{bmatrix} a & b-a \\ 0 & b \end{bmatrix} \begin{bmatrix} e \\ f \end{bmatrix} = \begin{bmatrix} a(e-f)+bf \\ bf \end{bmatrix} \qquad 2$$

We now look for ways to divide the general matrix product given in (9.4) into several steps of the types listed above. Since these types of products use less than the nominal number of multiplications, we may be able to save something at the end. It takes a lot of trial and error to reach the right combinations. This process is hardly straightforward or even clear, but it is somewhat less than magic. Let

$$B = \begin{bmatrix} b & b & 0 & 0 \\ b & b & 0 & 0 \\ 0 & 0 & 0 & 0 \\ 0 & 0 & 0 & 0 \end{bmatrix}, \quad C = \begin{bmatrix} 0 & 0 & 0 & 0 \\ 0 & 0 & 0 & 0 \\ 0 & 0 & c & c \\ 0 & 0 & c & c \end{bmatrix},$$

$$D = \begin{bmatrix} 0 & 0 & 0 & 0 \\ c-b & 0 & 0 & c-b \\ b-c & 0 & 0 & b-c \\ 0 & 0 & 0 & 0 \end{bmatrix}, \quad \text{and} \quad E = \begin{bmatrix} a-b & 0 & 0 & 0 \\ 0 & d-b & 0 & b-c \\ c-b & 0 & a-c & 0 \\ 0 & 0 & 0 & d-c \end{bmatrix}.$$

Then, $A = (B+C+D+E)$ and therefore $AX = BX + CX + DX + EX$. All the products above, except for EX, can be computed with one multiplication using types α or β. The only problem is to compute EX. But E can be divided into two matrices $E = F + G$, such that F is of type γ and G is of type δ:

$$F = \begin{bmatrix} a-b & 0 & 0 & 0 \\ 0 & 0 & 0 & 0 \\ c-b & 0 & a-c & 0 \\ 0 & 0 & 0 & 0 \end{bmatrix} \quad G = \begin{bmatrix} 0 & 0 & 0 & 0 \\ 0 & d-b & 0 & b-c \\ 0 & 0 & 0 & 0 \\ 0 & 0 & 0 & d-c \end{bmatrix}$$

So, overall, $AX = (B+C+D+F+G)X$, and we need two products of type α, and one product each of types β, γ, and δ, with a total of 7 multiplications (see also Exercise 9.10).

Complexity   We use 7 products of matrices of half the original size, and a constant number of additions of matrices. The additions are less important than the products, because addition of two $n \times n$ matrices can be done in time $O(n^2)$, which is basically a linear time in the size of the matrices. The $O(n^2)$ term is not the dominant factor in the recurrence relation, which is $T(n) = 7T(n/2) + O(n^2)$. The solution of this recurrence relation is $T(n) = O(n^{\log_2 7})$, which is approximately $O(n^{2.81})$. If we use the derivation described above, we obtain 18 additions (see Exercise 9.10). It is possible to reduce the number of additions to 15 (Winograd [1973]), but this reduction does not change the asymptotic running time.

Comments   There are three major drawbacks to Strassen's algorithm:
1.   Empirical studies indicate that n needs to be at least 100 to make Strassen's algorithm faster than the straightforward $O(n^3)$ algorithm (Cohen and Roth [1976]).
2.   Strassen's algorithm is less stable than the straightforward algorithm. That is, for similar errors in the input, Strassen's algorithm will probably create larger errors in the output.
3.   Strassen's algorithm is obviously much more complicated and harder to implement than the straightforward algorithm. Furthermore, Strassen's algorithm cannot be easily parallelized, whereas the regular algorithm can.

Nevertheless, Strassen's algorithm is important. It is faster than the regular algorithm for large n, and it can be used for other problems involving matrices, such as matrix inversion and determinant computation. We will see in Chapter 10 that several other problems are equivalent to matrix multiplication. Strassen's algorithm can be improved in practice by using it only for large matrices and stopping the recursion when the size of the matrices become smaller than about 100. This is similar to the idea of selecting the base of the induction with care, which we discussed in Section 6.4.4 and Section 6.11.3. Strassen's algorithm also opened the door to other algorithms and raised many questions about similar problems that seemed unsolvable.

9.5.3 Boolean Matrices

In this section, we consider the special case of computing the product of two $n \times n$ Boolean matrices. All elements are 0 or 1, and the sum and product are defined by the following rules (which correspond to *or* and *and* respectively):

+	0	1
0	0	1
1	1	1

×	0	1
0	0	0
1	0	1

These definitions of sum and product are of course different from the usual integer sum and product; hence, algorithms designed for integers normally cannot be used for Booleans. One problem with the definition of a Boolean sum is that subtraction is not well defined (both $0+1$ and $1+1$ are defined as 1; hence, $1-1$ can be both 1 and 0).

Therefore, Strassen's algorithm cannot be used for Boolean matrices, because it requires subtraction. However, there is a trick that allows us to use Strassen's algorithm. We consider every bit as an integer modulo $n+1$, where n is the size of the matrices, and we use the rules of addition and multiplication of such integers. So, for example, if $n=4$, then $1+1=2$, $1+1+1=3$, and $1+1+1+1+1=0$. It turns out that, if we compute the matrix product according to these rules and if we substitute every nonzero entry in the final result by a 1, then we get the Boolean product. This is so, essentially, because we will not "overflow" the number $n+1$ (we omit the proof). (More precisely, the integers modulo k form a **ring**, which is an algebraic structure with definitions of sums and products that satisfy certain properties; Strassen's algorithm can be applied to any ring; see Aho, Hopcroft, and Ullman [1974] for more details.) Thus, the complexity of Boolean matrix multiplication is also $O(n^{2.81})$. The use of Strassen's algorithm, however, requires integer operations rather than Boolean operations. Next, we present two algorithms that utilize the properties of Boolean operations to improve the running time of Boolean matrix multiplication. These algorithms are more practical in most situations than Strassen's algorithm for Boolean matrix multiplication.

Since Boolean operands require only one bit of storage, we can store k operands in one computer word of size k. In particular, since we assume that n is stored in one computer word, we can store k bits for $k \leq \log_2 n$ in one word. The regular algorithm for matrix multiplication consists of n^2 row-by-column products (or **inner products**), as defined in (9.3). The ijth inner product consists of computing $\sum_{m=1}^{n} a_{im} \cdot b_{mj}$. Assume, for simplicity, that k divides n. We can divide each inner product into a sum of n/k products, each of which involves Boolean vectors of size k. Finding the inner product of two Boolean vectors of size k is simpler than, say, multiplying two k-bit integers. We assume that a multiplication of k-bit integers takes one unit of time; thus, it is not unreasonable to assume that computing an inner product of two Boolean vectors of size k takes one unit of time. (For example, an inner product can be computed in two steps: first, we compute the *and* of the two vectors, then we check whether the result is all 0s.) Nevertheless, we usually do not want to make the algorithm dependent on special assumptions concerning the computer primitives (besides the four basic arithmetic operations). Next, we show how to avoid the need for such assumption. Then, we combine this idea with another idea to improve Boolean matrix multiplication even further. Both ideas illustrate interesting techniques for algorithm design.

The first idea is to precompute all possible Boolean inner products of size k. There are 2^{2k} possible products, since they involve two Boolean vectors of size k. We can compute all of them in time $O(k2^{2k})$ (we can actually do better than that; see Exercise 9.24), and store all the results in a two-dimensional table of bits of size $2^k \times 2^k$. The product of the two vectors a and b is stored at entry (i_a, i_b), where i_a is the integer represented by the k bits of a and i_b is the integer represented by the k bits of b. From now on, we will not make a distinction between i_a and a (or i_b and b), since they are represented in exactly the same way. Thus, given two Boolean vectors of size k, we can compute their product by simply looking at the table. If we can access a table of size 2^{2k} in $O(1)$ time, then each inner product of size k can be computed in constant time (once the table is constructed). For example, let $k = \lfloor \log_2 n / 2 \rfloor$. In that case, the size of the table is $O(n)$, and constructing it requires $O(n \log n)$ time. The assumption that we can access a table of size $O(n)$ in constant time is not unusual. We have already made this assumption (implicitly) many times before. We usually assume that, if n is the size of the input, then we can store a number with $\log_2 n$ bits in one computer word (or a constant number of computer words). Once the table is constructed, we can compute a Boolean inner product of size n in time $O(n/k) = O(n/\log n)$. Notice that the table depends only on the value of k and not on the matrices. So, computing the product of two Boolean matrices can be done in time $O(n^3/\log n)$ and extra storage of $O(n)$. We can also choose k to be $\lfloor \log_2 n \rfloor$, in which case the table size is $O(n^2)$, but we save an extra factor of 2 in the multiplication algorithm. However, if we can afford an extra space of size $O(n^2)$, we can find a faster algorithm.

Consider two $n \times n$ Boolean matrices A and B. The usual way to view matrix multiplication is as defined in (9.3): We perform n^2 inner products, each involves a row of A and a column of B. We can also multiply the two matrices by multiplying columns of A with rows of B in the following way. Denote the rth column of A by $A_C[r]$, and the rth row of B by $B_R[r]$. Consider $A_C[r]$ as an $n \times 1$ matrix, and $B_R[r]$ as a $1 \times n$ matrix. The product of $A_C[r]$ with $B_R[r]$ is an $n \times n$ matrix, whose ijth entry is the product of the ith entry of $A_C[r]$ with the jth entry of $B_R[r]$ (see Fig. 9.4). It is easy to see that

$$A \cdot B = \sum_{r=1}^{n} A_C[r] \cdot B_R[r]. \tag{9.5}$$

The expression (9.5) is equivalent to (9.3) in the sense that the same products and additions are performed, but they are performed in a different order.

We now partition the columns of A and the rows of B into n/k equal-sized groups. (We assume for simplicity that n/k is an integer; otherwise, there will be an extra smaller group.) In other words, we divide A into $A_1, A_2, ..., A_{n/k}$, such that each A_i is an $n \times k$ matrix, and we divide B into $B_1, B_2, ..., B_{n/k}$, such that each B_i is an $k \times n$ matrix. It is easy to see that

$$A \cdot B = \sum_{i=1}^{n/k} A_i \cdot B_i. \tag{9.6}$$

Figure 9.4 Multiplying matrices columns by rows.

The problem now is how to compute $C_i = A_i \cdot B_i$ efficiently. We describe this computation by an example (see Fig. 9.5).

The first row of C_i is exactly the same as the third row of B_i, because the first row of A_i has a 1 only in column 3. Similarly, the second row of C_i is the Boolean sum of the second and third rows of B_i. It is easy to see that the jth row of C_i is a Boolean sum of rows of B_i according to the jth row of A_i. Instead of computing each row of C_i in a straightforward way, we use a method, similar to the algorithm we described earlier, for precomputing all possibilities. There are k entries in each row of A_i, so there are 2^k possible combinations of rows of B_i. Let $k = \log_2 n$, and assume again that k is an integer. We precompute all $2^k = 2^{\log_2 n} = n$ combinations, and store the results in a table. In contrast to the first algorithm, this table contains n rows rather than n bits; thus, the storage requirement is $O(n^2)$. Also, this table depends on B_i, and must be constructed for each B_i. To find row j of C_i, we look at row j of A_i and see the combination of rows of B_i that need to be added. This combination can be represented as an integer corresponding to the binary representation of row j of A_i (e.g., the first row of A_i in Fig. 9.5 corresponds to 1, the second row corresponds to 3, the third row corresponds to 4, and so on). This integer is the address in the table where row j of C_i is stored. It takes $O(1)$ time to find a row of C_i in the table, and $O(n)$ time to copy this row to the appropriate row in C_i. Thus, computing C_i can be done in time $O(n^2)$.

We now show that all the combinations of sums of rows of B_i can be computed in time $O(n \cdot 2^k)$. Each combination of rows corresponds to a k-bit integer. We assume, by induction, that we know how to compute the sums of combinations of rows corresponding to integers that are less than i. Computing the sum corresponding to 0 is trivial. Assume that the binary representation of $i - 1$ is $xxxx\,011111$ — namely, its least significant 0 is followed by j 1s. The sum of rows corresponding to i is equal to the sum of rows corresponding to $xxxx\,000000$ plus the row corresponding to 0000100000. Since $xxxx\,000000$ is less than i, we know its corresponding sum by induction, and we need only to add one row to it. It takes n Boolean additions to add a row, and we have 2^k combinations. Hence, all the precomputing can be done with $O(n \cdot 2^k)$ operations. If $k = \log_2 n$, then the running time is $O(n^2)$. This algorithm is known as the **four-Russians**

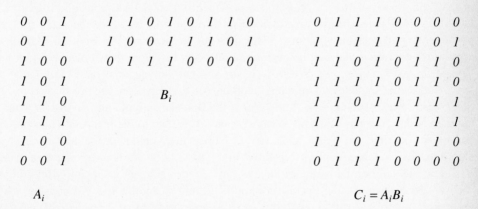

0	0	1		1	1	0	1	0	1	1	0		0	1	1	1	0	0	0	0
0	1	1		1	0	0	1	1	1	0	1		1	1	1	1	1	1	0	1
1	0	0		0	1	1	1	0	0	0	0		1	1	0	1	0	1	1	0
1	0	1											1	1	1	1	0	1	1	0
1	1	0				B_i							1	1	0	1	1	1	1	1
1	1	1											1	1	1	1	1	1	1	1
1	0	0											1	1	0	1	0	1	1	0
0	0	1											0	1	1	1	0	0	0	0

A_i $C_i = A_i B_i$

Figure 9.5 Boolean matrix multiplication.

algorithm (Arlazarov et al. [1970]), after the nationality and number of its inventors. The algorithm is given in Fig. 9.6.

Algorithm Boolean_Matrix_Multiplication *(A, B, n, k)* ;
Input: *A*, *B* (two $n \times n$ Boolean matrices), and *k* (an integer).
Output: *C* (the product of *A* and *B*).
    { we assume, for simplicity, that *k* divides *n* }

begin
    Initialize the matrix C to 0 ;
    for *i := 0* **to** *n/k − 1* **do**
        Construct Table$_i$;
        { Table$_i$ is an 2^k array of Boolean vectors of size n which contains
         all possible combinations of sums of k rows of B$_i$; see the text }
        m := i * k ;
        for *j := 1* **to** *n* **do**
            Let Addr be the k-bit number
                A[j, m+1] A[j, m+2] $\cdots$ *A[j, m+k]* ;
            add Table$_i$[Addr] to row j in C
    end

Figure 9.6 Algorithm *Boolean_Matrix_Multiplication*.

Complexity   To compute $A \cdot B$ we have to compute the n/k products $A_i \cdot B_i$. Since each such product takes $O(n^2)$ time and constructing the table takes $O(n \cdot 2^k)$ time, the total running time of the algorithm is $O(n^3/k + n^2 \cdot 2^k/k)$. If $k = \log_2 n$, then the running time is $O(n^3/\log n)$.

Next, we show how to combine the ideas of the first algorithm with the ideas of the second algorithm to improve the running time by another $O(\log n)$ factor. The main step in algorithm *Boolean_Matrix_Multiplication* (Fig 9.6) involves additions of a row from a table to *C*. We can perform this addition in time $O(n/m)$ by using the same trick of precomputing all possible additions. (This may not be necessary if a Boolean addition is a primitive operation that can be performed quickly; the algorithm, however, does not depend on this assumption.) We first construct a two-dimensional table *Add_Table* of size $2^m \times 2^m$ that includes all possible additions of two Boolean vectors of size *m*. In other words, the (i, j)th entry in *Add_Table* is the Boolean sum of *i* and *j*. (Again, *i* and *j* are used both as integers and as Boolean vectors.) It is easy to see that *Add_Table* can be constructed in time and space $O(m \cdot 2^{2m})$. Notice that, unlike the tables we used in algorithm *Boolean_Matrix_Multiplication* (Fig. 9.6), *Add_Table* is independent of *A* and *B*; it depends only on the value of *m*. We now divide each row of B_i into n/m groups, each of size *m* (we assume again, for simplicity, that *m* divides *n*). We consider each group as a *m*-bit integer; thus, each row of B_i is represented by an n/m-tuple of integers. All the steps of the algorithm will be performed on these tuples.

To add two vectors of size n, we use *Add_Table* to add the corresponding two n/m-tuples in n/m steps. Each step consists of taking two m-bit numbers and fetching the corresponding entry in *Add_Table* (which contains their sum). Such a step can be performed in constant time, as long as the size of the computer word is at most $2m$. We use this trick both for constructing the tables for the regular four-Russians algorithm, and for adding the rows during the execution of the algorithm. If we select m to be approximately equal to $\lfloor \log_2 n/2 \rfloor$, then $2^{2m} = O(n)$ and, since we assume that we can represent n in one computer word, we can represent a $2m$-bit number in one word. For this choice of m, the running time of the improved algorithm is $O(n^3/\log^2 n)$.

Comments   We presented an interesting method of computing all possibilities instead of the usual wisdom of computing only what is needed. We also demonstrated that changing the order of the computation can lead to a better algorithm. The trick of computing all possible combinations can be applied in the same manner to other algebraic functions on bit strings that cannot be performed directly by the hardware.

9.6 The Fast Fourier Transform

As an introduction to the fast Fourier transform, we quote from John Lipson's excellent book:

> An algorithm may be appreciated on a number of grounds; on technological grounds because it efficiently solves an important practical problem, on aesthetic grounds because it is elegant, or even on dramatic grounds because it opens up new and unexpected areas of applications. The *fast Fourier transform* (popularly referred to as the "FFT"), perhaps because it is strong on *all* of these departments, has emerged as one of the "super" algorithms of Computer Science since its discovery in the mid sixties. (Lipson [1981], page 293.)

The FFT algorithm is by no means simple, and its development is not straightforward. We concentrate on only one application of the FFT — polynomial multiplication.

The Problem   Given two polynomials $p(x)$ and $q(x)$, compute their product $p(x) \cdot q(x)$.

The problem, as stated above, is not well defined. We have not specified the representation of the polynomials. We usually represent a polynomial $P = a_{n-1}x^{n-1} + a_{n-2}x^{n-2} + \cdots + a_1 x + a_0$ by the list of its coefficients in increasing order of degrees. This representation is definitely adequate, but it is not the only one possible. Consider, for example, a polynomial of degree 1, which is a linear function $a_1 x + a_0$. This linear function is usually specified by the two coefficients a_1 and a_0. But, since the function corresponds to a line in the plane, it can also be specified by any two (nonequal) points on that line. In the same way, any polynomial of degree n is uniquely defined by $n+1$ points. For example, the second-degree polynomial $p(x)=x^2+3x+1$ is defined by the points $(1,5)$, $(2,11)$, and $(3,19)$, and it is the *only* second degree polynomial that includes all those points. These three points are not the only three points that define this polynomial; any three points on the corresponding curve will do.

This representation is attractive for polynomial multiplication because multiplying the values of points is easy. For example, the polynomial $q(x)=2x^2-x+3$ can be represented by $(1,4)$, $(2,9)$, and $(3,18)$. We right away know that the product $p(x)\cdot q(x)$ has the values $(1,20)$, $(2,99)$, and $(3,342)$. These three points are not enough to represent $p(x)\cdot q(x)$ since it has degree 4. We can overcome this problem by requiring five points from each of the smaller polynomials; for example, we can add the points $(0,1)$ and $(-1,-1)$ to $p(x)$, and $(0,3)$ and $(-1,6)$ to $q(x)$. We can then easily obtain five points that belong to the product — $(1, 20)$, $(2, 99)$, $(3, 342)$, $(0, 3)$, and $(-1, -6)$ — by making only five scalar multiplications! Using this idea, we can compute the product of two polynomials of degree n, given in this representation, with only $O(n)$ multiplications.

The main problem with this approach is that we cannot simply change the representation to fit only one application. We must be able, for example, to evaluate the polynomial at given points. This is much harder to do for this representation than it is when the coefficients are given. However, if we could convert efficiently from one representation to another, then we would have a very good polynomial multiplication algorithm. This is what the FFT achieves.

Converting from coefficients to points can be done by polynomial evaluation. We can compute the value of a polynomial $p(x)$, given by its list of coefficients, at any given point by Horner's rule (Section 5.2) using n multiplications. We need to evaluate $p(x)$ at n arbitrary points, so we require n^2 multiplications. Converting from points to coefficients is called **interpolation**, and it also generally requires $O(n^2)$ operations. The key idea here (as in so many other examples in this book) is that we do not have to use n *arbitrary* points; we are free to choose *any* set of n distinct points we want. The fast Fourier transform chooses a very special set of points such that both steps, evaluation and interpolation, can be done quickly.

The Forward Fourier Transform

We first consider the evaluation problem. We need to evaluate two $n-1$ degree polynomials, each at $2n-1$ points, so that their product, which is a $2n-2$ degree polynomial, can be interpolated. However, we can always represent an $n-1$ degree polynomial as a $2n-2$ degree polynomial by setting the first $n-1$ (leading) coefficients to zero. So, without loss of generality, we assume that the problem is to evaluate an arbitrary polynomial $P = \sum_{i=0}^{n-1} a_i x^i$ of degree $n-1$ at n distinct points. We want to find n points for which the polynomials are easy to evaluate. We assume, for simplicity, that n is a power of 2.

We use matrix terminology to simplify the notation. The evaluation of the polynomial P above for the n points $x_0, x_1, ..., x_{n-1}$ can be represented as the following matrix by vector multiplication:

$$\begin{bmatrix} 1 & x_0 & (x_0)^2 & \cdot & \cdot & (x_0)^{n-1} \\ 1 & x_1 & (x_1)^2 & \cdot & \cdot & (x_1)^{n-1} \\ \cdot & \cdot & \cdot & \cdot & \cdot & \cdot \\ \cdot & \cdot & \cdot & \cdot & \cdot & \cdot \\ \cdot & \cdot & \cdot & \cdot & \cdot & \cdot \\ 1 & x_{n-1} & (x_{n-1})^2 & \cdot & \cdot & (x_{n-1})^{n-1} \end{bmatrix} \begin{bmatrix} a_0 \\ a_1 \\ \cdot \\ \cdot \\ \cdot \\ a_{n-1} \end{bmatrix} = \begin{bmatrix} P(x_0) \\ P(x_1) \\ \cdot \\ \cdot \\ \cdot \\ P(x_{n-1}) \end{bmatrix} .$$

The question is whether we can choose the values of $x_0, x_1, ..., x_{n-1}$ in a way that simplifies this multiplication. Consider two arbitrary rows i and j. We would like to make them as similar as possible to save multiplications. We cannot make $x_i = x_j$, because the values must be different, but we can make $(x_i)^2 = (x_j)^2$ by letting $x_j = -x_i$. This is a good choice, because every even power of x_i will be equal to the same even power of x_j. We may be able to save one-half of the multiplications involved with row j. Furthermore, we can do the same for other pairs of rows. Our goal is to have n special rows for which the computation above requires only $n/2$ vector products. If we can do that, then we may be able to cut the problem size by half, which will lead to a very efficient algorithm. Let's try to pose this problem in terms of two separate subproblems of half the size.

We want to divide the original problem into two subproblems of size $n/2$, according to the scheme described above. This is illustrated in the following expression.

$$\begin{bmatrix} 1 & x_0 & (x_0)^2 & \cdot & \cdot & (x_0)^{n-1} \\ 1 & x_1 & (x_1)^2 & \cdot & \cdot & (x_1)^{n-1} \\ \cdot & \cdot & \cdot & \cdot & \cdot & \cdot \\ 1 & x_{n/2-1} & (x_{n/2-1})^2 & \cdot & \cdot & (x_{n/2-1})^{n-1} \\ 1 & -x_0 & (-x_0)^2 & \cdot & \cdot & (-x_0)^{n-1} \\ 1 & -x_1 & (-x_1)^2 & \cdot & \cdot & (-x_1)^{n-1} \\ \cdot & \cdot & \cdot & \cdot & \cdot & \cdot \\ 1 & -x_{n/2-1} & (-x_{n/2-1})^2 & \cdot & \cdot & (-x_{n/2-1})^{n-1} \end{bmatrix} \begin{bmatrix} a_0 \\ a_1 \\ \cdot \\ \cdot \\ \cdot \\ \cdot \\ \cdot \\ a_{n-1} \end{bmatrix} = \begin{bmatrix} P(x_0) \\ P(x_1) \\ \cdot \\ \cdot \\ \cdot \\ \cdot \\ \cdot \\ P(-x_{n/2-1}) \end{bmatrix} . \tag{9.7}$$

The $n \times n$ matrix in (9.7) is divided into two submatrices, each of size $n/2 \times n$. These two matrices are very similar. For each i, such that $0 \le i < n/2$, we have $x_i = -x_{n/2+i}$. The coefficients of the even powers are exactly the same in both submatrices, so they need to be computed only once. The coefficients of the odd powers are not the same, but they are exactly the negation of each other! We would like to write the expressions for $P(x_i)$ and $P(-x_i)$ for $0 \le i < n/2$ in terms of the even and odd coefficients:

$$P(x) = E + O = \sum_{i=0}^{n/2-1} a_{2i} x^{2i} + \sum_{i=0}^{n/2-1} a_{2i+1} x^{2i+1}.$$

The "even" polynomial (E) can be written as a regular polynomial of degree $n/2 - 1$

with the even coefficients of P:

$$E = \sum_{i=0}^{n/2-1} a_{2i}(x^2)^i = P_e(x^2).$$

The "odd" polynomial (O) can be written in the same way:

$$O = x \sum_{i=0}^{n/2-1} a_{2i+1}(x^2)^i = x P_o(x^2).$$

So, overall, we have the following expression:

$$P(x) = P_e(x^2) + x P_o(x^2), \tag{9.8}$$

where P_e (P_o) are the $n/2-1$ degree polynomials with the coefficients of the even (odd) powers of P. When we substitute $-x$ for x in (9.8), we get $P(-x) = P_e(x^2) + (-x) P_o(x^2)$. To avaluate (9.7), we need to compute $P(x_i)$ and $P(-x_i)$, for $0 \le i < n/2$. To do that, we need to compute only $n/2$ values of $P_e(x^2)$ and $n/2$ values of $P_o(x^2)$, and to perform $n/2$ additions, $n/2$ subtractions, and n multiplications. So, we have two subproblems of size $n/2$, and $O(n)$ additional computations.

Can we continue with the same scheme recursively? If we could, then we would get the familiar recurrence relation $T(n) = 2T(n/2) + O(n)$, resulting in an $O(n \log n)$ algorithm. But this is not so easy. We reduced the problem of computing $P(x)$ (a polynomial of degree $n-1$) at n points to that of computing $P_e(x^2)$ and $P_o(x^2)$ (both polynomials of degree $n/2-1$) at $n/2$ points. This is a valid reduction, except for one small thing. The values of x in $P(x)$ can be chosen arbitrarily, but the values of x^2, which are needed, for example, in $P_e(x^2)$, can only be positive. Since we obtained this reduction by using negative numbers, this poses a problem. Let's extract from (9.7) the matrix that corresponds to the computation of $P_e((x_i)^2)$:

$$\begin{bmatrix} 1 & (x_0)^2 & (x_0)^4 & \cdot & \cdot & (x_0)^{n-2} \\ 1 & (x_1)^2 & (x_1)^4 & \cdot & \cdot & (x_1)^{n-2} \\ \cdot & \cdot & \cdot & \cdot & \cdot & \cdot \\ \cdot & \cdot & \cdot & \cdot & \cdot & \cdot \\ \cdot & \cdot & \cdot & \cdot & \cdot & \cdot \\ 1 & (x_{n/2-1})^2 & (x_{n/2-1})^4 & \cdot & \cdot & (x_{n/2-1})^{n-2} \end{bmatrix} \begin{bmatrix} a_0 \\ a_2 \\ a_4 \\ \cdot \\ \cdot \\ a_{n-2} \end{bmatrix} = \begin{bmatrix} P_e(x_0) \\ P_e(x_1) \\ \cdot \\ \cdot \\ \cdot \\ P_e(x_{n/2-1}) \end{bmatrix}.$$

If we try the same trick on this subproblem, we need to set $(x_{n/4})^2 = -(x_0)^2$. Since squares are always positive, this seems impossible. But it is not impossible if we use complex numbers which include $\sqrt{-1}$. We again divide the problem into two parts and let $x_{j+n/4} = \sqrt{-1}\, x_j$, for $0 \le j < n/4$. This partition satisfies the same properties as did the first partition. Hence, we can solve the problem of size $n/2$ by solving two subproblems of size $n/4$ and $O(n)$ additional computation.

If we want to carry this process one step further, we need a number that is equal to $\sqrt{\sqrt{-1}}$; that is, a number z such that $z^8 = 1$, and $z^j \ne 1$ for $0 < j < 8$ (which implies that $z^4 = -1$, and $z^2 = \sqrt{-1}$). In general, we need a number that satisfies the condition above for n rather than for 8. Such a number is called a **primitive nth root of unity**. We denote it by ω. (We do not include n in the notation for simplicity; we will use the same n throughout this section.) ω satisfies the following conditions:

$$\omega^n = 1, \text{ and } \omega^j \neq 1 \text{ for } 0 < j < n. \tag{9.9}$$

The n points that we choose as $x_0, x_1, ..., x_{n-1}$ are $1, \omega, \omega^2, ..., \omega^{n-1}$. Therefore, we want to compute the following product:

$$
\begin{bmatrix}
1 & 1 & 1 & \cdot & \cdot & 1 \\
1 & \omega & \omega^2 & \cdot & \cdot & \omega^{n-1} \\
\cdot & \omega^2 & \omega^{2\cdot 2} & \cdot & \cdot & \omega^{2\cdot(n-1)} \\
\cdot & \cdot & \cdot & \cdot & \cdot & \cdot \\
\cdot & \cdot & \cdot & \cdot & \cdot & \cdot \\
1 & \omega^{n-1} & \omega^{(n-1)\cdot 2} & \cdot & \cdot & \omega^{(n-1)\cdot(n-1)}
\end{bmatrix}
\begin{bmatrix}
a_0 \\
a_1 \\
\cdot \\
\cdot \\
\cdot \\
a_{n-1}
\end{bmatrix}
=
\begin{bmatrix}
P(1) \\
P(\omega) \\
P(\omega^2) \\
\cdot \\
\cdot \\
P(\omega^{n-1})
\end{bmatrix}
$$

This product is called the **Fourier transform** of $(a_0, a_1, ..., a_{n-1})$. First, we notice that indeed for any j, $0 \leq j < n/2$, we have $x_{j+n/2} = \omega^{n/2} x_j = -x_j$. So the reduction that we applied initially to the problem of size n is still valid. Furthermore, the subproblems resulting from that reduction have $n/2$ points, which are $1, \omega^2, \omega^4, ..., \omega^{n-2}$. But this is exactly the problem of size $n/2$ in which we substitute ω^2 for ω. The conditions in (9.9) imply that ω^2 is a primitive $(n/2)$th root of unity. Therefore, we can continue recursively, and the complexity of the algorithm is $O(n \log n)$. A high-level view of the algorithm is presented in Fig. 9.7.

Algorithm Fast_Fourier_Transform $(n, a_0, a_1, ..., a_{n-1}, \omega, \textbf{var } V)$;
Input: n (an integer), $a_0, a_1, ..., a_{n-1}$ (a sequence of *elements* whose type depends on the application), and ω (a primitive nth root of unity).
Output: V (an array in the range $[0..n-1]$ of output elements).
{ we assume that n is a power of 2 }

begin
    if $n = 1$ **then**
        $V[0] := a_0$;
    else
        Fast_Fourier_Transform$(n/2, a_0, a_2, ..., a_{n-2}, \omega^2, U)$;
        Fast_Fourier_Transform$(n/2, a_1, a_3, ..., a_{n-1}, \omega^2, W)$;
        for $j := 0$ **to** $n/2 - 1$ **do** { *follow (9.8) for $x = \omega^j$* }
            $V[j] := U[j] + \omega^j W[j]$;
            $V[j+n/2] := U[j] - \omega^j W[j]$
    end

Figure 9.7 Algorithm *Fast_Fourier_Transform*.

☐ Example 9.2

We show how to compute the Fourier transform for the polynomial $(0, 1, 2, 3, 4, 5, 6, 7)$. To avoid confusion, we denote the subproblems by $P_{j_0, j_1, ..., j_k}(x_0, x_1, ..., x_k)$, where $j_0, j_1, ..., j_k$ denote the coefficients of the polynomials, and $x_0, x_1, ..., x_k$ denote the values for which we need to evaluate the polynomials. So, in particular, this example involves computing $P_{0,1,2,3,4,5,6,7}(1, \omega, \omega^2, ..., \omega^7)$. (This notation is quite awkward, but it contains all the information we need.) The main recurrence we use is (9.8).

The first step reduces $P_{0,1,2,3,4,5,6,7}(1, \omega, \omega^2, ..., \omega^7)$ to $P_{0,2,4,6}(1, \omega^2, \omega^4, \omega^6)$ and $P_{1,3,5,7}(1, \omega^2, \omega^4, \omega^6)$. We continue recursively and reduce $P_{0,2,4,6}(1, \omega^2, \omega^4, \omega^6)$ to $P_{0,4}(1, \omega^4)$ and $P_{2,6}(1, \omega^4)$. $P_{0,4}(1, \omega^4)$ is then reduced to $P_0(1)$, which is clearly 0, and $P_4(1)$, which is clearly 4. We can now combine the results to get

$$P_{0,4}(1) = P_0(1) + 1 \cdot P_4(1) = 0 + 1 \cdot 4 = 4,$$

and

$$P_{0,4}(\omega^4) = P_0(\omega^4) + \omega^4 P_4(\omega^4) = 0 + \omega^4 \cdot 4.$$

Since $\omega^4 = -1$, we get $P_{0,4}(\omega^4) = -4$, and, overall, $P_{0,4}(1, \omega^4) = (4, -4)$. In the same manner, we get $P_{2,6}(1, \omega^4) = (8, -4)$.

We now combine the two vectors above to compute $P_{0,2,4,6}(1, \omega^2, \omega^4, \omega^6)$:

$$P_{0,2,4,6}(1) = P_{0,4}(1) + 1 \cdot P_{2,6}(1) = 4 + 8 = 12.$$

$$P_{0,2,4,6}(\omega^2) = P_{0,4}(\omega^4) + \omega^2 \cdot P_{2,6}(\omega^4) = -4 + \omega^2(-4).$$

$$P_{0,2,4,6}(\omega^4) = P_{0,4}(\omega^8) + \omega^4 \cdot P_{2,6}(\omega^8) = P_{0,4}(1) - 1 \cdot P_{2,6}(1) = 4 - 8 = -4.$$

$$P_{0,2,4,6}(\omega^6) = P_{0,4}(\omega^{12}) + \omega^6 \cdot P_{2,6}(\omega^{12}) = P_{0,4}(\omega^4) - \omega^2 \cdot P_{2,6}(\omega^4) = -4 - \omega^2(-4).$$

So, overall

$$P_{0,2,4,6}(1, \omega^2, \omega^4, \omega^6) = (\ 12, -4(1+\omega^2), -4, -4(1-\omega^2)\ ).$$

In the same way, we find that

$$P_{1,3,5,7}(1, \omega^2, \omega^4, \omega^6) = (\ 16, -4(1+\omega^2), -4, -4(1-\omega^2)\ ).$$

To compute $P_{0,1,2,3,4,5,6,7}(1, \omega, \omega^2, ..., \omega^7)$, we need to compute 8 values. For example, $P_{0,1,2,3,4,5,6,7}(1) = 12 + 1 \cdot 16 = 28$, and, in the same manner, $P_{0,1,2,3,4,5,6,7}(\omega^4) = 12 - 1 \cdot 16 = -4$; $P_{0,1,2,3,4,5,6,7}(\omega) = (-4(1+\omega^2)) + \omega \cdot (-4(1+\omega^2))$, and, in the same manner, $P_{0,1,2,3,4,5,6,7}(\omega^5) = (-4(1+\omega^2)) - \omega \cdot (-4(1+\omega^2))$, and so on. We leave the rest to the reader.   ☐

The Inverse Fourier Transform

The algorithm for the fast Fourier transform solves only half of our problem. We can evaluate the two given polynomials $p(x)$ and $q(x)$ at the points $1, \omega, ..., \omega^{n-1}$ quickly, multiply the resulting values, and find the values of the product polynomial $p(x) \cdot q(x)$ at those points. But we still need to interpolate the coefficients of the product polynomial from the evaluation points. Fortunately, the interpolation problem turns out to be very similar to the evaluation problem, and an almost identical algorithm can solve it.

Consider again the matrix notation. When we are given the coefficients $(a_0, a_1, ..., a_{n-1})$ of the polynomial, and we want to compute the values of the polynomial at the n points $1, \omega, \omega^2, ..., \omega^{n-1}$, we compute the matrix by the following vector product:

$$
\begin{bmatrix}
1 & 1 & 1 & \cdot & \cdot & 1 \\
1 & \omega & \omega^2 & \cdot & \cdot & \omega^{n-1} \\
\cdot & \omega^2 & \omega^{2 \cdot 2} & \cdot & \cdot & \omega^{2 \cdot (n-1)} \\
\cdot & \cdot & \cdot & \cdot & \cdot & \cdot \\
\cdot & \cdot & \cdot & \cdot & \cdot & \cdot \\
1 & \omega^{n-1} & \omega^{(n-1) \cdot 2} & \cdot & \cdot & \omega^{(n-1) \cdot (n-1)}
\end{bmatrix}
\begin{bmatrix}
a_0 \\ a_1 \\ \cdot \\ \cdot \\ \cdot \\ a_{n-1}
\end{bmatrix}
=
\begin{bmatrix}
P(1) \\ P(\omega) \\ P(\omega^2) \\ \cdot \\ \cdot \\ P(\omega^{n-1})
\end{bmatrix}.
$$

On the other hand, when the values of the polynomial $(P(1), P(\omega), ..., P(\omega^{n-1})) = (v_0, v_1, ..., v_{n-1})$ are given, and we want to compute the coefficients, we need to solve the following system of equations for $a_0, a_1, ..., a_{n-1}$:

$$
\begin{bmatrix}
1 & 1 & 1 & \cdot & \cdot & 1 \\
1 & \omega & \omega^2 & \cdot & \cdot & \omega^{n-1} \\
\cdot & \omega^2 & \omega^{2 \cdot 2} & \cdot & \cdot & \omega^{2 \cdot (n-1)} \\
\cdot & \cdot & \cdot & \cdot & \cdot & \cdot \\
\cdot & \cdot & \cdot & \cdot & \cdot & \cdot \\
1 & \omega^{n-1} & \omega^{(n-1) \cdot 2} & \cdot & \cdot & \omega^{(n-1) \cdot (n-1)}
\end{bmatrix}
\begin{bmatrix}
a_0 \\ a_1 \\ \cdot \\ \cdot \\ \cdot \\ a_{n-1}
\end{bmatrix}
=
\begin{bmatrix}
v_0 \\ v_1 \\ v_2 \\ \cdot \\ \cdot \\ v_{n-1}
\end{bmatrix}.
\tag{9.10}
$$

Solving systems of equations is usually quite time consuming ($O(n^3)$ for the general case), but this is a special system of equations. Let's write this matrix equation as $V(\omega) \cdot \bar{a} = \bar{v}$, where $V(\omega)$ is the matrix in the left side, $\bar{a} = (a_0, a_1, ..., a_{n-1})$, and $\bar{v} = (v_0, v_1, ..., v_{n-1})$. The solution for $\bar{a}$ can be written as $\bar{a} = [V(\omega)]^{-1} \cdot \bar{v}$, provided that $V(\omega)$ has an inverse. It turns out that $V(\omega)$ always has an inverse; furthermore, its inverse has a very simple form (we omit the proof):

□ **Theorem 9.1**

$$
[V(\omega)]^{-1} = \frac{1}{n} V\left(\frac{1}{\omega}\right). \qquad \qquad \square
$$

Therefore, to solve the system of equations (9.10), we need to compute only one matrix by vector product. This task is greatly simplified by the following theorem.

□ **Theorem 9.2**

If ω is a primitive nth root of unity, then $1/\omega$ is also a primitive nth root of unity. □

Therefore, we can compute the product $V(1/\omega)\bar{v}$ by using the algorithm for the fast Fourier transform, substituting $1/\omega$ for ω. This transform is called the **inverse Fourier transform**.

Complexity   Overall, the product of two polynomials can be computed with $O(n \log n)$ operations. Notice that we need to be able to add and multiply complex numbers.

9.7 Summary

The algorithms presented in this chapter are a small sample of known algebraic and numerical algorithms. We have seen again that the straightforward algorithms are not necessarily the best. Strassen's algorithm is one of the most striking examples of a nonintuitive algorithm for a seemingly simple problem. We have seen several more examples of the use of induction, and, in particular, of the use of divide-and-conquer algorithms.

The four-Russians algorithm suggests an interesting technique, which is not based on induction. The main idea is to compute all possible combinations of certain terms, even if not all of them are needed. This technique is useful in cases where computing all (or many) combinations together costs much less than computing each one separately. Another technique, which is common particularly for problems involving matrices, is the use of reductions between problems. This method is described, with examples, in Chapter 10.

Bibliographic Notes and Further Reading

The best source for arithmetic and algebraic algorithms is Knuth [1981]. Other books include Aho, Hopcroft, and Ullman [1974], Borodin and Munro [1975], Winograd [1980], and Lipson [1981].

The algorithm for computing powers by repeated squaring is very old; it appeared in Hindu writings circa 200 B.C. (see Knuth [1981] page 441). The RSA public-key encryption scheme is due to Rivest, Shamir, and Adleman [1978]. The idea of public-key encryption schemes was introduced by Diffie and Hellman [1976]. Euclid's algorithm appeared first in Euclid's *Elements*, Book 7 (circa 300 B.C.), but it was probably known even before then (see Knuth [1981], page 318). The divide-and-conquer algorithm for multiplying two polynomials was developed by Karatsuba and Ofman [1962] (in the context of multiplying two large numbers).

Winograd's algorithm appeared in Winograd [1968] (see also Winograd [1970]). Strassen's algorithm appeared in Strassen [1969]. The constant c in the asymptotic running time $O(n^c)$ for matrix multiplication has been reduced several times since 1969 (first by Pan [1978]). The best-known algorithm at this time — in terms of asymptotic running times — is by Coppersmith and Winograd [1987], and its running time is $\mathcal{OO}(n^{2.376})$. Unfortunately, as the $\mathcal{OO}$ notation indicates, this algorithm is not practical. For more on the complexity of matrix multiplication and related topics see Pan [1984]. A discussion on the implementation of Strassen's algorithm can be found in Cohen and Roth [1976].

The four-Russians algorithm is due to Arlazarov, Dinic, Kronrod, and Faradzev [1970]. The improvement of the four-Russians algorithm by using addition tables has probably been observed by many people; it is mentioned, without details, in Rytter [1985], where a similar technique is used for context-free language recognition. The same idea was also used to improve sequence comparisons algorithms (Masek and Paterson [1983], Myers [1988]). The solution of Exercise 9.26 appears in Atkinson and Santoro [1988]. Fischer and Meyer [1971] showed a reduction between Boolean matrix multiplication and the transitive-closure problem.

The algorithm for the fast Fourier transform was introduced by Cooley and Tuckey [1965], although the origins of the method can be traced to Runge and König [1924]. For more information on the fast Fourier transform, see Brigham [1974] and Elliott and Rao [1982].

Drill Exercises

9.1　Discuss the relationship between the algorithm for computing n^k and the binary representation of k.

9.2　Algorithm *Power_by_Repeated_Squaring* (Fig. 9.2) for computing x^n does not necessarily lead to the minimal number of multiplications. Show an example of computing x^n ($n > 10$) with fewer number of multiplications.

9.3　Let x be a positive rational number that is represented by the pair (a, b) such that $x = a/b$. Design an algorithm to compute the smallest representation of x; that is, the representation (a, b) with the smallest possible values of a and b. For example, if $x = 24/84 = 6/21 = 2/7$, then $(2, 7)$ is the smallest representation of x.

9.4　Prove that the straightforward divide-and-conquer algorithm for polynomial multiplication that computes all four products of the smaller polynomials makes exactly the same operations as does the straightforward algorithm that follows (9.1). Assume that n is a power of 2.

9.5　Find the product $P(x) \cdot Q(x)$, by hand, using the divide-and-conquer polynomial multiplication algorithm presented in Section 9.4.

$P(x) = x + 2x^2 + 3x^3 + \cdots + 15x^{15}$.

$Q(x) = 16 + 15x + 14x^2 + \cdots + 2x^{14} + 1x^{15}$.

How many operations are required overall?

9.6　A divide-and-conquer technique can be used to multiply two binary numbers. Describe such an algorithm, and discuss the differences between it and the polynomial multiplication algorithm.

9.7 Use the algorithm discussed in Exercise 9.6 to multiply 10011011 by 10111010.

9.8 A divide-and-conquer technique can be used to multiply two numbers in any base b (not only $b = 2$). Use it to perform the decimal multiplication 4679×7114. Carry the recursion down all the way to 1-digit numbers.

9.9 Design an algorithm to multiply two complex numbers $(a + bi)(c + di)$ with only three multiplications. (i is the square root of -1.)

9.10 Derive the explicit expressions for Strassen's 2×2 matrix multiplication scheme described in Section 9.5.2.

9.11 Suppose that you find an algorithm to multiply 4×4 matrices with k multiplications. What would be the complexity of a general matrix multiplication algorithm based on the this algorithm? What is the maximal value of k that will lead to an asymptotic improvement over Strassen's algorithm?

Creative Exercises

9.12 Consider the two algorithms for computing n^k given in Section 9.2 (simple iteration, and repeated squaring). Let n be an integer with d digits. Assume that integer multiplications are performed by the regular algorithm, which requires $d_1 \cdot d_2$ *steps* to multiply two integers with d_1 and d_2 digits. What is the number of steps required to compute n^k by the two algorithms? (You can assume that k is a power of 2, and that a product of two integers with d_1 and d_2 digits is another integer with $d_1 + d_2$ digits.)

9.13 Design an algorithm to find the GCD of k integers.

9.14 The **least common multiple** (LCM) of m and n is the smallest integer that is a multiple of both n and m. Design an algorithm to find the LCM of two given integers.

9.15 Design an algorithm to find the LCM of k given integers. (The LCM of k integers is the smallest integer that is a multiple of all of them.)

9.16 The **Fibonacci numbers** are defined by the following recurrence relation:

$F(1) = 1, \quad F(2) = 1, \quad F(n) = F(n-1) + F(n-2) \ (n > 2)$.

a. Prove that every integer $n > 2$ can be written as a sum of at most $\log_2 n$ Fibonacci numbers.

b. Design an algorithm to find such a representation for a given number n.

9.17 Let $P(x)$ and $Q(x)$ be two polynomials. We say that a polynomial $D(x)$ **divides** $P(x)$ if there exists another polynomial $S(x)$ such that $P(x) = D(x) \cdot S(x)$. Similarly, we say that $Q(x) = R(x) \bmod P(x)$ if $R(x)$ has a smaller degree than $P(x)$, and there exists a polynomial $D(x)$ such that $Q(x) = D(x) \cdot P(x) + R(x)$. The GCD of two polynomials $P(x)$ and $Q(x)$ is a polynomial $R(x)$ such that $R(x)$ is the highest-degree polynomial that divides both $P(x)$ and $Q(x)$.

a. Show that the GCD of two polynomials is uniquely defined.

b. Extend Euclid's algorithm to find the GCD of two given polynomials.

9.18 Modify the polynomial multiplication algorithm described in Section 9.4 by dividing each polynomial into three equal parts (instead of two), and minimizing the number of multiplications involving smaller parts. You can assume that the size of the problem is a power of 3. What is the complexity of the algorithm?

9.19 Modify the polynomial multiplication algorithm described in Section 9.4 by dividing each polynomial into four equal parts, and minimizing the number of multiplications involving smaller parts. You can assume that the size of the problem is a power of 4. What is the complexity of the algorithm?

9.20 **Hamilton's quaternions** are vectors of the form $a + bi + cj + dk$, where a, b, c, and d are real numbers, and i, j, and k are special symbols. We add and subtract quaternions componentwise, and multiply them by using the following rules:

$$i^2 = j^2 = k^2 = -1$$
$$ij = -ji = k$$
$$jk = -kj = i$$
$$ki = -ik = j$$

(the symbols i, j, and k commute with real numbers and with themselves). How many multiplications of real numbers are required by the ordinary procedure for quaternion multiplication? Give an algorithm that reduces the number of multiplications to 12.

9.21 Show how to compute the square of a 2×2 matrix with only five multiplications.

9.22 A **permutation matrix** is an $n \times n$ matrix such that each row and each column has exactly one nonzero entry that is equal to 1. A permutation matrix can be represented by an array P such that $P[i] = j$ if the ith row contains a 1 in the jth column.

a. Prove that the product of two permutation matrices is another permutation matrix.

b. Design a linear-time algorithm to multiply two permutation matrices given by the array representation. The outcome should also be given in an array representation.

9.23 Consider the following suggestion to modify Strassen's algorithm. We can use Winograd's algorithm to compute the product of two $k \times k$ matrices with approximately $k^3/2$ multiplications. We can then use this product as the basis for the divide-and-conquer strategy instead of the one using 2×2 matrices. If k is large enough we get a better asymptotic time than Strassen's algorithm. What is wrong with this suggestion?

9.24 Design an algorithm to compute all possible Boolean inner products of two Boolean vectors of size k (see Section 9.5.3). The algorithm should create a table of size 2^{2k}. The product of the two vectors a and b should be stored at entry i, where i is an integer respresented by $2k$ bits such that the k most significant bits of i are those of a and the k least significant bits are those of b. The running time of the algorithm should be $O(2^{2k})$.

9.25 Complete the program for Boolean matrix multiplication (Fig. 9.6). Show how to build the tables explicitly, and how to handle the case where n/k is not an integer without a significant loss of efficiency.

9.26 Design an algorithm for Boolean matrix multiplication that divides the matrices into submatrices of size $k \times k$, and uses the idea of precomputing all possible products between such submatrices. The running time of the algorithm should be $O(n^3/(\log n)^{1.5})$, and it should require extra space of $O(n \log n)$. You can assume that you can perform basic operations on numbers with up to $\log_2 n$ bits in one step.

9.27   Let A and B be two $n \times n$ *random* Boolean matrices; each entry in each matrix is randomly chosen (independently) to be either 0 or 1 with probability $\frac{1}{2}$. Design an algorithm to find the product of A and B, such that the *expected* number of operations will be $O(n^2)$.

9.28   Let A and B be two $2n \times 2n$ Boolean matrices that represent **open Gray codes** (see Section 2.9) in the following way. The rows of each matrix correspond to the strings in the Gray code, such that two consecutive rows differ by exactly one bit (the first row and the last row may differ by more than one bit). Design an $O(n^2)$ algorithm to find the product of the two matrices.

*9.29   Let $M_1, M_2, ..., M_n$ be n matrices of real numbers. The dimensions of M_i are $a_i \times a_{i+1}$, so the product of $M_i \cdot M_{i+1}$ is defined for each $1 \leq i < n$. We want to compute the product $M_1 \times M_2 \times \cdots \times M_n$. Let's assume that it takes $a_i \, a_{i+1} \, a_{i+2}$ operations to multiply an $a_i \times a_{i+1}$ matrix by an $a_{i+1} \times a_{i+2}$ matrix. The problem is to find the right order in which to carry out the multiplications. For example, let $n = 3$, and let the matrices be of dimensions 10×2, 2×5, and 5×3. Finding the product of the first two matrices takes $10 \cdot 2 \cdot 5$ operations resulting in a matrix of dimensions 10×5. Finding the product of this matrix with the third one takes $10 \cdot 5 \cdot 3$ operations — overall, 250 operations. On the other hand, if we first find the product of the *last* two matrices and multiply the first matrix with that product, we end up with only 90 operations. Design an algorithm to find the optimal order of carrying out the matrix product above.

CHAPTER 10

REDUCTIONS

Knowledge is of two kinds.
We know a subject ourselves,
or we know where we can find
information upon it.

Samuel Johnson, 1775

10.1 Introduction

We start this chapter with an old joke. A mathematician and her husband are asked the following question: "Suppose that you are in the basement and you want to boil water, what do you do?" The mathematician says that she will go up to the kitchen and boil water there; her husband answers similarly. Now they are both asked the following question: "Suppose that you are in the kitchen and you want to boil water, what do you do now?" The husband says "it's easier — I'll just fill the kettle and boil the water." The mathematician answers "it's even easier than that — I'll go down to the basement and I already know how to solve that problem."

In this chapter, we will concentrate on the idea of reduction. We will show that besides being funny sometimes, reductions can be extremely useful. Here is another example of a reduction, this time a real one. When you send a package by Federal Express from uptown New York City to downtown New York City, the package will be routed through Memphis. Federal Express routes all packages through Memphis, so when they are faced with the special situation of delivering packages across town they "already know how to solve the problem." In this case, the solution makes sense. It may be much more difficult to identify a special situation and to build a mechanism to handle that situation more efficiently. It may be easier, and overall cheaper, to handle everything equally. This is also often true in algorithm design. When we encounter a problem that can be posed as a special case of another problem, whose solution is already known, then the known solution can be used. Such a solution may sometimes be too general or too expensive. But in many cases, using a general solution is the the easiest, the fastest, and the most elegant way to get a solution. We use this principle every day. For some computing problems — for example, a database query — it is usually not necessary to write a program that solves only this problem; it is sufficient to use general-purpose software that handles more general problems. The general-purpose solution may not be the most efficient solution, but it is much easier to use.

Suppose that we are given a problem P that seems complicated, but that also seems similar to a known problem Q. We can try to solve P from scratch, or we can try to borrow some of the methods used to solve Q and apply them to P. There is, however, a third way. We can try to find a **reduction** (or transformation) between the two problems. Loosely speaking, a reduction is a solution of one problem using a ''black box'' that solves the other problem. Reductions can achieve one of two goals depending on the direction in which they are done (i.e., which black box is used to solve which problem). A solution of P that uses a black box for Q can be translated into an algorithm for P if we know an algorithm for Q. On the other hand, if P is known to be a hard problem, or, in particular, if we know a lower bound for P, then the same lower bound may be applied to Q. In the former case, the reduction is used to obtain information about P, whereas, in the latter case, it is used to obtain information about Q.

For example, in Section 10.4.2, we discuss the problems of matrix multiplication and matrix squaring (i.e., multiplying the matrix with itself). Clearly, we can square a matrix with a matrix multiplication algorithm; therefore, the problem of matrix squaring can be reduced to the problem of matrix multiplication. We show in Section 10.4.2 that it is possible to multiply two matrices with the use of a matrix squaring algorithm; therefore, matrix multiplication is reduced to matrix squaring. The purpose of the latter reduction is to show that computing the square of a matrix cannot be done faster (by more than a constant) than computing the product of two arbitrary matrices (under some conditions that are discussed in Section 10.4.2)

We will see several examples of the use of reductions in this chapter. Finding a reduction between two problems is useful even if it does not lead directly to new upper or lower bounds on the complexity of the problem. The reduction helps us to understand both problems. The reduction may be used to find new techniques for attacking the problem or variations of it. For example, the reduction may be used to design a parallel algorithm for the problem.

An effective way to use reductions is to define a general problem to which many problems can be reduced. Finding such a general problem is not easy. This problem should be general enough to cover a wide variety of problems, but it must also be simple enough to have an efficient solution. We discuss one such problem, called linear programming, in Section 10.3.

We have already seen several examples of reductions in this book — for example, the reduction of the transitive-closure problem to the all-pairs shortest-paths problem (Section 7.8). Reductions are important enough, however, to deserve a special chapter. Reductions are also the cornerstone of the next chapter.

10.2 Examples of Reductions

In this section, we present four examples of using reductions to obtain efficient algorithms.

10.2.1 A Simple String-Matching Problem

We start with a simple variation of the string-matching problem.

The Problem   Let $A = a_0 a_1 \cdots a_{n-1}$ and $B = b_0 b_1 \cdots b_{n-1}$ be two strings of size n. Determine whether B is a cyclic shift of A.

The problem is to determine whether there exists an index k, $0 \le k \le n-1$, such that $a_i = b_{(k+i) \bmod n}$ for all i, $0 \le i \le n-1$. We call this problem CSM (for cyclic string matching), and we call the original string-matching problem (Section 6.7) SM. We can solve CSM, for example, by modifying the Knuth-Morris-Pratt algorithm that was described in Section 6.7. But there is a better way to arrive at a solution. The idea is to pose CSM as a *regular instance* of SM. In other words, we look for a certain *text T* and a certain *pattern P* such that finding P in T is equivalent to finding whether B is a cyclic shift of A. If we can do this, then a solution to SM involving T and P can be applied to solve CSM involving A and B. If one thinks about the problem in these terms it is easy to see the solution: We define the text T as AA (namely, A concatenated to itself). Clearly, B is a cyclic shift of A if and only if B is a substring of AA. Since we already know how to solve SM in linear time, we have a linear-time algorithm for CSM.

10.2.2 Systems of Distinct Representatives

Let $S_1, S_2, ..., S_k$ be a collection of sets. A **system of distinct representatives** (SDR) is a set $R = \{r_1, r_2, ..., r_k\}$ such that $r_i \in S_i$, for all i, $1 \le i \le k$, (notice that, since we require R to be a set, the r_is must be distinct). In other words, R includes exactly one representative from each set. It is not always possible to find an SDR of a given collection of sets. For example, an SDR for the collection of sets $S_1 = \{1,2\}$, $S_2 = \{2,3,4\}$, $S_3 = \{1,3\}$, and $S_4 = \{1,2,3\}$ is $\{1,4,3,2\}$, but there is no SDR for the collection of sets $S_1 = \{1,2\}$, $S_2 = \{2,3,4\}$, $S_3 = \{1,3\}$, $S_4 = \{1,2,3\}$, and $S_5 = \{2,3\}$.

The Problem   Given a finite collection of finite sets, find an SDR for the collection (any SDR will do), or determine that none exists.

There is a very elegant theorem, due to P. Hall, that gives necessary and sufficient conditions for the existence of SDRs. Let $card(S)$ be the number of elements of S.

□ Hall's Theorem

Let $S_1, S_2, ..., S_k$ be a collection of sets. This collection has an SDR if and only if the following condition is satisfied:

$$\text{card} \left[S_{i_1} \cup S_{i_2} \cup \cdots \cup S_{i_m} \right] \geq m$$

for every subset $\{i_1, i_2, ..., i_m\}$ of $\{1, 2, 3, ..., k\}$. In other words, every subcollection of m sets must contain altogether at least m distinct elements, for every $1 \leq m \leq k$. □

It is clear that the condition is necessary since, if there are m sets with altogether less than m elements, then they cannot have m distinct representatives. That the condition is also sufficient is harder to prove, and we leave it as an exercise.

Hall's theorem provides simple conditions but, unfortunately, they cannot be directly checked efficiently. We will have to check all possible subcollections, and there are 2^k of them. We need another approach. The idea is to pose this problem as a bipartite matching problem. Let $G = (V, U, E)$ be a bipartite graph such that there is a vertex v_i in V for each set S_i, and there is a vertex u_j in U for each possible element (i.e., for each element in the union of the sets). Each element is connected to all the sets containing it; that is, $(v_i, u_j) \in E$ if and only if $u_j \in S_i$. It is now easy to see that an SDR is simply a matching in G of size k. We can apply the algorithm discussed in Section 7.10 to solve this problem. Furthermore, the proof of Hall's theorem can be obtained from the properties of bipartite matching and network flows.

10.2.3 A Reduction Involving Sequence Comparisons

Consider the sequence-comparison problem discussed in Section 6.8: $A = a_1 a_2 \cdots a_n$ and $B = b_1 b_2 \cdots b_m$ are two strings of characters, and we want to edit A, character by character, until it becomes equal to B. We allow three types of edit steps, each involving one character — *insert*, *delete*, and *replace*. The cost of each of these steps is given, and our goal is to minimize the cost of the edit. The solution given in Section 6.8 was to construct a table of size n by m, where each entry corresponds to a *partial* edit. The *ij*th entry contains the cost of editing the first i characters of A into the first j characters of B. The goal is thus to compute the "bottom-right" entry (nm) of the table. We showed that each entry can be computed from only three other "previous" entries corresponding to the three different edit steps.

Another way to look at this problem is by considering the table as a directed graph. Each entry in the table corresponds to a vertex in the graph. A vertex thus corresponds to a partial edit. There is an edge (v, w) if the partial edit corresponding to w has one more edit step than the partial edit corresponding to v. An example of such a graph is given in Fig. 10.1, where $A = caa$ and $B = aba$. The horizontal edges correspond to insertions, the vertical edges to deletions, and the diagonal edges to replacements. For example, the shaded path in Fig. 10.1 corresponds to a deletion of c, a match of a, an insertion of b, and another match of a. In the basic problem, the cost of each edge is 1 except for diagonal edges that correspond to equal characters (i.e., no replacement is necessary)

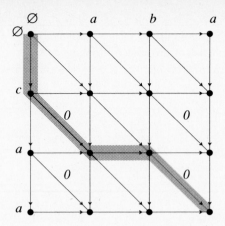

Figure 10.1 The graph corresponding to the sequences $A = caa$ and $B = aba$.

whose cost is 0. The problem now becomes a regular single-source shortest-paths problem. Each edge is associated with a cost (which is the cost of the corresponding edit step), and we are looking for the shortest path from vertex $[0, 0]$ to vertex $[n, m]$. We have reduced the string-edit problem to the single-source sortest-paths problem.

Finding shortest paths in general is not easier than solving this problem directly. Nevertheless, this reduction is useful. Consider, for example, the following variations of the sequence-comparison problem. The cost of editing is not necessarily per character. The cost of inserting a block of characters in the middle of another string may not be the same as that of inserting the same number of characters, one by one, in different places. The same may be true for deletions. In other words, instead of assigning a cost per insertion, deletion, and replacement, we may want to assign a cost per blocks of insertions, or deletions, regardless of their sizes. Alternately, we may want to assign a cost of say, $I + ck$, for inserting a block of k characters, where I is the "start-up" cost, and c is a cost per subsequent character. There are many other useful metrics. We can model them more easily by using the shortest-path formulation than by modifying the original problem. We can add edges anywhere we want and assign any cost to them, without changing the problem.

10.2.4 Finding a Triangle in Undirected Graphs

There is a strong correlation between graphs and matrices. A graph $G = (V, E)$ with n vertices can be represented by its **adjacency matrix** A, which is an $n \times n$ matrix in which the ijth entry is 1 if and only if $(v_i, v_j) \in E$. If G is undirected, then A is **symmetric**. If G is a weighted graph, then we define A as an $n \times n$ matrix such that the ijth entry is equal to the **weight** of edge (v_i, v_j) or to 0 if this edge is not in the graph. There are other ways to associate a matrix with a graph. For example, the **incidence matrix** of a graph $G = (V, E)$ with n vertices and m edges is an $n \times m$ matrix in which the ijth entry is 1 if and only if the ith vertex is incident to the jth edge.

The correlation goes beyond mere representation. Many properties of graphs can be better understood by looking at the corresponding matrices. Similarly, many properties of matrices can be discovered by looking at the corresponding graphs. Not surprisingly, many algorithmic problems can be resolved by making use of this analogy. Here is one example.

The Problem   Let $G = (V, E)$ be a connected undirected graph with n vertices and m edges. Design an algorithm to determine whether G contains three vertices all connected to one another.

The straightforward solution is to check all subsets of three vertices. There are $\binom{n}{3} = n(n-1)(n-2)/6$ subsets of three vertices, and each subset can be checked in constant time, so the running time of the resulting algorithm is $O(n^3)$. It is possible to design an algorithm whose running time is $O(mn)$ (Exercise 7.118), which is better if the graph is sparse. Can we do better than that? We proceed to show an algorithm, which is asymptotically faster, but is far from being intuitive. The main purpose of this discussion is to illustrate the relationships between graph algorithms and matrix algorithms.

Let A be the adjacency matrix of G. Since G is undirected, A is symmetric. Denote by A^2 the square of the matrix A, namely, $A^2 = A \times A$ (the product is the usual matrix product). We want to study the relationships between the entries of A^2 and the graph G. By definition of matrix multiplication,

$$A^2[i, j] = \sum_{k=1}^{n} A[i, k] \cdot A[k, j].$$

Therefore, $A^2[i, j] > 0$ if and only if there exists an index k such that both $A[i, k]$ and $A[k, j]$ are 1. In terms of the graph, $A^2[i, j] > 0$ if there exists a vertex k, such that $k \neq i$, and $k \neq j$, and both i and j are connected to k. (We assume that the graph does not contain self loops; hence, $A[i, i] = 0$ for all i.) However, that means that there exists a triangle involving i and j if and only if i is connected to j and $A^2[i, j] > 0$. Thus, there exists a triangle in G if and only if there are i and j such that $A[i, j] = 1$, and $A^2[i, j] > 0$.

The discussion above implies an algorithm. We first compute A^2 and then check the condition above for each pair i and j. It costs $O(n^2)$ to check all pairs, so the running time of the algorithm is dominated by the running time of matrix multiplication. We have thus reduced the problem of finding a triangle in a graph to that of Boolean matrix multiplication (more precisely to matrix squaring, but we will see in Section 10.4.2 that these two problems are equivalent). We can now use Strassen's algorithm for matrix multiplication and obtain an algorithm for finding a triangle whose running time is $O(n^{2.81})$. We can also use the algorithm in Section 9.5.3 for Boolean matrix multiplication, and obtain a practical algorithm for finding a triangle with a running time of $O(n^3/(\log n)^2)$. We have reduced this graph problem to Boolean matrix multiplication, so, in general, the complexity of this graph problem is $O(M)$, where M is the complexity of Boolean matrix multiplication.

10.3 Reductions Involving Linear Programming

The previous section included examples of reductions from different areas of algorithm design. We tried to map one problem to another so that we could use a known algorithm. This section also presents reductions, but with a slightly different approach. Instead of looking for a candidate for a reduction whenever a new problem arises, we explore some ''super-problems,'' to which many problems can be reduced. One such super-problem, perhaps the most important one, is **linear programming**. There are efficient algorithms for solving linear programming, although they are not simple. A thorough discussion of linear programming is beyond the scope of this book. In this section, we only define some variations of the problem, and show several examples of reductions to it.

10.3.1 Introduction and Definitions

There are many problems that involve maximizing or minimizing a certain function subject to certain criteria. For example, the network-flow problem involves maximizing the flow function subject to the capacity constraints and to the conservation constraints. Linear programming is a general formulation of such problems in cases where the function is a linear function and the constraints can also be written using linear functions in the following way. Let $\bar{x} = (x_1, x_2, ..., x_n)$ be a vector of *variables*. An **objective function** is defined as a linear function involving the variables of $\bar{x}$:

$$c(\bar{x}) = \sum_{i=1}^{n} c_i x_i, \text{ where the } c_i\text{s are constants.} \tag{10.1}$$

The goal of linear programming is to find the values of $\bar{x}$ that satisfy some constraints (listed below) and *maximize* the value of the objective function. We shall see later that, if necessary, it is easy to replace the maximization objective with a similar minimization objective. First, we define a general form of linear programming with three types of constraints, not all of which are needed for all problems. Later, we will show that the general problem can itself be reduced to a problem with only two types of constraints.

Let $\bar{a}_1, \bar{a}_2, ..., \bar{a}_k$ be vectors of real numbers, each of length n, and let $b_1, b_2, ..., b_k$ be real numbers. The **inequality constraints** are as follows:

$$\bar{a}_1 \cdot \bar{x} \leq b_1$$

$$\bar{a}_2 \cdot \bar{x} \leq b_2$$

$$\cdot \quad \cdot \quad \cdot \tag{10.2}$$

$$\cdot \quad \cdot \quad \cdot$$

$$\bar{a}_k \cdot \bar{x} \leq b_k.$$

(Except for $\bar{x}$, all other symbols are constants.)

The **equality constraints** are similar:

$$\overline{e}_1 \cdot \overline{x} = d_1$$

$$\overline{e}_2 \cdot \overline{x} = d_2$$

$$\cdot \quad \cdot \quad \cdot \qquad\qquad (10.3)$$

$$\cdot \quad \cdot \quad \cdot$$

$$\overline{e}_m \cdot \overline{x} = d_m,$$

where $\overline{e}_1, \overline{e}_2, ..., \overline{e}_m$ are also vectors of size n, and $d_1, d_2, ..., d_m$ are real numbers.

We also usually add the following **nonnegative constraints** separately (even though they can be represented as a special case of the previous constraints).

$$x_j \geq 0, \text{ for all } j \in P, \qquad\qquad (10.4)$$

where P is a given subset of $\{1, 2, ..., n\}$.

The linear programming problem can be formulated as follows: maximize the function $c(\overline{x})$ (10.1) subject to the inequality constraints (10.2), the equality constraints (10.3), and the nonnegative constraints (10.4). Of course, not all constraints must be used in all instances of the problem.

We first show that we can get rid of either the equality or the inequality constraints, but not both, without a loss of generality. Let

$$\overline{e}_i \cdot x = d_i \qquad\qquad (10.5)$$

be an arbitrary equality constraint. We can substitute for (10.5) the following two inequality constraints:

$$\overline{e}_i \cdot x \leq d_i, \qquad\qquad (10.6)$$

and

$$-\overline{e}_i \cdot x \leq -d_i. \qquad\qquad (10.7)$$

Alternately, we can replace the inequality constraints with equality constraints. Given a general inequality constraint

$$\overline{a}_i \cdot \overline{x} \leq b_i, \qquad\qquad (10.8)$$

we can introduce a new variable, y_i, and replace (10.8) with the following:

$$\overline{a}_i \cdot \overline{x} + y_i = b_i, \text{ and } y_i \geq 0. \qquad\qquad (10.9)$$

Such a variable is called a **slack variable**. A linear program with only equality constraints is said to be in **standard form**.

In both of these cases, replacing one set of constraints with another set of constraints may cause the number of constraints to increase. Therefore, it is not always a good idea to perform these transformations.

We will not describe any algorithm for solving linear programming. We only note here that the existing algorithms for linear programming are quite fast in practice, and thus a reduction to linear programming is not just an exercise but a good way to solve the problem.

10.3.2 Examples of Reductions to Linear Programming

Problems in real life are seldom given directly in linear programming formulation. One has to introduce the right definitions to make the problem fit this formulation. Here is one example.

The Network-Flow Problem

(This problem is discussed in detail in Section 7.11.) Let the variables $x_1, x_2, ..., x_n$ represent the values of the flow for all the edges (n is the number of edges here). The objective function is the value of the total flow in the network

$$c(\overline{x}) = \sum_{i \in S} x_i,$$

where S is the set of edges leaving the source. The inequality constraints correspond to the capacity constraints:

$$x_i \leq c_i \quad \text{for all } i, \ 1 \leq i \leq n,$$

where c_i is the capacity of edge i. The equality constraints correspond to the conservation constraints:

$$\sum_{x_i \text{ leaves } v} x_i \ - \sum_{x_j \text{ enters } v} x_j \ = 0 \quad \text{for all } v \in V - \{s, t\}.$$

Finally, the nonnegative constraints apply to all variables (i.e., the set P, as defined in (10.4), is the whole set $\{1, 2, ..., n\}$). We leave it to the reader to verify that the values of x that maximize the objective function under these constraints correspond indeed to a maximum flow.

A Static Routing Problem

Let $G = (V, E)$ be an undirected graph representing a communication network. Suppose that each node v_i in the network has a limited buffer space, and can receive only B_i messages in one unit of time (we assume, for simplicity, that all messages have the same size). Suppose further that there is no limit on the number of messages that can be transmitted through any link, and that each node has an infinite supply of messages. The problem is to decide how many messages each edge should carry in one unit of time in order to maximize the total number of messages on the network. (This is a static routing problem, since we assume that all nodes always want to transmit; usually, transmission needs are dynamically changing.) In a graph-theoretic formulation, the problem is to assign weights to the edges such that the sum of the weights of all edges incident to node v_i is $\leq B_i$, and the total sum of weights is maximized.

This graph-theoretic problem can be easily formulated as a linear programming problem. We can associate a variable x_i with each edge $e_i = (v, w)$, indicating the number of messages passing through e_i. The objective function is $c(\overline{x}) = \sum_i x_i$. The constraints are as follows:

$$\sum_{e_i \text{ is incident to } v_i} x_i \le B_i, \quad \text{for all } v \in V,$$

and

$$x_i \ge 0, \quad \text{for all } i.$$

The Philanthropist Problem

Suppose that there are n organizations that want to contributed money to k computer-science departments. Each organization i has a limit of s_i on its total contribution for the year, as well as a limit a_{ij} on the amount it is willing to contribute to department j (e.g., a_{ij} may be 0 for some departments). In general s_i is smaller than $\sum_{j=1}^{k} a_{ij}$; therefore, each organization has to make some choices. Furthermore, suppose that each department j has a limit of t_j on the total amount of money it can receive (this constraint may be unrealistic, but it is interesting nevertheless). The goal is to design an algorithm that maximizes the total contributions (with no regard to fairness).

This problem is a generalization of the matching problem introduced in Section 7.10. It can be solved by matching techniques, but it also has a simple linear programming formulation. There are nk variables x_{ij}, $1 \le i \le n$, $1 \le j \le k$, representing the amount of money organization i is willing to contribute to department j. The objective function is

$$c(\overline{x}) = \sum_{ij} x_{ij}.$$

The constraints are the following:

$$x_{ij} \le a_{ij} \quad \text{for all } i, j,$$

$$\sum_{j=1}^{k} x_{ij} \le s_i \quad \text{for all } i,$$

and

$$\sum_{i=1}^{n} x_{ij} \le t_j \quad \text{for all } j.$$

In addition, of course, all variables must be nonnegative.

The Assignment Problem

Let's change the philanthropist problem slightly by insisting that each organization donate money to only one department and that each department accepts money from only one organization. In other words, we make it a standard matching problem, but with weights. Each possible match has a dollar amount attached to it, and we want to find not only a perfect matching, but also one that maximizes the total donations. This problem is a bipartite weighted matching problem, or, as it is usually called, an **assignment problem**.

The variables for this problem must be different from those of the previous problem. We somehow have to capture the notion of a matching. We must insist that exactly one edge is connected to each node. We do so by assigning a variable x_{ij} for each edge (i, j) with a value of 1 when the edge is selected, and of 0 otherwise. The objective function becomes

$$c(\overline{x}) = \sum_{ij} a_{ij} x_{ij}. \tag{10.10}$$

The constraints are the following:

$$\sum_{j=1}^{k} x_{ij} = 1 \ \text{ for all } i,$$

and

$$\sum_{i=1}^{n} x_{ij} = 1 \ \text{ for all } j.$$

These constraints guarantee that no more than one edge is selected for each node. In addition, all variables must be nonnegative.

This formulation has one major deficiency. The variables represent a yes or no choice, but their optimal values may be real numbers! We have to add constraints that limit the values of the variables to either 0 or 1. This is generally very hard to do. Linear programs whose variables must be integers are called **integer linear programs**. Solving them involves **integer programming**. Many of the problems discussed in the previous chapters can be naturally formulated as integer linear programming problems. However, although linear programs can be efficiently solved, integer linear programs are usually (but not always) very difficult. We discuss this issue in the next chapter. (The assignment problem, by the way, can be solved efficiently by linear programming; see, for example, Papadimitriou and Steiglitz [1982].)

10.4 Reductions for Lower Bounds

If we can show that an algorithm for problem A can be modified — without adding too much to the running time — to solve problem B, then a lower bound for problem B applies to problem A as well. We present three examples of the use of reductions for lower bound proofs. Another example is presented in the next section, which deals with common errors in the use of reductions.

10.4.1 A Lower Bound for Finding Simple Polygons

Consider the problem of connecting a set of points in the plane by a simple closed polygon (see Section 8.3). We have seen how to solve this problem using sorting. It is also true that, under certain assumptions, this problem cannot be solved more quickly than sorting. Therefore, the algorithm we presented for the simple closed polygon problem cannot be improved without improving sorting. (When we say "improvement," we mean an improvement by more than a constant factor.)

□ Theorem 10.1

It is possible to sort in time $O(T+n)$, given a (black-box) algorithm for the simple polygon problem that runs in time $O(T)$.

Proof: Consider n points on a circle (see Fig. 10.2). The only way to connect these points into a simple polygon is to connect each point to its neighbor on the circle. Otherwise, if two points that are not neighbors are connected, the connecting line separates the rest of the points into two groups that cannot be connected without intersecting this line. Consider now an input $x_1, x_2, ..., x_n$ to the sorting problem. If we had a black box for the simple polygon problem, we could use it to sort in the following way: The input $x_1, x_2, ..., x_n$ is first converted to *yseqn*, such that the y_is are angles in the range -180 to 180 degrees, with the same relative order as the x_is. The angles are then converted to points all lying on the unit circle. The point corresponding to x_i is the point on the circle with angle y_i to some fixed line crossing the circle. These conversions can be done in linear time. We can now use the black box for constructing a simple polygon from a set of points in time $O(T)$. As we mentioned, this simple polygon must connect each point to its neighbor on the circle. But that means that we can scan the points in order and find the sorted order of the original sequence in time $O(T+n)$.   □

To obtain a lower bound for the simple polygon problem, we have to be careful about the model of computation that we assume. The $\Omega(n \log n)$ lower bound for sorting that was proved in Section 6.4.6 assumed the decision-tree model. To use this lower bound for the simple-polygon problem, we must use the same model. That is, we first must assume that the black box that solves the simple polygon problem uses $O(T)$ comparisons in a way that is consistent with the decision-tree model. The theorem must include this assumption. We then have to show that the reduction is also consistent with the decision-tree model. In this case, the reduction is valid since the proof of the lower bound for sorting did not make any restrictions on the type of queries allowed in the decision tree. Thus, a comparison involving the x or y coordinates of the point

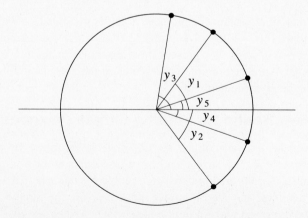

Figure 10.2 The conversion from numbers to points.

corresponding to the angle y_i is still counted as one comparison in the decision tree. A decision tree that solves the simple-polygon problem can be transformed into a decision tree that solves sorting, without significant change in height.

☐ Corollary 10.2

Under the decision-tree model, the problem of finding a simple polygon connecting a set of given points in the plane requires $\Omega(n \log n)$ comparisons in the worst case.   ☐

This reduction establishes the fact that sorting is really at the heart of solving the simple polygon problem.

10.4.2 Simple Reductions Involving Matrices

In Section 9.5, we saw very nonintuitive ways to multiply two matrices. Symmetric matrices (i.e., matrices in which the ijth entry is equal to the jith entry) occur commonly in practice. It is natural to ask whether it is easier to multiply symmetric matrices. It is entirely possible that symmetry helps in finding better expressions for multiplying, say, 3 by 3 matrices. This may lead to a better asymptotic algorithm for multiplying symmetric matrices. We now show that this is not the case. We prove that multiplying two symmetric matrices is as hard, to within a constant factor, as is multiplying two arbitrary matrices.

Let's denote the problem of computing the product of two arbitrary matrices by *ArbM*, and that of computing the product of two symmetric matrices by *SymM*. It is obvious that *SymM* is not *harder* than *ArbM* (since *SymM* is a special case of *ArbM*). Suppose now that we have an algorithm that solves *SymM*. We show that we can use this algorithm as a black box to solve the more general problem *ArbM*. Let A and B be two arbitrary matrices. Denote by A^T the **transpose** of A (i.e., the matrix obtained from A by exchanging every entry ij with the entry ji). We utilize the following expression, involving a product of two $2n \times 2n$ matrices, which is easy to verify:

$$\begin{bmatrix} 0 & A \\ A^T & 0 \end{bmatrix} \begin{bmatrix} 0 & B^T \\ B & 0 \end{bmatrix} = \begin{bmatrix} AB & 0 \\ 0 & A^TB^T \end{bmatrix}. \tag{10.11}$$

(The 0s stand for $n \times n$ matrices all of whose entries are 0.) The reduction follows from the fact that the two matrices on the left side are symmetric. We can find their product by using the algorithm for the problem *SymM*. But the upper-left side of their product contains exactly the product AB. Hence, we can solve *ArbM* by using the algorithm for *SymM* on two matrices of twice the size. This leads to the following theorem.

☐ Theorem 10.3

If there is an algorithm that computes the product of two symmetric $n \times n$ real matrices in time $O(T(n))$, such that $T(2n) = O(T(n))$, then there is an algorithm to compute the product of two arbitrary $n \times n$ real matrices in time $O(T(n) + n^2)$.

Proof: Given two arbitrary $n \times n$ matrices, we use the assumed algorithm to compute their product as shown in (10.11). It takes $O(n^2)$ steps to compute A^T and B^T and to construct the two symmetric matrices, and $T(2n)$ to multiply them. The theorem follows.   □

The assumption that $T(2n) = O(T(n))$ is not overly restrictive; for example, any polynomial satisfies it. This reduction is good only for establishing a lower bound. We do not suggest using it in practice to multiply. Theorem 10.3 tells us that it is impossible to utilize the symmetric properties of a matrix for a matrix multiplication algorithm that is faster asymptotically. Here is another similar reduction.

□ Theorem 10.4

If there is an algorithm that computes the square of an $n \times n$ real matrix in time $O(T(n))$, such that $T(2n) = O(T(n))$, then there is an algorithm to compute the product of two arbitrary $n \times n$ real matrices in time $O(T(n) + n^2)$.

Proof: As in the proof of Theorem 10.3, we need to find a matrix whose square contains enough information to obtain the product of two arbitrary matrices. This is done by the following expression:

$$\begin{bmatrix} 0 & A \\ B & 0 \end{bmatrix}^2 = \begin{bmatrix} AB & 0 \\ 0 & BA \end{bmatrix}. \tag{10.12}$$

The theorem follows immediately.   □

10.5 Common Errors

Reductions should be used with care. The following are examples of common errors one can make when attempting a reduction. The most common error is to apply the reduction in the wrong order. This mistake is more prevalent in reductions for lower bounds. The reduction should establish in this case that one problem P is at least as hard as another problem Q whose complexity we already know. We need to start with an *arbitrary* instance of Q and to show that it can be solved with a black-box solution for P. Consider, for example, the following attempt to reduce the problem of data compression via Huffman's encoding (Section 6.6) to the problem of sorting. The goal is to prove a lower bound of $\Omega(n \log n)$ for the complexity of Huffman's encoding.

The main observation is that, if the frequencies of the characters are wide apart, then the tree becomes so unbalanced that it can be used for sorting (see Fig. 10.3). In that case, the characters will appear in the tree in decreasing order of frequencies (with the highest-frequency character at the top of the tree). But that means that Huffman's encoding can be used to sort these frequencies. Therefore, building the tree is at least as hard as sorting, and a lower bound of $\Omega(n \log n)$ seems to be implied.

The error in this argument comes from the fact that we started with a special case of the sorting problem. We considered only those frequencies that that are wide apart.

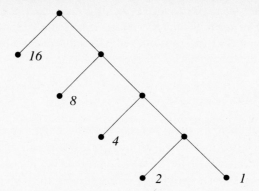

Figure 10.3 A Huffman tree for frequencies that are wide apart.

To prove a lower bound for sorting, we must start with an *arbitrary instance* of sorting. After all, the proof should show that Huffman's encoding can be used to perform *any* sorting. We must start with arbitrary numbers and show that these numbers can be sorted by the Huffman's encoding algorithm. We will discuss this error further in the next chapter.

As it turns out, we can modify the arguments above and save the proof. The trick is to spend some time changing the input of the sorting problem (which must be arbitrary) so that it conform with our goals. Let the input be a sequence of distinct positive integers $X = (x_1, x_2, ..., x_n)$. We can assume that the numbers are distinct, because the lower bound for sorting applies to distinct numbers as well (in fact, the lower bound was proved for distinct integers). The Huffman's encoding corresponding to frequencies that are equal to the numbers in X can be any general tree; thus, the arguments above cannot be used. However, we can replace each x_i with, say, $y_i = 2^{x_i}$. Since, for any positive integer m, we have $2^m > \sum_{i<m} 2^i$, the Huffman tree will have the form shown in Fig. 10.3. So, it is possible to use the Huffman's encoding algorithm to sort the y_is. We now must make sure that the extra computation involved in the reduction (computing the y_is from the x_is, in this case) is not prohibitive. Computing powers can be quite expensive, but that is irrelevant in this case, because the lower bound for sorting involves only comparisons. We made no assumptions about the number of other operations (see again Section 6.4.6). Therefore, we established that building the Huffman's encoding requires $\Omega(n \log n)$ comparisons in the worst case under the decision-tree model. (It may be possible to build the tree more quickly with an algorithm that does not conform to the decision-tree model.)

We also have to be careful that the reduction does not impose significant inefficiency. Consider the knapsack problem discussed in Section 5.11, and the extension to it addressed in Exercise 5.17. (The extension was to solve the knapsack problem where each item can be included in the knapsack an unbounded number of times.) A straightforward reduction of the extended problem to the original problem (in which each item appears at most once) is the following. Let the size of the knapsack be

K. An item of size s_i cannot be included more than K/s_i times. So, we can replace each item in the extended problem with $\lfloor K/s_i \rfloor$ items of the same size in the original problem. Although this reduction is correct, it is not very efficient, since we have increased the size of the problem considerably. This problem can be solved more efficiently.

10.6 Summary

It is always a good idea to look for similarities between problems. By studying differences and similarities between two problems, one usually gains insight into both problems. Given a new problem, the first thought should be (in almost all cases), ''Is this problem similar to a known problem?'' Sometimes, the similarities between two problems become apparent only after complicated reductions are exhibited. The reductions between matrix and graph algorithms are especially interesting. We have seen several examples of reductions in this chapter, and we will see more examples in the next chapter.

Linear and integer programming were described too briefly in this chapter. They are very important and should be studied in detail by anyone interested in algorithms.

Bibliographic Notes and Further Reading

Hall's Theorem is due to P. Hall [1935]. A detailed discussion of Hall's theorem can be found in almost any combinatorics book; see, for example, Brualdi [1977] or M. Hall [1986]. The relationships between finding small cycles — in particular, triangles — and matrix multiplications are discussed by Itai and Rodeh [1978]. The two reductions involving matrices (Section 10.4.2) are due to Munro [1971]. Similar, but more complicated, reductions can be obtained between Boolean matrix multiplication and the transitive-closure problem (Fischer and Meyer [1971]), and between matrix multiplication and matrix inversion (Winograd [1970b]).

Linear programming was first solved by Dantzig in 1947 (see Dantzig [1963] for detailed discussion and numerous examples). Dantzig's algorithm, called the **simplex algorithm**, has been in extensive use since the 1950s. It is fast and practical. Nevertheless, Klee and Minty [1972] proved that the worst-case running time of the simplex algorithm is exponential. Khachian [1979] was the first to exhibit an algorithm for linear programming whose running time is polynomial in the worst case. Khachian's algorithm, which is known also as the **ellipsoid algorithm**, works very poorly in practice. However, the ellipsoid algorithm has other applications (see, for example, Grötschel, Lovász, and Schrijver [1981]). Another polynomial-time algorithm for linear programming was introduced by Karmarkar [1984]. Karmarkar's algorithm received a lot of attention, and triggered extensive research, because of its potential for being superior to the simplex algorithm in certain cases. For more on linear and integer programming, see, for example, Papadimitriou and Steiglitz [1982], and Schrijver [1986].

A solution to Exercise 10.7 can be found in van Leeuwen [1986]. Exercise 10.8 is from Even [1979]. Exercise 10.11 is from Maggs and Plotkin [1988]. Exercise 10.22 is from Aho, Hopcroft, and Ullman [1974].

Exercises

10.1   Prove Hall's theorem by using the techniques developed in the sections on network flows and bipartite matching.

10.2   Solve the following variation of the sequence-comparison problem. The input is two sequences A and B, and the goal is to edit B so that it becomes equal to A. The edit steps are the usual ones: insert, delete and replace (or match). The cost of a step, however, depends on the position in the sequence of the corresponding characters. The cost of inserting a character at the ith position in B is ci, where c is a constant, and the cost of deleting the jth character of B is cj. The cost of replacing a character with another character is still 1. The algorithm should find the minimum-cost edit sequence.

10.3   Find a reduction (in some direction) between the problem of finding maximal points in the plane (Exercise 8.18) and that of marking intervals on the line for containment (Exercise 8.26).

10.4   Department D at University X administers a qualifying examination for its Ph.D. students. The examination consists of Q questions divided into n areas such that there are q_i questions in area i ($\sum_{i=1}^{n} q_i = Q$). There are k professors $P_1, P_2, ,..., P_k$ (these are not their real names) who write questions for the examination. Suppose that each professor P_i has overall p_i questions that can be used, and that $\sum_{i=1}^{k} p_i \geq Q$. A committee is responsible for selecting the questions for the examination from the questions supplied by the professors. We assume that all the questions are unique, and that they are all good. Assume, furthermore, that each professor insists that no more than r (where r is a constant independent of the professor) of his or her questions will be used (so that he or she can use the remaining questions in later years). Design an efficient algorithm to select the questions for the examination under these constraints, or to determine that it is impossible to do so.

10.5   Consider the following variation of the bipartite matching problem. Suppose that there are $2n$ students who want to be admitted to n universities. Consider the bipartite graph formed by having the students and the universities as the two sets of vertices and including an edge between a student and a university if the university agrees to admit that student. Find an algorithm to maximize the number of students that are admitted, such that no more than two students are admitted to each university (there are no preferences). Solve the problem by exhibiting a reduction to the regular bipartite matching problem.

10.6   Here is another variation of the bipartite matching problem. Suppose now that there are n training courses and n trainees. As usual, we consider the graph in which the courses and the trainees are the vertices and there is an edge between a trainee and a course if the trainee is qualified for the course. Each course can have at most two trainees, and each trainee can take at most two courses. Design an algorithm (by a reduction to a known problem) to maximize the registration. (Again, no preferences are given, and there are no scheduling problems.)

10.7   Let $G = (V, E)$ be an undirected graph such that each vertex v is associated with an integer

$b(v) \leq degree(v)$. A **b-matching** in G is a set of edges of E such that each vertex v has no more than $b(v)$ edges incident to it. (If $b(v) = 1$ for all v, then this is exactly the regular matching problem.) A **maximum** b-matching is one with maximum number of edges. Reduce the problem of finding a maximum b-matching to that of finding a maximum matching.

*10.8 Let $G = (V, E)$ be an acyclic directed graph. Design an algorithm to find a minimum number of vertex-disjoint paths that include all vertices of G.

10.9 Let $G = (V, E)$ be a network with source s and sink t. Assume that G is *planar*, namely, it can be laid out in the plane such that no edges intersect. Assume furthermore that such a layout is given to you (in a reasonable representation), and that both the source and the sink lie on the outside of the layout. Design an algorithm to find a minimum-cost *cut* in G without using the maximum-flow algorithm.

10.10 Exercise 8.40 can be solved by reducing the problem to that of minimum-weight matching. (In this case, the reduction leads to an inferior algorithm since minimum-weight matching is harder than a direct solution.) Show the reduction and prove its validity (i.e., prove that the corresponding minimum-weight matching satisfies the conditions of the problem).

10.11 Reduce the problem of finding an MCST in an undirected graph to a **bottleneck shortest-path problem**. (A bottleneck problem is a minimization problem in which we try to minimize the maximum value, rather than the sum of values; so, a bottleneck shortest-path problem involves paths whose maximal-cost edges are minimized, rather than the cost of the whole path.) As a result, show that the MCST problem can be solved by shortest-paths techniques. (Although shortest-paths algorithms are usually more expensive than MCST algorithms, the reduction can be helpful for parallel algorithms.)

10.12 The input is a directed graph $G = (V, E)$ with a distinguished vertex v, such that there is a positive cost $c(w)$ associated with each vertex w. The cost of a directed path $v, x_1, x_2, ..., x_k, u$ is defined as $\sum_{i=1}^{k} c(x_i)$. The costs of the two endpoints v and u are ignored, so if $(v, u) \in E$, the cost of getting from v to u is 0. Design an efficient algorithm to find the minimal-cost paths from v to all other vertices. (This exercise is identical to Exercise 7.47, but here we insist on a solution by reduction.)

10.13 An even more general formulation of linear programming than the one given in Section 10.3 allows two types of inequality constraints: The first type imposes the "$\leq$" relations, and the second type imposes the "$\geq$" relations (of course, with different coefficients). Show that this formulation can be reduced to the one in Section 10.3.

10.14 Suppose that you have a linear programming algorithm that can only handle nonnegative variables. (Recall that in our definition of linear programming not all variables were restricted to be nonnegative.) Show how to reduce the general problem to this one.

10.15 Show, by exhibiting a bad example, that constraints of the type $\bar{a} \cdot \bar{x} \neq b$ should not be allowed in a linear programming formulation.

10.16 Suppose that there are n people in a scientific conference whose goal is to maximize exchange of ideas. Not everyone can exchange ideas with everyone else. We represent the conference by an undirected graph, with the vertices associated with the people such that i is connected to j if i can exchange ideas with j. (One can also define a directed version.)

Suppose further that the number of hours for talking is limited. For simplicity, we assume that there is one global bound of h hours. That is, every person can spend at most h hours talking. We are not concerned here with scheduling. We assume that time is also spent on other activities, so there is sufficient flexibility to arrange any possible meeting. For example, suppose that there are three people, each "connected" to the others, and let $h = 1$. If two of them talk to each other for the whole hour, then there is only 1 hour of conversation. If, on the other hand, each one talks to each other for half an hour, then everyone exhausts his or her time and there is 1.5 hours of conversation. We want to maximize the total conversation time. Formulate this problem in terms of linear programming, or reduce it to another problem that we have already discussed.

10.17 Consider again the philanthropist problem of Section 10.3.2. Suppose that there are no limits on the amount of money each department is willing to accept. Solve this variation of the problem.

10.18 Consider the problem of arranging n players in an order consistent with the results of a round-robin competition (Exercise 7.104). Prove a lower bound of $\Omega(n \log n)$ for this problem by reducing it to sorting. Show that the reduction to sorting can also be helpful in finding a good algorithm for this problem.

10.19 Let S be a set of n points that are vertices of an arbitrary convex polygon. The points are given in an arbitrary order. Prove that it takes $\Omega(n \log n)$ time to arrange the points into the standard polygon representation (i.e., in consecutive order).

10.20 We have seen in Section 9.5.2 that 7 multiplications (instead of the nominal 8) are sufficient to compute the product of two arbitrary 2×2 matrices, and that this fact leads to a better matrix multiplication algorithm. It is possible to compute the square of an 2×2 real matrix with only 5 multiplications (Exercise 9.21). Discuss why this observation does not contradict Theorem 10.4.

10.21 A **lower triangular matrix** is a square matrix (a_{ij}) such that, if $j > i$, then $a_{ij} = 0$ (in other words, all nonzero entries are on or below the main diagonal). An **upper triangular matrix** is defined similarly, except that the nonzero entries are on or above the main diagonal. Prove that, if there exists an algorithm to multiply an $n \times n$ lower triangular matrix by an $n \times n$ upper triangular matrix, whose running time is $O(T(n))$, then there exists an algorithm to multiply two arbitrary $n \times n$ matrices whose running time is $O(T(n) + n^2)$. You can assume that $T(cn) = O(T(n))$ for any constant c.

10.22 Prove that if there exists an algorithm to multiply two $n \times n$ lower triangular matrices whose running time is $O(T(n))$, then there exists an algorithm to multiply two arbitrary $n \times n$ matrices whose running time is $O(T(n) + n^2)$. You can assume that $T(cn) = O(T(n))$ for any constant c.

10.23 The **transitive closure** A^* of an $n \times n$ matrix A is defined as follows:

$$A^* = I + A + A^2 + \cdots + A^{n-1},$$

where I is the $n \times n$ identity matrix.

a. Prove that, if A is a Boolean matrix corresponding to an adjacency matrix of a graph, then A^* corresponds to the adjacency matrix of the transitive closure of the graph. (Assume that multiplication is performed according to the Boolean rules.)

b. Prove that, if the transitive closure can be computed in time $T(n)$, where $T(n)$ is a polynomial in n, then matrix multiplication can be computed in time $O(T(n))$. You can assume that $T(cn) = O(T(n))$ for any constant c.

10.24 Let S be a set of n points in the plane. The points define a weighted undirected graph in the following way. The graph is the complete graph (i.e., every two vertices are connected), and the weight of an edge is equal to the Euclidean distance between the two corresponding points. Show a lower bound of $\Omega(n \log n)$ for the running time of an MCST algorithm for this case.

*10.25 Let S be a set of n points in the plane. The **diameter** of S is the maximal distance between two points in S. Denote the problem of finding the diameter by DM. Let A and B be two sets of n real numbers. Denote the problem of deciding whether A and B are disjoint by DJ. Prove that, if there exists an algorithm for DM that uses $O(T(n))$ arithmetic operations (you can assume any reasonable operations), then there exists an algorithm for DJ that uses $O(T(n) + n)$ operations.

CHAPTER 11

NP-COMPLETENESS

Give me where to stand, and I will move the earth.
Archimedes (287–212 B.C.)

11.1 Introduction

This chapter is quite different from other chapters. In the previous chapters, we mainly studied techniques for solving algorithmic problems and applied them to specific problems. It would be nice if all problems had elegant efficient algorithms that can be discovered by a small set of techniques. But life is rarely that simple. There are still many problems that do not seem to succumb to the techniques that we have learned so far. It is possible that we just have not tried hard enough, but we strongly suspect that there are problems that have no good general efficient solutions. In this chapter, we describe techniques for identifying some of these problems.

 The running times of most of the algorithms that we have seen so far were bounded by some polynomial in the size of the input. We call such algorithms **efficient** algorithms, and call the corresponding problems **tractable** problems. In other words, we say that an algorithm is efficient if its running time is $O(P(n))$, where $P(n)$ is a polynomial in the size of the input n. Recall that the size of the input is defined as the number of bits required to represent that input. The class of all problems that can be solved by efficient algorithms is denoted by P (for polynomial time). This may seem to be a strange definition. Surely, algorithms that run in time $O(n^{10})$ are not efficient by any standard (for that matter, algorithms that run in time $10^7 n$ are not efficient, even though they are linear). Nevertheless, this definition is valid for two reasons. First, it allows the development of the theory, which we are about to explore; second, and most important, it simply works in practice. It turns out that the vast majority of the tractable problems have practical solutions (of course, some are better than others). In other words, the running times of polynomial algorithms that we encounter in practice are mostly small-degree polynomials (seldom above quadratic). The opposite is also usually true: Algorithms whose running times are larger than any polynomial are not usually practical for large inputs.

There are many problems for which no polynomial-time algorithm is known. Some of these problems may be solved by efficient algorithms that are yet to be discovered. We strongly suspect, however, that many problems cannot be solved efficiently. We would like to be able to identify such problems, so that we do not have to spend time searching for a nonexistent algorithm. In this chapter, we discuss how to deal with problems that are not known to be in P. In particular, we discuss one special class of problems, called **NP-complete problems**. We can group these problems in one class because they are all equivalent in a strong sense — *there exists an efficient algorithm for any one NP-complete problem if and only if there exist efficient algorithms for* all *NP-complete problems*. There is a general belief that there is no efficient algorithm for any NP-complete problem, but no proof of that belief is known. Even if there were efficient algorithms for NP-complete problems, they would surely be very complicated, since they have eluded researchers for many years. So far, hundreds (maybe even thousands) of problems have been found to be NP-complete, which is why this subject is so important.

The chapter consists of two parts. First, we define the class of NP-complete problems and show how to prove that a problem belongs to the class. Then, we present several techniques and examples for solving NP-complete problems *approximately*. These solutions may not be optimal, and they may not always work, but they are better than nothing.

11.2 Polynomial-Time Reductions

We will restrict ourselves in this section to **decision problems**; that is, we consider only those problems whose answer is either yes or no. This restriction makes the discussion and the theory simpler. Most problems can be easily converted to decision problems. For example, instead of looking for the size of the maximum matching in a given graph, we can ask whether there exists a matching of size $\geq k$. If we know how to solve the decision problem, we can usually solve the original problem — for example, by binary search.

A decision problem can be viewed as a **language-recognition problem**. Let U be the set of all possible inputs to the decision problem. Let $L \subseteq U$ be the set of all inputs for which the answer to the problem is yes. We call L the **language** corresponding to the problem, and we use the terms *problem* and *language* interchangeably. The decision problem is to recognize whether or not a given input belongs to L. We now introduce the notion of polynomial-time reduction between languages, which is the main tool we use in this chapter.

> **Definition**: Let L_1 and L_2 be two languages from the input spaces U_1 and U_2. We say that L_1 is **polynomially reducible** to L_2 if there exists a polynomial-time algorithm that converts each input $u_1 \in U_1$ to another

input $u_2 \in U_2$ such that $u_1 \in L_1$ if and only if $u_2 \in L_2$. The algorithm is polynomial in the size of the input u_1. We assume that the notion of size is well defined in the input spaces U_1 and U_2, so, in particular, the size of u_2 is also polynomial in the size of u_1.

The algorithm mentioned in the definition converts one problem to another. If we have an algorithm for L_2, then we can *compose* the two algorithms to produce an algorithm for L_1. Denote the conversion algorithm by AC, and denote the algorithm for L_2 by AL_2. Given an arbitrary input $u_1 \in U_1$ we can use AC to convert u_1 to an input $u_2 \in U_2$; we then use AL_2 to determine whether u_2 belongs to L_2, which will tell us whether u_1 belongs to L_1. In particular, we have the following theorem.

□ Theorem 11.1

If L_1 is polynomially reducible to L_2 and there is a polynomial-time algorithm for L_2, then there is a polynomial time algorithm for L_1.

Proof: The proof follows from the preceding discussion.   □

The notion of reducibility is not symmetric; the fact that L_1 is polynomially reducible to L_2 does not imply that L_2 is polynomially reducible to L_1. This asymmetry comes from the fact that the definition of reducibility requires that *any* input of L_1 can be converted to an equivalent input of L_2, but not vice versa. It is possible, and in many cases likely, that the inputs of L_2 involved in the reduction are only a small fraction of all possible inputs for L_2. Thus, if L_1 is polynomially reducible to L_2, then we regard L_2 to be the *harder* problem.

Two languages L_1 and L_2 are **polynomially equivalent**, or simply equivalent, if each is polynomially reducible to the other. In particular, all nontrivial tractable problems are equivalent because all have polynomial-time algorithms (we leave the precise proof of this fact as an exercise). The relation of "polynomial reducibility" is transitive, as is shown in the next theorem.

□ Theorem 11.2

If L_1 is polynomially reducible to L_2 and L_2 is polynomially reducible to L_3, then L_1 is polynomially reducible to L_3.

Proof: We can compose the two conversion algorithms to form a conversion algorithm from L_1 to L_3. An input u_1 in L_1 will be converted first to an input u_2 in L_2 and then to an input u_3 in L_3. Since we use polynomial reductions and a composition of two polynomial functions is still a polynomial function, the result is a polynomial-time conversion algorithm. (This is one of the reasons we chose to use polynomials.)   □

The essence of the method we present in this chapter is to look for equivalent problems when an efficient algorithm cannot be found. When we are given a problem that we cannot solve efficiently, we try to find whether it is equivalent to other problems that are known to be hard. The class of NP-complete problems encompasses hundreds of such equivalent problems.

11.3 Nondeterminism and Cook´s Theorem

The theory of NP-completeness started with a remarkable theorem of Cook [1971]. Before we state the theorem, we must explain several notions. We will try to keep the discussion intuitive and will skip several technical details. An excellent reference book for this area is Garey and Johnson [1979]. The theory of NP-completeness is part of a large theory, called **computational complexity**, most of which is beyond the scope of this book. We limit the discussion to some parts that help us to *use* the theory.

We have not gone into great detail describing in precise mathematical terms what an algorithm is. This is not important for describing practical algorithms, as long as we use reasonable steps that are supported by all computers (e.g., additions, comparisons, memory accesses). A precise definition of an algorithm is very important, however, for proving lower bounds. (We have used decision trees to prove lower bounds in Chapter 6, but this is a very restricted model.) The most fundamental model of computation is a **Turing machine**. Another commonly used model is that of a **random access machine**. Fortunately, these and other reasonable models are equivalent for our purposes, because we can transform an algorithm from one model to another without changing the running time by more than a polynomial factor. Cook's theorem, for example, was proved with the use of Turing machines, but it is valid for other models as well. We will not use any specific model here, since we will not go into any details that require one.

We first need to discuss the notion of **nondeterminism**. This notion is rather non-intuitive, which leads many people to think that NP-completeness is something of a mystery. One should think of a nondeterministic algorithm as an abstract notion, and not as a realistic goal. Nondeterminism is more important to the development of the theory and the explanation of the existence of this class than it is to the techniques for using the theory. A **nondeterministic algorithm** has, in addition to all the regular operations of a deterministic algorithm, a very powerful primitive, which we will call *nd-choice*. As the name suggests, the *nd-choice* primitive is used to handle choices, but it does so in an unusual way. This primitive is associated with a fixed number of choices, such that, for each choice, the algorithm follows a different computation path. We can assume, without loss of generality, that the number of choices is always two. Let L be a language that we want to recognize. Given an input x, a nondeterministic algorithm performs regular deterministic steps interleaved with uses of the *nd−choice* primitive, and, at the end, it decides whether or not to accept x. The key difference between deterministic and nondeterministic algorithms lies in the way they recognize a language.

We say that the nondeterministic algorithm **recognizes** a language L if the following condition is satisfied:

> Given an input x, it is possible to convert each *nd−choice* encountered during the execution of the algorithm into a real choice such that the outcome of the algorithm will be to accept x, if and only if $x \in L$.

In other words, the algorithm must provide at least one possible way for inputs belonging to L to arrive at an accept outcome, and it must not provide any way for inputs not belonging to L to arrive at an accept outcome. Notice the asymmetry in the definition.

An input $x \in L$ may have many paths to a reject outcome. We require only that the algorithm has at least one "good" sequence of choices for every $x \in L$. On the other hand, for every input $x \notin L$, we must reach a reject outcome, no matter which choices we substitute for the nd–*choices*. The nd–*choice* primitive is sometimes called *guessing* for obvious reasons. The running time for an input $x \in L$ is the length of a minimum execution sequence that leads to an accept outcome. The running time of a nondeterministic algorithm refers to worst-case running time for inputs $x \in L$ (inputs not belonging to L are ignored).

Let's see an example of a nondeterministic algorithm. Consider the problem of deciding whether a given graph $G = (V, E)$ has a perfect matching. The following is a nondeterministic algorithm for this problem. We maintain a set M of edges, which is initially empty. We examine all the edges of G, one edge e at a time, and use an nd–*choice* corresponding to whether or not we include e in M. When we are done examining all the edges, we check to see whether M is a perfect matching. The checking can be done in linear time, since we have to determine only whether M contains exactly $|V|/2$ edges and whether each vertex is incident to exactly one edge from M. The output of the algorithm is yes if M is a perfect matching, and no otherwise. This is a correct nondeterministic algorithm for perfect matching because (1) if a perfect matching exists, then there is a sequence of choices that will put it in M; and (2) the algorithm outputs yes only if the existence of a perfect matching was proved (because of the checking). We will see more examples of nondeterministic algorithms in the next section.

Nondeterministic algorithms are very powerful, but their power is not unlimited. Not all problems can be solved efficiently by a nondeterministic algorithm. For example, suppose that the problem is to determine whether the maximum matching in a given graph is of size exactly k. We can use the nondeterministic matching algorithm to find a matching of size k if it exists, but we cannot easily determine (even nondeterministically) that there is no matching of a larger size.

The class of problems for which there exists a nondeterministic algorithm whose running time is a polynomial in the size of the input is called NP. It seems reasonable to believe that nondeterministic algorithms are much more powerful than deterministic algorithms. But are they? One way to prove that they are is to exhibit an NP problem that is not in P. Nobody has been able to do that yet. In contrast, if we want to prove that the two classes are equal (i.e., P = NP), then we have to show that every problem that belongs to NP can be solved by a polynomial-time deterministic algorithm. Nobody has proved that either (and few believe it to be true). The problem of determining the relation between P and NP is known as the **P = NP problem.**

We now define two classes, which not only contain numerous important problems (all equivalent to one another) that are not known to be in P, but also contain the **hardest** problems in NP.

Definition: A problem X is called an **NP-hard problem** if every problem in NP is polynomially reducible to X.

Definition: A problem X is called an **NP-complete problem** if (1) X belongs to NP, and (2) X is NP-hard.

The definition of NP-hardness implies that, if any NP-hard problem is ever proved to belong to P, then that proof would imply that $P = NP$.

Cook [1971] proved that there exist NP-complete problems; in particular, he exhibited one such problem, which we will describe shortly. Once we have found an NP-complete problem, proving that other problems are also NP-complete becomes easier. Given a new problem Y, it is sufficient to prove that Cook's problem, or any other NP-complete problem, is polynomially reducible to Y. This follows from the next lemma.

□ Lemma 11.3

A problem X is an NP-complete problem if (1) X belongs to NP, and (2') Y is polynomially reducible to X, for some problem Y that is NP-complete.

Proof: By condition 2 in the definition of NP-completeness, every problem in NP is polynomially reducible to Y. But since Y is polynomially reducible to X and reducibility is a transitive relation, every problem in NP is polynomially reducible to X as well.   □

It is much easier to prove that two problems are polynomially reducible than it is to prove condition 2 directly. Thus, Cook has found the anchor for the whole theory. And there is more good news. As we find more and more problems that are NP-complete we have more choices for proving condition 2'. Shortly after Cook's result became known, Karp [1972] found 24 important problems that he proved to be NP-complete. Since that time, hundreds of problems (maybe even thousands, depending on how we count variations of the same problem) have been discovered to be NP-complete. In the next section, we present five examples of NP-complete problems with their NP-completeness proof. We also list several other NP-complete problems without proof. The most difficult part of such proofs is usually (but not always) to verify condition 2 (or 2').

We now describe the problem that Cook proved to be NP-complete, and mention the idea of the proof. The problem is known as **satisfiability** (**SAT**). Let S be a Boolean expression in **conjunctive normal form** (**CNF**). That is, S is the product (*and*) of several sums (*or*). For example, $S = (x + y + \bar{z}) \cdot (\bar{x} + y + z) \cdot (\bar{x} + \bar{y} + \bar{z})$, where addition and multiplication correspond to the *and* and *or* Boolean operations, and each variable is either 0 (false) or 1 (true). (Any Boolean expression can be transformed into CNF.) A Boolean expression is said to be **satisfiable** if there exists an assignment of 0s and 1s to its variables such that the value of the expression is 1. The SAT problem is to determine whether a given expression is satisfiable (without necessarily finding a satisfying assignment). For example, the expression S is satisfiable, since the assignment $x = 1$, $y = 1$, and $z = 0$ satisfy it. We call an assignment of 0s and 1s to the variables of a Boolean expression a **truth assignment**.

The SAT problem is in NP because we can guess a truth assignment and check that it satisfies the expression in polynomial time. The idea behind the proof that SAT is NP-hard is that a Turing machine (even a nondeterministic one) and all of its operations on a given input can be described by a Boolean expression. By "described" we mean that the expression will be satisfiable if and only if the Turing machine will terminate at an accepting state for the given input. This is not easy to do, and such an expression becomes quite large and complicated, yet its size is no more than a polynomial in the number of steps the Turing machine makes. Therefore, any NP algorithm can be described by an instance of a SAT problem.

□ **Cook's theorem:**

The SAT problem is NP-complete.   □

11.4 Examples of NP-Completeness Proofs

In this section, we prove that the following five problems are NP-complete: vertex cover, dominating set, 3SAT, 3-coloring, and clique. Each of these problems is described in more detail below. The techniques we use for proving NP-completeness are typical, and they are summarized at the end of the section. To prove NP-completeness of a new problem, we must first prove that the problem belongs to NP, which is usually (but not always!) easy, then reduce a known NP-complete problem to our problem in polynomial time. The reduction order used for the five problems in this section is illustrated in Fig. 11.1. To make them easier to understand, we present the proofs in order of difficulty rather than the tree order. This order is indicated in Fig. 11.1 by the numbers of the edges.

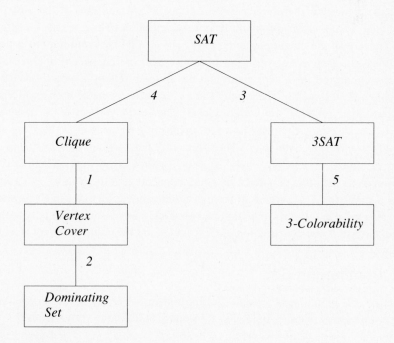

Figure 11.1   The order of NP-completeness proofs in the text.

11.4.1 Vertex Cover

Let $G = (V, E)$ be an undirected graph. A **vertex cover** of G is a set of vertices such that every edge in G is incident to at least one of these vertices.

> **The Problem**   Given an undirected graph $G = (V, E)$ and an integer k, determine whether G has a vertex cover containing $\leq k$ vertices.

☐ Theorem 11.4

The vertex-cover problem is NP-complete.

Proof: The vertex-cover problem belongs to NP, since we can guess a cover of size $\leq k$ and check it easily in polynomial time. To prove that the vertex-cover problem is NP-complete we have to reduce an NP-complete problem to it. We choose the clique problem, which is described next (the proof that the clique problem is NP-complete will be given in Section 11.4.4). Given an undirected graph $G = (V, E)$, a **clique** C in G is a subgraph of G such that all vertices in C are connected to all other vertices in C. In other words, a clique is a complete subgraph. The clique problem is to determine, given a graph G and an integer k, whether G contains a clique of size $\geq k$. We have to transform an arbitrary instance of the clique problem into an instance of the vertex-cover problem such that the answer to the clique problem is positive if and only if the answer to the corresponding vertex-cover problem is positive. Let $G = (V, E)$ and k represent an arbitrary instance of the clique problem. Let $\overline{G} = (V, \overline{E})$ be the **complement graph** of G; namely, $\overline{G}$ has the same set of vertices and two vertices are connected in $\overline{G}$ if and only if they are *not* connected in G. We claim that the clique problem is reduced to the vertex-cover problem represented by the graph $\overline{G}$ and $n - k$ (where n is the number of vertices in G). Suppose that $C = (U, F)$ is a clique in G. The set of vertices $V - U$ covers all the edges of $\overline{G}$, because in $\overline{G}$ there are no edges connecting vertices in U (they are all in G). Thus, $V - U$ is a vertex cover in $\overline{G}$. Therefore, if G has a clique of size k, then $\overline{G}$ has a vertex cover of size $n - k$. Conversely, let D be a vertex cover in $\overline{G}$. Then, D covers all the edges in $\overline{G}$, so in $\overline{G}$ there could be no edges connecting vertices in $V - D$. Thus, $V - D$ generates a clique in G. Therefore, if there is a vertex cover of size k in $\overline{G}$, then there is a clique of size $n - k$ in G. This reduction can obviously be performed in polynomial time, since it requires only the construction of G' from G (and the computation of $n - k$). ☐

11.4.2 Dominating Set

Let $G = (V, E)$ be an undirected graph. A **dominating set** D is a set of vertices in G such that every vertex of G is either in D or is adjacent to at least one vertex from D.

The Problem   Given an undirected graph $G = (V, E)$ and an integer k, determine whether G has a dominating set containing $\leq k$ vertices.

□ Theorem 11.5

The dominating-set problem is NP-complete.

Proof: The dominating-set problem belongs to NP since we can guess a set of size $\leq k$ and check that it is a dominating set easily in polynomial time. We reduce the vertex-cover problem to the dominating-set problem. Given an arbitrary instance (G, k) of the vertex-cover problem, our goal is to construct a new graph G' that has a dominating set of a certain size if and only if G has a vertex cover of size $\leq k$. We start with G, and add $|E|$ new vertices and $2|E|$ new edges to it in the following way (see Fig. 11.2). For each edge (v, w) of G, we add a new vertex vw and two new edges (v, vw) and (w, vw). In other words, we transform every edge into a triangle. Denote the new graph by G'. It is easy to construct G' in polynomial time.

We now claim that G' has a dominating set of size m if and only if G has a vertex cover of size m. Let D be a dominating set of G'. If D contains any of the new vertices vw, then it can be replaced by either v or w and the set will still be a dominating set (both v and w cover all the vertices that vw covers). So, without loss of generality, we can assume that D contains only vertices from G. But, since D dominates all the new vertices, it must contain at least one vertex from each original edge; hence, it is also a vertex cover for G. Conversely, if C is a vertex cover for G, then each edge is covered by C, so all the new vertices are dominated. The old vertices are also dominated since all the edges are covered.   □

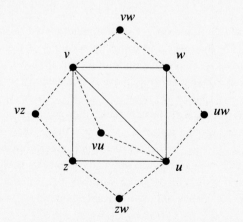

Figure 11.2   The dominating-set reduction.

11.4.3 3SAT

The 3SAT problem is a simplification of the regular SAT problem. An instance of 3SAT is a Boolean expression in which each clause contains exactly three variables.

> **The Problem**   Given a Boolean expression in CNF such that each clause contains exactly three variables, determine whether it is satisfiable.

□ Theorem 11.6

3SAT is NP-complete.

Proof: This problem seems easier than the regular SAT problem because there is the additional requirement of three variables per clause. We will show that a solution to 3SAT can be used to solve the regular SAT. First, 3SAT clearly belongs to NP. We can guess a truth assignment and verify that it satisfies the expression in polynomial time. Let E be an arbitrary instance of SAT. We will replace each clause of E with several clauses, each of which has exactly three variables. Let $C = (x_1 + x_2 + \cdots + x_k)$ be an arbitrary clause of E such that $k \geq 4$. We write each variable in its "positive" form (i.e., we do not use $\overline{x_i}$) only for convenience of notation. We now show how to replace C with several clauses, each with three variables. The idea is to introduce new variables $y_1, y_2, ..., y_{k-3}$ that transform the clause into a 3SAT formulation without affecting its satisfiability. We use new (and different) variables for each clause. C is transformed into C' such that

$$C' = (x_1 + x_2 + y_1) \cdot (x_3 + \overline{y_1} + y_2) \cdot (x_4 + \overline{y_2} + y_3) \cdots (x_{k-1} + x_k + \overline{y_{k-3}}).$$

We claim that C' is satisfiable if and only if C is satisfiable. If C is satisfiable, then one of the x_is must be set to 1. In that case, we can set the values of the y_is in C' such that all clauses in C' are satisfied as well. For example, if $x_3 = 1$, then we set $y_1 = 1$ (which takes care of the first clause), $y_2 = 0$ (the second clause is okay since $x_3 = 1$), and the rest of the y_is to 0. In general, if $x_i = 1$, then we set $y_1, y_2, ..., y_{i-2}$ to be 1, and the rest to be 0, which satisfies C'. Conversely, if C' is satisfiable, then we claim that at least one of the x_is must be 1. Indeed, if all x_is are 0, then the expression becomes $(y_1) \cdot (\overline{y_1} + y_2) \cdot (\overline{y_2} + y_3) \cdots (\overline{y_{k-3}})$. This expression is clearly unsatisfiable.

Using this reduction, we can replace any clause that has more than three variables with several clauses, each with exactly three variables. It remains to transform clauses with one or two variables. If C has only two variables, namely, $C = (x_1 + x_2)$, then

$$C' = (x_1 + x_2 + z) \cdot (x_1 + x_2 + \overline{z}),$$

where z is a new variable. Finally, if $C = x_1$, then

$$C' = (x_1 + y + z) \cdot (x_1 + \overline{y} + z) \cdot (x_1 + y + \overline{z}) \cdot (x_1 + \overline{y} + \overline{z}),$$

where both y and z are new variables.

Thus, we have reduced a general instance of SAT into an instance of 3SAT such that one instance is satisfiable if and only if the other one is. The reduction can clearly be done in polynomial time.   □

11.4.4 Clique

The clique problem was defined in Section 11.4.1, when we discussed the vertex-cover problem.

The Problem   Given an undirected graph $G = (V, E)$ and an integer k, determine whether G contains a clique of size $\geq k$.

□ Theorem 11.7

The clique problem is NP-complete.

Proof: The clique problem belongs to NP since we can guess a subset of $\geq k$ vertices and check that it is a clique in polynomial time. We reduce SAT to the clique problem. Let E be an arbitrary Boolean expression in CNF, $E = E_1 \cdot E_2 \cdots E_m$. Consider the clause $E_i = (x + y + z + w)$ (we use four variables only for illustration purposes). We associate a ''column'' of four vertices with the variables in E_i even if they also appear in other clauses. That is, the graph G will have a vertex for each appearance of each variable. The question is how to connect these vertices such that G contains a clique of size $\geq k$ if and only if E is satisfiable. Notice that we are free to choose the value of k because we want to reduce SAT to the clique problem, which means that we want to solve SAT using a solution of the clique problem. A solution of the clique problem should work for every value of k. This is an important flexibility that is used often in NP-completeness proofs. We will choose k to be equal to the number of clauses m.

The edges of G are as follows. Vertices from the same column (i.e., vertices associated with variables of the same clause) are not connected. Vertices from different columns are almost always connected unless they correspond to the same variable appearing in complementary form. That is, the only time we do not connect two vertices from different clauses is when one corresponds to a variable x and the other to $\bar{x}$. An example, which corresponds to the expression $E = (x + y + \bar{z}) \cdot (\bar{x} + \bar{y} + z) \cdot (y + \bar{z})$, is presented in Fig. 11.3. G can clearly be constructed in polynomial time.

We now claim that G has a clique of size $\geq m$ if and only if E is satisfiable. In fact, the construction guarantees that the maximal clique size does not exceed m independent of E. Assume that E is satisfiable. Then, there exists a truth assignment such that each clause contains at least one variable whose value is 1. We will choose the vertex corresponding to this variable for the clique. (If more than one variable in a clause is set to 1, we choose one arbitrarily.) The result is indeed a clique, since the only time two vertices from different columns are not connected is when they are the complement of

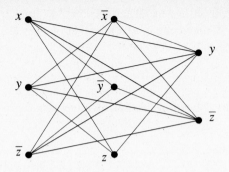

Figure 11.3 An example of the clique reduction for the expression
$$(x + y + \overline{z}) \cdot (\overline{x} + \overline{y} + z) \cdot (y + \overline{z}).$$

each other, which of course cannot happen in a consistent truth assignment. Conversely, assume that G contains a clique of size $\geq m$. The clique must contain exactly one vertex from each column (since two vertices from the same column are never connected). We assign the corresponding variables a value of 1. If any variables are not assigned in this manner, they can be assigned arbitrarily. Since all the vertices in the clique are connected to one another, and we made sure that x and $\overline{x}$ are never connected, this truth assignment is consistent. □

11.4.5 3-Coloring

Let $G = (V, E)$ be an undirected graph. A **valid coloring** of G is an assignment of colors to the vertices such that each vertex is assigned one color and no two adjacent vertices have the same color.

The Problem   Given an undirected graph $G = (V, E)$, determine whether G can be colored with three colors.

□ **Theorem 11.8**

3-coloring is NP-complete.

Proof: The 3-coloring problem belongs to NP since we can guess a 3-coloring and check that it is a valid coloring easily in polynomial time. We reduce 3SAT to the 3-coloring problem. This is a more complicated proof for two reasons. First, the two problems deal with different objects (Boolean expressions versus graphs). Second, we cannot just replace one object (e.g., vertex, edge) with another (e.g., clause); we have to deal with the whole structure. The idea is to use building blocks and then to tie them together. Let E be an arbitrary instance of 3SAT. We have to construct a graph G such that E is satisfiable if and only if G can be 3-colored. First, we build the *main triangle M*.

Since M is a triangle, it requires at least three colors. We label M with the "colors" T (for true), F (for false), and A (see the bottom triangle in Fig. 11.4). These colors are used only for the proof; they are not part of the graph. We will later associate these colors with the assignment of truth values to the variables of E. For each variable x, we build another triangle M_x whose vertices are labeled x, $\bar{x}$, and A, where A is the same vertex in M. So, if there are k variables, we will have $k+1$ triangles, all sharing one common vertex A (see Fig. 11.4). The idea is that, if x is colored with the color T, then $\bar{x}$ must be colored with F (since they are both connected to A), and vice versa. This is consistent with the meaning of $\bar{x}$.

We now have to impose the condition that at least one variable in each clause has value 1. We do that with the following construct. Assume that the clause is $(x+y+z)$. We introduce six new vertices and connect them to the existing vertices, as shown in Fig 11.5. (The labels are consistent, so that there is only one vertex in the whole graph labeled T, and one vertex for each x, y, or z.) Let's call the three new vertices connected to T and x, y, or z the *outer vertices* (they are labeled by O in the figure), and the three new vertices in the triangle the *inner vertices* (labeled by I in the figure). We claim that this construct guarantees that, if no more than 3 colors are used, then at least one of x, y, or z must be colored T. None of them can be colored A, since they are all connected to A (see Fig. 11.4). If all are colored F, then the three new vertices connected to them must be colored A, but then the inner triangle cannot be colored with three colors! The complete graph corresponding to the expression $(\bar{x}+y+\bar{z}) \cdot (x+\bar{y}+z)$ is given in Fig. 11.6.

We can now complete the proof. We have to prove two sides: (1) if E is satisfiable, then G can be colored with three colors; and (2) if G can be colored with three colors, then E is satisfiable. If E is satisfiable then there is a satisfiable truth assignment. We color the vertices associated with the variables according to this truth assignment (T if $x=1$, and F otherwise). M is colored with T, F, and A as indicated. Each clause must have at least one variable whose value is 1. Hence, we can color the corresponding outer vertex with F, the rest of the outer vertices with A, and the inner triangle accordingly. Thus, G can be colored with three colors. Conversely, if G can be colored with three

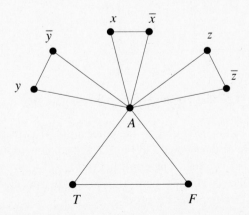

Figure 11.4 The first part of the construction in the reduction of 3SAT to 3-coloring.

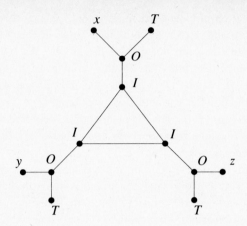

Figure 11.5 The subgraphs corresponding to the clauses in the reduction of 3SAT to 3-coloring.

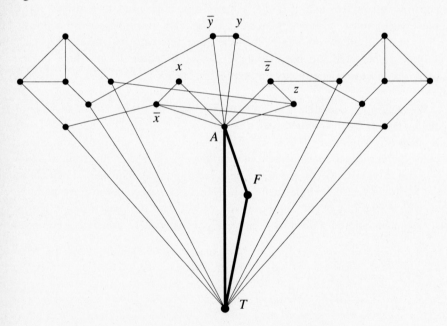

Figure 11.6 The graph corresponding to $(\bar{x}+y+\bar{z})\cdot(\bar{x}+\bar{y}+z)$.

colors, we name the colors according to the coloring of M (which must be colored with three colors). Because of the triangles in Fig. 11.4, the colors of the variables correspond to a consistent truth assignment. The construct in Fig. 11.6 guarantees that at least one variable in each clause is colored with T. Finally, G can clearly be constructed in polynomial time, which completes the proof.   □

11.4.6 General Observations

We discuss here briefly some general methods for proving that a problem Q is NP-complete. The first condition — showing that Q belongs to NP — is usually easy (but not always). Then, we have to select a known NP-complete problem that seems related or similar to Q. It is hard to define this "similarity" goal, since sometimes the problems look very different (e.g., the clique problem and SAT). Finding the right problem from which to reduce is sometimes a difficult task, which can be learned only by experience. It is a good idea to try several reductions with several problems until a successful one is found.

We stress that the reduction is done from *an arbitrary instance* of the known NP-complete problem to Q. The most common error in such proofs is to perform the reduction backward. One way to remember the right order is to ensure that the NP-complete problem can be solved by a black-box algorithm for Q. This is a little counterintuitive. The natural thing to do when given a problem Q is to try solve it. Here, however, we try to show that we can solve another problem (the NP-complete problem) using the solution of Q. We are not trying to solve Q!

There are several degrees of freedom that can be used in the reduction. For example, if Q includes a parameter, then its value can be set in any convenient way. (In contrast with the parameter in the problem that is reduced to Q, which cannot be fixed!) Again, Q is just a tool to solve the NP-complete problem; therefore, we can use it in any way we wish. Q can be restricted to special cases in other ways, besides fixing its parameter. For example, we may want to use only a certain types of input (e.g., regular graphs, biconnected graphs) for Q. Another important flexibility we have is the fact that the efficiency of the reduction is unimportant, as long as the reduction can be done in polynomial time. We can ignore not only constants and, for example, double the size of the problem, but we can also square the size of the problem! We can introduce polynomially many new variables, we can replace each vertex in a graph by a new large graph, and so on. There is no need to be efficient (within the bounds of a polynomial), since the reduction is not meant to be converted into an algorithm (at least not until P is found to be equal to NP, if ever).

There are some common techniques used in the construction of the reductions (again, Garey and Johnson [1979] provides many examples). The simplest one is showing that an NP-complete problem is a special case of Q. If it is, then the proof is immediate, since solving Q implies solving the NP-complete problem. For example, consider the **set-cover** problem. The input to the problem is a collection of subsets $S_1, S_2, ..., S_n$ of a set U, and an integer k. The problem is to determine whether there exists a subset $W \subseteq U$, with at most k elements, which contains at least one element from each set S_i. We can see that the vertex-cover problem is a special case of the set-cover problem in which U corresponds to the set of vertices V, and each set S_i corresponds to an edge and contains the two vertices incident to that edge. Thus, if we can solve the set-cover problem for arbitrary sets, then we can solve the vertex-cover problem.

We must be very careful, however, when using this approach. It is not true, in general, that adding more requirements to a problem makes that problem more difficult.

Consider the vertex-cover problem. Suppose that we add a constraint that the vertex cover must not include two adjacent vertices. In other words, we are looking for a small set of vertices that forms a vertex cover and an independent set at the same time. (An independent set is a set of vertices that are not adjacent to one another.) This problem seems more difficult than either the vertex-cover or the independent-set problem, because we have to worry about more requirements. In fact, however, this problem is an easier problem, and it can be solved in polynomial time (Exercise 7.115). It turns out that the extra requirements limit the candidate sets to such an extent that the minimum can be found easily.

Another relatively easy technique involves **local reductions**. In this case, an object in one problem is mapped into an object of the other problem. The mapping is done in a local manner, independently of the other objects. The NP-completeness proof of the dominating set problem followed that pattern. We replaced each edge in one graph by a triangle in the other graph. These local replacements were sufficient to reduce the problem. The difficulty in this technique is to define the objects in the best way.

The most complicated technique is to use building blocks as we did, for example, in the NP-completeness proof of the 3-coloring problem. The blocks usually depend on one another, and designing each one separately is impossible. We have to consider all the objectives of the problems in order to coordinate the design of the different blocks.

11.4.7 More NP-Complete Problems

The following list contains some more NP-complete problems that are useful as a basis for other reductions (e.g., the ones in the exercises). A very large list is given in Garey and Johnson [1979]. Finding the right problem for the reduction is sometimes more than half the work.

Hamiltonian cycle: A Hamiltonian cycle in a graph is a simple cycle that contains each vertex exactly once. The problem is to determine whether a given graph contains a Hamiltonian circuit. The problem is NP-complete for both undirected and directed graphs. (Reduction from vertex cover.)

Traveling salesman: Let $G = (V, E)$ be a weighted complete graph. A traveling-salesman tour is a Hamiltonian cycle. The problem is to determine, given G and a number W, whether there exists a traveling-salesman tour such that the total length of its edges is $\leq W$. (Straightforward reduction from Hamiltonian cycle.)

Hamiltonian path: A Hamiltonian path in a graph is a simple open path that contains each vertex exactly once. The problem is to determine whether a given graph contains a Hamiltonian path. The problem is NP-complete for both undirected and directed graphs. (Reduction from vertex cover.)

Independent set: An independent set in an undirected graph $G = (V, E)$ is a set of vertices no two of which are connected. The problem is to determine, given G and an integer k, whether G contains an independent set with $\geq k$ vertices. (Straightforward reduction from clique.)

3-dimensional matching: Let X, Y, and Z be disjoint sets of size k. Let M be a set of triples (x, y, z) such that $x \in X$, $y \in Y$, and $z \in Z$. The problem is to determine whether there exists a subset of M that contains each element exactly once. The corresponding two-dimensional matching problem is the regular bipartite matching problem. (Reduction from 3SAT.)

Partition: The input is a set X such that each element $x \in X$ has an associated *size* $s(x)$. The problem is to determine whether it is possible to partition the set into two subsets with exactly the same total size. (Reduction from 3-dimensional Matching.)

(Notice that this problem, as well as the next problem, can be solved efficiently by algorithm *Knapsack* (Section 5.10) if the sizes are all small integers. However, since the size of the input is the number of bits required to represent that input, such algorithms, which are called **pseudopolynomial algorithms**, are exponential in the size of the input.)

Knapsack: The input is a set X such that each element $x \in X$ has an associated *size* $s(x)$ and *value* $v(x)$. The problem is to determine whether there is a subset $B \subseteq X$ whose total size is $\leq s$ and whose total value is $\geq v$. (Reduction from partition.)

Bin packing: The input is a sequence of numbers $a_1, a_2, ..., a_n$, and two other numbers b and k. The problem is to determine whether the set can be partitioned into k subsets such that the sum of numbers in each subset is $\leq b$. (Reduction from partition.)

11.5 Techniques for Dealing with NP-Complete Problems

The notion of NP-completeness is a basis for an elegant theory that allows us to identify problems for which no polynomial algorithm is likely to exist. But proving that a given problem is NP-complete does not make the problem go away! We still need to solve it. The techniques for solving NP-complete problems are sometimes different from the techniques that we have previously seen. .We (most probably) cannot solve an NP-complete problem precisely and completely with a polynomial-time algorithm. So, we have to compromise. The most common compromises concern the optimality, robustness, guaranteed efficiency, or completeness of the solution. There are other alternatives as well, all of which sacrifice something. The same algorithm may be used in different situations, resulting in different compromises.

An algorithm that may not lead to the optimal (or precise) result is called an **approximation algorithm**. Of particular interest are approximation algorithms that can guarantee a bound on the degree of imprecision. We will see three examples of such algorithms later.

In Section 6.11, we discussed probabilistic algorithms that may make mistakes. The most famous such algorithms are the ones for primality testing, a problem that is not known to be in P, but is not believed to be NP-complete either. We will not describe primality-testing algorithms, because they requires knowledge of number theory. It is commonly believed that NP-complete problems cannot be solved by a polynomial-time probabilistic algorithm that make mistakes with low probability for all inputs. Therefore, such algorithms are more likely to be effective for problems that are not known to be in P but are not believed to be NP-complete. Such problems are not common. Probabilistic algorithms can be used as part of other strategies — for example, as part of approximation algorithms.

Another compromise involves the requirement for polynomial *worst-case* running times. We can try to solve NP-complete problems in polynomial time *on the average*. The problem with this approach is defining *average*. For example, it is difficult to exclude inputs for which the particular problem is trivial (e.g., a graph with only isolated vertices) from participating in the average. Such trivial inputs may lower the average significantly. Algorithms designed for certain types of random inputs can be useful if the actual distribution of inputs follows their assumption. Finding the right distribution, however, is usually very difficult. A major difficulty in designing algorithms that work well on the average is analyzing them, which is usually very complicated.

Finally, we can also compromise on the completeness of the algorithms; namely, we can allow the algorithm to work efficiently for only some special inputs. For example, the vertex-cover problem can be solved in polynomial time for bipartite graphs (Exercise 7.110). Therefore, when we abstract a problem from a real-life situation we should make sure that any extra condition involving the input is included in the abstract definition. Another example is algorithms whose running times are exponential, but they work reasonably well for small inputs, which may be sufficient.

We describe several of these techniques and illustrate them with examples in this section. We start with two general and useful techniques called **backtracking** and **branch-and-bound**. These techniques are similar. They can be used as a basis for either an approximation algorithm or an optimal algorithm for small inputs. We then give several examples of approximation algorithms.

11.5.1 Backtracking and Branch-and-Bound

We describe these techniques through an example. Consider the 3-coloring problem, which involves assigning colors, under certain constraints, to n vertices of a graph. This is an example of a problem that requires finding optimal *values* (colors in this case) for n parameters. In the 3-coloring example, there are three possible values for each parameter corresponding to the three colors. Therefore, the number of potential solutions is 3^n, which is the number of all possible ways of coloring n vertices with three colors. Of course, unless there are no edges in the graph, the number of possible *valid* solutions will be quite a bit smaller than 3^n, because the edges impose constraints on the possible colorings. To explore all possible ways of coloring the vertices, we can start by assigning an arbitrary color to one of the vertices and continue coloring the other vertices while maintaining the constraints imposed by the edges — namely, that adjacent vertices must be colored with different colors. When we color a vertex, we try all possible colors that are consistent with the previously colored vertices. This process can be performed by a tree-traversal algorithm, which is the essence of the backtracking and branch-and-bound techniques. To avoid confusion between the vertices of the graph and the tree, we will call the vertices of the tree *nodes*.

The root of the tree corresponds to the initial state of the problem, and each branch corresponds to a decision concerning one parameter. Denote the three colors by R(ed), B(lue), and G(reen). Initially, we can pick any two adjacent vertices v and w and color them, say with B and G. Since they will be colored differently in any valid coloring, it is not important which colors we choose (we can always permute the final coloring), which is why we can start with coloring two vertices instead of one. The coloring of these two vertices corresponds to the initial state of the problem, which is associated with the root. The tree is constructed as it is being traversed. At each node t of the tree, we select the next vertex u of the graph to color, and add one, two, or three children to t according to the number of colors that can be used to color u. For example, if our first choice (after v and w) is u, and if u is adjacent to w (which has already been colored G), then there are two possible ways of coloring u, B or R, and we add two corresponding children to the root. We then pick one of these children, and continue this process. After a vertex is colored, there is less flexibility in coloring the rest of the vertices; therefore, the number of children is likely to be smaller as we go deeper in the tree.

If we manage to color all the vertices of the graph, then we are done. More likely, however, we will reach a vertex that cannot be colored (since it has three adjacent vertices already colored with the three colors). At that point, we **backtrack** — we go up the tree and explore other children. An example of a graph and the corresponding 3-coloring backtrack tree is given in Fig. 11.7. Notice that, in this case, once the colors of vertices 1 and 2 are fixed, there is only one way to color the rest of the graph (which is found through the rightmost path in the tree).

We can think of this tree-traversal algorithm as an algorithm based on induction. We have to strengthen the hypothesis slightly to include coloring graphs some of whose vertices have already been colored. In other words, the induction hypothesis will have to deal not with coloring graphs from scratch, but with completing a partial 3-coloring:

> **Induction hypothesis:** *We know how to complete the 3-coloring of a graph that has $< k$ vertices that are not already colored, or to determine that the 3-coloring cannot be completed.*

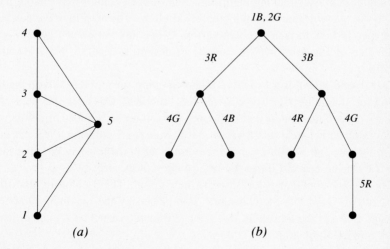

Figure 11.7 An example of backtracking for 3-coloring. (a) The graph (b) The backtrack tree.

Given a graph with k vertices that are not yet colored, we pick one of them and find all possible colors that can be assigned to it. If all colors have already been used for its neighbors, then the 3-coloring cannot be completed. Otherwise, we color the vertex with the possible colors (one at a time) and solve the remaining problems (which now have $k-1$ uncolored vertices) by induction. The algorithm is given in Fig. 11.8.

Algorithm 3-coloring (G, var U) ;
Input: $G = (V, E)$ (an undirected graph), and U (a set of vertices that have
      already been colored together with their colors). { U is initially empty }
Output: An assignment of one of three colors to each vertex of G.

begin
    if $U = V$ *then* print "coloring is completed"; *halt*
    else
        pick a vertex v not in U ;
        for C := 1 to 3 do
            if no neighbor of v is colored with color C then
                add v to U with color C ;
                3-coloring(G, U)
    end

Figure 11.8 Algorithm *3-coloring*.

It is not hard to come up with a graph and an order of traversal for the 3-coloring problem that results in a tree with an exponential number of nodes (Exercise 11.34). This is quite common in backtracking algorithms. Our hope is that, by traversing the tree in a "good" order, we will find the solution early enough. The algorithm we described so far does not specify how to pick the next vertex. Since any vertex can be chosen next, we have a degree of freedom that we can use to design heuristics. We will return to this point shortly.

Branch-and-bound is a variation of backtracking for problems involving finding the minimum (or maximum) of some objective function. Consider the general coloring problem — we are now interested in finding the minimum number of colors required to color the graph rather than just a yes or no answer for 3-coloring. We can build a tree similar to the one for 3-coloring, but the number of branches may be quite large. Each new vertex can be colored either by one of the colors already used (unless one of its neighbors already uses that color), or by a new color. The 3-coloring algorithm is thus modified in two ways: (1) the constant 3 is replaced by the maximal number of colors used so far, and (2) the algorithm does not terminate when $V = U$, since there may be better ways to color the graph.

The problem is that this algorithm backtracks only when a leaf is reached (i.e., $V = U$), since a new color can always be assigned to the vertex. Thus, the algorithm is almost guaranteed to have poor performance (unless the graph is very dense). We can improve the performance of this algorithm by the following observation, which is the basis of the branch-and-bound method. Suppose that we traverse the tree all the way to a leaf and find a valid coloring with k colors. Suppose further that, after backtracking several steps up the tree, we traverse another path and reach a vertex that requires color number $k+1$. At this point, we can backtrack, since we already know a better solution. Thus, k serves as a **bound** for backtracking. At each node, we compute a lower bound on the best solution that can be found farther down the tree. If that lower bound is greater than a known solution, we backtrack. One key to making a branch-and-bound algorithm efficient is computing good lower bounds (or upper bounds, if we want to *maximize* the objective function). Another key is finding a good traversal order so that good solutions are found fast, in which case we can backtrack earlier.

We illustrate this idea through the problem of **integer linear programming** (which is also mentioned in Section 10.3). The problem is similar to linear programming, but with the extra constraints that the values of the variables are integers. Let $\bar{x} = (x_1, x_2, ..., x_n)$ be the vector of *variables*; $\bar{a}_1, \bar{a}_2, ..., \bar{a}_k$ be vectors of real numbers, each of size n; and $b_1, b_2, ..., b_k$ and $c_1, c_2, ..., c_k$ be real numbers. The problem is to maximize the value of the **linear objective function**

$$z = c_1 x_1 + c_2 x_2 + \cdots + c_n x_n \tag{11.1}$$

under the integrality constraints of $\bar{x}$ and the following constraints

$$\bar{a}_1 \cdot \bar{x} \leq b_1$$

$$\bar{a}_2 \cdot \bar{x} \leq b_2$$

$$\cdot \quad \cdot \quad \cdot \tag{11.2}$$

$$\cdot \quad \cdot \quad \cdot$$

$$\bar{a}_k \cdot \bar{x} \leq b_k.$$

(All $\bar{a}_i$s and b_is are constants.) Many NP-complete problems can be easily posed as integer programming problems (we show one example below). Therefore, integer programming is NP-hard. It is in fact NP-complete, but the proof that it belongs to NP is quite complicated.

The following is an integer linear programming formulation of the clique problem. (The problem here is to find the maximal clique, rather than to decide whether a certain sized clique exists.) There are n variables $x_1, x_2, ..., x_n$, corresponding to the vertices, such that $x_i = 1$ if v_i belongs to the maximum clique, and $x_i = 0$ otherwise. The objective function is

$$z = x_1 + x_2 + \cdots + x_n,$$

which implies that we want to select as many vertices as we can. There is one constraint per vertex

$$0 \leq x_i \leq 1 \quad \text{for all } 1 \leq i \leq n,$$

and one constraint for each pair of nonadjacent vertices

$x_i + x_j \leq 1$ for each pair of vertices v_i and v_j such that $(v_i, v_j) \notin E$.

The first set of constraints restrict the variables to either 0 or 1. The second set of constraints guarantee that two vertices that are not adjacent cannot both be selected; therefore, the vertices that are selected form a clique.

Integer linear programming can be solved with branch-and-bound by using the corresponding linear program (which is the same problem without the restriction to integers) to compute the bounds. The solution of the linear program may consist of only integers, in which case we are done. More likely, however, the solution will include some noninteger values. For example, assume that the solution of the linear program associated with the clique problem is $(0.1, 1, ..., 0.5)$ and $z = 7.8$. Since the linear program maximizes the objective function with less restrictions than the integer linear program, the maximum it finds is an upper bound on the maximum possible for the integer linear program. Therefore, we cannot hope for a clique of size greater than 7. This kind of information can be helpful farther down the tree. As in regular backtracking, we make some choices as we go down the tree, and a node lower in the tree corresponds to a subproblem of the original problem. For example, the subproblem may correspond to selecting v and w to the clique, and eliminating u and x, in which case we are trying to find the maximal clique that includes v and w and excludes u and x. If at that point the solution of the linear program gives us a bound that is *less than* a size of an already-known clique, then we can backtrack. This is the essence of the branch-and-bound method. We are trying to find upper bounds (or lower bounds, if the objective function is supposed to be minimized) that will allow us to backtrack as early as possible.

We can also use the result of the linear program to help us choose the branching. For example, since $x_2 = 1$ in the noninteger solution, we may guess that $x_2 = 1$ is the integer solution as well. This may not be a good guess, but it is an example of the kind of heuristics that we are looking for. We try to increase the probability of finding the optimal solution quickly. (We know that being ''right'' all the time is probably impossible, since the problem is NP-complete.) We can set $x_2 = 1$, update the constraints (e.g., set the values of all vertices not adjacent to v_2 to 0), and solve the resulting linear program. If at some point the modified linear program has a maximal value of $z = a$, where a is smaller than the maximal clique known so far, we can backtrack.

Thus, the linear program serves two purposes: It gives upper bounds and thus allows us to backtrack, and it also hints at which choices to make next. We hope that, when we are done with the ''most likely to succeed'' subproblem, we will be able to prune the other subproblems substantially. The amount of pruning — and the efficiency of the whole algorithm — depends on the heuristic to divide the problems and to choose the next subproblem to explore. This heuristic depends on the particular application. Extensive research has been done in this area.

Branch-and-bound algorithms lead to the optimal solution when all subproblems are explored or pruned. If this takes too long, we can terminate the algorithm and obtain an approximation that consists of the best solution found so far. The traversal of the tree can be done by breadth-first search, depth-first search, or a combination. An extreme example of terminating early is taking the first path (chosen by a certain heuristic) that leads to a feasible solution (usually at a leaf) as the outcome of the algorithm. For example, in the coloring algorithm, we can color the vertices in reverse order of degree (the idea being that we lose less flexibility by fixing the color of a small-degree vertex). This is a simple greedy algorithm.

11.5.2 Approximation Algorithms with Guaranteed Performance

In this section, we discuss approximation algorithms for three NP-complete problems: vertex cover, bin packing, and the Euclidean traveling salesman problem. All these approximation algorithms have guaranteed performance. That is, we can prove that the solution they produce is not too far from the optimal solution.

Vertex Cover

We start with a simple approximation algorithm for finding the minimum vertex cover of a given graph. The algorithm is guaranteed to find a cover that contains no more than twice the number of vertices contained in a minimum cover. Let $G = (V, E)$ be a graph and let M be a maximal matching in G. Since M is a matching, its edges have no vertex in common, and since M is maximal, all other edges have one vertex in common with at least one of the edges in M.

□ **Theorem 11.9**

The set of all vertices incident to the edges of a maximal matching M is a vertex cover with no more than twice the number of vertices of a minimum-size vertex cover.

Proof: The set of vertices that belong to M forms a vertex cover, because M is maximal. Every vertex cover must cover all the edges — in particular, the edges of M. But, since M is a matching, a vertex of M cannot cover more than one edge of M. Therefore, at least half of the vertices of M must belong to every vertex cover.   □

We can find a maximal matching by simply collecting edges until all edges are covered. Since the vertex cover includes all the vertices in the matching, we would like to find a small maximal matching. Unfortunately, the problem of finding the minimum maximal matching (i.e., a maximal matching with smallest number of edges) is also NP-complete (Garey and Johnson [1979], problem [GT10]). Exercise 11.35 discusses another approximation algorithm with guaranteed performance for the vertex-cover problem.

One-Dimensional Bin Packing

The **bin packing problem** is concerned with packing different-sized objects into fixed-sized *bins* using as few of the bins as possible. For example, we may want to move the contents of a house using as few cars (or the same car as few times) as possible by packing the cars as densely as possible. Moving is a 3-dimensional problem, but we will concentrate on the one-dimensional version. We will also assume for simplicity that all the bins have size 1.

The Problem   Let $x_1, x_2, ..., x_n$ be a set of real numbers each between 0 and 1; partition the numbers into as few subsets as possible such that the sum of numbers in each subset is at most 1.

The one-dimensional bin packing problem arises, for example, in memory-management problems in which there are requests for many different-sized blocks of memory, and the blocks need to be allocated from several large chunks of available memory. Bin packing is an NP-complete problem (Exercise 11.8).

One heuristic for this problem is to put x_1 in the first bin, and then, for each i, to put x_i in the first bin that has room for it, or to start a new bin if there is no room in any of the used bins. This algorithm is called the **first fit** algorithm. First fit is not "too bad" in the worst case, as is shown in the next theorem.

□ Theorem 11.10

The first fit algorithm requires at most 2OPT bins, where OPT is the minimum number of bins.

Proof: First fit cannot leave two bins less than half full; otherwise, the items in the second bin could be placed in the first bin. Therefore, the number of bins used is no more than twice the sum of the sizes of all items (rounded up). The theorem follows from the fact that the number of bins in the best solution cannot be less than the sum of all the sizes (in which case all items are perfectly packed).   □

It turns out that the bound given by Theorem 11.10 is quite conservative. The constant of 2 in the theorem can be reduced to 1.7, by a much more complicated analysis. The 1.7 constant is tight, since there exist cases in which first fit requires 1.7 times the optimal.

First fit can be improved with the following simple modification. The worst case occurs when many small numbers appear at the beginning. Instead of placing the numbers in the bins in the order they appear, we sort them first in decreasing order, and then use first fit. This modified algorithm is called **decreasing first fit**, and, in the worst case, its solution comes within a constant of about 1.22 from the optimal (we omit the proof).

□ Theorem 11.11

The decreasing first fit algorithm requires at most $\dfrac{11}{9}$ OPT $+ 4$ bins, where OPT is the minimum number of bins.   □

This constant is also tight. First fit and decreasing first fit are both simple heuristics. There are other methods leading to better constants. In most cases, the analysis is complicated.

The strategies we described are typical of heuristics algorithms. They present natural approaches corresponding to what one would probably do by hand. We have seen many times, however, that straightforward approaches can perform quite poorly for large inputs. Therefore, it is very important to analyze the performance of these algorithms.

Euclidean Traveling Salesman

The **traveling salesman problem (TSP)**, is an important problem with many applications. We discuss here a variation of TSP with the additional constraint that the weights correspond to Euclidean distances:

> **The Problem** Let $C_1, C_2, ..., C_n$ be a set of points in the plane corresponding to the location of n cities; find a minimum-distance Hamiltonian cycle (traveling salesman tour) among them.

The problem is still NP-hard, but we will see that the Euclidean assumption helps in designing an approximation algorithm for the problem. (We can relax this assumption somewhat by assuming only that the distances satisfy the **triangle inequality**, which states that the direct distance between any two points is shorter than any route through other points.)

The algorithm starts by computing the minimum-cost spanning tree (here, cost = distance), which is a much easier problem (see Section 7.6). We claim that the cost of the tree is no more than the length of the best TSP tour. This is so because a TSP tour is a cycle containing all vertices; therefore, removing any edge from a TSP tour makes it a spanning tree, whose cost is thus at least that of the minimum-cost spanning tree.

A spanning tree, however, does not correspond directly to a TSP tour. We need to modify it. First, consider the circuit that consists of a depth-first search traversal of the tree (starting from any city), and includes an edge in the opposite direction whenever the search backtracks. (This circuit corresponds, for example, to traversing a tree-shaped gallery, with exhibits on both sides of every hall, by always going to the right.) Every edge will be traversed exactly twice, so the cost of this circuit is twice the cost of the minimum-cost spanning tree, which is no more than twice the cost of the minimum TSP tour. We can now convert this circuit into a TSP tour by taking direct routes instead of always backtracking (see Fig. 11.9). That is, instead of backtracking using the same edge, we go directly to the first new vertex. The assumption that the distances are Euclidean is important, because it guarantees that the direct route between any two cities is always at least as good as the nondirect route. The length of the resulting TSP tour is thus still no more than twice the length of the minimum TSP tour, although it is often less than that.

Complexity The running time of this algorithm is dominated by the running time of the minimum-cost spanning tree algorithm, which, in the case of Euclidean graphs, is $O(n \log n)$ (see, for example, Preparata and Shamos [1985]).

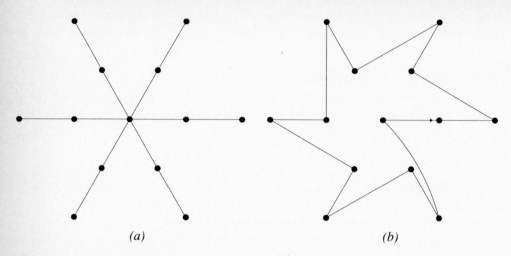

Figure 11.9 (a) A spanning tree. (b) A TSP tour obtained from the tree by starting at the middle point, and going right first.

Improvement

The algorithm we have just described can be improved in the following way. The "sloppiest" part of the algorithm is the conversion from the tree traversal into a TSP tour. Another way to look at this conversion is that it builds an Eulerian circuit on top of the tree, by repeating each edge twice. We then obtain the TSP tour by taking shortcuts from the Eulerian circuit. We can convert the tree into an Eulerian graph more effectively. An Eulerian graph must include only even-degree nodes. Consider all the odd-degree nodes in the tree. There must be an even number of them (otherwise, the total sum of all degrees would be odd, which is impossible, since this sum is exactly twice the number of edges). If we add enough edges to the tree to make the degrees of all nodes even, then we get an Eulerian graph. Since the TSP tour will consist of the Eulerian circuit (with some shortcuts) we would like to minimize the length of the additional edges. Let's abstract the problem.

We are given a tree in the plane and we want to add edges to it, minimizing their total length, such that the resulting graph is Eulerian. We must add at least one edge to each vertex of odd degree. Let's try to add exactly one. Suppose that there are $2k$ vertices of odd degree. If we add k edges, each connecting two odd-degree vertices, then all vertices will have even degree. The problem thus becomes a *matching* problem. We want to find a minimum-length matching that covers all odd-degree vertices. Finding a minimum-weight perfect matching can be done in $O(n^3)$ for general graphs (see Gabow [1976] or Lawler [1976]). There is a recent algorithm, due to Vaidya [1988], that works for the special case of Euclidean distances in time $O(n^{2.5} (\log n)^4)$. (Whether this is a better algorithm in practice is not clear.) The final TSP tour is then obtained from the Eulerian graph (which includes the minimum-length spanning tree plus the minimum-length matching) by taking shortcuts. The TSP tour obtained by this algorithm for the tree in Fig. 11.10 is given in Fig. 11.11.

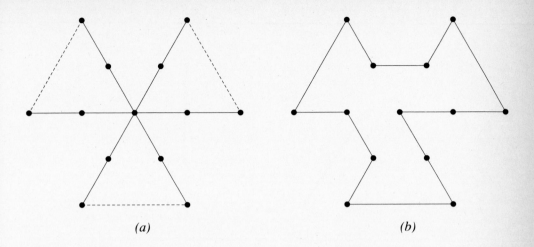

(a)   *(b)*

Figure 11.11 The minimum Eulerian circuit and its corresponding TSP tour. (a) The spanning tree plus the matching. (b) The tour obtained from the Eulerian circuit.

□ Theorem 11.12

The improved algorithm produces a TSP tour whose length is at most 1.5 times the length of the minimum TSP tour.

Proof: We will ignore the shortcuts (since there may not be any in the worst case), and will concentrate on the length of the Eulerian circuit. The circuit consists of the tree and the matching. We have already seen that the length of the tree is at most the length of a minimum TSP tour; hence, it is sufficient to prove that the length of the matching is at most half the length of a minimum TSP tour. Let Q be a minimum TSP tour. Q is a cycle containing all vertices. Let D be the set of odd-degree vertices in T. We can obtain two disjoint matchings of D such that the sum of their lengths is no more than that of Q in the following way (see Fig. 11.12). We start with an arbitrary vertex v of D and match it to a vertex of D that is its closest neighbor clockwise in Q. We then continue matching in a clockwise direction. If the matched vertices are not neighbors in Q, then the distance between them is no more than the length of the path connecting them in Q (by the triangle property). This process gives us one matching. The second matching is obtained by repeating the same process counterclockwise. The sum of the lengths of both matchings is at most the length of Q, as is shown in Figure 11.12. But, since M was a minimum-weight matching of D, its length is at most half the length of Q.   □

Finding a minimum-weight perfect matching takes much longer than finding a minimum-cost spanning tree, but it results in a better bound. It is still an open problem whether it is possible either to improve the constant of 1.5, or to find a faster algorithm achieving this constant. This algorithm illustrates one of the main characteristics of this type of algorithm: We abstract an easier problem — or relax some parts of the original problem — and then design the heuristic accordingly.

Figure 11.12 Two matchings whose sum is at most that of the TSP tour.

11.6 Summary

The previous chapters should have generated some deserved optimism about our ability to design good algorithms. This chapter should bring us closer to reality. There are many important problems that unfortunately cannot be solved with elegant, efficient algorithms. We have to be able to recognize these problems and to solve them with a less than optimal solution. When a problem is given to us, we have two possible lines of attack. We can try to use the techniques introduced in the previous chapters to solve the problem, or we can try to use the techniques introduced in this chapter to show that the problem is NP-complete. To avoid making many wrong turns before we take the right approach, we need to develop an intuition for the difficulty of problems.

Bibliographic Notes and Further Reading

The notion of NP-completeness was introduced in the seminal paper of Cook [1971] (a similar result was discovered in the Soviet Union independently by Levin [1973]). Karp [1972] presented a list of 24 important NP-complete problems (some of which are included in Section 11.4). Both Cook and Karp received the Turing award in part due to this work, and their Turing award lectures were published in Cook [1983], and in Karp [1986]. Several other notable classes of problems that are not known to be in P have been studied. One such class is co-NP, which contains the complements of all problems in NP. For example, the problem of deciding whether a Boolean expression is always false belongs to co-NP. The reason co-NP is different from NP is that the definition of acceptance of languages by a nondeterministic algorithm is asymmetric; there are different requirements for accepting and for rejecting an input. Another important class is PSPACE, which contains all problems that can be solved using polynomial space. It turns out that nondeterminism does not add more power when an algorithm is limited to polynomial space [Savitch 1970]. In other words, any problem that can be solved in polynomial space by a nondeterministic algorithm can also be solved in polynomial space by a deterministic algorithm. The generalized HEX game is an example of a problem that is *complete* for PSPACE (Even and Tarjan [1976]), where completeness is defined similarly to the way it is defined for the class NP, except that the reductions can use polynomial space. There is a hierarchy of classes between P and PSPACE called the **polynomial-time hierarchy**. It is important to note that at present *there is no proof that any of the classes mentioned above is different from P!* We do not know of any problem that belongs to PSPACE and does not belong to P. There are, however, problems that are known to require exponential time and space (Meyer and Stockmeyer [1972]), or even more (Fischer and Rabin [1974]).

There are several problems that are not known to be either in P or in NP-complete. The most notable ones are the **graph isomorphism** and **primality testing**. Graph isomorphism can be solved in polynomial times for many special cases (see, for example, Luks [1982]), but the general problem is still open. Rabin [1976] and Solovay and Strassen [1977] present Monte Carlo probabilistic algorithms for primality testing. (These algorithms determine that a number is prime with very little error probability, and they make no error when they determine that a number is not a prime.) Goldwasser and Killian [1986] present a Las Vegas probabilistic algorithm that tests primality, without errors, whose expected running time is polynomial. Another seemingly simple problem that is still open is the even-cycle problem, which is to determine whether a given directed graph contains a (simple) even-length cycle (see Klee, Ladner, and Manber [1984]). A wealth of information about NP-completeness and related subjects can be found in Garey and Johnson [1979] and in an NP-completeness column by Johnson that has been appearing in the *Journal of Algorithms* since 1981. A natural question to ask is whether all problems in NP are either NP-complete or are in P. This question was partially answered by Ladner [1975] who proved that, unless P = NP, there are infinitely many classes in between.

An algorithm that runs in polynomial time on the average for the Hamiltonian cycle problem is described in Angluin and Valiant [1979], and one for satisfiability is described in Purdom and Brown [1985b]. An approximation algorithm for the weighted vertex-cover problem is given in Bar-Yehuda and Even [1981]. The algorithm finds a vertex cover whose weight is at most twice that of the minimum-weight cover. Gusfield and Pitt [1986] present a more intuitive explanation of this algorithm. Heuristics for coloring graphs with k colors (for fixed k) are given by Brélaz [1979], and by Turner [1988]. These heuristics are proven successful for "almost all" graphs (see Turner [1988] for a precise definition). In fact, Wilf [1984] proved that the average size of the simple backtrack tree for graph k-coloring (for a fixed k) is a constant independent of n. (It is less than 200 for $k = 3$, and is 1 million for $k = 5$.) However, it is likely that the good performance of these algorithms are due more to the definition of the *average* than to the strength of the algorithms (see, for example, Franco [1986]). The best known guaranteed bound for approximate graph coloring is given by Wigderson [1983]. Backtrack techniques are described in Golomb and Baumert [1965] (see also Bitner and Reingold [1975] and Horowitz and Sahni [1978].) Knuth [1975] describes a technique for estimating the running time of backtrack programs. A general discussion on heuristics is given by Pearl [1984].

The bounds on the performance of first fit and decreasing first fit given in Section 11.5.2 are proved in Johnson et al. [1974]. For another heuristic that comes very close to an optimal solution of the bin-packing problem, see Karmarkar and Karp [1982].

The traveling salesman problem is probably the most studied NP-complete problem in terms of proposed solutions. An approximation algorithm for the general problem is given by Lin and Kernighan [1973]. The algorithm achieving the bound of 1.5 for the Euclidean problem, which is the best bound currently known for a polynomial algorithm, is due to Christofides [1976]. A book edited by Lawler, Lenstra, Rinnooy Kan, and Shmoys [1985] contains 12 articles covering most aspects of this problem, including heuristics and their analysis, branch-and-bound algorithms, special cases, and applications.

Drill Exercises

You can complete these exercises using only the NP-complete problems discussed in the text or in other exercises from this chapter.

11.1   Prove that all problems in P are polynomially equivalent according to the definition given in Section 11.2.

11.2   Prove that the definition of how a nondeterministic algorithm recognizes a language does not allow one algorithm to recognize two different languages.

11.3   Consider the following algorithm to determine whether a graph has a clique of size k. First, we generate all subsets of the vertices containing exactly k vertices. There are $O(n^k)$ subsets altogether. Then, we check whether any of the subgraphs induced by these subsets is complete. Why is this not a polynomial-time algorithm for the clique problem, which implies that $P = NP$?

11.4   Write the 3SAT expression that is obtained from the reduction of SAT to 3SAT (given in Section 11.4.3) for the expression

$$(x + y + \bar{z} + w + u + \bar{v}) \cdot (\overline{x + \bar{y} + z} + \bar{w} + u + v) \cdot (x + \bar{y} + \bar{z} + w + u + \bar{v}) \cdot (x + \bar{y}).$$

11.5   Draw the graph that is obtained from the reduction of SAT to the clique problem (given in Section 11.4.4) for the expression

$$(x + \bar{y} + z) \cdot (\overline{x + y + z}) \cdot (\overline{x} + y + z) \cdot (x + \bar{y} + \bar{z}).$$

11.6   Draw the graph that is obtained from the reduction of 3SAT to the 3-coloring problem (given in Section 11.4.5) for the expression

$$(x + \bar{y} + z) \cdot (\overline{x + y + \bar{z}}) \cdot (\overline{x} + y + z).$$

11.7   Prove that the knapsack problem is NP-complete.

11.8   Prove that the bin packing problem is NP-complete.

11.9   Pose the 3-coloring problem as an integer linear program.

Creative Exercises

You can complete these exercises using only the NP-complete problems discussed in the text or in other exercises from this chapter.

11.10 Prove that the following problem is NP-complete: Given an undirected graph $G = (V, E)$ and an integer k, determine whether G contains a spanning tree T such that each vertex in T has degree $\leq k$.

11.11 Prove that the vertex-cover problem remains NP-complete even if all the vertices in the graph are restricted to have even degree.

11.12 Consider again the problem of finding large induced subgraphs discussed in Chapter 5. Suppose that, instead of the requirement that each vertex in the induced subgraph has degree $\geq d$, we require that its degree be $\leq d$. Here is the formulation of the problem in terms of a decision problem. Given an undirected graph $G = (V, E)$, and two integer parameters d and k, determine whether G contains an induced subgraph H with at least k vertices, such that the degree of each vertex in H is $\leq d$. Prove that this problem is NP-complete.

11.13 Prove that the following problem is NP-complete: Given an undirected connected graph $G = (V, E)$ and an integer k, determine whether G contains a clique of size k *and* an independent set of size k.

11.14 Prove that the following problem is NP-complete: Given an undirected graph $G = (V, E)$ and an integer k, determine whether G contains a subset of k vertices whose induced subgraph is acyclic.

11.15 Let E be a CNF expression such that each variable x appears exactly once as x and exactly once as $\bar{x}$. Either find a polynomial-time algorithm to determine whether such expressions are satisfiable or prove that this problem is NP-complete.

11.16 Prove that the following variation of 3SAT, called 1-in-3SAT, is NP-complete. The input is the same as the one for 3SAT. The problem is to determine whether there exists a satisfying assignment such that in every clause *exactly* one of the 3 variables is true.

11.17 Prove that 2-in-4SAT is NP-complete: The input is a Boolean expression in CNF with exactly 4 variables per clause, and the problem is to determine whether there exists a satisfying assignment such that in every clause exactly 2 of the 4 variables are true. (Hint: Use Exercise 11.16.)

*11.18 The input is again a Boolean expression in CNF. The problem is to determine whether there exists a satisfying assignment such that every clause contains an *odd* number of variables whose values are 1. For example, if the input is a 3SAT input, then we are looking for assignments such that, in every clause, either 1 or 3 variables have value 1.

(Another way to look at this problem is that the *or* operations are replaced with *exclusive or* operations.) This may seem like another variation of the problems in Exercises 11.16 and 11.17, but in fact this problem can be solved in polynomial time! Find a polynomial-time algorithm for it.

11.19 The input is an undirected *regular* graph (i.e., a graph in which all vertices have the same degree). Prove that the clique problem remains NP-complete for regular graphs.

11.20 The **exact cover by 3-sets** (X3C) problem is the following. The input is a set S with $3n$ elements and a collection of subsets of S, $S_1, S_2, ..., S_k$, each containing exactly three elements. The problem is to determine whether there exists a subcollection of subsets $S_{i_1}, S_{i_2}, ..., S_{i_n}$ such that each element of S is contained in exactly one subset S_{i_j}. Prove that X3C is NP-complete.

11.21 Prove that the following problem is NP-complete: Given an undirected graph $G = (V, E)$ with $3n$ vertices, determine whether the vertices of G can be partitioned into n groups, such that each group contains three elements, each connected to each other. In other words, the question is to determine whether the graph can be partitioned into n triangles.

11.22 Let $G = (V, U, E)$ be a bipartite graph such that V is the set of vertices on one side, U is the set of vertices on the other side, and E is the set of edges connecting them. V corresponds to a set of *machines* and U to a set of *parts*. A machine v_i is connected to a part u_j if the machine is used to work on that part. Suppose that a room can accommodate at most K machines and unlimited number of parts (for simplicity, we assume that all machines have the same size). We assume that we have as many rooms as needed, but we want to minimize the movements of parts from one room to another. Each edge (v_i, p_j) is associated with a cost $c(v_i, p_j)$, which is the cost of moving part u_j to machine v_i if the part and the machine are not in the same room. We define the cost of a partition of machines and parts into rooms as the sum of the costs of the edges connecting parts to machines that are not in the same room. Prove that the following problem is NP-complete: Given the graph G, the parameter K, and another parameter C, determine whether it is possible to partition the machines and parts into rooms with cost $\leq C$. (In other words, the set of vertices should be partitioned into subsets, each with at most K vertices from V, such that the sum of the costs associated with the edges that connect vertices in two different subsets does not exceed C.)

11.23 Let S be a set, and $C = \{C_1, C_2, ..., C_k\}$ be a collection of subsets of S each with four elements. Two subsets of S are said to be *connected* if they contain a common element. A collection C is said to be a *cycle* if C_i is connected to C_{i+1} for all i, $1 \leq i \leq k-1$, and C_1 is connected to C_k. An subcollection $C' \subseteq C$ is called *acyclic* if it does not contain a cycle. Prove that the following problem is NP-complete: Determine whether a given collection C contains an acyclic subcollection C' such that (1) every two subsets in C' have at most one element in common, and (2) every element of S is included in at least one subset of C'.

11.24 Assume that the Hamiltonian path problem for undirected graphs is NP-complete. Prove that the Hamiltonian cycle problem for undirected graphs is also NP-complete. (Both problems are defined in Section 11.4.)

11.25 The input is an undirected graph $G = (V, E)$ and two distinguished vertices v and w in G. Prove that there is no polynomial-time algorithm to determine whether G contains a Hamiltonian path whose end vertices are v and w unless P = NP.

11.26 Consider again the problem of determining whether a graph $G = (V, E)$ contains a Hamiltonian path with given end vertices v and w (see Exercise 11.25). Let G' be the graph obtained by adding two new vertices $\bar{v}$ and $\bar{w}$ and two new edges $(v, \bar{v})$ and $(w, \bar{w})$. If G' contains a Hamiltonian path, then its two end vertices must be $\bar{v}$ and $\bar{w}$. Therefore, such a path corresponds to a Hamiltonian path in G with the end vertices v and w. What have we just proved?

11.27 Prove that graph k-coloring is NP-complete. The problem is to determine, given an undirected graph $G = (V, E)$ *and* an integer k, whether G can be colored with at most k colors.

11.28 Prove that, if there is a polynomial-time approximation algorithm that can color any graph with less than 4/3 times the minimal number of colors required to color that graph, then P=NP.

11.29 Prove that the following problem, called **feedback edge set**, is NP-complete: Given a directed graph $G = (V, E)$ and an integer parameter k, determine whether G contains a set F of at most k edges such that every directed cycle in G contains at least one edge from F.

11.30 Let Q be some NP-complete problem involving undirected graphs. Suppose that you find a polynomial-time algorithm that solves Q for some particular restricted class of graphs (e.g., planar graphs, graphs containing perfect matchings, Eulerian graphs). Does this algorithm imply that all NP-complete problems involving undirected graphs can be solved in polynomial time when restricted to that class?

11.31 Let $G = (V, E)$ be an undirected graph, and let $(v_1, w_1), (v_2, w_2), ..., (v_k, w_k)$ be k pairs of distinct vertices of G. Prove that the following problem is NP-complete: Determine whether there exist k paths in G such that path i connects v_i to w_i, and all paths are vertex disjoint.

11.32 Let $G = (V, E)$ be an undirected graph, such that each vertex is associated with some task. Two vertices are connected if the corresponding tasks *cannot* be performed at the same time (e.g., they need the same resource). This is the only limit on concurrency. Any set of tasks such that no two of them are connected can be performed in one step. Prove that the following problem is NP-complete: Given a graph $G = (V, E)$, and an integer parameter k, determine whether all corresponding tasks can be performed in at most k steps.

*11.33 Let $G = (V, E)$ be an undirected graph such that the edges incident to each vertex are ordered in a cyclic order. There is no relationship between ordering at different nodes. Suppose further that G is Eulerian. The problem is to find an Eulerian tour covering G that satisfies the following "noncrossing" property: If the tour enters a vertex v at an edge e, then the next edge in the tour must be adjacent to e in the cyclic order imposed on the edges incident to v (from either side of e). One way to view this property is to look at a road map. The goal is to travel through all the edges (road segments) such that an intersection (vertex) is never crossed except from one edge to its neighbor. Prove that determining whether such an Eulerian tour exists for a given graph and cyclic orderings is NP-complete. (The problem remains NP-complete for planar graphs, but the proof is more difficult.)

11.34 Show an example in which the simple backtracking algorithm described in Section 11.5 for 3-coloring a graph results in exponential number of nodes.

11.35 The following is a simple heuristic for finding a vertex cover. In each step of the algorithm, the vertex of highest degree (ties are broken arbitrarily) is added to the cover, then it is removed from the graph together with all its incident edges. The algorithm terminates when no more edges remain. Since an edge is removed only after a vertex incident to it is included in the cover, the algorithm indeed finds a vertex cover. This is a greedy algorithm since it always selects the vertex with the highest "payoff." The worst-case behavior of this algorithm is not very good. Show an example of a graph and an order of execution of this algorithm that leads to a vertex cover with more than twice the number of vertices of the minimum cover.

11.36 Show an instance of the bin packing problem for which the first-fit algorithm gives a solution using 5/3 times more bins than the optimal solution.

11.37 You are a traveling salesman of the 1980s. Your boss has asked you to visit n cities, and you are planning your flight itinerary. You do not care about the cost of travel — the company is going to pay your expenses anyway. What you want to maximize is the benefits you will receive as a frequent flyer! In other words, you want to *maximize* the length of the entire trip. You can assume that the mileage computed by the airlines is actual mileage, so this is an Euclidean problem. Also, do not worry about choosing different airlines. You just want to maximize the total mileage. Prove that this problem is NP-complete, and suggest approximation algorithms for it.

11.38 Let $C_1, C_2, ..., C_n$ be a set of courses offered at a certain university, and let $t_1, t_2, ..., t_n$ be the time intervals (not necessarily disjoint) during which the courses are offered. For example, t_1 may be Tuesday from 10:00 to 11:00, t_2 may be Tuesday from 10:30 to 12:00, and so on. Your job is to assign classrooms to the courses. The only requirement is that no two courses overlap at the same time at the same room. The goal is to use the minimal number of classrooms that satisfies the requirement.

a. Reduce this problem to a coloring problem, and design an efficient algorithm to solve it.

b. Discuss why your solution does not imply that P = NP (even though coloring is an NP-complete problem).

CHAPTER 12

PARALLEL ALGORITHMS

A person with one watch knows what time it is;
a person with two watches is never sure.

Anon

In the first place, it is to be remarked that, however small
the republic may be, the representatives must be raised to a
certain number, in order to guard against the cabals of the
few; and that, however large it may be, they must be limited
to a certain number, in order to guard against the
confusion of the multitude.

James Madison, 1787

12.1 Introduction

The subject of parallel computing has moved from the exotic to mainstream computer science within a decade. It is expanding very fast (even relative to other areas of computer science). There are numerous types of parallel computers in operation, ranging from 2 to 65,536 processors. The differences between the various existing parallel machines, even as far as the naive user is concerned, are major. We can no longer adopt one ''generic'' model of computation and hope that it adapts to all parallel computers. Designing parallel algorithms, analyzing them, and proving them correct is much more difficult than the corresponding steps for sequential algorithms.

We cannot hope in this short chapter to cover all (or even most) areas in parallel computing. We present a variety of examples using different models of computation and different techniques. We try to give the flavor of parallel algorithms and to explore the difficulties in designing them. We start with some common characteristics. We then briefly describe the main models of parallel computing used in this chapter, and follow with examples of algorithms and techniques.

The main measures of complexity for sequential algorithms are running time and space utilization. These measures are important in parallel algorithms as well, but we must also worry about other resources. One important resource is the number of processors. There are problems that are inherently sequential, and they cannot be "parallelized" even if an infinite number of processors is available. Most other problems, however, can be parallelized to a degree. The more processors we use — up to a certain limit — the faster the algorithm becomes. It is important to study the limitations of parallel algorithms, and to be able to characterize the problems that have very fast parallel solutions. Since the number of processors is limited, however, it is also important to use the processors effectively. Another important issue is communication among the processors. Generally, it takes longer to exchange data between two processors than it does to perform simple operations on the data. Furthermore, some processors may be "close" to one another, whereas other processors may be farther apart. Therefore, it is important to minimize communication, and to arrange it in an effective way. Yet another important issue is synchronization, which is a major problem for parallel algorithms that run on independent machines connected by some communication network. Such algorithms are usually called **distributed algorithms**. For lack of space, we will not consider distributed algorithms in this book. We discuss only models that assume full synchronization.

Some models of parallel computation restrict all processors to execute the exact same instruction in each step. Parallel computers that follow this restriction are called **SIMD** (Single-Instruction Multiple-Data) machines. The **connection machine** is a prominent example of such computers. Parallel computers in which each processor can execute a different program are called **MIMD** (Multiple-Instruction Multiple-Data) machines. Unless specified otherwise, we will assume the MIMD model.

12.2 Models of Parallel Computation

A comprehensive survey of parallel machine models is beyond the scope of this book. We mention only a few major models, with emphasis on those that are used in this chapter. We include, in this section, some general discussion and definitions that apply to many models. Each of the following sections covers one type of model, and includes a more detailed description of the model and examples of algorithms for it.

We denote the running time of an algorithm by $T(n, p)$, where n is the input size and p is the number of processors. The ratio $S(p) = T(n, 1)/T(n, p)$ is called the **speedup** of the algorithm. A parallel algorithm is most effective when $S(p) = p$, in which case we say that the algorithm achieves a **perfect speedup**. The value of $T(n, 1)$ should be taken from the *best* known sequential algorithm. An important measure of the utilization of the processors is the **efficiency** of a parallel algorithm, which is defined as

$$E(n, p) = \frac{S(p)}{p} = \frac{T(n, 1)}{pT(n, p)}.$$

The efficiency is the ratio of the time used by one processor (with a sequential algorithm) and the *total time* used by p processors. (The total time is the actual elapsed time multiplied by the number of processors.) The efficiency indicates the percentage of the processors' time that is not wasted, compared to the sequential algorithm. If $E(n, p) = 1$, then the amount of work done by all processors throughout the execution of the algorithm is equal to the amount of work required by the sequential algorithm. In this case, we get the optimal use of the processors. Obtaining such an optimal efficiency is rare, because most of the time the parallel algorithm introduces some overhead that was not required by the corresponding sequential algorithm. One of our goals is to maximize the efficiency.

When we design a parallel algorithm we could fix p, according to the number of processors available to us, and try to minimize $T(n, p)$. But, doing so would potentially require a new algorithm whenever the number of processors changes. It is more desirable to find an algorithm that works for as many values of p as possible. We discuss next how to translate an algorithm that works for a certain value of p to algorithms for smaller values of p, without changing the efficiency significantly. In general, we can modify an algorithm with $T(n, p) = X$ to an algorithm with $T(n, p/k) \approx kX$, for any constant $k > 1$. In other words, we can use a factor of k less processors running for a factor of k more time. We construct the modified algorithm by replacing each step of the original algorithm with k steps in which one processor *emulates* the execution of one step of k processors. This principle cannot be applied to all situations. For example, k may not divide p, the algorithm may depend on a certain interconnection pattern of the processors (as discussed in Section 12.4), or the decision concerning which processors to emulate may require computation time. However, this principle, called the **parallelism folding principle,** is quite general and useful. It shows that we can reduce the number of processors without changing the efficiency significantly. If, for example, the original algorithm (which was designed for a large p) exhibits a good speedup, then we can obtain algorithms achieving about the same speedup for any smaller value of p. Therefore, we should try to get the best speedup with the maximal number of processors, provided that the efficiency is good (i.e., close to 1). Then, if we have fewer processors, we can still use the same algorithm. On the other hand, parallel algorithms with small efficiency are useful only for a large number of processors. For example, suppose that we have an algorithm with $T(n, 1) = n$ and $T(n, n) = \log_2 n$, which implies that the speedup $S(n) = n/\log_2 n$ — a very impressive speedup — and the efficiency $E(n, n) = 1/\log_2 n$. Suppose now that the number of processors available to us is $p = 256$, and that $n = 1024$. The running time of the parallel algorithm is $T(1024, 256) = 4\log_2 1024 = 40$ (assuming that folding is possible), which is a speedup of about 25 over the sequential algorithm. On the other hand, if $p = 16$, then the running time would be 640, which is not a good speedup (less than 2 with 16 processors).

The various models of parallel computation differ mainly in the way the processors communicate and synchronize. We will consider only models that assume full synchronization, and concentrate on different communication paradigms. The **shared-memory** models assume that there is a random-access shared memory, such that any processor can access any variable with unit cost. This assumption of unit-cost access regardless of the number of processors or the size of the memory is unrealistic, but it is a good first approximation. The shared-memory models differ in the way they handle access conflicts. We discuss several different alternatives in Section 12.3.

Shared memory is usually the easiest way to model communication, but it is the most difficult model to implement in hardware. Other models assume that the processors are connected through an **interconnection network**. An interconnection network can be represented by a graph, such that the vertices correspond to the processors and two vertices are connected if the corresponding processors have a direct link between them. Each processor usually has a local memory that it can access quickly. Communication is done through messages, which may have to traverse several links to arrive at their destinations. Therefore, the speed of the communication depends on the distance between the communicating processors. Many different graphs have been studied as interconnection networks. We will mention several popular ones in Section 12.4. Parallel computers based on interconnection networks with message passing are sometimes called **multicomputers**.

Another model that we discuss is that of **systolic computation**. A systolic architecture resembles an assembly line. The data move through the processors in a rhythmic fashion, and very simple operations are performed on them. Instead of having to access a shared (or nonshared) memory, the processors receive their input from their neighbors, operate on it, and pass it on. Systolic algorithms are discussed in Section 12.5.

A basic theoretical model that we will use only for illustration purposes is that of a **circuit**. A circuit is a directed acyclic graph in which the vertices correspond to simple operations and the edges show the movement of the operands. For example, a Boolean circuit is one in which all indegrees are at most 2 and all operations are Boolean operations (*or*, *and*, and *not*). There are designated vertices for input (with indegree of 0), and for output (with outdegree of 0). The depth of a circuit is the longest path from an input to an output. The depth corresponds to the parallel running time.

12.3 Algorithms for Shared-Memory Machines

A shared-memory computer consists of several **processors** and a **shared memory**. We use only fully synchronized algorithms in this section. We assume that the computation consists of *steps*. In each step, each processor performs an operation on the data it possesses, reads from the shared memory, or writes into the shared memory. (In practice, each processor may also have local memory, but we assume that all memory is global.) The shared-memory models differ in the way they handle memory conflicts. The Exclusive-Read Exclusive-Write (EREW) model does not allow more than one processor to access the same memory location at the same time. The Concurrent-Read Exclusive-Write (CREW) model allows several processors to read from the same memory location at the same time, but only one processor can write. Finally, the Concurrent-Read Concurrent-Write (CRCW) model poses no restrictions on memory conflicts.

The EREW and CREW models are well defined, but it is not clear what is the result of two processors writing at the same time to the same location. There are several alternatives to handle concurrent writes. The weakest CRCW model — and the only

CRCW model we utilize in this book — allows several processors to write to the same location at the same time only if they all write the same thing. If two processors attempt to write different values to the same location at the same time, the algorithm halts. Surprisingly, as we will see in Section 12.3.2, this feature is very powerful. Another alternative is to assume that the processors are labeled, and that, when several processors write to the same location at the same time, the highest-labeled processor succeeds. Yet another possible assumption is that an arbitrary processor succeeds.

12.3.1 Parallel Addition

We start with a simple example of a parallel algorithm, developed by induction, for a problem that looks inherently sequential at first glance.

The Problem   Find the sum of two n-bit binary numbers.

The regular sequential algorithm starts at the least significant bits, and adds two bits at a time with a possible carry. It seems that we cannot be sure of the outcome of the ith step until the two $i-1$ least significant bits are added, since there may or may not be a carry. Nevertheless, it is possible to design another algorithm.

We use induction on n. It will not help much to go from $n-1$ to n, since this implies an iterative sequential algorithm. The divide-and-conquer approach has a much better potential for parallel algorithms, since it may be possible to solve all smaller parts in parallel. Suppose that we divide the problem into two subproblems of size $n/2$ (we assume that n is a power of 2 for simplicity). We can find the sums of the two pairs in parallel. But we still have the problem of the carry. If the sum of the least significant pair has a carry, we have to change the sum of the most significant pair.

The key observation here is that there are only two possibilities — we either have a carry or we do not. Therefore, we can *strengthen the induction hypothesis* to include both cases. The modified problem is to find the sum of the two numbers with *and* without an initial carry. Suppose that we now solve this modified problem for both pairs. We get four numbers: L, L_C, R, and R_C, which correspond to the sum of the least significant pair with no initial carry, the same sum with an initial carry, and the corresponding sums for the most significant pair, respectively. For each of these sums, we also find whether it generates a carry. The final sum S, without initial carry, is L and either R or R_C, depending on whether L had a carry. The final sum S_C is the same as S, except that L is replaced by L_C.

We solve a problem of size n by two subproblems of size $n/2$ and a constant number of (conquer) steps. Since both subproblems can be solved in parallel — assuming that the processors can access different bits independently — we obtain the recurrence relation $T(n, n) = T(n/2, n/2) + O(1)$, which implies that $T(n, n) = O(\log n)$. Furthermore, since both subproblems are completely independent, this algorithm assumes only the EREW model. This algorithm may not be the best one for parallel addition (see, for example, Ladner and Fischer [1980]), but it is a good example of an easy parallelization of an algorithm. Once it becomes clear that the problem can be solved very quickly in parallel, the solution can be further improved.

12.3.2 Maximum-Finding Algorithms

> **The Problem**   Find the maximum among n distinct numbers, given in an array.

We solve this problem for two different shared-memory models — EREW and CRCW. The algorithms for both models use techniques that are used for many other problems.

EREW Model

The straightforward sequential algorithm for finding the maximum requires $n-1$ comparisons. We can think of a comparison as a game played between the two numbers, with the larger of the two winning. The maximum-finding problem is thus equivalent to running a tournament with the winner being the maximum of the whole set. An efficient way to run a tournament in parallel is to use a tree. The players are divided into pairs for the first round (with possibly one player sitting out, in case of an odd number of players), all the winners are again divided into pairs, and so on, until the finals. The number of rounds is $\lceil \log_2 n \rceil$. We can obtain a parallel algorithm from the tournament by assigning a processor to every game (think of the processor as the referee of the game). We have to ensure, however, that each processor knows the two competing numbers. This can be arranged by putting the winner of the game in the larger indexed position of the two players. That is, if the game is played between x_i and x_j such that $j > i$, then the maximal of x_i and x_j is put in position j. In the first round, processor P_i compares x_{2i-1} to x_{2i} ($1 \le i \le n/2$), and exchanges them if necessary; in the second round, P_i compares x_{4i-2} to x_{4i} ($1 \le i \le n/4$), and so on. Since each number is involved in only one game at a time, an EREW model is sufficient. The running time of this simple algorithm is clearly $O(\log n)$. Let's try now to minimize the number of processors.

The algorithm we just presented requires $\lfloor n/2 \rfloor$ processors, and we have $T(n, \lfloor n/2 \rfloor) = \lceil \log_2 n \rceil$. Since the sequential algorithm achieves $T(n, 1) = n - 1$, the efficiency of the parallel algorithm is $E(n, n/2) \approx 1/\log_2 n$. If $n/2$ processors are available anyway (e.g., if the maximum-finding algorithm is a part of another algorithm that requires them), then this algorithm is simple and efficient. With some modifications, however, we can achieve a parallel time of $O(\log n)$ with $O(1)$ efficiency.

The total number of comparisons required for this algorithm is $n-1$, the same as the sequential algorithm. The reason for the low efficiency is that many processors are idle in later rounds. We can improve the efficiency by reducing the number of processors and performing load balancing in the following way. Suppose that we use only about $n/\log_2 n$ processors. We divide the input into $n/\log_2 n$ groups, with about $\log_2 n$ elements per group, and assign a group to each processor. In the first phase, each processor finds the maximum in its group, using the sequential algorithm that takes about $\log_2 n$ steps. It remains now to find the maximum among about $n/\log_2 n$ maximums, but there are now enough processors to use the tournament algorithm. The running time of this algorithm (assuming that n is a power of 2) is $T(n, \lceil n/\log_2 n \rceil) \approx 2\log_2 n$. The corresponding efficiency is $E(n) \approx \frac{1}{2}$. Next, we formalize the idea we just used for saving processors.

We call a parallel algorithm **static** if the assignment of processors to actions is predefined. We know apriori, for each step i of the algorithm and for each processor P_j, the operation and the operands P_j uses at step i. The maximum-finding algorithm, for example, is a static algorithm, because all the "games" are prearranged.

□ Lemma 12.1

If there exists an EREW static algorithm with $T(n, p) = O(t)$, such that the total number of steps (over all processors) is s, then there exists an EREW static algorithm with $T(n, s/t) = O(t)$.

(Notice that, if s is equal to the sequential complexity of the problem, then the modified algorithm has an efficiency of $O(1)$.)

Proof: Let a_i ($i = 1, 2, ..., t$) be the total number of steps performed by all processors in step i of the algorithm. We have $\sum_{i=1}^{t} a_i = s$. If $a_i \leq s/t$, then there are enough processors to perform step i, and we do not have to change it. Otherwise, we replace step i with $\lceil a_i/(s/t) \rceil$ steps in which the available s/t processors emulate the steps taken by the p processors in the original algorithm (following the folding principle). The total number of steps is now

$$\sum_{i=1}^{t} \left\lceil \frac{a_i}{(s/t)} \right\rceil \leq \sum_{i=1}^{t} \left(\frac{a_i \cdot t}{s} + 1 \right) = t + \frac{t}{s} \cdot \sum_{i=1}^{t} a_i = 2t.$$

Hence, the running time of the modified algorithm is still $O(t)$. □

Lemma 12.1 is known as **Brent's lemma** after Brent [1973] (which contains a proof of the same spirit of a more complicated case). Brent's lemma shows that, in some cases, the efficiency of a parallel algorithm depends mainly on the ratio between the total number of operations performed by all processors and the running time of the sequential algorithm.

We need the restriction to static algorithms because we must know which processors to emulate. Lemma 12.1 is valid for nonstatic algorithms as well, provided that the emulation can be done quickly. An example of a case where Lemma 12.1 is not valid is as follows. Suppose that there are n processors and n elements. After the first step, some of the processors decide (based on the results of the first step) to withdraw. The same thing happens after the second step, the third step, and so on. This algorithm is similar to the tournament algorithm, except that, in this case, we do not know which processors withdraw. If we try to emulate the remaining processors, say, after the first step, we need to know which of them are still active. But, it may require some computation time to find that out.

CRCW Model

It may seem at first that a parallel algorithm cannot find the maximum in less than $\log_2 n$ steps if only comparisons are used. But this is not so. The following algorithm, whose parallel running time is $O(1)$, illustrates the power of concurrent writes. We use the version of concurrent writes in which two or more processors can write to the same location at the same time only when they write the same thing.

We use $n(n-1)/2$ processors, and assign a processor P_{ij} to each *pair* $\{i, j\}$ of elements. We also allocate another shared variable v_i for each element x_i, and initialize v_i to 1. In the first step, each processor compares its two elements and writes a 0 in the shared variable associated with the smaller element. Since only one element is larger than all others, only one v_i remains 1 (see also Exercise 12.12). In the second step, the processors associated with the winner can determine that it is the winner and can announce this fact. This algorithm requires only two steps, independent of n; its efficiency, however, is very poor, since it requires $O(n^2)$ processors. We call this algorithm the *two-step algorithm*.

We can improve the efficiency of the two-step algorithm by using a method similar to the one for the EREW model. We divide the inputs into groups such that we can allocate enough processors to find the maximum of each group by the two-step algorithm. As the number of candidates declines, the number of available processors per candidate increases, and the group size can be increased. The two-step algorithm shows that, if the size of a group is k, then $k(k-1)/2$ processors are sufficient to find the group's maximum in constant time. Assume that we have n processors overall, and that n is a power of 2. In the first round, the size of each group is 2, and the maximum of each group can be found in one step. In the second round, only $n/2$ elements are left, and we still have n processors. If we set the size of each group to be 4, then we have $n/8$ groups, allowing us to allocate 8 processors per group. This is sufficient, since $4 \cdot (4-1)/2 = 6$. In the third round, we have $n/8$ remaining elements. Let's calculate the maximal group size that we can afford. If the group size is g, then the number of groups is $n/8g$, and there are $8g$ processors available per group. To use the two-step algorithm, we need $g(g-1)/2$ processors for a group of size g; therefore, we must have $g(g-1)/2 \le 8g$, which implies that $g \le 17$ (it is simpler to use $g = 16$). We leave it to the reader to verify that the size of the group can be *squared* in each round, leading to an algorithm that requires $O(\log \log n)$ rounds.

Although this algorithm is slightly slower that the two-step algorithm ($O(\log \log n)$ versus $O(1)$), its efficiency is much better. It is $O(1/\log \log n)$, versus $O(1/n)$ of the two-step algorithm. This technique has been called **divide and crush**, since we divide the input into groups of size small enough that we can "crush" them with lots of processors. This technique is not limited to the CRCW model.

12.3.3 The Parallel-Prefix Problem

The parallel-prefix problem is important because it serves as a major building block in the design of numerous parallel algorithms. Let $\bullet$ be an arbitrary *associative* binary operation — namely, it satisfies $x \bullet (y \bullet z) = (x \bullet y) \bullet z$ — which we will simply call *product*. For example, ● can represent addition, multiplication, or maximum of two numbers.

> **The Problem**   Given a sequence of numbers $x_1, x_2, ..., x_n$, compute the products $x_1 ● x_2 ● \cdots ● x_k$, for all k, such that $1 \le k \le n$.

We denote by $PR(i, j)$ the product $x_i ● x_{i+1} ● \cdots ● x_j$. Our goal is to compute $PR(1, k)$ for all k, $1 \le k \le n$. The sequential version of the prefix problem is trivial — we simply compute the prefixes in order. The parallel-prefix problem is not as easy to solve. The method we use is divide and conquer. As usual, we assume that n is a power of 2.

> **Induction hypothesis:** *We know how to solve the parallel-prefix problem for n/2 elements.*

The case of one element is trivial. The algorithm proceeds by dividing the input in half, and solving each half by induction. Thus, we obtain the values of $PR(1, k)$ and $PR(n/2+1, n/2+k)$, for all k, $1 \le k \le n/2$. The values for the first half can be used directly. The values $PR(1, m)$, for $n/2 < m \le n$ can be obtained by computing $PR(1, n/2)$ ● $PR(n/2+1, m)$. Both terms are known by induction (notice that we use the associativity of the operation). The algorithm is given in Fig. 12.1.

Complexity   The input is divided into two disjoint sets in each recursive call of the algorithm. Both subproblems can thus be solved in parallel under the EREW model. If we have n processors for the problem of size n, then one-half of them can be allocated to each subproblem. The combining step requires $n/2$ steps, and they can also be performed in parallel, but an CREW model is required because they all use $x[Middle]$. Although several processors must read $x[Middle]$ at the same time, they all write to distinct locations, so a CRCW model is not required. Overall, $T(n, n) = O(\log n)$, and $E(n, n) = O(1/\log n)$ (since the sequential algorithm clearly runs in $O(n)$ steps).

Unfortunately, we cannot improve the efficiency of this algorithm by using Brent's lemma. The total number of steps used in the algorithm is $O(n \log n)$. The waste comes from the second recursive call. A sequential algorithm can compute all the prefixes without the second recursive call. Therefore, if we want to improve the efficiency, we must improve the algorithm such that the total number of steps is reduced. We do that next. An EREW algorithm for this problem (with the same resource bounds) is the subject of Exercise 12.18.

Improving the Efficiency of Parallel Prefix

The trick is to use the same induction hypothesis, but to divide the input in a different way. Assume again that n is a power of 2 and that there are n processors. Let E denote the set of all x_is with i even. If we find the parallel prefixes of all elements in E, then finding the rest of the prefixes (those with odd indices) is easy: If $PR(1, 2i)$ is known for all i such that $1 \le i \le n/2$, then, for each odd prefix $PR(1, 2i+1)$, we need to compute one

---

***Algorithm Parallel_Prefix_1** (x, n)* ;
Input: *x* (an array in the range 1 to *n*).
  { we assume that *n* is a power of 2 }
Output: *x* (the *i*th element contains the *i*th prefix).

begin
  PP_1(1, n) ;
end

procedure PP_1 *(Left, Right)* ;

begin
  if *Right - Left = 1* **then**
    x[Right] := x[Left] ● *x[Right]* *{ ● is an associative binary operation }*
  else
    Middle := (Left + Right − 1)/2 ;
    do in parallel
      PP_1(Left, Middle) ; *{ assigned to P_1 to $P_{n/2}$ }*
      PP_1(Middle + 1, Right) ;   *{ assigned to $P_{n/2+1}$ to P_n }*
    for *i := Middle + 1* **to** *Right* **do in parallel**
      x[i] := x[Middle] ● *x[i]*
end

Figure 12.1 Algorithm *Parallel_Prefix_1*.

---

more product ($PR(1, 2i)$ ● x_{2i+1}). We can find the prefixes of the elements in E in two phases. First, we compute (in parallel) x_{2i-1} ● x_{2i} for all $1 \leq i \leq n/2$, and we store the result in x_{2i}. In other words, we compute the products of all elements of E with their left neighbors. Then, we solve the $n/2$-sized prefix problem for E (by induction). The result for each x_{2i} is the correct prefix, since each x_{2i} already includes the product with x_{2i-1}. And if we know the prefixes of all the even indices, then we have already seen how to compute the odd prefixes in one more parallel step. We leave it to the reader to verify that this algorithm requires only the EREW model. The algorithm is given in Fig 12.2 (see also Exercise 12.17)

Complexity Both loops in algorithm *Parallel_Prefix_2* can be performed in parallel in $O(1)$ time with $n/2$ processors. The recursive call is applied to a problem of half the size, so the running time of the algorithm is $O(\log n)$. The total number of steps $S(n)$ satisfies the recurrence relation $S(n) = S(n/2) + n - 1$, $S(2) = 1$, which implies that $S(n) = O(n)$. But, this implies that we can now use Brent's lemma to improve the efficiency. By Brent's lemma, we can modify the algorithm to run in time $O(\log n)$ with only $O(n/\log n)$ processors, leading to an $O(1)$ efficiency. The key to this improvement is using only one recursive call (instead of two) while still being able to perform the merge step in parallel.

***Algorithm Parallel_Prefix_2** (x, n)* ;
Input: *x* (an array in the range 1 to *n*).
 { we assume that *n* is a power of 2 }
Output: *x* (the *i*th element contains the *i*th prefix).

begin
    PP_2(1) ;
end

procedure PP_2 *(Inc)* ;

begin
    if *Inc = n/2* **then**
        $x[n] := x[n/2] \bullet x[n]$ *{ $\bullet$ is an associative binary operation }*
    else
        for $i := 1$ **to** $n/(2 \cdot Inc)$ **do in parallel**
            $x[2 \cdot i \cdot Inc] := x[2 \cdot i \cdot Inc - Inc] \bullet x[2 \cdot i \cdot Inc]$;
        PP_2(2·Inc) ;
        for $i := 1$ **to** $n/(2 \cdot Inc) - 1$ **do in parallel**
            $x[2 \cdot i \cdot Inc + Inc] := x[2 \cdot i \cdot Inc] \bullet x[2 \cdot i \cdot Inc + Inc]$
end

Figure 12.2 Algorithm *Parallel_Prefix_2*.

12.3.4 Finding Ranks in Linked Lists

Generally, it is much more difficult to deal with linked representations in a parallel environment than with arrays. Linked lists, for example, are inherently sequential. If the only access to the link list is through the head of the list, then we have to traverse the list one element at a time with no possibility of parallelism. In many cases, however, the elements of the list (or pointers to them) are actually stored in a contiguous array; the order imposed on the elements by the list is independent of the array. In such cases, where parallel access to the list is possible, there is hope for fast parallel algorithms.

The **rank** of an element in a linked list is defined here as the distance of the element from the end of the list (thus, the head has rank *n*, the second element has rank $n - 1$, and so on).

The Problem   Given a linked list of *n* elements, all of which are stored in an array *A* [1..*n*], compute for each element its rank in the list.

We can solve the sequential problem by simply traversing the list. The method we will use for designing a parallel algorithm for this problem is called **doubling**. We assign a processor to each element. Initially, each processor knows only the right neighbor of its element in the list. In the first step, each processor finds the neighbor of its neighbor. After the first step, each processor knows the element at distance 2 from its element. If, at step i, each processor knows the element at distance k from its element, then in one step each processor can find the element at distance $2k$. This process continues until the end of the list is reached. Let $N[i]$ be the farthest element to the right of i in the list that is known to P_i at a given moment. Initially, $N[i]$ is i's right neighbor (except for the last element whose right neighbor is nil). Basically, in each step, P_i updates $N[i]$ to $N[N[i]]$ until the end of the list is reached. Let $R[i]$ be the rank of i. Initially, $R[i]$ is set to 0, except for the last element in the list, for which it is set to 1 (this element is detected by its nil pointer). When a processor encounters a neighbor with a nonzero rank R, this processor can determine its own rank. Initially, only the element of rank 1 knows its rank. After the first step, the element of rank 2 finds that its right neighbor has rank 1, so it knows that its own rank is 2. After the second step, rank 3 and rank 4 are determined, and so on. If P_i finds that $N[i]$ points to a "ranked" element of rank R after d doubling steps, then i's rank is $2^{d-1}+R$. The precise algorithm is given in Fig 12.3. This algorithm can be easily adapted to the EREW model (Exercise 12.4).

Algorithm List_Rank (N) ;
Input: N (an array in the range 1 to n of indices).
Output: N (the rank of each element in the array).

begin
    $D := 1$;
    { *each processor can have its own local D variable;*
     we use only one D variable }
    do in parallel { *processor P_i is active until $R[i]$ becomes nonzero* }
       $R[i] := 0$;
       if $N[i] = nil$ *then* $R[i] = 1$;
       while $R[i] = 0$ *do*
          if $R[N[i]] \neq 0$ *then*
             $R[i] := D + R[N[i]]$
         else
            $N[i] := N[N[i]]$;
            $D := 2D$
    end

Figure 12.3 Algorithm *List_Rank*.

Complexity   The doubling process guarantees that each processor will reach the end of the list in at most $\lceil \log_2 n \rceil$ steps. Therefore, $T(n, n) = O(\log n)$. The efficiency is $E(n, n) = O(1/\log n)$. Reducing the efficiency requires making a major modification to the algorithm, since the total amount of work is $O(n \log n)$. (See the Bibliography section for a discussion on recent results.)

The rank computation allows us to convert a linked list into an array in $O(\log n)$ time (even though with less than perfect efficiency). After all the ranks are computed, the elements can be copied into the appropriate locations in the array, and the rest of the computation can then be performed directly on the array, which is much easier.

12.3.5 The Euler's Tour Technique

We can parallelize many types of algorithms on trees by operating on a whole level of the tree in parallel (e.g., the tournament algorithm to find the maximum). The running time of such an algorithm is proportional to the height of the tree. If the tree is reasonably balanced, and its height is $O(\log n)$ (where n is the number of nodes), then this approach is quite good. However, when the tree is not balanced, the height may be as high as $n-1$, and we need another approach. The *Euler's tour technique* is instrumental in designing parallel algorithms on trees, and especially on unbalanced trees.

Let T be a tree. We assume that T is represented by the regular adjacency-list representation, with one additional feature. As usual, there is a pointer $E(i)$ to the start of the list of edges incident to the vertex i ($E(i)$ nil if this list is empty). Each list contains records that include the corresponding edge (i, j) (it is sufficient to store only j, since i is known), and a pointer to the next edge in the list $Next(i, j)$. Each (undirected) edge (i, j) is represented by two (directed) copies, one for (i, j) and one for (j, i). The additional feature is an extra pointer for each edge that points to the other copy of that edge. We need that extra pointer to find the edge (j, i) quickly when edge (i, j) is given. This representation is illustrated in Fig. 12.4 (the pointers connecting the copies are not shown).

The key idea behind the Euler's tour technique is to construct a list of edges of the tree that forms an Euler's tour of the directed version of the tree (in which every edge appears twice). Once this list is built, many operations on the tree can be performed

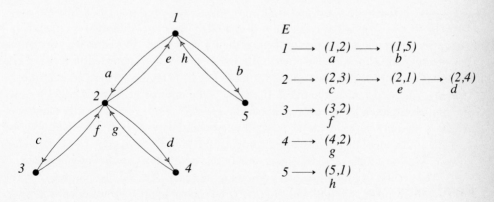

Figure 12.4 The representation of the tree.

directly on the list almost as though the list was linear. A sequential algorithm can always traverse the tree and perform operations together with the traversal. This "linearization" of the tree allows us to perform such operations on the tree efficiently in parallel. We will see two examples of such operations. But first we discuss how to construct the Euler's tour.

It is easy to find an Euler's tour of T (with every edge appearing twice) sequentially. We can traverse the tree using depth-first search, taking the opposite order of an edge whenever the search backtracks. We will do a similar thing in parallel. Let $NextTour(i, j)$ denote the edge following edge (i, j) in the tour. We claim that $NextTour$ is defined by the following rule, which can be easily computed in parallel:

$$NextTour(i, j) = \begin{cases} Next(j, i) & \text{if } Next(j, i) \text{ is not nil} \\ E(j) & \text{otherwise.} \end{cases}$$

In other words, the list of edges incident to a vertex is considered in a cyclic order, such that, if (j, i) is the last on j's list, then the first edge on that list, pointed to by $E(j)$, is taken. For example, if we start with edge a in Fig. 12.4 (we assume that the edges incident to each vertex are ordered clockwise), then the tour consists of the edges a, d, g, c, f, e, b, h, and back to a. By choosing $Next(j, i)$ to follow (i, j) in the tour, we guarantee that (j, i) will be chosen only after all other edges incident to j are chosen. Therefore, the subtree rooted at j will be completely traversed before we backtrack to i. We leave the proof that this procedure is correct as an exercise.

Once the list is constructed, we can choose a starting edge (r, t) (any edge will do), and mark the edge before it in the tour as the end of the list. The vertex r is chosen as the *root* of the tree. We can now number the edges according to their position in the list by algorithm *List_Rank* (Fig. 12.3). Let $R(i, j)$ denote the rank of edge (i, j) in the list (e.g., $R(r, t) = 2(n - 1)$, where n is the number of vertices). We now show two examples of operations on the tree — ordering the vertices in preorder traversal, and computing, for all vertices, the number of their descendants.

Let (i, j) be an edge in the tour. We call (i, j) a *forward edge* if it points away from the root, and a *backward edge* otherwise. The numbering of the edges allow us to distinguish between forward and backward edges: An edge (i, j) is a forward edge if $R(i, j) > R(j, i)$. Since the two copies of the edge (i, j) are connected by a pointer, we can easily determine which one of them is the forward edge. Furthermore, we can make this determination for all edges quickly in parallel. We are interested in forward edges because they impose preorder on the vertices. Let (i, j) be the forward edge leading to j (namely, i is j's parent in the tree). If $f(i, j)$ is the number of forward edges following (i, j) in the list, then the preorder number for j is $n - f(i, j)$. (The preorder number of r, which is the only vertex with no forward edge pointing to it, is 1.) We can now use a variation of the doubling algorithm to compute, for each forward edge (i, j), the value of $f(i, j)$. We leave the exact implementation of this doubling algorithm as an exercise.

The second example involves computing, for each vertex j, the number of vertices below j (descendants) in the tree. Let (i, j) be the (unique) forward edge leading to j. Consider the edges following the edge (i, j) in the list. The number of vertices below j in the tree is equal to the number of forward edges that are below j in the tree. We already know how to compute in parallel the value of $f(i, j)$, which is the number of forward edges that are after (i, j) in the list. We can similarly compute the number of forward edges $f(j, i)$ following (j, i) in the list. It is easy to see that the number of descendants of j is equal to $f(i, j) - f(j, i)$, which can be found again by the doubling technique. The algorithms for preorder numbering and for finding the number of descendants can both be performed in time $T(n, n) = O(\log n)$ under the EREW model.

12.4 Algorithms for Interconnection Networks

Interconnection networks can be modeled by graphs (almost always undirected). The processors correspond to the nodes and two nodes are connected if there is a direct link between the corresponding processors. Each processor has local memory, and can also access, through the network, the local memories of other processors. Thus, all memory can be shared, but the cost of accessing a variable depends on the locations of the processor and the variable. A shared-memory access may be as quick as a local access (if the variable happens to be in the same processor), or as slow as a traversal of the whole network (in case the graph is a simple chain). It is usually somewhere in between. Processors communicate by messages. When a processor wants to access a shared variable that is located at another processor, it sends a message asking for this variable. The message is routed across the network.

Numerous graphs have been suggested as interconnection networks. The simplest ones include linear arrays, rings, binary trees, stars, and two-dimensional meshes (grids). The more edges we add to the graph, the better the communication becomes. But edges are expensive (e.g., edges increase the area required for the layout of the wires, which increases the time for communication). We have to find the right tradeoff. There is no one type of graphs that is good for all purposes. The performance on a certain graph depends heavily on the communication patterns of the particular algorithm. There are, however, several properties that are very useful. We list some of them below, together with examples of interconnection networks.

The **diameter** of the graph is of great importance. (The diameter is the maximum of all the shortest distances between any two nodes.) It determines the maximum number of hops that a message may have to take. An $n \times n$ grid has diameter $2n$, whereas an n-node balanced binary tree has diameter $2\log_2(n+1) - 2$. A tree can thus deliver a message (in the worst case) much faster than a grid. On the other hand, the tree has a major bottleneck. All traffic from one half of the tree to the other half must pass through the root. The two-dimensional mesh has no such bottlenecks, and it is very symmetric, which is important for algorithms that communicate in a symmetric fashion.

A *hypercube* is a popular topology that combines the benefits of high symmetry, small diameter, many alternate routes between two nodes, and no bottlenecks. A d-dimensional hypercube consists of $n = 2^d$ processors. The addresses of the processors are integers in the range 0 to $2^d - 1$. Therefore, each address contains d bits. Processor P_i is connected to processor P_j if and only if i differs from j by exactly one bit. The distance between two processors is never more than d, since we can go from P_i to P_j by changing at most d bits (one bit at a time). A four-dimensional hypercube is shown in Fig. 12.5.

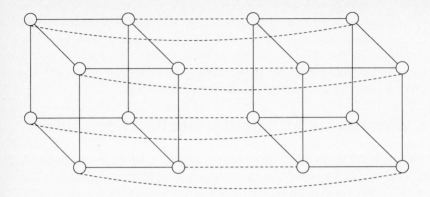

Figure 12.5 A four-dimensional hypercube.

The hypercube provides a rich connection, since there are many different routes between any two processors (e.g., we can change the appropriate bits in any order). We can also combine the hypercube with the mesh architecture by, for example, embedding meshes in the faces of the hypercube. Other suggested networks include the perfect shuffle, cube-connected cycles, quad and octal trees, mesh of trees, butterfly, and more.

12.4.1 Sorting on an Array

We start with the relatively simple problem of sorting on an array of processors. There are n processors $P_1, P_2, ,..., P_n$, and n inputs $x_1, x_2, ..., x_n$. Each processor holds one input. The goal is to distribute the input among the processors such that the smallest input is in P_1, the second smallest is in P_2, and so on. In general, we may want to assign more than one input to each processor. We will see that the same algorithm can be adapted to this case as well. The processors are connected in a linear fashion. Each processor P_i is connected to P_{i+1}, $1 \leq i < n$.

Since each processor can communicate only with its neighbors, the only comparisons and possible exchanges can be done with elements that are consecutive in the array. In particular, in the worst case, the algorithm must allow $n-1$ steps, which is the time it takes for an input to move from one end of the array to the other. The algorithm is basically as follows. Each processor compares its number to the number of one of its neighbors, exchanges the numbers if they are in the wrong order, and then does the same with the second neighbor. (We must alternate neighbors, because otherwise the same numbers will be compared again.) The same process continues until all numbers are in the correct order. The steps are divided into *odd* steps and *even* steps. In the odd steps, the odd-numbered processors compare their numbers with those of their right neighbors; in the even steps, the even-numbered processors compare their numbers with those of their right neighbors (see Fig. 12.6). This way, all processors are synchronized and a comparison always involved the correct processors. If a processor does not have

x_1 x_2 x_3 x_4 x_5 x_6 x_7 x_8

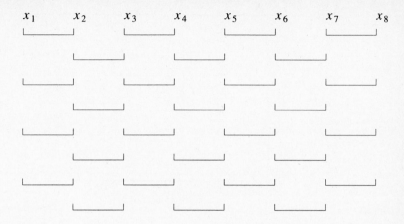

Figure 12.6 Odd–even transposition sort.

the corresponding neighbor (e.g., the first processor in the second step), it remains idle through this step. This algorithm is called the **odd–even transposition sort**. It is given in Fig. 12.7. A numeric example of the algorithm is presented in Fig. 12.8. Notice that the sort in the example is complete after only six steps. However, early termination can be very hard to detect in a network. Therefore, in many cases it is better to let the algorithm run to its worst-case completion.

Algorithm *Sorting_on_an_Array* seems natural and clear, but its proof of correctness is far from obvious. For one thing, an element may move *away* from its final destination. For example, in Fig. 12.8, 5 moves to the left for two steps before it starts moving to the right, and 3 moves to the leftmost position and stays there for three steps before it moves back to the right. Proving the correctness of parallel algorithms is difficult, because of the interdependencies among the actions of the different processors.

Algorithm *Sorting_on_an_Array* (x, n)
Input: x (an array in the range 1 to n, such that x_i resides at P_i).
Output: x (the array in sorted order, such that the ith smallest element is in P_i).

begin
    do in parallel $\lceil n/2 \rceil$ **times**
        P_{2i-1} *and* P_{2i} *compare their elements and exchange them*
            if necessary ; {for all i, such that $1 \leq 2i \leq n$ *}*
        P_{2i} *and* P_{2i+1} *compare their elements and exchange them*
            if necessary ; {for all i, such that $1 \leq 2i < n$ *}*
            { if n is odd, then this step is done only $\lfloor n/2 \rfloor$ *time }*
end

Figure 12.7 Algorithm *Sorting_on_an_Array*.

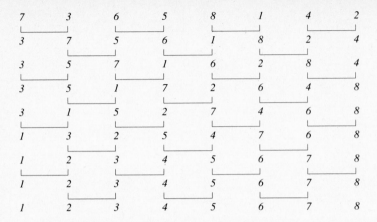

Figure 12.8   An example of odd–even transposition sort.

The behavior of one processor affects all other processor, and it is usually hard to focus on only one processor and prove that its actions are correct; we have to consider all processors together.

□ Theorem 12.2

When algorithm Sorting_on_an_Array terminates, the numbers are sorted.

Proof: The proof is by induction on the number of processors (or elements). If there are only two processors, then one comparison sorts the two numbers. We assume that the theorem is true for n processors and consider the case of $n + 1$ processors. Let's focus our attention on the maximum element and assume that it is x_m (e.g., x_5 in Fig. 12.8). In the first step, x_m will be compared to either x_{m-1} or to x_{m+1}, depending on whether m is even or odd. If m is even, then no exchange will take place because x_m is greater than x_{m-1}. But this is exactly the same as the case of x_m residing initially at P_{m-1} (and an exchange taking place). Therefore, we can assume, without loss of generality, that m is odd. In this case, x_m is compared to x_{m+1}, exchanged, and moved step by step (diagonally) to the right (since it is greater than all other numbers) until it arrives at x_{n+1} and stays there. This is its correct position, so the sort works correctly for the maximum element.

We now must show that the rest of the elements are sorted correctly too. There are n other elements, and we would like to use induction. To do that, we have to map the execution of the n processors in the array of size $n + 1$ to a possible execution of $n - 1$ processors in an array of size n. This mapping is done as follows. Consider the diagonal formed by the movement of the maximum element (see Fig. 12.9). The comparisons involving the maximum element (i.e., those that are on the diagonal) are ignored. We divide the other comparisons into two groups, the one below the diagonal and the one above it. We then "move" the triangle above the diagonal one step down. In other words, for the comparisons in the upper triangle, step i is now called step $i + 1$. For example, consider the comparisons 1 versus 8 and 4 versus 2 in the first step of Fig. 12.8.

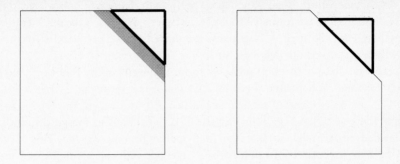

Figure 12.9 The induction step in the proof of theorem 12.2.

The first comparison is on the diagonal, so it is ignored; the second one is above the diagonal, so we consider it to be part of step 2 (instead of step 1). Therefore, step 2 consists of 7 versus 5, 6 versus 1, and (from step 1) 4 versus 2. But, this is a valid even step involving only n elements. We can now simply ignore step 1 (i.e., row 1) on the left side of the diagonal and all comparisons involving the maximum element (the last column), and the rest is exactly a sequence of comparisons that can result from running the algorithm for n elements. By the induction hypothesis, the sort on n elements is correct; therefore, this sort is correct too, and it requires only one more step.   □

So far, we have discussed the case of one input per processor. Suppose now that each processor holds k inputs and consider first the case of only two processors. We assume that the goal is to redistribute the elements such that the smallest k elements reside at P_1, and the largest k elements reside at P_2. It is clear that in the worst case all elements must be moved, so we cannot do better than $2k$ element movements. One way to achieve the sort is to repeat the following step until the sort is completed: P_1 sends its largest element to P_2 and P_2 sends its smallest element to P_1. The process terminates when the largest element in P_1 is not greater than the smallest element in P_2. This step is called *merge-split*. If we use this step as the basic step in the odd–even transposition sort, we can extend the sort to many elements per processor. Instead of a comparison and possibly an exchange of neighboring elements, a merge-split operation is done.

Although the sorting algorithm presented in this section is optimal for an array, its efficiency is low. We have n processors each running for n steps; therefore, the total number of steps is n^2. The low efficiency is not surprising, since an efficient sorting algorithm must be able to exchange elements that are far away. The array cannot support such an exchange. In the next section, we present interconnection networks that are designed specifically for efficient sorting.

12.4.2 Sorting Networks

When we design an efficient sequential algorithm, we are concerned only with the total number of steps. In a design of a parallel algorithm, we must also try to make the steps as independent as possible. Consider mergesort (Section 6.4.3). The two recursive calls are completely independent, and they can be performed in parallel. However, the merge part of the algorithm is performed in a serial manner. We place the ith element in the final array only after the first $i-1$ elements are placed. If we can parallelize the merge, then we will be able to parallelize mergesort.

We now describe a different merge algorithm, developed by Batcher [1968], using divide and conquer. We assume for simplicity that n is a power of 2. Let $a_1, a_2, ..., a_n$ and $b_1, b_2, ..., b_n$ be two sorted sequences that we want to merge, and let $x_1, x_2, ..., x_{2n}$ be the final merged order (e.g., $x_1 = min(a_1, b_1)$). We want to merge disjoint parts of these sequences in parallel so that the final merge becomes easy. This is done by dividing the two sequences into two parts — the odd-indexed elements and the even-indexed elements. Each part is merged with the corresponding part of the other sequence, then a final merge is performed. Let $o_1, o_2, ..., o_n$ be the merged order of the odd subsequences $a_1, a_3, ..., a_{n-1}$ and $b_1, b_3 ..., b_{n-1}$, and let $e_1, e_2, ..., e_n$ be the merged order of the even subsequences $a_2, a_4, ..., a_n$ and $b_2, b_4 ..., b_n$. Clearly, $x_1 = o_1$ and $x_{2n} = e_n$. The rest of the merge is also easy to obtain, as can be seen by the following theorem (see also Fig. 12.10).

□ Theorem 12.3

Following the notation above, for all i such that $1 \leq i \leq n-1$, we have $x_{2i} = min(o_{i+1}, e_i)$ and $x_{2i+1} = max(o_{i+1}, e_i)$.

Proof: Consider e_i. Since e_i is the ith element in the merged order of the even sequences, e_i is greater than or equal to at least i even elements from both sequences.

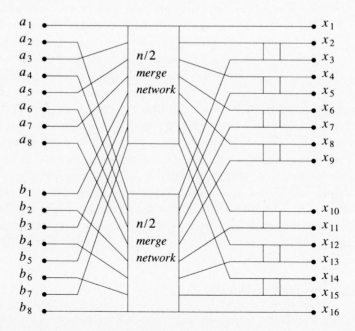

Figure 12.10   The circuit for odd–even merge.

But, for each even element, we can add one more odd element that e_i is greater than (since we started with two sorted sequences). Therefore, e_i is greater than or equal to at least $2i$ elements from both sequences. In other words, $e_i \geq x_{2i}$. By the same argument, o_{i+1} is greater than or equal to $i+1$ odd elements, which implies that it is greater than or equal to at least $2i$ elements altogether. (We have to subtract 2 from the index, because the first elements in both odd sequences do not add any more elements.) Hence, $o_{i+1} \geq x_{2i}$. But now, by a variation of the pigeonhole principle, both e_i and o_{i+1} *must* be equal (in some order) to x_{2i} and x_{2i+1}. This is so because only e_1 and o_2 can be equal to x_2 and x_3, and that makes only e_2 and o_3 fit x_4 and x_5, and so on. □

The important property of Theorem 12.3 is that the final merge can be obtained in one parallel step. The rest is done by induction. The parallel algorithm follows directly from the theorem. Figure 12.10 illustrates the recursive merge construction, and Fig. 12.11 shows the complete sort, which is called **odd–even mergesort**. The seemingly small boxes on the left side of Fig. 12.11 (marked ''$n/2$ sort'') are recursive constructions of the whole sort. The numbers on the right side are the input in the sorted order.

Complexity   The recurrence relation for the total number of steps $T_M(n)$ for the merge procedure is $T_M(2n) = 2T_M(n) + n - 1$, $T_M(1) = 1$. Therefore, the total number of comparisons is $O(n \log n)$, in contrast to the sequential algorithm that requires only $O(n)$ steps. The depth of the recursion, which corresponds to the parallel time, is $O(\log n)$. The recurrence relation for the total number of steps $T_S(n)$ for odd–even mergesort is

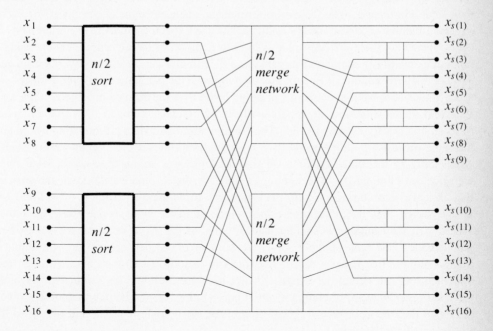

Figure 12.11   The circuit for odd–even merge sort.

$T_S(2n) = 2T_S(n) + O(n \log n)$, $T_S(2) = 1$, which implies that $T_S(n) = O(n \log^2 n)$. The circuit contains n processors in each "column" and its depth is $O(\log^2 n)$, so overall there are $O(n \log^2 n)$ processors in the circuit. (Notice that although the same processors can be used for all columns, they will have to be almost fully connected.) The only type of computation in the circuit is a comparison, and the only processors needed are comparators with two inputs and two outputs.

12.4.3 Finding the kth-Smallest Element on a Tree

We now assume that the interconnection network is a complete binary tree with $n = 2^{h-1}$ leaves. There are $2^h - 1$ processors, each associated with a node in the tree. The input is a sequence $x_1, x_2, ..., x_n$, such that x_i resides initially at leaf i. Tree machines have been suggested mainly for image-processing applications, where the leaves correspond to the inputs (e.g., pixels in a picture) and the algorithms for manipulating them are hierarchical (see, for example, [Uhr 1987]). In this section, we consider the problem of finding the kth-smallest element. This example illustrates the translation of a sequential algorithm to a parallel algorithm, and the use of pipelining (which is described in more detail in Section 12.5).

First, we recall the sequential algorithm for finding the kth-smallest element described in Section 6.5. We assume, for simplicity, that the elements are distinct. The algorithm is a probabilistic one. In each step, a random element x is chosen as the **pivot**. The rank of x is computed by comparing x to all other elements and, according to whether the rank is smaller or greater than k, the elements that are less than x or greater than x are eliminated. The algorithm terminates when the rank of the pivot is k. The expected number of iterations is $O(\log n)$, and the expected number of comparisons is $O(n)$. There are three different phases in each iteration of the algorithm: (1) choosing a random element, (2) computing its rank, and (3) eliminating. We first describe efficient parallel implementations of each phase, then improve the parallelization even further.

Choosing a random element can be achieved by a tournament arranged on the tree. Each leaf sends its number to its parent where the number "competes" with the number of its sibling leaf by flipping a coin. The winning number is then promoted up again, and the same process continues up the tree until the root chooses the overall winner. (This works only in the first iteration; we discuss later how to make it work after some elements are eliminated.) The winning number is then "broadcast" down the tree, so that all leaves can compare it with their number. If the identity of the pivot is known at all the leaves, they can all compare their numbers to the pivot in one step. They then send a 1 (if their number is smaller than or equal to the pivot) or 0 (otherwise) to their parent node. The rank of the pivot is the number of 1s that are sent up. Summing n numbers up the tree is easy to do. The root can then broadcast the rank down the tree, and each leaf can determine whether or not its number should be eliminated. Overall, there are four "waves" of communication per iteration: (1) up the tree to choose a pivot; (2) down the tree to broadcast it; (3) up the tree to compute its rank; and (4) down the tree to broadcast the rank.

The problem is that, after some elements are eliminated, the tournament is no longer fair. In the extreme case, all elements in one-half of the tree, except for one, are eliminated. The remaining element in that half will be promoted to the root without competition. It will then be chosen with probability ½, while other elements are chosen with much smaller probabilities. We want to preserve the uniform randomness of the choice. We can preserve it in the following way. Processors associated with values that have been eliminated in previous rounds send up a nil value. Any element always wins against a nil value. Every competing element has an associated counter, which is initially 1. The counter indicates the number of (real) "opponents" that participated in the part of the tournament involving this element (i.e., the number of elements in the subtree that have not yet been eliminated). When an element wins a game at some node in the tree, it is promoted upward, and the losing element's counter is added to its counter. Every game is now played with a biased coin according to the counters of the competing elements. For example, if x wins its first game (say, against y) and z advances by default, then x's counter is 2 and z's counter is 1. If x now plays against z, then the game is played with 2:1 bias toward x. Overall, z has a probability of ⅓ of winning this game, and both x and y have probability of $½ \cdot ⅔ = ⅓$ of winning both their games. This process guarantees that the final choice is uniformly selected among the participating elements.

Complexity   The number of (parallel) steps involved in each phase is equal to four times the height of the tree. Since this algorithm eliminates elements in exactly the same way as the sequential algorithm, the expected number of phases is still $O(\log n)$. The expected running time is thus $O(\log^2 n)$.

A Sketch of an Improved Algorithm

The root of the tree is a major bottleneck in the computation. Most of the information must pass through the root, but the root has only two connections and all leaves are at distance $h - 1$ from it. If we cannot improve the connections, we should at least make the root as busy as possible. In the algorithm we just described, the root and the leaves are active for one step and then remain idle for about $2h$ steps. We can improve this algorithm by making all processors busy all the time. We do that by initiating new iterations in every step even before the previous iterations are completed. All those iterations will proceed in a pipeline fashion up and down the tree. The reason this pipeline improves the running time is the following. It takes $2h - 2$ steps to select one pivot ($h - 1$ steps to reach the root, and $h - 1$ steps for the root to broadcast the result). If we start another tournament in the second step and run it in parallel to (but one step behind) the first one, then we can select two pivots in $2h - 1$ steps. We can select h pivots in $3h - 2 = O(\log n)$ steps. All those pivots can be used to eliminate elements. Thus, instead of cutting the search space by about half with one pivot, we cut it to about $1/(h + 1)$ of its original size with h pivots, and we do it without spending significantly more time. We can also interleave the different phases. The leaves start a new tournament at each step (until the k smallest is found) and the tournament pushes the rest of the computation.

□ Example 12.1

An example of this process is given in Fig. 12.12 (which proceeds from left to right top down). The elements are the numbers from 1 to 8, and we are looking for the fourth-smallest number. (In this case, the rank of each number is equal to that number's value, so we do not show both ranks and numbers.) For each step, the contents of all nodes is shown. The numbers inside the nodes are the ones obtained from below, and the numbers outside the nodes are those that are broadcast down. The first chosen pivot is 3 (Fig. 12.12d), the second one is 5 (Fig. 12.12e), and then 4, 3, 1, and 4. In Fig. 12.12(g), the first pivot (3) arrives at the leaves, and from then on they start the second phase, which is computing the rank. The fact that 3 has rank 3 is discovered in Fig. 12.12(j), and the fourth smallest element is discovered by the root at Fig. 12.12(l). Once the element is broadcast to the nodes (which we do not show), the algorithm terminates. In this case, there was no need to run another set of iterations (or eliminate any element); in general, however, this process should be run several times and elements should be eliminated until the kth-smallest element is found.   □

Complexity   The regular algorithm requires $O(\log n)$ steps to eliminate elements with one pivot. Since we can generate $O(\log n)$ pivots at about the same time, we save a factor of $O(\log \log n)$ overall. The expected running time is reduced to $O(\dfrac{\log^2 n}{\log \log n})$.

The proof of this fact, as well as the details of the algorithm, simulation results, and some slight improvements, can be found in Greenberg and Manber [1987].

12.4.4 Matrix Multiplication on the Mesh

The interconnection graph we consider now have is a two-dimensional $n \times n$ mesh (grid). Processor $P[i, j]$ is the processor at row i and column j, and it is connected to $P[i-1, j]$, $P[i, j+1]$, $P[i+1, j]$, and $P[i, j-1]$. We assume that the boundaries of the mesh are wrapped around, so that, for example, $P[0, 0]$ is connected to $P[0, n-1]$ and $P[n-1, 0]$, in addition to $P[0, 1]$ and $P[1, 0]$ (see Fig. 12.13). In other words, all additions and subtractions of indices are done modulo n. The algorithm we present is more symmetric and elegant with this assumption; it has the same running time (to within a constant) without the wrap around.

> **The Problem**   Given two $n \times n$ matrices A and B, such that initially $A[i, j]$ and $B[i, j]$ reside at $P[i, j]$, compute $C = A \cdot B$, such that $C[i, j]$ resides at $P[i, j]$.

We use the regular matrix multiplication algorithm. The problem is to move the data such that the right numbers are at the right place at the right time. Consider $C[0, 0] = \sum\limits_{k=0}^{n-1} A[0, k] \cdot B[k, 0]$, which is the inner product of the first row of A and the first

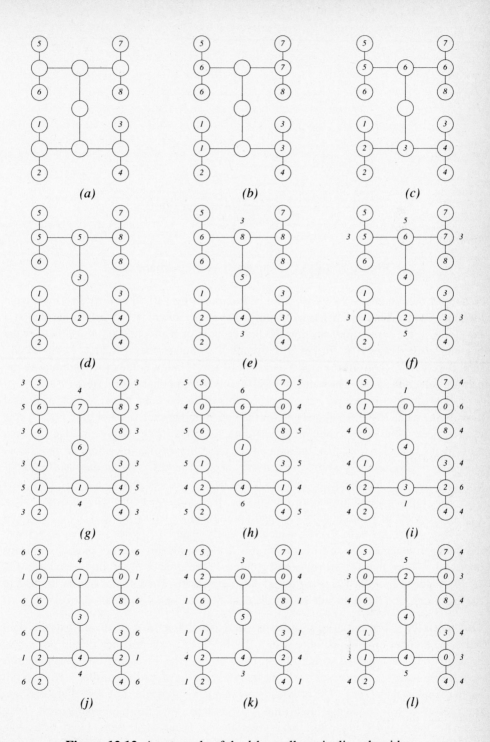

Figure 12.12 An example of the *k*th-smallest pipeline algorithm.

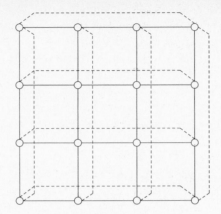

Figure 12.13 A two-dimensional wrap-around mesh.

column of B. We would like $C[0, 0]$ to be computed by $P[0, 0]$ (which also must have the final result). This can be done by shifting the first row of A to the left one step at a time, and, at the same time, shifting the first column of B up one step at a time. At the first step, $P[0, 0]$ has $A[0, 0]$ and $B[0, 0]$, and it computes their product; in the second step, it gets $A[0, 1]$ (from the right) and $B[1, 0]$ (from below), adds their product to the partial result, and so on. The value of $C[0, 0]$ will be computed after n steps.

The problem is that we need all processors to do the same thing, and they all need to share the data. We have to arrange for the data to move such that not only $P[0, 0]$ gets what it needs, but every other processor does too. The trick is to rearrange the data movements in such a way that, throughout the execution of the algorithm, all processors always have two numbers whose product they need. The key is the initial distribution of the data. We will rearrange the data such that each processor $P[i, j]$ has $A[i, i+j]$ and $B[i+j, j]$ (again, all additions are modulo n). If we can do that, then afterward every step will consist of simultaneous row and column shifts, which bring $A[i, i+j+k]$ and $B[i+j+k, j]$, $1 \leq k \leq n$, to $P[i, j]$, which is exactly what $P[i, j]$ needs. We can achieve the initial arrangement by shifting the ith row i steps to the left and the jth column j steps up, and by doing that for all rows and columns. The precise algorithm is given in Fig 12.14. Figure 12.15 illustrates the initial data movement. The left side shows the data at the beginning, and the right side shows the data after the initial shifts are performed.

Complexity   The initial row shifts take $n/2$ parallel steps (we can shift to the right when the number of shifts is more than $n/2$); the same is true for the column shifts. No computations are involved so far. Then, there are n steps, involving both computations and shifts, for each processor. All these steps can be done in parallel. The overall running time is thus $O(n)$. The efficiency is $O(1)$ if we compare the parallel algorithm to the regular $O(n^3)$ sequential algorithm. The efficiency is (asymptotically) less if we compare the parallel algorithm to asymptotically faster algorithms (e.g., Strassen's algorithm).

Algorithm Matrix_Multiplication (A, B)
Input: *A* and *B* ($n \times n$ matrices).
Output: *C* (the product of *A* and *B*).

begin
    for *all rows* **do in parallel**
        shift row i of A to the left i steps
        { namely, perform $A[i, j] := A[i, (j+1) \bmod n]$ i times }
    for *all columns* **do in parallel**
        shift column j of B upwards j steps
        { namely, perform $B[i, j] := B[(i+1) \bmod n, j]$ j times }
    { the data is now in the proper starting positions }
    for *all i and j* **do in parallel**
        $C[i, j] := A[i, j] \cdot B[i, j]$;
    for *k := 1 to n − 1* **do**
        for *all i and j* **do in parallel**
            $A[i, j] := A[i, (j+1) \bmod n]$;
            $B[i, j] := B[(i+1) \bmod n, j]$;
            $C[i, j] := C[i, j] + A[i, j] \cdot B[i, j]$
end

Figure 12.14 Algorithm *Matrix_Multiplication*.

a_{11} b_{11}	a_{12} b_{12}	a_{13} b_{13}	a_{14} b_{14}		a_{12} b_{21}	a_{13} b_{32}	a_{14} b_{43}	a_{11} b_{14}
a_{21} b_{21}	a_{22} b_{22}	a_{23} b_{23}	a_{24} b_{24}		a_{23} b_{31}	a_{24} b_{42}	a_{21} b_{13}	a_{22} b_{24}
a_{31} b_{31}	a_{32} b_{32}	a_{33} b_{33}	a_{34} b_{34}		a_{34} b_{41}	a_{31} b_{12}	a_{32} b_{23}	a_{33} b_{34}
a_{41} b_{41}	a_{42} b_{42}	a_{43} b_{43}	a_{44} b_{44}		a_{41} b_{11}	a_{42} b_{22}	a_{43} b_{33}	a_{44} b_{44}

Figure 12.15 The initial data placement and the result of the initial shifts.

12.4.5 Routing in a Hypercube

The examples we have seen so far illustrate the difficulty of adapting even a simple algorithm to an algorithm that runs on an interconnection network. If algorithms depend so heavily on the architecture, then programming becomes very difficult. Another approach to designing algorithms for interconnection networks is to define some powerful primitives, to implement these primitives on the network, then to design the algorithms using these primitives. We have to implement only the primitives on another network to translate all algorithms that use these primitives. The problem with this approach is the definition of the primitives. After all, there are major differences between the topologies, and we cannot hope to find primitives that are good for all topologies. Yet another approach is to design algorithms that emulate one network using another. This technique will allow an easy translation of algorithms between the two networks, but the translation may not yield an efficient algorithm. In this section, we briefly discuss a general routing scheme that allows us to design algorithms for interconnection networks as though shared memory is available.

We assume a hypercube connection (similar schemes have been designed for other topologies). In an EREW shared-memory algorithm, the different processors can in one step access arbitrary variables. Suppose that each processor P_i is responsible for one variable x_i. Since an EREW algorithm does not have any read or write conflicts, a step in the algorithm consists of processors accessing distinct variables. Another way to look at a step is as a permutation σ, such that processor P_i accesses variable $x_{\sigma(i)}$. (Not all processors may be accessing variables all the time, but in the worst case we can assume that they do.) We concentrate on one (arbitrary) step of the EREW algorithm, and try to emulate it using several steps of a hypercube. We now have a **routing problem**. We assume that each processor P_i on the hypercube wants to send a message to processor $P_{\sigma(i)}$ (which holds variable $x_{\sigma(i)}$). All messages are sent at the same time, and our goal is to route all of them through the hypercube quickly. We assume that each edge of the hypercube can deliver only one message at a time. Therefore, the problem is not only to find short routes between sources and destinations, but also to minimize the conflicts arising from trying to use the same edge at the same time. If two messages try to use the same edge at the same time, one of them must be buffered. We also want to minimize the buffer space requirements.

The best routing obviously depends on the particular permutation. However, it is generally not possible to analyze the permutation to find the best routing, since the permutation is distributed among the processors. Therefore, we are looking for a scheme that works well on the average. The following routing scheme was suggested by Valiant [1982]. The key idea is to use randomization. The routing consists of two phases. In the first phase, each processor P_i sends its message to a *random* processor, chosen uniformly (independently of the destination) among all other processors. (In a moment, we will describe how to select this random processor and how to route the message to it.) In the second phase, the message is sent along a shortest route between the random processor that received the message and the final destination.

All messages are sent in the same way, so we can concentrate on one message — say, that from i to j. Let the binary representation of i be $b_1 b_2 \cdots b_d$ (with possible padding of 0s at the beginning), and that of j be $c_1 c_2 \cdots c_d$. In the first phase, we need to find a random processor r. We find it by considering the bits representing i one by one, and deciding randomly with probability ½ whether to route to the corresponding neighbor or not. For example, consider Fig. 12.16, and let $i = 000$ and $j = 110$. First, we randomly choose whether or not to send the message to 100. Suppose that we decide not to send it to 100. Then, we consider the second bit and decide whether to change it; in

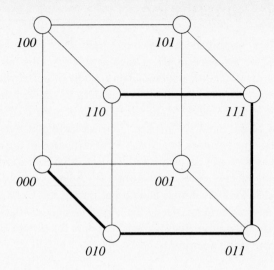

Figure 12.16 An example of random routing in a 3-cube.

other words, we decide whether or not to send the message to 010. Finally, we consider the third bit. In Fig. 12.16, the random processor is 011 and the route (marked in bold lines) passes through it. If we decide not to send a message, we immediately make the next choice without waiting for the next round; we assume that local computation is much faster than message passing. When the choice concerning the last bit is made, the random routing is done. Each choice is made locally.

Since all processors send messages at the same time, a processor may have more than one message waiting to be sent along the same edge. In this case, the messages are put in a queue (in a random order, if there is more than one) and are sent when the edge becomes available.

It is not difficult to see that every number k (in the appropriate range) has the same probability of being chosen as the random destination. The routing from the random chosen processor r to j is done deterministically. Suppose that r and j differ in t bits with the indices $k_1 < k_2 < \cdots < k_t$. The message is sent by changing bit k_1, then bit k_2, and so on. In the example of Fig. 12.16, the message will be sent first from 011 to 111 (since the destination 110 has a 1 in the first bit), and then to 110 (the second bit is not changed).

This routing scheme is simple to implement. The routes are not necessarily the shortest routes (in the example above, the route took four edges versus two edges of the shortest route). The length of each route, however, is not too large; it is at most $2d$. The main property of these routes is that, with very high probability, they have few conflicts; thus, the permutation is expected to be completed in $O(d)$ steps. Similar routing schemes have been suggested for other topologies. There are also efficient algorithms, based on such schemes, to map shared-memory algorithms to algorithms for interconnection networks automatically.

12.5 Systolic Computation

A systolic architecture resembles an assembly line. The processors, usually called **processing elements**, are arranged in a very regular way (usually, but not always, as one or two dimensional arrays), and the data move through them in a rhythmic fashion. Each processor performs very simple operations on the data it received in the previous beat, and moves the result(s) to the next "station." Each processor contains very limited (if any) memory. Most of the input is "pushed" one variable at a time, rather than being loaded all at once to some memory locations. The advantage of systolic architecture is efficiency, both in terms of the hardware (which is specialized and simple), and speed (the number of memory access cycles is minimized). As in assembly lines, the key is to avoid the need to fetch tools, material, and so on, during the work. Everything that is required to perform an operation arrives on the line. The big drawback is the inflexibility of such schemes. Systolic architectures are efficient only for certain algorithms. We will see three examples of systolic algorithms.

12.5.1 Matrix-Vector Multiplication

We start with a straightforward example, then use it to develop more complicated algorithms.

The Problem   Find the product $x = Ab$ of an $m \times n$ matrix A with a column vector b of size n.

There are n processors (stations), such that P_i is responsible for adding to the partial product the term involving b_i. The data movements and the actions of each processor for the case of $n = m = 4$ are illustrated in Fig. 12.17. We assume that b resides in the appropriate processors (or is pumped into them regularly). The results are accumulated as they move from left to right through the processors. The x_is are initially 0. In the first step, $x_1 (= 0)$ together with a_{11} move into P_1, and all the other inputs move closer. P_1 computes $x_1 + a_{11} \cdot b_1$, and moves the result to its right. In the second step, P_2 receives $x_1 = a_{11} \cdot b_1$ from the left, together with a_{12} from above; it computes $x_1 + a_{12} \cdot b_2$, and moves the result to its right, and so on. In each step, processor P_i receives a partial result, which is equal to $\sum_{k=1}^{i-1} a_{jk} b_k$, from the left, the appropriate entry of the matrix from above, and the appropriate element of b from either local memory (as it is in the figure) or from below. P_i computes $x + a_{ji} b_i$ and passes it to its right. When x_i leaves the array, it clearly has the right value. The whole product is computed in $m + n$ steps.

The main problem in designing systolic algorithms is the data movement. Each data element must be at the right place at the right time. The only trick in this example was to introduce delays so that column i of the matrix arrives at P_i in step i. This example is simple, since each element of A was used only once. When the same value is

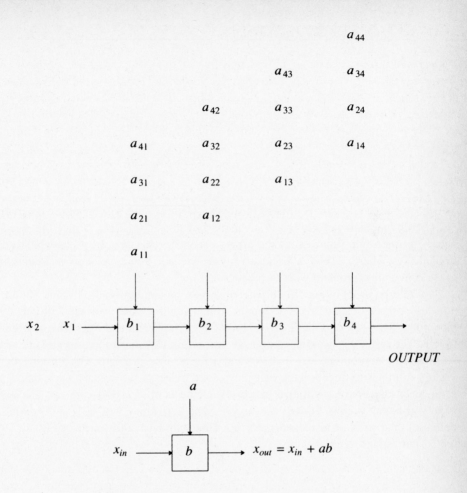

Figure 12.17 Matrix-vector multiplication.

used several times (as is usually the case), it is much more complicated to design its movement, as is illustrated in the next example.

12.5.2 The Convolution Problem

Let $x = x_1, x_2, ..., x_n$ and $w = w_1, w_2, ..., w_k$ be two sequences of real numbers with $k < n$.

The Problem   Compute $y_1, y_2, ..., y_{n+1-k}$, such that $y_i = w_1 x_i + w_2 x_{i+1} + \cdots + w_k x_{i+k-1}$.

The vector y is called the **convolution** of x and w. We can reduce the convolution problem to a matrix-vector product as follows.

$$
\begin{bmatrix}
x_1 & x_2 & x_3 & \cdot\cdot & x_k \\
x_2 & x_3 & x_4 & \cdot\cdot & x_{k+1} \\
x_3 & x_4 & x_5 & \cdot\cdot & x_{k+2} \\
\cdot & \cdot & \cdot & \cdot\cdot\cdot & \cdot \\
\cdot & \cdot & \cdot & \cdot\cdot\cdot & \cdot \\
\cdot & \cdot & \cdot & \cdot\cdot\cdot & \cdot \\
x_{n+1-k} & x_{n+2-k} & x_{n+3-k} & \cdot\cdot & x_n
\end{bmatrix}
\cdot
\begin{bmatrix}
w_1 \\ w_2 \\ w_3 \\ \cdot \\ w_k
\end{bmatrix}
=
\begin{bmatrix}
y_1 \\ y_2 \\ y_3 \\ \cdot \\ \cdot \\ y_{n+1-k}
\end{bmatrix}
\qquad (12.1)
$$

We can obtain the systolic algorithm for this problem by simply substituting the matrix in (12.1) with the matrix of Fig. 12.17. This is shown in Fig. 12.18. Notice that each x_i is needed at the same time across the array (except for the first $k-1$ x_is which are not needed everywhere). Thus, a broadcast line is needed. Next, we show another solution to the convolution problem with no broadcast.

The processors in Fig. 12.18 receive several inputs, but send only one output. We now use processors that receive inputs from two directions and send output to two directions. The idea is to move the vector x from left to right and the vector w from right to left. The result y is accumulated in the processors. We have to design this movement such that the appropriate values of w and x meet. The problem with moving the two vectors in opposite directions is that they move twice as fast toward each other. As a result, each element of x will miss half of the elements of w, and vice versa. The solution is to move the vectors at *half the speed*. The left input will be "x_1, nothing, x_2, nothing," and so on, and the same for w. This solution is illustrated in Fig. 12.19 (the bullets correspond to empty slots).

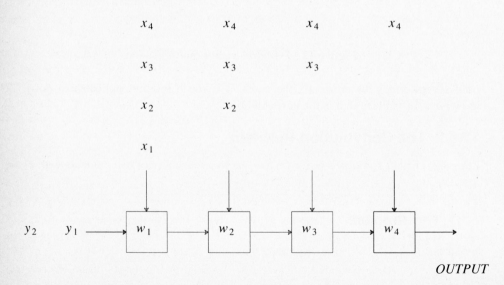

Figure 12.18 Convolution using broadcast.

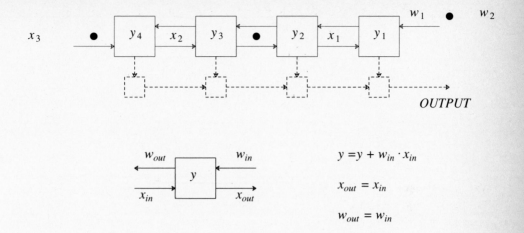

Figure 12.19 Convolution using a bidirectional array.

We leave it to the reader to verify that each P_i collects the value of y_i. When w_k leaves P_i, the final value of y_i is computed, and it can move out of the array through the data path illustrated below the array in Fig. 12.19. The main drawback to moving data at half speed is, of course, that the computation takes twice as long.

12.5.3 Sequence Comparisons

Let $A = a_1 a_2 \cdots a_n$ and $B = b_1 b_2 \cdots b_m$ be two strings of characters. Our goal is to find the minimal edit distance between A and B (see Section 6.8 and Section 10.2). A dynamic programming algorithm was presented in Section 6.8 to solve this problem. We first discuss general ways to parallelize this algorithm, then present a systolic array solution.

The algorithm proceeds by filling a table, such that the solution appears at the bottom right of the table. The value of the ijth entry depends on three entries surrounding it, the $(i-1)j$th, $(i-1)(j-1)$th, and $i(j-1)$th entries. Suppose first that we have nm processors arranged according to the table (see Fig. 12.20). Each processor P_{ij} gets input from three processors — above it, to the left of it, and diagonally from it — and sends output to three processors similarly. Each character from B moves down the table, and each character from A moves to the right. Let's see which of the algorithm's steps can be performed in parallel. The labels on the squares in Fig. 12.20 indicate the level of this square, such that squares with the same level can be computed in parallel. We can compute the whole table in $O(n+m)$ steps by computing one level at a time. It is not necessary, however, to have nm processors. The same processors that handled level i can also handle level $i+1$, level $i+2$, and so on. Therefore, $\min(n, m)$ processors are sufficient. The problem is to arrange the data movement.

For simplicity, we assume that $n = m$. We use $2n$ processors arranged in a one-dimensional bidirectional array (see Fig. 12.21). We have to ensure that every pair of characters a_i and b_j meets at some processor at some time, and that the three values

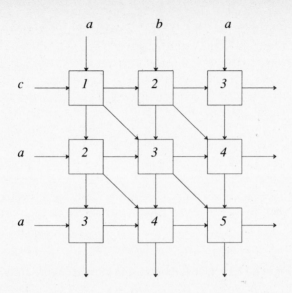

Figure 12.20 Sequence comparisons by a two dimensional array.

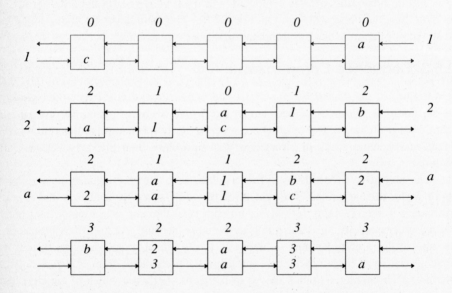

Figure 12.21 Sequence comparisons by a one-dimensional array.

needed to process these characters are known to the processor. This is achieved by moving A from left to right, B from right to left, both at half speed, and having one memory cell per processor which is used for the diagonal connection. We use half speed not only to ensure that the corresponding characters meet, but also to allow the costs computed so far to use the empty slots between two adjacent characters. For example, let $A = caa$ and $B = aba$ (see also Section 10.2.3). The first row (and column) in the matrix is

123 (corresponding to the costs of inserting or deleting those characters). The input from the right side will be $a\,1b\,2a\,3$, and that from the left side will be $c\,1a\,2a\,3$. The memories of all processors are initialized to 0. When two characters a_i and b_j meet at, say, P_k, they are compared; in the next beat, the two numbers following them meet at P_k, and P_k now has all the information needed to compute the corresponding entry in the matrix. The minimal cost of matching $A[1..i]$ to $B[1..j-1]$ comes from P_{k-1}, the minimal cost of matching $A[1..i-1]$ to $B[1..j]$ comes from P_{k+1}, and the minimal cost of matching $A[1..i-1]$ to $B[1..j-1]$ comes from P_k's memory. This new entry will then be moved both left and right in the next step, and so on. Figure 12.21 shows four different steps: The first row is the initial step, the second row is the third step, the third row is the fourth step, and the last row is the seventh step. The values of the memories and costs are shown *before* the step. When the last character leaves the last processor (in either side), the number that follows it is the minimal edit cost.

12.6 Summary

Since parallel algorithms are even more complicated to design than sequential algorithms, we have to make good use of building blocks. The parallel-prefix paradigm is a powerful building block. It was even suggested as a primitive machine operation (for example, Blelloch [1987]). The same is true for the routing through permutations (Section 12.4.5). It is still too early to know which of the suggested parallel architectures (if any) will dominate in the future. Therefore, it is important to identify design techniques that are common to many models. We have seen four techniques (and there are, of course, others that we have not seen): *doubling* (list ranking and other operations on linked lists), *parallel divide and conquer* (addition, parallel prefix, sorting), *pipelining* (finding k-smallest on the tree, and systolic computation in general), and the *Euler's tour* technique (which is helpful for a variety of tree and graph algorithms). Induction, again, plays a major role.

Bibliographic Notes and Further Reading

The area of parallel computing is expanding rapidly, as is evidenced by the number of books that have appeared in the last few years. Books describing parallel computing include Akl [1985], which is devoted to parallel sorting; Jia-Wei [1986] and Parberry [1987], which include theoretical models of parallel computation and their relationships; Quinn [1987] and Gibbons and Rytter [1988], which are general books on parallel algorithms; Hwang and Briggs [1984], Lipovski and Malek [1987], and Almasi and Gottlieb [1989], which describe different parallel architectures and parallel software; Ullman [1984], which deals mainly with VLSI; Gehringer, Siewiorek, and Segall [1987], which describes experience with Cm[*]; Fox et al. [1987], which describes experiments with the hypercube; Reed and Fujimoto [1987], which includes models, architectures, and several detailed applications; Bertsekas and Tsitsiklis [1989], which deals mainly with numerical and optimization methods; and others. Chandy and Misra [1988] present a general methodology for writing parallel (and sequential) programs. A survey on parallel graph algorithms is given by Quinn and Deo [1984], and on general parallel algorithms by Moitra and Iyengar [1986]. Richards [1986] contains a large bibliography on parallel sorting. The classification of machines according to Single/Multiple-Instruction Single/Multiple-Data is due to Flynn [1966]. Modeling algorithms by circuits is described, for example, in Borodin [1977].

Valiant [1975] is an early work on parallel maximum finding, merging, and sorting, from which some of the material in Section 12.3.1. is taken. Other parallel algorithms for these problems appear in Shiloach and Vishkin [1981], and in Borodin and Hopcroft [1985]. Additional algorithms for list ranking appear in Kruskal, Rudolph, and Snir [1985] (where parallel prefix is used), in Vishkin [1987] (where a randomized algorithm is presented), and in Cole and Vishkin [1986] (where a general technique for converting randomized parallel algorithms to deterministic ones is presented). Cole [1988] presents an elegant parallelization of mergesort which has $T(n, n) = O(\log n)$ under both the CREW and EREW models (although the CREW algorithm is much simpler and involves smaller constants). Attalah, Cole, and Goodrich [1987] includes several other applications of Cole's technique, in particular to parallel geometric algorithms.

Algorithms for the parallel-prefix problem and applications, including parallel addition, appeared in Ladner and Fischer [1980]. Fich [1983] provides upper and lower bounds for the number of gates in parallel-prefix circuits. Beame, Cook, and Hoover [1986] describe parallel algorithms for division and related problems. The Euler's tour technique, as well as the algorithms presented in Section 12.3.5, are from Tarjan and Vishkin [1985]; see also Kruskal, Rudolph, and Snir [1986]. Divide and conquer for parallel computing is discussed in Horowitz and Zorat [1983], and in Stout [1987]. Exercise 12.24 is from Kruskal, Rudolph, and Snir [1987]; Exercise 12.15 is from Cook and Dwork [1982].

Sorting networks, including the odd–even mergesort, were introduced by Batcher [1968]. It was an open problem for a long time whether there exist sorting networks with depth $O(\log n)$. Ajtai, Komlós, and Szemerédi [1983] proved that such networks exist (even though their network was definitely an impractical $O(\log n)$ — see Section 3.2). Reif and Valiant [1987] exhibit a network with a randomized $O(\log n)$ sort. The connection machine is described by Hillis [1985], and various algorithms for it are given in Hillis and Steele [1986]. The improved algorithm for finding the kth-smallest element on a tree is due to Greenberg and Manber [1987] (the regular algorithm appeared in Shrira, Francez, and Rodeh [1983]). A deterministic algorithm whose running time is $O(\log^3 n)$ in the worst case is given by Frederickson [1988]. The algorithm for matrix multiplication on a mesh can be adapted to run on a hypercube and other interconnection networks (Dekel, Nassimi, and Sahni [1981]). Experimental results for matrix multiplication on a hypercube are given in Fox et al. [1988]. The routing scheme presented in Section 12.4.5 is from Valiant [1982] and Valiant and Brebner [1981] (the former was actually developed earlier). (Valiant [1982] suggested to choose the order of the bits at random; it was shown in Valiant and Brebner [1981] that the bits can be considered in order, which is how we described it in Section 12.4.5.) Similar schemes appear in Aleliunas [1982] and Upfal [1982]. Schemes for emulating shared memory in networks appear in Karlin and Upfal [1986], Upfal and Wigderson [1987], and Ranade [1987]. For more on interconnection networks see, for example, Feng [1981], Siegel [1985], or Ullman [1984].

More on systolic computing can be found in Kung [1979], Kung and Leiserson [1980], and Kung [1982]. Systolic arrays for matrix multiplication using Winograd's algorithm (Section 9.5.1) are presented in Jagadish and Kailath [1989]. The systolic array algorithm for sequence comparisons in Section 12.5.3 is from Lipton and Lopresti [1985]. The July 1987 issue of *Computer* is devoted to systolic arrays.

"Thinking in parallel" is difficult, and designing parallel algorithms is usually significantly more difficult than designing the corresponding sequential algorithms. Nevertheless, Megiddo [1983] has found an ingenious technique to design some types of sequential algorithms by using parallel algorithms. An improvement of this technique was given by Cole [1984].

Drill Exercises

12.1 Draw the circuit corresponding to the parallel addition discussed in Section 12.3.1.

12.2 Design an algorithm to add k binary numbers, each with n bits. The running time should be $O(\log n \log k)$ using nk processors.

12.3 Draw the circuit that corresponds to algorithm *Parallel_Prefix_2* of Section 12.3.3.

12.4 Prove that algorithm *List_Rank* (Fig. 12.3) requires only the EREW model.

12.5 Prove that the rules for constructing an Euler's tour given in Section 12.3.5 are correct.

12.6 Complete the details of the doubling algorithm to find the preorder numbering of all vertices in a tree (Section 12.3.5).

12.7 Figure 12.22 is an example of a graph representing an interconnection network that we discussed in this chapter. Identify the network, and label the nodes appropriately.

12.8 Consider the proof of correctness of the odd–even transposition sort. The proof uses induction, and shows that, when an additional processor (and input) is added, the number of steps is incremented by 1. The base case, $n = 2$, uses exactly one comparison. Hence, the total number of steps seems to be $n - 1$ and not n. Show an example that requires n steps, and discuss why the proof does not show that $n - 1$ steps are sufficient.

12.9 a. Draw the full circuit for merging two sequences of size 8.

b. Draw the full circuit for sorting 16 inputs.

c. Draw the full circuit for sorting 10 inputs.

12.10 Complete Fig. 12.21 by showing all the steps until the two sequences are separated.

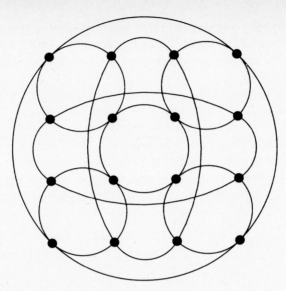

Figure 12.22 An example of an interconnection network.

Creative Exercises

12.11 Design an CREW algorithm for matrix multiplication that can multiply two n by n matrices in time $O(\log n)$ using $O(n^3/\log n)$ processors.

12.12 Modify the CRCW algorithm for finding the maximum (Section 12.3.2) to work in the case where the numbers are not distinct. The parallel running time should still be $O(1)$.

12.13 Let $A[1..n]$ be an array of values. We want to copy the value $A[1]$ to all other locations in the array (i.e., *broadcast*).

   a. Design an EREW algorithm with $T(n, n) = O(\log n)$ for this problem.

   b. Design an EREW algorithm with efficiency $O(1)$ and running time $O(\log n)$.

12.14 Parallelize Horner's rule to evaluate a polynomial of degree n under the EREW model in time $O(\log n)$ and efficiency $O(1)$.

*12.15 The input is an array of n Boolean variables. The output is the *or* function of all of them. In other words, the output is 1 if and only if at least one of the variables is 1. It is straightforward to compute the *or* of n variables in $\lceil \log_2 n \rceil$ steps by an EREW algorithm with n processors. It seems fairly obvious that doing better than $\lceil \log_2 n \rceil$ is impossible. But this is not the case. Design an EREW algorithm whose running time is less than $\lceil \log_2 n \rceil$. You can assume an unlimited number of processors and space. (This algorithm is not practical, but it shows that simple "obvious" lower bounds are not always so obvious.)

12.16 Solve Exercise 12.15 (computing *or* of n Boolean variables) in time $O(1)$ under the CRCW model.

12.17 Draw a circuit with $O(n \log n)$ vertices that solves the parallel-prefix problem with depth $O(\log n)$, such that the fan-in and fan-out of every processing element is no more than 2 and every processing element is involved in exactly one operation.

12.18 Use the circuit of Exercise 12.17 to design an EREW algorithm for the parallel-prefix problem with $T(n, n) = O(\log n)$.

12.19 Let $x_1, x_2, ..., x_n$ be a sequence of distinct numbers. Design a CREW algorithm to sort the sequence in time $O(\log n)$. You can assume an unlimited number of processors and space.

12.20 Design a CRCW algorithm to merge two sorted arrays A and B into one sorted array in time $O(1)$. You can assume an unlimited number of processors and space.

12.21 Let S be a set of size n and let $k > 1$ be a constant. Design a CRCW algorithm to find the maximum in S with $T(n, n^{1+1/k}) = O(1)$.

12.22 Let $x_1, x_2, ..., x_n$ be a sequence of (not necessarily distinct) integers in the range 1 to n. Design a CRCW algorithm to find the maximum in the sequence with $T(n, n) = O(1)$.

12.23 Let $x_1, x_2, ..., x_n$ be a sequence of real numbers, let S be a subset of $\{1, 2, ..., n\}$, and let $\bullet$ be an associative binary operation on real numbers. The set S partitions the sequence into groups, such that the first group contains $x_1, x_2, ..., x_i$, where i is the smallest element in S, the second group contains $x_{i+1}, ..., x_j$, where j is the second smallest element of S, and so on (the last group contains the rest of the elements in case n does not belong to S). The **group parallel-prefix problem** is to compute parallel prefixes separately for all groups. Show that the group parallel-prefix problem can be solved with the same resources as are used for the regular parallel-prefix problem.

12.24 The **cross product** of two arrays $A[0..n-1]$ and $B[0..m-1]$ is an array $C[0..nm-1]$ such that, if $i = k \cdot m + r$, $0 \le k \le n-1$, $0 \le r \le m-1$, then $C[i] = A[k] \cdot B[r]$. (In other words, C is a row representation of an $n \times m$ matrix whose ij entry is the product of $A[i]$ and $B[j]$.) Design an EREW parallel algorithm to compute C with p processors and time $O(mn/p + \log p)$. You can use $O(nm)$ space. (For simplicity, you can assume that n, m, or p is a power of 2.)

12.25 The input is an array of records. Each record contains some data (which is immaterial for this exercise) and a Boolean variable *Mark*. The goal is to pack all records whose *Mark* value is 1 into the beginning of the array. (For example, these records may be selected for some purpose and some more work has to be performed on them; it is better to have them in a contiguous area.) The order among the records that are moved should not be changed. Design an EREW algorithm for this problem with $T(n, n) = O(\log n)$.

12.26 The input is a linked list such that all of its elements are stored (in an arbitrary order) in an array. Let $F[i]$ be a Boolean flag associated with the elements. Design an EREW algorithm with $T(n, n) = O(\log n)$ to construct another linked list consisting of only the elements with $F[i] = 1$ in the same order they appear in the original list. (This algorithm is needed, for example, in computing preorder in Section 12.3.5.)

12.27 The input is a linked list such that all of its elements are stored (in an arbitrary order) in an array. Design an efficient parallel algorithm to construct a linked list in the opposite order of the original list (i.e., reverse the list), without moving any element. You can assume that sufficient space is allocated to hold the extra pointers.

12.28 Design an EREW algorithm with $T(n, n) = O(\log n)$ to rank the forward edges in the list obtained by the Euler's tour method. In other words, for each forward edge you should find the number of forward edges that follow it in the list. (This number is denoted by $f(i, j)$ in the text, and it is needed to compute the preorder associated with the Euler tour; see Section 12.3.5.)

12.29 Suppose that a tree T is given in the regular adjacency-list representation without the extra pointers connecting the two copies of each edge. Design a fast and efficient EREW algorithm to construct these pointers. You can assume that you have as much work space as you want.

12.30 Let T be a tree represented by adjacency lists in the same way as described in Section 12.3.5. Design an $T(n, n) = O(\log n)$ EREW algorithm to find, for each vertex i, the number of ancestors of i in the tree (i.e., the length of the path to the root).

12.31 Construct a **counter circuit**: The input consists of n binary numbers, and the output is the binary representation of the number of 1s in the input.

12.32 Consider the following attempt to prove the correctness of the odd–even transposition sort. We have seen that the maximum element gets to the right position. Without it there are $n-1$ numbers. But the maximum number adds at most one idle step to each number. Since we have a step to spare, the algorithm terminates on time. Discuss why this proof is not a valid.

12.33 Consider the binary tree topology and assume that each leaf i has a number x_i. Solve the parallel-prefix problem under this model. At the end of the computation, each leaf i should have the sum $x_1 \bullet x_2 \bullet \cdots \bullet x_i$ (where $\bullet$ is an associative binary operation that can be computed in one step). The running time of the algorithm should be $O(\log n)$.

12.34 Consider the parallel algorithm for finding the kth-smallest element on a tree described in Section 12.4.3. Suppose that the elements are not distinct. Describe the modifications to the algorithm required to deal with this case.

12.35 Design a sorting algorithm for processors connected through a complete binary tree as described in Section 12.4.3. Each leaf contains a number, and the goal is to get the kth smallest element to the kth leaf. Show that the running time of your algorithm is optimal to within a constant.

12.36 The processors are arranged in a ring. Each processor P_i holds the ith row of an $n \times n$ matrix A and the ith element of the vector $b = (b_1, b_2, ..., b_n)$. We want to compute the matrix vector product $x = Ab$ such that x_i is stored in P_i at the end. $(x_i = \sum_{k=1}^{n} a_{ik} \cdot b_k.)$ Design an $O(n)$ algorithm for this problem.

12.37 Solve Exercise 12.36, except that initially each processor P_i holds the ith *column* of the matrix (and b_i).

12.38 The **transpose** of a $n \times n$ matrix A is the matrix A^T such that $a_{ij}^T = a_{ji}$. Suppose that A is initially stored in an $n \times n$ mesh such that $P[i, j]$ holds a_{ij}. Design an $O(n)$ algorithm to compute the transpose of A.

12.39 Suppose that you are given a mesh of $n \times n$ processors, each holding a pixel of an $n \times n$ black-and-white picture. In other words, each processor holds one binary number where 1 corresponds to black and 0 corresponds to white. We would like to find the *connected components* of the picture. Two black pixels belong to the same component if there is a black path connecting them (horizontally or vertically; diagonals are not considered connected). All pixels in the same component should be labeled with a unique component label. Initially, the (ij)th pixel is labeled $i \cdot n + j$. Consider the following algorithm that labels each component with the smallest label of a pixel in it. In each step, each processor holding a black pixel looks at the current labels of its black neighbors. If any of them is smaller than its own label, then it updates it own. Prove that this algorithm will eventually label the components correctly, but that it may require $c \cdot n^2$ parallel steps for some input (where c is a constant). How would you terminate the algorithm?

12.40   Let A be an $n \times n$ matrix stored in an $n \times n$ mesh in the usual way. Let σ and π be two permutations of $(1, 2, ..., n)$, such that σ is stored in the first row of the grid and π is stored in the second row. Design an $O(n)$ algorithm to permute the rows of A according to σ and the columns of A according to π (starting with the rows). In other words, row i should move to row $\sigma(i)$ and column j should move to column $\pi(j)$.

12.41   Consider the n-dimensional hypercube topology and assume that each processor holds one element. Design an $O(n)$ parallel algorithm to find the maximum of the 2^n elements.

12.42   Design a fast algorithm to solve the parallel-prefix problem on an n-dimensional hypercube. Each processor holds one number. You can assign indices to the processors in any way you want. At the end of the algorithm, each processor should have the value of the prefix associated with its index.

12.43   Let $G = (V, E)$ be a directed weighted graph with positive weights. Design a CREW algorithm to compute the costs of all shortest paths in G in time $O(\log^2 n)$ where n is the number of vertices of G. You can use as many processors as you want, and any reasonable graph representation.

12.44   Design parallel algorithms for the following problem when an adjacency matrix is given. Use as many processors as you can while preserving an efficiency of $O(1)$.

     a.   Design an algorithm to determine whether a given undirected graph contains a triangle as a subgraph.

     b.   Design an algorithm to determine whether a given undirected graph contains a square as a subgraph (namely, a cycle of length 4).

12.45   A common way to generate integer random numbers is to use the recurrence $x_i = a \cdot x_{i-1} + b \ (mod \ n)$, where a, b, and n are constants, and x_1 is the *seed*. Design an EREW parallel algorithm for computing the first n numbers from this sequence when the seed is given. The running time of the algorithm should be $T(n, n) = O(\log n)$.

12.46   a.   Prove that a complete binary tree of height $n > 1$ (which has $2^n - 1$ nodes) cannot be embedded in an n-dimensional hypercube (with 2^n nodes). (Embedding one graph G in another graph H involves mapping every vertex of G to a unique vertex of H such that two adjacent vertices of G are mapped into two adjacent vertices of H.)

     b.   Find ways to embed complete binary trees in hypercubes *approximately*; that is, some of the tree edges may be mapped to short paths rather than to edges. The goal is to be able to map algorithms designed for complete trees to hypercubes with little effort (and with reasonable efficiency).

12.47 Show how to embed a two-dimensional grid of size 2^k by 2^m in the $(k+m)$–dimensional hypercube.

12.48 This is a parallel **gossip problem**. Suppose that there are $n = 2^k$ persons, each with a certain item of information. In each step, each person can communicate with another person and share all the information he or she knows (including information learned in previous steps). A person cannot communicate with more than one person in any step. Design a communication (gossip) pattern such that after $\log_2 n$ steps, everyone knows everything.

12.49 Design another systolic array for the convolution problem such that both the x vector and the w vector move in the same direction (say, from left to right). Each processor will have two inputs from the left and two outputs to the right. The partial values are accumulated at the processors. (Hint: Move the two vectors at different speeds.)

12.50 Design a two-dimensional systolic array for matrix multiplication. The connections are the same as a two-dimensional mesh. The first matrix arrives from the top row, and the second matrix arrives through the first column. The result moves from right to left starting from the last column.

12.51 In some biology applications of sequence comparisons, there are only four different characters (corresponding to four types of nucleotides). In that case, each character can be represented by two bits. Show that it is possible to encode the numbers associated with the costs that move following the characters in the systolic implementation given in Section 12.5.3 with only two bits as well. (This short encoding is important, since it reduces the required bandwidth between the processors.)

SKETCHES OF SOLUTIONS
TO SELECTED EXERCISES

You know my methods. Apply them.

Sir Arthur Conan Doyle

Chapter 1

1.13   There are quite a few possible ties. The following states have 269 electoral votes overall: California, New York, Illinois, New Jersey, Massachusetts, Wisconsin, Maryland, Minnesota, Washington, Iowa, Connecticut, Rhode Island, Washington DC, Ohio, Michigan, North Carolina, Oregon, and West Virginia.
(Note: This is written well before the 1988 election.)

Chapter 2

2.1   The base case of $n = 1$ is trivial. The induction hypothesis states that $x^{n-1} - y^{n-1}$ is divisible by $x - y$ for all natural numbers x and y $(x \neq y)$. We try to write $x^n - y^n$ in terms of $x^{n-1} - y^{n-1}$:

$$x^n - y^n = x(x^{n-1} - y^{n-1}) + y(x^{n-1} - y^{n-1}) + x \cdot y^{n-1} - y \cdot x^{n-1}$$

$$= x(x^{n-1} - y^{n-1}) + y(x^{n-1} - y^{n-1}) + xy \, (x^{n-2} - y^{n-2}).$$

The first two terms in the expression above are divisible by $x - y$ by the induction hypothesis; the third term includes $x^{n-2} - y^{n-2}$. Therefore, we use the strong induction principle by changing the hypothesis to state that $x^k - y^k$ is divisible by $x - y$ for all natural numbers x, y $(x \neq y)$, and k, such that $k < n$.

2.6   The base case is $k = 1$, and indeed $1^2 = 1(1+1)/2$. Assume that the claim is true for $k - 1$. The sum for k is the sum for $k - 1$, which by the induction assumption is $(-1)^{(k-1)-1}(k-1)k/2$, plus the kth element, which is $(-1)^{k-1}k^2$. This sum is

$$(-1)^{k-1}k^2 + (-1)(-1)^{k-1}(k-1)k/2 \; = \; (-1)^{k-1}(k^2 - k(k-1)/2) = (-1)^{k-1}k(k+1)/2.$$

2.8   The proof is by induction on n. The case of $n = 1$ is trivial. Assume that the claim is true for n and consider $n + 1$. We have to prove that

$$2^n(a^{n+1} + b^{n+1}) \geq (a+b)^{n+1}.$$

We start with the right side.

$$(a+b)^{n+1} = (a+b)(a+b)^n \leq (a+b)2^{n-1}(a^n + b^n),$$

by the induction hypothesis. We now rearrange the expression to make it as close as we can to the desired result $(2^n(a^{n+1} + b^{n+1}))$.

$$(a+b)2^{n-1}(a^n + b^n) = 2^{n-1}(a^{n+1} + b^{n+1} + b\,a^n + a\,b^n)$$

$$= 2^n(a^{n+1} + b^{n+1}) + 2^{n-1}(b\,a^n + a\,b^n - a^{n+1} - b^{n+1}).$$

The left term is what we want, so it is sufficient to prove that the right term is at most 0. In other words, we need to prove that

$$2^{n-1}(b\,a^n + a\,b^n - a^{n+1} - b^{n+1}) \leq 0.$$

The 2^{n-1} factor can be ignored, and without it the expression becomes

$$b\,a^n + a\,b^n - a^{n+1} - b^{n+1} = a^n(b-a) + b^n(a-b) = (b-a)(a^n - b^n).$$

If $a = b$, then the expression above is equal to 0. Otherwise, if $a < b$, then the left factor is positive but the right factor is negative, and vice versa if $a > b$. In either case, the expression is no more than 0, and the proof is complete.

2.9   There are several ways to prove this theorem. We present a proof of a slightly more general theorem. We say that an integer n is **congruent** to k modulo 3, written $n \equiv k$ (modulo 3), if k is the remainder when we divide n by 3. (k can be any one of 0, 1, or 2.) We prove the following stronger theorem.

   □ **Theorem A.1**

   A number n, given in its decimal representation, is congruent to k modulo 3 if and only if the sum of its digits is congruent to k modulo 3.

   Proof: The claim can be easily checked for small numbers. Assume that it is true for $n - 1$, and consider n. The difference between the decimal representations of $n - 1$ and n is only in the last digit, unless the last digit of $n - 1$ is 9. If the last digit of $n - 1$ is not 9, then when we go from $n - 1$ to n, we increment both the number and the sum of its digits; thus, the congruence remains the same. If the last digit of $n - 1$ is 9, then it changes to 0 and 1 is added to the second digit. The change of 9 to 0 does not change the congruence of the sum of digits (since both are divisible by 3), and the addition of 1 to the second digit has the same effect on the congruence of the sum of digits as that of the addition of 1 to the first digit (e.g., it may cause another 9 to change to 0).

2.15   The subtle point is that, when we subtract a element, say a_i, from the list to reduce the size of the number in question n, we must make sure that $n - a_i \leq a_i$; otherwise, the induction hypothesis cannot be used on $n - a_i$ since it may require another use of a_i in its representation. But the requirement was that the sum use distinct numbers from the list.

2.26   The only tree with two vertices is a single edge, in which case both degrees are 1. Assume that the theorem is true for $n - 1$ vertices, and consider the case of n vertices. Since all degrees are positive and their sum is $2n - 2$, at least one of them, say d_i, must be equal to 1 and at least one of them, say d_j, must be greater than 1. We can now remove d_i from the sequence and decrement d_j by 1. There are now $n - 1$ numbers whose sum is $2n - 4$; therefore, by the induction hypothesis, there exists a tree with these degrees. We can add one additional vertex to this tree and connect it to the vertex whose degree is $d_j - 1$ to obtain the desired tree.

2.29 If two balls are put inside one box, then the box contains more than one ball. Assume that the principle is true for $n + 1$ balls and consider putting $n + 2$ balls inside $n + 1$ boxes. Assume the contrary; namely, no box contains more than one ball. But then, there exists a box with one ball, and if we remove both the box and the ball we get a contradiction to the induction hypothesis.

2.34 The claim is clearly true for $n = 2$. Assume that it is true for n and consider $n + 2$. Take any two vertices v and u. The graph without them is K_n, and by the induction hypothesis it can be partitioned into $n/2$ spanning trees. We need to extend those spanning trees to include v and u, and to add one more spanning tree. The edges included in K_{n+2} that are not covered by K_n are those that are connected to v and u. We partition the set of n vertices into two equal-sized groups X and Y. The new spanning tree contains the edge (v, u) and all edges from v to vertices in X and from u to vertices in Y. Each of the previous spanning trees includes all vertices in K_n. Therefore, we can extend each of these spanning trees to span K_{n+2} by adding an edge from a vertex of X to u and an edge from a vertex of Y to v. We will choose different vertices of X and Y for each spanning tree.

2.38 We added a subtle implicit assumption in the proof: We took it for granted that a maximum always exists. If all the x_is are positive integers, then there are finitely many possible sets whose sum is S, and so a maximum always exists. However, if some of the x_is are real numbers, then a maximum may not exist. Hence, the proof, as is, is valid only for integers.

Chapter 3

3.6 It is easy to remove the recursion:

$$T(n) = T(n - 1) + n/2 = T(n - 2) + (n - 1)/2 + n/2 = \cdots =$$

$$1 + 2/2 + 3/2 + \cdots + n/2 = n(n + 1)/4 + 1/2.$$

3.8 Let n be a power of 2. We guess that $T(n) \le cn (\log_2 n)^2$. We have to verify (see Section 3.5.1) that (1) $c2 (\log_2 2)^2 \ge 4$, and that (2) $c(2n)(\log_2(2n))^2 \ge 2cn (\log_2 n)^2 + 4n \log_2(2n)$, for some value of c. We can simplify (2) to

$$2cn (\log_2 n)^2 + 4cn \log_2 n + 2cn \ge 2cn (\log_2 n)^2 + 4n \log_2 n + 4n.$$

Both inequalities clearly hold for $c \ge 2$.

3.14 We have

$$\sum_{i=1}^{n} i^k \log_2 i \le \int_{x=1}^{x=n+1} x^k \log_2 x \, dx = \frac{\log_2 e}{k+1} \left[x^{k+1} \log x - x^{k+1} \right]_{x=1}^{x=n+1} = O(n^{k+1} \log n).$$

3.15 The functions $f(n) = 3n$, $g(n) = 2n$, and $s(n) = r(n) = n$ form a counterexample to the claim.

3.17   We can construct the two functions by letting one of them grow fast for all even numbers and the other one grow fast for the odd numbers. We define the functions recursively. Let $f(1) = g(1) = 1$.

$$f(n) = \begin{cases} f(n-1)+1 & \text{when } n \text{ is odd} \\ f(n-1)+(g(n-1))^2 & \text{when } n \text{ is even} \end{cases}$$

and

$$g(n) = \begin{cases} g(n-1)+1 & \text{when } n \text{ is even} \\ g(n-1)+(f(n-1))^2 & \text{when } n \text{ is odd} \end{cases}$$

$f(n)$ is about the square of $g(n)$ for all even numbers, and $g(n)$ is about the square of $f(n)$ for all odd numbers. Therefore, $f(n) \neq O(g(n))$ and $g(n) \neq O(f(n))$.

3.19   We can use Theorem 3.4, since m and c are constants. The result is

$$S(n) = O\left[n^{\log_m(cm \log m)}\right].$$

3.21   The solution is $T(n) = O(n)$. To prove it, we guess that $T(n) \leq dn$ for some constant d. We have to show that

$$dn \geq \sum_{i=1}^{k} a_i(dn/b_i) + cn = dn \sum_{i=1}^{k} a_i/b_i + cn.$$

Since $f = 1 - \sum_{i=1}^{k} a_i/b_i > 0$, the inequality above holds for $d \geq c/f$.

3.25   If we replace the term $T(\lfloor \sqrt{n} \rfloor)$ with $T(n/2)$, then we get the typical divide-and-conquer recurrence relation, whose solution, by Theorem 3.4, is $O(n \log n)$. Thus, since $\sqrt{n}$ is no greater than $n/2$ for $n \geq 2$, $T(n) = O(n \log n)$. However, it is possible that $T(n)$ is smaller than that. Let's try $T(n) = cn$. The base case implies that $c \geq 1$. Consider $2n$. We have to prove that

$$2cn \geq cn + \sqrt{cn} + n,$$

which is clearly true for $c = 2$ and $n \geq 2$.

3.29   a. If n is a power of 2, then the upper part of the recurrence will always be used. In this case, we can substitute k for n, and obtain the following recurrence relation for $T'(k) = T(2^k)$.

$$T'(k) = T'(k-1) + 1, \quad T'(0) = 1.$$

The solution of this recurrence relation is clearly $T'(k) = k+1$.

b. Consider now $n = 2^k - 1$. If we use the bottom part of the recurrence, then $T(n)$ is replaced by $T((n-1)/2)$, and $(n-1)/2 = 2^{k-1} - 1$. In other words, if we start with $n = 2^k - 1$, then we will always use the bottom part of the recurrence relation, because the numbers involved will always be of the form $2^j - 1$ for some j. We can now define $T'(k) = T(2^k - 1)$, and obtain the recurrence relation

$$T'(k) = 2T'(k-1), \quad T'(1) = 1.$$

The solution of this recurrence relation is clearly $T'(k) = 2^{k-1}$. The recurrence relation behaves differently for powers of 2 and for nonpowers of 2, because its definition is vastly different between even numbers and odd numbers. We can restrict ourselves to powers of 2 if the solution of the recurrence relation is a function that behaves "nicely." In particular, the expressions for the running times of most algorithms are monotonically increasing functions. If the difference between the value of $T(n)$ and $T(2n)$ is no more than a constant and if $T(n)$ is monotonically increasing, then $T(m)$ for $n < m < 2n$ is no more than a constant times $T(n)$. Therefore, the analysis for powers of 2 is sufficient in that case.

Chapter 4

4.5   Since 16 is occupied, 8 (16's parent) must be occupied. By the same argument, 4, 2, and 1 must be occupied. Thus, 5 is the minimal number of heap elements in an array of size 16.

4.12   We will use an array of size n and store element i at location i. Therefore, insertions are easy. A removal is more complicated, since i is not specified and we do not know which locations are occupied. We handle removals by linking all the occupied locations in a linked list. An insertion of i thus involves marking the ith location *and* inserting i to the list. A removal deletes the first element from the list and unmarks that element.

4.13   We first remove an arbitrary element from one of the heaps (e.g., the top of one of them), and rearrange this heap. We then insert the removed element as a new root such that the roots of the two heaps are connected to it as its children. The new root may not be in its appropriate place, but it takes $O(\log(m+n))$ steps to move it down the combined heap to a correct place.

4.15   We use AVL trees so that insertions and deletions can be done in $O(\log n)$ steps. To perform *Find_Next(x)* we use the regular search algorithm for x, except that we branch right if we meet x and x is not a leaf. If x is not a leaf, then the search leads us to the desired element. If x is a leaf, then the element for which we are looking is the last node on the path from the root to x where we branch to the left (if we always branch to the right, then x is the largest element in the tree). We can, during the search, store a pointer to the last node from which we branch left and use it if x is found to be a leaf.

4.17   We use AVL trees so that insertions and deletions can be done in $O(\log n)$ steps. We add a new field to every node v, denoted by $v.D$, which contains the number of descendants of v (including v). We can use this field to find the *rank* of a node v (namely, the number of elements in the tree that are smaller than or equal to $v.Key$) during the search. This is done by the use of induction as follows. We assume that we know the ranks of all nodes on the path from the root to some node w, and show how to find the ranks of the children of w. Denote the rank of node v by $v.Rank$.

$$w.Left.Rank = w.Rank - w.Left.Right.D - 1.$$

$$w.Right.Rank = w.Rank + w.Right.Left.D + 1.$$

(If any of the children does not exist, the D value is taken as 0.) To perform *Find_Next(x, k)* we first find v such that $v.Key = x$ (if there is no such node, then the search is unsuccessful). We then search for the node with rank $v.Rank + k$. It is as easy to search according to ranks as it is according to keys. We are not yet done, however. Since we have introduced a new field, we must show how to maintain this field when insertions or deletion take place. This is done as follows. When we insert (delete) an element we increment (decrement) the descendant fields in all nodes along the search path. (Notice that, if the insertion or the deletion is unsuccessful, we must redo these changes.)

Here is another question: Why did we add a descendant field instead of a rank field, which would have made the search for a key with a specified rank much easier?

4.20   Let the height of the "left" tree (i.e., the tree with the smaller elements) be h_1 and the height of the right tree be h_2. Assume that $h_1 \geq h_2$ (the other case is similar). First, delete the maximal element from the left tree. Denote this element by r. Then, use r as a new root for the right tree, and insert this root in the appropriate place on the right side of the left tree. More precisely, traverse the left tree, taking only right branches, for $h_1 - h_2$ steps. Let the node at that place be v, and its parent p. The new concatenated tree will have r in place of v as the right child of p, v as the left child of r and the root of the right tree as the right child of r (the right tree remains below its root on the right side of r). It is easy to verify that this is a consistent binary search tree. This insertion may invalidate the AVL property, in which case we can use the usual remedy of a rotation.

4.23   Let T_h be the worst AVL tree of height h (namely, the tree with the fewest nodes). T_1 is clearly a tree with a root and one child. T_2 is a tree with a root and two children such that one of the children has one child of its own, and the other child is a leaf. In general, we assume that we know how to construct T_h and consider T_{h+1}. T_{h+1} must have a child that is a root of a subtree of height h. Since this subtree must satisfy the AVL property and we want a tree with fewest nodes, we should use T_h. Furthermore, since the AVL property must also be satisfied at the root, the other child of the root must be the root of a subtree of height at least $h - 1$. The subtree with fewest nodes for this child is thus T_{h-1}. Therefore, T_{h+1} consists of a root connected to T_h and T_{h-1}. The number of nodes $N(h+1)$ in T_{h+1} satisfies

$$N(h+1) = N(h) + N(h-1) + 1.$$

This is the Fibonacci recurrence relation. Its solution leads to the lower bound on the number of nodes in an AVL tree. This lower bound can then be used to prove the upper bound on the height of an AVL tree with n nodes given in the theorem.

4.27   We use the extra array, denoted by S, to store sums of numbers in a special way. Let's assume first that $n = 2^k - 1$ for some k. We store in $S[2^{k-1}]$ the sum of all numbers from 1 to 2^{k-1}. By doing so, we have divided the problem into two subproblems of half the size — maintaining the left side of the array (from 1 to $2^{k-1} - 1$), and the right side of the array (from $2^{k-1} + 1$ to $2^k - 1$). Each subproblem can be solved by induction. The first subproblem can be solved independently, except that every time an *Add* operation is performed, the appropriate change in $S[2^{k-1}]$ must be made. The second subproblem can also be solved independently, except that we add the value of $S[2^{k-1}]$ to the returned value of *Partial_sum*. If we look beyond the recursion, what happens is that $S[i]$ holds the sum of the numbers from $A[j]$ to $A[i]$, where j is the closest index to i that is divided by a higher degree of 2 than i. For example, $S[12]$ holds the sum $A[9] + A[10] + A[11] + A[12]$, and $S[6]$ holds the value of $A[5] + A[6]$. We leave the exact details to the reader.

4.29   We can implement all the operations in the exercise, except for *Add_all*, in a straightforward way by using AVL trees. To support *Add_all(y)*, we associate one more global variable, *Scale*, with the tree. *Add_all(y)* simply adds y to *Scale*. *Find_value(x)* adds *Scale* to the value associated with x. *Insert(x, Value)* sets the value of x as $Value - Scale$.

Chapter 5

5.4   The loop invariant is the following:

> *Only one person among the first next − 1 persons can be the candidate, and that person is i if next = j, or j if next = i.*

5.12   The solution is similar to that of the maximum consecutive subsequence problem, except that we strengthen the induction hypothesis even further. We assume that we know (1) the subsequence with the maximal product, (2) the subsequence that ends at the end with the maximal product, (3) the subsequence with the minimal negative product, and (4) the subsequence that ends at the end with the minimal negative product. We leave it to the reader to handle all these cases.

5.14   The solution is trivial for a tree with one or two vertices. Suppose that we know how to solve the problem for a tree with n vertices, and consider a tree T with $n + 1$ vertices. Let v be an arbitrary leaf in T, and let w be the only vertex connected to v. If we remove v, we are left with a smaller tree T'. The distance between v and any vertex u in T' is 1 plus the distance between w and u.

5.15   Let v be an arbitrary vertex in G, which we designate as the *root* of the tree. If we remove v from the tree, we obtain several smaller trees whose roots are the vertices that were adjacent to v. We can repeat this process, each time obtaining new roots and smaller trees, until all edges are removed. We will solve the problem by induction on the number of times we have to perform this process until all edges are removed. If the path corresponding to the diameter of the tree does not contain the root, then the diameter of the tree is also the diameter of one of the smaller trees, which we find by induction. If the root is contained in the path corresponding to the diameter, then this path connects two vertices in two separate smaller trees that are farthest away from the root. This observation suggests the following induction hypothesis (which is stronger than the straightforward one).

> **Induction hypothesis:** *We know how to find the diameter of subtrees with* $<$ n *vertices, and how to find the maximal distance from a fixed root.*

The base case is trivial. Given a tree with n vertices, we designate v as the root, and solve the problem by induction for all the subtrees rooted at the children of v. Notice that the distances we find are those to the children of v, and not those to v. However, to find the distances to v, we need only to add 1 to all the distances. After doing that, we compare the maximum diameter found among the subtrees with the sum of the two maximum distances from v. The larger of the two is the diameter.

5.21   We assume that a subset whose sum is k exists. Use the black box for the input set without one of the elements. If the answer is yes, then there is a solution without this element; if the answer is no, then the element is necessary. In either case, the problem has been reduced, since the status of one element has been determined.

Chapter 6

6.3   We can use binary search by cutting the text in half and running the program on one half. If an error occurs, then we know that it is in that half and we can continue in the same manner; if no error occurs, then it is in the other half. (We assume that the offending string has not been cut.)

6.11   We first modify algorithm *Partition* (Fig. 6.9) such that, if the pivot is not equal to $X[Left]$, then the pivot is first exchanged with $X[Left]$. Let $X[1]=1$, $X[n]=2$, and let all other elements be greater than 2. In this case, the pivot will clearly be $X[n]$. Algorithm *Partition* will first exchange $X[1]$ with $X[n]$ as mentioned above, then exchange $X[n]$ with $X[2]$ (since $X[n]$ is now <2 and $X[2]>2$). Since all other elements are greater than 2, no other exchanges will take place. The result of the partition is to put 1 and 2 at their correct places in the beginning of the array. Quicksort will then recursively sort the array from the third index to the last one. To continue this pattern, we need to put the third smallest element in the third position, and, since the element in the last position in the array after the partition was originally in the second position, we need to put the fourth smallest element in the second position. For example, if $n=8$, then a bad order will be 1, 4, 3, 6, 5, 8, 7, 2.

6.14   Divide the set into two equal-sized subsets (or into two sets with sizes different by 1 if the size of the original set is odd). Solve each subproblem recursively, and merge the results. Each recursive solution produces two results, the maximal and minimal element. Only two comparisons are required to merge the two solutions; one to compare the two maximals, and one to compare the two minimals. The following recurrence relation is obtained:

$$T(n) = 2T(n/2) + 2, \quad T(2) = 1.$$

It is easy to verify by induction that $T(n) = 3n/2 - 2$: $T(2) = 3 \cdot 2/2 - 2 = 1$, and $T(2n) = 2T(n) + 2 = 2(3n/2-2) + 2 = 3n - 2$. The savings come from the base case! It takes only one comparison to find both minimum and maximum between two numbers. We do it (at the final unfolding of the recursion) for $n/2$ pairs, so we save about $n/2$ comparisons. It is interesting to note that more than $3n/2 - 2$ comparisons may be needed if n is not a power of 2. For example, since $T(3) = 3$, we have $T(6) = 8$, $T(12) = 18$, and so on. The algorithm suggested in Section 6.5.1 is better in this case.

6.19   Consider $w = A[n/2]$ (we assume without loss of generality that n is even). If $w \geq z$, then z must appear in the array between $A[1]$ and $A[n/2]$. This is true because the difference between consecutive elements in the array is at most 1, and therefore no number can be skipped. If $w < z$, then, by a similar argument, z must appear between $A[n/2+1]$ and $A[n]$. In either case, we cut the search space in half with each comparison. The maximal number of comparisons is thus $\lceil \log_2 n \rceil$.

6.20   We can use the simple information-theoretic bound. The number of possible answers to the question posed by Exercise 6.19 is n (z can be equal to $A[1]$, $A[2]$, and so on). Therefore, any decision tree that solves this problem must have at least n leaves (where the ith leaf corresponds to the answer "z is equal to $A[i]$"). The height of such a decision tree must be at least $\lceil \log_2 n \rceil$.

6.22   a. Sort the set S; then, for each element z of S, perform binary search for the number $x - z$.

       b. We use induction.

           Induction hypothesis: *We know how to solve the problem for a sorted set of $<n$ elements.*

           Assume that S is sorted in increasing order. Consider $S[1]$ and $S[n]$, and let $y = S[1] + S[n]$. If $y = x$, then we are done. If $y > x$, then clearly $S[n]$ cannot be part of the solution because $S[n] + S[i] > x$ for all i. Therefore, we can eliminate $S[n]$ from consideration and solve the remaining problem by induction. If $y < x$, then, by a similar argument, we can eliminate $S[1]$.

6.26 Sort the set, and pair the smallest element with the largest, the second smallest with the second largest, and so on. This procedure is correct for the following reasons. Suppose that there is another partition with a better bound, in which x_1 and x_n are not matched. Let x_1 be matched in this partition with x_i and x_n with x_j. But then, we can change the partition so that x_1 is matched with x_n and x_i is matched with x_j, without increasing the maximal sum, which is a contradiction.

6.28 The permutation $a_1, a_2, ..., a_n$ defines a total order on $x_1, x_2, ..., x_n$. That is, we can "compare" any pair of elements x_i and x_j by comparing a_i to a_j. We want to rearrange the x_is such that the a_is will appear in order. Therefore, any sorting algorithm that sorts according to the values of the a_is and moves both x_i and a_i together will lead to the desired outcome. Since we want an in-place algorithm, we can use, for example, heapsort.

6.29 Initially, put all the d minimal elements of the sequences in a heap. Then, in each step, remove the minimal element in the heap and insert the next element from the corresponding sequence.

6.31 a. Insert each element into a balanced binary search tree (e.g., an AVL tree). Each node of the tree has a key and a pointer to a linked list of all the elements with the same key. Since the number of different keys is $O(\log n)$, the number of nodes in the tree is $O(\log n)$ and therefore the tree's height is $O(\log \log n)$. After we construct the tree we can append the different linked lists to one list by performing inorder traversal of the tree.

   b. The lower bound for sorting does not apply to this problem, because the lower bound proof assumed that all permutations are possible valid inputs. In this problem, we restrict the possible inputs to only those with $O(\log n)$ different values.

6.33 The sum of heights is at most

$$T(n) = 2 \sum_{i=1}^{n} \lceil \log_2((n+1)/i) \rceil.$$

To evaluate $T(n)$ we start with a small concrete example. Consider $T(7)$:

$$T(7) = \log_2 8 + \log_2 4 + \lceil \log_2 8/3 \rceil + \log_2 2 + \lceil \log_2 8/5 \rceil + \lceil \log_2 8/6 \rceil + \lceil \log_2 8/7 \rceil$$

$$= 3 + 2 + 2 + 1 + 1 + 1 + 1.$$

There are 4 ($=(n+1)/2$) terms of size 1, two terms of size 2, and one term of size 3. Let's assume that $n+1 = 2^k$. It is not difficult to see that $T(n)$ will consist of $(n+1)/2$ terms of size 1, $(n+1)/4$ terms of size 2, and so on, up to one term of size k. (This is exactly the heights of all nodes in a complete binary tree.) So, overall

$$T(n) = \sum_{i=1}^{k} i 2^{k-i}.$$

This sum was shown to be $O(n)$ in Section 3.4. If $n+1$ is not a power of 2, then there can be at most an extra contribution of 1 to each term, adding no more than n.

6.36 Suppose that algorithm A finds that x_i is the kth largest element by making a series of comparisons whose results cannot determine whether a certain element x_j is greater or smaller than x_i. This implies that the outcome of the comparisons is consistent with x_j being equal to a value $y > x_i$ and to a value $z < x_i$. But both cases lead to a different kth largest element, which is a contradiction.

6.38   The idea is to consider $2k$ elements at a time. We start with the first $2k$ elements, and find their median. All elements greater than the median can be eliminated. We now look at the next k elements and do the same. This process requires approximately n/k phases, each consisting of computing the median of $2k$ elements.

6.41   There are exactly $n+1$ possible answers to this problem, so every decision tree that solves the problem must have at least $n+1$ leaves. The claim follows immediately.

6.44   This problem is discussed in Section 10.2.

6.46   The basic idea is to construct the *next* table for the part of the pattern that is known, and to extend it as more characters of the pattern become known. This is not hard to do, since the construction of the *next* table is similar to the regular pattern matching problem (see also Takaoka [1986]).

6.51   Part b serves as a good hint for the solution of part a. We find the minimal edit distance (and the minimal edit sequence) between T and P under the assumption that no replacements are allowed (the same algorithm can be used, except that the cost of a replacement is set to 2). The LCS of the two sequences is the set of characters that are matched in the minimal edit sequence (i.e., those that are not involved in the insertions or deletions). The SCS is the LCS plus all the insertions and deletions. We leave the proof to the reader.

6.54   The easiest way to solve this problem is to use the regular sequence comparison algorithm, except that the initial values of $C(i, 0)$ (see algorithm *Minimal_Edit_Distance*) are 0. In other words, inserting the beginning of A does not cost anything, which is exactly what we want.

6.60   The (not surprising) answer is that it is better to be correct than to be fast. Given a Las Vegas algorithm that runs in expected time $T(n)$ and always produces the correct result, we can transform it into a Monte Carlo algorithm by enforcing termination of the algorithm after $4T(n)$ steps, if it has not already terminated. Since its expected running time is $T(n)$, the probability that it does not terminate after $4T(n)$ steps is no more than 1/4. When we enforce termination, we output an arbitrary answer. The algorithm now runs in (guaranteed) time $O(T(n))$ and no more than 1/4 probability of error.
A little harder question: Show that it is sufficient to run the algorithm for $2T(n)$ steps.

6.61   We use the majority algorithm, except that we keep up to three different candidates. Each element is compared to the candidates, and if it is equal to one of them, then the corresponding multiplicity is incremented. Otherwise, if the new element is different from the existing three candidates, then we can decrement the multiplicity of all candidate (by the same argument as in the majority algorithm — we can eliminate four distinct values from consideration). If there are less than three candidates, we add the current element as a new candidate. At the end, all remaining candidates are compared to all the elements.

Chapter 7

7.4   Let T be a tree that satisfies the conditions of the problem, and consider the rest of the graph. Let e be an edge not in T. Since T is a DFS tree, e must be a back edge; that is, e must connect a vertex to its ancestor. However, since T is also a BFS tree, e must connect two vertices at the same level or at neighboring levels. This is a contradiction; hence, the only graphs that satisfy the constraints of the problem are trees.

7.8   The claim is wrong.

7.24   The conditions of the problem imply that G is Eulerian. Consider an Eulerian circuit C in G, and its traversal.

7.27   Perform a DFS (a BFS will do just as well), and construct the DFS tree. Prove that any leaf in that tree satisfies the conditions of the problem.

7.29   The solution is by induction. The base case is simple. We want to reduce the problem to one with $n-1$ numbers, and still have the same constraints. Since all d_is are positive and their sum is $2n-2$, there exists at least one k such that $d_k = 1$. There also exists j such that $d_j > 1$. So, we can remove d_k from the list and subtract 1 from d_j. This is a valid problem of size $n-1$ (everything is still positive and the sum is $2n-4$), which we solve it by induction. We find a tree T with the corresponding degrees. We need only to add a leaf to the vertex corresponding to d_j in T to find the tree that solves the original problem.

7.34   We use the KMP pattern-matching algorithm (Section 6.7) in combination with a DFS-like (preorder) traversal of the tree. During the traversal, we maintain the status of each vertex in regard to current potential matching. That is, we define $v.match$ to be equal to the size of the maximal prefix in the pattern that matches the suffix of the path from the root to v. (This is exactly the same information that is maintained by the KMP algorithm.) *preWORK* for v is defined by including v's character as the next step in the KMP algorithm, and computing $v.match$. *postWORK* is defined by restoring the status of v — that is, by continuing the matching from v using $v.match$. The running time of this algorithm is linear in the number of vertices in the tree.

7.35   Without the cycle, the graph would have been a tree for which the problem is easy (pick a root and direct all edges away from it). We can discover the cycle by DFS when the first (and only) edge leading to a previously visited vertex is found. The cycle can be directed so that it becomes a directed cycle and all its vertices have indegree 1. All other edges should be directed away from the cycle. This can be achieved by starting another DFS from any vertex on the cycle and directing all edges in the direction they are visited during the search. The single back edge will point to the root of the search which will have indegree 1 (as will all other vertices).

7.37   Perform DFS on the graph, and build a DFS tree T. Since all the other edges in the graph are back edges relative to T, we can direct all edges of T to point away from the root and all other edges to point toward vertices that are closer to the root (i.e., toward the ancestors).

7.40   Modify the topological sort algorithm so that all vertices of indegree 0 are removed together from the queue and are put in one group. The algorithm handles these vertices as before (i.e., it removes their emanating edges by decrementing the corresponding indegrees), and then again all vertices of indegree 0 are removed. Prove that the groups satisfy the conditions of the problem, and that there are no more than $k+1$ of them.

7.42   Use BFS starting at v. Each edge (x, y) encountered through the search, such that y is a new vertex, is part of a shortest path from v to y. A common error is to increment the count of shortest paths to y when (x, y) is encountered. However, there may already be several known shortest paths to x, and each one of them is a part of a shortest path to y (ending with the edge (x, y)). Hence, the correct solution is to *add* the number of shortest paths to x (which is already known) to the count of shortest paths to y. All counts are initialized to 0.

7.43   The main idea is not to use a heap. Instead, we find a new minimum path by looking at *all* the vertices. This takes $O(|V|)$ time, but now the update for each edge takes only constant time (since no heap is maintained).

7.45   Add to each edge a weight of $1u$ where u stands for a *unit*. Use the same algorithm, except that the length of a path is its regular length plus the sum of units. The units are used to compare two paths with the same regular weight. Instead of using artificial units, it may be possible to add a very small number x to the weight of each edge. The value of x must be small enough that it does not affect paths with different regular weight. For example, x can be taken as $m/(|V|+1)$, where m is the precision of the weights (e.g., if they are integers, then $m = 1$).

7.48   We use induction on k, and find not only the path to w, but also the paths to all other vertices. For simplicity, we discuss finding only the lengths of the paths, rather than the paths themselves. The case of $k = 1$ is obvious. Denote by $w.SP_k$ the length of the shortest path from v to w which contains exactly k edges. Assume that we know the shortest paths, which contain exactly $k - 1$ edges, from v to all other vertices. That is, we know the values of $w.SP_{k-1}$ for all w. We now need to consider all edges, and for each edge (x, y) set $y.SP_k$ to $x.SP_{k-1} + length(x, y)$ if it is smaller than the current $y.SP_k$. The running time is thus $O(|E| \cdot |V|)$.

7.50   Algorithm *Improved_Acyclic_Shortest_Paths* (Fig. 7.16) works for negative-cost edges as well. (Hint for a proof: Whenever a vertex is considered, all the paths leading to it from the source have been compared.)

7.52   The graph must be Eulerian, since each cycle adds a degree of 2 to each of its vertices. On the other hand, the edges of an Eulerian graph can always be partitioned into a set of cycles. It is enough to note that there exists at least one cycle in an Eulerian graph, and that removing a cycle from an Eulerian graph gives a set of (possibly one) connected Eulerian graphs.

7.55   This is an excellent example for a solution by induction. The induction will be on the number of vertices. The base case is simple. Let v be any leaf in the tree. We would like to remove v, to solve the problem for the remaining tree, and to find a value of $S(v)$ that satisfies the requirements. If the edge connected to v points toward v, then the reduction is simple: Let the edge be (w, v); then, $S(v)$ can be set to $S(w) \cup \{\lambda(w, v)\}$, and it is easy to see that the requirements are satisfied. The difficult case is when the edge is (v, w). In that case, we set $S(v)$ to be equal to $S(w)$ and change all the other subsets by adding the label $\lambda(v, w)$ to them. It is easy to verify that all the requirements are satisfied.

7.60   Start with F as the current "minimal" spanning tree and add edges to it according to the algorithm in Exercise 7.59.

7.64   First find the MCST, call it T. (The answer for all edges of T is obviously T itself.) For each pair of vertices v and w, find the maximum-cost edge in the (unique) path connecting v to w in T. This is a preprocessing step. We may not need the information for all pairs, but it is simpler to compute it for all of them. A minimum-cost spanning tree containing the edge (x, y) is obtained by adding the edge (x, y) to T, then removing the maximum-cost edge from the unique cycle that is formed (or the second largest, if (x, y) is the maximum). This edge is the maximum-cost edge on the path from x to y in T, whose identity we obtained in the preprocessing step. The preprocessing step can be done by using DFS on T for $|V|$

times, each time starting from another vertex.

7.67   Increasing all costs by a constant does not change an MCST, because only the *relative order* of the costs is important for the algorithm. Whenever costs are used in the algorithm, they are compared to each other with a simple comparison (''<'' or ''>''). They are not used (or manipulated) in any other way. Therefore, since adding a constant to all costs does not change the order of the costs, it also does not change the result.

7.68   (This is just a sketch of a rather complicated algorithm.) First, we notice that we can concentrate on T and ignore the rest of the graph. Since T has already been found to be an MCST, every other edge in G completes a cycle with the edges of T in which it is a maximum-cost edge. Adding another vertex does not change that fact. We will also assume, for simplicity, that v is connected to all vertices in T (e.g., we can add dummy edges with infinite cost). We use induction on the number of vertices in T. Consider T as a rooted tree (with an arbitrary root), and look at an internal vertex w connected to several leaves. Each pair of leaves x and y connected to w defines a cycle of four edges with v and w (containing the edges (w, x), (x, v), (v, y), and (y, w)). The maximum-cost edge of this cycle should be deleted, which creates a new leaf in the new graph. This leaf is guaranteed to be in the new MCST, which will reduce the size of the problem. We are not quite done, since w may have only one leaf z. In that case, the cycle is a triangle consisting of (w, z), (z, v), and (v, w). The difficult case is when (v, w) is the maximum-cost edge in this cycle and needs to be removed. This case is difficult because no new leaf is found. However, we can still reduce the problem by ''compressing'' w. We replace the two edges (w, z) and (w, p) (where p is the parent of w in the rooted tree) by one edge (p, z), and set the cost of this new edge as the maximal cost of the two old edges. We leave it to the reader to complete this argument into an algorithm. One needs to prove that the compression is valid, and to design the appropriate data structure to maintain the necessary information during the running of the algorithm.

7.70   The main idea is to solve the problem backward. Instead of deleting vertices in the way the problem is stated, we add vertices in the opposite order. We use the union-find data structure (Section 4.5) to maintain the set of components currently in the graph. We start with vertex n and add it as one component to the data structure. We then consider vertices $n-1$, $n-2$, and so on. For each vertex i, we first add it as a component, then check all edges (i, j) such that $j > i$. For each such edge (i, j), we check whether i and j belong to the same component (using the find operation), and, if not, we join the two corresponding components (using the union operation). We stop when one component contains more than $n/2$ vertices.

7.71   Since every cycle in G must contain an edge from the feedback-edge set F, the set of edges $E - F$ cannot contain a cycle. We want to minimize the size of F, which is the same as maximizing the size of $E - F$. The largest set of edges with no cycle in a graph corresponds to a spanning tree (or spanning forest, if the graph is not connected). Hence, the minimum-size feedback-edge set in an undirected graph is a complement of a spanning tree of the graph, and its size is $|E| - |V| + 1$ (assuming that the graph is connected). The corresponding problem for directed graphs is NP-complete (see Chapter 11).

7.74   Check all the edges not in the tree. If there is an edge (v, w) such that $v.SP + cost(v, w) < w.SP$ (where $x.SP$ is the length of the shortest path to x via the tree), then the tree is obviously not a shortest-path tree. It remains to prove that, if no such edge exists, then the tree is indeed a shortest-path tree.

7.79   Find a topological order, and then check, for all vertices with consecutive labels, if they are connected in the graph. If they are, then the topological order gives a Hamiltonian path. On the other hand, if there exists a Hamiltonian path, then any topological order will sort the vertices according to their place in that path.

7.84   We proved in Section 7.9 that two edges are contained in a cycle if and only if they are in the same biconnected component. Hence, we need only to remove c from the graph and to run the biconnected components algorithm to determine whether a and b belong to the same biconnected component in the graph without c.

7.85   We will prove a slightly stronger theorem (and leave it to the reader to show that it implies the claim in the exercise).

□ **Theorem A.2**

If v and w are two vertices of the same biconnected component B, then any simple path between v and w is contained in B.

Proof: There is obviously at least one simple path between v and w in B. If there is path that is not contained in B, then it has to leave B and to come back. It has to leave B from one component and to come back through another (since it is simple, and two components can be connected only through one articulation point). But that would imply the existence of a cycle involving more than one biconnected component, which is impossible.

7.87   Pick an arbitrary articulation point v. Remove v and its incident edges from the graph and find the different connected components of the resulting graph. Then put back the removed edges into the appropriate components. Consider now each component separately, and perform the same procedure by picking another articulation point, and so on.

7.89   A first approach may be to try to modify the strongly connected component algorithm to update the *High* values more accurately. For example, instead of using DFS numbers, we can use the currently known *High* values. In other words, when an edge (v, w) is considered for the purpose of computing $v.High$, we use $w.High$ instead of $w.DFS$ in the computation. However, $w.High$ may be updated later (e.g., one of its other children may have a path to a higher vertex). Updating all the vertices that used the previous value of $w.High$ may be too costly. We use another approach.

Denote the largest DFS number reachable from v by $v.Real\_High$. All the vertices in the same strongly connected component have the same characteristics as far as reachability is concerned. That is, if any of them can reach a vertex w, then all of them can reach w. Hence, it is sufficient to compute $v.Real\_High$ for one representative of each strongly connected component. We first use the strongly connected component algorithm to construct the SCC graph SG. Each node in SG is marked with the DFS number of the root of the corresponding strongly connected component (this is the vertex with the highest DFS number in the component). SG must be acyclic, so we have reduced the problem to that of finding the *Real_High* values of acyclic graphs. The advantage of this reduction is that it solves the problem with repeated updating that we had before. Since SG is acyclic, there are no back edges. Therefore, at the time the edge (v, w) (in SG) is used to update $v.Real\_High$, the value of $w.Real\_High$ is the correct final value. We leave it to the reader to prove this fact — for example, by induction (the proof is not trivial).

7.92   a. Suppose that v belongs to a vertex basis B. If v is not on a cycle and v has a nonzero indegree, then there exists a vertex w such that (w, v) is an edge and w is not reachable from v. For B to be a vertex basis, either w belongs to B or there is a path from some vertex in B to w. In either case, however, there is also a path from a vertex in B to v, and v can be removed from B. This contradicts the minimality of B.

   b. Since no vertex is on a cycle in an acyclic graph, it follows from part a that only the vertices of indegree 0 can be in a vertex basis. But, it is also true that each vertex of indegree 0 *must* be in any vertex basis, since there is no path leading to it. Hence, the unique vertex basis of an acyclic graph is the set of vertices of indegree 0 (we proved in Section 7.3 that this set is not empty).

   Given a general graph now, we first find the SCC graph (see Section 7.9). As we have shown, the SCC graph is acyclic. Any vertex in a strongly connected component covers all other vertices in this component. Hence, it is sufficient to choose one of the vertices in each component. Thus, a vertex basis consists of one vertex (any vertex) from each component that corresponds to a node of indegree 0 in the SCC graph.

7.95   Consider the tree as a rooted tree with an arbitrary root. Take an arbitrary leaf v and match it to its parent w. Remove both from the tree (and all other "brothers" that become disconnected). Solve the resulting problem by induction. We need to prove that the edge (v, w) indeed belongs to a maximum matching. Let M be a maximum matching. If M does not contain (v, w), then v is not matched (it is connected only to w). If (u, w) is in the maximum matching, then simply replace it with (v, w). It is still a matching, and it has the same cardinality.

7.99   a. A graph must not include a vertex of degree 0 to have such a cover. When we remove an arbitrary vertex, we may end up with a component that consists of only one vertex.

   b. We now assume that the graph contains only vertices of degree > 0, and we make sure that the reduced graph satisfies this condition. Only vertices of degree 1 pose any problem. So, if the graph contains any vertex of degree 1, we remove one such vertex with its edge and add this edge (which is a star graph by itself) to the cover. Only one degree of one other vertex is reduced by 1. It is easy to see that this is now a valid reduction.

7.100 We use binary search in combination with the maximum-matching algorithm described in Section 7.10. Let's solve first the problem of *verifying* whether there exists a maximum matching such that all of its edges have weights $\leq x$ (for some given x). This problem can be solved by removing from the graph all edges of weight $> x$ and applying the maximum-matching algorithm to see whether the maximum matching in the remaining graph has the same number of edges as the maximum matching in the original graph. The cost of this verification is dominated by the cost of the maximum-matching algorithm, which is $O(\sqrt{n}\, m)$. There are m edges in G, so there are at most m different possibilities for weights. We can now use binary search to find the smallest x such that x is a weight of some edge and there is a maximum matching such that all of its edges have weights $\leq x$. (For an algorithm with a lower time complexity, see Gabow and Tarjan [1988].)

7.104 We use divide and conquer. We divide the players into two equal-sized groups and construct a chain as required for each group. We then *merge* the two chains in exactly the same way as regular merge. We leave it to the reader to verify the correctness of this procedure. The similarity of this algorithm to mergesort is not incidental; see Exercise 10.18.

7.106   Clearly, at least k colors are necessary, since all edges incident to the same vertex must be colored differently. We will show that k colors are also sufficient. We want to use divide and conquer, but we have to divide the problem such that the subproblems are the same as the original problem. If we divide into two smaller subgraphs, we have to ensure that the degrees of all vertices in each subgraph are equal and that they are a power of 2. This is achieved by finding an Eulerian circuit of the graph (such a circuit exists, since all degrees are even). Then, we traverse the circuit and divide the edges into two groups by alternating between the two groups (i.e., the first edge goes to the first group, the second to the second group, the third to the first group, and so on). Each group defines a subgraph with all the original vertices and one-half of the original edges. The degree of each vertex in each subgraph is exactly $k/2$, since whenever an edge entering a vertex is put in one group, the next edge (which is leaving the vertex) will be put in the second group. The rest can be done by induction. We now have graphs with fewer edges and, more important, smaller degrees. We color all the edges of the two subgraphs separately, but we use distinct colors for each group. Therefore, we can just put the two colorings together. The complexity of this algorithm is dominated by the algorithm for finding Eulerian circuits, which takes linear time but which has to be performed for each subgraph. The number of stages of this algorithm is $\log_2 k$ (since k is halved at each stage); hence, the total running time is $O(|E| \log k)$. (It is interesting to note that every graph whose maximal degree is k can be edge-colored with at most $k+1$ colors; see, for example, Chartrand and Lesniak [1986].)

7.108   A common approach to this problem (judging from students' examinations) is to consider a root of the tree (any vertex can serve as the root), to find minimum vertex covers for all the subtrees below the root, and then to include the root in the vertex cover unless all its children are already included in the vertex covers of the subtrees. This seems like a good approach, since the root must indeed belong to the vertex cover if any of its children does not belong. However, there may be many different minimum vertex covers (see Fig. S.1). For a given subtree, it is possible that there is a minimum vertex cover that includes its root and one that does not include the root. Therefore, this approach does not necessarily lead to minimum vertex covers (unless more precautions are taken). A different reduction can be achieved by considering a leaf first. The edge from a leaf to its parent must be covered, and can be covered by either the leaf or its parent. There is no advantage to choosing the leaf,

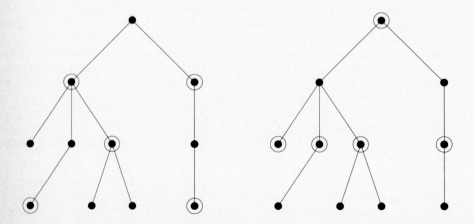

Figure A.1 A tree with two minimum vertex covers.

since it does not cover anything else. More precisely, *there is a minimum vertex cover that includes the parent.* Therefore, if we choose the parent (of any arbitrary leaf), remove it and all its incident edges, and then solve the remaining problem by induction, we are guaranteed to have a minimum vertex cover. It is not difficult to implement this algorithm in linear time.

7.109   It is easy to see that the weight of a vertex cover in this case must be equal to at least the number of edges (since all edges must be covered and each contributes at least a cost of 1 to the cover). A cover that includes exactly one vertex from each edge is thus the minimum-weight cover. We will show that such a cover can always be found.

Solution 1: Perform a BFS with an arbitrary vertex v as the root, and assign each vertex a level number according to its distance from v. Now add all vertices with odd level numbers (even level numbers will do just as well) to the vertex cover. The result will be a vertex cover, since every edge connects vertices from two adjacent levels, so one of them has odd level number. Furthermore, each edge is covered by exactly one vertex, so the cover is minimum.

Solution 2: The induction hypothesis states that we know how to solve the problems for all trees with $< n$ vertices. Pick an arbitrary leaf v and remove it (and its incident edge) from the tree. Let the only vertex adjacent to v be w, and let G' be the remaining tree. Solve the problem for G' by induction. Consider again the original tree G. If w is used in the minimum-weight vertex cover of G', then this cover is still valid; otherwise, include v in the cover for G. We have to prove that in both cases the cover of G is minimal. But, the size of a minimum-weight vertex cover of G must be at least 1 more than the minimum-weight cover of G', since the extra edge must be covered by either v or w (and it costs 1 more in either case, since the degree of w is increased). We achieve this bound, so the resulting vertex cover is minimal.

7.114   Let v be an arbitrary vertex of G. Denote the set of vertices adjacent to v by $N(v)$. If v belongs to the vertex cover, then none of the vertices in $N(v)$ can belong to the vertex cover (since the vertices in the cover should be independent). Furthermore, all the vertices adjacent to vertices from $N(v)$ *must* belong to the cover, since that is the only way to cover those edges. In particular, if any two vertices of $N(v)$ are adjacent, then the edge between them cannot be covered, and the procedure fails. This procedure is continued until either it fails, in which case v cannot belong to the vertex cover, or a vertex cover is found. All the steps of the procedure are determined by the choice of v; hence, the vertex cover that is found is the only one containing v that satisfies the conditions of the problem. If this cover is not too large, then we are done; otherwise, v cannot belong to the vertex cover. But, if we determine that v cannot belong to the vertex cover, then all its adjacent vertices must belong to the cover, and we can apply the same procedure.

7.116   Each interval I_j is represented by two numbers (l_j, r_j) (the left and right endpoints). Sort the intervals according to the r_js. Denote the intervals in the sorted order by $I_1, I_2, ..., I_n$ (i.e., r_1 is the minimum among the right endpoints). We claim that there is a maximum independent set that includes I_1. To prove it, take any maximum independent set and consider the interval I_j in it such that r_j is minimum among all other right endpoints in the set. Since r_1 is the global minimum, $r_j \geq r_1$. But that implies that I_1 does not intersect with any other interval in the set (except possibly with I_j); hence, I_1 can replace I_j, and the modified set is still maximum independent set. The algorithm follows directly by induction, because we know how to handle I_1.

7.119 a. Let v_1, v_2, v_3, and v_4 be a cycle of length 4 (in that order). Consider the adjacency matrix of the graph, and assume that the main diagonal is 0 (i.e., a vertex is not considered adjacent to itself). The rows corresponding to v_1 and v_3 both contain 1s corresponding to v_2 and v_4. This is, is some sense, a characterization of a cycle of length 4. (Notice that the matrix is symmetric since the graph is undirected.) We can look at all pairs of rows, and for each pair check its intersection. In other words, for each pair of vertices, we check all the other vertices that are adjacent to both of them. There is a square if and only if any such intersection contains at least two vertices. Any row intersection (which is basically a row *and* operation) can be performed in linear time. There are $O(|V|^2)$ pairs of vertices, so the overall running time is $O(|V|^3)$.

b. Use an adjacency-list representation. First sort all the edges in all the lists. Then show that the intersection between two rows described in part a can be performed in time proportional to the number of edges incident to the two corresponding vertices.

7.120 Compute the maximum number of squares that can be contained in a graph with $|V|$ vertices, and show that it may be more than $O(|V| \cdot |E|)$. Therefore, just listing all squares may take more than $O(|V| \cdot |E|)$ time.

Chapter 8

8.6 The counterexample is given in Fig. A.2. The circled point will be removed by Graham's scan even though it is on the hull.

8.11 Sort the vertices of the polygon in a cyclic order according to the angles of the line segment they make with q (and a fixed line). Then scan these vertices in that order. Start with an arbitrary vertex v, and determine the number of edges of the polygon that intersect with the half-line passing through q and v using the algorithm presented in Section 8.2. Then, whenever a vertex w is visited, one can in constant time determine whether the line through q and w intersects one more edge, one less edge, or the same number of edges.

8.16 Divide the plane into vertical columns of width d starting with the minimal x coordinate among the points and ending with the largest x coordinate. Find the points with the minimal

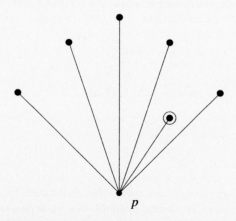

Figure A.2 A counter example for Exercise 8.6.

and maximal y coordinates in each of the columns. This can be done in time $O(n + X/d)$ since the column that contains a given point can be found in constant time. Apply a procedure similar to Graham's scan to all the minimal points and then to all the maximal points. This results in two convex paths, which can easily be connected at both ends to form a convex polygon C. C is not necessarily the convex hull of the points, but it is easy to show that the distance of any point from the set outside the hull to the hull is at most d.

8.17   The gift-wrapping algorithm can be applied to this problem without additional complexity. The necessary observation here is that each point is compared against all other *remaining* points. Thus, the algorithm requires $n - 1$ comparisons to find the first vertex of the hull, $n - 2$ comparisons to find the second, and so on. After the hull is discovered, all its vertices are marked with the appropriate depth, and removed. The same algorithm continues. The first vertex on it requires $n - k$ comparisons (where $k - 1$ is the number of vertices removed so far), and so on. Overall, $O(n^2)$ steps are required.

8.22   The only difficult case is that of finding intersections between all vertical line segments and the segments with 45-degree angle (the other cases are either symmetric or can be handled by the algorithm in Section 8.6). We use the same approach as the intersection algorithm of Section 8.6. The segments are sorted according to the x coordinates of their endpoints. The line-sweep algorithm is performed in the same way. A segment with 45-degree angle is inserted when its left endpoint is meeting the sweeping line, and is deleted when its right endpoint is meeting the sweeping line. We now have to find intersections between a new vertical line and several candidate segments with 45-degree angles. This is done as follows. For each segment with 45-degree angle, we compute the intersection of the full line overlapping the segment with the x axis. We use this value when we perform the range queries. The range is set as follows. The left point of the range is the intersection between the line with 45-degree angle that contains the top endpoint of the vertical line and the x axis. The right point of the range is the intersection between the line with 45-degree angle that contains the bottom endpoint of the vertical line and the x axis. We have converted the problem to a one-dimensional range query, and the complexity remains the same.

8.26   We strengthen the induction hypothesis a little.

> **Induction hypothesis:** *We know how to mark all the intervals contained in other intervals among a set of $< n$ intervals, and how to find the largest right endpoint among them.*

We first sort the intervals according to their left endpoints. Assume that we solved the problem for the first (leftmost) $n - 1$ intervals, and consider the nth interval. If its right endpoint is larger than the largest right endpoint so far, then it is not contained in any interval; we update the largest right endpoint. Otherwise, it is contained in another interval; we mark it.

8.28   The intersection of two rectangles whose edges are parallel to the axes can be computed in constant time. Furthermore, either this intersection is empty or it is a rectangle. Hence, we can solve the problem in linear time by intersecting one rectangle after the other in any order.

8.31   We give only a rough sketch of a solution. The basic idea is to divide each polygon into *slabs* and to intersect the slabs separately. First, we sort all the vertices according to their x coordinates. This sorting can be done in linear time, because the cyclic order of the vertices in each polygon is known. We associate with each vertex a vertical line, and we use these vertical lines to divide the two polygons into slabs, as in shown in Fig. A.3. Since we know the sorted order of the vertical lines, we need only to compute intersections between disjoint pairs of slabs. An intersection between two slabs can be computed in constant time, because each slab has at most four edges. We can then assemble the corresponding intersections into a polygon in linear time.

8.34   An intersection of triangles is a convex polygon. We can intersect two triangles in constant time, and we can intersect two convex polygons in linear time (Exercise 8.31). Thus, a divide-and-conquer algorithm that divides the set of triangles into two sets, computes the intersection of all triangles in each set recursively, and then intersects the two resulting convex polygons has a running time of $O(n \log n)$.

Chapter 9

9.2   One example is $n = 15$. The method presented in Section 9.2 requires 6 multiplications $(x^{15} = (((x^2 \cdot x)^2)^2 \cdot x)^2 \cdot x)$. It is possible to compute x^{15} with only 5 multiplications $(x^{15} = ((x \cdot x)^2 \cdot x)^3)$. See [Knuth 1981, p. 443] for a detailed discussion of this issue.

9.10   We use the notation of Section 9.5.2. We need to compute $(B + C + D + F + G)X$. We make the following definitions, which correspond directly to the seven multiplications in the four types of products introduced in Section 9.5.2: $z_1 = b(e+f)$, $z_2 = c(g+h)$, $z_3 = (c-b)(e+h)$, $z_4 = (a-b)e$, $z_5 = (a-c)(g-e)$, $z_6 = (d-c)h$, and $z_7 = (d-b)(f-h)$. We now look at the contribution of each of the matrices. B contributes $[z_1, z_1, 0, 0]$ (we write it as a row matrix instead of as a column matrix for convenience); C contributes $[0, 0, z_2, z_2]$; D contributes $[0, z_3, -z_3, 0]$; F contributes $[z_4, 0, z_4+z_5, 0]$; and G contributes $[0, z_6+z_7, 0, z_6]$. So, overall, we have $p = C_{1,1} = z_1+z_4$, $r = C_{2,1} = z_1+z_3+z_6+z_7$, $s = C_{1,2} = z_2+z_3+z_4+z_5$, and $t = C_{2,2} = z_2+z_6$. There are 18 additions and 7 multiplications.

9.16   The hard part of this problem is proving that such a representation always exists. We prove that it does by induction. It is easy to verify the base case. Let $n > 2$ be an integer, and let $F(k)$ be the largest Fibonacci number not larger than n (i.e., $F(k) \leq n$ and $F(k+1) > n$). We claim that $F(k) > n/2$, since otherwise $F(k+1) = F(k) + F(k-1) < n$. By the induction hypothesis, $n - F(k)$ can be represented as a sum of at most $\log_2(n - F(k))$ Fibonacci

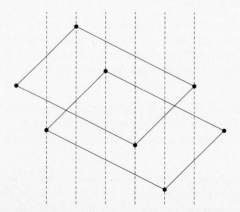

Figure A.3   Intersection of two convex polygons by the slab method.

numbers. But, since $n - F(k) < F(k)$, adding $F(k)$ to the representation of $n - F(k)$ still keeps the numbers distinct; furthermore, it is easy to see that $\log_2(n - F(k)) + 1 < \log_2 n$. To find the representation we need, we compute all Fibonacci numbers until we reach one that is larger than or equal to n; we can then follow the proof given here.

9.19   We denote the four parts of the first polynomial by a_1, b_1, c_1, and d_1, and the four parts of the second polynomial by a_2, b_2, c_2, and d_2. We can illustrate the problem using a 4×4 table as shown in Fig. A.4. This table is similar to the 2×2 table that was given in Section 9.4. Each entry in the table corresponds to a product of two parts of the polynomials. We do not have to compute the value of each entry, only the sum of values in each of the diagonals shown in the figure. Each of these diagonals corresponds to the coefficient of a certain degree in the product of the polynomials. The following 9 products are sufficient to compute the values of all the diagonals: (1) $a_1 \cdot a_2$, (2) $b_1 \cdot b_2$, (3) $(a_1 + b_1) \cdot (a_2 + b_2)$, (4) $c_1 \cdot c_2$, (5) $d_1 \cdot d_2$, (6) $(c_1 + d_1) \cdot (c_2 + d_2)$, (7) $(a_1 + c_1) \cdot (a_2 + c_2)$, (8) $(b_1 + d_1) \cdot (b_2 + d_2)$, and (9) $(a_1 + b_1 + c_1 + d_1) \cdot (a_2 + b_2 + c_2 + d_2)$. We leave it to the reader to verify that all diagonals can be computed from these 9 products. The corresponding recurrence relation is $T(n) = 9T(n/4) + O(n)$, which implies that $T(n) = O(n^{\log 9}) = O(n^{\log 3})$, which is the same as the running time of the algorithm that divides each polynomial into two parts. Is that equality coincidental, or is there a good reason for it? In other words, what are the similarities between the two algorithms?

9.23   Winograd's algorithm assumes commutativity of multiplication (i.e., it assumes that $x \cdot y = y \cdot x$). If we use Winograd's algorithm as the base of the recursion, we have to be able to substitute matrices for elements, but we cannot do that because matrix multiplication is not commutative.

9.29   We solve the problem by induction on n. The case of $n = 1$ is trivial. Assume that we know the solution for $n > 1$, and consider $n + 1$. Denote by $M[i..j]$ the product $M_i \times \cdots \times M_j$. The best way to compute $M[1..n + 1]$ is first to compute $M[1..i]$ and $M[i + 1..n + 1]$, for some (as yet unknown) i, and then to multiply the two products. We can find the value of i that leads to the minimum cost by trying all possibilities. We know the best way to compute $M[1..i]$ by induction. However, we need to know how to compute $M[i + 1..n + 1]$. To do that, we strengthen the induction hypothesis.

> **Stronger induction hypothesis**: *We know the best way to compute M[i..j] for all $1 \le i < j \le n$.*

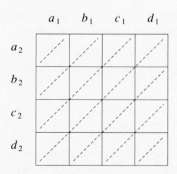

Figure A.4 Finding the product of two polynomials by dividing them into four parts.

To extend this hypothesis to $n+1$, we need to compute $M[i..n+1]$ for all $1 \le i \le n$. We solve this problem by yet another (nested) induction, this time on i in a reversed order. For $i = n$, there is only one way to compute the product $M[n..n+1]$; hence, the problem is trivial. Assume that we know the best way to compute $M[i..n+1]$ and consider $i-1$. We can now perform the reduction. We check for each j, $i < j < n+1$, the cost of computing $M[i-1..j]$ (which we know by the original induction), the cost of computing $M[j+1..n+1]$ (which we know by the nested induction), and the cost of multiplying both products. We then choose the j that minimizes this cost. Overall, the two induction processes correspond to two loops, the first of size n, the second of size $n-i$, and the inside loop consists of $n-i$ steps. The total number of steps is thus $\sum_{k=1}^{n} \sum_{i=k}^{n} \sum_{j=i}^{n} O(1)$, which is $O(n^3)$.

Chapter 10

10.3 We show that the interval-containment problem can be solved by using the maximal-points algorithm. For each interval $I_j = (L_j, R_j)$, we define a point in the plane such that its x coordinate is $-L_j$ and its y coordinate is R_j. We leave it to the reader to verify that an interval is contained in another interval if and only if the corresponding point is not maximal.

10.5 Split each vertex that corresponds to a university into two vertices. Connect both of those vertices to all the students who were admitted to that university. This is a regular bipartite matching problem.

10.12 The simplest solution to this problem is by reduction. We construct a new graph H with two vertices w_1 and w_2 for each vertex w of G. We call w_1 the *tail* vertex of w, and w_2 the *head* vertex of w. The edges of H are the following. For each edge (w, u) in G, we add the edge (w_2, u_1) with cost 0 to H. In other words, we make all edges go from head vertices to tail vertices. In addition, we add an edge (u_1, u_2) with cost $c(u)$ for each vertex u in G. The problem becomes the regular single-source shortest-paths problem from v_2 to all tail vertices.

10.15 The simplest counterexample involves only one variable x. The objective function, which we try to maximize, is simply x, and the only two constraints are $x \le 0$ and $x \ne 0$. This problem has no solution, since there is no maximum number smaller than 0.

10.17 The linear program can be changed easily, but it is much easier to notice that the best solution is for every organization to donate its maximum.

10.20 To compute the square of a matrix, we indeed need only five multiplications of matrices half its size. However, these are multiplications of two *arbitrary* matrices, not squarings of matrices of half the size.

10.24 We show how to use such an algorithm to sort. Given a sequence $x_1, x_2, ..., x_n$ of distinct numbers that we wish to sort, we associate a point p_i with each x_i such that all points lie on a fixed line and the distance of point p_i from a fixed origin is x_i. It is easy to see that the minimum-cost spanning tree must connect each point to its neighbors on the line — namely, the tree is a chain. The tree has two leaves, which are the maximum and minimum elements of the sequence. If we know the minimum-cost spanning tree, then we can find the sorted order of the points in linear time as follows. First, we find the minimum among the points, say x_i. The chain defined by the tree gives us the sorted order, and we can follow it in linear time. Thus, we have a lower bound of $\Omega(n \log n)$ for this problem under the decision tree model (which is the model under which the lower bound for sorting was proved).

Chapter 11

11.3 $O(n^k)$ is a polynomial in n, but it is an exponential function in k. Since k is part of the input (and may be as high as n), this is not a polynomial-time algorithm.

11.11   We use a reduction from the regular vertex-cover problem. Let $G = (V, E)$ be an arbitrary undirected graph, and let U be the set of vertices of odd degree in G. We modify G by adding three new vertices, x, y, and z, which are connected to each other (in a triangle). We also connect x to all vertices in U. It is now easy to prove that the modified graph has a vertex cover of size K if and only if G has a vertex cover of size $K - 2$.

11.14   The problem is obviously in NP, since we can guess the subset and check its induced subgraph in polynomial time. We use a reduction from 3SAT. Let $E = C_1 \cdot C_2 \cdot \cdots \cdot C_n$ be an arbitrary instance of 3SAT. We construct a graph $G = (V, E)$ with $4n + 1$ vertices as follows. For each clause C_i, we include four vertices, one associated with the clause itself, and the other three associated with the corresponding variables. The four vertices associated with a clause are fully connected to one another. We also connect any two vertices in the graph that are associated with x and $\bar{x}$ for any variable x. Finally, we add one additional vertex r which is connected to all vertices associated with variables (but not to the vertices associated with the clauses themselves). We claim that the graph has a subset of size $2n + 1$ that induces an acyclic graph if and only if the expression is satisfiable.

1. If the expression is satisfiable, then we can find a consistent truth assignment satisfying every clause. The subset will consist of the vertex r, the n vertices corresponding to the clauses, and one vertex for each clause corresponding to the variable that satisfies the clause (ties are broken arbitrarily). This subset induces an acyclic graph since r is connected only to variables, and two variables are not connected if they belong to a consistent truth assignment.

2. If there exists a subset S with $2n + 1$ vertices that induces an acyclic graph, then we claim that S includes r and exactly two vertices from every clause. Indeed, S cannot include more than two vertices from one clause, since such vertices are connected (and thus form a triangle). Also, since S includes r, it cannot include two vertices that correspond to x and $\bar{x}$ for some variable x. Therefore, it is possible to obtain a truth assignment for E.

11.16   We use a reduction from 3SAT. Let $C = (x + y + z)$ be a clause in an arbitrary 3SAT problem. We replace C with the following three clauses (the a_is are all new variables): $(x + a_1 + a_2)$, $(y + a_3 + a_4)$, and $(z + a_5 + a_6)$. In the 1-in-3–SAT problem, exactly one of the variables in each of the three clauses above must be satisfied. We want to guarantee that at least one of x, y, or z is satisfied. We do that by adding more clauses that guarantee that no more than one of a_1, a_3, and a_5 is satisfied, and no more than one of a_2, a_4, and a_6 is satisfied. The clauses are $(a_1 + a_3 + a_7)$, $(a_3 + a_5 + a_8)$, $(a_5 + a_1 + a_9)$, $(a_2 + a_4 + a_{10})$, $(a_4 + a_6 + a_{11})$, and $(a_6 + a_2 + a_{12})$. We leave the verification to the reader.

11.19   We reduce the clique problem to this problem. Let $G = (V, E)$ and k be an arbitrary instance of the clique problem. We need to convert G into a regular graph R such that the clique problem for G can be solved by solving a clique problem for R. We cannot simply add edges to G until G becomes regular, because this would potentially increase the sizes of the cliques of G. We must add vertices and edges to G such that no new cliques are formed. Let d be the maximal degree of G if it is even or the maximal degree plus 1 otherwise, and let n be the number of vertices of G. For each vertex v of G with degree $d(v) < d$, we add $d - d(v)$ vertices and connect each of them to v. The total number of additional vertices is $dn - \sum_{i=1}^{n} d(v_i) = dn - 2|E|$. This number is even since we chose d to be even. Notice that all the original vertices now have the same degree d, and that no new cliques were added (since each new vertex is connected to only one vertex). The only problem is that the new vertices have a degree of 1. We can change their degrees to d without introducing more cliques by adding edges between them in the following way. We divide the set of new vertices to two equal sets. We then connect each vertex of one set to exactly $d - 1$ vertices of the other set. The new vertices thus induce a bipartite graph, which does not contain cliques of size > 2. We leave it to the reader to verify that it is possible to construct this bipartite graph in the desired way.

11.25   If we could determine whether there exists a Hamiltonian path with specified end vertices, then we could determine whether there exists any Hamiltonian path by just trying all pairs of vertices. Therefore, a polynomial-time algorithm for this problem leads to a polynomial-time algorithm for the Hamiltonian path problem, which in turn leads to polynomial-time algorithms for all NP problems. Notice that this is not a pure reduction as defined in Section 11.2, but it is sufficient.

11.29   We use a reduction from the vertex-cover problem. Let $G = (V, E)$ and K be an arbitrary instance of the vertex-cover problem. We construct a directed graph G' by replacing every vertex v in G with two vertices v_1 and v_2 connected by a directed edge (v_1, v_2). We replace each edge (v, w) of G with two directed edges, (w_2, v_1) and (v_2, w_1). We now claim that G' contains a feedback-edge set of size K if and only if G contains a vertex cover of size K.

11.33   We sketch a reduction from SAT. Let v be a vertex in G and let the edges adjacent to v be (in the cyclic order) $e_1, e_2, ..., e_k$. The Eulerian tour defines a *pairing* among the edges of v, such that the consecutive edges in the tour used to enter and leave v are paired. By the conditions of the problem, an edge e_i can be paired either with e_{i-1} or with e_{i+1} (additions and subtractions are done modulo k). The main observation is that, if e_i is paired with e_{i+1}, then the pairings for all other edges of v are fixed (e_{i+2} must be paired with e_{i+3}, and so on). The same is true if e_i is paired with e_{i-1}. In other words, there are only two ways of pairing the edges of v. We will associate a vertex with each variable in the SAT expression, such that the value of this variable in the truth assignment will correspond to the way the pairing is done for this vertex in the tour. We have to make sure that the truth assignment is consistent (i.e., the values of x and $\bar{x}$ are complementary), and that every clause is satisfied. We will have one vertex v_x for every variable x, and one vertex $\overline{v_x}$ for $\bar{x}$, and we will connect them such that a pairing for v_x forces a certain pairing for $\overline{v_x}$. We associate the truth values accordingly. Then, for each clause $(x + y + z)$, we connect the corresponding three vertices such that at least one of the pairings that is associated with one the variables being true must be taken. We leave the details (which are not straightforward) to the reader. The planar case, which is more complicated, is proved in Bent and Manber [1987].

Chapter 12

12.13   We use the doubling method. In the first step, only one processor P_1 participates: P_1 simply copies $A[1]$ to $A[2]$. In step i, there are 2^{i-1} participating processors, and they copy the array $A[1..2^{i-1}]$ to $A[2^{i-1}+1..2^i]$. To improve the efficiency, use Brent's lemma.

12.16   This problem can be solved in exactly the same way as the problem of finding the maximum.

12.17   The circuit for $n=8$ is given in Fig. A.5.

12.20   Assign one processor P_{ij} to every pair of elements $A[i]$ and $B[j]$. P_{ij} first compares $A[i]$ to $B[j]$, then compares $A[i]$ to $B[j+1]$. If $A[i]$ is between $B[k]$ and $B[k+1]$, then P_{ik} will find that out and conclude that $A[i]$'s place in the final array is in the $(i+k)$th position. The same procedure can be applied to B.

12.25   We sketch an elegant solution using parallel prefix (the problem can also be solved directly). We first compute the parallel prefix on the *Mark* array with the $+$ operation. The prefix value of each record whose *Mark* value is 1 will be equal to its place in the compacted array. We can then complement the *Mark* array to do the same for the other elements. Once all the indices are computed, the actual movement can be done in one (parallel) step, since there are no conflicts.

12.27   If we associate a processor with each record, then in one step each processor can write its index in the appropriate field of its successor. Each processor now knows its predecessor in the list.

12.32   We cannot concentrate on each number separately. It is true that each number incurs at most one more idle step, but a delay for one processor can cause more delays at other processors if the numbers do not arrive there fast enough.

12.33   We use induction. If the height of the tree is 2, then the left leaf sends its number x_1 to the root, which then sends it down where it can be added to x_2. Suppose that we have an algorithm for height h, and consider height $h+1$. (We will consider only the case of complete binary trees. It is easy to modify the algorithm to the general case.) Let R be the root, and R_L and R_R be the root's left and right children. We call the sum over all the leaves in a particular subtree the *sum of the subtree*. A straightforward solution is to solve the

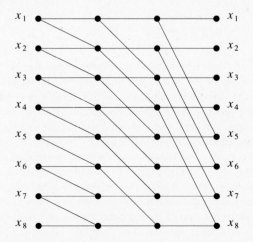

Figure A.5 A parallel-prefix circuit.

problem separately for the left and right subtrees, then to broadcast the sum of the left subtree to all the leaves of the right subtree. Each leaf in the right subtree simply adds the sum of the left subtree to the prefix it computed so far. The problem with this solution is that its running time is $O(h^2)$, because the recurrence relation is $T(h+1)=T(h)+h$. We can improve this solution by noticing that there is no need to wait until the left subtree has finished its computation. The right subtree needs to obtain the sum of the left subtree, and this sum can be available at the root at step $h+1$. Thus, the requirement from R_L is that it receives the sum of all its descendants and sends it up to the root. The requirement from R_R is that it receives the sum from the root and sends it down to all its descendants. This leads directly to the following rules: (1) each leaf starts by sending its value up (we have to modify the simple solution for height 2 slightly, since the root needs to know the sum); (2) the internal nodes, when receiving values from below, add those values and send them up; (3) the internal nodes, when receiving values from above, send those values down to both children; and (4) the internal nodes also act as the roots of their own subtrees and send the value they receive from their left children to their right children. We leave it the the reader to verify that this is a correct algorithm and that its running time is $2h$.

12.37 Suppose first that we are interested only in computing x_1. Processor P_2 computes $a_{12} \cdot b_2$, which is its contribution to the value of x_1, and sends it to P_3; processor P_3 adds to the value it receives $a_{13} \cdot b_3$ and forwards that value to P_4, and so on. After $n-1$ steps, P_1 will receive from P_n the value of $x_1 - a_{11} \cdot b_1$, and it will be able to complete the computation. Now, to compute all the x_is, we pipeline this process. In the first step, each processor P_i computes $a_{(i-1)i} \cdot b_i$ (all index calculation are done modulo n), and sends it to P_{i+1}. In the jth step, P_i receives the value $\sum_{k=1}^{j-1} a_{(i-j)(i-k)} \cdot b_{i-k}$, adds to it $a_{(i-j)i} \cdot b_i$, and sends it to P_{i+1} (again, all index calculations are modulo n).

12.40 This problem can be solved directly, but it is easier to use a reduction to matrix multiplication. We first use the the the σ permutation to build a *permutation matrix* S such that, for each column i, only the entry at the $\sigma(i)$th row has a value of 1, and all other entries at that column have a value of 0. We can easily build this matrix and distribute it to the appropriate processors in n steps. Permuting all the rows according to the permutation σ is the same as computing the product $S \cdot A$, which we already know how to do in $O(n)$ steps. Permuting the columns can be done in the same way with the permutation matrix Q, except that the product is $A \cdot Q$.

12.42 The straightforward induction solution is to compute the parallel prefix in each half-cube separately in parallel, then to broadcast the largest prefix in one half-cube (designated as the smaller one) to the other. (The base case of one dimension is trivial.) Broadcast in a d-dimensional cube takes d steps. Thus, the running time of this algorithm satisfies the following recurrence relation: $T(d+1)=T(d)+d$, which implies that $T(d)=O(d^2)$. We can improve this algorithm by strengthening the induction hypothesis. We assume that every processor not only computes its corresponding prefix, but also computes the sum of all numbers in the cube. The base case of one dimension is still easy: The two processors simply exchange their values. Given a $(d+1)$–dimensional cube, we divide it into two d-dimensional cubes, and solve the problem by induction in both of them. But now, we do not have to broadcast the sum of the left cube. Since each node in the left cube knows the sum, it can send the sum in one step to its neighbor in the right cube. All the prefixes can thus be computed in one more step. Furthermore, the sum of everything can also be computed in one more step if the nodes in the right subtree send their (global) sum to their neighbors in the left subtree. The recurrence relation is thus $T(d+1)=T(d)+2$, which implies that $T(d)=O(d)$. The assignment of indices to processor should be clear from this description.

12.48 There is a rich literature on the subject of gossip as it is related to computer networks; see, for example Hedetniemi, Hedetniemi, and Liestman [1988] for a survey. The exercise presents a relatively simple gossip problem. It can be solved by the pattern shown in Fig. A.6, called **butterfly**, which has many other uses (the most notable is the parallel computation of the FFT). Figure A.6 shows the solution for $n=8$.

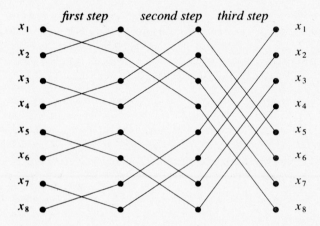

Figure S.6 The solution of the gossip problem (Exercise 12.48) for $n=8$.

BIBLIOGRAPHY

Adel'son-Vel'skii G. M., and Y. M. Landis, "An algorithm for the organization of information," *Soviet Math. Dokl.*, **3** (1962), pp. 1259–1262.

Aho A. V., and M. J. Corasick, "Efficient string matching: An aid to bibliographic search," *Communications of the ACM,* **18** (June 1975), pp. 333–340.

Aho A. V., J. E. Hopcroft, and J. D. Ullman, *The Design and Analysis of Computer Algorithms,* Addison-Wesley, Reading, MA, 1974.

Aho A. V., J. E. Hopcroft, and J. D. Ullman, *Data Structures and Algorithms,* Addison-Wesley, Reading, MA, 1983.

Ajtai M., J. Komlós, and E. Szemerédi, "An $O(n \log n)$ sorting network," *15th Annual ACM Symposium on Theory of Computing,* Boston (April 1983), pp. 1–9.

Akl S. G., *Parallel Sorting Algorithms,* Academic Press, New York, 1985.

Aleliunas R., "Randomized parallel communication," *First ACM Symposium on Principles of Distributed Computing,* Ottawa (August 1982), pp. 60–72.

Almasi G. S., and A. Gottlieb, *Highly Parallel Computing,* Benjamin/Cummings, Redwood City, CA, 1989.

Angluin D., and L. G. Valiant, "Fast probabilistic algorithms for Hamiltonian circuits and matchings," *Journal of Computer and System Sciences,* **18** (April 1979), pp. 155–193.

Apostolico A., and Z. Galil, *Combinatorial Algorithms on Words,* Springer-Verlag, New York, 1985.

Arlazarov V. L., E. A. Dinic, M. A. Kronrod, and I. A. Faradzev, "On economical construction of the transitive closure of a directed graph," *Soviet Math Dokl,* **11** (May 1970), pp. 1209–1210.

Atkinson M. D., and N. Santoro, "A practical algorithm for Boolean matrix multiplication," *Information Processing Letters,* **29** (September 1988), pp. 37–38.

Attalah M. J., R. Cole, and M. T. Goodrich, "Cascading divide–and–conquer: A technique for designing parallel algorithms," *28th Annual Symposium on*

Foundations of Computer Science, Los Angeles (October 1987), pp. 151–160.

Auslander L., and S. V. Parter, "On imbedding graphs in the plane," *J. Math. and Mech.,* **10** (May 1961), pp. 517–523.

Bach E., G. Miller, and J. Shallit, "Sums of divisors, perfect numbers and factoring," *SIAM Journal on Computing,* **15** (November 1986), pp. 1143–1154.

Baer J.-L., and B. Schwab, "A comparison of tree–balancing algorithms," *Communications of the ACM,* **20** (May 1977), pp. 322–330.

Bar-Yehuda R., and S. Even, "A linear time approximation algorithm for the weighted vertex cover problem," *Journal of Algorithms,* **2** (1981), pp. 198–203.

Batcher K. E., "Sorting networks and their applications," in *Proceedings AFIPS 32nd Spring Joint Computer Conference,* (1968), pp. 307–314.

Bates J. L., and R. L. Constable, "Proofs as programs," *ACM Transactions on Programming Languages and Systems,* **7** (January 1985), pp. 113–136.

Bavel Z., *Math Companion for Computer Science,* Reston Publishing Company, Reston, Virginia, 1982.

Beame P. W., S. A. Cook, and H. J. Hoover, "Log depth circuits for division and related problems," *SIAM Journal on Computing,* **15** (February 1986), pp. 994–1003.

Beckenbach E., and R. Bellman, *An Introduction to Inequalities,* New Mathematical Library, Random House, New York, 1961.

Bellman R. E., *Dynamic Programming,* Princeton University Press, Princeton, NJ, 1957.

Bent S. W., and J. John, "Finding the median requires $2n$ comparisons," *17th Annual ACM Symposium on Theory of Computing,* Providence, RI (May 1985), pp. 213–216.

Bent S. W., and U. Manber, "On non-intersecting Eulerian circuits," *Discrete Applied Mathematics,* **18** (1987), pp. 87–94.

Bentley J. L., *Programming Pearls,* Addison-Wesley, Reading, MA, 1986.

Bentley J. L., M. G. Faust, and F. P. Preparata, "Approximation algorithms for convex hulls," *Communication of the ACM,* **25** (January 1982), pp. 64–68.

Bentley J. L., D. Haken, and J. B. Saxe, "A general method for solving divide-and-conquer recurrences," *SIGACT News,* (Fall 1980), pp. 36–44.

Bentley J. L., and B. W. Kernighan, "Tools for printing indexes," *Electronic Publishing,* **1** (1988), pp. 3–17.

Bentley J. L., and T. Ottmann, "Algorithms for reporting and counting geometric intersections," *IEEE Transactions on Computers,* **C-28** (Sept. 1979), pp. 643–647.

Berge C., *The Theory of Graphs and Its Applications*, John Wiley and Sons, New York, 1962.

Berge C., *Graphs and Hypergraphs*, North Holland, London, 1973.

Bertsekas D. P., and J. N. Tsitsiklis, *Parallel and Distributed Computation, Numerical Methods*, Prentice-Hall, Englewood Cliffs, NJ, 1989.

Bitner J. R., and E. M. Reingold, "Backtrack programming techniques," *Communications of the ACM*, **18** (November 1975), pp. 651–656.

Blelloch G., "Scans as primitive parallel operations," *1987 International Conference on Parallel Processing*, (August 1987), pp. 355–362.

Blum M., R. W. Floyd, V. R. Pratt, R. L. Rivest, and R. E. Tarjan, "Time bounds for selection," *Journal of Computer and System Sciences*, **7** (1972), pp. 448–461.

Bollobás B., *Graph Theory: An Introductory Course*, Springer Verlag, New York, 1979.

Bollobás B., *Combinatorics*, Cambridge University Press, Cambridge, 1986.

Bondy J. A., and U. S. R. Murty, *Graph Theory with Applications*, Elsevier, New York, 1976.

Borodin A., "On relating time and space to size and depth," *SIAM Journal on Computing*, **6** (December 1977), pp. 733–744.

Borodin A., and J. E. Hopcroft, "Routing, merging and sorting on parallel models of computation," *Journal of Computer and System Sciences*, **30** (1985), pp. 130–145.

Borodin A., and I. Munro, *The Computational Complexity of Algebraic and Numeric Problems*, Elsevier Computer Science Library, New York, 1975.

Boyer R. S., and J. S. Moore, "A fast string searching algorithm," *Communications of the ACM*, **20** (October 1977), pp. 762–772.

Brélaz D., "New methods to color the vertices of a graph," *Communications of the ACM*, **22** (April 1979), pp. 251–256.

Brigham E. O., *The Fast Fourier Transform*, Prentice-Hall, Englewood Cliffs, NJ, 1974.

Brualdi R. A., *Introductory Combinatorics*, North Holland, New York, 1977.

Burge W. H., *Recursive Programming Techniques*, Addison-Wesley, Reading, MA, 1975.

Bussey W. H., "Origin of mathematical induction," *American Mathematical Monthly*, **24** (1917), pp. 199–207.

Capobianco M., and J. C. Molluzzo, *Examples and Counterexamples in Graph Theory*, North-Holland, New York, 1978.

Carter J. L., and M. N. Wegman, "Universal classes of hash functions," *Journal of*

Computer and System Sciences, **18** (April 1979), pp. 143–154.

Chand D. R., and S. S. Kapur, "An algorithm for convex polytopes," *Journal of the ACM,* **17** (January 1970), pp. 78–86.

Chandy K. M., and J. Misra, *Parallel Program Design: A Foundation,* Addison-Wesley, Reading, MA, 1988.

Chartrand G., *Graphs as Mathematical Models,* Wadsworth International Group, Belmont, CA, 1977.

Chartrand G., and L. Lesniak, *Graphs & Digraphs,* Second Edition, Wadsworth & Brooks/Cole, Monterey, CA, 1986.

Cheriton D., and R. E. Tarjan, "Finding minimum spanning trees," *SIAM Journal on Computing,* **5** (December 1976), pp. 724–742.

Choueka Y., A.S. Fraenkel, S.T. Klein, and Y. Perl, "Huffman coding without bit-manipulation," *Proceedings of the Eighth Annual ACM-SIGIR Conference,* Montreal, Canada (1985), pp. 122–130.

Christofides N., *Graph Theory: An Algorithmic Approach,* Academic Press, London, 1975.

Christofides N., "Worst-case analysis of a new heuristic for the traveling salesman problem," Technical Report, Graduate School of Industrial Administration, Carnegie-Mellon University, Pittsburgh, PA, 1976.

Cohen J., and M. Roth, "On the implementation of Strassen's fast multiplication algorithm," *Acta Informatica,* **6** (1976), pp. 341–355.

Cole R., "Slowing down sorting networks to obtain faster sorting algorithms," *25th Annual Symposium on Foundations of Computer Science,* Singer Island (October 1984), pp. 255–259.

Cole R., "Parallel merge sort," *SIAM Journal on Computing,* **17** (August 1988), pp. 770–785.

Cole R., and U. Vishkin, "Deterministic coin tossing and accelerating cascades: micro and macro techniques for designing parallel algorithms," *18th Annual ACM Symposium on Theory of Computing,* Berkeley (May 1986), pp. 206–219.

Cook S. A., "The complexity of theorem proving proceudres," *Third Annual ACM Symposium on Theory of Computing,* New York (1971), pp. 151–158.

Cook S. A., "An overview of computational complexity," *Communications of the ACM,* **26** (June 1983), pp. 400–408.

Cook S. A., and C. Dwork, "Bounds on the time of parallel RAMs to compute simple functions," *14th Annual ACM Symposium on Theory of Computing,* San Francisco (May 1982), pp. 231–233.

Cooley J. M., and J. W. Tuckey, "An algorithm for the machine calculation of complex Fourier series," *Math. Comp.,* **19** (1965), pp. 297–301.

Coppersmith D., and S. Winograd, "Matrix multiplication via arithmetic progressions," *19th Annual ACM Symposium on Theory of Computing,* New York (May 1987), pp. 1–6.

Culberson J., "The effects of updates in binary search trees," *17th Annual ACM Symposium on Theory of Computing,* Providence, RI (May 1985), pp. 205–212.

Dantzig G. B., "On the shortest route through a newtwork," *Management Science,* **6** (1960), pp. 187-190.

Dantzig G. B., *Linear Programming and Extensions,* Princeton University Press, Princeton, NJ, 1963.

Dekel E., D. Nassimi, and S. Sahni, "Parallel matrix and graph algorithms," *SIAM Journal on Computing,* **10** (November 1981), pp. 657–675.

Denardo E. V., *Dynamic Programming,* Prentice-Hall, Englewood Cliffs, NJ, 1982.

Deo N., *Graph Theory with Applications to Engineering and Computer Science,* Prentice-Hall, Englewood Cliffs, NJ, 1974.

Deo N., and C. Pang, "Shortest-path algorithms: Taxonomy and annotation," *Networks,* **14** (1984), pp. 275–323.

Dershowitz N., *The Evolution of Programs,* Birkhauser, Boston, 1983.

Diffie W., and M. E. Hellman, "New directions in cryptography," *IEEE Transactions on Information Theory,* **IT-22** (June 1976), pp. 644–651.

Dijkstra E. W., "A note on two problems in connexion with graphs," *Numerische Mathematik,* **1** (1959), pp. 269–271.

Dijkstra E. W., *A Discipline of Programming,* Prentice-Hall, Englewood Cliffs, NJ, 1976.

Dobkin D. P., and J. I. Munro, "Determining the mode," *Theoretical Computer Science,* **12** (1980), pp. 255–263.

Dreyfus S. E., and A. M. Law, *The Art and Theory of Dynamic Programming,* Academic Press, New York, 1977.

Dvorak, S., and B. Durian, "Unstable linear time $O(1)$ space merging," *The Computer Journal,* **31** (1988), pp. 279–283.

Ebert J., "Computing Eulerian trails," *Information Processing Letters,* **28** (June 1988), pp. 93–97.

Edelsbrunner H., *Algorithms in Combinatorial Geometry,* Springer-verlag, Berlin, 1987.

Edmonds J., and R. M. Karp, "Theoretical improvements in algorithmic efficiency for network flow problems," *Journal of the ACM,* **19** (1972), pp. 248–264.

Elliott D. F., and K. R. Rao, *Fast Transforms: Algorithms Analyses, Applications*, Academic Press, New York, 1982.

Eppinger J. L., "An empirical study of insertion and deletion in binary search trees," *Communications of the ACM*, **26** (September 1983), pp. 663–669.

Erdös P., and A. Szekers, "A combinatorial problem in geometry," *Compositio Mathematica*, **2** (1935), pp. 463–470.

Erdös P., and J. Spencer, *Probabilistic Methods in Combinatorics*. Academic Press, New York, 1974.

Euler L., "Solutio problematis ad geometriam situs pertinentis," *Commentarii Academiae Scientiarum Petropolitanae*, **8** (1736), pp. 128–140.

Even S., *Graph Algorithms*, Computer Science Press, Rockville, MD, 1979.

Even S., and R. E. Tarjan, "A combinatorial problem which is complete in polynomial space," *Journal of the ACM*, **23** (1976), pp. 710–719.

Fagin R., J. Nievergelt, N. Pippenger, and H. R. Strong, "Extendible hashing — a fast access method for dynamic files," *ACM Transaction on Database Systems*, **4** (September 1979), pp. 315–355.

Feng T., "A survey of interconnection networks," *Computer*, **14** (December 1981), pp. 12–27.

Fich F. E., "New bounds for parallel prefix circuits," *15th Annual ACM Symposium on Theory of Computing*, Boston (April 1983), pp. 100–109.

Fischer M. J., "Efficiency of equivalence algorithms," in *Complexity and Computations*, R. E. Miller and J. W. Thatcher, eds., Plenum Press, New York, 1972, pp. 153–168.

Fischer M. J., and A. R. Meyer, "Boolean matrix multiplication and transitive closure," *IEEE 12th Annual Symposium on Switching and Automata Theory*, East Lansing, MI (October 1971), pp. 129–131.

Fischer M. J., and M. O. Rabin, "Super-exponential complexity of Presburger arithmetic," in *Complexity of Computation*, R. M. Karp Ed., SIAM–AMS, 1974.

Fischer M. J., and S. L. Salzberg, "Finding a majority among n votes," *Journal of Algorithms*, **3** (1982), pp. 375–379.

Flajolet P., and J. S. Vitter, "Average-case analysis of algorithms and data structures," Technical Report 718, INRIA, France, August 1987.

Floyd R. W., "Algorithm 97: Shortest paths," *Communications of the ACM*, **5** (June 1962), pp. 345.

Floyd R. W., "Assigning meanings to programs," *Symposium on Appllied Mathematics*, American Mathematical Society (1967), pp. 19–32.

Floyd R. W., and R. L. Rivest, "Expected time bounds for selection," *Communication of the ACM,* **18** (March 1975), pp. 165–172.

Flynn M. J., "Very high-speed computing systems," *Proceedings of the IEEE,* **54** (1966), pp. 1901–1909.

Ford L. R., "Network flow theory," The Rand Corporation P-293, Santa Monica, CA (1956).

Ford L. R., and D. R. Fulkerson, "Maximal flow through a network," *Canadian Journal of Mathematics,* **8** (1956), pp. 399–404.

Ford L. R., and D. R. Fulkerson, *Flows in Networks,* Princeton University Press, Princeton, NJ, 1962.

Ford L. R., and S. M. Johnson, "A tournament problem," *American Mathematical Monthly,* **66** (1959), pp. 387–389.

Fortune S., and J. Hopcroft, "A note on Rabin's nearest-neighbor algorithm," *Information Processing Letters,* **8** (1979), pp. 20–23.

Fox G. C., M. A. Johnson, G. A. Lyzenga, S. W. Otto, J. K. Salmon, and D. W. Walker, *Solving Problems on Concurrent Processors, Volume 1: General Techniques and Regular Problems,* Prentice-Hall, Englewood Cliffs, NJ, 1988.

Franco J., "On the probabilistic performance of algorithms for the satisfiability problem," *Information Processing Letters,* **23** (August 1986), pp. 103–106.

Frederickson G., "Distributed algorithms for selection in sets," *Journal of Computer and System Sciences,* **37** (December 1988), pp. 337–348.

Fredman M. L., and R. E. Tarjan, "Fibonacci heaps and and their uses in network optimization," *Journal of the ACM,* **34** (July 1987), pp. 596–615.

Gabow H. N., "An efficient implementation of Edmonds's algorithm for maximum matching on graphs," *Journal of the ACM,* **23** (1976), pp. 221–234.

Gabow H. N., Z. Galil, T. H. Spencer, and R. E. Tarjan, "Efficient algorithms for finding minimum spanning trees in undirected and directed graphs," *Combinatorica,* **6** (1986), pp. 109–122.

Gabow H. N., and R. E. Tarjan, "Algorithms for two bottleneck optimization problems," *Journal of Algorithms,* **9** (September 1988), pp. 411–417.

Galil Z., "On improving the worst case running time of the Boyer-Moore string searching algorithm," *Communications of the ACM,* **22** (September 1979), pp. 505–508.

Galil Z., "Efficient algorithms for finding maximum matching in graphs," *Computing Surveys,* **18** (March 1986), pp. 23–38.

Galler B. A., and M. J. Fishcer, "An improved equivalence algorithm," *Communications of the ACM*, **7** (1964), pp. 301–303.

Garey M. R., and D. S. Johnson, *Computers and Intractability, A Guide to the Theory of NP-completeness*, W. H. Freeman, San Francisco, CA, 1979.

Gehringer E. F., D. P. Siewiorek, and Z. Segall, *Parallel Processing: The Cm** *Experience*, Digital Press, Bedford, MA, 1987.

Gibbons A., *Algorithmic Graph Theory*, Cambridge University Press, Cambridge, 1985.

Gibbons A., and W. Rytter, *Efficient Parallel Algorithms*, Cambridge University Press, Cambridge, 1988.

Goldberg A. V., and R. E. Tarjan, "A new approach to the maximal-flow problem," *Journal of the ACM*, **35** (October 1988), pp. 921–940.

Goldwasser S., and J. Killian, "Almost all primes can be quickly certified," *18th Annual ACM Symposium on Theory of Computing*, Berkeley (May 1986), pp. 316–329.

Golomb S., and L. Baumert, "Backtrack programming," *Journal of the ACM*, **12** (1965), pp. 516–524.

Golovina L. I., and I. M. Yaglom, *Induction in Geometry* (translated from Russian), D. C. Heath, Boston, 1963.

Golumbic M., *Algorithmic Graph Theory and Perfect Graphs*, Academic Press, New York, 1980.

Gondran M., and M. Minoux, *Graphs and Algorithms*, John Wiley & Sons, New York, 1984.

Gonnet G. H., *Handbook of Algorithms and Data Structures*, Addison-Wesley, Reading, MA, 1984.

Graham R. L., "An efficient algorithm for determining the convex hull of a planar set," *Information Processsign Letters*, **1** (1972), pp. 132–133.

Graham R. L., D. E. Knuth, and O. Patashnik, *Concrete Mathematics*, Addison-Wesley, Reading, MA, 1989.

Gray F., *Pulse Code Communication*, US Patent 2632058 (March 1953).

Greenberg A., and U. Manber, "A probabilistic pipeline algorithm for k-selection on the tree machine," *IEEE Transactions on Computers*, **C-36** (March 1987), pp. 359-362.

Greene D. H., and D. E. Knuth, *Mathematics for the Analysis of Algorithms*, Birkhauser, Boston, 1982.

Gries D., *The Science of Programming*, Springer-Verlag, New York, 1981.

Grötschel M., L. Lovász, and A. Schrijver, "The ellipsoid method and its consequences in combinatorial optimization," *Combinatorica*, **1** (1981) pp. 169–197.

Guibas L. J., and A. M. Odlyzko, "A new proof of the linearity of the Boyer-Moore string searching algorithm," *SIAM Journal on Computing*, **9** (1980), pp. 672–682.

Gusfield D., and L. Pitt, "Equivalent approximation algorithms for node cover," *Information Processing Letters*, **22** (May 1986), pp. 291–294.

Guting R. H., and D. Wood, "Finding rectangles intersections by divide-and-conquer," *IEEE Transactions on Computers*, **C-33** (July 1984), pp. 771–775.

Hall M., *Combinatorial Theory*, Second Edition, John Wiley and Sons, New York, 1986.

Hall P., "On representatives of subsets," *Journal of the London Mathematical Society*, **10** (1935), pp. 26–30.

Hamming R. W., *Coding and Information Theory*, Second Edition, Prentice-Hall, Englewood Cliffs, NJ, 1986.

Harary F., *Graph Theory*, Addison-Wesley, Reading, MA, 1969.

Hedetniemi S. T., S. M. Hedetniemi, and A. L. Liestman, "A survey of broadcasting and gossiping in communication networks," *Networks*, to appear (1989).

Hibbard T. N., "Some combinatorial properties of certain trees with applications to searching and sorting," *Journal of the ACM*, **9** (January 1962), pp. 13–28.

Hillis W. D., *The Connection Machine*, MIT Press, Cambridge, MA, 1985.

Hillis W. D., and G. L. Steele, "Data parallel algorithms," *Communications of the ACM*, **29** (December 1986), pp. 1170–1183.

Hinrichs K., J. Nievergelt, and P. Schorn, "Plane-sweep solves the closest pair problem elegantly," *Information Processing Letters*, **26** (1988), pp. 255–261.

Hirschberg D. S., "A linear-space algorithm for computing maximal common subsequences," *Communications of the ACM*, **18** (June 1975), pp. 341–343.

Hirschberg D. S., "Recent results on the complexity of common-subsequence problems," in *Time Wraps, String Edits, and Macromolecules: The Theory and Practice of Sequence Comparison*, D. Sankoff and J. B. Kruskal, eds., Addison-Wesley, Reading, MA, 1983.

Hoare C. A. R., "Quicksort," *The Computer Journal*, (1962), pp. 10–15.

Hoffman C. M., *Group Theoretic Algorithms and Graph Isomorphism*, Lecture Notes in Computer Science, **136**, Springer-Verlag, New York, 1982.

Hofri M., *Probabilistic Analysis of Algorithms*, Springer-Verlag, New York, 1987.

Hopcroft J. E., and R. M. Karp, "An $n^{5/2}$ algorithm for maximum matchings in bipartite graphs," *SIAM Journal on Computing*, **2** (December 1973), pp. 225–231.

Hopcroft J. E., and R. E. Tarjan, "Dividing a graph into triconnected components," *SIAM Journal on Computing*, **2** (September 1973), pp. 135–158.

Hopcroft J. E., and R. E. Tarjan, "Efficient planarity testing," *Journal of the ACM*, **21** (October 1974), pp. 549–568.

Hopcroft J. E., and J. D. Ullman, "Set-merging algorithms," *SIAM Journal on Computing*, **2** (December 1973), pp. 294–303.

Horowitz E., and S. Sahni, *Fundamentals of Computer Algorithms*, Computer Science Press, Rockville, MD (1978).

Horowitz E., and A. Zorat "Divide and conquer for parallel processing," *IEEE Transactions on Computers*, **C-32** (June 1983), pp. 582–585.

Hu T. C., *Integer Programming and Network Flows*, Addison-Wesley, Reading, MA, 1969.

Huang B. C., and M. A. Langston, "Practical in-place merging," *Communications of the ACM*, **31** (March 1988), pp. 348–352.

Huffman D. A., "A method for the construction of minimum redundancy codes," *Proceedings of the IRE*, **40** (September 1952), pp. 1098–1101.

Hunt J. W., and T. G. Szymanski, "A fast algorithm for computing longest common subsequences," *Communications of the ACM*, **20** (May 1977), pp. 350–353.

Hwang K., and F. A. Briggs, *Computer Architecture and Parallel Processing*, McGraw-Hill, New York, 1984.

Incerpi J., and R. Sedgewick, "Practical variations of shellsort," *Information Processing Letters*, **26** (1987) pp. 37–43.

Itai A., and M. Rodeh, "Finding a minimum circuit in a graph," *SIAM Journal on Computing*, **7** (November 1978), pp. 413–423.

Jagadish H. V., and T. Kailath, "A family of new efficient arrays for matrix multiplication," *IEEE Transactions on Computers*, **C-38** (January 1989), pp. 149–155.

Jia-Wei H., *Computation: Computability, Similarity and Duality*, Pitman, London, 1986.

Johnson D. S., A. Demers, J. D. Ullman, M. R. Garey, and R. L. Graham, "Worst case performance bounds for simple one-dimensional packing algorithms," *SIAM Journal on Computing*, **3** (1974), pp. 299–325.

Johnson D. B., "Efficient algorithms for shortest paths in sparse networks," *Journal of the ACM*, **24** (January 1977), pp. 1–13.

Jones D. W., "An empirical comparison of priority–queue and event–set implementations," *Communications of the ACM*, **29** (April 1986), pp. 300–311.

Karatsuba A., and Yu. Ofman, "Multiplication of multidigit numbers on automata," translated in *Sov. Phys. Dokl.*, **7** (1963), pp. 595–596. Originally appeared in *Dokl. Akad. Nauk SSSR*, **145** (1962), pp. 293–294.

Karlin A. R., and E. Upfal, "Parallel hashing — An efficient implementation of shared memory," *18th Annual ACM Symposium on Theory of Computing,* Berkeley (May 1986), pp. 160–168.

Karmarkar N., "A new polynomial time algorithm for linear programming," *Combinatorica,* **4** (1984), pp. 373–395.

Karmarkar N., and R. M. Karp, "An efficient approximation scheme for the one-dimensional bin packing problem," *23th Annual Symposium on Foundations of Computer Science,* (November 1982), pp. 312–320.

Karp R. M., "Reducibilities among combinatorial problems," in *Complexity of Computer Computations,* R. E. Miller and J. W. Thatcher, eds., Plenum Press, New York (1972), pp. 85–103.

Karp R. M., M. Saks, and A. Wigderson, "On a search problem related to branch-and-bound procedures," *27th Annual Symposium on Foundations of Computer Science,* Toronto (October 1986), pp. 19–28.

Karp R. M., "Combinatorics, complexity, and randomness," *Communications of the ACM,* **29** (February 1986), pp. 98–109.

Karp R. M., and M. O. Rabin, "Efficient randomized pattern-matching algorithms," *IBM Journal of Research and Development,* **31** (March 1987), pp. 249–260.

Khachian L. G., "A polynomial algorithm in linear programming," *Soviet Math. Dokl.,* **20** (1979), pp. 191–194.

King K. N., and B. Smith-Thomas, "An optimal algorithm for sink-finding," *Information Processing Letters,* **14** (May 1982), pp. 109–111.

Klee V., and G. L. Minty, "How good is the simplex algorithm?" in *Inequalities III,* O. Shisha, ed., Academic Press, New York (1972), pp. 159-175.

Klee V., R. E. Ladner, and R. Manber, "Signsolvability revisited," *Linear Algebra and its Applications,* **59** (1984), pp. 131–157.

Knuth D. E., *The Art of Computer Programming, Volume 1/ Fundamental Algorithms,* Second edition, Addison-Wesley, Reading, MA, 1973a.

Knuth D. E., *The Art of Computer Programming, Volume 3/ Sorting and Searching,* Addison-Wesley, Reading, MA, 1973b.

Knuth D. E., "Estimating the efficiency of backtrack programs," *Mathematics of Computation,* **29** (1975), pp. 121–136.

Knuth D. E., "Big omicron and big omega and big theta," *SIGACT News,* (April–June 1976), pp. 18–24.

Knuth D. E., *The Art of Computer Programming, Volume 2/ Seminumerical Algorithms,* Second edition, Addison-Wesley, Reading, MA, 1981.

Knuth D. E., ''Dynamic Huffman coding,'' *Journal of Algorithms,* **6** (1985), pp. 163–180.

Knuth D. E., J. H. Morris, and V. R. Pratt, ''Fast pattern matching in strings,'' *SIAM Journal on Computing,* **6** (June 1977), pp. 323–350.

Kronrod, M. A., ''An optimal ordering algorithm without a field of operation,'' (in Russian), *Dok. Akad. Nauk. SSSR,* **186** (1969), pp. 1256–1258.

Kruskal J. B., ''On the shortest spanning subtree of a graph and the traveling salesman problem,'' *Proceedings of the American Mathematical Society,* **71** (1956), pp. 48–50.

Kruskal C. P., L. Rudolph, and M. Snir, ''The power of parallel prefix,'' *IEEE Transactions on Computers,* **C-34** (November 1985), pp. 965–968.

Kruskal C. P., L. Rudolph, and M. Snir, ''Efficient parallel algorithms for graph problems,'' *1986 International Conference on Parallel Processing,* (August 1986), pp. 869–876.

Kruskal C. P., L. Rudolph, and M. Snir, ''Techniques for parallel manipulation of sparse matrices,'' IBM Research report RC-13364, (December 1987).

Kung H. T., ''Let's design algorithms for VLSI systems,'' *Proceedings of the Caltech Conference on VLSI,* (1979), pp. 65–90.

Kung H. T., ''Why systlic architecture,'' *Computer,* **15** (January 1982), pp. 37–46.

Kung H. T., and C. E. Leiserson, ''Algorithms for VLSI processor arrays,'' in *Introduction to VLSI Systems,* C. Mead and L. Conway, eds., Addison-Wesley, Reading, MA, (1980), pp. 271–292.

Kurtz T., and U. Manber, ''A probabilistic distributed algorithm for set intersection and its analysis,'' *Theoretical Computer Science,* **49** (1987), pp. 267–282.

Ladner R. E., ''On the structure of polynomial time reducibility,'' *Journal of the ACM,* **22** (January 1975), pp. 155–171.

Ladner R. E., and M. J. Fischer, ''Parallel prefix computation,'' *Journal of the ACM,* **27** (October 1980), pp. 831–838.

Lakatos I., *Proofs and Refutations: The Logic of Mathematical Discovery,* Cambridge University Press, Cambridge, 1976.

Lawler E. L., *Combinatorial Optimization: Networks and Matroids,* Holt, Rinehart & Winston, New York, 1976.

Lawler E. L., J. K. Lenstra, A. H. G. Rinnooy Kan, and D. B. Shmoys, *The Traveling Salesman Problem,* John Wiley & Sons, New York, 1985.

Lempel A., S. Even, and I. Cederbaum, ''An algorithm for planarity testing of graphs,'' *Theory of Graphs: An International Symposium,* Rome (July 1966), pp. 215–232.

Levin L. A., "Universal sorting problems," *Problemy Peredaci Informacii,* **9** (1973), pp. 115–116. English translation in *Problems of Information Transmission,* **9** (1973), pp. 265–266.

Lin S., and B. W. Kernighan, "An effective heuristic for the traveling salesman problem," *Operations Research,* **21** (1973), pp. 498–516.

Lipovski G. J., and M. Malek, *Parallel Computing: Theory and Comparisons,* John Wiley & Sons, New York, 1987.

Lipson J. D., *Elements of Algebra and Algebraic Computing,* Bejamin Cummings, Menlo Park, CA, 1981.

Lipton R. J., and D. Lopresti, "A systolic array for rapid string comparison," *Proceedings of the 1985 Chapel Hill Conference on VLSI,* (1985), pp. 363–376.

Litwin W., "Linear hashing: A new tool for file and table addressing," *Proceedings of the Sixth Conference on Very Large Databases,* Montreal, Canada (1980) pp. 212–223.

Lovász L., "Coverings and colorings of hypergraphs," *Proceedings of the Fourth Southeastern Conference on Combinatorics, Graph Theory, and Computing,* Utilitas Mathematica, Winnipeg (1973), pp. 3–12.

Lovász L., *Combinatorial Problems and Exercises,* North Holland, Amsterdam, 1979.

Lovász L., and M. D. Plummer, *Matching Theory,* North Holland, Amsterdam, 1986.

Lucas E., *Recreations Mathematiques,* Paris, 1882.

Lueker G. S., "Some techniques for solving recurrences," *Computing Surveys,* **12** (December 1980), pp. 419–436.

Luks E. M., "Isomorphism of graphs of bounded valence can be tested in polynomial time," *Journal of Computer and System Sciences,* **25** (1982), pp. 42–65.

Lynch T. J., *Data Compression Techniques and Applications,* Van Nostrand Reinhold, New York, 1985.

Maggs B. M., and S. A. Plotkin, "Minimum-cost spanning tree as a path-finding problem," *Information Processing Letters,* **26** (January 1988), pp. 291–293.

Manacher G. K., "The Ford–Johnson sorting algorithm is not optimal," *Journal of the ACM,* **26** (July 1979), pp. 441–456.

Manber U., "On maintaining dynamic information in a concurrent environment," *SIAM Journal on Computing,* **15** (November 1986), pp. 1130–1142.

Manber U., "Using induction to design algorithms," *Communications of the ACM,* **31** (November 1988), pp. 1300–1313.

Manber U., and L. McVoy, "Efficient storage of nonadaptive routing tables," *Networks,* **18** (1988), pp. 263–272.

Manber U., and E. Myers, "Suffix arrays: A new method for on-line string searches," to appear.

Manna Z., *Lectures on the Logic of Computer Programming*, CBMS–NSF Regional Conference series in Applied Mathematics, SIAM, Philadelphia, PA, 1980.

Manna Z., and R. Waldinger, "The origin of a binary search paradigm," *Science of Computer Programming*, **9** (1987) pp. 37–83.

Masek W. J., and M. S. Paterson, "How to compute string-edit distances quickly," in *Time Warps, String Edits, and Macromolecules: The Theory and Practice of Sequence Comparison*, D. Sankoff and J. B. Kruskal, eds., Addison-Wesley, Reading, MA (1983), pp. 337–349.

McCreight, E. M., "A space-economical suffix tree construction algorithm," *Journal of the ACM* **23** (1976), pp. 262–272.

Megiddo N., "Applying parallel computation algorithms in the design of serial algorithms," *Journal of the ACM*, **30** (October 1983), pp. 852–865.

Mehlhorn K., *Data Structures and Algorithms 3: Multi-Dimensional Searching and Computational Geometry*, Springer-Verlag, Berlin, 1984.

Menger K., "Zur allgeminen Kurventheorie," *Fund. Math.*, **10** (1927), pp. 95–115.

Meyer A. R., and L. Stockmeyer, "The equivalence problem for regular expression with squaring requires exponential space," *13th Annual Symposium on Switching and Automata Theory*, (1972), pp. 125–129.

Minieka E., *Optimization Algorithms for Networks and Graphs*, Marcel Dekker, New York, 1978.

Mirzaian A., "A halving technique for the longest stuttering subsequence problem," *Information Processing Letters*, **26** (1987), pp. 71–75.

Misra J., and D. Gries, "Finding repeated elements," *Science of Computer Programming*, **2** (1982), pp. 143–152.

Moffat A., and T. Takaoka, "An all pair shortest path algorithm with expected time $O(n^2 \log n)$," *SIAM Journal on Computing*, **16** (December 1987), pp. 1023–1031.

Moitra A., and S. S. Iyengar, "Discussion of parallel algorithms," Technical Report TR-86-759, Department of Computer Science, Cornell University (June 1986).

Moret B. M. E., "Decision trees and diagrams," *Computing Surveys*, **14** (December 1982), pp. 593–623.

Munro I., "Problems related to matrix multiplication," in *Computational Complexity*, R. Rustin, ed., Algorithmics Press, New York, 1971.

Myers E. W., "An *O(ND)* difference algorithm and its variations," *Algorithmica*, **1** (1986), pp. 251–266.

Myers E. W., "A four-Russians algorithm for regular expression pattern matching," Technical Report #88-34, Deperment of Computer Science, University of Arizona, October 1988.

Nishizeki T., and N. Chiba, *Planar Graphs, Theory and Algorithms,* Annals of Discrete Mathematics, **32**, North Holland, Netherlands, 1988.

Ore O., "Note on Hamiltonian circuit," *American Mathematical Monthly,* **67** (1960), p. 55.

Ore O., *Graphs and Their Uses,* Random House, New York, 1963.

Pan V., "Strassen's algorithm is not optimal," *19th Annual Symposium on Foundations of Computer Science,* Ann Arbor, MI (October 1978), pp. 166–176.

Pan V., *How to Multiply Matrices Faster,* Lecture Notes in Computer Science, Volume 129, Springer-Verlag, Berlin, 1984.

Papadimitriou C. H., and K. Steiglitz, *Combinatorial Optimization: Algorithms and Complexity,* Prentice-Hall, Englewood Cliffs, NJ, 1982.

Parberry I., *Parallel Complexity Theory,* John Wiley & Sons, New York, 1987.

Paull M. C., *Algorithm Design: A Recursion Transformation Framework,* John Wiley & Sons, New York, 1988.

Pearl J., *Heuristics — Intelligent Search Strategies for Computer Problem Solving,* Addison-Wesley, Reading, MA, 1984.

Perl Y., A. Itai, and H. Avni, "Interpolation search — A $\log \log N$ search," *Communications of the ACM,* **21** (July 1978), pp. 550–553.

Polya G., *Induction and Analogy in Mathematics,* Princeton University Press, Princeton, NJ, 1954.

Polya G., *How to Solve It,* Second Edition, Princeton University Press, Princeton, NJ, 1957.

Polya G., *Mathematical Discovery,* Combined Edition, John Wiley & Sons, New York, 1981.

Polya G., and G. Szego, *Aufgaben und Lehrsatze aus der Analysis,* Volume I, Berlin, Springer, 1927, p. 7.

Polya G., and G. Szego, *Problems and Theorems in Analysis I,* Springer-Verlag, Berlin, 1972.

Preparata F. P., and M. I. Shamos, *Computational Geometry: An Introduction,* Springer-Verlag, New York, 1985.

Prim R. C., "Shortest connection networks and some generalizations," *Bell System Technical Journal,* **36** (1957), p. 1389.

Purdom P. W., and C. A. Brown, *The Analysis of Algorithms*, Holt, Rinehart & Winston, New York, 1985a.

Purdom P. W., and C. A. Brown, "The pure literal rule and polynomial average time," *SIAM Journal on Computing*, **14** (November 1985b), pp. 943–953.

Quinn M. J., *Designing Efficient Algorithms for Parallel Computers*, McGraw-Hill, New York, 1987.

Quinn M. J., and N. Deo, "Parallel graph algorithms," *Computing Surveys*, **16** (September 1984), pp. 319–348.

Rabin M. O., "Probabilistic algorithms," in *Algorithms and Complexity, Recent Results and New Directions*, J. F. Traub, ed., Academic Press, New York, 1976, pp. 21–39.

Raghavan P., "Probabilistic construction of deterministic algorithms: Approximating packing integer programs," *27th Annual Symposium on Foundations of Computer Science*, Toronto (October 1986), pp. 10–18.

Ranade A. G., "How to emulate shared memory," *28th Annual Symposium on Foundations of Computer Science*, Los Angeles (October 1987), pp. 185–194.

Reed D. A., and R. M. Fujimoto, *Multicomputer Networks: Message-Based Parallel Processing*, MIT Press, Cambridge, MA, 1987.

Reif J. H., and L. G. Valiant, "A logarithmic time sort for linear size networks," *Journal of the ACM*, **34** (January 1987), pp. 60–76.

Reingold E. M., and W. J. Hansen, *Data Structures*, Little, Brown, Boston, MA, 1983.

Richards D., "Parallel sorting — A bibliography," *SIGACT News*, **18** (Summer 1986).

Rivest R. L., A. Shamir, and L. M. Adleman, "A method for obtaining digital signatures and public-key cryptosystems," *Communications of the ACM*, **21** (February 1978), pp. 120–126.

Roberts F. S., *Applied Combinatorics*, Prentice-Hall, Englewood Cliffs, NJ, 1984.

Rodeh M., "Finding the median distributively," *Journal of Computer and System Sciences*, **24** (1982), pp. 162–166.

Ronse C., "A bibliography on digital and computational convexity," Manuscript M185, Philips Research Laboratory, Brussels, (February 1987).

Rosenberg A. L., "On the time required to recognize properties of graphs," *SIGACT News*, (1973), pp. 15–16.

Runge C., and H. König, *Die Grundlehrn der mathematischen Wissenschften*, Springer, Berlin, 1924.

Ryser H. J., "Combinatorial properties of matrices of zeros and ones," *Canadian Journal of Mathematics*, **9** (1957), pp. 371–377.

Rytter W., "Fast recognition of pushdown automaton and context-free languages," *Information and Control,* **67** (1985) pp. 12–22.

Sankoff D., and J. B. Kruskal, *Time Wraps, String Edits, and Macromolecules: The Theory and Practice of Sequence Comparison,* Addison-Wesley, Reading, MA, 1983.

Savitch W. J., "Relationships between nondeterministic and deterministic tape complexities," *Journal of Computer and System Sciences,* **4** (1970), pp. 177–192.

Schaback R., "On the expected sublinearity of the Boyer-Moore algorithm," *SIAM Journal on Computing,* **17** (August 1988), pp. 648–658.

Schönhage A., M. S. Paterson, and N. Pippenger, "Finding the median," *Journal of Computer and System Science,* **13** (October 1976), pp. 184–199.

Schrijver A., *Theory of Linear and Integer Programming,* John Wiley & Sons, Chichester, 1986.

Sedgewick R., *Quicksort,* Garland, New York, 1978.

Sedgewick R., *Algorithms,* Second Edition, Addison-Wesley, Reading, MA, 1988.

Sedgewick R., and J. S. Vitter, "Shortest paths in Euclidean graphs," *Algorithmica,* **1** (1986), pp. 31–48.

Shamos M. I., and D. Hoey, "Closest-point problems," *16th Annual Symposium on Foundations of Computer Science,* Berkeley (October 1975), pp. 151–162.

Shamos M. I., and D. Hoey, "Geometric intersection problems," *17th Annual Symposium on Foundations of Computer Science,* Houston (October 1976), pp. 208–215.

Shell D. L., "A high-speed sorting procedure" *Communications of the ACM,* **2** (July 1959), pp. 30–32.

Shiloach Y, and U. Vishkin, "Finding the maximum, merging, and sorting in a parallel computation model," *Journal of Algorithms,* **3** (March 1981), pp. 88–102.

Shrira L., N. Francez, and M. Rodeh, "Distributed *k* selection: From a sequential to a distributed algorithm," *Second ACM Symposium on Principles of Distributed Computing,* Ottawa (August 1983), pp. 143–153.

Siegel H. J., *Interconnection Networks for Large Scale Parallel Processing: Theory and Case Studies,* Lexington Books, Lexington, MA, 1985.

Sleator D. D., and R. E. Tarjan, "Self-adjusting binary search trees," *Journal of the ACM,* **32** (July 1985), pp. 652–686.

Smit G. V., "A comparison of three string matching algorithms," *Software — Practice and Experience,* **12** (1982), pp. 57–66.

Solovay R., and V. Strassen, "A fast Monte-Carlo test for primality," *SIAM Journal on Computing*, **6** (March 1977), pp. 84–85; erratum (February 1978), p. 118.

Sominskii I. S., *The Method of Mathematical Induction*, (translated from Russian), D. C. Heath, Boston, 1963.

Spafford E. H., "The Internet worm program: An analysis," Technical Report CSD-TR-823, Department of Computer Science, Purdue University (November 1988).

Spira P. M., "A new algorithm for finding all shortest paths in a graph of positive arcs in average time $O(n^2\log^2 n)$," *SIAM Journal on Computing*, **2** (1973), pp. 28-32.

Standish T. A., *Data Structure Techniques*, Addison-Wesley, Reading, MA., 1980.

Stanton D., and D. White, *Constructive Combinatorics*, Springer-Verlag, New York, 1986.

Stout Q. F., "Supporting divide-and-conquer algorithms for image processing," *Journal of Parallel and Distributed Computing*, **4** (1987), pp. 95–115.

Strassen V., "Gaussian elimination is not optimal," *Numerische Mathematik*, **13** (1969), pp. 354–356.

Takaoka T., "An on-line pattern matching algorithm," *Information Processing Letters*, **22** (May 1986), pp. 329–330.

Tarjan R. E., "Depth first search and linear graph algorithms," *SIAM Journal on Computing*, **1** (June 1972), pp. 146–160.

Tarjan R. E., "Efficiency of a good but not linear set union algorithm," *Journal of the ACM*, **22** (April 1975), pp. 215–225.

Tarjan R. E., "Amortized computational complexity," *SIAM Journal on Applied and Discrete Mathematics*, **6** (1985), pp. 306–318.

Tarjan R. E., *Data Structures and Network Algorithms*, SIAM, Philadelphia, PA, 1983.

Tarjan R. E., and J. van Leeuwen, "Worst case analysis of set union algorithms," *Journal of the ACM*, **31** (April 1984), pp. 245–281.

Tarjan R. E., and U. Vishkin, "An efficient parallel biconnectivity algorithm," *SIAM Journal on Computing*, **14** (November 1985), pp. 862–874.

Tarry G., "Le probleme des labyrinths," *Nouvelles Ann. de Math*, (1895), p. 187.

Toussaint G., *Computational Geometry*, North Holland, Amsterdam, 1984.

Turner J. S., "Almost all k-colorable graphs are easy to color," *Journal of Algorithms*, **9** (1988), pp. 63–82.

Tutte W. T., *Graph Theory*, Encyclopedia of Mathematics, Volume 21, Addison-Wesley, Reading, MA, 1984.

Uhr L., *Parallel Computer Vision*, Academic Press, New York, 1987.

Ukkonen E., "Algorithms for approximate string matching," *Information and Control*, **64** (1985), pp. 100–118.

Ullman J. D., *Computational Aspects of VLSI*, Computer Science Press, Rockville, MD, 1984.

Upfal E., "Efficient schemes for parallel communication," *First ACM Symposium on Principles of Distributed Computing*, Ottawa (August 1982), pp. 55–59.

Upfal E., and A. Wigderson, "How to share memory in a distributed system," *Journal of the ACM*, **34** (January 1987), pp. 116–127.

Vacca G., "Maurolycus, the first discoverer of the principle of mathematical induction," *Bulletin of the American Mathematical Society*, **16** (1909), p. 70.

Vaidya P. M., "Geometry helps in matching," *20th Annual ACM Symposium on Theory of Computing*, Chicago (May 1988), pp. 422–425.

Valiant L. G., "Parallelism in comparisons problems," *SIAM Journal on Computing*, **4** (September 1975), pp. 348–355.

Valiant L. G., "A scheme for fast parallel communication," *SIAM Journal on Computing*, **11** (May 1982), pp. 350–361.

Valiant L. G., and G. J. Brebner, "Universal schemes for parallel communication," *13th Annual ACM Symposium on Theory of Computing*, Milwaukee (May 1981), pp. 263–277.

van der Nat M., "On interpolation search," *Communications of the ACM*, **22** (December 1979), p. 681.

van Leeuwen J., "Graph algorithms," Technical Report RUU-CS-86-17, Department of Computer Science, University of Utrecht, Utrecht, The Netherlands, (October 1986).

von Neumann J., *Collected Works*, **5**, Macmillan, New York, 1963, pp. 91–99.

Vishkin U., "Randomized parallel speedups for list ranking," *Journal of Parallel and Distributed Computing*, **4** (1987), pp. 319–333.

Vitter J. S., "Design and analysis of dynamic Huffman coding," *26th Annual Symposium on Foundations of Computer Science*, Portland, OR (October 1985), pp. 293–302.

Vitter J. S., and W. C. Chen, *Design & Analysis of Coalesced Hashing*, Oxford University Press, New York, 1987.

von Neumann J., *Collected Works*, **5**, Macmillan, New York, 1963.

Wagner R. A., and M. J. Fischer, "The string-to-string correction problem," *Journal of the ACM*, **21** (January 1974), pp. 168–173.

Warren H. S., "A modification of Warshall's algorithm for transitive closure of binary relations," *Communications of the ACM*, **18** (April 1975), pp. 218–220.

Warshall S., "A theorem on Boolean matrices," *Journal of the ACM*, **9** (January 1962), pp. 11–12.

Wegman M. N., and J. L. Carter, "New classes and applications of hash functions," *20th Annual Symposium on Foundations of Computer Science*, (October 1979), pp. 175–182.

Weiner, P., "Linear pattern matching algorithm," *14th IEEE Symposium on Switching and Automata Theory*, Iowa City, Iowa (October 1973), pp. 1–11.

Whitney H., "Congruent graphs and the connectivity of graphs," *American Journal of Mathematics*, **54** (1932), pp. 150–68.

Wigderson A., "Improving the performance guarantee for approximate graph coloring," *Journal of the ACM*, **30** (October 1983), pp. 729–735.

Wilf H. S., "Backtrack: An $O(1)$ expected time algorithm for the graph coloring problem," *Information Processing Letters*, **18** (1984), pp. 119–121.

Williams J. W. J., "Algorithm 232: Heapsort," *Communications of the ACM*, **7** (June 1964), p. 701.

Winograd S., "A new algorithm for inner product," *IEEE Transactions on Computers*, **C-17** (1968), pp. 693–694.

Winograd S., "On the number of multiplications necessary to compute certain functions," *Communications on Pure and Applied Mathematics*, **23** (1970a), pp. 165–170.

Winograd S., "The algebraic complexity of functions," *Proceedings of the International Congress of Mathematicians*, **3** (1970b), pp. 283–288.

Winograd S., "Some remarks on fast multiplication of polynomials," in *Complexity of Sequential and Parallel Numerical Algorithms*, J. F. Traub, ed., Academic Press, New York (1973), pp. 181–196.

Winograd S., *Arithmetic Complexity of Computations*, SIAM, Philadelphia, PA, 1980.

Wirth N., *Algorithms & Data Structures*, Prentice-Hall, Englewood Cliffs, NJ, 1986.

Yao A., "An $O(|E|\log\log|V|)$ algorithm for finding minimum spanning trees," *Information Processing Letters*, **4** (1975), pp. 21–23.

Yao A., "Probabilistic computations — toward a unified measure of complexity," *18th Annual Symposium on Foundations of Computer Science*, Providence, RI (October 1977), pp. 222–227.

Ziv J., and A. Lempel, "Compression of indiviual sequences via variable-rate coding," *IEEE Transactions on Information Theory*, **IT-24** (September 1978), pp. 530–536.

INDEX

o 41
O 39
OO 41–42, 174, 316, 410
Θ 41
Ω 41
ω 41

Aanderaa, S. O. 113
Abstract data types 62
Ackerman's function 86
Acyclic collection of sets 372
Acyclic graph, *see* Directed acyclic graph
Addition, parallel 379–380, 411
Adel'son-Vel'skii, G. M. 75
Adjacency list representation 84
Adjacency matrix representation 84
Adleman, L. M. 295, 316
Aho, A. V. 85, 174, 175, 305, 316, 336
Ajtai, M. 410
Akl, S. G. 409
Aleliunas, R. 411
Algebraic algorithms 293–320, 436–438
Algorithm
    algebraic 293–320, 436–438
    analysis of 37–60
    approximation 357, 363–367
    definition of 1
    distributed 208, 376
    divide-and-conquer 103–104, 113–114,
        131, 137, 141, 144, 158, 169, 172,
        176, 183, 264, 278–281, 286, 287,
        289, 299–304, 311–314, 316–319,
        379–380, 383, 394–396, 409–410, 431
    efficient, definition of 341
    geometric 102–104, 265–291, 331–333,
        434–436
    graph 95–96, 98–101, 185–264, 325–326,

347–349, 351–354, 356–363, 369,
    370–374, 414–415, 426–434
    greedy 210–211, 235, 237, 363
    for interconnection networks 378,
        389–403
    notation for 4
    numeric 293–320, 379–380, 398–401,
        404–407
    parallel 214, 216, 304, 375–416
    probabilistic 158–164, 175, 287, 320,
        402–403
    running time of an 42
    sequences and sets 119–183
    systolic 404–409, 411, 416
All shortest paths problem 212–214, 322
Almasi, G. S. 409
Alternating path 236
Amortized complexity 55, 83, 86
Analysis of algorithms 37–60
Ancestor (in a tree) 193
Angluin, D. 369
Anti-Gray codes 33
Apostolico, A. 175
Approximate convex hull 289
Approximation algorithms 357, 363–367
Arborescence 66, 186
Arithmetic geometric mean theorem 24–26,
    35–36
Arithmetic sum 11–12, 31, 53
Arlazarov, V. L. 317
Array, definition of 63
Articulation point 218, 223, 260, 430
ASCII 146
Assembly line 404
Assignment problem 330–331
Asymptotic complexity, definition of 38
Atkinson, M. D. 317